Letter from the Publisher

Welcome to IDG Books Online!

Thank you very much for selecting the first in a new series of books, a unique blend of paper and online publishing. We hope you'll not only enjoy the contents of the book you now hold in your hands but also take advantage of the wealth of information related to this title that we'll be publishing on our Web site in the months to come.

At the back of this book you'll find a CD-ROM containing everything you need to access the IDG Books Web site. If you've never connected to the Web, simply follow the easy sign-on procedures to obtain an Internet account. If you're already online and connected to the Web, you can go directly to the IDG Books Online area of our Web site:

> http://www.idgbooks.com/

The online medium is still evolving, and we believe it will enable us to deliver the highest quality information to you in the fastest way possible. To help us improve our future products, we encourage you to send your suggestions and comments to us at this address: online@idgbooks.com.

We hope you'll enjoy and benefit from this title and future titles we'll be publishing in the months to come. We look forward to hearing from you. Our goal is to make each and every title in our line a quality, information-rich reading experience both online and in print.

David Ushijima
Vice President and Publisher
IDG Books Online

Yahoo!™
UNPLUGGED

Your Discovery Guide
to the Web

Yahoo!™
U N P L U G G E D

Your Discovery Guide to the Web

By David Filo and Jerry Yang

**with Karen Heyman, Paul Hoffman,
Tom Negrino, Richard Raucci, Anne Ryder,
Charles Seiter, Dave Taylor, and Karen Wickre**

**IDG
BOOKS
WORLDWIDE**

IDG Books Worldwide, Inc.
An International Data Group Company

Foster City, CA ◆ Chicago, IL ◆ Indianapolis, IN ◆ Braintree, MA ◆ Dallas, TX

Yahoo!™ Unplugged: Your Discovery Guide to the Web

Published by
IDG Books Worldwide, Inc.
An International Data Group Company
919 E. Hillsdale Blvd., Suite 400
Foster City, CA 94404

Library of Congress Catalog Card No.: 95-81104
ISBN: 1-56884-715-7
Printed in the United States of America
10 9 8 7 6 5 4 3 2 1
1M/QR/RR/ZV
Distributed in the United States by IDG Books Worldwide, Inc.

Distributed by Macmillan Canada for Canada; by Computer and Technical Books for the Caribbean Basin; by Contemporanea de Ediciones for Venezuela; by Distribuidora Cuspide for Argentina; by CITEC for Brazil; by Ediciones ZETA S.C.R. Ltda. for Peru; by Editorial Limusa SA for Mexico; by Transworld Publishers Limited in the United Kingdom and Europe; by Al-Maiman Publishers & Distributors for Saudi Arabia; by Simron Pty. Ltd. for South Africa; by IDG Communications (HK) Ltd. for Hong Kong; by Toppan Company Ltd. for Japan; by Addison Wesley Publishing Company for Korea; by Longman Singapore Publishers Ltd. for Singapore, Malaysia, Thailand, and Indonesia; by Unalis Corporation for Taiwan; by WS Computer Publishing Company, Inc. for the Philippines; by WoodsLane Pty. Ltd. for Australia; by WoodsLane Enterprises Ltd. for New Zealand.

For general information on IDG Books Worldwide's books in the U.S., please call our Consumer Customer Service department at 800-762-2974. For reseller information, including discounts and premium sales, please call our Reseller Customer Service department at 800-434-3422.

For information on where to purchase IDG Books Worldwide's books outside the U.S., contact IDG Books Worldwide at 415-655-3021 or fax 415-655-3295.

For information on translations, contact Marc Jeffrey Mikulich, Director, Foreign & Subsidiary Rights, at IDG Books Worldwide, 415-655-3018 or fax 415-655-3295.

For sales inquiries and special prices for bulk quantities, write to the address above or call IDG Books Worldwide at 415-655-3200.

For information on using IDG Books Worldwide's books in the classroom, or ordering examination copies, contact Jim Kelly at 800-434-2086.

For authorization to photocopy items for corporate, personal, or educational use, please contact Copyright Clearance Center, 222 Rosewood Drive, Danvers, MA 01923, or fax 508-750-4470.

is a trademark under exclusive license to IDG Books Worldwide, Inc., from International Data Group, Inc.

About the Authors

David Filo, Chief Yahoo Filo, 28, a native of Moss Bluff, Louisiana, co-created the Yahoo! online guide in April 1994 and took a leave of absence from Stanford University's Electrical Engineering Ph.D. program in April 1995 to co-found Yahoo! Corporation. Filo received a B.S. in Computer Engineering from Tulane University and an M.S. in Electrical Engineering from Stanford University. He sleeps every third night.

Jerry Yang, Chief Yahoo Yang, 26, is a Taiwanese native who was raised in San Jose, California. He co-created the Yahoo! online guide in April 1994 and co-founded Yahoo! Corporation in April 1995. Yang is currently on a leave of absence from Stanford University's Electrical Engineering Ph.D. program and holds B.S. and M.S. degrees in Electrical Engineering from Stanford University. Jerry is a total hack at the game of golf but likes to play in his spare time anyway.

Karen Heyman started out life wanting to be a medievalist, but then aliens kidnapped her and transmogrified her brain, and suddenly she found herself at COMDEX. She has been West Coast Editor of *Web Week,* has lectured and consulted on the Internet and chaired panels at industry conferences. She currently writes for *NetGuide, Home Office Computing*, and other industry publications. She celebrated finishing this book by changing her .SIG file, which once read: "Latest Internet Statistic: One in five people who have used the Internet have written a book about it." She dedicates this book to her nephews Nate and Ben and her niece/goddaughter Libby, for setting the pace.

Paul Hoffman has written more than a dozen books about computers, including many about the Internet. His most recent book, *Netscape and the World Wide Web For Dummies,* is the best-selling book on the topic. He has been on the Internet for more than 15 years and oversees the popular Internet Computer Index site on the Web.

Tom Negrino is a Los Angeles-based writer and consultant. He has worked exclusively with the Macintosh since its introduction in 1984 and has been writing and reviewing Mac products since 1986. Mr. Negrino is a Contributing Editor to *Macworld*. He has also written for *Digital Video, Mac Guide,* and *Mac Computing* magazines. He is the author of *Upgrading Your Mac Illustrated* and coauthor of several other books. Mr. Negrino has been both moderator and panelist on the conference faculty at the Macworld Expo trade shows in San Francisco and Boston. He has also served on the Board of Directors of the Los Angeles Macintosh Group (LAMG) for the past nine years; he is currently the group's Vice President. The LAMG is the largest Mac-specific user group in the United States, serving more than 5,000 members in the greater L.A. area. Prior to 1984, Mr. Negrino worked in the film business as a videotape editor and production coordinator for industrial films, music videos, and commercials.

Richard Raucci lives in a beautiful house in San Francisco's Noe Valley with his wife, writer Elizabeth Crane, and their son, Philip. A former computer magazine editor, Richard turned to full-time book writing when the opportunity to make it a profession arose. Besides this book, he has written two books for Springer Verlag on World Wide Web browsers. His freelance work has appeared in numerous magazines, including *Publish, SunWorld, PCWorld/MultiMediaWorld,*

NeXTWorld, Electronic Entertainment, Mac Computing, UnixWorld, Open Computing, and *InfoWorld.* He regularly chairs Internet sessions at major industry conferences and volunteers as an Internet teacher at the Exploratorium Museums Multimedia Playground exhibits. He is a graduate in English from the University of Pennsylvania, and he grew up in South Philadelphia. Past occupations have included Psychiatric Technician (at the Bethesda Naval Hospital), Department of Justice Court Clerk (processing political asylum applications for the Executive Office for Immigration Review in San Francisco), magazine editor (for IDG and McGraw-Hill), and the usual round of temp jobs and chain store idiocy. His interests include reading, architecture, photography, design, movies, technology, and the Internet, not necessarily in that order. Reach him at rraucci@well.com. To Liz and Philip with love.

Anne Ryder is an online editor at *InfoWorld* and has created several Web sites. She has also worked as a market research analyst, librarian, bus driver, pizza cook, copy editor, and English teacher in Japan. Her favorite foreign capital is Kathmandu, and her favorite band is King Sunny Ade and his African Beats. Originally a Massachusetts Yankee, she is now enjoying the climate in Silicon Valley.

Charles Seiter, Ph.D., is a *Macworld* contributing editor and *PC World* contributor, mostly covering technical topics such as software development, science, and engineering. He's the author of *The Internet For Macs For Dummies* (IDG Books, 1994), and this is his 20th computer book. He lives in a place that, until the Web developed, was approximately the middle of nowhere. Now there is no nowhere.

Dave Taylor is President of Intuitive Systems (http://www.intuitive.com/), a consulting firm helping companies build smarter and easier systems both online and off. He is author of the best-selling *Creating Cool Web Pages with HTML* (IDG Books, 1995), coauthor of *The Internet Business Guide* (Sams.Net, 1995), and proprietor of The Internet Mall™ (located on the Web at http://www.iw.com/imall). To Nero.

Karen Wickre cowrote *Atlas to the World Wide Web* (Ziff-Davis Press, 1995) and is a contributing editor to the U.S. edition of *The Net* magazine.

Steve Arbuss, who generously donated his time to consult on the legal section, is a partner in the Los Angeles law firm of Pircher Nichols & Meeks. Mr. Arbuss lectures on the Internet at UCLA Extension and elsewhere. Jennifer McRae, responsible for research and additional writing on the Arts section, is Information Manager at the Interactive Center, an Internet consultancy in Marina Del Rey, California.

Welcome to the world of IDG Books Worldwide.

IDG Books Worldwide, Inc., is a subsidiary of International Data Group, the world's largest publisher of computer-related information and the leading global provider of information services on information technology. IDG was founded more than 25 years ago and now employs more than 7,700 people worldwide. IDG publishes more than 250 computer publications in 67 countries (see listing below). More than 70 million people read one or more IDG publications each month.

Launched in 1990, IDG Books Worldwide is today the #1 publisher of best-selling computer books in the United States. We are proud to have received 8 awards from the Computer Press Association in recognition of editorial excellence and three from Computer Currents' First Annual Readers' Choice Awards, and our best-selling ...*For Dummies*® series has more than 19 million copies in print with translations in 28 languages. IDG Books Worldwide, through a joint venture with IDG's Hi-Tech Beijing, became the first U.S. publisher to publish a computer book in the People's Republic of China. In record time, IDG Books Worldwide has become the first choice for millions of readers around the world who want to learn how to better manage their businesses.

Our mission is simple: Every one of our books is designed to bring extra value and skill-building instructions to the reader. Our books are written by experts who understand and care about our readers. The knowledge base of our editorial staff comes from years of experience in publishing, education, and journalism — experience which we use to produce books for the '90s. In short, we care about books, so we attract the best people. We devote special attention to details such as audience, interior design, use of icons, and illustrations. And because we use an efficient process of authoring, editing, and desktop publishing our books electronically, we can spend more time ensuring superior content and spend less time on the technicalities of making books.

You can count on our commitment to deliver high-quality books at competitive prices on topics you want to read about. At IDG Books Worldwide, we continue in the IDG tradition of delivering quality for more than 25 years. You'll find no better book on a subject than one from IDG Books Worldwide.

John J. Kilcullen

John Kilcullen
President and CEO
IDG Books Worldwide, Inc.

Acknowledgments

Karen Heyman: Thanks to Randy Haykin for introducing me to the project. To Corbin, Erfert, and Tim for their guidance. To Jim Sabo for keeping me from tying the computer to my ankle and jumping off the Santa Monica Pier when Windows crashed. To Irene "Believe me, you're not alone" Kaufman and to John "Trust that Instinct!" Sheehan, for love, support, and perfect timing. And especially to Jerry and David — I still remember when I first heard, "These two grad students at Stanford came up with a way to search the Web. . ."

Tom Negrino: I'd like to thank Dori for help way above and beyond the call; you're the best. I couldn't have done it without you. Thanks also to Erfert Fenton, for getting me involved in this project; and Tim Brady, David Ushijima, and Corbin Collins, for their patience.

Richard Raucci: I'd like to thank David Ushijima at IDG Books Online for inviting me to be a part of this project, and Tim Brady and the rest of the people at Yahoo! for their support and encouragement.

Charles Seiter: Surfing the Web is fun. Picking up every rock on the floor of the Web ocean to see if it's a gem is not. Loretta Toth deserves a lot of credit for not strangling me with a mouse cord during this fast-paced project.

Dave Taylor: Thanks as always to Linda for her help and support. Thanks also to the teams at Best Communications and NETCOM for the online resources needed to keep things up and running.

(The Publisher would like to give special thanks to Patrick J. McGovern, without whom this book would not have been possible.)

Contents at a Glance

Table of Contents

Yahoo!

Yahoo!

Yahoo!

Yahoo!

Ƴ𝖺𝗁𝗈𝗈!

Ya**h**oo!

Yahoo!

Foreword by David and Jerry

It wasn't so long ago that we were trying out this new thing on the Net called Mosaic. Talk about an instant diversion . . . from our Ph.D.s.

Work quickly took a backseat while we went madly surfing computer info sites, reading up on obscure music lyrics, virtually visiting Paris, and trying our hand at hacking up some HTML code.

Before we knew it, our theses became distant memories as we were sucked further and further into the far reaches of cyberspace. In a matter of months, we lost any lingering hope of turning our doctoral candidacies into doctoral degrees as we spent all our time combing the Web, devoting ourselves to becoming full-fledged yahoos.

The Web craze still rages a full 20 months later, with no slowdown in sight. We never thought we'd jump from specialists in integrated circuit design to *cybrarians,* but that's where we find ourselves today and it continues to be a thrilling ride.

What's most exciting to us isn't what's on the Web already. It's really the potential and promise of what's yet to come. The Web today is just a hint of what digital connectivity and interactivity can bring. While a lot still is uncertain, several trends are evident: Bandwidth will continue to increase; access will become simpler and, in turn, more pervasive; content will diversify even more; interactivity will only get better; and customization will allow people to enjoy a unique and individualized experience. The Internet will cease to be a mysterious, unchartered "other world" and begin to seamlessly integrate into *our* world.

The biggest hurdles we've faced so far with Yahoo! have not been technical but rather practical: understanding and interpreting the various social and ethical ramifications of this new medium. The Web is a global, dynamic, heterogeneous place that has something for everyone. Maintaining a broad, comprehensive information base has been and will continue to be important, but as the Web continues to grow, providing *context* for the content will become increasingly essential. It is through context that Yahoo! has been able to direct people with similar interests to the same place.

It is to all Web users that we owe our eternal gratitude. Yahoo! would not have been possible without the incredible amount of support we received from users of all walks of life. The contributions of individual users — educators, engineers, business people, elderly folks, and kids alike — have helped shape and will continue to help shape the Yahoo! directory. We promise to keep striving to build an even better, free online guide that is based on the users who use it.

We hope you enjoy this book. It is designed to give you a highlight of the breadth of subjects that are available on Yahoo!. And where the book leaves off, you'll have the Yahoo! categories to keep you going. We hope this book will get you on the Web and enrich your experiences using it.

Our Best,

David Filo and Jerry Yang — September 1995

Introduction to This Book

Welcome to *Yahoo! Unplugged: Your Discovery Guide to the Web!* Yahoo! is the premier online database of the best of the ever-expanding Internet, cataloging more than 80,000 sites and growing. This book puts the best of Yahoo! into a form that you can take to class, to work, to bed, to the bathroom, or to the beach. You can use this book to find online resources cataloged on Yahoo! while you relax in your favorite chair. After you find what you're looking for, *then* go log on. In other words, if you often find yourself surfing around the Web trying to find stuff, this book can save you time and money, and a bit of your sanity, too.

What This Book Is

Yahoo! Unplugged is cutting-edge publishing. It comes in three flavors: paper, plastic, and electrons.

Paper

The book you're holding is designed to get you up to speed on how to get the most out of the Internet, the Web, and Yahoo!. It's full of entertaining, expert reviews of the best sites on the Web and describes what you can expect to find when you visit them with your Web browser. The five introductory chapters will give you a good background on what exactly the Internet, the Web, and Yahoo! are and how you can use Yahoo! to make your information hunting more effective and to enhance your online experiences.

The rest of the book is divided up just like Yahoo! divides up the World Wide Web: into 14 subject categories. The 14 Yahoo! categories are:

Arts	**News**
Business and Economy	**Recreation**
Computers and Internet	**Reference**
Education	**Regional**
Entertainment	**Science**
Government	**Social Science**
Health	**Society and Culture**

The book contains one more chapter, called Business Directory. In Yahoo!, online businesses selling products and services are found under Business and Economy, but because of the rapidly expanding size of the section, we chose to give these businesses their own chapter. Therefore, the Business Directory chapter is sort of a Yellow Pages for the Web, where you'll find businesses selling everything from bumper stickers to airplanes.

Plastic

Bound into the back of this book is a specially developed CD-ROM disc that contains portions of the book integrated into an attractive presentation. The CD-ROM presentation of *Yahoo! Unplugged* is a fun way to get started learning about Yahoo! and the Internet. Also on the CD-ROM is the complete Yahoo! database in searchable format, which enables you to quickly find what you're looking for before you even log on!

The CD-ROM disc also contains the latest Windows *and* Macintosh versions of Quarterdeck Mosaic, the acclaimed, powerful Web browser software from Quarterdeck Corporation, with a full three months of VIP prepaid technical support. You can install the Quarterdeck Mosaic software on your PC or Macintosh and be surfing the World Wide Web in minutes! All you need is a modem, preferably 14.4K or 28.8K. And a credit card.

If you already have an account with an Internet Service Provider, simply configure the software to work with your provider. If you don't already have Internet access, you can choose from a number of preconfigured Internet Service Providers during the installation process. In most cases, you simply follow the online instructions, fill out the online forms (including your credit card information), and click on a button to connect via modem with your chosen provider. Note: Your credit card information is *not* transferred over the Internet but is submitted over a private, direct dial-up line — the process is as secure as ordering from a catalog over the phone.

Once Quarterdeck Mosaic is installed and configured, you can begin surfing the World Wide Web at Yahoo! For more information on installing and using the Quarterdeck Mosaic software, see the Installing and Using the CD-ROM and the Passport to Quarterdeck Technical Support sections near the back of this book.

Electrons

This book also has a Web page, located at the IDG Books World Wide Web site:

http://www.idgbooks.com/

The *Yahoo! Unplugged* Web page is located in the IDG Books Online area of the IDG Books site. Visit the book's Web page to view book-related news, online portions of the book, elements from the CD-ROM, and lots more up-to-date information about this book and events related to Yahoo!.

Of course, you also should visit Yahoo! itself. Yahoo! is located on the Web at the following address:

http://www.yahoo.com/

That may just be the most useful address to memorize in all of cyberspace, because you can get just about everywhere else *from* there. For extra convenience, if you make http://www.yahoo.com/ your Web browser's home page (starting point), you don't even have to remember it.

How to Use This Book

You can browse through this book at your leisure, letting your mind wander, looking up whatever you like, or just start reading anywhere. This book, like Yahoo!, is chock-full of amazingly useful information relating to just about every subject imaginable. Read the first five chapters to get your bearings on how the Internet, the World Wide Web, and Yahoo! work. Read the subject category chapters to see the vast amount of stuff waiting for you out there on the Web.

Use this book as a reference. A good way to start is to look up your topic in the table of contents or the index and follow from there.

Sooner or later, you're going to want to log on and start cruising the Web online. Read Installing and Using the CD-ROM, located in the back of this book, to see how to install the Quarterdeck software. If you already have access to the Web and Yahoo!, well, you know what to do.

URLs

This book is just bursting with URLs (Uniform Resource Locators). They look like this:

http://www.loop.com/~raw/TV/abfab/abfab.htm

All Web browsers allow you to type in a URL to go directly to that address on the Web. Be sure to type it exactly as you see it. Spelling counts. Capitalization counts. All the funny characters you'll see (like ~ and % and @ and #) — they all count, so type carefully.

D & J

On some site reviews in this book, you'll see a graphic element that looks like this:

The D & J stands for Dave and Jerry, the founders of Yahoo!, and that little circle indicates that the site in question receives their official seal of coolness.

Let us explain: Not every site on the Web gets listed in Yahoo!, and not every site listed in Yahoo! wound up in this book. Dave and Jerry and the gang at Yahoo! try to allow only good and useful sites into the Yahoo! universe. And only the best of *them* made it into this book. And only the best of the ones in this book are good enough to get the D & J stamp of approval.

Errors

Sometimes, you may get an error message when you try to call up a Web page. That doesn't necessarily mean that the Internet is broken or that the page has been removed from its site or that you typed it wrong (but do double-check your typing). Sometimes it just means that something between your machine and the page is temporarily out of order, and it will be fixed shortly. It could be any number of things, and what they might be is not important. What's important is that you go do something else for awhile and then come back later and try to load the page again. Often, you'll be relieved to discover that the page pops right up as if nothing was ever wrong. Just one of the mysteries of the Web that we all must deal with.

Of course, the Web is ever-changing, and Web pages do come and go. In fact, there's no guarantee that any of the sites in this book will still be up six months or a year from now. That's because the Web is a distributed system of autonomous participants who are free to discontinue or move their Web pages whenever they feel like it. That's just the way it goes. Of course, by the time one goes down, *quite a few* have come up. The Web is certainly not shrinking by any means — it's growing by leaps and bounds (for details and stats, see the chapter titled Introduction to the World Wide Web).

Yahoo! is also changing, and although *most* of the structure of subject categories within Yahoo! is stable, Yahoo! may opt to make changes in the future to better serve its users. In other words, some sites in this book may change locations within Yahoo!. To see the latest Yahoo! subject category listings, simply visit Yahoo! online.

Feedback

We love to hear from our readers. If you want to contact us, please feel free to do so. The following information will help you determine the appropriate folks to contact.

For questions or concerns regarding Yahoo! itself (the *plugged* version, not this book), first check Yahoo!'s extremely helpful list of Frequently Asked Questions (FAQs) at http://www.yahoo.com/docs/info/faq.html. If your problem isn't addressed in that document, click on the "Write Us" button in Yahoo! and follow the instructions to narrow down what you should send and where to send it.

To submit corrections or comments about this book, send e-mail to online@idgbooks.com.

For questions or feedback regarding the IDG Books Home Page on the Web, send e-mail to webmaster@idgbooks.com.

For questions or concerns regarding the Quarterdeck Mosaic software, please see the section in the back of this book called Passport to Quarterdeck Technical Support to find out whom to contact. In many cases, the best thing to do is to send e-mail describing in detail the problems you are having to support@qdeck.com. Then be patient! Don't send multiple e-mails.

For questions or problems with anything else on the CD-ROM *except* the Quarterdeck software, call IDG Books customer service at 1-800-434-3422.

If you just love the U.S. Postal Service and want to give them something to do, send correspondence regarding this book to:

Yahoo! Unplugged
Online Press
IDG Books Worldwide
919 East Hillsdale Blvd.
Suite 400
Foster City, CA 94404

The Story of Yahoo!

Graduate school is a strange time. As such, it induces strange psychological states. One of them is the manic desire to do practically anything rather than write up a doctoral dissertation once coursework and research are finished. Faced with the prospect of showing up every day at a small desk and laboriously manufacturing a lengthy document with hundreds of footnotes, the human spirit seems to gravitate toward other distractions. Graduate students find an amazing variety of ways to pass the time while they avoid getting on with the Final Task.

In 1994, David Filo and Jerry Yang were graduate students in electrical engineering at Stanford University, living in a world of irregular schedules, odd diet, and distinctly informal attire. By late 1994, they were both about six months away from finishing their dissertations and collecting Ph.D.s in computer-assisted integrated-circuit design. Six months away from a degree is, in fact, the dangerous time described above. Uh-oh.

To their credit, and unlike generations of students before them, David and Jerry avoided the obvious and classic time-wasters. They did not engage in countless Frisbee contests, hone their rock-climbing skills on the rocky edifices of the Stanford campus, start a home-brew club, or attend horror-film marathons. Instead, they became interested in the World Wide Web, just as it was becoming the world's deepest electronic bottomless pit.

Our heroes, David Filo (right) and Jerry Yang.

The Early Days of the Web

In 1992, you could have kept a list of all World Wide Web sites on a neatly printed card in your shirt pocket, using just one side of the card. For quite a long time after its debut in 1990, the Web had stabilized at approximately 12 sites worldwide, nearly all of them at research or educational institutions.

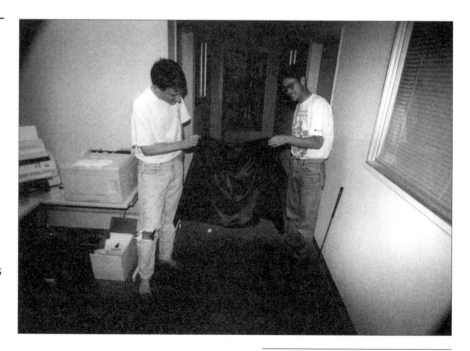

Will our heroes "go corporate"? Not a chance.

Then in 1993, the Web began its relentless expansion into the real world. Software for marking up Web pages began making its way into more institutions; more places had Internet-connected graphic terminals so that Web sites could feature pictures as well as text; the Web browser Mosaic started appearing everywhere; and individuals — not just institutions — began putting up informative, interesting, and just plain silly things on the Web. (Note: The Internet and the World Wide Web are discussed in more detail in the next two chapters.)

Enter David and Jerry.

If soon-to-be-Drs. Filo and Yang had just kept a list of 20 or 100 or even a few hundred Web sites as a hobby, they would have just now been released from educational servitude in the trailer that served as their offices, and

> **In 1992, you could have kept a list of all World Wide Web sites on a neatly printed card in your shirt pocket, using just one side of the card.**

This humble site housed the workstations that ran David and Jerry's early Web index.

would probably be chip designers somewhere in Silicon Valley.

What happened instead was that the boys went completely over the top with this Web business. They started putting in 20 — sometimes 40 — hours a week collecting and classifying Web sites. Thesis productivity languished. But their site at Stanford, which they called Yahoo!, just kept growing. (Depending on whom you ask, Yahoo! either stands for Yet Another Hierarchical Officious Oracle or reflects the fact that its creators consider themselves to be a couple of yahoos.)

They developed their own software to help them locate, identify, and index sites, and continued to spend hour after hour amassing information. The Yahoo! directory resided on Jerry's student workstation, dubbed *akebono* (after the legendary Hawaiian Sumo wrestler), and the Web-searching software was located on David's workstation, *konishiki* (named after another Sumo wrestling giant — come to think of it, they're all giants).

Sumo!

The starting point of Yahoo! was a Sumo-wrestling page created by Jerry Yang. This page illustrates one of the great features of the World Wide Web: If you're the only person in, say, Mitchell, South Dakota who is interested in Sumo wrestling, you can have access to all the latest Sumo news anyway, just as if you were in Los Angeles or Tokyo.

As an almost-forgotten bit of Yahoo! heritage, from way back in early 1995, here's a look at Jerry's Sumo page:

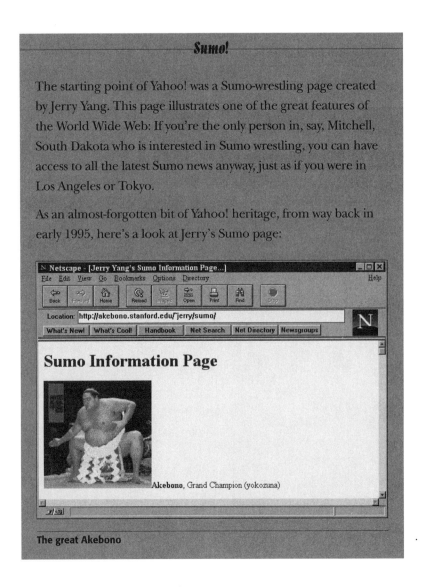

The great Akebono

Jerry's mom, as well as assorted academics at Stanford, failed to see how all this Web activity was connected to producing acceptable electrical-engineering Ph.D. dissertations. (Picture yourself explaining to your graduate advisor why you have indexed a site that periodically updates a video image of a coffee pot, and you'll see the considerable courage the original Yahoo! operation required.) To give these skeptics some credit, there *was* no connection between surfing the Web and graduating. But as you will soon see for yourself when you start using Yahoo!, the Web is simply more interesting than practically anything else — at least, anything else you can do with a computer.

As humorist Robert Benchley once said, "Anyone can do any amount of work, provided it isn't the work he's supposed to be doing at that moment." Looking back at what they actually had been doing for a year instead of what they were supposed to be doing, David and Jerry found that they had assembled the hottest index on the Web, and that index was being accessed by thousands of people a day.

> *To give these skeptics some credit, there was no connection between surfing the Web and graduating.*

Out of the Trailer . . .

Now, consider their situation. Having constructed an extremely popular Web index site, David and Jerry had something that could potentially turn into a viable business. After all, for all practical purposes, it was already a full-time job for both of them. Part of their success was due to the intensity with which they tracked down Web pages, and part of it was due to their timing. Two years earlier, nobody needed a Web index; two years later, someone else would have been forced to make some sort of comparable index. (Although it must be stated here that any other index almost certainly would have lacked the indefinable quality of *cool* that has made Yahoo! a hit.)

But the time was right, and the service exploded to the point where serious hardware limitations started to emerge. Just as our heroes were starting to confront problems in managing both the size of Yahoo! index files and the port-choking flood of daily access, they got an e-mail message from Marc Andreessen at Netscape Communications Corporation.

Marc was probably the one person in the world who could appreciate their situation *exactly*. As a student at the University of Illinois, Marc had written the now-famous Web browser called Mosaic. The success of Mosaic led eventually to the formation of Netscape Communications. As a result of the experience, Marc knew a lot about taking a project from small university beginnings to an independent commercial enterprise.

Marc offered David and Jerry the computing facilities they needed to keep Yahoo! growing. At 10,000–15,000 hits per day, fast PCs could keep up with the traffic. (Hits refer to individual accesses by folks on the Web.) As of summer 1995, Yahoo! gets about 7,000,000 hits per day, which calls for another level of hardware entirely. Thus the current Yahoo! site consists of ten workstations located at Yahoo!'s offices.

At nearly the same time, Randy Adams, president of the Internet Shopping Network, called Mr. Filo and Mr. Yang and introduced them to Sequoia Capital, a company that has helped launch new high-tech enterprises since the dawn of the PC age. A service that was seen by millions of people every day had the potential of generating some advertising revenue, and in the spring of 1995 Sequoia financed Yahoo! as a commercial operation.

David and Jerry moved off campus to an unassuming building in an industrial park in Mountain View, California, and became *yahoo.com* on the Internet, instead of being part of *stanford.edu*. They hired an energetic staff with a median age of about 25. Now, between the efforts of the human staffers and a tireless band of automated search robots, hundreds of sites are added to the Yahoo! index every week — sometimes as many as 1000 sites are added in a single day.

The humans behind the Yahoo! index. These tireless staffers work day and night to keep the Yahoo! directory up and running and up to date.

. . . and into the World

We're talking here about an enterprise that started out in a trailer, which a year later became a full-tilt, venture capital-funded business a sign on the office door with and a refrigerator full of sodas. Does all this profession-alism mean that future versions of Yahoo! won't be as cool? Will the next edition of this book show photos of David and Jerry in suits? Don't bet on it.

Despite their headlong leap from academia to Corporate America, David and Jerry are still intent on main-taining the Yahoo!-ness of Yahoo!. The two have a simple and elegant way of telling what would be acceptable to you, the Yahoo! user: "If we don't like it, we figure you won't like it." Remember: They created the Web index more or less for their own amusement, and they know what they like.

"If we don't like it, we figure you won't like it."

David and Jerry seem to be taking their success in stride. "I think being a core part of a business that affects many people is different and takes some getting used to, but I am surprised at how little has changed in my life," says Jerry. "I think Dave and I are still the same old guys who dress badly and drive beat-up cars."

Naughty Bits

A nonnegligible fraction of Internet bandwidth is devoted to transmitting pornographic pictures, probably because the demographic profile of the typical Internet user a few years ago was a 25-year-old male.

Contrary to popular belief, these naughty pictures are not necessarily easy to find. Most of the legislators currently calling for Internet censorship to protect children wouldn't be able to set up a connection and download anything themselves, for example. In fact, they have admitted as much and explained that they had to hire outside Internet consultants to help them locate offensive pictures online. Bottom line: Kids are probably more likely to come across strange pictures in their older brother's sock drawer than on the Web.

And you can't find any of that stuff on Yahoo!. As a service, it's not practicing censorship. It just turns out that when porno sites were indexed on Yahoo! in the early days, the access demand for those sites would go through the roof, servers would crash from the strain, and the sites would have to be removed from the index. So, as far as Yahoo! is concerned, porno sites fall into the category "more trouble than they're worth" rather than "too hot to handle."

If the World Wide Web can grow in five years from a dozen sites to a global labyrinth of millions of sites, who knows what it will be like in another five years? Five years is pretty much a geological era in the world of computers. In the meantime, Yahoo! has already done a pretty good job of taming the Web, and you can rest assured that David and Jerry and staff will do their best to keep up with whatever twists and turns the Web may take in the coming years.

Whither Yahoo!? Whither the Web?

The next two chapters deal with the history of the Internet and the World Wide Web. After that, you'll learn how to use Yahoo! to search for information. Whether you're a serious researcher or a casual browser, you've come to the right place.

Introduction to the Internet

The Internet has expanded so fast that it may be difficult for newcomers to figure out how any of it got here in the first place. Our tale begins with a branch of the U.S. government. Of course, these days it's fashionable to regard almost any government program as a form of waste. Although people are familiar with such space program spin-off products as Tang and Teflon, it seems likely that those admirable products *could* have been developed by cheaper means than a full-blown rocket fleet with manned space flights.

Sometimes, though, research—even military research—pays off with amazing benefits to civilian life. The Internet is a prime example. It will be the biggest force in world business by the year 2000, and yet the whole network infrastructure was put in place by government-funded researchers who never once gave a thought to commerce.

Who Operates the Internet?

Way back when, in the coldest days of the Cold War, when American military planners felt that they had just escaped a close call, the need for a bomb-proof communications system became apparent. Would it be possible to maintain some form of national communications system if New York, Washington, D.C., and most other major cities were nuked into oblivion? It would be difficult to tell which phone exchanges worked, radio communications wouldn't work at all in a highly ionized atmosphere, and mail delivery might even be two or three days slower.

Dr. Strangelove's network

The Department of Defense asked the Rand Corporation and others to make a study of the communications problem. After some consideration, they came up with an ingenious solution. If you had teletype machines (remember, this was the mid-1960s) and connected them to computers, you could then link the computers together over a private dial-up network.

In such a system, if you were trying to send a message from computer A to computer B, you could have computer A use a list of all computers it could reach directly and then give all those computers lists of their own, and if there were a network path from A to B, the computers could find it for themselves (see Figure A). Whole sections of the two coasts and the Midwest could be bombed out, but the network designers could guarantee with nearly 100 percent certainty that a teletype message could still get through.

So, in the beginning, the Army operated the Internet, more or less. The details were contracted out to defense think tanks and a handful of universities, but it was really an emergency military communications system. This bit of heritage comes in handy even now, in that big chunks of the Net can "go down" without disrupting message flow very much. The next Internet operator was the Department of Defense's Advanced Research Project Agency (ARPA); the whole operation was called ARPANET.

Dr. Wizard's network

A funny thing happened to the ARPANET. ARPANET-connected computers were installed at every university in the United States that had defense-related funding, which pretty much meant every university with a national reputation. As ARPANET grew, more and more of its actual usage was

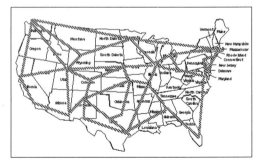

Figure A: An "unbombable" network.

devoted to scientific information exchange, and eventually administration of the whole show was turned over to the National Science Foundation (NSF).

By the early 1980s, most graduate students in computer science were attending schools with departmental Internet connections. Although the hardware that served as terminals was pretty wretched (there aren't going to be point-and-click graphic interfaces for teletypes — ever), students began quietly programming their own Internet software.

You may have concluded from the preceding chapter that graduate students in engineering and the sciences have a lot of spare time for programming. Actually, they're a pretty harassed bunch of characters, but some of them are as smart as it gets, and they can write a useful program in a weekend. Consider this: In the first days of the Internet explosion, practically every piece of useful Internet software, from programs for searching to file transfer to e-mail, was written by graduate students and distributed free or as shareware. As you'll recall, even Yahoo! started as an after-hours school project. This is *not,* to press the point, how word processors or spreadsheets have been developed, and to this day the values of freedom and sharing give the Internet some of its unique flavor.

The Net goes commercial

When scientific information became the main traffic on the Net, ARPA turned the system over to the NSF. Then, years later, when businesses began filling up Internet bandwidth, the NSF decided it was time to move along and find another administrative scheme. In the spring of 1995, the NSF quietly slipped out of the Internet business. An organization called Merit Network Inc. is managing the transition that assigns responsibility for different parts of the old NSFNET backbone (the computers plus the interconnection network) to a consortium of private firms.

AT&T is a major player in the transition of the Net from research to commercial use, as are the regional Bell operating companies. Internet service providers such as NETCOM and nonprofit services such as the Internet Society also participate in decision-making in the new, decentralized Net. So, finally, after all that preamble, the answer to the question, "Who operates the Internet?" is this: nobody. The most important communications system in the world just manages itself, as originally envisioned, as a set of computers that have each other's network addresses. It's hard to believe, but it's true: There really is no single, overall authority over the Internet. But it seems to be doing just fine so far.

There really is no single, overall authority over the Internet.

What about the Web?

The World Wide Web has helped put the Internet on the map for common folks. Those who never bothered to learn UNIX programming commands can now cruise the Net with the best of them, accessing information from all over the globe. The Web is discussed in the following chapter. For now, all you have to know is that a person, organization, or business can place information on a *page* or *site,* which can include text, graphics, and sound. A page can have *links* to other pages. Select a link, and you're whisked to another page, which can be anywhere in the world.

What Can You Do with the Internet?

You can do almost anything with the Internet, as long as it concerns information. That's why, in a burst of enthusiasm about information technology fueled more by love of futurism than detailed social planning, the Speaker of the U.S. House of Representatives recently advocated a program for giving laptops with modems to homeless people. Although there probably are a few other services more urgently needed than modems (some form of housing with RJ-11 jacks might help), it's true that people without Internet access are rapidly becoming marginalized, in the workplace and in many kinds of public discourse.

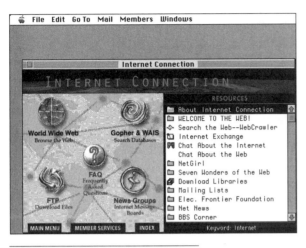

Figure B: Typical online-service Internet functions.

A simple way to show what you can do with the Internet is to display America Online's Internet-connection setup (see Figure B), in which separate functions have their own somewhat Star-Trekkie symbols.

The Internet provides four basic functions: e-mail, Usenet newsgroups, FTP, and Gopher. AOL is as good an example of those basic functions as any other service.

Here's a quick rundown on the Big Four. First we'll look at the tools, and then you'll see what you can do with them.

E-mail

Just about everyone on the Internet has an address to which you can send text files online. With a little finagling, you can also send formatted files (word-processor documents, for example), pictures, and sounds via e-mail. But although the situation is improving, you *may* run into problems sending files other than text from one Internet address to another.

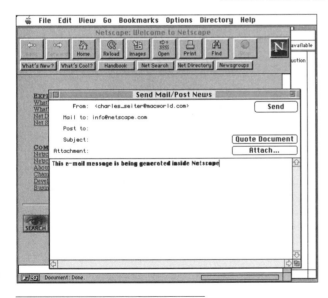

Figure C: An e-mail address inside a Web page.

From Yahoo!'s perspective, most of your e-mail use will involve built-in e-mail addressing in Web pages. Most Web pages include a link to the page author's e-mail address (see Figure C); just click on the address, and then compose and send your message. The recipient will automatically get your return e-mail address in the message.

Usenet newsgroups

If that were the whole story on e-mail, it would be exactly as exciting as a high-speed version of the U.S. Postal Service (well OK, a high-speed post office would be mildly exciting, but it would still be mostly business). What makes e-mail fun is that it can be used to construct two other services: *list servers* and *newsgroups.*

With outgoing e-mail, people can make list servers, which send messages to everyone on a list of interested parties. With incoming e-mail, people can establish *Usenet newsgroups*, where people with mutual interests contribute items to a "bulletin board," which can then be read by other newsgroup members. Before the World Wide Web became so popular, newsgroups were the principal source of hilarity on the Net. In the notorious *alt* (alternative) newsgroups, not much of the content has to do with *news,* per se. The *alt* groups include everything anyone has ever been interested in, from *alt.sex* to *alt.spam.*

FTP

Everything you put on your computer is a file of some sort. Files are also all over the Internet. You can go online and collect pictures, shareware business programs, book-length documents, games, and much, much more.

In the bad old days (which ended approximately a few months ago), getting files from a remote computer to your computer required you to learn and use a special FTP (file transfer protocol) program, which had its own rules and commands. But now, in the modern, streamlined approach to file transfer over the World Wide Web, you count on internal procedures in the design of the Web itself to accomplish a transfer. As you can see in Figure D, a Yahoo! search may lead you to pages with FTP links. Click on the link, and you'll get the file.

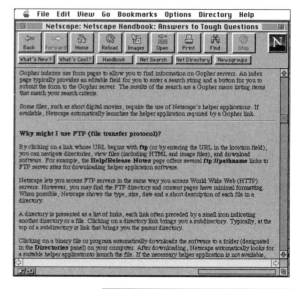

Figure D: The new look of FTP.

Gopher

The Internet used to be very texty. Even so, you could use a special progam called Gopher to browse collections of files, most of which were located at universities, and Gopher would organize everything it found into menus. Select a menu item, and you get another menu. The program is called Gopher not just for the little pun on the idea of a "go-fer" (it goes fer your files) but because the original program was written at the University of Minnesota, home of the fabulous Golden Gophers.

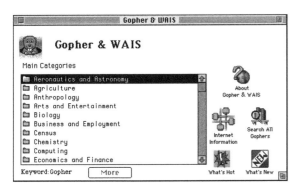

Figure E: A new look for Gopher.

In a conventional Gopher, you're connected to a big hard drive at some remote site and are simply looking at a list of its contents. But Gophers represent a conceptual step up from FTP programs, because they incorporate searching *and* file transfer. Gopher is sort of a poor man's Web.

There's not much programming involved in replacing this relatively spartan interface with a Web page (nowhere near as much programming as it took to design the Gopher system in the first place). Thus, when you use Yahoo! to find a Gopher site, you can start with a relatively self-explanatory screen in a familiar environment (see Figure E).

These days, of course, the World Wide Web incorporates many of the Internet services just described and makes them easier to use besides. Yahoo! includes file-searching capabilities (more on searching the Web in the chapter Surfing and Searching) and e-mail can be added to Web pages themselves.

Yes, but what can you actually do?

Here's a short rundown on just a handful of things you can do with the Internet features just described.

- **Make yourself famous to a specific list of people.** If you're a college student majoring in chemistry, you can join a few interesting chemistry newsgroups, make a few months' worth of intelligent comments as a newsgroup participant, and you may then find that when you apply to graduate school the professors screening your application already know who you are — a tremendous advantage.

- **Find out everything you want to know about Orson Welles.** That is just one example; you can get a huge quantity of details about practically any person whose name has ever been known, even to specialists in tiny, obscure fields. You can find the names of all the Munchkins who appeared in the *Wizard of Oz.* You can find out the name of the make up people in the original *Star Trek* TV series. You can look up your own ancestors. You get the idea.

- **Become an online consultant.** Start a small computer-consulting business, get it indexed in the Business section of Yahoo!, and start taking in consulting assignments from anywhere in the country. You may find that it's cheaper to advertise on the Web than in your local Yellow Pages, and the people who access your Web site are essentially prequalified as being interested in computing.

- **Find those elusive front headlights for a 1959 Austin-Healey "bug-eye" Sprite.** And you can do this from your desk in Waterloo, Iowa, where most 35-year-old British sports cars have long since rusted into oblivion. The parts dealer in Phoenix will be delighted to hear from you.

- **Find a job.** At this point, a large percentage of jobs posted on the Internet are computer related, but you must have some interest in computers if you're reading this book, so you may qualify.

- **Work hard and/or goof off.** Shove your career into high gear, wheeling and dealing like a demented yuppie full of Starbuck's coffee. Or waste 24 hours a day surfing around to "goof" sites, which are present in glorious abundance. (The Entertainment chapter of this book lists many such sites, but you can find them in just about every category.)

Internet Statistics

Take a look at the graph in Figure F. Businesspeople love to look at graphs like this and *extrapolate*, which means to expect that things will keep going the way they have been going. In the case of the Internet, that is not what is going to happen.

The situation looks like explosive growth, but in this case there is a definite limit on the horizon. Here are the four stages of Internet growth, with an educated guess as to what will happen in the next few years.

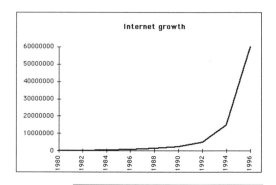

Figure F: Internet growth in number of users from prehistory to late 1994.

1982 to 1992

In the first part of the curve, almost nobody outside of a few hundred thousand UNIX jockeys at universities around the world even knew that the Internet existed. Things *were* growing, but slowly.

1992 to 1994

Newspaper articles start to appear that suggest that you are a hopeless loser and way behind the times if you don't know about this amazing new thing called the Internet. Pioneers cobble together do-it-yourself Internet connections, driving the population on the Net into the millions.

1995 to 1999

Major national online services in the United States and elsewhere begin to offer real Internet connections rather than just e-mail. The Net population soars into the tens of millions. Old-timers complain about the barbarian invasion of newcomers putting up home pages about their pets.

Around the year 2000, the growth curve of the Net starts to match the number of computers worldwide.

2000 and beyond

Around the year 2000, the growth curve of the Net starts to match the number of computers worldwide. In other words, it won't be possible to buy a PC that doesn't have some kind of Internet-connection hardware and software included. The Net is still growing, but the curve doesn't look like the straight-up rocket trajectory of the late 1990s. It looks like the numbers for worldwide sales of personal computers.

Privatizing the Internet

Earlier in this chapter, you read about how the U.S. government slipped out of its original role as the funding source for the Internet. In most places, this is going to mean that businesses are going to be operating the Internet network backbone.

Businesses are already influencing the look and feel of the Internet by dominating the content of the World Wide Web. The first commercial sites appeared on the Web around 1994. In August 1995, the number of Internet sites with the zone identifier *.com* (commercial) passed the 75,000 mark. Compare that to the 1,000 or so *.edu* (education) sites, which used to be the main inhabitants of the Internet. And because business means advertising, many of these businesses have sites full of graphics designed by advertising agencies.

It's not just that businesses now outnumber every other type of organization on the Internet by a huge margin, either — the gap itself is growing. Business presence on the Internet, and therefore on the World Wide Web, is growing at the rate of *12 percent a month*. That means the number of businesses on the Internet is doubling every six months or so, or increasing by a factor of 4 every year, or factor of 16 every two years.

If you look in the Yellow Pages of a big-city phone book and count the number of businesses (*.com*) and compare it to the number of educational institutions (*.edu*), military facilities (*.mil*), government agencies (*.gov*), nonprofit organizations (*.org*), and computer networks of various kinds (*.net*), you will see at once that businesses make up more than 95 percent of the listings. That's exactly where the Internet is headed.

The Net may have been started by a group of people involved with *.mil* and *.edu* places, but it's going to be a statistical representation of society at large by mid-1996, and that means *.com* places. Calvin Coolidge once remarked that "The business of America is business," and with the demise of the state-directed economies of Eastern Europe and elsewhere, that's becoming true of the whole world as well.

Yahoo!

The International Internet

The Internet is necessarily a study in extreme cosmopolitanism; anyone with a phone line, a computer, and a reasonably accommodating national telecommunications system is the equal of any other Net citizen, both as a Net user and an information provider. Political, military, and economic factors still determine which nations are world powers in the real world, but on the Net countries such as Finland and Norway are as important in most respects as countries many times larger. And Finland and Norway are *more* important on the Net than big countries that still exercise tight political control and suffer from telecomm paranoia.

Right now, Asian countries are a big presence on the Net. The Asian economy currently is dominated by Japan and smaller countries sometimes called the *tigers:* Taiwan, Singapore, Korea, and Malaysia are examples of tigers. More tigers are joining the action every year, and the big economic dragon of mainland China is not just

The smaller, high-tech Asian economies are among the most wired in the world.

waking up but is taking amphetamines. The smaller, high-tech Asian economies are among the most wired in the world. Singapore and Taiwan in particular were getting online to the max while many American companies were still trying to decide whether this Internet thing was a fad.

Yahoo!'s Business section will rapidly lead you out of the country, and you could find yourself checking out not just the splendors of duty-free shopping (see Figure G) but serious business as well (Figure H). Some of the material available in the Asia Trade site is an indication of the way business will be conducted in the year 2000. There are plastics parts manufacturers with sites on that page which promise to turn around sample parts via Federal Express within a few days of receiving an AutoCAD file for the parts e-mailed via their Web page. Manufacturing — not just of plastic parts but of everything from televisions to water pumps — will soon be so efficiently organized that traditional methods of doing business will, in some industries, disappear overnight.

Figure G: Cruise into this pricey boutique in Singapore and order anything you like.

Fast-moving small countries aren't found only in Asia, either. The Netherlands, for example, put a map of the whole country on the Web, complete with hypertext links at every point on the map — and it did this when the entire Web consisted of only a few hundred sites. The map is still there, but the number of sites in the Netherlands has grown so rapidly that it's easier to see what's available in Holland's own Yahoo!-style index, which offers information in several languages. The Dutch have been open for business since the late Middle Ages, they went all over the globe looking for trade in the 1500s, and they're ready to roll right now as Internet pioneers.

Faster, Better, Smaller, Cheaper

Until recently, all that was needed to make the Internet the main means of information exchange were fast-enough input/output speeds for computers connected through modems or other special hardware. In 1992, the computers were already fast enough to work miracles, but the transfer speed was lagging behind. It was still considered perfectly respectable, for example, for Jane Q. Public to have a 2400 bps modem, which might fairly be described as close to useless for download-ing still pictures, much less video images.

Figure H: The Asia Trade home page, a model business site of the future, except that it's already here.

In a few short years, modems went from 2400 bps to 9600 bps to 14.4 Kbps (kilobits per second) to 28.8 Kbps as a standard. That's a factor of ten in access-speed improvement for the average user. National online services such as America Online and Prodigy offer 28.8K-modem access in most big cities, and will have

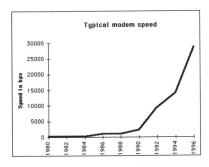

Figure I: History of modem speeds (does this curve remind you of another you've seen recently?).

service at that speed in smaller towns within a year. Internet connection at 56.6 Kbps is becoming commonplace among business users, and that's just the beginning (see Figure I).

ISDN (Integrated Services Digital Network), a method of data transmission that requires special hardware costing quite a bit more than a modem, gives you speed around 150 Kbps for data transfer. That's not bad; it's about the speed of an early floppy disk drive. But telephone companies have not yet set the price of ISDN connection over their lines to prices that are likely to attract anyone but hard-core Internet hipsters. You can get ISDN in most U.S. cities right now, but it will produce fairly hefty monthly connect-time bills, not to mention the also-hefty setup charges.

But there are plenty of clever people out there who foresee large profits in faster Internet connection. In mid-1995, a division of AT&T called Paradyne Corporation announced a chip set called GlobeSpan that can support downloads at 6.312 Mbps (megabits per second) over standard copper phone lines. You don't need coaxial cabling, you don't need as much hardware as for ISDN, and regional Bell operating companies are already planning implementation of GlobeSpan equipment in their switching branches.

The new modems based on this chip set will use asymmetric digital subscriber lines (ASDL) into the phone company centers, but these will be implemented at the phone company end of the scheme and won't require modification of your home telephone wiring. (The scheme is asymmetrical in that you can perform downloads at a high speed and uploads at a slower — but still impressive — 64 Kbps.)

Perhaps the GlobeSpan chip set will dominate, or perhaps its competitors will. But because of the recent explosion of interest in the Internet, the fact that a well-designed compression and coding scheme *can* get you megabits-per-second transmission rates over standard phone lines means that this *is* going to be done, and soon. And when it is done, there will be strong economic pressures to use the Internet as the principal distribution mode for any sort of information of commercial value.

At 6 Mbps, IDG Books could sell you this book online, as several modules with a custom search engine and automatic updates, and you could have it in a matter of minutes. If you had a connection to the Internet that didn't charge hourly fees, you could download live video at these data rates and watch a TV show right on your computer screen (GlobeSpan was originally designed for exactly that purpose). Given the rapidly rising cost of a college education, it's reasonable to expect that any computer-related portions of that education could be conducted mostly over the Internet (publishers are busily designing Web-page textbooks even now).

And although some of the growth of commerce on the Internet has been slowed by problems relating to the transmission speed of graphics, higher-speed communication makes everything different. You can have not just catalogs but videos demonstrating products; not just software to order but a chance to try it out online; not just pictures of resorts but travel videos. Inevitably, some clever marketer is likely to start offering substantial discounts for merchandise ordered over the Internet, and *then* watch the fun. Once your Internet connection has nearly the same communications bandwidth as your television set, it's a whole new world.

Introduction to the World Wide Web

Unless you have embarked upon a life of tranquil meditation beside remote mountain streams, you've heard of the World Wide Web, increasingly called just the Web. Come to think of it, the fact that you're reading this book probably means that you've opted out of the tranquil meditation scene and jumped into the Web with both feet, yelling "Yahoo!"

Unlike the first versions of Internet software, which were really just e-mail and file-search-and-transfer programs, Web software is distinguished by two simple but powerful features:

- The Web lets you jump from one place to another on the Internet with a clear picture of where you're going.

- The Web is basically the illustrated version of the Internet, in which you can see pictures immediately rather than downloading them and viewing them later.

Before we plunge into the ins and outs of Web navigation, it's worth it to look into the Web's history. The history of the Web makes a strong case for the support of basic research, because what started out as a literature-exchange system for physicists is turning into the big news of the decade for communication and business.

Why the Web? A Short Story

Well, it's a *pretty* short story, but we have to break it into two parts to provide dramatic emphasis.

Ground zero

You may not have given the matter much thought, but all sciences are not created equal, and that fact has some interesting consequences. If you come to the United States and get a Ph.D. in chemistry, you can go back home to Singapore and get a job as a chemist. That's because you can do professional, internationally accepted research in chemistry with quite modest equipment that barely fills a single room.

In contrast, high-energy physics requires facilities that are beyond the budget of most countries. Seven or eight really important centers for high-energy physics research exist in the world, from Argonne National Laboratories in the U.S. to the European Center for Nuclear Research (CERN) in Switzerland. If you are a research physicist but don't have access to one of these centers, you're just not in the game.

Therefore, a degree in high-energy or particle physics qualifies you to be a kind of scientific gypsy, traveling from one of the big research centers to another in search of a permanent home. And that's how the foundations for the World Wide Web came to be developed by Dr. Tim Berners-Lee, an Englishman living in Switzerland and working at CERN.

Around 1989, practically the Pleistocene Epoch in Internet history, Dr. Berners-Lee wrote a modest computer program for his own use in research. It was basically a notepad program with the interesting wrinkle that individual pages of notes were linked by keywords. You could call up a page about a scientific conference, for example, and click on the title of a particular lecture, and the program would then call up an abstract of the lecture. The abstract itself might contain other links to articles or reference tables.

Dr. Berners-Lee's supervisors thought it would be interesting to develop this idea into a general-purpose way of exchanging information among the far-flung physics labs around the globe. If you could dial up a central computer, and if you had one starting-point page with an index, it would be possible to access all the latest in physics research from anywhere (assuming that some laudable soul had done all the heavy lifting involved in setting up the information and establishing the links). A group at CERN did just that, and in 1991 the first World Wide Web site was set up as a service to the world's physicists.

Along the way, Dr. Berners-Lee modified a document-formatting language called SGML (Standard Generalized Markup Language), which is an established publishing format for book-length documents. In this new version of SGML, he created a formatting language that supported hypertext links *as well as* marking up plain text to indicate headings, subheadings, lists, and so on, and called it HTML (Hypertext Markup Language). HTML is still the underlying language of the World Wide Web. Dr. Berners-Lee is now at M.I.T., overseeing a study group that's trying to define standards for the future of the Web.

Down on the farm

The first version of the Web was essentially a text-based affair, with hypertext links scattered throughout long passages of scientific literature. Physicists are generally quite serious people, so the physics community was unlikely to clamor for color graphics and animation. But on the other side of the world from CERN, in the cornfields of downstate Illinois at the National Center for Supercomputing Applications at the University of Illinois, another lone ranger named Marc Andreessen decided to do something amazing.

The amazing thing he did was produce a program called NCSA Mosaic — available in three flavors: UNIX, Macintosh, and Windows — and then *give it away!* It is important to realize that this one act, giving away copies of Mosaic, more than any other, put the Web at the center of Internet computing.

Mosaic is a *Web browser,* a program that enables you to get around on the World Wide Web. The program has an interface that's fun to use, that encourages the use of pictures, and that can be adapted to all styles of Internet access — from phone-line dialup to high-speed direct connection. In fact, when Mosaic was originally developed in 1992, it was running on an incredibly fast network that was connected to the world's biggest supercomputers. Hence, the programming efforts for subsequent offspring of Mosaic — such as Quarterdeck Mosaic (a copy of which you have on the CD-ROM in the back of this book), AIR Mosaic, Spry Mosaic, Spyglass Mosaic, and Andreessen's own Netscape Navigator — have focused on making a graphical Web browser work over the puny 14.4 Kbps modems most home users have. Compared to the original Mosaic software, running on some of the fastest hardware around, the new browsers are much, much more efficient, simply because they have to be.

Dr. Andreessen is now one of the principals of Netscape Communications, which in turn is the benevolent uncle of Yahoo! (see The Story of Yahoo! chapter).

@ Addresses vs. http:// Addresses

Before 1995, when you heard someone talk about an "Internet address," the person meant a designation such as

stephen@wri.com

or

topgun@miramarnas.mil

Note the @ symbol that separates the two parts of the address. The part before the @ symbol is the *username;* the part after it is called the *domain.* The last three letters of the domain name (*.gov, .mil, .com, .edu, .net,* and a few special others) specify the *zone* (government, military, commercial, educational, or network).

Since 1995, however, an Internet "address" on a business card is more and more likely to be a *Uniform Resource Locator* (URL), also known as an *http address. Http* stands for *hypertext transfer protocol,* which is the way Web documents are passed between computers.

The World Wide Web, amazing as it is, is actually just one type of Internet service. *FTP (file transfer protocol)*, is another service, and there are computers with addresses such as

ftp.mich.edu

that exist only to support file transfers.
When you look at a URL such as

http://www.yahoo.com/

you can decode it as follows:

- The *http* designation means that communications will employ hypertext transfer protocol, which means dealing with Web documents.

- The *www* designation points to the computer that's acting as a Web server.

- *yahoo.com* is the domain name, which specifies the particular company (in this case, Yahoo!) where the Web server is.

- The // (slashes), colon, and other odd punctuation you may encounter within a URL are telltale signs of the Internet's underlying UNIX structure.

There really isn't any particular mystery to Web addresses, except perhaps the mystery of the amount of redundant typing that's necessary (you can get *really* tired of entering the *http://www* part of Web addresses).

How the Web Works

HTML is actually a pretty straightforward affair. The Web browser software on your computer, such as Mosaic or Netscape, calls up the HTML document from the Web and interprets HTML *tags* embedded in the document. HTML documents are ordinary text files that have been marked up with these tags. The browser displays fonts, formatting, pictures, links, and all other aspects of the document according to how it interprets the document's tags.

The Web works the way it does for a couple of reasons. First, it means that the documents going over the wires are mostly text files, and error-checking protocols for text were perfected years ago. Second, text and text tags for formatting are very efficient (compare the tiny size of a formatted word-processor file to the multimegabyte-sized graphic image file of the same page). That makes the Web fast.

The world's smallest HTML example

Here's a little sample of HTML:

```
<HTML>

<HEAD>

<TITLE>cat page</TITLE>

</HEAD>

<BODY>

<BR>

<BR>

The Tale of the Cat<BR>

<BR>

This looks like a harmless illustration, but<BR>

<BR>

<H2>Beware!</H2>

<BR>

<BR>

<IMG SRC="cat_page1.gif"><BR>

The End.

</BODY>

</HTML>
```

Take a look at this simple example and you can see a bit of the machinery behind the World Wide Web (for a complete reference, check out *Creating Cool Web Pages with HTML* by Dave Taylor or *HTML For Dummies* by Ed Tittel and Steve James, both published in 1995 by IDG Books Worldwide).

- The tag <HTML> at the beginning of the document tells the Web browser that a standard-format Web document is coming (rather than, for example, an FTP transfer or Gopher menu).

- The tags <HEAD> and </HEAD> mark the beginning and end of the head part of the page, which usually contains little more than the title of the page. The title of this page is *cat page* and is embedded in the pair of tags <TITLE> and </TITLE>.

- <BODY> indicates the start of the main part of the page, the part you see on the screen.

-
, which you'll see a lot, indicates a line break.

- <H2> and </H2> indicates a level 2 heading, which the browser displays as larger, bolder text (probably).

- <IMG SRC> is an image tag and it points to an *image source,* a graphic file named *cat_page1.gif.* By changing your browser's settings, you can choose to view the images in Web pages, which is pretty, or to not view them, which is fast.

- </BODY> tells the browser that the end of the page has been reached.

The image tag demonstrates the key concept of the Web. It refers to another file, the graphic image file, which in this case is presumed to exist in the same subdirectory (or folder) as the original HTML document. If the file is located elsewhere, the Web-page designer must include a pathname so that the browser can find it. The image file doesn't *have* to reside on the same computer as the HTML document, just as long as there's a way of specifying its location — and with HTML, there almost always is.

And that brings up another kind of tag — an essential part of the Web — the link to another document, called an *anchor* or *hypertext reference.* As long as you can tell a browser to look up a file, there's no reason the file can't be another HTML document anywhere on the Web.

The tag pair <A> and </A> serves just that purpose. In the "cat" document, the following link would take you to the main page of Yahoo!:

<A HREF ="http://www.yahoo.com/">Yahoo!</A>

Web reality

In principle, all word processors could offer automatic translation of their documents into HTML. Most already are or will be offering such services soon. In principle, automatic translation is not a problem and should produce perfectly respectable Web pages. But in practice, most of the pages you see on the Web were laboriously and manually coded by people who know their way around HTML coding. Look at Figure A, for example.

Now look at the HTML coding that lurks behind Figure A. You can probably pick out many of the same elements that were used in the simple "cat" page example, except this more complex page underwent considerable fine-tuning by hand after it was translated to HTML.

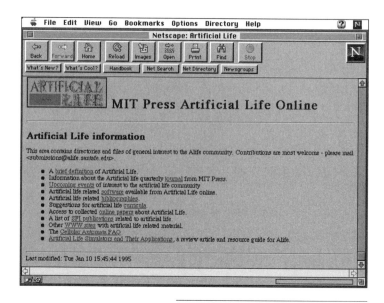

Figure A: The Artificial Life page from MIT Press.

<html> <head><title>Artificial Life</title></head>

<body>

<h1>

<a href="http://alife.santafe.edu/"><img src="../images/ALIcon.gif"></a>

MIT Press Artificial Life Online</h1> <hr>

<h2>Artificial Life information</h2>

This area contains directories and files of general interest to the Alife community. Contributions are most welcome - please mail <submissions@alife.santafe.edu>.<p><ul> <li> A

<a href="alife-def.html">brief definition</a> of Artificial Life.

<li> Information about the Artificial life quarterly

<a href="journal/">journal</a> from MIT Press. <li>

<a href="events/">Upcoming events</a> of interest to the artificial life community <li> Artificial life related

<a href="software/">software</a>

available from Artificial Life online. <li>

Artificial life related <a href="biblio.html">bibliographies</a>. <li> Suggestions for artificial life <a href="curricula/">curricula</a>. <li> Access to collected <a href="papers.html">online papers</a>

about Artificial Life. <li> A list of <a href="sfi-pub.txt">SFI publications</a> related to artificial life. <li> Other

<a href="../network/www.html">WWW sites</a> with artificial life related material. <li> The

<a href="topics/cas/ca-faq/ca-faq.html">Cellular Automata FAQ</a> <li>

<a href="/alife/topics/simulators/dret/dret.html">Artificial Life Simulators and Their Applications</a>, a review article and resource guide for Alife.</ul><hr><!– hhmts start –>Last modified: Tue Jan 10 15:45:44 1995<!– hhmts end –></body></html></html>

A Web browser takes the preceding marked-up text and displays Figure A.

E-mail Inside a Web Browser

Anyone with a choice in the matter (some people are, alas, still stuck with text-only Internet access) would find graphics-rich pages such as Figure B to be the preferred method of Internet information exchange. But other communications needs still have to be filled. Great e-mail programs are available for all platforms, and there are some lovely programs for managing newsgroup downloads, but it's a nuisance to keep switching from one program to the next.

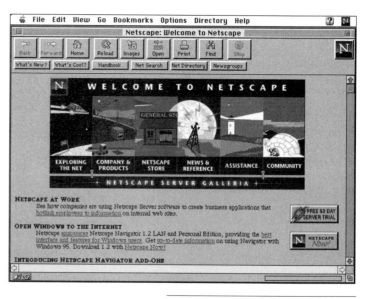

Figure B: Netscape Navigator, the most popular Web browser.

So the developers of Web browsers have been obliged to provide other services as part of their programs' built-in functionality. When you use Netscape Navigator, for example, you can use its Preferences setting to configure your mail server and ID. Then you can send e-mail from Netscape.

Similarly, as a closely related text-file handling operation, you can also select Usenet newgroups of interest and browse their contents directly from Netscape (see Figure C). Given that most people outside of universities pay for on-line time, such features save you money by allowing quicker access to these other services. Right now, Netscape is one step ahead of most other browsers at e-mail and Usenet news access, and the next revision of Netscape is likely to maintain this lead.

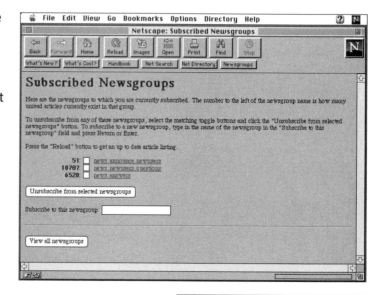

Figure C: Newsgroup access via Netscape Navigator.

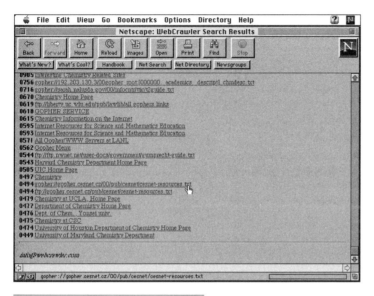

Figure D: Gopher city but still in Netscape; check out the URL at the bottom.

Web Searches vs. Gopher Searches

Yahoo! can pretty much point you anywhere on the Net where there is information to be found. That often means Web pages, but not always. Sometimes, especially when you're pursuing scholarly topics, you'll find that your travels lead you to Gopher sites. Gopher, as you may recall from the preceding chapter, is an Internet search utility created at the University of Minnesota. Before the advent of the World Wide Web, Gopher was the best browsing utility on the Net because it organizes everything into easily navigable menus.

Although people are busily converting their archives to Web format, often you'll come across a Web page that is just a list of Gopher sites (see Figure D). The good news is that you don't have to know how Gopher works. When you select a Gopher site, you'll see a menu screen that looks like a file or folder directory — click on folders to open them and you'll see the files they contain. Remember: When it's connecting to a site, your browser handles all the details.

One thing you should know is that, because they've been around longer, Gopher sites tend to be deeper than Web sites; typically you'll find hundreds of files at a Gopher site, but just a few Web pages at a Web site.

FTP and the Web

Besides Gopher and Usenet news, another link between the Web and older Internet services is FTP. FTP can be used as a URL. Just as the people who maintain Gopher servers are making http links to the archives at their sites, so too are the folks at FTP sites. Many of the best FTP file collections have put up index pages in Web-page format (see Figure E).

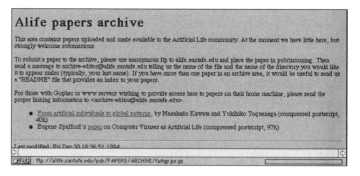

Figure E: An FTP file archive in Netscape Navigator.

So when you cruise around with Yahoo! and find a pointer to an FTP archive, you can confidently expect your browser to present the contents of that file collection in an accessible style. Sooner or later, the Web simply will have gobbled up these earlier kinds of services because, like the Blob, it can absorb anything. For another year or so, though, you'll find yourself taking side trips to FTP land. Don't be alarmed — if nothing else, FTP side trips will give you a glimpse of Net archaeology.

Now that you are familiar with the basics of the Internet and the World Wide Web, it's time to dive into Yahoo! and start exploring the vast territory of cyberspace. In the next chapter, you'll learn how to use Yahoo! as a starting point for finding information on just about any topic you can dream of.

Surfing and Searching

You can find lots of information on the Web just by clicking on hypertext links in Yahoo!, and there's nothing wrong with surfing around to get yourself oriented. If you want to find a lot of information in a hurry, however, you are going to need a strategy. That's what this chapter is about — finding all the available information on the Web about a specific topic as quickly as possible. Dozens of different techniques have been developed for searching, and you can save yourself lots of online time by checking out these techniques here in print before starting an online search.

A Few Precautions

Just a few short years ago, the Internet was entirely dominated by nonprofit organizations, with universities being the largest part of the mix. Now the Internet and Web are exploding with information from businesses and individuals.

If you stop for a minute and think about what these businesses and individuals have to communicate, you will see that the overall information content of the World Wide Web is going to be quite different from the content in traditional information providers such as libraries. In the reference part of a library, you see the accumulated effort of centuries of work, aimed at providing standard resource material that's been organized and screened by experts. On the Web, you see anything anybody cared to post. No guarantees are given that the Web material is correct, or even useful. Much of it is simply advertising, personal or corporate, and if you are over the age of six you probably have your own set of expectations about the accuracy of advertising.

Under most circumstances, a search that returns 50,000 hits is almost as useless as a search that turns up nothing at all.

Nonetheless, plenty of valid reference information resides on the Web, and Yahoo! represents the quickest path to most of it. In fact, there's so much information on the Net that the sheer scope of everything presents a problem in itself. For example, if you do a search of the whole Web on a single vague keyword, you're going to get pointed to zillions of documents. Under most circumstances, a search that returns 50,000 hits is almost as useless as a search that turns up nothing at all. So designing searches that return a *usable amount* of information is a big priority in Web searching. You may as well learn to search properly now, because the growth of the Web is only going to aggravate the 50,000-hit problem.

Yahoo!

First Steps in Yahoo!

It helps to think about numbers a bit before setting out on your search. Suppose that you are looking at a hierarchical set of choices such as Yahoo!'s. (Hierarchical just means that the choices are arranged in layers rather than presented all at once.) The first layer might contain fifteen choices, and when you pick one of those choices, the next layer might offer twenty choices, and then the third layer might give you a list of fifty choices. This example is in fact very close to the way Yahoo! is arranged. Looking at the numbers, when you pick something at the third level you have selected from 15,000 possibilities.

Choices = 15 x 20 x 50 = 15,000

If there's an option for a *fourth* layer of fifty choices after you pick something from layer three, then you have negotiated your way at level four through roughly 500,000 possibilities. One of the things that sets Yahoo! apart from other Web directory services is Yahoo!'s exceptionally well-thought-out set of choices at each level, which allows you to pick your way through the Web quickly and efficiently.

Missing a branch

What happens if you take a wrong turn at one of the forks in the search path? It means you probably won't find the information you wanted. And that's exactly why all Web browsers since the earliest days have included icons for both backward and forward navigation. You may have to back up a step or two steps or three steps, but backing up is not particularly time consuming. Usually, in fact, your Web browser will have stored most of the pages on the backward path temporarily on your system, so you can back out of a page a lot faster than you got there in the first place.

The other issue in what you might call a manual search — since you're pointing and clicking with your own hand on a mouse rather than asking a machine to do searching for you — is this:

You don't know what you want until you get there and you have it.

Very often, stuff that you turn up in the course of a search turns out to be more interesting than the topic you were investigating when you started! That's one of the great advantages of poking around a page at a time — the rate at which you see information is a rate at which you can actually evaluate it for yourself. You'll find that using keyword searches sometimes makes it *more* difficult to manage and evaluate information than does using manual searches. A search can turn up all sorts of irrelevant pages, and too many of them besides.

Man vs. machine

One of the reasons Yahoo! has been such a roaring success is that it's a friendly place to look around, leafing through Web pages at your own pace. Even so, Yahoo! also provides keyword searches with its own search form and leads you to other search engines available on the Net.

Some of these other search engines seem very impressive. There's a search facility called Savvy Search, for example, that activates a search across all popular search engines at the same time. One enterprising fellow has put together a Web page that contains links to all other search facilities. But there are some precautions to be taken with any of these.

Precaution 1: "I'd like to talk to Mr. Hernandez in Mexico City."

Um, which Mr. Hernandez was that exactly? If you don't specify your request fairly sharply, you'll get flooded with junk. Use your imagination: What do you think would happen if you were to search the Web on the keyword *computer*?

Precaution 2: "Did you mean & or * or /p?"

Some of the most efficient search engines have a language all their own for wildcards and linked keywords and other specialty tricks. The language is based on traditional search techniques in UNIX utilities, and, after all, UNIX is still the "operating system of the Internet" at most big sites. If you propose to do lots of searching, or set yourself up as a professional information agency, these are well worth learning. If you're only doing a few kinds of searches, or if you're in a hurry, learning special codes or the lingo of the *grep* (general regular expression parser) utility or the Perl programming language won't be worth the effort.

Precaution 3: "A blind Venetian isn't the same as a Venetian blind."

Search engines, interacting with the wild world of the Web, do odd things. A search for *Jefferson AND Adams* will not always return the same set of hits as a search for *Adams AND Jefferson.* Some search engines treat the first word in a set as more important than the other words. Nobody tells you they're doing this, but it explains why engines that give you a score for relevance are typically the engines with this symmetry problem. Yahoo!, by the way, is set up so that a keyword search gives the same result, no matter what the word order.

If you're going to use your search results for anything other than mere curiosity, it's a good idea to formulate your query more than one way. Most of the things you may have read in recent years about artificial intelligence in computer software don't seem to have drifted down yet to actual application in current Web search engines.

Online with Yahoo!

These humble precepts simply cry out for illustration in real-world examples. So, just to pick one example that you would imagine to be pathetically simple, try the case of finding a map of Washington, DC.

Searching with simple clicks

You sign on to Yahoo!, and the first thing you see will be a screen like that in Figure A. The people at Yahoo! do some minor tinkering from time to time, and the numbers in the categories will change, but this is the starting point for a topic search. In this example you are looking for that map of Washington, DC, so it's appropriate to scroll down the list and think a bit about where such a document might be found.

One of the items on the opening list, near the bottom, is called Regions. This sounds promising — after all, you're not going to find maps under Health, presumably. Click on Regional, and you see the screen in Figure B, offering an assortment of geographical choices. One of the things you might find, in poking around the regions of the world, is that there are a lot of well-organized, high-tech countries, such as the Netherlands or Taiwan, that have a big-time Web presence. On the Web in 1995, Singapore is a bigger country than mainland China, mainly because Singapore is "wired" as a matter of government policy.

Well, it's not really a state exactly, but you might well guess that Washington, DC will be filed under U.S. States. They have to put it somewhere, right? And although it may seem like a foreign country when you're lost there at night, it's more like a U.S. state than anything else. It's worth keeping in mind that the people making all the decisions for classification at Yahoo! are just like you, except perhaps that they get less sleep because they're always at work. But your guesses about the way Yahoo! has organized things will be right more often than not.

Click on U.S. States and see what happens. There it is, a page of state site listings, but also one for Washington, DC. The obvious choice now is to click on the DC site and see what happens. You guessed it: You get a whole raft of DC possibilities. The gang's all there, from the White House to the Smithsonian to dozens of places you may not know. But there's also a site called Area Map (Figure C).

Bingo!

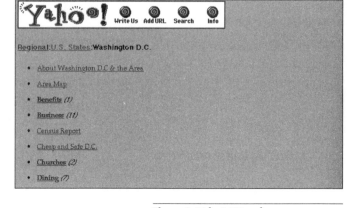

Figure A: Your basic Yahoo! starting point.

Figure B: Exploring the world's regions with Yahoo!.

Figure C: At last, DC and a map.

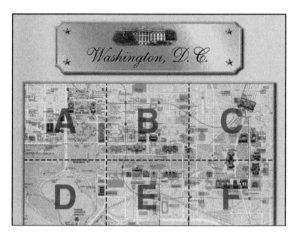

Figure D: An online junior-high field trip.

The map, as it happens, is a bit of a disappointment (Figure D). You can tell that it's Washington DC, but there are few PCs around that can display a map of Washington you could actually use if you were trying to negotiate America's Capital in a rent-a-car. The sheer dots-per-inch resolution and size of a $2.49 map from a gas station will put to shame the picture on a $2000 monitor. Also, a map of DC that would let you pick out 501 K Street easily would take an hour to download with a fast modem. This map, at any rate, lets you pick out individual big buildings.

Clicking on the NASA headquarters building gets you to another map (Figure 4-5), one more appropriate for the resolution available on today's Web. And all these sites on the map are clickable, leading you into the many mysteries of NASA and its current mission and perhaps pondering the need for the agency to have so many different sites.

Searching Yahoo! with keywords

Finding the map of DC took a little bit of intelligent decision-making on your part (you're obviously intelligent anyway, since you bought this book), plus a few clicks. But perhaps there's a faster way to find things — you might want to check out the standard Yahoo! search form (see Figure F). Later in this chapter there will be more discussion of the options built into this form, but for now why not just try to type *Washington DC map* into the space provided and see what the search engine finds.

So you type *Washington DC map,* click on the Search button, and then stand back and wait a few seconds for results. What happens?

At the time this was written, almost *nothing* happens. The search reports that it found no matches. Huh? What? How could it miss the Washington, DC map that you found just by clicking through a few lists?

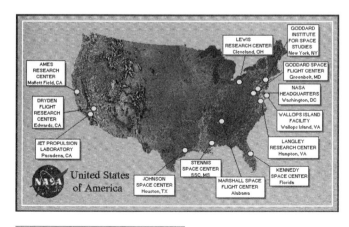

Figure E: Maps upon maps.

The answer is that the contents of all Web index sites are registered in a database which may or may not have the exact keyword you expect.

In the original version of Yahoo!, a keyword search looks at the URL, the title, and the comments on a Web page. If your keywords are buried somewhere in the text contents of the page, the search doesn't find them. Right now there's a plan to index all the text in the Web pages covered by Yahoo! Other services (Lycos is one example) use a program that indexes everything on a page. As you will see when we tackle a few examples, there are times when you may want as much data as you get from an indexed-everything search, and there are times when you'd rather have less.

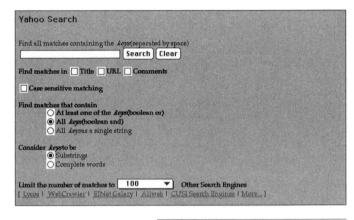

Figure F: Starting the search.

Instant Term Paper

To see Web searching in action, it helps to have a topic in mind. The topic for this term paper will be *asthma* (we were recently asked to do this by a friend who was diagnosed as having asthma and who required medication). This choice should turn up a goodly amount of information, because medical data is a hot Web topic, for companies and nonprofit organizations.

A few clicks away

The standard Yahoo! startup screen at *www.yahoo.com* gives you a nice, manageable set of choices, one of which is Health. (By the way, if you have been searching Yahoo! for the Internet's severely exaggerated stocks of pornography, some items are innocently stashed under Health: Sexuality.) Right near the top of the selections on the Health page you will find a choice called Diseases and Conditions (see Figure G). Sounds like a reasonable place to look, doesn't it?

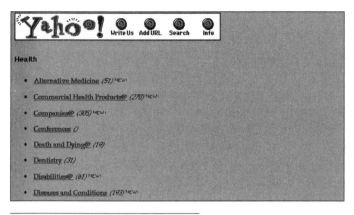

Figure G: Health, and unhealth too.

Figure H: Lots of diseases.

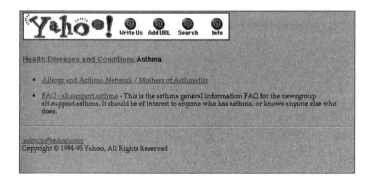

Figure I: The two best asthma references.

So, you click on Diseases, and you get to the Diseases and Conditions page. Look down the list, and you'll find Asthma almost immediately (see Figure H). Notice that — at least this was the case in late September 1995 — there are only two pages indexed by Yahoo! for asthma. You might guess that there must be hundreds of Web documents that mention asthma in some way. And you would be right.

But it just so happens that the Yahoo! staff does a lot of information filtering, and the two sites presented here are essentially the most useful references on asthma currently available (see Figure I).

A short, sweet search

You usually don't have to be afraid of being flooded with results in a Yahoo! keyword search, mainly because the contents of Yahoo! are carefully edited and because Yahoo! doesn't index all text elements. A search on the keyword *asthma* turns up ten hits (your mileage may vary — every search is a sort of snapshot-in-time of Web contents). The hits are an interesting assortment, and because for a topic this straightforward the title and comments are almost certain to contain the keyword, the search finds the two items (see Figure J) that were recovered just by the tree search, and also finds some items *besides* just plain medical information on asthma. For example, the keyword search finds businesses that offer different products for management of asthma.

Term paper considerations

You may have memories, if you are older than 25, of sitting in a library copying over information from an encyclopedia for an elementary school assignment. If you're younger than that, you probably have memories of printing a file from a CD encyclopedia.

If you were preparing a report from the asthma FAQ that turns up in both the tree search and the keyword search, you could try one of two strategies. You could save the whole FAQ as text, which in this case turns out to be a reasonable thing to do because it consists mostly of long blocks of text (some pages, saved as text, are interrupted every line or so by an HTML tag, making cut-and-paste reconstruction of a formatted document a very annoying activity). Or you could save it as an HTML document, preserving the original formatting.

There are shareware programs for converting HTML to word-processor formats and vice versa, and as this is being written most major word processors are starting to accommodate HTML documents by doing the conversion directly. The HTML conversion system in ClarisWorks for both Windows and Mac is particularly effective at dealing with captured Web documents, and you can expect that WordPerfect and Microsoft Word will have their acts together by late 1995. As a last consideration, you are, of course, on the honor system here and must give your solemn promise that you will *read* the documents you find rather than just assemble them and hand them in (if you're doing a school report, that is).

Yahoo Search

[*Yahoo* | Up | Search | Suggest | Add | Help]

10 matches were found containing the substring (**asthma**).

Business and Economy:Products and Services:Health

- Asthma Systems Kits - disease management program to aid in the mangement of **asthma** whether mild moderate or severe.

Business and Economy:Products and Services:Health:Allergies

- Allergy Clean Environments - State-of-the-art products to **asthma** and allergy sufferers to assist you in allergy proofing your home.
- Allergy Supply Company - Quality Allergy & **Asthma** Equipment & Hard to Find Supplies

Entertainment:People

- Muzzo, Elizabeth - a 10 year old girl with Down Syndrome, Cerebral Palsy, and **Asthma**.

Figure J: Keyword: asthma.

All Those Other Indexes

Yahoo! has very efficient tree searches, or quick keyword searches if you prefer. The other services on the Web are a mixed collection: some offer trees, others offer keywords, a few offer both. Yahoo! offers an Options link to all these other services, and they all represent slightly different approaches to the large and growing problem of information collection from the Web.

While not disparaging the fine efforts of many dedicated people, you should always try Yahoo! first. Why? Because it's fast, it's the easiest to use, and it has minimal junk content. If you find some leads on your topic from Yahoo!, you can follow up the links on these pages to expand your search. But the main point is that Yahoo! won't waste your time. You may need to use other search engines eventually, especially for scholarly topics, but it can't hurt to try good old Yahoo! before you turn to the others.

The following is a short review of other search facilities you can reach from Yahoo!. Since most of this book is a review of Web sites, it makes sense to give you a review of the ways to get there.

Galaxy

EINet Galaxy, located at http://www.einet.net, was one of the first index services to offer a tree search through the Web. This service is also the home of the software products winWeb and MacWeb, which are both fast, compact Web browsers available free at this nonprofit site.

The Galaxy style is quite a bit different from the Yahoo! style in that it usually presents you with more choices per page (see Figure K). Taking the case of asthma as a search topic again, you face the question of which one of these looks like a likely place for the next step of the search? Human Biology? Medical Specialties? It isn't actually quite as clear here in Galaxy as in Yahoo!, where at least you can guess that asthma is likely to be classified as a "Disease or Condition." Looking at this Galaxy page, you can see that it's a terrifically efficient way to find Scuba pages, or information on Military Law, but on a number of other topics things are considerably cloudier.

Your choice is to spend some time poking around in these categories or to bail out and try a keyword search on Galaxy's entries. The search option (see Figure L) lets you choose *titles* (Galaxy pages) or *content* (Galaxy entries) as a search basis.

Figure K: Galaxy choices: where's asthma?

It would be nice to be able to report to you that you would find all the asthma information you need just with that bit of effort, but you're not quite there yet. This search returns a list of Galaxy links with scores, ranging from 1000 down to 0, that indicate degree of likely relevance (see Figure M).

Plowing ahead, you may as well click on the link, Community Health, with a score of 1000 (hey, at 1000, it's gotta work!). Sure enough, if you scroll down, past rather a lot of stuff you aren't trying to find, you'll find one of the items (Figure N) from the Yahoo! asthma search (the Mothers of Asthmatics information page). With a little more looking around, you can find the Asthma FAQ page too.

The problem here is not that Galaxy doesn't have lots of interesting material (it certainly does), but that Galaxy seems to be better organized for surfing or random exploration than for find-it-in-ten-seconds access like Yahoo!. Somehow, plowing through titles for mental health institutes and DeathNET to look for asthma information almost seems to defeat the purpose of indexing.

WebCrawler

WebCrawler is a formidable keyword search engine that can access giant amounts of indexed data on the Web. The indexing is done by a program that searches out URLs and their contents, and because of the scope of WebCrawler's activities the starting WebCrawler page (see Figure O) gives you a pop-up box for limiting the number of hits it returns.

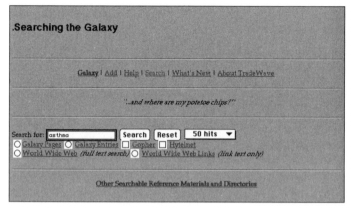

Figure L: Setting up a Galaxy search.

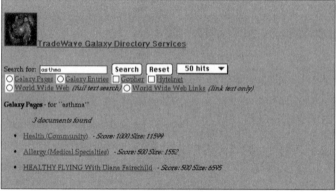

Figure M: Asthma hits, with scores, from Galaxy.

Figure N: Everything, and more.

WebCrawler™

To search the WebCrawler database, type in your search keywords here. Type as many relevant keywords as possible; it will help to uniquely identify what you're looking for. **Last update:** August 14, 1995.

> asthma

[Search]   ☒ AND words together

Number of results to return: [25 ▼]

News | Home | Random Links | FAQ | Top 25 Sites | Submit URLs | Simple Search

Figure O: Welcome to WebCrawler.

WebCrawler **Search Results**

The query "asthma" found 144 documents and returned 25:

```
1000  http://www.meddean.luc.edu/lumen/Medicine/Allergy/Asthma/asthmatoc.html
0713  Are You Breathing Free?
0627  National Jewish Center Med Facts Subject List
0561  Asthma Advice
0550  What is Asthma>
0481  http://www.asthma.com/stats.html
0284  Antony Rowstron
0284  http://www.w2.com/asthma.html
0267  Asthma and Climate
0210  BWH Pulmonary/Critical Care Division: Attendings
0203  The Lung Line® at National Jewish Center
0189  BWH Pulmonary/Critical Care Division: Asthma Clinical Research Center
0189  Asthma Zero Mortality Coalition (AZMC)
0189  Pulmonary and Critical Care Medicine
0145  National Jewish Center Information
0141  BWH Pulmonary/Critical Care Division: Introduction
```

Figure P: The first 25 WebCrawler asthma hits.

ASTHMA ADVICE:
JUST IN TIME FOR THE WHEEZIN' SEASON

By Michael LeNoir, M.D.
Chairman, Asthma Zero Mortality Coalition
Regional Chairman, National Medical Association

My mother is fifty-one years old and was just diagnosed with asthma. Is asthma contagious and isn't it more common in children?

Figure Q: The 1000-point asthma site.

If this feature weren't built in, you could pick an injudicious set of keywords and find yourself in the middle of an all-night download at 14.4K.

Well, WebCrawler has the stuff, all right. The search finds 144 asthma hits, of which 25 are presented (the default for a small search was left at 25 hits). Curiously, none of the hits at the top of this first batch (see Figure P) finds the meticulously maintained FAQ site at CalTech that Yahoo! finds. Note also how the relevance scores start dropping like a stone after the first few — it's something of a puzzle how some right-on-the-money asthma information sites rank lower than 200 in the scores returned.

Just for kicks, check out the 1000-score site, a valuable reference for sure (see Figure Q) but not an obvious 1000 compared to some others. The computer algorithm that ranks the sites at least works away in the background, day and night, but often produces conclusions that may not match what a human looking at the same material would find. The Web is a place of many mysteries, and is likely to continue as such for awhile.

Despite these apparent inconsistencies, WebCrawler is an excellent place to see if there's anything you missed in a Yahoo! search. And you almost certainly will miss a few things, partly because Yahoo! has screened some of the material that has been automatically indexed elsewhere.

Lycos

The true Monster of the Web is Lycos. No matter how many sites any other service has indexed, Lycos has more. No matter how many hits you find in a keyword search elsewhere, Lycos can top them. Lycos is maintained by the Computer Science department at Carnegie Mellon University (see Figure R), and like WebCrawler is an automated operation.

Figure R: The Lycos home page.

The true Monster of the Web is Lycos.

If you are interested in the Maritime Archaic culture of the shores of Labrador and Maine, or want to look up references to maximum-entropy signal processing in nuclear magnetic resonance spectroscopy, or wonder if texts in Luvian are available somewhere on the Web (rise to the challenge! find out about the Luvians! really!), you are going to find that Lycos is your most valuable resource. Lycos indexes every scrap of every Web site and by the time you read this will have about 1,000,000 URLs on tap.

Its depth suggests that on popular topics you'll find more material than you can use, but as a resource for rarities, it's fantastic. As an illustration, in the now familiar asthma search you will find (see Figure S) a total of 394 hits. Lycos returns the 85 hits with scores of 0.010 or better (here 1.000 is a perfect score, rather than 1000) but also gives you a set of scored-for-relevance links to a variety of sites that represent variations on the original keyword.

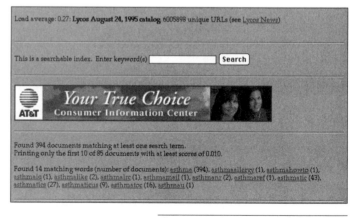

Figure S: A rather large assemblage of asthma sites.

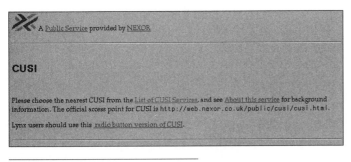

Figure T: CUSI greets you.

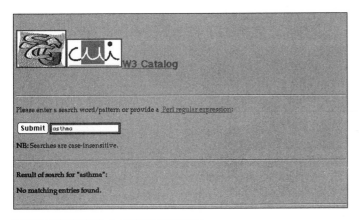

Figure U: CUSI sites in the U.S.

CUSI

This option (see Figure T) is actually a big collection of index sites maintained by Nexor in the United Kingdom. It encompasses almost every Web index, and in fact leads back to Yahoo!, if that's what you would like. Some of the sites represented here are among the earliest Web pioneers at indexing, which *could* mean they have lots of great stuff, but in practice *tends* to mean that they are old-fashioned, clunky, UNIX-oriented sites with lackadaisical maintenance at a university somewhere.

CUSI is mirrored all over the globe — the people at Nexor encourage you to find a site near you (see Figure U). This minimizes traffic to a certain extent, but in fact you might have better results picking a site where it's 3 o'clock in the morning.

There are probably some resources you will find with CUSI that you won't find elsewhere, but most of these have to do with academic research databases. Amazingly, a search on the simple keyword *asthma* for this project turned up exactly nothing (Figure V), indicating that the indexing engines are getting a little behind in their labors. If you strike out elsewhere, you can always check here for the sake of completeness, but it probably isn't the right choice for square one in your progress through the Web.

Harvest

Harvest (see Figure W) is one of the few really new services on the Web, an integrated tool set for developing indexes of Web information. It's offered to developers by the Computer Science Department at the University of Colorado at Boulder.

Figure V: Huh? Nothing??!!

Those people should have lots of relevant experience for the chore, having maintained the Internet White Pages service called Netfind for years.

The plan here is to offer a consistent interface for commercial services, directories, and special-purpose information collection. Right now, several useful services (see Figure X) are organized with Harvest software; the AT&T 800-number directory is a stand-out. This is a site worth checking every few weeks or so during the next few years, because Harvest's role as a directory of directories will make it a resource for some specialist sites that might get overlooked by Yahoo!.

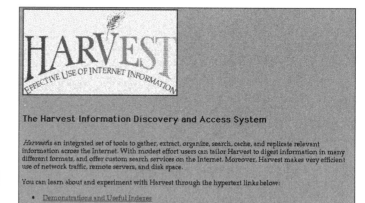

Figure W: Harvest, a new approach.

SavvySearch

Savvy searches (see Figure Y) fire up every popular keyword-searching engine on the Web in parallel. If you haven't found anything after a good long look on Yahoo!, this might be your best bet. You should be warned in advance, however, that a vague search on this service (that is, a search on a single general keyword like *disease* or *network*) will take a very long time and produces giant piles of useless or marginally useful information. This is the right service for really obscure topics (Byzantine coinage after 1200, for example), but it's the equivalent of a 200-mile-long drift net in ocean fishing. You'll take in lots of stuff, but most of it won't be edible.

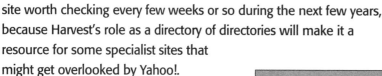

Figure X: Some Harvest sites, circa 1995.

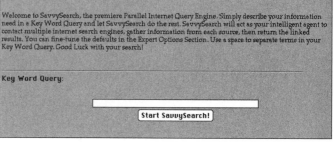

Figure Y: Savvy searching.

Optimizing Yahoo! Searches

The original Internet searching tools (Lycos, for example) required quite a bit of planning for effective use. They were designed in an Internet world where most users were connected at universities, were looking mostly for text-based information, and were familiar with the search protocols of UNIX tools. The main search optimization techniques involved formulation searches like:

John AND Adams ANDNOT Quincy AND President

so that you could extract only information about the President named John Adams, and not the President J. Q. Adams or random computer-science graduate students or others named John Adams.

Yahoo! is different. Yahoo!'s tree directory structure already has been carefully designed to yield very fast results with almost no planning on your part. When you click on a link in the directory, you get back only one or two pages of results. That means you are positively encouraged to click around at random, since you won't be punished with an unstoppable twenty minute download for clicking on a topic that's too vague.

> **Yahoo!'s tree directory structure already has been carefully designed to yield very fast results with almost no planning on your part.**

To determine the procedure for an optimal Yahoo! search for this book, ten different users were commissioned to look up information on four topics, ranging from very simple (finding a New York subway map) to esoteric (finding online the works of the classical author Lucian). Five users *only* searched by clicking through the tree structure, and the other five *only* by using keywords and combinations of keywords.

The short notes on this investigation are: Point-and-click beat keyword searching every time, both for speed and information quality. In fact, several of the test subjects came to the same conclusions: First, spend ten or fifteen minutes just clicking your way through a Yahoo! tree. Then when you're done, and have a nice list of Web pages, try one or two keyword searches on WebCrawler to see if you missed anything. Those two steps constitute a pretty thorough search by themselves, and shouldn't take you more than half an hour. That's pretty impressive!

Software Tools

In the bad old days, as recently as early 1995, software for information retrieval on the Web pretty much consisted of browsers. Your best bet for saving information was probably to save any Web pages you found in their original HTML format and then look at them again off-line in the same browser. Saving a document as text only worked for very plain, mostly-text pages, since an abundance of formatting tags in a page would make it nearly unreadable as a text document.

Text, though, has the advantage that you can cut and paste it into word-processing documents, although you lose formatting information. There are two software tools you might want to consider, especially if you are reluctant to upgrade every time the major software vendors snap their fingers.

GrabNet

The first is called GrabNet, a little $19.95 utility for either Windows or Mac systems from the Forefront Group (713-961-1101). You can run GrabNet concurrently with Netscape, and when you use it to select text directly on a "live" Web page, it stores the text, formatted, along with the page's URL and title. If you're going to be doing a lot of research, GrabNet is just the ticket.

ClarisWorks

The second is ClarisWorks, and it also is available in Mac and Windows versions. Basically, it has the most compact word-processor that can do competent HTML-to-formatted text translation. If you are running Netscape Navigator on a minimal system (4MB RAM, for example), you can use ClarisWorks while you're online as a repository of documents for later off-line searching. Most other word processors are simply too big and slow to use in this mode.

You Are Ready to Surf

The rest of the chapters here explore Yahoo! and the World Wide Web. Good luck and happy surfing!

Arts

So maybe you're an art director, a sketch artist, a production designer, an architect, or an interior decorator, and your study is filled with art books, along with your living room, your bedroom, and your kitchen, and you would put them in the bathroom if not for all that nasty moisture. It's 2 a.m., and even with all those books, you *still* can't find the image you need for tomorrow's (oops, today's) 9 a.m. meeting.

Try clicking around in Yahoo!'s Arts section.

Even if you don't have a meeting at 9 a.m., it's fun to see the amount and variety of arts offering. Not only will you probably find what you're looking for, from Arts & Crafts lamps to classical sculptures, online art could save you from those embarrassing "It's the books or me!" fights with the significant other.

Architecture

From professional specifications to historical information, something for everyone, even if the closest you ever came to a blueprint was the directions for Barbie's dreamhouse.

AEC InfoNet: Architecture, Engineering, Building Construction

http://www.inforamp.net/~aec/

Need a bathtub faucet? Or an architect? Wide-ranging database has products and services for architects and builders.

Arcat's Spec Disk

http://ideanet1.ideanet.com/~arcat/

Free to architects, engineers, contractors, designers, and other construction industry professionals, Spec Disk contains construction product manufacturers' specifications ready to edit for actual construction projects. They're downloadable from the site in either WordPerfect 5.1 or Microsoft Word 6.0 formats.

ArchiWeb

http://www.archiweb.com

More than 500 links to the best architectural sites on the Internet. The Virtual Lab is for students or studios and the Architecture Yellow Pages is for companies.

ALSO RECOMMENDED:

Arcosanti

http://www.getnet.com/~nkoren/arcosanti/

It's architecture, it's ecology, it's archeology. It's Paolo Soleri's visonary habitat in the Arizona desert.

Architects

Art Nouveau Architects

http://www-stud.enst.fr/~derville/AN/authors.html

This site contains a listing of Architects such as Berlage (Dutch), Gaudi (Spanish), Guimard (French), Mackintosh (Scottish), Sauvage (French), and Viollet le Duc (French), as well as examples of their work.

Tracking Hector Guimard in Paris

http://www.etca.fr/Users/
Sylvain%20Meunier/Guimard/
baladepseizeAGL/

And just in case you didn't get enough Art Nouveau, this site offers a virtual walking tour of Guimard's work in Paris.

Plecnik, Joze

http://www.ijs.si/slo/ljubljana/
plecnik.html

The now world-renowned architect who transformed the provincial town of Ljubljana into the capital of the Slovene nation.

Architects: Wright, Frank Lloyd

Yes, Wright has his own subsection. It would have pleased him, and Ayn Rand would have it no other way.

Index - Frank Lloyd Wright Source Page

http://www.mcs.com/~tgiesler/
flw_home.htm

This site contains links to all known pages that either display the architecture of Frank Lloyd Wright or have content about Frank Lloyd Wright.

Archives

ArchiGopher

gopher://libra.caup.umich.edu/

Gopher archive with text background and many GIFs on varied topics,

among them: The Palladio Image Archive, Images of 3-D CAD Models, Musings on Lunar Architecture, Greek Architecture, and Tunisian Architecture.

Architecture Database, ANU

http://rubens.anu.edu.au/
architecture_form.html

Researcher heaven. Extremely detailed, searchable database of classical architectural images. Need an example of the difference between Corinthian and Ionic at 4 a.m.? Go to this place. Mostly JPEGs.

Bridges

Covered Bridges

http://william-king.www.drexel.edu/
top/bridge/CB1.html

A guide to old covered bridges of southeastern Pennsylvania and surrounding areas. No guarantees that Clint Eastwood will be found inside.

Institutes

Fifty-six schools are listed, U.S. and international. The offerings vary from schools that link to libraries and collections, to others that merely give admissions information, to others that without irony say they're "under construction."

American Institute of Architects

http://www.aia.org/

Includes information on Selecting an Architect, K-12 resources, a list of research centers, and some fascinating architectural links.

Columbia University - Architecture, Planning and Preservation

http://www.cc.columbia.edu/
~archpub/

Check out the Digital Design Lab (DDL), which "focuses on the development of intuitive three-dimensional interfaces for multimedia and on-line learning environments. . . Who will design this virtual space? We have already seen what computer scientists, animators, and media people have conjured up, and we are not impressed."

Japanese-style modern architecture in NAGOYA

http://www.tcp-ip.or.jp/~csakao/
index-eg.html

The site also includes links to many other Japanese architectural sites.

MIT School of Architecture and Planning

http://alberti.mit.edu/ap/

As one would expect from MIT, an excellent site, incorporating full multimedia. Be sure to see the fascinating Projects page.

Princeton University School of Architecture

http://www.princeton.edu/~soa/
ginfo.html

A university that has some of the finest examples of neo-Gothic architecture in the world on its campus — and Michael Graves on its faculty. Go figure.

Landscapes

Index - Landscape Architecture - WWW Virtual Library

http://www.clr.toronto.edu:1080/VIRTUALLIB/larch.html

Searchable database of Internet resources includes lists of events and competitions as well as research sources.

Lighthouses

Lighthouses over the World

http://www.ivg.com/~derks/

Historical and technical background and graphics of lighthouses from around the world.

Indices

PAIRC - Planning and Architecture Internet Resource Center

http://arch.buffalo.edu:8001/internet/h_pa_resources.html

This site at the University of Buffalo offers comprehensive resources for architectural students and professionals.

Art History

A collage of Western Art from Greco-Roman ruins and unicorn horns at the Liverpool Museum (http://www.bbk.ac.uk/Departments/HistoryOfArt/narwhal.html) to Degas and Munch.

ANU Art History Top Level Menu Page

http://rubens.anu.edu.au/

A true gift to the Web, Michael Greenhalgh, The Sir William Dobell Foundation Professor of Art History at Australian National University, has put up a searchable collection of nearly 11,500 images and a tutorial on The "Palace" of Diocletian at Split.

The site also contains the complete text of his own *The Greek and Roman Cities of Western Turkey*, a fascinating guide to visiting ancient ruins, written in lay language. "Turkey is today a foremost country in which to study the remains of both Greek and Roman civilization (to say nothing of the Hittites, of course) ... for variety and completeness, nowhere can compete with Turkey. And if anyone should wish to dispute just how little has changed at some sites over the past one or two hundred years, let him visit the sites with an 18th or 19th century traveller's account to hand."

Genres: Surrealism

Surrealist imagery

http://pharmdec.wustl.edu/juju/surr/images/surr-imagery.html

Comprehensive links to Surrealist sites throughout the Web, well organized by artists considered to be related to the movement.

Indices

Index - Art History - WWW Virtual Library

http://www.hart.bbk.ac.uk/VirtualLibrary.html

Links to a varied assortment of museums and university programs worldwide.

Body Art

In the '60s, *body art* used to mean painting flowers on your tummy. In the '90s, people seem to be going for more permanent enhancements. The sites here answer those needling questions about tattoos and body piercing from hygiene to aesthetics. Given the subject matter, and the appearance of certain, er, *sensitive* body parts, this entire category is not recommended for children or squeamish adults.

Body Modification

http://www.io.org/~bme/

"Piercing, cutting, branding, tattooing, surgery, stretching, bodybuilding as art, transhumanism, and any other aesthetically inspired body modifications." Definitive, if you're into that sort of thing. A very large selection of very graphic graphics.

Christiaan's Piercing Page

http://stripe.colorado.edu/~vanwoude/piercing.html

Includes links to many related pages, including one that suggests witty replies to the oft-heard question, "Does it hurt?"

Children

A digital refrigerator door on which proud parents display their children's artwork. Some pages invite you to submit your own children's efforts. Hey, why else did you spend all that money on a scanner?

Kids' Space

http://plaza.interport.net/kids_space/

A friendly environment that helps kids get to other fun sites. Includes an art gallery and an interactive storybook.

The Refrigerator

http://users.aimnet.com/~Ejennings/refrigerator/

Brought to you on a "Frigidaire Avocado" background, a charming collection of kid's drawings.

Cinema

Lists educational resources, institutes, and other resources for filmmakers and film students. For movie reviews, please see the Entertainment chapter, under Movies and Films.

Cinema News

http://www.sf.co.kr/c.cinema/cinema.html

Includes a number of Internet cinema resources, including a link to the 1995 International Cannes Film Festival. The link called Current Movies in Korea connects you to detailed information about Hollywood movies that are currently running in Korea, with no mention of Korean titles or Korean playing times.

Institutes

NYU - Media Research Lab

http://found.cs.nyu.edu/MRL/

NYU's departmental structure is even more confusing to the uninitiated than are New York's subway maps. If you're interested in studying Interactive Multimedia, you should also check the two NYU sites: the Interactive Telecommunications Program of the Tisch School of the Arts (http://www.itp.tsoa.nyu.edu/) and the NYU Center for Digital Multimedia (http://found.cs.nyu.edu/CAThome_new.html). Pack black clothes.

Index - Cinema/TV/Radio/Multimedia Schools

http://www.gu.edu.au/gwis/cinemedia/CineMedia.schools.html

From the Institut for *film og medievidenskab* in Copenhagen, to the Queensland, Australia College of Art, to the University of Alabama at Tuscaloosa, links to film schools in the United States and worldwide.

Index - Film School Confidential

http://wavenet.com/~tomedgar/fsc/fsc.html

If you're really thinking of going to film school, for godsakes, *read this first.* Okay, now go spend your money on an engineering degree. (The Film School Confidential Web site was created by two NYU film grads, and a

third NYU film school grad just wrote part of *Yahoo! Unplugged* … get it now?)

Collectives

A cross-section of artists, from serious work to people just taking themselves too seriously.

OTIS

OTIS

http://sunsite.unc.edu/otis/otis.html

From the site's disclaimer: "OTIS is in NO WAY related to the following organizations: Otis College of Art & Design, Otis Elevators, the estate of Otis Redding, Otis Design, Otis the town-drunk on Andy Griffith, the bands Otis or Otis13, or any other 'Otis.' OTIS is an acronym for "Operative Term Is Stimulate." OTIS is also famous on the Web, fabulous, and just has to be experienced.

ALSO RECOMMENDED:

Women Artists Archive

http://www.sonoma.edu/library/waa/

A Web-based brochure for the Women Artists Archive at Sonoma State University. The Web site is currently spotlighting works from Bay Area women artists. It also has an unannotated list, divided by period, of the more than 1,000 artists included in the offline collection.

Computer Generated

The images on these sites will leave you saying "wow," but unless you're a computer art professional, most of the *text* will leave you saying "huh?" If you *are* a computer art professional, this is Graphic Heaven.

Fractals

Fractals

http://www.uncg.edu:80/~amralph/fractals/

A collection of shareware-created, fractal images by Randy D. Ralph, Ph.D. The site also includes links to other fractal sites.

Mandelbrot Exhibition

http://www.comlab.ox.ac.uk/archive/other/museums/computing/mandelbrot.html

An excellent introductory and advanced site with information, images, and software for Mandelbrot and Julia sets.

Morphs

3-D volume morphing

http://www-graphics.stanford.edu/~tolis/morph.html

From Stanford, images that are impressive to the layperson, with information that is only comprehensible to professionals.

ALSO RECOMMENDED:

Stereograms

3-D and SIRDS images

http://www.comlab.ox.ac.uk/archive/3d.html

Although this site itself is not visually spectacular, it has good links to other stereograms, 3-D images, and SIRDS.

3-D art

http://www.ionet.net/~mw0811/index.shtml

Contains interesting links to sites containing computer-generated graphics.

Courses

Can you draw Lucky?

Artist's Way 12-Week Course On-Line

http://www.waterw.com/~lucia/aw.html

This popular 12-step art recovery book has been developed as a free online course.

Design

From the new car color you can't take seriously (*Barney purple?*) to the Web pages you can't read for the life of you, design permeates our lives. (In addition to the listings here, check also Science: Engineering: Mechanical Engineering.

UI World

http://www.io.tudelft.nl/uiworld/intro.html

A resource of publications, schools, jobs, and other listings for designers involved in the creation of GUIs, kiosks, CD-ROMs, CD-Is, ITV, consumer electronic products, and games.

Exhibits

Damp Squib

http://www.pavilion.co.uk/medianet/dampsquib/welcome.htm

An intriguing application of RayGun-type graphics to a Web site structured as an unfolding pamphlet.

Design in Sports

http://www.commerce.wca95.org/design/

The world's largest exhibition on design in sports.

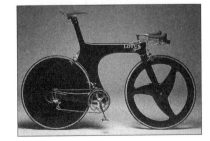

Graphic design

Graphion's online type museum

http://www.slip.net/~graphion/museum.html

A superlative example of resources donated freely to the Net by a Web site established for commercial purposes, the Web site at Graphion Typesetting of San Francisco presents a complete history of type design, including font examples, biographies of designers, an excellent glossary, and an anecdotal history of the change from hot lead typesetting to phototypesetting to desktop publishing.

Organizations

OBD - Organization of Black Designers

http://www.core77.com/OBD/

A beautifully designed Web site with an excellent collection of links for design professionals, including upcoming events and job postings from well-known recruiter Rita Sue Siegel. Should be on any design professional or student's bookmark list.

Drama

Tempting as it may be to define *high drama* as the thing that happens when you have a book deadline and your Internet connection goes down, the sites here run the gamut from interactive collaborations to individual performances to internationally renowned companies.

Theatre Central

http://www.mit.edu:8001/people/quijote/theatre-central.html

Excellent, comprehensive, extremely well-organized hypertext listings of amateur, scholastic, and professional groups, services, and resources.

Magazines

Playbill On-Line

http://www.webcom.com/~broadway/

An extremely rich site featuring a search engine, theatre history, trivia, contests, job listings, and, of course, theatre listings. All that and more, without the people next to you rustling their copies during the quiet scenes.

Opera

The Opera Schedule Server

http://www.fsz.bme.hu/opera/main.html

A large collection of opera-related links, historical information about opera houses worldwide, and yes, worldwide schedules. Note that it does come with a disclaimer regarding accuracy.

Playwrights' Resources

Screenwriters and Playwrights HomePage

http://www.teleport.com/~cdeemer/scrwriter.html

The granddaddy of drama sites, Charles Deemer's Screenwriters and Playwrights HomePage has become justly famous as a comprehensive resource. In addition to copies of works by great playwrights, the site also includes lists of seminars, playwrights' tips, marketing tips, and discussions of hypertext as a literary form.

ALSO RECOMMENDED:

TDR: The Drama Review

http://www-mitpress.mit.edu/jrnls-catalog/tdr.html

Read *TDR* and you too can use phrases such as *Morphing Borders: The Remanence of MTV. TDR* is an excellent resource for those in the jargon-rich field of Performance Studies. For others, memorize the table of contents listed here and never again lose at charades.

Ethnic

By which is meant "Non-Western."

African

African Art: Aesthetics and Meaning

http://www.lib.virginia.edu/dic/exhib/93.ray.aa/African.html

"An Electronic Exhibition Catalog" includes pictures from the exhibit at The University of Virginia's Bayly Art Museum, elements of African Aesthetics, and a bibliography of offline texts.

Asian

Asian Arts

http://www.webart.com/asianart/index.html

A likely nominee for "Best of the Web" lists, the online journal *Asian Arts* includes scholarly articles on all aspects of Asian art, lists of exhibitions, a choice of thumbnail GIFs or larger JPEG images, and some of the most articulate letters ever posted on a Web site.

Chinese

Feng Hua Gallery of Computer Arts

http://eddy.me.utoronto.ca/gallery.html

Traditional Chinese images created with the most modern of mediums.

Filipino

CAI Art Gallery

http://www.usc.edu.ph/cai/

Artworks by contemporary Cebuano artists.

Japanese

MINGEI: Two Centuries of Japanese Folk Art

http://www.star.net/salem/pem/mingei/

If you're lucky enough to have a monitor with great resolution, this is probably one of the most beautiful sites on the Net. Sit back and watch gorgeous JPEGs of Japanese folk art unfold in pixels. Or turn off the computer and go see the exhibition live at the listed museums.

ALSO RECOMMENDED:

International Netsuke Kenkyukai Society

http://www.hooked.net/netsuke/

Comprehensive for collectors.

Indian

Digital Avatar

http://www.charm.net/~nayak/avtar2.html

Eclectic and very beautiful offerings.

ALSO RECOMMENDED:

Batish Records

http://hypatia.ucsc.edu:70/1/RELATED/Batish

Yes, now you too can learn the sitar over the Internet. This site includes the Indian Music journal *RagaNet* and audio files of sitar sounds.

Middle Eastern

interARTisrael

http://www.macom.co.il/interart/

Stuck for a Hanukkah gift? Perhaps an original $3,000 sculpture is just the thing. Beautiful examples of Israeli art, many of them available for sale.

Native American

National Museum of the American Indian

http://www.users.interport.net/~logomanc/heye.html

An excellent link page for American Indian art and research.

Wingspread Collectors Guide to Southwest Art

http://www.wingspread.com/

Wow, this was selected as Glenn Davis's Cool Site of the Day and as Spider's Pick of the Day within days of each other ... and, amazingly, you can still get in to see it. It features searchable information on Southwestern artists, plus artists' techniques, materials, history, and visitor's information. Essential if you're planning to visit New Mexico, and probably pretty amazing even if you live there.

Events

From the Appalachian Fair to the Viennal Biennenal, a changing list of sites for upcoming events. (Note: Sites often stay up as archives once their respective events have taken place.)

Art DEADLINES List, The

http://rtuh.com/adl

Lists competitions, contests, calls for entries/papers, grants, scholarships, fellowships, jobs, internships, etc., in the arts or arts-related areas around the world.

Index - FineartForum Online Art Resources: Events, Conferences, Associations

http://www.msstate.edu/ Fineart_Online/art-resources/events-conf.html

Lists upcoming art events worldwide.

Exhibits

More than 200 exhibit sites are listed in this section of Yahoo!, covering every possible taste, school, style, and medium, from prehistoric cave paintings to whatever digital artists put up on the Web so far today. Take a day (or more) out of your life to sit back and explore, for these brief entries are but a small sample of a tsunami of creativity.

A Hundred Highlights from the Koninklijke Bibliotheek (The Netherlands)

http://www.konbib.nl/100hoogte/hh-en.html

A virtual exhibition, including the *Delft Bible,* the *Blaeu* atlas, sheet music in manuscript from Willem Pijper.

Alt.art - A Compendium of Bad Art Form

http://www.power.net/users/janet/ alt.art.html

Hysterically funny photo montage parodies of Michelangelo's painting on the ceiling of the Sistine chapel. Writes the site's creator, Janet McAndless: "I'd always been struck by the unusual poses given his frescoed Sistine chapel ceiling subjects by Michelangelo. And it occurred to me that many appeared to be caught in the act of doing something they should not …."

Sistine Chapel (Cappella Sistina)

http://www.christusrex.org/www1/ sistine/0-Tour.html

And now that you've had your slightly blasphemous fun, here's the real thing. Note: This is not an academic site; it is deeply Catholic, and the images are reached by scrolling down past several papal encyclicals.

Artists

Denton, Andrew H - Art Gallery

http://www.eunet.ch/People/ahd/ home.html

Get to the text pre-home page and click on it. It takes a while for the home page to load, so go get a refreshment and then come back.

Magritte, René - Art Gallery

http://www.westwind.be/magritte/

He's been on every college dorm wall, he's featured in Michael Jackson's new video, so naturally everybody's favorite surrealist is now on the Web.

Fine Arts

To quote one site: *"Voila! les images!"*

Leonardo da Vinci Museum

http://www.leonardo.net/museum/ main.html

Considered a Top Ten Site of 1995 by the ubiquitous Point Communications. Many images from Leonardo's work, divided into "galleries" of clickable thumbnails with brief explanatory notes.

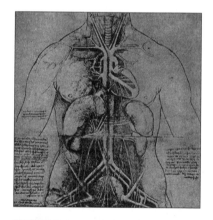

Artists

Homer, Winslow

http://web.syr.edu/~ribond/ homer.html

An interesting site for its addition of links to other sites that relate to 19th-century American history and culture, as well as the work of the great painter of the sea.

Yahoo!

Salvador Dali's Homepage

http://www.mercon.com/mercon/carl/dalilink.html

Yahoo! lists ten sites for Dali. This tribute to Dali was created by a docent at the Salvador Dali Museum.

Picasso, Pablo

http://www.oir.ucf.edu/wm/paint/auth/picasso/

One of several comprehensive sites of great artist's works presented by the WebMuseum, Paris.

Kahlo, Frida

http://www.cascade.net/kahlo.html

Devoted to the disturbing work of the currently enormously popular artist Frida Kahlo. Many pictures with accompanying biographical notes.

Journals

In one corner, ladies and gentlemen, prolix and arcane academic publications, in the other, sardonic and arcane alternative publications. Anyone for a copy of *Entertainment Weekly*?

Acid-free Paper

http://tnt.vianet.on.ca/pages/smithk/

Thoughts to ponder from the aptly named and cleverly designed inaugural issue of *Acid-free Paper*: "This is a sight, not a site...And why do I call this a *sight,* as opposed to the traditional *site* of the cyber-culture? By definition, a site is a place or location. A sight is something that is visual, viewed or looked at. If you have

bought into the cyberspace illusion, then you're free to believe that you're travelling through your computer from site to site. In truth, you are just looking at your monitor. This, my friend, is simply a sight."

Literature

The "geek factor" of Internet culture explains the presence of more than 200 sites dealing with science fiction, fantasy, and horror. But of course, other genres and literary topics are represented too. But not quite as much.

Awards

Pulitzer Prizes

http://www.pulitzer.org/

It not only lists the winners but reprints their work in its entirety, which is especially welcome, because you'll undoubtedly wish you could have seen the articles. Now you can, including two landmark series from *The Wall Street Journal*: Ron Suskind's on the struggles of inner-city honors students trying to get into M.I.T. and Tony Horowitz's on low-wage jobs, which may go down as *The Jungle* of the '90s (it was the basis of a really gross chicken plant in an *X Files* episode).

Children

IPL Story Hour

http://ipl.sils.umich.edu/youth/StoryHour/

Illustrated children's stories presented by the Internet Public Library (for many offerings, you will need a fast connection). One selection called "Do

Spiders Live on the World Wide Web?" is a child's introduction to computer terms that adults also can appreciate.

Children's Literature

http://www.ucalgary.ca/~dkbrown/index.html

Superb site with extensive links. Features hypertext subject organization to resources on children's literature for parents and professionals. Uses a delightful "bouquet" icon to indicate particularly valuable links.

The Realist Wonder Society

http://rrnet.com/~nakamura/

A journal geared more toward the child in adults, which restores "wonder" to its rightful meaning.

Classics

Shakespeare Web

http://www.shakespeare.com

Can't remember how that favorite quote went? Here's the easiest URL to remember for finding *everything* about the Bard on the Net, including links to several sites with search engines for the complete works, and a link to Joey's Personalized Shakespearean Insult Server (http://kite.ithaca.ny.us/insult.html). An example: "Thou art an impertinent reeling-ripe pigeon-egg."

Electronic Literature

Western European Literature

http://www.lib.virginia.edu/wess/
etexts.html

Guide to collections of literary texts in languages other than English, predominantly Nordic and Romance. Hypertexted, organized by country.

ALSO RECOMMENDED:

Tim Ware's Hyper-Concordance to Gravity's Rainbow

http://www.crl.com/~timware/
gravity.html

A hyperlinked index to Thomas Pynchon's encyclopedic novel, *Gravity's Rainbow*, containing pictures, maps, historical asides, and so on.

Fiction

What if Nietzsche Worked at a Convenience Store?

http://www.well.com/user/xkot/
whatif.htm

Anthony Gancarski's cynical send-up "What if Nietzsche Worked at a Convenience Store?" may be one of the few Web novels to show off a talent worth paying for. An excerpt: "So I walk in the front door at home, and my mother's playing her Melissa Etheridge cd. It's always, always a bad sign when she's playing dyke music. It means that she's, yet again, re-crafting her poem. Her ONE poem, entitled 'vaginal discharge,' which she wrote in the early 1970s and subsequently parlayed into a series of poetry readings, including a one-woman show at a Native American Lesbian Coffeehouse in New York City."

LitLinks, University of Alberta

http://www.ualberta.ca/~amactavi/
litlinks.htm

Extensive list of literary links.

Museums

There are two advantages to seeing museum collections on the Web. One: You have much more text background than you normally would (or normally could stand to read) during the real-life exhibition. Two: You won't strain your back from lifting the glossy coffee table book version.

Yahoo! - Le Louvre

http://www.yahoo.com/Arts/
Museums/Le_Louvre/

Way back in the spring of 1994, when the graphical Web was still in its infancy, and a 14.4K modem was considered blazingly fast for a home connection, what blew everyone away was that the Louvre was on the Web. It still does. One of the most frequently demoed areas was *Les très riches heures du Duc de Berry.* It's awe-inspiring to see one of the greatest medieval illuminated manuscripts materialize on your computer screen.

Art Deco Museum of Fashion and Theatre Designs

http://www.webcom.com/~tuazon/
ajarts/erte.html

Featuring Erte, Alphonse Mucha, James Rizzi. Historical background and gorgeous images.

Treasures of the Czars exhibition

http://www.sptimes.com/Treasures/
Default.html

Fabulous pictures and descriptive text from the catalogue of the exhibition of Romanov artifacts.

Museums - WWW Virtual Library

http://www.comlab.ox.ac.uk/archive/
other/museums.html

A very large index of art links.

Organizations

Despite their presence on the Web, many of the organizations listed have local flavors and goals. However, many invite the wider world community to exchange ideas.

Women's Studio Workshop

http://www.webmark.com/wsw/
wswhome.htm

A charming site. It describes not just the organization but the entire Catskills-Woodstock region, including the history of the area. The site is as much a cultural and tourist guide as it is a brochure, and it's perfect for urban artists procrastinating by dreaming of sylvan artist hideaways. There's also the lovely irony in its giving grants to creators of handmade paper.

Art & Science Collaborations, Inc.

http://nttad.com/asci/index.html

An organization that believes it may have come up with a movement name for the conjunction of art and technology: The new computer artists are the Digitalists. Hmmm, maybe, but couldn't that also be interpreted as "fingerpainters"?

Performing Arts

For Dance, please see the Recreation chapter. For Drama, please see Arts: Drama. For Music, please see the Entertainment chapter.

UNLV Performing Arts Center

http://hch4.lv-hch.nevada.edu/

It would seem that there are performing artists in Las Vegas who don't wear sequins. The site offers a mailing list to upcoming events, a list of links to other university performing arts centers on the Net, and a varied list of professionally oriented performing arts-related links, including the Center for Safety in the Arts with its online information about chemicals, motion risks, and so on (http://gopher.tmn.com:70/1/Artswire/csa).

Currency Press

http://www.currency.com.au/

Currency Press presents original plays and produced screenplays from Australian writers. Among those available for sale: *Muriel's Wedding* and *Priscilla, Queen of the Desert*.

Photography

A profuse variety of photographs are available for viewing on the Net, from the earliest days of the medium to the very latest in digital manipulation. Just be aware: Some sites come perilously close to global vacation-slide torture.

Exhibits

Adams, Ansel

http://bookweb.cwis.uci.edu:8042/AdamsHome.html

America's photographer laureate. These photos, however, are not the familiar images of Yosemite and New Mexico. This is a series commissioned by the University of California for its Centennial celebration in 1968. Not to worry, though, it is Ansel Adams after all.

Altman, Robert

http://www.cea.edu/robert/

As in the cover photographer for *Rolling Stone*, not that other guy. This is one of the last sites on the Net you should ever visit, because once you see it, nearly everything else will be a disappointment. (You'll need Netscape to fully appreciate every trick.)

CELLS alive!

http://www.whitlock.com/kcj/quill/

Fascinating, beautiful, creepy, stunning. See it. Microscopy and 3-D computer animation images, with explanatory text.

Cemetery, The

http://loki.stockton.edu/~whitew/cemetery/cemetery.html

A photograpic and text essay that is nearly novelistic in its unfolding of the lives in the historically African-American communities of southern New Jersey.

Photo Perspectives

http://www.i3tele.com/photo_perspectives_museum/faces/perspectives.home.html

Varying exhibitions of superior quality. Among its current offerings are heartrending images of the war in the former Yugoslavia (the section titles alone are difficult to view). On another part of the site (http://www.i3tele.com/photo_perspectives_museum/faces/abt.html), soaring images celebrate the 55th anniversary of The American Ballet Theatre, one of the greatest ballet companies in the world. An exhibition that should complement any dance researcher's or balletomane's Web tour.

Stacey, Dennis

http://www.infi.net/~dennys/

A varying and wondrous display of rare photographs from his collection of the Victorian era, including stereoscopic images.

Chip Shots Calendar of Microprocessors

http://micro.magnet.fsu.edu/micro/products/chipshot.htm

Centerfolds that nerds can really drool over. Fear not, these aren't so much product shots as they are gorgeous, crystalline neon images.

Publications

It has been said there may be more people in the United States writing poetry than reading it. It may be the same way with e-zines. An astonishing selection is out there on the Net, ranging from those that will only be published until their editors start dating to professional journals for working artists — even *The Paris Review*. Aesthetically, you'll find an interesting mix of those that are merely digital versions of paper zines to those working exclusively with electrons to those trying to extend electronic publishing as far as Photoshop can go.

eye WEEKLY's eye.net

http://www.interlog.com/eye/

The Web component of the Toronto alternative *eye Weekly*, *eye.net* is the online publication *HotWired* wants to be. Simply one of the best on the Net.

Dance Ink Magazine

http://www.webcom.com/~ink/

Alternative online journals can start looking pretty much the same after a while. And then you see *Dance Ink*. In these days of nipple piercing, its black and white cover of a Charles James evening gown may be a radical statement. It features top writers in the fields of dance and costume criticism, such as Tobi Tobias, Elizabeth Kendall, and Anne Hollander.

On Line Design

http://www.cea.edu/online.design/

Essential reading for anyone already in the field, and a great peek behind the curtain for anyone wanting to know about the art and business of designing for the Web.

RANT

http://www.clark.net/pub/rant/rant/

Give 'em points for truth in advertising and then read their rants, taking on American Consumer Culture. Very funny, in a Fran Liebowitz-meets-Andy Rooney kind of way. "Any similarities between persons living and/or dead and/or resembling Albert Einstein are purely coincidental."

Sculpture

From ancient sculpture to contemporary art to contemporary reproductions of ancient art.

Kutani-Yaki - Japan's traditional and most famous pottery

http://www.njk.co.jp/kutani/

Although this site can load slowly, there are lovely images throughout from serene pictures of Japan to overviews of technique.

New England Wood Carvers Web Site

http://www.tiac.net/users/rtrudel/

Both a commercial site (you can buy or sell woodcarvings) and an enthusiast's site with links and background information on woodcarving. A nice, tactile activity after all that surfing.

Gargoyles

Gargoyle

http://ils.unc.edu/garg/garghp4.html

Fortunately, one site here links to the other, so you'll get a chance both to see the contemporary work of Walter S. Arnold, (http://www.mcs.net/~sculptor/GARGOYLE.HTML), who worked on the National Cathedral, and this site with its clickable Gargoyle tour map of the Duke University campus. Both sites give detailed information on Gargoyles and Grotesques and the differences between them.

Yahoo!

Indices

Stay tuned — if this category gets any bigger, someone will surely come up with an Index to the Indices. These are just a few examples from many excellent mega-sites.

ArtSource

http://www.uky.edu/Artsource/artsourcehome.html

Attractive and well-organized, annotated, hypertext selections.

Voice of the Shuttle

http://humanitas.ucsb.edu/

Particularly eclectic and unique listings covering general culture and humanities, as well as arts listings. Apparently *techgender* is now an academic term.

Index - World Wide Arts Resources - Galleries

www.concourse.com/wwar/default.html

Extraordinarily ambitious, this site has an alphabetical index *by individual* of any artist appearing on any Web site. The site includes other searchable art resources and links as well. Definitely a bookmark site for artists, critics, and researchers.

ALSO RECOMMENDED:

Arts, Humanities, and Social Sciences Resources

http://lib-www.ucr.edu/rivera/

Searchable database of Net resources in these areas.

Art - WWW Virtual Library

http://www.w3.org/hypertext/DataSources/bySubject/Literature/Overview.html

Not quite its usual definitive self in this category, this W3 collection nevertheless is still very good.

Business and Economy

The Business and Economy section of Yahoo! is where you'll find a large amount of information on business and financial matters, including business schools, various consortia and financial institutions, economic foundations, and market-trend analysis pages.

There are also stock market and mutual-fund sites featuring places to directly check performance (including dynamic charts) and tax sites with IRS forms that you can download directly. The IRS even provides tax advice on the Web.

Consumer economy sites include the Consumer Information Center from Pueblo, Colorado, now offering free booklets over the Internet, a legal self-help center, and employment information. Find out how to post your resume on the Internet and how to conduct a job search via the World Wide Web.

You can also look at in-depth MIS technology sites, with information on new forms of electronic commerce, including digital cash payments and secure credit card usage over the Internet. There's even an electronic grocery store demo for you to try out.

Trade and International Economy sites cover international trade issues. There are links to large econometric databases, trade law institutes, and global trade centers.

Look for interesting sites in marketing, real estate, and small business, including information on running a home office and entrepreneuring on the Web, and the U.S. Small Business Administration. You can find out about mortgage loans here and use online calculators to figure out mortgage payments.

Transportation sites include train information and rail schedules, an interactive subway route planner, and up-to-date regional traffic information.

Organizations listed at Yahoo! include business development groups, social and cultural societies, economic foundations such as the World Bank, political organizations, and a whole lot of public interest groups. Here's where you'll find NOW, Greenpeace, the Sierra Club, and the Peace Corps, among others. There's also information on missing children organizations, philanthropic foundations, and student groups.

Business Schools

A wide range of business schools have home pages on the Web, offering information ranging from program descriptions and faculty/student directories to interactive hypertext courses. This is a good place to research business schools before applying, and it's also easy to request catalogs and admission applications via e-mail directly from most of the schools' Web sites.

Brigham Young University - Marriott School of Management

http://www.byu.edu/acd1/msm

The Marriott School of Management Information Network is a well-organized Web site with

information on various programs available in business management, as well as faculty and student home pages. The site also features a good collection of business resources and general Internet information in a good Web-browser format.

California Polytechnic at San Luis Obispo - Graduate Management Programs

http://www.calpoly.edu/~mgt/gmp/

The Cal Poly Graduate Management site offers information on programs for graduate business study in specialty areas such as agribusiness, architecture, and engineering. It also features a link to a student organization that offers online resumes of students in the program.

CMU Graduate School of Industrial Administration

http://www.gsia.cmu.edu/

This site offers an in-depth look at Carnegie-Mellon's Graduate School of Industrial Administration, including course and program descriptions and a well-indexed community "phone book" of faculty and student home pages. It also has information on outreach programs (including pictures from a community help program called "Dare To Share") and research centers on subjects such as financial analysis, technology management, and an ecologically sound Green Design initiative.

Columbia University - Graduate School of Business

http://www.cc.columbia.edu:80/~sbw17/business/

The Columbia Business School Web site has sections leading to an interactive tour, admissions

information, campus life, career opportunities, and an alumni register, all available from the top page via button bar. There's also a direct link to an interactive Web course called Information Technology in Marketing.

Defense Business Management University

http://sm.nps.navy.mil/DBMU/tom.html

The Defense Business Management University online information system contains listings of military-related courses on financial administration as well as a Department of Defense business newsletter. It also vies for the title of Most Acronyms at a Single Web Site. A downloadable offline copy of the course catalog is available for PC users.

Embry-Riddle Aeronautical University - Aviation Business Administration

http://155.31.1.1/~bizweb/

The Embry-Riddle Aviation Business Administration site delivers information on graduate and undergraduate programs, faculty home pages, and a departmental newsletter. It's also linked to the Avion student newspaper and a great graphically oriented aviation/aerospace Web magazine.

Escuela de Administracion de Negocios para Graduados (ESAN)

http://www.esan.edu.pe

ESAN, the first Latin American business school, has a Peruvian-based Web site with information on specialized master's programs and research opportunities pertaining to the Latin American community. The page has versions in Spanish and English.

Harvard University Business School

http://www.hbs.harvard.edu/index.html

The Harvard Business School sites offer some of the best presentations of information on the Internet. Besides listing courses and degree programs, they feature interactive courses with dynamic links to PowerPoint slides and pertinent World Wide Web links in an easy-to-use table format. A faculty directory is available, along with working papers on business subjects and seminar information. The entire MBA admissions catalog is also online.

MCDM WorldScan

http://www.cba.uga.edu/mcdm.html

WorldScan is a journal from the International Society on Multiple Criteria Decision Making. It focuses on an organizational approach to decision support systems, multiobjective optimization, and negotiation. The WorldScan site also features a member directory and conference information.

MIT Sloan School of Management

http://www-sloan.mit.edu/SloanHome.html

The Sloan School at MIT has an interesting mix of business and technology degree programs, and its Web site reflects this combination. Here you'll find not only course and program descriptions but also a Dean's Gallery of artists in the MIT community, news and current events pages, working papers and handbooks, and community resource information.

Nanyang Technological University - Business School

http://www.ntu.ac.sg/nbs/index.shtml

The Nanyang Business School in Singapore has a very clean, nicely laid-out Web site. Information on degree programs and courses is balanced with sections on the school's history, collaborative projects, and research centers. This site also has links to more information on Singapore, including interactive maps and Web servers.

New York University - Leonard N. Stern School of Business

http://www.stern.nyu.edu/

The Stern School of Business Web page at NYU is set up to take full advantage of World Wide Web technology. Besides the usual graphical Web page format, you can also find out about the school's offerings via a hypertext menu and a Yahoo!-like search engine. Another interesting page at Stern is the Management Communication Program page. This features a breathtaking view of the InfoBahn Diner and in-depth course information.

Northeastern University's Center for Family Business

http://nmq.com:80/fambiznc/cntprovs/orgs/necfb/

This site offers information for family-owned businesses, including education programs and membership opportunities. It also features an indexed *Family Business Quarterly* newsletter, with articles ranging from joint property and planning to sexual harassment in family businesses.

Rensselaer Polytechnic Institute - School of Management

http://www.rpi.edu/dept/mgmt/SOM.pages/SOM_home.html

The RPI School of Management Web server features a large amount of information on courses, degree programs, and faculty in Technology and Management. It also goes a bit further into the Web than do most business school sites, offering interactive course material on business sites on the Web and a repository that features case studies of small businesses on the Internet with links to the relevant sites. Also particularly useful at this site are collections of links to management and economics information.

Stanford University - Graduate School of Business

http://gsb-www.stanford.edu/home.html

Stanford University's Graduate School of Business puts multimedia into the forefront of its Web site, including a QuickTime movie from the Dean of the school extolling its virtues and an audio clip from a representative MBA student. The site also features information on degree programs and a faculty directory. Also useful is a Web version of the *Stanford Business School Magazine,* and a newspaper, *The VIRTUAL Reporter,* which features student experiments in electronic publishing.

U.C. Berkeley - Walter A. Haas School of Business

http://haas.berkeley.edu/

The Haas School of Business site is one of the best business school Web sites. From its graphically stunning

main menu to the great layout of the course descriptions and campus information, this Web site really stands out. What makes it even more compelling are the links to the Haas Interactive Tour CD, a series of multimedia modules about resources and offerings at the school, some of which are readable by Web browsers, or downloadable (for Macintosh).

University of Cape Town

http://www.os2.iaccess.za/gsb/index.htm

The University of Cape Town Graduate Business School is Africa's first business school on the Web. It offers a dynamic look at the changes in Africa today by employing a mix of information on diverse programs such as foreign student exchange and Association In Management, a degree program specifically designed for apartheid victims. You'll also see a beautiful vista of the school, which was a turn-of-the-century prison, against Table Mountain in South Africa.

Wharton School of the University of Pennsylvania

http://www.wharton.upenn.edu/

The Wharton Information Network is an excellent collection of information from one of the nation's top business schools. It is well maintained, frequently updated, and features information on faculty members, course offerings, and MBA programs.

The dynamic use of Web technology includes many documents in Adobe Acrobat format (PDF files), liberal use of icon buttons, and an integrated help page.

ALSO RECOMMENDED:

University of Chicago - Graduate School of Business

http://www-gsb.uchicago.edu/

The University of Chicago Graduate School of Business features hypertext information on admissions, degree programs, and faculty, as well as a link to a Gopher site with information on the Chicago area.

American University Kogod School of Business

http://www.american.edu:70/1/academic.depts/kogod

This site features a look at programs such as MoGIT (Management of Global Information Technology), faculty publications, and student projects in international business.

Tulane University Freeman School of Business

http://freeman.sob.tulane.edu

An interesting mix of two pages, an "official" school site with information on business degree programs and an "unofficial" student-run site with a free-form style.

MBA International Register

http://www.webcom.com/~thames/mba/

The MBA Register is a Web site where MBA graduates can record information about themselves, post articles, and network.

Index - Business Schools from Tuck

http://www.dartmouth.edu/pages/tuck/bschools.html

An alternative list of business school sites across the globe and related places of interest.

Index - Marr's Official Internet Rating Guide to Management Education Around the Globe

http://www.crimson.com/fen/bus.html

An independent rating of business school Web sites.

Classifieds

Yahoo! lists a huge variety of classified ads for everything from helicopters to horses, and more.

BarterNet

http://www.teleport.com/~dtpdx/bnhome.htm

How to reach bartering groups all across the world, listed by city. This site also lists items to barter of all types, from personal services and business opportunities to recreational vehicles and computer equipment. By using a simple form interface from particular items' descriptions, you can receive information directly via e-mail.

Beer Classifieds

http://www.mindspring.com/~jlock/beerads0.html

Suds listings by category, including brewing supplies, magazine and book publishers, brewers, and pubs. The listings are free (you can add your own), and most contain e-mail/Web site links.

Business and Income Solutions Classifieds

http://www.magi.com/~bizsol/enter.html

Listings for business opportunities, products, and services. Caveat emptor.

Emporium

http://www.atw.fullfeed.com/emporium/

Items for sale or barter, including computers, demo software (available for downloading), and environment-friendly products. You can request information on a specific purchase via a forms interface and receive more information via e-mail.

EPages Internet Classifieds

http://ep.com/

Free classifieds listed by region or subject, in areas such as merchandise, personals, jobs, and services. The regional listing page has a form where you can enter your area code and then view a list of available items in your area. You can also send e-mail directly to persons offering items from the item description page and post your own ads.

For Sale By Owner

http://www.teleport.com/~filmnw/
4_sale_by_owner.html

Classifieds by categories such as collectibles, jewelry, sporting goods, music, and computers. There's also a Want To Buy section where you can post an inquiry, and a form to use to place your own ad. This is where you could find that signed James Brown poster.

Fun City Free Classified Advertising

http://www.funcity.com/

Free listings in several categories, including art and collectibles, aviation and automobiles, electronics and computers, books, business, and clothing. Each listing includes an e-mail link, and you can use a form at the site to place your own ad.

Global Marketing Classifieds

http://www.indy.net/~bbrat/
global.html

Basic listings in the areas of automobiles, business opportunities, music, and computer hardware. Classifieds include price information and a contact phone number.

Highway Classifieds

http://www.tiac.net/users/pwb/
hwctop.html

Classifieds for books, emergency equipment, home entertainment, and household items. There's also information available directly from advertisers for shoes, screwdrivers, and skeleton keys (amaze your friends!).

iMALL Classifieds

http://www.imall.com/ads/ads.shtml

A nicely laid out site, iMALL has direct links to a good classified ad search mechanism, or you can browse the listings directly in a hierarchical listing (categories range from Automobiles and Real Estate to Pets and Personals). We found a Bugs Bunny sweater, used, $20, no problem. Each listing has a dynamic e-mail link that you can use to contact the poster directly.

Internet Ad Pages

http://netmar.com/mall/ads/

Listings by category, including miscellaneous items, real estate, software, and employment. You can also browse a list of miscellaneous items wanted and post your own ads by filling in an online order form.

Internet Classifieds

http://ad.wwmedia.com/classified/
main.html

Media Xpress's ads include primary classifications for autos and aircraft, business and collectibles, investment and real estate, and employment. You can also search the entire list by keyword (type of job) and location.

Ithaca Internet Classifieds

http://wordpro.com/classifieds

Ithaca, New York, regional ad site, with many categories (including jobs, restaurants, lodging, personals, and

real estate) and a good table-based interface for general categories. There's also a complete linked category list with visual feedback on whether there are any current ads posted in that section.

JJ Electronic Plaza Classifieds

http://www.jjplaza.com/onlinead/
welcome.html

Basic classifieds for businesses, entertainment, help wanted, merchandise, and personals, with contact information.

Laran Communications

http://www.web-ads.com/

This site's listings are in an easy-to-use table format, which also shows the number of ads currently available. Categories include computers and software, business opportunities, vehicles, employment, and real estate.

National InterAd

http://www.nia.com/

Illustrated classifieds for real estate, travel, marine equipment, vehicles, and business opportunities. There are explicit search forms for each category, allowing you to narrow your search. You can also browse the listings directly in a number of different ways.

Net-AD

http://www1.mhv.net/~intercity/
netad.htm

This is a direct link to a form used to submit an ad to the InterCity Net-AD service. There's also a link to the service's main home page.

On-Line Trader

http://www.onlinetrader.com/closeouts/index.html

Closeouts, surplus, government-seized merchandise, and department store returns. You can access an index of these here, including items like *The Dust Bunny Chronicles,* Suzanne Somers exercise videos, handheld sewing machines, and odd-lot African dolls.

Public Service Announcements

http://webnetserv.com/psa

A place to post free public service ads, this site has included information on new computer viruses and announcements about upcoming film showings and festivals. There's also information on whom to contact to submit your own ad.

Traders' Connection

http://www.trader.com/

Half a million ads online, available through telnet or direct-dialup via modem (not on the Web). This site explains the service and how to connect to it.

Trading Post

http://www.tradingpost.com/TradingPost/

Business-to-consumer and personal ads, in areas such as employment and education, automotive, sporting goods, and jewelry. You can also use HTML markup in your own Web ads. The Trading Post FAQ outlines services offered and fees.

Visual Marketplace Online, Inc.

http://www.forman.com/v20/

Fine autos, boats, motor homes, and real estate for sale, including photo galleries of items offered with pricing and contact information.

WebBarter

http://www.ultranet.com/~bellvill/webbarter.html

Individuals bartering goods and services. Each listing includes items offered or wanted and an e-mail contact link. You can register directly here.

World Wide Web Classified Ads

http://www.commercial.net/vault/ads/classifi.html

Miscellaneous classifieds from around the world. Categories include animals and livestock, property rentals, machinery, employment, money, aviation, and boats.

World-Wide Classifieds

http://www.world-wide.com/wwa/

Forms-based classified ad search mechanism. You can search by a wide range of classifications (automotive, general merchandise, real estate, and more) via a scrolling menu. There's also information on placing your own free ad on the service.

WorldPort Classifieds

http://www.worldport.com/classified

Free classifieds browsable by category (including areas such as business, computer, employment, and real estate). You can also search for a specific item, view all of the listings at once, or request classifieds be sent to you directly via e-mail.

WorldWide Classifieds

http://www.worldwide-classifieds.com/classifieds/

Paid ads for items in categories such as automobiles, boats, finance, computers, medical services, real estate, and personals. You can browse each category and view the listings in a number of ways, including by subject, location, or price.

Adoption

Adoptee Classifieds

http://www.law.cornell.edu/~shelden/adoption.html

A searchable index to the Internet newsgroups focused on adoptees searching for birth parents and vice versa. It's an interesting project with a basic search interface, along with a hyperlinked list of recent articles you can browse directly.

Aircraft

Aviation from the *big* (commercial airliners) to the *small* (single-pilot craft and ultralights). You'll also find a site specifically for helicopter sales.

Aircraft Shopper Online

http://www.sonic.net/aso/

A site to find aircraft-related items in a large number of categories, including new and used planes, manufacturers, dealers, and service providers. You can place an ad for 30 days for free, and plane listings can also include several images.

Warbirds

http://www.sonic.net/aso/74.html

Aircraft Shopper Online's Web page devoted specifically to fighter aircraft. Pick up a P51D Mustang or an ex-Soviet Yak fighter for your backyard.

Aviation Classifieds

http://haven.uniserve.com/~aircraft/welcome.html

Listings for preowned aircraft and parts, including homebuilts and ultralights. There's also a section where you can look for pilots and aviation mechanics (and read their resumes).

Commercial Aircraft for Sale

http://corp.intergal.com/aircraft/

The *big* ones. This site has a nice table view of several larger commercial aircraft for sale, including details on mileage, seating, and price, with linked inline images. Interesting to know you can *buy* a 737 over the Internet! Just scrape together $25.5 million with your pals.

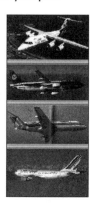

NorthStar's Aircraft for Sale

http://www.toronto.com/flyer/northstar/index.htm

This site has a good index of planes for sale by category, including the number available at the current time. This makes for easy browsing. There's also a glossary of aviation terms used in the listings.

RotorNet Helicopters

http://www.ftech.co.uk/~retford

A basic site for international used helicopter sales. There's a simple e-mail interface for submitting an inquiry after you've read the listings and information on how to place an ad.

Arts and Crafts

The arts section, where you can find that Erte vase and that Picasso lithograph for the rec room.

Art Cellar Exchange Classified Ads

http://www.artcellarex.com/ace/classifieds.html

Fine art listings, including limited-edition lithographs, etchings, paintings, and sculpture, with price and date information. There's an alphabetical index that lets you jump to a section by letter, and some of the listings include beautiful images. You can use a form to directly request a price quote on an art item or to make a bid.

Automotive

Australian Classic Cars

http://www.wps.com.au/

Australian Classic Cars Monthly's site featuring used cars from Down Under and New Zealand as well, including for-sale listings, wanteds, and miscellaneous free classifieds.

Auto View

http://www.well.com/user/av062813/autoview.htm

Nice-looking site for used car ads. Each listing includes a small color graphic and a full description, plus contact information.

autoBANK

http://cygnus.igs.net/autobank/

This site allows you to search for a specific car type, model year, and price range, and will then present you with a list of models you can choose from. Then it looks up a number of particular dealer offers and gives you a list to choose from.

Automobile Buyers' Network

http://www.dmssoft.com/

This site features a database of car listings you can search via an interactive form or directly. You can also browse all of the listings by area code and view dealer information.

Automotive Online

http://www.nando.net/classads/auto/

Car listings for North Carolina, from the *News and Observer.* You can look at dealer inventory, or check out the *News and Observer* used car classifieds by category. This site also includes a good search mechanism.

AutoNetwork

http://www.autonetwork.com/

A comprehensive search index highlights this site. It allows you to search by make and model and provides a good hyperlinked list of what's currently available. You'll also find a link to the *African Americans On Wheels* automotive newsletter.

AutoPlus

http://www.tiac.net/users/autoplus/

New England car listings, including dealer offerings and free used car classifieds. You'll also find special deals (most prices lowered for Internet users), an online new car showroom, and links to the Massachusetts Executive Office of Consumer Affairs and Business Regulation.

AutoWeb Interactive For Sale By Owner

http://www.autoweb.com/byowner.htm

Cars for sale by private owner, listed by area code. Click on your area code to go directly to that section. Most car descriptions also include an e-mail link. There's also a link to a search mechanism called AutoFinder, which you can use to look for a car by make, model, and price range.

Bugattis For Sale

http://dutoc74.io.tudelft.nl/bsale.htm

This Netherlands site features European Bugatti-for-sale listings culled from various magazines and other sources and a link to the Bugatti home page (with pictures).

C.A.R.S.

http://www.elysian.net/cars/

Classic Auto Registry Service provides classic car listings by make, from Buicks and Chevys to Nash Ramblers and Hudson Hornets. Most include color graphics.

C.A.R.S. Net Auto Swapmeet

http://www.carsnet.com/

An extension of San Diego's CARS auto swap meet, this site features car listings, information on car videos, and an events page. Um, there's also a "car babe of the month" section.

Calling All Cars Marketplace

http://www.cacars.com/cac/cachome.html

Car listings from this magazine are arranged by make in a hyperlinked index, which leads to a model list you can choose from to see an individual listing (including pictures). Here's where you'll find that Delorean or Monster Truck. There's also a sample of the *Calling All Cars* magazine online and a section listing Recreational Vehicles.

Car-Link

http://www.bdt.com/car-link/

Information on the CAR-LINK ISDN dialup database. It's not currently on the Internet, and it's only for PCs running Windows, and you have to have an ISDN connection for your system, and it's only available in California. But if you meet those criteria, it *will* connect you to a large database of car information.

Hotrods World Wide

http://www.america.net/com/hotrods/hrhome.html

Street rods, including great listings with graphics on specialty cars and events. There's also an advertiser's index and a coming events section.

Internet Classic Car Connection

http://www.primenet.com/~dadalus/classic.html

A site for international car listings, including information on car auctions and tours, and a guide to used car buying.

internetAUTOMOTIVE

http://www.internetautomotive.com/

Car ads and catalogs, some in Adobe Acrobat format (which makes them look almost like the print versions). You can browse via a regional list. There's also a classic car section with full-color images.

Marques and Sparks

http://www.innotts.co.uk/~margin/MandS

Car and bike listings from the U.K., including new makes, classics, and specials. Each listing has a color graphic and a link to more information on the dealer or other contacts.

MG Classifieds

http://www.ipl.co.uk/MG/classified.html

Worldwide MG listings, including cars and parts for sale, and links to other MG-oriented sites and the MG home page.

MotorCity

http://www.motorcity.com/

This site features an interactive graphical map leading to information on upcoming auto events and dealer offerings. There's also a global vehicle search linked here that lets you look for a car by make, class, and price range.

Swap Meet

http://www.mm.com/swapmeet/

This site includes car and motorcycle listings, vendor and dealer information, and free listings for cars and parts wanted. There's also information on upcoming events and rallies.

UsedCar Net

http://www.rezn8.com/usedcars/

A database of used cars that allows you to search by make, model, price, and even mileage. Results include dealer contact information, and some also have pictures of the cars described.

Vettes On The Net Classifieds

http://www.bcd.com/bcd/votn/forsale/default.html

A place to list your Corvette on the Web. Ads can include stunning full-color graphics. There's also a link to the Vettes On The Net Corvette home page.

Webfoot's Used Car Lot

http://www.webfoot.com/lots/international.car.lot.html

The Webfoot has a very useful set of links to used car lot pages across the Internet arranged by two-letter state abbreviations at this site. There are also Canadian provinces listed.

Wheels On-Line

http://www.snsnet.net/wol/

The place that states, "If it has wheels, we'll advertise it!" Here you'll find great listings by make ranging from Rolls Royces to Yugos. Each listing has a full-color graphic, complete descriptions, and contact information.

Boats

Used boats for sale, including listings by powerboat and sailboat classifications and specific regional information.

National Boat Listing Service - Pacific NW

http://www.marinenetwork.com/~marinent/nblspnw.html

This site features boat listings (with color pictures) and marine products and services, searchable via menu selections, for the Pacific Northwest region. There's also information on clearing U.S. Customs and schedules for the Washington State ferry system.

National Boat Listings - East Coast, Great Lakes, Heartland River System, Canada

http://www.marinenetwork.com/~marinent/blonlhp.html

This part of the National Boat Listing features boats from the East Coast, the Heartland river system, the Great Lakes area, and Canada. You can search boats by type, and marine products and services from a pull-down menu.

Western Boat Listing

http://www.gsn.com/bin/welcome.exe??Western_Boat_Listing?/sports/boating/usedboat/usedboat.htm?Yahoo

More than 2000 used boats are listed at this impressive West Coast site. You can search by extensive pull-down menu criteria (several types of boats are listed), type of construction material, date of manufacture, and price. Listings include full details and contact information, and some include color pictures.

Collectibles

Not just Hummel figurines, but also trading cards and items of general interest to collectors. (OK, you'll also find Hummel stuff here too.)

The Collectors Network

http://www.xmission.com/~patco/collect.html

This site features an e-mail Internet collectors information exchange (you'll have to subscribe first), links to other, related home pages, and a gateway to Usenet newsgroups especially focused on collector topics (indexed by several categories).

The Trading Card Classifieds

http://www.teleport.com/~filmnw/tradingcards.html

A short listing of trading cards available from a private collector, with scanned images. There's also a link to a site for prepaid phone card collectors.

CyberPages Classifieds

http://www.cyberpages.com/classifieds/

Personal ads for items under $100. You can jump to a city listing by a first-letter index, browse items for sale, and you can also add items yourself via a forms interface.

Employment

Mineralogy, education, and scientific job specialties listings. There's also a career-placement site for promoting yourself in more general classifications.

Classified Ads from JOM

http://www.tms.org/pubs/journals/JOM/classifieds.html

Job listings from the *Journal Of Mineralogy*. These include industrial and academic positions. There's also a link to the main JOM site, with a current copy of the journal online.

EDNET

http://pages.prodigy.com/CA/luca52a/bagley.html

This site provides information on how to connect to the Educator's Network BBS, a dial-up (non-Internet) classifieds listing for jobs in education in several Southern California counties.

Science JobNet

http://sgcn.aaas.org/sgcn/

An index of current job listings from the journal *Science,* in many scientific fields. The fields are listed by organization and job title, allowing

you to search them using the Find or Search function of your Web browser. The job links lead to scanned copies of the journal ads, an interesting approach.

Employment Edge

http://sensemedia.net/sprawl/employment.edge

At this site, click on icons for accounting, auditing, engineering, legal, management, and programming/MIS to reach job listings by category. There's also a Help Wanted section, and you're encouraged to post your resume (or your job offering) to the site.

Horses

EQuest Classifieds

http://www.mindspring.com/~gary/equest.html

Hunters, jumpers, and ponies are listed here. Each category has a list of available horses by name, including descriptions and terms offered. Most include links to full-color images. There's also information on how to add your own horse.

HORSES!

http://horses.product.com/

Equinet has a large amount of information on horses listed here, including for sale and wanted lists, a foal showcase, and stallion procurement ads. There are also listings for horse property, products, and services, as well as information on books and publications on the subject.

Music

Music Gear Marketplace

http://indyunix.iupui.edu/~badrian/
list.html

The Big Used Gear List, where you can find personal ads for drums, bass, guitar, amps, and outboard gear. Listings are free (but no businesses) and include e-mail links so you can negotiate directly. You can use a direct form to post your own stuff.

PFF Music Co.

http://www.escape.com/~sequence/

This company offers custom music design, including jingles, scoring, and music for CD-ROMs. Its site includes sample WAV audio files you can check out.

SoundWave

http://soundwave.com

The professional audio industry's link to the Internet. This site features a music industry guide, a compact disc report, and an upcoming trading post (for music equipment buyers and sellers). There's also a current events and news section.

Personals

match.com

http://www.match.com/

Find your perfect match here. Guests can browse new member profiles and register for an anonymous membership for free. Members can match their profiles to other members. There's also an online romance magazine and an advice section.

Ottawa/Hull Contact Pages Index

http://lyra.newforce.ca/

Groovy site with strong graphics and links to classifieds for gay, lesbian, straight, couples, bisexual, and fetish interests. You can also post a free ad here.

Regional

Classifieds by country and state. You can use this category to narrow your search to a specific place close to you.

Countries

Australian Directory of Travel, Real Estate, Business and Classifieds

http://www.wps.au

World Publishing Systems' site features the World Of Classifieds, arranged by state. These include listings for vehicles, appliances, business equipment, and livestock. New Zealand is also included.

Canada - ICE Online's Classified Ads

http://www.iceonline.com/
classified.html

Free classifieds for British Columbia, in areas such as accommodations, real estate, employment, services, and personals. Each ad contains a direct e-mail link.

Canada - Internet Buy, Sell & Directory Service

http://www.isisnet.com/ibs/

Nova Scotia classifieds, arranged in a nice alphabetical list by category. The listings include ads for furniture, automobiles, dolls, books, camping supplies, and more.

Canada - NetAdsR'us Classifieds

http://www.iceonline.com/home/
davide/deversweb/main.html

Vancouver Lower Mainland site with paid advertising. Here's where you'll find architecturally beautiful treehouses, chefs who will work in your home, psychics, skydiving lessons, and business card listings.

Canada - Vancouver Island Classifieds Online

http://www.islandnet.com/~willard/
html/homepage.html

VICO has free ads in areas such as finance, employment, and merchandise, listed by category. The main category view also shows how many ads are currently available, making browsing more efficient.

United Kingdom - FLUTE

http://www.internetweb.co.uk/
centres/classifi/flute/flute.htm

A free classified index, categories include antiques, clothing, household items, appliances, property, and pets. You can also check for vacancies and look at personal messages. There are easy-to-use forms you can use to enter your own ad.

United Kingdom - InternetWeb

http://www.internetweb.co.uk/
centres/

Paid advertisements in areas such as professional services, cars, shopping, travel and hotel information, and leisure. There's an easy-to-use button map interface that also includes a guided tour of the site.

United Kingdom - Net Classifieds

http://www.net-classifieds.co.uk/

International classifieds for a number of countries. Click on the flag of your choice to go to that category. The U.K. section includes listings for vehicles, property, and small advertisements.

States

Ads for several U.S. states, from coast to coast and Hawaii as well.

California - Classified Flea Market

http://www.cfm.com/cfm

East Bay/Oakland advertisements, with more than 90 categories to choose from, including antiques, art, clothing, home furnishings, jewelry, and garage sales. There's also a special music section and a Kid's Column for children's items.

California - Coolware

http://none.coolware.com/

This site features Bay Area employment listings from a number of sources, and features a great search page that makes it easy to look for a particular job. There are also property ads.

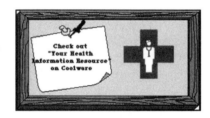

California - Mercury Center Web Classified Search

http://www.sjmercury.com/
searchc1.htm

Ads from the *San Jose Mercury News* in employment, real estate, event announcements and tickets, transportation, and merchandise. This site is linked directly to the newspaper host, and you can search the classifieds in today's paper or last Sunday's or place an ad online.

California - Palo Alto Weekly Classifieds

http://www.service.com/PAW/
thisweek/classifieds.html

Listings each week include personals, merchandise for sale or rent (including kids' stuff), business and home services, and rental properties.

California - Potpourri's Bay Area Cybershopper

http://ww.netview.com/pp/

The Buy And Sell Connection features a wide range of ad categories, including auto sales and services, employment, real estate, and home services. You can also search the Cybershopper listings directly.

California - San Mateo Times Classifieds

http://www.baynet.com/smtimes/
market/classified/index.html

Listings directly from the newspaper, in categories such as Help Wanted, Real Estate, and Automobiles. You can also search the ads by keyword.

California - SF Gate Classified Ads Directory

http://sfgate.com/classifieds/

Ads from San Francisco newspapers in real estate, employment, garage sales, personal computers, musical equipment, and more.

Colorado - FreeAdz Classifieds

http://www.freeadz.com/classifieds/

Regional Boulder listings in areas such as farm animals, autos, child care, finance, metaphysics, and travel. There's an alphabetical index you can jump to by letter, and you can browse all of the ads directly. Personal ads are free.

Colorado - WebTix Ticket Exchange

http://www.inetmkt.com/webtix/

Electronic ticket listings to sporting events and concerts in Colorado. Areas are divided by sport (college and pro) and different types of events (concert, theater, or special event), and there are also online schedules. You can post an ad directly using a Web form.

Florida - Sunday Paper

http://www.sundaypaper.com/

Turbo-powered buttons lead you to a list of classified ads that includes categories for 900 numbers (live astrologers!), advertising, AIDS awareness, business opportunities, and employment for the Florida area.

Hawaii - PennySaver Classifieds Hawaii

http://www.pennysaver.com

Ads for goods and services in Hawaii in a number of categories, including business and personal, real estate, and employment.

Maryland - Chesapeake Ads Online

http://www.cybersoft.com/pub/cybersoft/home.html

Real estate listings for Maryland's Chesapeake Bay area, available from a comprehensive search form that lets you search by specific house type, area and minimum acreage, and price. It works well and returns a list of entries that includes contact information and links to pictures.

Massachusetts - NETIS Classifieds

http://www.netis.com/forsale

Ad listings in areas such as aircraft, automobiles and boats, computers, and real estate. Each listing includes a photograph and contact information.

Massachusetts - Newburyport Classifieds

http://www.shore.net/~gacjr/class.html

Local listings for Newburyport and Boston include items for sale and employment ads. There's also a more general, worldwide classifieds listing.

New Jersey - National Internet Source Classifieds

http://aayt.nis.net/nis/niscom.main.html

The NIS Commerce Bulletin Board has free classifieds for merchandise and services, and also company listings in areas such as business and computer services (including a miscellaneous products section where you'll find Artifacts R Us, a company that will sell you a dinosaur egg with embryo intact for only $1.6 million).

Washington - ByDesign Classifieds

http://pacificrim.net/~bydesign/

General classifieds for the San Juan Island area, including information on tourist services, realty offerings, computer assistance, and music.

Washington - Exchange Nickel Want Ads

http://www.iea.com/~adlinkex/

Electronic edition of classifieds for the Spokane area. Categories include animals, boats, business equipment, child care, cars, motorcycles, and personals.

Washington - Seanet Classifieds

http://www.seanet.com/classified/

For sale and want ads for items in the Seattle area, including camera equipment, computers, furniture, cars, motorcycles, and tickets. There are also local housing and personal ads available.

Software

Used Software Exchange

http://www.hyperion.com/usox/

A great place to buy or sell used software. The showroom is easy to navigate — all you have to do is use the menus or fill out the forms for the type of software you're looking for, your computer platform, titles, publisher, and price range. The search engine then gives you a list of what's available, including contact information.

Sports

19th Hole Classifieds

http://www.sport.net/golf/classifd.html

Golf-related for-sale and items-wanted listings, including clubmaker ads. You can place ads for free using an online form.

Ski Web Classified Ads

http://www.skiweb.com/
classifieds.html

Ski rentals in Nevada, including contact information and a list of classified ad rates.

Tecnet

http://www.tecnet.com

A database of new and used equipment you can search using a simple form.

Consortia

Consortia on Yahoo! is where you'll find business groups affiliated around a particular subject. These include research and development organizations centering on information technology, computer science, cable television, financial services, climate assessment, and publishing. Consortium Web sites often feature important links to their respective members, as well as useful seminar information and position papers.

Cable Television Laboratories

http://www.cablelabs.com/

CableLabs is an international organization of cable system operators. This site features interesting documents in Adobe Acrobat format, including an RFP (request for proposal) for CableNET (cable meets Internet), an overview of cable television in the United States, as well as a hypertext White Paper on Cable and the National Information Infrastructure. There's also a member directory and a calendar of events.

CIESIN - Consortium for International Earth Science Information Network

http://www.ciesin.org/

These sites feature information on the Earth Sciences for the global community in several formats, including a Web site, two Gopher servers, and an FTP server, allowing you to look for information in a variety of ways. There's also an interesting kiosk of unpublished papers, newsletters, and global change declarations. CIESIN is active in assessing the global changes needed to cope with our changing environment.

GamePC Consortium

http://www.mmwire.com/gamepc/
gpchome.html

The GamePC Consortium is active in trying to turn a pig's ear into a silk purse — making the IBM-compatible platform into a serious game machine. This site has information on joining the consortium, conference dates, and special programs for developers, including the GamePC Demo CD-ROM.

Information Worker 2005

http://www.nidl.org/

The Information Worker site at the Sarnoff Research Center is a collaborative look at how information technology will change in the future. It includes strange scenarios of the near future (imagine a tour bus filled with remotely operated video binoculars and no people, or a corny vision of a "home shopper" buying real estate over the National Real Estate Network), an analysis of different functions of information technology

work, and an interactive tour. The site's most interesting aspect is that it actively seeks out participation from visitors, inviting writing and interactive demo submissions.

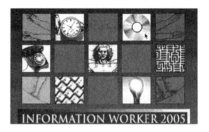

The AstroWeb Consortium

http://fits.cv.nrao.edu/www/
astroweb.html

AstroWeb is a consortium designed to pool the resources of several astronomical institutions. It maintains a large database of links to astro information on the Web, which is fairly comprehensive. This is where you'll find those cool space pictures and interactive NASA sites.

The MIT World Wide Web Consortium

http://www.w3.org/

As close to the Official Web Control Center as a site can get. Here's where you'll find out what's really going on with the Web. The W3 Consortium is dedicated to promoting stable development of software and protocols for the Internet Web, and the site provides reference material on hot WWW topics, as well as conference details and membership information.

Yahoo!

UBC MultiCentre Research Network

http://unixg.ubc.ca:780/~emerg_vh/ubc_multicentre.html

The University of British Columbia MultiCentre Research Network site is a collaboration of three Emergency Service teaching hospitals in Canada. It's a good site to find medical and emergency service-related information via a comprehensive list of links, and you can also jump to the member hospitals' and departments' respective home pages.

ALSO RECOMMENDED:

The ATM Forum

http://www.atmforum.com/

Companies and institutions looking to provide better, faster networking hardware and software.

MAGIC - Multidimensional Applications and Gigabit Internetwork Consortium

http://www.magic.net/

Sites connected by a *2.4 Gigabyte/second network,* like none of us has — yet. A peek into the future.

Consumer Economy

This is where you'll find help on consumer issues such as product safety, legal rights, and ecologically sound buying practices. Also look for the Consumer Information Center online, a legal self-help center, and consumer brochures from the Federal Trade Commission and the Consumer Product Safety Commission.

Consumer Information (from the U.S. Postal Service)

http://www.usps.gov/consumer/

The USPS maintains a good collection of documents at its main site on subjects such as mail fraud and common postal scams. There's also information on upcoming postal auctions of unclaimed property, a section on how to file change-of-address forms when you move, and a postal FAQ (which finally explains why you get your mail so late in the day).

Consumer Information Center

http://www.gsa.gov/staff/pa/cic/cic.htm

This is the big Pueblo, Colorado, center you may have seen on TV. The site's interface is very good, with subject categories arranged around an easy-to-navigate street sign map. The whole catalog is here, with hypertext versions of government pamphlets available to view and text versions for downloading.

European Consumer Policy Service

http://www.cec.lu/en/comm/spc/spc.html

The European Commission maintains this site as a way for customers to understand their rights in the new Common Market. It's well laid out and features sections on cross-border shipping, taxes, product safety, and contracts. There's also specific information on food and drink, pharmaceuticals, cosmetics, travel, and housing. It's interesting to see how the European Common Market is striving to provide answers to consumers doing business with new countries for the first time. With a site such as this, it's easy for consumers to find out what they need to know in order to reassure and protect themselves.

FTC Consumer Brochures

http://www.webcom.com/~lewrose/brochures.html

The U.S. Federal Trade Commission provides more than 100 brochures on subjects relevant to consumers at this site. There's information on car buying, telemarketing scams, home financing, credit lines, infomercials, and more. We were especially impressed by the brochure offering parents instructions on how to cope with toy advertising at the child level (as in, *sorry, the toy robot won't morph or fly by itself once you get it home*).

Home Recording Rights Coalition

http://www.digex.net/hrrc/hrrc.html

The HRRC has an impressive site dedicated to the protection of "home-use" video and audio recording rights. You can view a timeline of events in the chronology of home recording rights and also access an interactive White Paper on Digital Video and the National Information Infrastructure (with links to relevant Gopher sites). Find out what's up with digital recording rights before you wind up having to *pay* to tape that soap opera.

Nolo Press's Self-Help Law Center

http://gnn.digital.com/gnn/bus/nolo/

Nolo Press is dedicated to legal reform and self-help for individuals, and its site reflects this commitment. This is a good spot to find out how to keep your legal costs in control. There are special Web books such as *Fed Up With The Legal System: What's Wrong And How To Fix It,* and articles on trademark rights, child custody planning, and how to cope with an IRS audit. You can also read plain-English legal briefs on law issues and access a large hypertext list of insensitive lawyer jokes. (Q: What's the difference between a lawyer and a tick? A: The tick drops off when you die.)

The EnviroProducts Directory

http://envirolink.org/products/

The Progressive Businesses Web Page offers a direct link to the Internet Green Marketplace, a small list of environmentally conscious businesses on the Internet. There are also links to Students for Responsible Business (SRB) chapters across the Internet, progressive publications, mailing lists, and government support agencies. This is a good site for consumers interested in getting involved in eco-conscious activities on the Web.

U.S. Consumer Product Safety Commission

gopher://cpsc.gov/

This Gopher site has a large amount of information on consumer products and health matters, including press releases announcing product recalls, consumer hotline numbers, a CPSC calendar of events, and a series of product safety publications designed to keep parents awake at night (try "Bunk Bed Entrapment Hazard"). Seriously, it's a good place to keep abreast of manufacturer recalls and general product safety guidelines.

Economics

The technical aspects of financing and marketing are located here, with sites focusing on economic policies and regulations, accounting and auditing, and game theory. You'll also find an interesting set of economic time series charts from various government agencies, and even some economist jokes.

Economic Bulletin Board - EBB

gopher://una.hh.lib.umich.edu/11/ebb

EBB is a U.S. government Gopher server with a wide range of economic information from several different agencies, including statistics on agriculture, defense conversion, energy, foreign trade, U.S. income levels, and more. You can also search here for a specific document topic (find out what your disposable income *should* be!).

Antitrust Policy

http://www.vanderbilt.edu/Owen/froeb/antitrust/antitrust.html

This site features a hypertext journal (in table format) on the subject of antitrust policy. It has links to economic research, government policies, and other antitrust sites. The journal also has links to specific case histories and an online discussion group area. We bet Microsoft stops by here a lot.

Berkeley Roundtable on the International Economy

http://server.berkeley.edu/BRIE/

The Berkeley Roundtable on the International Economy (BRIE) focuses on the areas of international competitiveness and the development and implementation of advanced technologies. Its site offers working papers, research notes, and works in progress. The attention to file formats is especially good: The working paper on Interoperability and the National Information Infrastructure is available in PostScript, MS Word, WordPerfect, and ASCII formats.

Federal Reserve Board Data

gopher://town.hall.org/1/other/fed

This Gopher site features table data on subjects such as the flow of funds in money markets, selected interest rate charts, asset and liabilities studies of large commercial institutions, and industrial productivity/capitalization reports. There's also a link to other Federal Reserve data tables containing more of the same.

Yahoo!

Economist Jokes

http://www.etla.fi/pkm/joke.html

If you get tired of tons of flat statistics, pop over to this site. You'll find a fair amount of economist-oriented jokes, some of which are even comprehensible by noneconomists. Q: How many economists does it take to screw in a light bulb? A: One to prepare the proposal, an econometrician to run the model, one each MS and Ph.D. students to write the theses and dissertations, two more to prepare the journal article (senior authorship not assigned), four to review it, and at least as many to refine the model and replicate the results.

History Of Game Theory

http://william-king.www.drexel.edu/top/History.html

Game Theory is a favorite of economists, and this site provides an interesting timeline look at how the theories involved in games of chance got folded into economics and decision-support theory. Take this lovely abstract, from a 1962 paper: "In their paper College Admissions and the Stability of Marriage, D. Gale and L. Shapley asked whether it is possible to match m women with m men so that there is no pair consisting of a woman and a man who prefer each other to the partners with whom they are currently matched. Game theoretically the question is, does the appropriately defined NTU coalitional game have a non-empty core? Gale and Shapley proved not only non-emptiness but also provided an algorithm for finding a point in it." Game theoretically, indeed!

University of Maryland, InforM EconData

http://info.umd.edu:86/ Educational_Resources/ AcademicResourcesByTopic/ EconomicsResources/EconData/ .www/econdata.html

InforM is a valuable resource of economic time series information presented in a variety of layouts, including national income, balance of payments, employment statistics, and consumer price indices. All of the data is in G format, a specialized data set. You'll need to use the commercial G reader version or the public-domain program PGS to view the information. PGS is available to download from this site (PC version only). The data also needs to be downloaded before use and can't be viewed directly in your Web browser.

ALSO RECOMMENDED:

Government

http://www.yahoo.com/ Business_and_Economy/Economics/ Government/

This section offers links to a full-text version of President Clinton's economic plan, and a site for the Office of Economic Conversion Information, a government agency working with industry on defense conversion (beating swords into plowshares).

Institutes

http://www.yahoo.com/ Business_and_Economy/Economics/ Institutes/

The Economic Institutes section on Yahoo! features research organizations in the business of economic study and

forecasting. Here you'll also find direct links to many university economics departments.

Finance

http://www.yahoo.com/ Business_and_Economy/Economics/ Finance/

The Finance section is where you'll find information on conferences and courses in financial management, as well as journals, organizations, and institutes centered on the subject. It has links to the WWW Virtual Library Finance index (even more financial sites) and the KiwiClub Financial Web server at the University of Texas.

Education

Michigan State University - School of Hotel, Restaurant and Institutional Management

http://www.bus.msu.edu/broad/hri/hri.htm

Hospitality is the name of the game, and Michigan State's site gives a good look at one of the only Institutional Management programs located at a business school. The site has information on degree programs and courses and an independently ranked hypertext list of hospitality organizations and schools across the Internet.

Electronic Commerce

Digital cash, virtual transactions, cybercash, secure credit card use on the Internet — here's where you'll find the real information on this very important subject. Find out how to get involved in the new frontier of commerce and even try out some of the first interactive catalogs and shopping agents available. There's also a site with government resource information for businesses implementing EC and one on the legal aspects of transacting business without paper.

BargainFinder Shopping Agent

http://bf.cstar.ac.com/

Andersen Consulting's Bargain Finder Web page features an electronic software agent that searches for bargains from several online vendors. From the top level, you can test drive the service by entering a sample music CD query directly into a form and retrieve a list of linked sites that have what you're looking for at the best prices. This is a very interesting example of the new forms of electronic commerce. It found Frank Zappa's *ThingFish* on the first try, at Music Connection, for $30!

CommerceNet

http://www.commerce.net/

CommerceNet is a very well-organized Web site featuring corporations doing business over the Internet. Crisp graphics and an excellent layout make it very easy to navigate. It also features well-placed information and help screens, search panels, and links to news resources. CommerceNet is a good place to find companies that are proactive in providing a service over the Internet.

Digital Money

This section takes you right into the heart of the digital cash world. It includes indices to a large number of electronic payment scheme sites and direct connections as well.

Commerce on the Internet

http://gopher.econ.lsa.umich.edu/ EconInternet/Commerce.html

This is an excellent site for finding out about digital commerce. It has several links to electronic payment sites, and also has links to explanatory texts, related marketing and business sites, and legal info. This site is not too flashy, but it is quite useful.

Network Payment Mechanisms and Digital Cash

http://ganges.cs.tcd.ie/mepeirce/ project.html

This is another site filled with connections to articles, position papers, and research information about digital commerce on the Internet (and beyond), including electronic cash payments using secure newsgroups. It also has a comprehensive list of worldwide secure private banks.

Electronic Auction

http://www.primenet.com/~auction/ index.html

Electronic Auction has gone head over heels into trading over the Internet. Featuring closeout and overstock inventory, this is the place to check for bargain-basement deals on the Web. The site is basically a front end to a text-based FTP server, but it works.

Here's where to find that Suzanne Somers exercise video you've been looking for, a cheap joystick for your PC, or a closeout wedding gown.

Marketer's Help Desk

http://www.activmedia.com/

ActivMedia's online Marketer's Help Desk is a very useful site for Internet entrepreneurs. It features abstracts and ordering information for online surveys of companies on the Net, with topics such as content, management, and monthly sales distribution. There's also a linked list of sites accepting paid advertising, and a Net directory of places to promote your business site.

San Antonio Electronic Commerce Resource Center

http://www.saecrc.org/

This is where you'll find out how to do business electronically with the U.S. federal government. This site has an interactive map that leads to a lot of information on Electronic Data Interchange and how it relates to several federal agencies. There are also a few PC-compatible interactive courses available to download.

Versatile Virtual Vending

http://rainer.bnt.com/

This is a great demo of an interactive grocery store, with an easy-to-use Web browser format. You can browse food categories, search for specific items, keep track of your selections in your digital shopping cart, and even choose paper or plastic when you check out.

Buying via the Internet - An Academic Research Survey

http://www.rit.edu/~dbgacc/survey.html

Participate in a survey on how you shop over the Web.

Electronic Commerce Resource Center

http://www.ecrc.ctc.com/

A federal site for conducting electronic commerce within the military-industrial complex.

EM Electronic Markets Newsletter

http://www-iwi.unisg.ch/iwi4/cc/em/emnewsl.html

This is a good-looking professional quarterly on electronic marketing presented by the University of St. Gallen in Switzerland.

The CAFE project

http://www.digicash.com/products/projects/projects.html

A European project for standardizing electronic commerce.

Employment

Need a job? Looking to hire someone? Here's where you go. There are sites for job seekers, professional resume writers, employment agencies, and recruitment firms. The information is also broken down regionally at a number of sites, making the search easier. Some interesting links to relevant Net newsgroups and newspaper classifieds are also available. Look for sites that offer interactive search panels and good indices to help sort out what you're looking for, as well as places where you can submit your resume as a Web document.

Careers

This section deals with preparing for a career, including specifics on employment in various fields, job lists, and sales/marketing opportunities.

Careers In Finance, Accounting and Consulting

http://www.cob.ohio-state.edu/dept/fin/osujobs.htm

The Ohio State Business Job Finder is a great site with lots of information on employers in the business markets. You can look up accounting, for example, and find a list of standard job requirements and skill levels, current salary levels, and downloadable information disks. There's also a directly accessible section of prominent business firms offering multimedia links to presentations about themselves and hotlists of worldwide employers and job search aids. If you look closely, you'll find a link to a list of nonprofits on the Net as well.

CareerWEB

http://www.cweb.com/

The premier stop for job searchers on the Internet, CareerWEB features a searchable employment index, a list of employers, and library resources. You can also browse a list of career fairs to find one in your area, and take a "career fitness test" to rate yourself (Are You Weary Or Tired, Despite A Decent Night's Sleep, Before You Even Get To Work?).

Nontraditional career resources for young women

http://www.ksu.edu/~dangle/

Look here for a good list of education and career Internet resources for women looking for employment. There's also a list of women-oriented general links and an interest assessment study with direct links to nontraditional careers in several fields.

Getting Past Go

http://lattanze.loyola.edu/MonGen/home.html

An interactive career and resume planning site for job seekers just out of college.

HEART (Human Resources Electronic Advertising And Recruiting Tool)

http://www.career.com

A searchable index of job offerings where you can also attach a resume and apply for a job directly from the site.

Jobs

This is a large section of information on that eternal subject, *the job*. Look here for resources from employment agencies, sites with listings by state and regional areas, and direct connections to employers.

America's Job Bank

http://www.ajb.dni.us/

This place links the electronic listings of 1,800 state and federal employment agencies and features an easy-to-use search mechanism. Here's where you'll find that Center for Disease Control job you've been dreaming about.

Career Magazine

http://www.careermag.com/careermag/

A full-featured career center, this site has a good visual menu with links to job openings, employer profiles, and a resume bank. There's also an interactive career forum where you can participate in discussions on job search and employment issues.

E-Span Employment Database Search

http://www.espan.com/cgi-bin/ewais/

A direct search index into several job categories. Use the scrolling menu to quickly find your area and search using job specifics, regions, and dates. We found an administrative assistant position in Lake Tahoe just by searching for *legal* and *CA* and are leaving immediately.

Entry Level Job Seeker Assistant

http://galaxy.einet.net/galaxy/Community/The-Workplace/joseph-schmalhofer/jobs.html

Everyone has to start somewhere, and this is the site to do it from. Find out how to get a job without experience. There's a good hotlist of companies offering entry-level employment and a subject-oriented resume index you can link to your own page. This is a good place to point employers to as well.

Intellimatch

http://www.intellimatch.com/intellimatch/

An interactive database of resumes and employers, this site has candidates enter their resume information into a WATSON database and then matches it to a HOLMES database of employers. Intellimatch also offers an Online Job Center with alphabetical job listings, articles on high-tech careers, and a list of professional associations and job help centers.

JobCenter

http://www.jobcenter.com/

JobCenter features places to post job ads or resumes directly on the site. The service then matches resumes to jobs (or vice versa) via a database and e-mails responses back to you. You'll also get new responses when new posts that match your criteria come in. You can also search postings directly.

The Monster Board

http://199.94.216.72:81/

The Monster Board is a great site for job searchers. The impressive graphics help you to find your way around, and you can access a career-search mechanism and an online-resume section with ease. Also look for employer profiles, career events, and the CyberZone (where you can ask the monsters job-related questions and check out articles on the frontiers of online job searching). Equating monsters with employment is brilliant, and you'll enjoy this site.

The Catapult

http://www.wm.edu/catapult.html

A collaborative effort between career service professionals, this site features a clear chapter format with links to employment centers, relocation resources, and professional associations. You'll also find help guides, library resources, and special information for people with disabilities. Resources for career practitioners include a career office home page showcase, a list of course syllabi, and a section on career-assessment tools.

VISTA (Volunteers In Service To America) Online

gopher://gopher.hanover.edu/11/Hanover_College_Information/Career_Planning_and_Placement/jobs/vista

VISTA Online is a Gopher server with text copies of the *VISTA Newsletter*. Find out how to take part in increasing the capability of low-income individuals. The biweekly online journal offers updated assignment openings, program updates, and items of interest to potential volunteers.

Government

http://www.yahoo.com/
Business_and_Economy/
Employment/Jobs/Government/

A list of governmental sites with job listings for federal agencies, including regional information.

Indices

http://www.yahoo.com/
Business_and_Economy/
Employment/Jobs/

The Employment:Jobs indices on Yahoo! range from Rensselaer Polytechnic Institute's Career Resource home page to a University of Michigan guide to employment opportunities on the Net. These have more links to job information and services.

Usenet

http://www.yahoo.com/
Business_and_Economy/
Employment/Jobs/Usenet/

This is where you'll go to find more than 40 Usenet job newsgroups, mostly laid out by specific regions. Although not as attractive as Web listings, these can still be very useful for job seekers.

Resumes

Dust it off, polish it up, and put it on the Internet. You'll be surprised at how extensively helpful the Net can be for

a job applicant, and this section is where you go to show yourself off. You can also use it to look for people to hire.

CybeRezumes for Personal Marketing

http://www.seanet.com/HTML/
Vendors/raj/cyberez.html

A place to look for information on job listings, companies looking to hire, and employment resources. Special sections include a rundown on what to expect on a job interview, and how to present yourself.

Get A Job!

http://sensemedia.net/getajob

You can't get much clearer than that, can you? This site for hypermedia professionals features a nicely laid-out job board with links to prospective employers and other career sites, and a list of hypermedia professionals' resumes. You can add yours to this list by sending it in HTML format to the site maintainer. It'll post it for free!

Shawn's Internet Resume Center

http://www.website.net/sirc/

This is also a good place to post your resume. Resumes are listed by subject matter, making them easy to find, and there's also an Employer's Guest Book.

Interactive Resume Search

http://www.tisny.com/tis/
tis_form.html

Transaction International Systems offers an interesting forms-based selection mechanism for hiring computer consultants across the Internet. You can search a resume database by multiple criteria, including platform experience, type of occupation, and professional skills, via scrolling menus. You can also select a fax, phone, or e-mail response from the service, and browse a list of contract positions available.

Resumes and More

http://www.tiac.net/users/rooftop/
index.html

A place to find out about a professional resume writing service (and have yours critiqued), with links to other job-related sites, not to mention the coolest t-shirts on the Net. Bow to Spammon!

Usenet - resumes

news:misc.jobs.resumes

The Usenet newsgroup for posting resumes directly to the greater Internet community.

Individual resumes

If you've got your own home page, you might want to attach your resume to it. This is the section on Yahoo! that you can register it with. It's also a good place to check out other individuals' Net resumes, and to look for qualified job seekers. Also see the Student Resumes section for resume links directly from colleges and universities.

History

Movies of Financial Executives and Speakers

http://www.cob.ohio-state.edu/dept/fin/clips.htm

The Clipmedia In Finance site from the Fisher Business School at Ohio State University is an interesting way to preserve business history through multimedia. This site features pictures from historical stock markets showing how trading was performed in the past, links to other sites with business multimedia files, and movies from financial bigwig T. Boone Pickens (see him give career advice and equate large shareholders with camels) and executives from Allstate Insurance and JC Penney.

International Economy

International finance by country is located here, as well as information on trade conferences and governmental agencies promoting international business. You'll find good sites with lots of information, including Pacific Rim business and management data and opportunities in the new Russian Republic. There's also a link to a site with a large amount of World Bank socioeconomic data.

Conferences

Mostly information on the G7 Economic Summit (centered in 1996 on the Global Information Infrastructure), sites under this heading include a daily Internet update, detailed conference information, a chronology of summit meetings, and lists of member organizations.

Development

Virtual Libraries On International Development

http://www.synapse.net/~acdi03/indexg/welcome.htm

This site has a clickable world map that leads to a sampling of Internet resources for International Development, including regional information, networking, and international organization links. There's also a section on social indicators and trends and a scrolling menu of Internet search engines.

Pacific Region Forum on Business and Management Communication

gopher://hoshi.cic.sfu.ca/11/dlam/business/forum

A number of texts on business concerns in the Pac Rim markets are located here, including future forecasts for China, comments on the importance of cross-cultural face-negotiation techniques, investor relations in Japan, the emergence of Vietnam as a business market, and more.

Russian and East European Studies Business and Economic Resources

http://www.pitt.edu/~cjp/rsecon.html

Part of the World Wide Web Virtual Library, this site has a good set of links to business, economic, and legal information about the Russian Republic. These include trade journals, e-mail discussion lists, stock and commodities markets, travel-related sites, and development studies.

The Japan That Can Say No

gopher://hoshi.cic.sfu.ca/1m/dlam/business/japan

The full text of Akito Morita's famous book, where the chairman of Sony Corporation sits anywhere he wants. It's in a format any browser can read, and provides an interesting insight into Japanese business philosophy.

US Council for International Business

http://www.uscib.org/

This U.S. agency site explains what an ATA Carnet happens to be. That's a Merchandise Passport, which facilitates Customs clearances for import/exporters. Coverage ranges from ordinary goods such as computers and cameras to extraordinary items such as Van Gogh's self-portrait, Ringling Brothers tigers, satellites, and the New York Philharmonic. Electronic application and fee information is also available here.

World Bank socio-economic data

http://www.cc.ukans.edu/hytelnet_html/FUL030.html

A gateway into a telnet site with a large range of economic data from countries around the world, ranging from 1960-1986. The information covers 126 countries and tracks 126 socioeconomic indicators.

Labor

This area contains links to other spots on Yahoo! with labor information on education, health and employment issues, including the US Department of Labor. You'll find a good amount of information on the Internet about workers' rights and professional concerns arranged here. There's also a link to an interesting site focusing on workplace issues.

Workplace Labor Update

http://venable.com/wlu/wlu3.htm

This site contains a hypertext labor law newsletter. A recent issue centered on violence in the workplace, civil rights, and medical coverage issues, not to mention Kitchengate (where the White House French chef got the boot after the Clintons moved in — not enough fried chicken and black-eyed peas on the menu).

Magazines

Magazines for the business community. These range in subject from farm information and home buying to mutual-fund and stock market performance. There are also magazines focusing on new product trends, technology, and innovation. There are only a few fully blown Web versions of business magazines located here, but the larger ones (such as *Fortune* and *Mutual Fund Magazine*) are very well done, and even the smaller sites are worth a look.

Farmer To Farmer

http://www.organic.com/Non.profits/F2F/

A look at farming in California. Sections of the first issue include a farm profile, a pesticide report, a study on the demands for organic cotton products, and an editorial on the move toward natural farming.

For Sale By Owner Magazine

http://www.human.com/mkt/fsbo/

How to sell your own house, and where to advertise the sale on the Internet. This publication includes interactive house listings by state and location (with pictures), area maps (mostly California), and a form you can use to place your own ad. There's also a link to free home buyer qualification and refinancing software packages, so you can get your sweating done in the privacy of your own home (or apartment).

Fortune 500

http://www.pathfinder.com/fortune/fortune.html

The big list. This interactive version features an index that lets you view the list by rankings in sales/revenue, profits, assets, equity, or market value. You can also search for a particular company directly, and look at group listings by industry and state. There are also articles on the development of the Fortune 500 list, and on trends that the editors feel lead to getting your company ranked.

Ideas DIGest ONLINE

http://www.ideas.wsi.net/

A small business magazine on developing creative ideas for the marketplace. There are articles on the invention process, special reports on trademarks and idea presentation, as well as an events calendar and a classified section. You can also read a summary of innovation in the news (check out the Feb./Mar. 95 report on "Gusty," the umbrella that can withstand hurricane-force winds).

It'sNEW!

http://www.cts.com/~itsnew/

Everything under the sun (Shakespeare notwithstanding). Here you'll find brief selections from the newsstand version of this trend and innovation magazine. A recent "Environmental" issue featured an interesting look at an electric bicycle being produced in Malibu, future light bulb technology, and a new Rolls Royce jet engine (environmental? It uses more fuel per hour than an average family car does in two years — but it's efficient!). There's also information on how to get your product listed.

Mutual Funds Magazine

http://www.mfmag.com/

Find out about mutual funds and their performance here. This is a very good-looking online magazine. You can use a visual table of contents reproduced from the print magazine to reach any article, or use a search mechanism to get to an area of interest. There are also Adobe Acrobat versions of articles available to download. Use the database to access information on over 6000 funds, including daily performance rankings, a phone directory, and fund reports. You can also submit letters to the editor and story ideas here, and subscribe to the magazine via a secure form.

NASDAQ Financial Services Journal

http://www.law.cornell.edu/nasdaq/v3n4%2f

A journal on financial issues affecting the NASDAQ stock market, this version features articles on employee stock option programs, interviews with financial leaders, and corporate strategy reports.

Stellar Business

http://corp.tig.com/stellar/global/index.html

Practical business information with a touch of magic. This magazine features reports on what's new in the business community, editorial departments on marketing, corporate finance, and human resources, a section on personal business items (for the busy exec), and regional information.

Management Information Systems

Sites on the subject of MIS include conference information, interactive course materials, direct links to institutes and universities, and online journals. There are also sites with links to more information on MIS on the Web and on how MIS will relate to the new National Information Infrastructure.

MIS WEB

http://www.smeal.psu.edu/misweb/

A good site for jumping into the Web of MIS (the picture of a black hole representing the Internet is particularly appropriate). There are a lot of links to IS sites, including news sections, a library, and interactive course materials.

Institutes

This section features institutes for MIS training, industry and academic conferencing, and IS technology management. There are also experimental electronic forums you can access.

Loyola College in Maryland - Center for Executive Studies in Information Systems

http://ignatius.lattanze.loyola.edu/lattanze

The David D. Lattanze Center at Loyola provides a forum for executives and academics to confer on issues in MIS and information technology. This site features membership and program information, working papers, and a member directory.

MIS Training Institute

http://www.bitwise.net/misti/MIS-I.HTML

This site features a list of training seminars by subject and location, including course summaries and fees. There's also course outline information and information on how to request (via e-mail) a specific course not listed here.

University of Texas - Information Systems Management

http://cism.bus.utexas.edu/

The Center for Information Systems Management site is an intellectual indexing of subjects related to MIS at the Graduate Business School of the University of Texas. You can access the MIS Collaboratory, an interactive representation of the relationship of MIS to organizational technology, and post comments in its electronic forums. There are also research papers on MIS topics available.

ISWorld Net

http://www.isworld.org/isworld.html

A great site for MIS matters, this is a single entry point into multiple resources for information technology. An easy-to-use button map leads to MIS information from several sites, including research and scholarship information, teaching and learning sites, electronic journals, and a What's New list.

MISQ Central

http://www.cox.smu.edu/mis/misq/central.html

This is an electronic extension of the *MIS Quarterly,* a journal focusing on research into information technology. This site features an experimental electronic forum (currently featuring a Call for Papers from MIS professionals) and a system archivist that you can use to search past issue abstracts. There are also a few full-text articles available, on subjects such as CASE tools and business reengineering.

Organizations

Society for Information Management

http://www.simnet.org/

A professional organization for information executives, SIM's site has a section on upcoming conferences and forums on management and technology, a list of member chapters and working groups, and membership information. There's also a section on IS advocacy and outlines of companies successfully implementing Total Quality Management in their IS business.

Strictly Business! Web

http://www.uni.com/

Here's where you'll find an information exchange between entrepreneurs, managers, and business professionals. The site offers an online newsletter (check out articles on how to protect yourself from a bad investment, organizing the home office, and avoiding creative block) and a catalog system with direct links to business opportunities, products, and services arranged by subject.

ALSO RECOMMENDED:

Index - Information Systems

http://rampages.onramp.net/
~mnixon/isr.htm

Mark Nixon's list of IS links is worth checking out. It includes links to vendors and products, technical publications and White Papers, and user groups.

Marketing

Sites that will help you get your product marketing done right. There are sites ranging from conference and organization information to demographics, advertising, and mailing lists. This also the place to find out about how to use the Internet as a business market. Also see the Advertising Parody Hall of Iniquity for a good lesson on how *not* to do it.

Advertising Age

http://www.adage.com

The leading publication on advertising and marketing, *Ad Age*'s site features a database of advertising and marketing firms (you can also register yourself), a graphical section of portfolios and awards, and a collection of up-to-date industry news stories. You can also join in an interactive discussion on topics such as digital media, customer loyalty, and marketing.

American Business Information Marketing and Credit Information

http://www.abii.com

A site with information on obtaining directory information to 11 million businesses, with credit rating codes. You can't access the database directly from here, but there's information on how to use the service, including different ways to access data and fees charged.

Consumer Marketing

http://turnpike.net/metro/tuvok/
index.html

A guide for marketing to consumers, this interactive outline has sections on customer and competitor analysis, product strategy, and promotion. It's a good way to focus on issues of consumer marketing for small businesses.

Internet Resource Pages

http://www.netresource.com/

A great site for accessing information on Internet services and marketing resources. You can also find out about a secure transaction robot, view Internet marketing reports, and access a list of Net resources. This is a good site for businesses looking to establish a presence on the Internet to find out what's up.

MouseTracks - NSNS Marketing Resources

http://nsns.com/MouseTracks/

MouseTracks offers an interactive commentary on the state of marketing on the Internet. Check out the Hall of Malls (a collection of Internet storefronts), read about videoconferencing efforts, even find out about sites marketing to marketers. There's also sections on academic marketing studies and mailing lists (the kind you buy, not the kind you subscribe to).

Sharrow's Advertising & Marketing BizInfo Resource Center

http://www.dnai.com/~sharrow/register.html

An irreverent look at advertising and marketing on the Internet, this is the place to separate the reality from the hype. There's a section on marketing ideas and a business information resource list. Article topics include database marketing, sex as an advertising ploy, and effective sales management. It's all written in a clear, intelligent style, and there are direct links to the subjects covered. Don't forget to look up the Advertising Hall of Shame, a hilarious series of real and parody ads. Can you tell which is which?

Web Digest For Marketers

http://www.advert.com/wdfm/wdfm.html

WDFM is a biweekly executive summary of the latest marketing sites to appear on the World Wide Web. It's a good place to stay on top of businesses with an emerging Internet presence. Brief summaries of the new sites are arranged under headings such as "Fortune 500," and each includes a direct site link.

Web InSight for Marketers

http://www.webinsight.com/

This site is designed to provide Web resources for marketing professionals. Topics include "How The Web Was Won" (on marketing ideas), a tutorial on Web basics, and a guide to professional services. There's also a list of Insightful Sites and a section on the future of the Internet.

Demographics

UpClose Demographic Summaries 1994

http://www.upclose.com/upclose/demomenu/demomenu.htm

Population demographics information for U.S. state, metropolitan, and city areas. Listings for 1990, 1994, and projections about the year 2000 are included, with information on average household size, average age, and median income. Find out how your target area stacks up.

Institutes

Institute for the Study of Business Markets

http://www.psu.com/isbm/

This Penn State University site has information on ISBM membership, events, and upcoming seminars on subjects such as marketing strategy in business markets. There are also lists of free working papers and academic research fund programs, and an interactive tour of marketing Web sites.

Organizations

Sales and Marketing Exchange

http://www.sme.com

This is a prime spot for online sales and marketing professionals looking for services to hire or to advertise themselves. There are links to sites for sales and marketing, advertising and public relations, and design. You can also register your own service. We liked the fact that design firms were included; it's one of the most important concerns in online marketing.

Markets and Investments

The world of finance on the Internet is here. You'll find a wealth of information on stocks and bonds, mutual funds, and currency exchange. There are interactive stock quote generators, analytical data sets on market performance, and sites on personal finance.

Form for Mortgage Payment Query

http://ibc.wustl.edu/mort.html

A neat Web application for calculating mortgage rates on a primary loan amount. This gadget can figure out payment rates at any amortization schedule you enter. You can also plug in prepayment plans and adjust the annual interest rate. It also understands the Canadian monetary system.

Corporate Reports

This section contains direct links to corporate reports from a number of businesses, including IBM, Bank of America, Intel, Motorola, Boeing, and National Semiconductor. It's a good way to go right to corporate performance information without having to wade through a company home page.

Currency Exchange

Here's where you'll find daily foreign exchange rates for a number of different currencies. There's also interactive currency conversion sites, an FAQ on using money abroad, and an online discount foreign exchange.

Koblas Currency Converter

http://bin.gnn.com/cgi-bin/gnn/currency

This one shows the relative value of currency for over 40 countries in a single chart. Selecting a country name resets the chart relative to that country. The U.S. dollar is the default.

Online Discount Foreign Exchange

http://magic.winnet.net/c/feller

Korth Feller & Company's site has an updated currency exchange chart and an online ordering system for buying and selling currency over the Net.

EDGAR Database

http://www.yahoo.com/
Business_and_Economy/
Markets_and_Investments/
Edgar_Database/

A number of sites for getting information from the Securities and Exchange Commission's EDGAR database of corporate financial filings, and for submitting reports. These include interactive forms and search tools. Did you know that Apple stockholders had $4 billion worth of voting stock as of December 1994? Find out who's worth what.

Futures and Options

It's good to have both of these, and here's where you'll find sites on projected commodities trading and historical performance indicators.

Chicago Mercantile Exchange

http://www.cme.com/

The world's largest marketplace. This is where the hog bellies live. Find out how the exchange works and what its background is, and learn about new currency and commodity initiatives. There's a glossary of futures and options terms (find out the difference between a *long* and a *short* hedge), and video clips of the "feeding-frenzy" trading pits. You'll also find the related CME Marketing page full of useful information.

Historical Commodities Price Data

http://www.best.com/~pierre/invest/data/

Raw table data on commodities performance for items ranging from Japanese yen to coffee. Plug this info into your spreadsheet and see what you can come up with.

International Finance & Commodities Institute

http://finanace.wat.ch/IFCI/

This organization promotes the understanding of financial risk management instruments and commodities. Its site includes Financial Wat.ch, a hypertext review of finance subjects (including information on financial and commodity derivatives and an industry index), and selected research papers. There's also a helpful, top-level search engine.

Mutual Funds

The art of managed investing. These sites will help you track fund performance via various indicators, and also provide background information and historical analysis of mutual funds in several markets.

100% No-Load Mutual Fund Council

http://networth.galt.com/council

No-load mutual funds don't charge you a service fee per transaction. The council site provides information on more than 200 of them and also includes a hypertext investment guide.

Yahoo! - Funds

http://www.yahoo.com/
Business_and_Economy/
Markets_and_Investments/
Mutual_Funds/Funds/

This Yahoo! area is where specific funds have their home pages. If you want to find out about a particular fund, this is a good place to go. It's also a good place to browse through the available mutual funds and their offerings on the Web.

Mutual Fund Charts (MIT)

http://www.ai.mit.edu/stocks/mf.html

The MIT Artificial Intelligence Laboratory's charts are a great way to view fund performance. A graph chart is generated on the fly when you select a particular fund from the list provided, so you can quickly analyze how the fund performs over time.

The Mutual Funds Home Page

http://www.ultranet.com/~marla/funds.html

A good stop for fund info on the Web. This site contains information on resources and databases available online, a discussion on upcoming legislation, and fund manager profiles. It also has a tutorial on how to search the Internet for fund information.

ALSO RECOMMENDED:

Usenet - Investment funds

news:misc.invest funds

The Usenet newsgroup on investment funds. This is where you can request information from the greater Internet community on fund performance and investment opportunities and participate in general discussions.

Personal Finance

Everything from auto finance sites to an interactive debt reduction calculator, plus an investment guide for beginners.

Debt Calculator

http://uclc.com/uclc/debt.html

This interesting forms-based calculator has sections for car payments, credit card debt, and your mortgage. It calculates for you a reduced refinancing debt rate and pitches you an online loan at the same time.

Investing For The Perplexed

http://www.inch.com/~robertny/invest/menu.html

Kelly & O'Sullivan Financial Services Group's site is for people who want to invest but " ... have no interest in investments, find business boring, have no idea what the current prime rate is, and don't care." Sound familiar? You'll find a guide to investing in the 90s here, as well as a FAQ list with general financial information, and several low-cost investment advice options.

Personal Finance Center

http://gnn.com/meta/finance/

This Global Network Navigator site is a good collection of links to personal finance news and information. You'll also find selections from investment books (such as "Qualifying For The Loan" from *The Mortgage Applicant's Bible*) and a financial columnist.

Auto Financing

Boss guides to valuing used cars, plus interactive loan calculators, incentive plans, and finance/used car centers.

Edmund's Guide to Used Car Buying

gopher://gopher.enews.com:2100/11/showroom/edmunds/usedmake

The definitive guide to used cars. This Gopher server is arranged alphabetically and also by year, making it easy to find information on a specific model. You can also submit your own review.

Webfoot's Useful Automotive Information

http://www.webfoot.com/lots/info/useful.info.html

A good collection of tips on buying a car and links to car finance pages. You'll also find information on basic auto operations and a collection of Internet magazines and newsgroup related to (you guessed it) cars.

Stocks

Stock sites on Yahoo! range from S&P's 500 Index to interactive quote generators. Exchanges listed here include the American Stock Exchange (AMEX), and world stock exchanges from Johannesburg, Vancouver, Vienna, and Warsaw. There are also electronic stock guides and market simulators you can use to "play the market" without risking your cash.

American Stock Exchange

http://www.amex.com

This is the big place to be. The site includes an updated market summary, an industry news section, and a list of affiliated companies. There's also an informational section explaining options and securities, including structured derivatives. You can check out the Gallery to see pictures of the market in action, and participate in an online Information Exchange.

Holt's Stock Market Reports

gopher://wuecon.wustl.edu:671/11/holt/

A comprehensive daily list of stock performance in various markets, also arranged by level of activity. This is presented in straight-text format but contains a lot of useful data nonetheless.

Onramp Access, Inc.

http://www.onr.com/stocks.html

Onramp offers several lists of links to sites on investment research, securities performance, and small business assistance, as well as online brokerage firms. Each list of sites is well annotated, making it easy to find specific information on a particular topic.

PC Quote/Spacecom Systems Stock Quote Server

http://www.spacecom.com:8001/
Participants/pcquote/qmaster.html

A stock quote server, this site allows you to enter a ticker symbol, and returns a 15-minute delayed quote. Even better, there's a panel that allows you to enter a normal language company name, and returns the correct ticker symbol. There's also a helpful symbol format guide with detailed information on how to submit correct queries.

Security APL Quote Server

http://www.secapl.com/cgi-bin/qs

Another quote server, this site also allows you to enter a ticker symbol and receive a report (this one's delayed by five minutes). You'll also find links to financial documents for the relevant ticker symbol/company right at the report page. Other features include a Market Watch report with a detailed look at market activity and an interactive forum for investors.

Stock Market Charts

http://www.ai.mit.edu/stocks/
graphs.html

Interactive daily graph charts of stock market performance. This site features

overall market coverage, as well as an indexed corporate site list. No ticker symbol to remember; just scroll down to the company you want to look up and bang on the name.

Stock Market Simulations

This collection of sites provides you with a place to exercise your market skills. Several portfolio management contests and stock trading challenges are available at any given time.

Index - Financial Resource Guide

http://www.libertynet.org/
~beausang/aaafrg.html

This index, from LibertyNet in Philadelphia, is a well-organized, brief set of links to trader information on the Web, including stocks, options, and currency information, and stock exchanges.

ALSO RECOMMENDED:

Remedies

http://www.li.net/~gdecamp/
remedies.html

A quirky collection of financial links, market analysis tools, and up-to-date stock charts.

Usenet - Stocks

news:misc.invest.stocks

The Usenet newsgroup for discussing stock information across the Internet.

Indices

These sites have further lists of links to market information on the Internet. Use them to explore a wider range of subjects in the finance world.

FILL Financial Information Link Library

http://www.mbnet.mb.ca:80/
~russell/

A comprehensive collection of links arranged by country. This site has an easy-to-browse format and allows you to add your own links. This is where you'll go to find the Hong Kong Bank of New Zealand and other esoteric sites.

NCSA What's New: Investment and Personal Finance

http://gnn.com/gnn/meta/finance/
res/ncsa/ncsa.index.html

The list of new sites in finance and marketing, arranged by date, and linked directly from the site. A good place to come to find out what recently became available. It's also a good "last resort" — if other finance site collections don't have what you're looking for, it just might be here.

Ohio State University Financial Data Finder

http://www.cob.ohio-state.edu/dept/
fin/osudata.htm

This index has sites listed by provider and Net presence and also includes downloadable financial datasets (for example, an Excel file on Corporate Debt Issues over a ten-year period). You'll also find a helpful list of online business libraries.

Usenet - General investment

news:misc.invest

The Usenet newsgroup on general investment topics, news, and discussion.

Miscellaneous

These sites run the gamut from interactive bar code generators to information on duty-free shopping, commercial business services, and even a service that can Remember It For You Wholesale.

The Barcode Server

http://www.milk.com/barcode/

This is an interesting business utility: If you enter an 11- or 12-digit number into the form field on this page and press the Encode It button, a graphic of the barcode is returned to you in your Web browser. Possible uses include coding postal envelopes for bulk mailings. This is a good example of a simple service that the Web can provide.

Duty-Free Shopping Information

http://www.webscope.com/duty_free

Find out about the duty-free shopping world at the Alexander Dun & Sons Web site. It features good explanations of duty-free particulars for international travelers in an easy-to-use hypertext format. Sites such as this one can be used to learn more about complex subjects, and make good reference bookmarks.

Commercial Business Information Center

http://tig.com/IBC/Pay-Info-Services.html

A short list of commercial services on the Net, this site includes links to Dialog, Dun and Bradstreet, Lexis-Nexis, and other pay-for-use financial information sites. Each link is annotated, and includes pricing and contact information.

Rachael's Reminders

http://heinlein.k2nesoft.com/~rar/rates.html

What's that thing we were supposed to do? Oh yeah, we wanted to register for this inexpensive online reminder service and receive e-mail and/or postal reminders of important dates before they happen. Now, what was that URL again?

Organizations

Business organizations of all types, running from development agencies to cultural facilities. You'll also find international trade and relations groups, science and technology organizations, and professional interest outfits. Check out the large number of public interest groups available online and also see the rapidly developing social interest sites.

Business Development

Development agencies, including the Better Business Bureau, can be found here. There are industrial organizations, guides to nonprofit resources, and small business advocacy centers.

Better Business Bureau

http://www.bbb.org/bbb/

This site is a joint effort of the Council of Better Business Bureaus and provides information on BBB services and support. There are sections on advertising self-regulation guidelines, alternative dispute resolution systems, and consumer/business education programs. We especially liked the reliability reports on businesses section and the updated scam advisory alerts.

National Center for Nonprofit Boards - NCNB

gopher://ncnb.org:7002/

A Gopher server with information on NCNB's organizational goals, the strengthening of nonprofits' boards of directors to augment their growth and stability. This site has sections on common questions about nonprofits, publications and resource lists, and upcoming conferences and events.

Small Business Advancement National Center

http://161.31.2.174/

This site contains a great deal of informational links to proceedings, bulletins, databases, and publications on small business in the Southwest U.S. You can also find out about the Small Business Institute Directors Association and read the center's quarterly newsletter.

Small Business Foundation of America

http://web.miep.org/sbfa/

A research institute for emerging enterprise, the SBFA site provides information on research projects, export fact sheets, and executive summary position papers. You can also find out about *Exportise,* an international trade source book for smaller company executives, and order it online.

The Industrial Research Institute

http://www.iriinc.org/

A nonprofit organization of more than 260 industrial companies involved in enhancing the effectiveness of technological innovation in industry, IRI's site has copies of the institute's newsletter, lists of members and committees, and a subscription form for the *Research-Technology Management* journal.

ALSO RECOMMENDED:

Industrial Technology Institute

http://www.iti.org/

ITI provides services to manufacturers in the areas of electronic commerce, energy and environmental services, and machine vision application.

Cultural

Cultural organizations listed on Yahoo! include sites for Palestine and Arabic cultures, the India Student Organization, a German-Japanese society, a chapter of the NAACP, and more. It's a very interesting side of the World Wide Web.

Tomodachi Online

http://server.Berkeley.EDU/tomodachi/

A great-looking site for Japanese and Japanese-American culture at UC Berkeley. It has information on cultural

and community service events, a photo gallery, and links to related sites.

ALSO RECOMMENDED:

Ethnic Heritage Council

http://www.eskimo.com/~millerd/ehc/

Promoting ethnic diversity and cross-cultural understanding in the Pacific Northwest.

NAACP Rockford Chapter

http://www.misha.net/~desktop/naacp.htm

A branch of the National Association for the Advancement of Colored People.

Economics

World Bank

http://www.worldbank.org

The global lending agency. This nicely crafted site has information about the Bank and its departments, current events and press releases, research studies and publications, and country/project information. You can also look at an independent inspection panel list, where disputed World Bank projects are evaluated.

Foundations

Philanthropic organizations, now on the Web. Find out how to apply for that basket-weaving grant, or check out foundations dedicated to providing humanitarian grants and aid.

Carnegie Corporation of New York

gopher://tigger.jvnc.net:3000/11/Carnegie_Corporation_of_New_York

The educational foundation's Gopher server contains information on how to submit a proposal, grant restrictions, and recent publications. There's also information on different Carnegie commissions and task forces, including ones on "Preventing Deadly Conflict" and "Meeting The Needs Of Young Children."

John Simon Guggenheim Memorial Foundation

http://www.gf.org

Fellowship information, including contact information, how to apply for a grant, lists of advisory board and selection committee members, and practical advice.

Alfred P. Sloan Foundation

http://www.sloan.org/

This site provides an interesting look into several programs supported by the foundation, including promoting the success of underrepresented minorities in mathematics, science, and engineering (with tables of grant recipients and their affiliations), and on the Asynchronous Learning Networks (a distance learning initiative).

Philanthropy

Philanthrophy Related Links

http://www.duke.edu/~ptavern/
Pete.Philanthropic.html

A well-annotated collection of links to philanthropic foundations and related sites. You can also find out about Impact On Line, an Internet service that helps nonprofits maintain a Web presence.

International Development

This is where the global community comes together. You'll find sites centering on the U.S. role in the world economy, international agricultural research, and global developmental aid.

Alliance for a Global Community

gopher://vita.org/11/intl/interaction/
alli

This Gopher server has information on alliance members, an event calendar, and copies of the alliance's newsletter. You'll also find media background guides to developing countries, a list of volunteer opportunities, and information on socially responsible shopping.

CGIAR

http://www.worldbank.org/html/
cgiar/HomePage.html

The World Bank's Consultative Group on International Agriculture Research site has press releases on the efforts to use technology to improve worldwide agriculture efforts, program information, and an interactive map of worldwide research centers.

International Trade

International trade organizations listed on Yahoo! include chambers of commerce from cities and countries around the world. This is a good place to find out about contacting countries directly for business purposes.

American Chambers of Commerce

http://www1.usa1.com/~ibnet/
usachams.html

A state-by-state listing of commerce and industry groups in the United States that have sites on the Internet.

European Chambers of Commerce

http://www1.usa1.com/~ibnet/
eurocham.html

A country and commonwealth listing of commerce and industry groups across the world that have sites on the Internet.

United States Chamber Of Commerce

http://www.uschamber.org/chamber/

A great site, with a large amount of information arranged around an interactive map. You can find out about training and education programs, nonprofit services, and association relations. There's also membership information available.

Political Groups

The art of politics on the World Wide Web is defined by these sites. Yahoo! has links to left, right, and every-which-way organizations, plus sites for voter registration efforts.

Congressional Black Caucus

http://drum.ncsc.org/~carter/
CBC.html

A nice-looking site for the Caucus, this place has legislative agenda reports, member reports, and representative contact information. A valuable news media e-mail address list is also here.

The League of Conservation Voters

http://www.econet.apc.org/lcv/
scorecard.html

The group that uses politics to help the environment. Its site features an interactive scorecard map of the impact of the U.S. Congress on the environment — just select an area to see how your representatives shape up. Follow the links from there to see how the votes on specific issues affect us all.

Project Vote Smart

http://www.vote-smart.org/

As they say, "It's time to check up on the hired help." Find out what the people who work for you are up to. This site has information on congressional performance, full-text books on political subjects such as immigration, and information on upcoming elections.

Professional

Professional organizations of all types, from aeronautics and astronautics to zookeepers. Also you'll find relevant professional groups on marketing, science, and self-employment.

American Association for the Advancement of Science

http://www.aaas.org/

Information available includes a Web tour of the journal *Science*, information on education and human resource programs, and information on science and public policy initiatives (including a hypertext report on the Global Information Infrastructure project).

American Marketing Association (AMA)

http://www.ama.org/

The AMA Marketing Mix site has membership information, a list of special interest groups, and contact information for professional chapters, including links to upcoming marketing events and chapter home pages.

Association of Support for Graduate Students

http://www.vpm.com/asgs/

Good help for people working on advanced degrees. ASGS's site offers a moderated e-mail discussion list about doing a thesis, a dissertation news bulletin, and a professional consultant directory. You can also find out about low-cost word-processing templates on disk and read student surveys about the graduate degree process.

College Board

http://hub.terc.edu/ra/ceeb/fall94.html

Back issues of the College Board's *Equity 2000* newsletter, about the program to increase the number of academically prepared minority and disadvantaged students who will graduate from college.

American Medical Informatics Association

http://amia2.amia.org/overview.html

A society focusing on the information sciences in medicine. The site has information on upcoming events, an interactive membership application form, and an overview of the society's publications.

American Philosophical Society

http://www.oxy.edu/apa/apa.html

Here's where you'll find a philosopher's link to the Internet, including a list of Web sites with philosophical content, proceedings of the association, and links to philosophy-related software projects.

National Academy of Sciences

http://www.nas.edu/

Press releases and program information from several committees at the NAS, as well as membership information and an e-mail directory of the National Research Council.

National Association for the Self Employed

http://www.awa.com/nase/nase.html

A detailed list of membership benefits is available at this site. There's also information on NASE's advocacy programs and a list of fees.

Public Interest Groups

Interest groups ranged on a number of topics, including human rights and child advocacy, environment and volunteerism issues, charities, and public service organizations.

Charities

Groups such as the United Way and the Make A Wish foundation are listed here, as well as America's Charities, a central point for finding out about a large number of U.S. charitable organizations.

Children

Easter Seals Online

http://www.cyberplex.com/CyberPlex/Kids/Seals/News.html

The Ontario chapter of the charity that helps children with physical disabilities. You'll find infomation on special programs, an online newsletter, and volunteer/donation information here.

Missing Children

http://www.yahoo.com/
Business_and_Economy/
Organizations/Public_Interest_Groups/
Children/Missing_Children/

A subsection listing sites for information on missing children, including specific searches and the National Center for Missing & Exploited Children (NCMEC) database.

Electronic Freedom

Where the Internet community protects itself. Find out about how to keep the Web free for all.

Electronic Frontier Foundation

http://www.eff.org/

The organization at the forefront of the fight to keep civil liberties alive on the Net. Check here for action bulletins, news alerts, and an online newsletter. There's also a multimedia section and a file archive. You might also find the *(Extended) Guide to the Internet* and the *Virtual World Tour of Cyberspace* helpful.

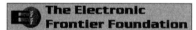

Environment

There are a strong number of environmental organizations listed on Yahoo!, including groups working to protect the rainforests, develop sustainable agriculture methods, and conserve national parklands.

Earth First!

gopher://gopher.igc.apc.org/11/orgs/
ef.journal

This site contains information on the organization's fight to protect the environment, including the *Earth First Journal* and action bulletins.

EcoNet

http://www.econet.org/

EcoNet provides electronic resources and support for environmental groups. Check out its site for a Gopher browser on environment issues and links to ecological resources on the Internet.

Greenpeace International

http://www.greenpeace.org/

The international organization using direct, peaceful action to save the environment. The Greenpeace site has information on membership, campaign updates, and links to local Greenpeace offices. See beautiful pictures of the Rainbow Warrior, too.

Rainforest Action Network

http://www.ran.org/ran/

An extensive visual site for RAN, this features action alerts, an online membership form, and rainforest information. You'll also find a Kids Corner with illustrated rainforest stories and guides to responsible action children can take to protect the environment.

Sierra Club

http://www.sierraclub.org/

A well-organized site for the Sierra Club, this offers membership information, action alert bulletins, and information on specific regional programs. You can also find out about local chapters, student organizations, and member outings. The site is searchable and also provides a list of links to other environmental places on the Net.

Health

Organizations for health concerns, including AIDS/HIV information, cerebral palsy, Lyme disease, sickle cell anemia, psychiatric disorders, and dyslexia. You'll also find the Red Cross listed here.

Human Rights

Protecting the rights and lives of people everywhere, these organizations work to elevate the status of individuals in society.

Amnesty International

http://www.io.org/amnesty/
overview.html

The premier human rights organization's site contains information on international campaigns, country reports, and news reports. There's also information on worldwide appeals (letter-writing campaigns in which you can participate) in English, French, and Spanish, and a search engine for the local Amnesty International document archive.

Refuse And Resist!

http://www.calyx.com/~refuse/

The home page of the "climate of resistance." Find out about protests against capital punishment, the abortion rights movement, and more. There's also a good set of links to activism sites across the Internet.

United States Holocaust Memorial Museum

http://www.ushmm.org/

An impressive site from this national museum. It has information on research opportunities and special collections, an online education section, and an extensively searchable research database.

Service

Groups involved in service to local and global communities.

International Service Agencies

http://www.charity.org/

Affiliated service agencies in the United States listed by subject groups and alphabetically. You can find out how each organization contributes to its community here.

Internet NonProfit Center

http://www.human.com/inc/

A nice site to find nonprofit service organizations on the Net. There are geographical, subject, and purpose indices, library sections, and places to find out about volunteer opportunities.

Peace Corps

http://www.clark.net/pub/peace/PeaceCorps.html

This site has information on how to volunteer, details about the Corps, and a list of domestic programs. There's also information on specific countries where Peace Corps volunteers serve.

Technology

Technological organizations working on public policy issues in several fields.

Alliance for Public Technology - APT

http://apt.org/apt/index.html

This site has information on the alliance's programs designed to make technology available for public use, including position papers, conference announcements, and a newsletter index.

Computer Professionals for Social Responsibility

http://snyside.sunnyside.com/home/

A professional society dedicated to improving the interaction between information technology and individuals. Its site has information on potentially harmful Internet legislation (and online petitions that can help stop such legislation), upcoming conferences, and related issues.

Women

National Organization of Women

http://now.org/now/home.html

NOW's site is a focal point on the Internet for information about women's rights. There's information on individual chapters and membership, action issue reports and position papers, and an online version of the *National NOW Times*.

Global Fund for Women

http://www.igc.apc.org/gfw/

An international grant foundation, the GFW site has information on grant programs, international recipients, and application guidelines.

Science and Technology

American Academy of Arts and Sciences

http://www.amacad.org

The academy's site features abstracts of the *Daedalus* journal, membership information, and a list of recent publications.

The Planetary Society

http://planetary.org/tps/

A great site for the interplanetary exploration society, it features news bulletins on the current state of space activities, an interactive e-mail dialog system, online surveys and petitions, and a kids' section (featuring programs like a Lego Red Rover Mars study simulation).

Biology and Genetics

National Center for Genome Resources

http://www.ncgr.org/

A link to the Genome Sequence Database and the Human Genome Project. There's also information on small business opportunities (creating life, perhaps?) and a discussion on the ethical, legal, and social implications of biotechnology.

Social

Social organizations, including a large number of fraternities and sororities, not to mention secret-handshake societies such as the Freemasons and MENSA.

United States Junior Chamber of Commerce (Jaycees)

http://www.galstar.com/~jaycees/index.html

The Jaycees site offers membership information and reports on community programs such as Outstanding Young Farmer, Jaycees Against Youth Smoking, Shooting Education, and KidCare.

Fraternities and Sororities

Look for individual chapters of fraternities and sororities from several colleges and universities around the globe. These sites offer information on chapter activities and community programs and a look into campus life.

Freemasonry

Hiram's Inner Chamber

http://international.com/hiram/hiramhome.html

Scottish Rite, York Rite, Shrine, The International Order of Job's Daughters, Order of DeMolay. Be thankful there's a Freemasonry FAQ here as well. Find out about that 33rd degree.

Student

Student organizations, including medical groups, residence hall associations, and honor societies.

Premedical Chapter at University of Pennsylvania

http://dolphin.upenn.edu/~amsa/

Information on the American Medical Student Association Premedical program at Penn, with links to other chapters and AMSA document archives. There are also links to interesting medical sites and resources and to vital statistics for all U.S. medical schools.

Trade

Trade organizations, centered on subjects ranging from lambs and agriculture to computer software.

Association of Shareware Professionals

http://www.msen.com/~rgharper/homeasp.html

News and information, online membership kits, and links to member sites with interesting shareware.

Institute for Agriculture and Trade Policy

gopher://gopher.igc.apc.org:70/11/trade/iatp

A Gopher server with information on IATP's efforts in the field of international trade and agriculture, including reports on biodiversity and hazardous waste handling.

North American Electric Reliability Council (NERC)

http://www.nerc.com/

Founded by a group of regional power providers, NERC works "to keep the lights on." You'll find newsletters and publications on electric power issues at this site, including ordering information.

Software Publishers Association

http://www.spa.org/

The SPA site has information on anti-piracy efforts, research, and publications in the software publishing field.

Real Estate

Sites for calculating your mortgage payments, applying for loans, and general information about real estate matters.

Mortgage Loans

Homebuyer's Fair Obtain a Mortgage Site

http://www.homefair.com/homefair/mortgage.html

Answers to mortgage questions. This site also includes an electronic postcard you can use to request information from several vendors, up-to-date regional financial tables, and links to mortgage calculator pages.

HSH Associates

http://www.hsh.com/

Up-to-date national mortgage rate charts, online mortgage calculators, and pamphlets for prospective homebuyers. There's also a downloadable PC Mortgage Update program for viewing rates and lender terms offline (PC-based).

Organizations

Appraisal Institute

http://www.realworks.com/ai/

Find out what it's *really* worth. This site gives you information on the appraisal process, including how to find a registered appraiser in your area.

Who's Who In Luxury Real Estate

http://www.luxury-realestate.com/jbl/

If you have to ask, you can't afford it. Find firms and view properties by an interactive map, regional listing, or index.

Women In Real Estate (WIRE)

http://www.hia.com/hia/wire/

This site provides membership information, reports on special events and activities, and a job bank.

Small Business Information

Home office and independent entrepreneurs, this is the place for you. Find sites with information about federal and state small business programs, business resources, and legal guides.

Advanced Business Consulting

http://addcom.clever.net/abc/

Links to articles for small business owners, including how to determine whether you really *want* to have a home-based business, and also an annotated list of links to sites on home-based business and entrepreneurial topics.

Entrepreneurs on the Web

http://sashimi.wwa.com/~notime/eotw/EOTW.html

A guide to entrepreneurial activity on the Internet. This site has an annotated list of sites of interest to small businesses and a form for sponsoring the site with your own business ad for a small fee.

Franchise Source

http://www.axxs.com/source.htm

A comprehensive list of franchise opportunities arranged by alphabetical index, industry list, and (most helpful) start-up cost.

Small Business Administration (SBA)

http://www.sbaonline.sba.gov/

A branch of the U.S. government dedicated to promoting small business. SBA Online is a great addition to the SBA list of business programs, and this Web site features good hyperlinked guides to the SBA's available services, including tutorials on small business topics and a multimedia help page. You can also check on current SBA events or search for a particular employee.

Products

The Big Wind Kite Factory

http://planet-hawaii.com/bigwind/

This site features a service for small businesses that offers custom-made kites and windsocks for promotions, sales events, and personal use. Available here are full-color illustrations of different kite models, an illustrated, *easy* kite-building tutorial, a frequently asked-questions list, and a printable fax payment form.

Venture Capital

Price Waterhouse Venture Capital Survey

http://www.sjmercury.com/features/venture/menu.htm

This is a quarterly survey of entrepreneurial investment activity in major business areas. You can retrieve information from the survey by company, industry, amount invested, or ZIP code. This allows a business user to quickly sort the information in the study by a particular region or business type. The site also includes a comprehensive fact sheet on how the survey was performed.

Taxes

The thing besides death that is certain. At least Yahoo!'s collection of sites offers useful information, including interactive workbooks, downloadable forms and instructions from the IRS, and updates on new tax laws.

Income Tax Information

http://www.best.com/~ftmexpat/notebook.html

This interactive notebook provides a lot of information on the subject of income tax, including relevant sites on the Web, tax software reviews, and Excel spreadsheet templates for tax calculation. It's in a very useful chapter format, too.

Internal Revenue Service

http://www.ustreas.gov/treasury/bureaus/irs/irs.html

The site provides direct links to a searchable tax form and instruction list. The forms are in Adobe Acrobat format (PDF), and you can download and use some of them for filing purposes. There's also a list of filing centers, a section on where to get help, and a FAQ list.

Taxing Times

http://www.scubed.com/tax/tax.html

Maxwell Labs' alternative site for tax information. You'll find a good list of electronic forms, links to tax e-mail discussion lists and Usenet newsgroups, and a collection of public-domain tax software available by FTP. There's also a link to the entire U.S. Tax Code online, for your bedside reading enjoyment.

Trade

Trade information from federal agencies and business institutions, tracking import and export statistics and development.

Foreign Trade Division (U.S. Census Bureau)

http://www.census.gov/ftp/pub/foreign-trade/www/

U.S. international trade statistics, including a list of the United States' top ten trading partners, an overview of the International Trade Program, and a guide to foreign trade statistics. There's also a section on Who's Who in foreign trade and instructions on the correct way to fill out the *Shipper's Export Declaration* (with interactive examples).

Global Trade Center

http://www.tradezone.com/tz/

Information on worldwide business opportunities. This site has good links to a lot of information on international trade, including banks and resource centers, trade directories and law centers, conference announcements, and publications. There are also links to worldwide government and embassy/consulate sites.

National Trade Data Bank on Internet

http://www.stat-usa.gov/BEN/Services/ntdbhome.html

Fee-based access to a database with trade information from over 26 different federal agencies. The site has detailed information on what's contained in the Data Bank, and you can run a sample query on a small database at no charge.

International Trade Law Home Page

http://ananse.irv.uit.no/trade_law/nav/trade.html

A great site, this place offers a lot of information on international trade law, including European Community links, a list of NAFTA sites on the Internet, access to international trade pages at the UN, WTO/GATT links, and more. There's also a helpful subject outline, liberal use of icons, and a local search function.

Yahoo!

Transportation

Planes, trains, and other transportation systems. There are also interactive train timetables and subway route planners you can use and current traffic report and travel advisory sites.

Air Travel

Airline History Archives

http://fohnix.metronet.com/~olesen/aha.html

A great site for commercial aviation buffs, this one has links to other aviation and airline sites (with pictures you can download), a family tree of U.S. airlines, a list of recommended books, and a brief history of PeoplExpress (Holy Eighties!).

Intelligent Transportation Systems

ITS (Intelligent Transportation Systems) Online

http://www.io.com/~itsol/

The art of bringing technology to the highways and other transportation systems. This site is an independent forum with information on federal initiatives, links to transportation news, and hypertext versions of ITS mailing lists.

Traffic Reports

http://www.yahoo.com/Business_and_Economy/Transportation/Traffic_Reports/

Real-time traffic reports from a number of U.S. cities, including Houston, San Diego, Seattle, and Los Angeles. Most have interactive maps that can show you just how bad it is at a given time.

Trains and Railroads

Lots of sites on railroading, including model railroad outfits, historical associations, and train information. Here's where you'll also find interactive train timetables and subway route generators.

Amtrak

http://www.amtrak.com/

Information from the largest U.S. passenger train service, including routes, travel and vacation planning tips, and information on special promotions and package deals.

Cyberspace World Railroad

http://www.mcs.com/~dsdawdy/cyberoad.html

Tons of stuff for the railroad buff. Coverage of special events (such as the opening of the Steamtown Railroad Museum) with pictures, weekly news updates, editorials on international railroading topics, and links to other railroading sites. There's also a complete set of Amtrak timetables, an online schedule and maps for Chicago's Metra system, and Canadian Rail timetables. You can also download train clip art and browse an extensive library of railroading documents.

MERCURIO - The European Railway Server

http://mercurio.iet.unipi.it/home.html

Another railroading mega-site, this features European train information, including selected schedules and histories, color liveries and paint schemes for international train lines, links to more train information, and technical data for the entire European rail system.

Subway Navigator

http://metro.jussieu.fr:10001/bin/cities/english

A utility that plots a transit route in world cities, it also tells you the estimated time of travel and which line to take. All you have to do is select a city, and enter a departure and arrival station. It even helps with your spelling! Some city results will also generate a map of your route.

Truckers/Transportation Homepage

http://www.truckers.com

This site has a list of services for folks out on the road, including traffic conditions and weather reports, driver alerts, and a transportation phone book. There's also a linked list of transportation-related sites, a job section, and the Road Kill Cafe (fine dining on the road).

Indices

Interesting Business Sites on the Web

http://www.rpi.edu/~okeefe/business.html

A short, well-annotated list of top business-related Web pages arranged by category.

IOMA Business

http://www.ioma.com/ioma/

A comprehensive list of sites, including news sources, business documents, newsgroups, and databases.

Thomas Ho's favorite Electronic Commerce WWW resources

http://www.engr.iupui.edu/~ho/
interests/commmenu.html

A mega-list of business and financial links from around the world. There's a whole lot of useful information linked here.

FINWEB

http://riskweb.bus.utexas.edu/
finweb.htm

A great set of annotated Financial Economics links at the University of Texas.

RISKWEB

http://riskweb.bus.utexas.edu/
riskweb.htm

A great set of annotated risk-management and insurance links at the University of Texas.

Computers and Internet

Because you are reading this book, you probably have a computer, and you probably also use the Internet. Thus, it is likely that you are interested in finding out more about your computer (at least enough to keep it from getting in your way) and about what's on the Internet.

Since the earliest days of the Internet's existence, a great deal of the discussion and information on the Internet has revolved around the Internet itself. That may seem a bit odd to you — after all, you don't find many television shows about the technology of television or newspaper articles about how to operate a newspaper.

But the Internet is different in that it is a two-way medium in which anybody can say what they want with very little expense. You don't have to buy a television station or newspaper to take part. To publish on the Net, you don't even need to buy an Internet host. All you need is a low-cost or free Internet connection.

The low cost of participation leads many people to talk about almost anything, particularly what they know about. And what does everyone on the Internet know about? And what do they have in common? The Internet, of course, and the computers they use to connect to the Internet. Although a relatively small number of

Internet users know much about, say, football, they all know at least something about the Net, and in many cases that's what they want to talk about.

The Web sites devoted to computer- and Internet-related topics discussed in this chapter run the gamut from those run by computer companies, professionally maintained by their technical support staff, to pet projects of individuals. The corporate sites tend to be less freewheeling than the personal sites, but both kinds offer a huge amount of useful information on how to get around the Internet and how to use your computer — no matter which brand it is or how expensive or cheap it is.

Conferences

In many professions, the best places to find out about exciting new things are conferences. The computer industry thrives on conferences because that's where you can force vendors to show their products next to their competitors' products.

Computer conferences can be small affairs with just a few hundred people, or they can be massive trade shows such as PC Expo and Macworld Expo that attract many tens of thousands of people. In fact, the computer trade show Comdex is one of the largest trade shows in the world of *any* kind, with well over 100,000 people attending each year.

CeBIT

http://www.datamation.com/cebit/

One of the largest conferences of any sort in the world, Hannover, Germany's CeBIT is an incredible experience. Multimillion dollar (or pound or mark or yen) deals are made, novice users wander around aimlessly, and the booths offer everything from the gaudy to the austere.

Comdex

http://www.comdex.com/

The United States' version of CeBIT is Comdex. Every fall, just before Thanksgiving, more than 125,000 people descend on Las Vegas, Nevada for a week of wheeling and dealing, becoming lost, and walking way too much. The Comdex Web site provides information about the thousands of vendors exhibiting at the show.

ONE BBSCON

http://www.one.bbscon.com/

The growing BBS (bulletin-board service) industry is one of those "who would have guessed it" successes. Recently, the BBS world has started merging with the Internet industry. ONE BBSCON is the premier show for anyone who runs or wants to run a BBS.

Computer Events Directory

http://www.kweb.com/

Put together by KnowledgeWeb, Inc., this Web site keeps track of many international and United States computer shows and trade conferences. You can search the site by date, name, or location, which makes it easy to find interesting conferences near you.

ALSO RECOMMENDED:

Wescon

http://wescon.com/wescon/

A show that is more about electronics than about just computers, Wescon still has lots to interest the computer hardware buff.

Desktop Publishing

Created as a marketing term a decade ago, *desktop publishing* (DTP) means using computers to create good looking, printed documents without going to an outside typesetting or design service. These days, all one really needs in order to get going in desktop publishing is a PC, some word-processing software, and a laser printer.

Because so many people are now creating their own documents instead of sending them out to be prepared, typeset, and printed, desktop publishing has flourished as its own niche within the computer market. Many Web sites and other Internet resources exist to help novices and advanced users deal with the host of difficulties involved in getting the printed word to look exactly right.

Desktop Publishing Discussion on Usenet

news:comp.text.desktop

Because desktop publishing is a combination of hardware and software from a variety of manufacturers, users often get confused about where they should ask questions. The comp.text.desktop newsgroup is a catch-all discussion of desktop publishing, and the conversations can get pretty lively if the topic is controversial (such as "which is the best …").

Adobe Systems

http://www.adobe.com/

Probably the biggest player in the desktop publishing software market is Adobe Systems. The company started out by inventing PostScript, the language used by most laser printers, and rapidly moved into developing application software such as Acrobat, Illustrator, and Photoshop. The Adobe Web site is a good place to look for technical support and product announcements.

DTP Internet Jumplist

http://www.cs.purdue.edu/homes/gwp/dtp/dtp.html

This is a great collection of pointers to desktop publishing resources on the Internet, including a superb bunch of pointers to FAQs about various desktop publishing software and hardware. There are also good lists of places to look for free fonts and clip art.

Fonts Home Page

http://jasper.ora.com/comp.fonts/

Want to know anything about fonts? It's certainly here. A long and detailed site with hundreds of pointers to most if not all of the font libraries on the Internet, font company resources, obscure tidbits such as how to name fonts, and so on.

A First Guide To PostScript

http://www.cs.indiana.edu/ docproject/programming/postscript/ postscript.html

A wonderful introduction to PostScript internals. This document is of value to any DTP enthusiast who has to fight with PostScript to get documents to look just right (which means almost everyone in the DTP world).

Internet PostScript Resources

http://yoyo.cc.monash.edu.au/~wigs/ postscript/

More than you could ever want to know about PostScript. Here you'll find pointers to other Internet sites with sample files, printer descriptions, and lots of other odd bits of PostScript knowledge that can help you when you are in a jam.

TEI Guidelines for Electronic Text Encoding and Interchange

http://etext.virginia.edu/TEI.html

If you are serious about text and computers, you should certainly know about TEI, the Text Encoding Initiative. TEI is a standardized method for telling a computer about the formatting and content of your text. Using TEI lets you exchange text with other people in a way where you will

both understand the structure and display of the information.

ALSO RECOMMENDED:

XWord

http://www.cs.uidaho.edu:8000/ hungry/microshaft/xword.html

A free DTP program that works with X Windows terminals.

Thoughts on Scientific HTML Documents

http://rascals.stanford.edu/~mcgrant/ equations/

A short essay on the many problems that can crop up when using HTML for scientific documents.

Documentation and Publications

What's a computer or its software without a manual? Computer documentation can be well-organized and clear, or obtuse and confusing. A few manufacturers have started putting their documentation online, which may or may not be of help if you are having an emergency.

BugNet Online

http://www.bugnet.com/~bugnet/

You rarely find any mention of bugs or misfeatures in the documentation that comes with software because, of course, that would be admitting imperfection — not good. BugNet Online is a great list of known bugs in popular (and not-so-popular) software. Before tearing your hair out trying to figure out whether it is you or the software, check out this site.

PC Lube and Tune

http://pclt.cis.yale.edu/pclt/ default.htm

The Internet is at its best when people *volunteer* to help others who are experiencing vexing problems, with no remuneration involved. This site is a great example of that spirit. It contains simple and funny introductions to computer networking topics such as Ethernet, TCP/IP, and SNA, as well as a few other dweeby (but important) topics.

Graphics

Ten years ago, computer graphics was an esoteric field which mostly promised things for the future. Now, it's hard to find computers that do not use graphics (although a number of Unix sites have only a character-based interface). The subject of computer graphics spans everything from animation to color drawings to photography to graphical interfaces.

Because of the lack of standardization in the field of computer graphics, the topics in this area are very diverse. Also, the field of computer graphics is still moving ahead rapidly, fueled by continuously improved hardware and continuously falling prices.

Digital Illusions Magazine

http://www.mcs.com/~bcleach/ illusions/

A top-notch information and news site that covers all sorts of topics related to computer graphics and pictures. The site is updated weekly, and you can find new and older articles on all sorts of graphics topics, such as hardware scanners and animation.

3DSite

http://www.3dsite.com/3dsite/

Three-dimensional graphics has always held a fascination for many artists, and the computer can be a powerful tool for creating realistic pictures of objects in three dimensions. This site provides a great index of other Internet sites with information on 3-D systems and software for a variety of computers.

Animation Master Hobbyist

http://www.xmission.com/~gastown/animation/

Animation Master is one of the more popular high-end animation programs available for Windows and Macintosh users. Although it costs over $500, lots of folks who want to play with serious animation tools use Animation Master to create their own cartoons and videos. This site is a great resource for users of this program.

Animator's Booklist

http://www.xmission.com/~grue/animate/books.html

If you're interested in getting into animation — particularly computer animation — there are dozens of good books on the subject. The list maintained on this site is taken from comments on an animation mailing list and comes with comments from people on the list about the value of each book.

Computer Animation Index

http://skynet.oir.ucf.edu/~suzan/companim/companm2.shtml

A comprehensive list of Internet sites and companies with animation interest. The site also has many examples of computer animation, but viewing the animations may be difficult due to the need for special software for some of the programs.

Scientific Visualization

http://www.nas.nasa.gov/NAS/Visualization/visWeblets.html

Computer graphics is much more than entertainment and art. Scientists use computer graphics to display results and models of their experiments. This site has pointers to Web sites all over the world that describe different uses for computer graphics for visualizing data.

Silicon Surf

http://www.sgi.com/

Although most computers today can display graphics, a few computers are specifically designed to create and display high-quality graphics as fast as possible. Among these computers, the best known are from Silicon Graphics. You know those amazing scenes in *Jurassic Park*? They were done on SGI computers. Their systems are much more expensive than standard PCs, but graphics professionals are often willing to pay the price for such power and speed.

Holography Domain

http://www.holo.com/holo/gram.html

One of the fringes of computer graphics that has never quite caught on is holography, the production of three-dimensional images. You see small representations of these everywhere these days, such as on credit cards and jewelry, but the untapped potential for computer-controlled holography is still huge. This site has lots of information about holography and its relation to computers.

Organitecture

http://www.uio.no/~mwatz/art/gallery/

A gallery of the computer graphics of Marius Watz, an artist who uses organic material as inspiration for his pieces. The site includes not only his works but explanations and commentaries on the work and his creative process.

ALSO RECOMMENDED:

INRIA graphics index

http://www-inria-graphlib.inria.fr:8000/

Yet another index of graphics links, this French site has an index with many more European sites than its US-based counterparts.

RayTracing Rules!

http://tahoma.cwu.edu:2000/~mcknight/raytrace.html

This site gives lots of pointers to resources for ray-tracing rendering of graphics.

Computer graphics list

http://mambo.ucsc.edu/psl/cg.html

A jumbled mishmash of links to dozens of interesting graphics sites on the Web.

GOOD Project

http://metallica.prakinf.tu-ilmenau.de/GOOD.html

A public domain software environment for interactive programming of 3-D graphics. Cute name, no?

Pixel-Planes

http://www.cs.unc.edu/~pxpl/home.html

An academic project to build graphics engines with an emphasis on scalability and real-time rendering.

Hardware

It is easy to forget how important your computer's hardware is ... until it either breaks or you begin thinking of buying a better/faster/smaller system. Your hardware is an important part of the way you compute.

Because of its seemingly less important status, there is not nearly as much hardware information on the Web as there is software information. However, you can still find a great deal about non-PC computers and peripherals by browsing just a few sites (PCs are covered in their own section later in the book).

Benchmark Discussion on Usenet

news:comp.benchmarks

Everyone wants to know how fast his or her computer is relative to the rest of the world. Benchmarks are programs that help rate computer speeds under realistic conditions. The comp.benchmarks newsgroup is the best place to find out about which benchmark programs are right for the type of computer you have and the kind of work you do.

Snake Oil, Miracle Cures, and Computer Monitors

http://hawks.ha.md.us/hardware/monitors.html

A great treatise on computer monitors, how to buy them, and how to rate them. The author clearly has researched the field thoroughly and makes even the most technical details understandable. A great place to go before plunking down $500 (or much more) on your next purchase.

ChipList

http://einstein.et.tudelft.nl/~offerman/chiplist.html

Not many of us can tell one chip from another, but there are certainly folks who can. This list gives exquisite detail about every kind of CPU chip that you might find in your PC or Macintosh, as well as all the FPUs for those systems.

CPU Info Center

http://infopad.eecs.berkeley.edu/CIC/

A great central repository of information about CPUs. The site is very up-to-date, enough so to have a news section that actually seems

newsy. There's everything here from press releases to serious academic papers about CPU architecture.

SCSI Discussion on Usenet

news:comp.periphs.scsi

SCSI (for *small computer system interface,* pronounced "scuzzy") has a long history of being a fast peripheral bus for hard disks and other peripherals. Apple has standardized on SCSI for most of the Macintosh's lifetime, and many high-speed PC systems also rely on SCSI drives. Here's a good place to find out about what makes SCSI work.

VITA

http://www.vita.com/

Much less popular than SCSI, the VME bus is still used in many control applications. The VME International Trade Association (VITA) keeps the VME flame alive and helps users find vendors who still support this particular bus.

SPARC International

http://www.sparc.com/

Users of SPARC-based computers (mostly Sun Microsystems computers) will find a wealth of information about their CPU here. Because Sun is not the only manufacturer of SPARC systems, this is also a great place to shop for alternate manufacturers.

Newton Archive

http://newton.uiowa.edu/

If you use an Apple Newton PDA (*personal digital assistant*), this site is a must. It has pointers to all the shareware and freeware available for the Newton, as well as listings for almost anyone who has produced commercial software.

Drive Specs

http://www.cs.yorku.ca/People/frank/

An incredible collection of technical information about hard drives and CD-ROMs. There is also hard-to-find information on such black magic as boot sectors and the differences between various types of hard drives.

A L S O   R E C O M M E N D E D:

Slide Rule Home Page

http://photobooks.atdc.gatech.edu/~slipstick/slipstik.html

The original computer hardware.

HP 48 Calculator Site

http://kahless.isca.uiowa.edu/hewlett_packard.html

The venerable Hewlett-Packard 48 series calculators still do more number-crunching that many PCs.

History

The somewhat short history of computers is much shorter than the history of other sciences but is fascinating nonetheless. Much of early computing was funded by the U.S. government as part of its research in atomic weapons. By the late 1960s, there was a strong commercial market for computers which supplanted much of the government research.

Given that most computers can be used as tools of creativity, the history of computers is filled with twists caused by people using computers and software for things that their creators didn't expect. Entire markets appeared out of nowhere, and many expected advances never appeared due to customer indifference.

Charles Babbage Institute

http://fs1.itdean.umn.edu/cbi/cbihome.htm

The University of Minnesota is home to the Charles Babbage Institute, one of the premiere collections covering the history of information processing. You'll find much more than just computers here: the collection covers the history of information processing back hundreds of years.

Historic Computer Images Archive

http://ftp.arl.mil/ftp/historic-computers/

A large collection of pictures of old computers. The pictures are stored in a variety of formats and sizes, making it a great place to find small images for Web pages as well as full-sized pictures.

IEEE Annals of the History of Computing

http://www.computer.org/pubs/annals/annals.htm

The IEEE (the Institute of Electrical and Electronics Engineers) is one of the largest academic and computing groups in the country, and their *Annals of the History of Computing* is perhaps the best known magazine about computer history. Although articles are not online, you can look through tables of contents of old issues and find out how to subscribe.

Museum of Obsolete Computers

http://www.ncsc.dni.us/fun/user/tcc/cmuseum/cmuseum.htm

A great place to find photos and descriptions of recent but no-longer-sold computers. The focus is on personal computers from the last 20 years, but the collection is expanding, and the site maintainer solicits pictures and stories about other computers as well. Be glad they don't have a museum for obsolete computer *owners.*

The Computer Museum

http://www.net.org/

This aptly-titled museum is probably the largest walk-in collection of computers and historical information anywhere in the world. The museum is much more than a place of history: It has plenty of exhibits about the current technology and manufacturing as well.

Virtual Museum of Computing

http://www.comlab.ox.ac.uk/archive/
other/museums/computing.html

A great index to other Internet sites with historical computing information. The list is kept up to date, and even includes things like a list of books on the history of computing and galleries that sell historical photographs that include computers.

ALSO RECOMMENDED:

Unisys History Newsletter

http://www.cc.gatech.edu/services/
unisys-folklore/

A collection of stories about Unisys computers, IBM's most notable competitor in the 1950s and 60s.

Computer History Association of California

gopher://gopher.vortex.com/11/
comp-hist

A small collection of information about computer history.

Internet 25th Anniversary

http://www.amdahl.com/internet/
events/inet25.html

An overview and pointers to sites discussing the recent 25th anniversary of the birth of the Internet.

Internet

You wouldn't be reading this book unless you were interested in the Internet (well, you probably *shouldn't* be reading this book if you aren't interested in the Internet). The Internet is the current media darling, the amazing, hip, magical thing that will tell us everything we want to know and entertain us at the same time. A bit of skepticism is in order.

Yet the Internet is clearly a great tool that does have lots going on. For the tens of millions of current users, it has some attraction, and many of those users are finding great things to do on the Internet. Hopefully, you now realize that Yahoo! is one of those great things. But there is oh so much more.

Archie

If you want to find something at a public FTP site, Archie is your tool. Archie is a search program that has indexes of over 1000 of the known anonymous FTP sites around the world. Although the database has some big holes, it is clearly the most powerful way of finding files on the Internet.

SURANET's Guide to the Archie Service

http://www.sura.net/archie/Archie-
Usage.html

This is probably the best written explanation of Archie available. It covers both the simple how-to parts as well as giving a deeper technical explanation for those who like that sort of thing.

Archie files

ftp://ftp.bunyip.com/pub/

This archive, maintained by Archie's authors at Bunyip Information Systems, has many files of interest to Archie users, including Archie client programs, information about getting your FTP site listed in the Archie database, and the future of Archie.

ALSO RECOMMENDED:

List of WWW Archie Services

http://pubweb.nexor.co.uk/public/
archie/servers.html

A nicely-organized list of all the public Archie sites on the Internet, with emphasis on the sites that have a forms interface.

Beginner's Guides

We were all beginners once.

Beginner's Guide to Effective Email

http://www.webfoot.com/advice/
email.top.html

A very nice, real-world guide to using email. Instead of telling you how to use your email program, it explains how to create messages that get your point across. Much more than just netiquette, it covers things like thinking about the context of your messages and the person who receives them.

Complete Internet Beginner's Guide

http://www.futurenet.co.uk/netmag/Issue1/Easy/index.html

Refreshingly irreverent, this guide gives you the basics on many of the parts of the Internet without fluffing them up too much. The dry British humor helps, as does the acknowledgment that the Internet takes more technical understanding than most other topics thrown at novice computer users.

EFF's (Extended) Guide to the Internet.

http://www.eff.org/papers/bdgtti/eegtti.html

A gentle overview of the Internet, from the folks who are fighting to keep the Internet a hospitable place for everyone. Previously called "Big Dummy's Guide to the Internet", this seems to be aimed at novices who aren't sure whether they even want to get on the Internet.

Internet Tour

http://www.globalcenter.net/gcweb/tour.html

This one uses a different method for introducing the Internet: a day-in-the-life description of what you might use the Internet for and the tools you need for each task. It is well laid-out and somewhat fun to follow.

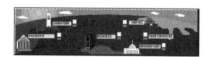

ALSO RECOMMENDED:

Glossary of Internet Terms

http://www.matisse.net/files/glossary.html

Nice, simple definitions of most of the buzzwords that you might come across.

How to Set Up a Winsock Connection

http://sage.cc.purdue.edu/~xniu/winsock.htm

A good guide for Windows 3.1 users on how to set up a Winsock connection without going crazy.

Roadmap

http://ua1vm.ua.edu/~crispen/roadmap.html

A tutorial on how to get on the Internet and what to do when you get there.

Business and Economics

One of the biggest debates in the Internet world is whether the new commercialization of the Internet is a Good Thing or a Bad Thing. As more money flows into the Internet, the business end becomes much more important to investors and other folks who want to make money from Internet users.

20 Reasons to Put Your Business on the World Wide Web

http://www.net101.com/reasons.html

If you feel like you need a justification for giving your business exposure on the Internet, you'll find it here. Created

by an Internet marketing company, this is a fairly compact list of good ideas of what you might get out of an Internet presence.

Setting Up Shop on the Internet

http://www.netrex.com/business.html

A beginner's guide, but with a business flavor. This document assumes that you don't understand much about what the Internet is, but want to know whether it is a viable option for your company.

World Wide Web Market Report

http://www.jpmorgan.com/MarketDataInd/Research/WebReport/TOC.html

This is an analysis of the Web from the standpoint of a market researcher for a major investment company. The emphasis is on major players in the Web market and how the market might tend to favor one company over another.

Advertising on the Internet

http://www.missouri.edu/internet-advertising-guide.html

Whether or not you have your own site on the Internet, you may be interested in advertising on someone else's site. This list has many pointers to articles and other resources relating specifically to advertising, mostly on the Web.

The Internet Advertising Resource Guide

Internet Business Center

http://www.tig.com/IBC/index.html

Good set of links to examples of interesting business sites on the Web.

Print Publications Related to Business Use of the Internet

http://arganet.tenagra.com/Tenagra/books.html

A place to go when you want to use paper to read about the commercial side of the Internet.

Chatting

IRC (Internet Relay Chat) is a popular service for those who like their communication to happen in real time. With IRC, you get on the equivalent of a telephone party line and start talking with everyone and anyone. Most Internet chatting is done on IRC, although other chat forums are starting to emerge as well.

Synchronous communications on the Net

http://sunsite.unc.edu/dbarberi/chats.html

This site has logs of some timely chats, such as the Oklahoma City bombing and the 1994 California earthquake. Reading these logs gives you an idea of what IRC is like, particularly when folks have something immediate on their minds.

Internet Relay Chat FAQ

http://www.kei.com/irc.html

The best introduction to IRC and associated chat systems. It covers how to get on IRC, the different client software you can use, and all the fancy types of add-ons that people have devised for their chatting. Novices should certainly read this before they go on the first time.

Index of IRC Nets

http://uptown.turnpike.net/L/Larry14/irc.html

A well-organized list of the different IRC servers and their differences. If you plan on chatting much, you should certainly read through this list to get a feeling for what kind of servers have what kind of chat channels.

Global Stage

http://prospero.com/globalstage/

If you're a Windows user who uses IRC, you should certainly look into Global Stage, a free chat client. It has good links to Web clients, lets you chat on multiple channels at the same time, and has lots of advanced features that you'll want on busy channels.

Undernet

http://www.undernet.org/

One of the main networks for IRCing, Undernet is newer than the larger EFnet, but is quickly becoming popular.

Bots and Games

http://calypso.cs.uregina.ca/Games/

An overview of the few games you can play on IRC.

Channels on WWW

http://www.uni-karlsruhe.de/~Urs.Janssen/irc/channels.html

Many IRC channels have their own unofficial Web pages, which is an odd combination when you think about it.

Internet Citizen's Band

http://icb.sjsu.edu/~kzin/icb.html

An alternative to IRC that uses different Internet technology.

Directory Services

The classical wisdom is that the Internet is too big to be indexed, but that doesn't stop some folks (like Yahoo) from trying. Creating directories and indexes of the Internet can be done with enough resources and a good dollop of creativity.

Access, Searching and Indexing of Directories

http://www.ietf.cnri.reston.va.us/html.charters/asid-charter.html

This is the IETF working group that deals with the weighty issues of how you let others query your directories in a standard fashion. An Internet directory is no good unless everyone can get access to it, and this group discusses the many methods to give people such access.

whois++

http://vinca.cnidr.org/protocols/
whoispp/whoispp.html

This is a good location for information about whois++, a promising candidate to become the next popular protocol for Internet directory services. Sites with whois++ directories can share information with other sites in a secure but easy fashion.

ALSO RECOMMENDED:

Publicizing Your Home Page

http://www.ntg-campus.com/ntg/
public.htm

A list of sites that let you list your home page.

Domain Registration

Domain names turn out to be a Big Thing for the Internet. In many people's minds, you've got to have the right domain name in order to be successful on the Internet. In the US, getting a domain name is easy, and it's free (at least for now).

InterNIC Directory and Database Services

http://www.internic.net/

These are the folks who hand out domain names in the United States. At this site, you can find the official form you need to fill out, as well as detailed instructions as to what you need to have before you can get a domain name.

Table of Global and Country Top Level Internet Domains

http://www.isoc.org/domains.html

If you've ever wondered what countries some of the non-US top-level Internet domains represent, you should have a copy of this table. It is updated often, since the domains change from time to time based on countries being formed and other political changes.

ALSO RECOMMENDED:

Association of Internet Users

http://usa.net/welcome/domain.html

A group that will register a domain name for you if you join.

Guides and Publications

Aether Madness

http://www.aether.com/Aether/

The electronic version of the popular book about odd things you can find on the Internet. The book is full of links, which makes the electronic version much more useful than the print version; on the other hand, the weird pictures don't fare well on the computer screen.

Clearinghouse for Subject-Oriented Internet Resource Guides

http://www.lib.umich.edu/
chhome.html

The Internet is full of guides to particular subjects, and this is a guide to those guides. The lists are more academic than other such lists, and they are categorized by traditional academic boundaries, but you can

generally find a guide to almost any subject here.

ALSO RECOMMENDED:

Canadian Internet Handbook

http://www.csi.nb.ca/handbook/

If you have anything to do with the Internet in North America, you should read this book.

Mapping the Internet

http://www.uvc.com/gbell/
promo.html

An interesting talk about how to figure out the extent of the Internet and how big it is.

Interesting Devices Connected to the Net

One of the best things about the Internet is that you can hook almost anything to it. The device doesn't even need to speak TCP/IP: it just needs to be connected to a computer that does. Some of the devices listed here are pretty silly, but others should give you an idea of what's to come for the Internet.

Australia's Telerobot On The Web

http://telerobot.mech.uwa.edu.au/

Given the great time lag, it may seem a bit odd to be moving a robot over the Web. This experiment lets you open and close the jaws of a robot arm, grab blocks, move them around, and so on. Each time you change the robot, you get a new picture of what is happening.

Bradford Robotic Telescope

http://www.telescope.org/rti/index.html

This represents a somewhat more realistic use of robots on the Web. After getting authorized, you can position the telescope and get the image relayed to you. This starts to show that devices which aren't used that often can be shared.

Internet-To-Real-World Gadgets

http://csclub.uwaterloo.ca/gadgets.html

The University of Waterloo's Computer Science Club has a bunch of different devices hooked up to a Web server, and you can see what the devices are up to at any given moment. You can see what they're listening to on the CD player, or even listen in to what is happening in the office (there's a microphone taped to the wall).

Streamflow Conditions at Selected Sites in California

http://s101dcascr.wr.usgs.gov/sites/sites.html

The U.S. Geological Survey measures the rate of flow of rivers and streams all over the country. This site shows a clickable map of California, and you can see a current flow graph for any of the streams measured.

Peeping Tom

http://www.ts.umu.se/~spaceman/camera.html

This is a fairly long list of Web sites that have live cameras. The list is organized by type of location (outdoors, indoors, on animals), and has good descriptions of what is being shown.

ALSO RECOMMENDED:

Anthony's List of Internet Accessible Machines

http://www.dsu.edu/~anderbea/machines.html

There are hundreds of sites with machines and devices attached to them, and this list describes most of them.

Automatic Talking Machine

http://www.inference.com/~hansen/talk.html

You type a message into the window, and it is spoken to this person in his office. Politeness counts.

Barcode Server

http://www.milk.com/barcode/

Wanna see what the stripes for a barcode number you enter will look like?

Brian's Lava Lamp

http://www.arl.wustl.edu/~brian/Office/LavaLamp/

Brian's camera, which is connected to Brian's computer, is pointed at Brian's lava lamp.

FallsCam

http://fallscam.niagara.com/

An up-to-the-minute picture of Niagara Falls; looks pretty much the same most of the time, eh?

Interactive Model Railroad

http://rr-vs.informatik.uni-ulm.de/rr/

A model railroad you can control and watch. This site is also an advertisement for better video over the Internet.

Paul's (Extra) Refrigerator

http://hamjudo.com/cgi-bin/refrigerator

How cold is it in the refrigerator? Is the door open or closed? Why do we care?

REINAS Project's Instrumentation Tour

http://sapphire.cse.ucsc.edu/MosaicMet/

Look at real-time weather pictures around the Monterey Bay area of California.

Internet Resources

Sometimes you just want a generalized way of finding sites and resources on the Internet, regardless of the type of Internet service that is used. There are a few sites with these kinds of lists, usually based at universities.

NCSU Libraries Collection of Internet Resources

http://dewey.lib.ncsu.edu/disciplines/index.html

This is a great list of academic topics and the dozens or hundreds of Internet resources that relate to each. Many of the entries are for lesser-known mailing lists and Gopher servers, which are often ignored by indexes of Web sites.

Internet Training Resources

http://www.brandonu.ca/~ennsnr/Resources/Welcome.html

People who train others how to use the Internet love to find other folk who have already written training materials. This is a good list of such materials, and is a good way to find other Internet trainers.

Internet Web Text

http://www.rpi.edu/Internet/Guides/decemj/text.html

This is probably one of the best-known resource lists on the Internet. Its author, John December, has been making it public for many years, and it comes in many formats. The information here comes both from his extensive searching on the Internet and from contributions from hundreds of people.

Special Internet Connections

http://www.uwm.edu/Mirror/inet.services.html

This is the other well-known resource list that has been around for many years. Between this and Internet Web Text, you should be able to find at least one site about almost any topic, assuming that such a site even exists.

News and Newspapers Online

http://www.uncg.edu/~cecarr/news/

Keeping up with the news is very important to many people. More and more newspapers are getting on the Internet, and many alternative news services are also setting up Web sites. This is an extensive list of many newspapers and news organizations with Internet access.

Usenet Archives List

http://starbase.neosoft.com/~claird/news.lists/newsgroup_archives.html

For most people, Usenet seems very transitory. Few sites keep more than a week or two's worth of news. However, a few places keep years worth of postings for specific news groups. This site lists all the known Usenet archives and describes different ways to access and use them.

ALSO RECOMMENDED:

InterNIC Directory of Directories

http://ds.internic.net/ds/dsdirofdirs.html

Not as complete as it should be, but a very good attempt at making a searchable index of resources.

Netlink

http://netlink.wlu.edu:1020/

Another academic resource list, hosted at Washington and Lee University.

Internet Voice

In the past year, there has been a surge of interest in using the Internet as an alternative to the long-distance phone system. Many new freeware and commercial packages now allow two Internet users with low-speed modem lines to converse over the Internet. It remains to be seen whether or not this will take off.

Internet Phone

http://www.vocaltec.com/

A commercial package that runs under Windows from VocalTec. This popular program is also bundled in with some Internet services, making it a contender for becoming a leader in the field. It has some advanced features like full-duplex operation.

NetPhone

http://www.emagic.com/netphone/mainblurb.html

A Macintosh phone program that has many extensions, such as group talking areas and an equivalent of Caller ID. It is compatible with CU-SeeMe so you can chat with videophone users as well. The freeware version has a commercial companion product with more features.

Yahoo!

IPhone User Directory

http://www.pulver.com/iphone/

Lists of people who you can chat with using various Internet phone products, and good links to information resources.

CyberPhone

http://magenta.com/cyberphone/

A free software package that runs on Sun workstations.

Mailing Lists

If you like two-way interaction with lots of people, mailing lists are a great way to go. Some are very active, with dozens or even hundreds of messages a day, while others have only a few messages a week. Mailing lists are quite established as a communication medium, and there are thousands of topics to chose from.

Internet Tour Bus

http://csbh.mhv.net/~bobrankin/tourbus/

An interesting way to find out more about the Internet through a mailing list. The list consists of information about various Internet sites, most available by email, and is an easy way to find out more about the Internet without having to use the Web.

The Internet TourBus!

LISTSERV Index at tile.net

http://tile.net/listserv/

A complete list of all the mailing lists that use the LISTSERV mailing list software. The list is searchable, and you can see how many people are on a particular list as well as where the list is located. The Web interface for subscribing is also nice.

Publicly Accessible Mailing Lists

http://www.neosoft.com/internet/paml/

This is the probably the best list of mailing lists. It is kept up to date, the subject indexes are much better than the LISTSERV ones, and the descriptions of the lists are generally much more readable. A good first stop when looking for a mailing list.

E-Mail Discussion Groups

http://www.nova.edu/Inter-Links/listserv.html

An introduction to e-mail, and a searchable index to the Dartmouth mailing list archive.

Lesbian Gay, Bisexual and Transgendered Mailing Lists

http://www.qrd.org/qrd/electronic/email/

A large collection of information about mailing lists (many of them regional) on queer issues.

ListWebber

http://www.lib.ncsu.edu/staff/morgan/about-listwebber2.html

This software lets you search through mailing list archives using a nice Web interface.

Maps

Many Internet users have a hard time conceiving the Internet without a map; maybe that says something about the way we learned about places as kids. Unfortunately, there is no really good way to "map" the Internet in the geographic sense. However, a few people have put together reasonable attempts at mapping parts.

Connectivity Maps

ftp://ftp.cs.wisc.edu/connectivity_table/

These maps show which countries have what kinds of Internet connections. Not surprisingly, there is an almost direct correlation with the GNP of a country and whether or not it has a high level of Internet connectivity. The maps are kept in PostScript format.

Host Name to Latitude/Longitude

http://cello.cs.uiuc.edu/cgi-bin/slamm/ip2ll/

Not really a map, but a way to create your own. You can enter a host name, a domain name, or an IP address, and the server will return to you a latitude and longitude. It even has links to the Xerox map server so you can see a map of the location you got back.

Matrix Maps Quarterly (MMQ)

http://www.zilker.net/mids/mmq/index.html

A commercial map service that has maps of the entire Matrix, not just the Internet. The maps show the density of the number of hosts in various areas, and give some analysis of changes between issues.

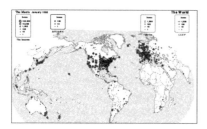

Newsletters

EduPage

http://www.educom.edu/edupage.new

A great newsletter about information technology in general, with a recent emphasis about the Internet. EduPage is put together by Educom, a consortium of universities looking for better ways to use computers in education, so the articles in the newsletter are slanted towards those aspects.

Mr. Media

http://www.review.net/cool/mrmedia.html

Don't let the title put you off: this is a great newsletter based on the weekly column that appears in many local newspapers. The sites covered are fairly light-weight, and the site reviews are often entertaining. Easy to read, easy to digest.

Scout Report

http://rs.internic.net/scout_report-index.html

This is a wonderful weekly newsletter with interesting Internet sites. It is one of the few newsletters that pays attention to Gopher sites and mailing lists, and emphasizes non-commercial sites and good sites for kids.

ALSO RECOMMENDED:

Cowles/SIMBA Media Daily: Internet Information

http://www.mecklerweb.com/simba/internet.htm

A good selection of recent stories concerning the Internet, with an emphasis on the business side of things.

Linx

http://www.sol.sarasota.fl.us/guest.html

A nice little newsletter for a local ISP. Definitely aimed and novices and intermediate users.

The Stick

http://www.vpm.com/tti/stick.html

Fun things to do on the Internet, although the writing is a tad overenthusiastic.

Internet Week

http://www.phillips.com:3200/

Very newsy and very business-oriented. Lots of small articles about what is happening in the business of the Internet.

The Scalzi Report

http://www.cybergate.com/~scalzi/tsr.html

A fun everyman's view of the Internet business scene. The articles have lots of opinion, which makes it less dry than many similar newsletters.

Organizations

African Internet Development Action Team

http://www.africa.com/pages/aidat/

A group aimed at developing the Internet in Africa. Many African countries don't even have rudimentary e-mail, while others have fairly good Internet connections, so this group has to also coordinate varying levels of technologies at the same time as it works around political roadblocks.

Yahoo!

IETF

http://www.ietf.cnri.reston.va.us/home.html

The IETF (more formally known as the Internet Engineering Task Force) is the main body that makes Internet standards and guidelines. Anyone can read what's going on, and people interested in doing the hard work of design, research, and implementation are encouraged to participate in the online discussions.

Current Internet Drafts

http://www.ietf.cnri.reston.va.us/1id-abstracts.html

As ideas and proposals move through the IETF, they are stated as Internet Drafts. This site has links to all the active drafts, categorized by the IETF Working Group to which the draft was proposed. Some of these are quite dense, others easy to read and even fun.

Internet Society

http://www.isoc.org/

The Internet Society (sometimes called "ISOC") is the umbrella society for many groups working on the Internet. It is a membership organization, and publishes a magazine. The Web site has links to many of the best resources on how the Internet works and who keeps it going.

ALSO RECOMMENDED:

Center for Cyber Communities Initiative

http://www.ccci.or.jp/

An interesting group in Janpan is doing research on how you create online communities for regular folks.

Internet Software Consortium

http://www.isc.org/isc/

A nonprofit group that will create and maintain reference software for the Internet.

Statistics and Demographics

The Internet is a magnet for big numbers. "Look at this huge growth!" "Millions and millions!" It is easy to count big things on the Internet, but it isn't always easy to interpret what the numbers mean. The sites here are good sources of information on what the big numbers mean.

Commercial Domains

http://www.webcom.com/~walsh/

One of the most overused Internet numbers bounced around the press is the number of commercial domains, which really means the number of domain names, not actual hosts. This site has good, up-to-date summaries of which commercial domains are being added, and where they are located.

NSFNET Backbone Statistics Page

http://www.cc.gatech.edu/gvu/stats/NSF/merit.html

A good historical review of the amount of information that traveled over the NSFnet backbone. This is now historical data, since there is no more backbone, but it gives some idea of the growth in the amount of information being passed around the US part of the Internet.

Coolest Hostnames On The Net

http://www.seas.upenn.edu/~mengwong/coolhosts.html

A very silly list of some of the funnier names for Internet hosts. Why name your system "www.something.com" when you can have a name like "pong.ping.com" or "dysfunctional-relationship.ecst.csuchico.edu"?

Internet Domain Survey

http://www.nw.com/zone/WWW/top.html

If you start to hear one too many discussions of the number of domain names, this is the place to go. This site has very good statistical analysis of many domains, the subdomains, and an explanation of what (if anything) the numbers mean.

Survey-Net

http://www.survey.net/

A place to go when you want to participate in Internet surveys, and view the results of previous surveys. Scientific methodology goes out the window here, but then again there really aren't many other sources of data for things like how much people shop on the Internet.

ALSO RECOMMENDED:

U-Do-It Internet Estimator

http://www.gnn.com/gnn/news/
feature/inet-demo/web.size.html

A great set of links (and a fair amount of skepticism) about the number of people on the Internet.

InterMania

http://www.webcom.com/~walsh/
million.html

Some very funny and scary stories about how many billions of dollars Wall Street is throwing at Internet companies.

Irresponsible Internet Statistics Generator

http://www.anamorph.com/docs/
stats/stats.html

How to extrapolate numbers over time and get really wrong results about the growth of the Internet.

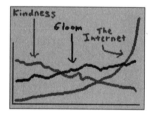

Internet Index

http://www.openmarket.com/info/
internet-index/

A knockoff of the Harper's Index, this site has some cute lists of Internet factoids and demistatistics.

Internet Business Statistics

http://www.tig.com/IBC/
Statistics.html

Many pointers and summaries of business-related Internet statistics.

Veronica

Gopher servers are much more amenable to searching than their Web counterparts. Veronica is an organized effort to let Gopher users search for information at any of the public Gopher servers throughout the world.

Veronica FAQ

gopher://gopher.scs.unr.edu/00/
veronica/veronica-faq

Although Veronica is fairly easy to use, there are still many common questions about it. This document, written by Steve Foster, also known as "Mr. Veronica", tells you how to use Veronica most effectively.

ALSO RECOMMENDED:

How To Compose Veronica Queries

gopher://veronica.scs.unr.edu/00/
veronica/how-to-query-veronica

Not everyone understands boolean searches. This short guide tells you how to use Veronica's search system.

Assorted Internet-related Sites

Building Internet Servers

http://www.charm.net/~cyber/

If you want to become an Internet publisher, as compared to just being a user, you have to learn a bit about Internet servers and how they operate. Even if you never run a server yourself, this site has lots of good information about what servers are, the kind of software they use, and so on.

Internet Fax Server

http://town.hall.org/fax/

Here's an interesting experiment that might turn into something real: the ability to send faxes on the Internet for free. The basic idea is that your fax goes to the closest participating host, which prints it and faxes it to the desired phone number. Will it work? Time will tell.

Church of Scientology vs. the Net

http://www.cybercom.net/
~rnewman/scientology/home.html

This is an interesting ongoing documentary of how the Church of Scientology is trying to inhibit discussion of its practices on the Internet. The church has sued a number of people, and has tried to pressure some sites from carrying church-related Usenet newsgroups.

ALSO RECOMMENDED:

Jughead

gopher://gopher.utah.edu/11/
Search%20menu%20titles%20using%
20jughead

A hierarchical client for searching
Gopher menus.

Chicago Area Internet Society (CAIS)

http://www.cais.org/

One of the few user's groups with a
really useful site.

Languages

All computers need to be
programmed in order to work, and
there is a huge variety of languages
that can be used for the task of
programming. Many people think that
programming is a black art which can
only be performed by a few rocket
scientists, but in fact many computer
languages can be picked up with only
a bit of reading.

Just as human languages differ in
structure and size of vocabulary,
computer languages can be incredibly
different from each other. Some read
almost like English; others look like a
jumble of numbers and punctuation
with only a few letters thrown in.

Every programmer has her or his
favorite language, although most
programmers know at least two or
three different languages. Yahoo has
listings for more than 50 computer
languages, but only the more popular
ones are shown here.

Catalog of Free Compilers and Interpreters

http://remarque.berkeley.edu/~muir/
free-compilers/

A comprehensive and up-to-date list
of most of the free language compilers
available on the Internet. The catalog
is arranged so that you can easily find
out which languages have free
compilers and when they were last
updated.

Ada

Best known because it is a U.S.
military standard, Ada has a wide
variety of applications. It has only
caught on in niche markets, however.
The language is named after the
woman widely recognized as the first
computer programmer ever, Countess
Augusta Ada Lovelace.

Ada Pointers

http://www.cs.kuleuven.ac.be/~dirk/
ada.html

A fairly complete list of places on the
Internet with Ada information. This site
has a strong emphasis on European
Ada sites, which often have more
nonmilitary information than similar
U.S. sites.

SIGAda

http://info.acm.org/sigada/

The home site for the ACM
(*Association for Computing
Machinery*) Ada group. SIGAda is a
very active group of Ada programmers
and a very good source of information
for finding out about current Ada
implementations.

APL

APL is a great language for processing
symbols and arbitrary-sized numbers,
but it requires a different character set
than what you see on your keyboard
and thus has been doomed to relative
obscurity. Still used by some
programmers for a small number of
applications.

APL Pointers

http://grover.jpl.nasa.gov/~sam/

This site is probably the best place to
find out about APL. It is maintained by
the same person who writes the APL
FAQ, so you can always get the latest
copy of the FAQ here.

awk

One of the mainstays of many Unix
programmers, awk is great for looking
for patterns in text files and returning
the parts that matches those patterns.
Although mostly superseded by the
Perl language these days, there are
still many fervent awk programmers
around.

TAWK compiler

http://www.mbnet.mb.ca/~natewild/awk/awk.html

Thompson Automation has created a PC-compatible awk compiler, TAWK (yet another cute name for a fairly dweeby product). TAWK extends the features of the original awk and makes the programs very fast. This site also has pointers to other awk-related Internet sites.

Basic

Given that millions of people learned to program starting with Basic, usually in a high school curriculum, it is somewhat sad that there are so few Internet resources for Basic. Perhaps this is due to the popularity of newer dialects of Basic, such as Visual Basic, which is covered later in this section.

Basic Archives

http://www.fys.ruu.nl/~bergmann/basic.html

This is the best index to Internet resources on Basic, of which there are only a few. This site also serves as a FAQ file for the comp.lang.basic.misc Usenet newsgroup.

Liberty Basic

http://world.std.com/~carlg/basic.html

If you use Windows or OS/2, you should definitely check out this shareware Basic. It has many of the features of Visual Basic, but costs much less. And of course it also has a much nicer interface than non-GUI Basic.

BETA

Object-oriented languages are all the rage these days, and BETA is one of the better ones to compete with C++. A compiled language, BETA programs run fairly quickly on most hardware. BETA comes from Denmark, and most of the development of the language is based there as well.

BETA index

http://www.daimi.aau.dk/~beta/

The central site for information on BETA and its derivative languages. BETA has its own Usenet newsgroup, and there are many papers on the language that are stored on this server.

ALSO RECOMMENDED:

Mjolner BETA

http://www.mjolner.dk/

A commercial implementation of the BETA language.

C and C++

By far, the most popular programming languages for writing common applications are C and C++. C has long been a mainstay of the Unix community, but has now migrated to all computer platforms. C++, the object-oriented dialect of C, is gaining a new following as more people are drawn towards object-oriented systems.

Coding Convention for C++

http://www.cs.princeton.edu/~dwallach/CPlusPlusStyle.html

If you work with other programmers, it is often difficult to understand bits of the code they write. This paper is a good set of guidelines for standardized naming and usage in C++.

ANSI-C Collection

http://gcn.scri.fsu.edu/~jamie/ansi_c.html

Everything you wanted to know about ANSI-C, mostly formatted in HTML for easier reading on the Web. Although the graphics are a bit tacky, the site has lots of good information in a format that Web users will certainly appreciate.

C and C++ Resources

http://www.cyberspace.org/u/viking1/www/progra.htm

A good collection of pointers to other Internet resources on C and C++, including many college-level courses in programming in these languages.

C++ Archive

http://www.quadralay.com/www/CCForum/CCForum.html

This archive is supported by Quadralay because they do all their programming in C++ and wanted to have the latest information for their own programmers. A good, nonacademic site.

G++

http://www.ai.mit.edu/!info/g-whiz/
!!first

The GNU Project's free C++ compiler, called G++, is considered to be better than many C++ compilers that can cost thousands of dollars. Not surprisingly, G++ is used by many major companies because the source code is free (making bugs easier to fix) and because G++ is being supported by thousands of other programmers throughout the world.

GCC

http://www.ai.mit.edu/!info/gcc.info/
!!first

If you use C but not C++, you should look at GCC, also from the GNU Project. It compiles to an incredible range of hardware, and is fairly well supported by its users.

Introduction to C Programming

http://www.iftech.com/classes/c/
c0.htm

Interface Technologies offers the sourcebook for its C programming class, which is offered free to the Internet. This tactic is interesting in that it lets you see how they teach before signing on for their courses. They offer other sourcebooks for their other courses free as well.

International Obfuscated C Code Contest

ftp://ftp.uu.net/pub/ioccc/

One of those dweeby things some programmers like to do. This contest honors the people who can take a simple task and code it in such a way that no one can figure out what is going on in the program.

A L S O R E C O M M E N D E D:

C++ Virtual Library

http://info.desy.de/user/projects/
C++.html

Another index of C++ resources, this one with a German slant and more emphasis on external tools.

COBOL

Although it is still heavily used in the financial industry, many people consider COBOL a dinosaur that refuses to die. However, with literally tens of thousands of COBOL programs still running (and gazillions of dollars being transferred though its code every day), it is still a programming force to be reckoned with.

COBOL Index

http://www.cs.indiana.edu/hyplan/
mayer/cobol/cobol.html

One of the few index sites that also serves double-duty as a reference manual. There is a good list of COBOL books here and a plea to help make the page more useful.

Dylan

Apple often comes out with advanced tools (although not *always* too useful to their users) and a few years ago the company decided to publish the specification for Dylan, an new object-oriented language that looks a bit like Lisp. Dylan is meant to be more modular and flexible than its predecessors, although so far it has not gotten much attention.

DylanWorks

http://www.harlequin.com/full/
dylan.html

Apple, of course, puts most of its initial efforts on its own computer platforms. DylanWorks is an implementation of Dylan for PCs running under Windows.

A L S O R E C O M M E N D E D:

Dylan Index

http://www.cambridge.apple.com/
dylan/dylan.html

This site points to the surprisingly large number of Dylan sites on the Internet.

Forth

Fifteen years ago, many computer dweebs predicted that Forth would be the next popular language; so much for the ability of computer dweebs to predict the future. Forth is still somewhat popular for people writing programs that control machines, as well as a variety of other niche applications.

Forth Interest Group

http://taygeta.oc.nps.navy.mil/
fig_home.html

FIG has been around for almost as long as Forth has and is one of the last keepers of the flame for true Forth believers. There are links here to many articles about Forth as well as lists of hardware and software implementations you can still buy.

ALSO RECOMMENDED:

Forth, Inc.

http://www.earthlink.net/~forth/

The last sizable developer of Forth compilers and related software.

Fortran

Like COBOL, Fortran has outlasted many other languages in part due to the continued existence of a huge number of programs written in it. Unlike COBOL, though, Fortran still attracts many new users due to the fact that it is optimized for numerical and scientific tasks.

Fortran 90 Software Repository

http://www.nag.co.uk:70/1h/
nagware/Examples

A public site where people can put their Fortran code for others to browse. This can help reduce duplication of effort and give Fortran programmers a way to optimize their current code.

Fortran Market

http://www.fortran.com/fortran/
market.html

This is an interesting site that caters to the Fortran community by listing commercial software of interest to Fortran programmers. They also list Fortran users groups, training companies, and so on.

Java

Few new languages get as much instant attention from the press as Sun's Java got in the months since it was announced. Java programs enable Internet users to download standardized programs that they can run from their Web browsers and other Internet clients.

Sun's HotJava Home

http://java.sun.com/

Because Java was developed at Sun, Sun is still the primary source for information about the language. This site has the language specification, examples of using Java in Web browsers, and news of who else is working on Java.

Lisp

Originally hailed as *the* language of artificial intelligence, Lisp was probably the most hyped language that never really went anywhere. Part of the reason it failed to catch on is that Lisp uses a very different structure for its commands than most other computer languages; another part of the reason was that no one could figure out what else Lisp was good for.

Common Lisp manual

http://www-cgi.cs.cmu.edu/afs/
cs.cmu.edu/project/ai-repository/ai/
html/cltl/clm/clm.html

A complete reference to Common Lisp, the dialect most popular among Lisp users. This is clearly a reference manual, not a learning guide. The book is fully rendered for the Web in HTML.

Association of Lisp Users

http://www.cs.rochester.edu/users/
staff/miller/alu.html

The folks who are still trying to keep Lisp alive. This is the best index of Lisp resources and the Lisp-related companies that have not yet gone out of business.

Literate Programming

A name that sounds like an oxymoron. Literate programming is a style of programming that incorporates the program's documentation into the source code. Made popular by programming guru Donald Knuth, this style of programming challenges the programmer to actually describe what is going on in the code.

Literate programming course

http://info.desy.de/user/projects/
LitProg/Course.html

This site features a complete, online course in literate programming. It includes many examples and references to Knuth's book and is appropriate for anyone who knows a bit about the LaTeX formatting language and at least one programming language.

Literate programming index

http://info.desy.de/www/LitProg.html

The central spot for finding resources about literate programming.

Logo

An offshoot of Lisp, Logo is a very simplified language that is supposed to be easy for kids to understand. Logo was developed to help teach simple programming concepts using computer graphics and is still used in a few schools today.

Kids Learning Programming

http://www.inasec.ca/com/logo/mainpb.htm

An extensive site dedicated to teaching logo to children. Parents are encouraged to submit the programs that their kids create.

Logo archives

ftp://cher.media.mit.edu/pub/logo/

An FTP archive of Logo information (that is getting a bit dusty …).

Pascal

Popular in the academic world during much of the 1980s, Pascal is still in use today on several platforms. Programs written in Pascal are less likely to have logic errors than their counterparts written in C, although C compilers are usually much more optimized and have better tools than their Pascal counterparts.

Online Pascal course

http://www.cit.ac.nz/smac/pascal/default.htm

This is a great introduction to Pascal. It can be easily browsed by anyone who wants to learn Pascal in a nonclassroom setting. The examples are quite simple, making it easy for even novices to get the hang of Pascal.

Turbo Pascal index

http://www.cs.vu.nl/~jprins/tp.html

Turbo Pascal is probably the most popular commercial dialect of Pascal. This page has dozens of resources for Turbo Pascal users, as well as news about recent products and new books.

Perl

Perl has become the new darling of the programming world, catching many people's fancy as a great language suitable for many tasks. It excels at string handling, has very

powerful search-and-replace functions, and works well with almost all common Unix systems (as well as with other platforms).

Perl archive

http://www.metronet.com/perlinfo/perlinfo.html

One of the more up-to-date indexes of Perl information, this site also has many examples of Perl programs and fragments. There is also lots of information about the newest version of Perl, Perl5.

MacPerl

http://err.ethz.ch/members/neeri/macintosh/perl-qa.html

Perl is not for Unix only. MacPerl works well as an advanced scripting language for the Macintosh and can be integrated with other Mac programming tools. Many folks swear that it is easier to write little scripts in MacPerl than in any other Macintosh language.

Perl for NT

ftp://ftp.intergraph.com/pub/win32/perl/

Because of Windows NT's similarities to Unix, Perl for NT can make creating NT programs much easier because so many useful programs have already been written in Perl. This port of Perl5 has a fairly sparse interface but it certainly gives the NT programmer a good tool for creating powerful programs easily.

Crypto-in-short-Perl

http://dcs.ex.ac.uk/~aba/rsa-perl.html

A really cute hack: three lines of Perl code that perform RSA cryptography which is illegal (at the time of this writing) to export from the United States.

Rexx

IBM created Rexx as a scripting language similar to Basic, but Rexx is much more robust. Rexx took over a decade to catch on, but it is now gaining popularity on many of IBM's platforms, as well as on non-IBM computers. It is fairly easy to learn and reasonably powerful.

Rexx index

http://www2.hursley.ibm.com/rexx/

The best site for information about what is happening with Rexx. There are lists of implementations of Rexx for many computers (even the Amiga!) as well as news about what IBM is doing to move the language forward.

Rexx Language Association

http://www.pvv.unit.no/RexxLA/index.html

The international user's group for Rexx programmers and developers. They even have annual meetings, a rarity for such programmer's associations.

VX-Rexx

http://www.watcom.on.ca/vxrexx/vxrexx.html

A high-quality commercial implementation of Rexx for OS/2.

Scheme

Probably the most common variant of Lisp being used today, Scheme is still used in a few environments, particularly in artificial intelligence (whatever that means this year). They are so similar, if you know Lisp, you can pick up Scheme in a matter of minutes.

Scheme 48

http://www-swiss.ai.mit.edu/~jar/s48.html

This is an implementation of Scheme that has extensions for many modern features, notably multitasking, exception handling, and hash tables. It also handles modules in a new fashion with which the authors are particularly enamored.

Scheme Repository

http://www.cs.indiana.edu/scheme-repository/home.html

The central storage location for sample Scheme source code samples, fragments, and fully-functional modules. There are dozens of useful programs here, and some of them are even well documented.

Tcl/Tk

Tcl is a new programming language that is quite good at creating small graphical programs. It is essentially a mini-language, but it has been extended by many people and can interface with other languages like C and C++. Tk is a toolkit of graphical objects that work with Tcl. Together, they make quite a good programming environment for small applications.

Brief Introduction to Tcl

http://http2.brunel.ac.uk:8080/~csstddm/TCL2/TCL2.html

A pretty complete guide to getting started wit Tcl and Tk. Laid out in a textbook-like fashion, this introduction walks you through all the language's features as well as provides many short examples and tips.

Tcl/Tk at Sun

http://www.sunlabs.com/research/tcl/

The originator of Tcl/Tk, John Ousterhout, works for Sun Microsystems and is in charge of maintaining Tcl/Tk and moving them forwards. This is by far the best site to get the latest versions of the software and to find out what will be happening in the near future with the language.

The Tcl War

http://www.utdallas.edu/acc/glv/Tcl/war/

What's a good language without some petty fighting about what's wrong with it? This is an archive of some of the major arguments and counter-arguments that happened after Richard Stallman, a somewhat famous programmer, suggested that people shouldn't program with Tcl.

Tcl/Tk Style Guide

http://www.atd.ucar.edu/jva/TCL.style.html

An excellent little list of suggestions for making your Tcl/Tk programs more understandable.

Tcl Index

http://www.sco.com/Technology/tcl/

This site has a list of sites on the Web which have Tcl information.

Tcl/Tk Resources

http://web.cs.ualberta.ca/~wade/HyperTcl/

Another index site, but this one has many more programming examples.

Visual Basic

Microsoft has certainly created a very useful tool with Visual Basic. Although clearly more complex than vanilla Basic, Visual Basic enables you to create complete, usable Windows programs with very little effort. Many programmers have found Visual Basic to be a great way to create utilities quickly.

Ask Dr. VB

http://www.crl.com/~cicero/drvb/askdrvb.html

Amazing as it may seem, here's someone who's willing to answer your Visual Basic programming questions without charging you for his time. Of course, you probably should peruse the answers already on the site before asking your question.

VB Junction

http://www.ticllc.net/~bobrob/vbj/

More than just an index, this site also includes a question-and-answer board as well as many pointers to sites off the Internet. People who create Visual Basic extensions can also advertise them here.

VBxtras

http://www.vbxtras.com/

Serious Visual Basic programmers don't want to reinvent the wheel, so buying existing tools often makes more sense than creating your own. This site gives reviews of over 100 tools and offers many of them for sale.

Carl and Gary's Visual Basic

http://www.apexsc.com/vb/

A complete and well-organized index to the Visual Basic world.

Other Languages

There are dozens of other programming languages, some of them quite obscure. Yet many people find these to be even more interesting than the mainstream languages. A few are described here.

ABC

http://www.cwi.nl/~steven/abc.html

A small Basic-like language for teaching.

Assembly language tips

http://www.fys.ruu.nl/~faber/Amain.html

Quite a large collection of resources for 80x86 assembly language programming.

Cecil

http://www.cs.washington.edu/research/projects/cecil/cecil/www/cecil-home.html

Another object-oriented language, this one with classless object for easier prototyping.

Delphi Connection

http://www.pennant.com/delphi.html

A magazine for Delphi users. (Delphi is a popular database language from Borland.)

Eiffel

http://arachnid.cm.cf.ac.uk/CLE/

An object-oriented language that emphasizes code reuse (don't they all?).

Haskell at Yale

http://www.cs.yale.edu/HTML/YALE/CS/haskell/yale-fp.html

A purely functional programming language, for the purely functional at heart.

Icon

http://www.cs.arizona.edu/icon/www/index.html

This was one of the first great languages for handling strings and arbitrary data structures.

IDL Discussion on Usenet

news:comp.lang.idl

If you are prototyping a user interface, IDL (Interface Description Language) may help you get going quickly.

Infer

http://www.cs.indiana.edu/hyplan/chaynes/infer.html

A derivative of Scheme/LISP, Infer is statically based, which makes it easier to debug as well as to throw together programs that work right the first time.

LIFE (Logic, Inheritance, Functions, and Equations)

http://brie.cs.sfu.ca/life/

A really odd programming language with an excessively cute name.

Magma

http://www.maths.usyd.edu.au:8000/comp/magma/Overview.html

Serious mathematicians need their own programming language, and this one fits the bill. Not for the faint of heart.

ML

http://www.cs.cmu.edu/afs/cs.cmu.edu/user/jgmorris/web/sml-faq.html

MLs are meta-languages that define their own structures. They are mostly of interest to computer science folks.

Modula

http://www.research.digital.com/SRC/modula-3/html/home.html

Modula is considered to be a more modern dialect of Pascal with many of the inconsistent parts removed.

Obliq

http://www.research.digital.com/SRC/Obliq/Obliq.html

Obliq is an experiment in distributed, object-oriented computation.

Occam

http://www.comlab.ox.ac.uk/archive/occam.html

A wonderful little language that is optimized for parallel computing (particularly with Transputer CPUs).

Prograph

http://msor0.ex.ac.uk/Prograph_Talk/StartTalk.html

Another fad come and gone: dataflow languages.

Prolog Discussion on Usenet

news:comp.lang.prolog

A great language for those who like to deal with mathematical logic problems.

Proteus

http://www.cs.unc.edu/proteus-intro.html

The designers hope that this will be the end-all language for parallel programming on any platform.

Python

http://www.python.org/

Another pretender to the object-oriented throne.

Sather

http://http.icsi.berkeley.edu/Sather/

You want the best of every possible language in one? According to this site, Sather "… aims to be as efficient as C, C++, or Fortran, as elegant as and safer than Eiffel or CLU, and support higher-order functions and iteration abstraction as well as Common Lisp, Scheme, or Smalltalk." Um, OK.

ScriptX Technical Reference Series

http://www.kaleida.com/reference/index.html

Possibly the Next Big Thing in multimedia: a programming language with an open standard interface.

SDL

http://www.tdr.dk/public/SDL/SDL.html

SDL is an object-oriented language optimized for real-time systems such as telecommunications and networking.

Self

http://self.smli.com

If you like your objects more malleable and self-configuring than standard OOPs, check out Self, now being supported by Sun Microsystems.

Smalltalk

http://st-www.cs.uiuc.edu/

One of the first object-oriented languages, Smalltalk is popular for rapid prototyping of programs.

SR (Synchronizing Resources)

http://www.cs.arizona.edu/sr/www/index.html

Using a paradigm only a computer scientist could love, SR treats resources as objects and lets you manipulate them in odd and fascinating ways.

Visual languages

http://union.ncsa.uiuc.edu/HyperNews/get/computing/visual.html

An introduction and index to languages that manipulate visual information.

Z Users Group

http://www.comlab.ox.ac.uk/archive/z/zug.html

This language (which the British authors point out is pronounced "zed") describes predicate logic, set theory, and other bits of higher mathematics.

Magazines

For decades, the computer market has always enjoyed a parallel magazine market. This has particularly been true of the PC industry, where magazines in the late 1970s spoke breathlessly of new computers with more RAM and faster CPUs as if they were the solutions to all our problems. Today, there are magazines for just about everyone, with topics from the incredibly technical to fluffy, lightweight "lifestyle" coverage.

Amiga Report Magazine

http://www.omnipresence.com/Amiga/News/AR/

One of the great things about publishing on the Internet is that you can do frequent issues at very little cost. *Amiga Report Magazine* is a great example of a frequently updated resource that would make little sense on paper, especially given the uncertain status of how long the Amiga will be around.

Black Boxes

http://gagme.wwa.com/~pancho/bbox1.htm

A small, opinionated magazine about Microsoft Windows and related products, with an emphasis on using Windows and the Internet. There are usually a few articles, reviews of Windows Internet software, and pointers to related Web sites.

BYTE

http://www.byte.com/

The venerable dweeb magazine, long a mainstay of computer users who want to keep up on the technical side of the PC market. The *BYTE* Web site has a searchable index of past issues as well as almost-current ones.

Search CMP Magazines

http://techweb.cmp.com/techweb/
programs/registered/search/cmp-
wais-index.html

You can search many computer
magazines published by CMP from a
single search. CMP publishes general
computer magazines such as
Windows Magazine and *Home PC* to
narrowly-focused ones such as
Electronic Engineering Times and *VAR
Business.*

Computer-Mediated Communication Magazine

http://sunsite.unc.edu/cmc/mag/
current/toc.html

A somewhat academic journal
covering how people use computers
and networks to talk to each other.
Each issue has a few long articles as
well as news and other features. This
is a good place to look if you're
thinking about how computers have
changed the way we interact.

DevelopNet News

gopher://vita.org/11/intl/dnn

If you are interested in how
technology affects developing
countries and regions, this is definitely
a great monthly magazine. It covers
technology transfer, development
costs, and so on for computer and
noncomputer technology.

G-Web

http://www.cinenet.net/GWEB/

Creating animation is a popular
activity for many computer users. *G-
Web* covers the field for both
amateurs and professionals, with an
emphasis on the software and

hardware tools used. This is also a
good place to browse if you just like
to see some fun new animations.

HyperZine

http://www.hyperzine.com/

This is where consumer electronics
meets the Web. *HyperZine* reviews
and previews audio and video
equipment, as well as covering their
respective industries. The articles have
many links to other Web sites, which
makes them useful if you're planning
on buying what's covered.

In, Around and Online

http://www.clark.net/pub/robert/
home.html

This one-person powerhouse is by far
one of the best weekly
newsmagazines in the
communications business. Robert
Seidman reviews the major online
services, talks honestly about their
faults, looks at how the Internet will
change them, and even talks finance.
A must-read.

Inter@ctive Week

http://www.zdnet.com/~intweek/

You can't get much better than this for
the interactive services industry. There
is plenty of coverage of the Internet,
private services, and the telephone
and cable companies.

Boardwatch

http://www.boardwatch.com

Anyone interested in the BBS (bulletin
board system) world should read
Boardwatch, period. It is a great
magazine, and their Web site is
improving by the month. The
magazine covers the world of the
Internet from a provider's perspective,
which makes for interesting reading.

Internet and Comms Today

http://www.atlas.co.uk/paragon/
ict1.html

A great British monthly magazine with
a fairly lively Web site. The magazine is
often much more interesting than its
American counterparts, although the
articles can be a bit sensationalistic.
Still, it offers quite a good perspective
on the people side of the Internet.

Develop

http://www.info.apple.com/dev/
develop.html

Folks who develop software for
Macintosh computers should certainly
be reading this magazine. Produced
by Apple, *Develop* is slick, somewhat
funny (considering the terribly dry
topic), and is quite responsive to
questions posed by readers.

Technology Review

http://web.mit.edu/techreview/www/

Yet another paper-magazine-on-the-Web, this one is probably more interesting to computer users because of its in-depth coverage of many science and technology issues. One of the few magazines aimed at technical readers which is still willing to cover policy and ethics.

NCT

http://www.awa.com/nct/

This magazine has a bit of everything for computer users: articles on Macs, PCs, using the Web, office tips, you name it. *NCT* is perhaps too liberal with its use of formatting, but the content is fun and informative.

PC Magazine

http://www.zdnet.com/~pcmag/

The Web version of *PC Magazine* has many of the articles from the very popular print version, although they are at least one issue behind. The Web site also has recent news, and you can download programs described in the print magazine.

Perforations

http://noel.pd.org/perforations/perforations.html

One of the more interesting technology-and-society journals. It covers how humans and machines interact and how we view the interactions. A little heady at times, it is still very fulfilling and well thought-out.

Flames: The Science And Technology Magazine

http://www.gold.net/flames/st.html

Every scientist who also uses computers should be reading this magazine. It demystifies PCs for scientists and talks about such issues as the computers becoming more important than the research they're being used on. Great stuff.

Upside

http://www.upside.com/upside/upside.html

The business of the computer industry can be just as fun or boring as any other industry. *Upside* covers the computer industry in all its glitz and greed. The Web site has only one article from each issue, which is unfortunate since many folks will find all the articles of interest.

ALSO RECOMMENDED:

.net

http://www.futurenet.co.uk/netmag/net.html

A droll British Internet magazine with an odd slant on the news.

cc:browser

http://www.faulkner.com/

Interesting coverage of the computer and communications industries, with frequent updates.

Computer Life

http://www.ziff.com/~complife/

Excerpts from the monthly print magazine, with special weekly updates.

Future Music

http://www.futurenet.co.uk/music/futuremusic.html

A British magazine covering high-tech music, including computer-generated and played music.

Computer Sun Times

http://www.rmii.com/cstimes/

A fun online zine with a local feel but professional-level articles.

c|net online

http://www.cnet.com/

An eclectic collection of articles and interaction with its readers.

d.Comm

http://www.d-comm.com/

Mostly text-based computer news magazine that is updated often.

Datateknik

http://www.et.se/datateknik/

Swedish magazines, computer style. This is the online version of Sweden's largest computer magazine.

elektra

http://www.digitas.org/

This is a well-designed small magazine of technology news from the perspective of Harvard students.

Error 404

http://cban.worldgate.edmonton.ab.ca/error404/

A good place to find technology news with a Canadian perspective.

Harvard Computer Review

http://hcs.harvard.edu/~hcr/

A bit less trendy than *elecktra,* this Harvard student magazine also covers technology news.

Meeker

http://www.winternet.com/~chada/meeker.html

Young'uns should have a good time with this one, written by and for kids.

Planete Internet

http://www.netpress.fr/

French-language Internet magazine with a wide range of topics.

Where It's @

http://www.mistral.co.uk/wia/

Sometimes too cute for its own good, an all-Web magazine on the Web.

Iway News

http://www.iway.de/

And, checking in from Germany, an Internet news-and-reviews Web site for the print magazine of the same name.

Macintosh Online Magazine Database

http://tkb.colorado.edu/olm/zines.html

A list of other Mac magazines with descriptive information about each.

Popular Mechanics

http://popularmechanics.com/

Yep, that *Popular Mechanics,* just the way it has been for 50 years, but this time on the Web.

The Way

http://theway.com/

Very New York, very computerphilic, very fun.

WindoWatch

http://www.channel1.com/users/winwatch/WindoWatch.html

As good as many mainstream print magazines, this online journal has news and reviews for the typical Windows user.

MagNet

http://www.cris.com/~milewski/magnet.html

A simple list of dozens of Web-accessible magazines.

Mobile Computing

Taking your computer on the road ain't what it used to be. Just a few years ago, it usually meant that you could either not communicate with the network at the office, or you could only do very simple e-mail or file transfers. Now, it is quite common to be able to hook into the office network as if you were local, even if you are a continent or two away.

This section covers many aspects of mobile computing, including the remote access software as well as the hardware you use when you're on the road.

Mobile Wireless Computing at Rutgers

http://paul.rutgers.edu/~acharya/dataman.html

Although this is quite an academic site, you can find a great deal here about the future of wireless networks. Some of the papers cover the difficult issues that are normally glossed over at some of the other sites covering the same subject.

Yahoo!

Mobile Office Magazine

http://www.mobileoffice.com

As you might guess, a magazine devoted to mobile computing. The Web site has links to some recent articles. The content is a bit too fluffy and breathlessly excited about fairly mundane parts of the industry.

Mobile Planet

http://www.mplanet.com/

This is quite a specialized store, only carrying items for the mobile computer user. However, their selection is good and they appear to have a great deal of pre-sale information on the items they sell.

ALSO RECOMMENDED:

Mobile and Wireless Computing Index

http://snapple.cs.washington.edu:600/mobile/mobile_www.html

A very complete listing of Internet resources, part of the Web's Virtual Library.

Multimedia

Buzzword alert! What started off as a definable part of the computer industry has recently become such a magnet for hype that almost anything can be called "multimedia" if it has graphics and text, graphics and sound, or has anything to do with CD-ROMs.

Parents who don't want their kids to be left behind blindly buy "multimedia upgrade kits" for their computers, and novices buying new systems ask with a tone of insecurity, "will it do multimedia?"

What we've been promised is great entertainment from our PCs, more compelling than what we see on television. After five years of such promises, it seems like we're no closer to it.

Archives

Science Multimedia

http://www.ncsa.uiuc.edu/SDG/DigitalGallery/DG_science_theater.html

Selections from a CD-ROM of scientific uses for multimedia. This is probably meant to show that multimedia is useful for non-entertainment purposes, but the video clips here seem not that much more interesting than still pictures.

ALSO RECOMMENDED:

Rob's Multimedia Lab

http://www.acm.uiuc.edu/rml/

A hodgepodge of clips and sound bytes, vaguely arranged by category.

Multimedia in Japan

http://sunsite.sut.ac.jp/multimed/multimed.html

A good collection of pictures and sounds, as well as pointers to other international sites.

CD-ROM

Because of the size of most multimedia content, you can't easily distribute it on floppy disks. Thus, CD-ROM has become a required element for a multimedia system, particularly if you want to view video images.

CD-ROM Software Reviews

http://falcon.cc.ukans.edu/~dj

This is a very personal site: one guy's reviews of a slew of CD-ROMs. Fortunately, they're not all in one category, and he really does try to make the reviews fair.

Go Digital Magazine

http://www.godigital.com/

These folks are really obsessed with CD-ROMs. The magazine, which is itself on a CD-ROM, explores the exciting wonders of the digital age using multimedia to an extreme. They also proudly proclaim that they have a scantily-clad multimedia centerfold with no staples and folds; ooh, ahh.

Channel Watch

http://www.laig.com/dcweb/tamer.htm

An in-depth discussion of which multimedia software titles get into the stores and which don't. A bit highbrow for some folks, but an interesting view of how stores choose what they want to sell when they can't really judge what buyers want to buy.

Compact Disc Formats

http://cuiwww.unige.ch/OSG/ MultimediaInfo/Info/cd.html

Ever get confused about what makes CD-DA, CD-ROM, CD-ROM/XA, and CD-I different? This paper is a great explanation of them all and gives a good review of the history that lead to the different formats. A must-read for people serious about CD-ROM.

ALSO RECOMMENDED:

Synapse

http://www.tricon.net/Comm/ synapse/index.html

Yet another very heady analysis of the world of multimedia.

Demos

Young, mostly European programmers get together and show off their graphical and musical prowess in short clips called "demos." They do it for the glory and ego of having the best demo of the minute and for proving that you can make large programs in a tiny amount of space. Most of these only run on Amiga hardware, although some run on PCs.

DemoLinks

http://www.cs.msu.su/~gong/ demoscene/demolinks.html

A fairly extensive site with links to many kinds of demos, arranged by the group of people who put together the demos. There are also links to general information about the demo movement.

PC Demo Scene

http://www.mcs.net/~trixter/html/ demos.html

A U.S.-based site with lots of information about the demo scene and the folks who put them together. There is also a fair amount about what goes on in the minds of demo writers and how they compete for non-existent prizes.

Joey's 4K Demos

http://www.preferred.com/~joey/ 4kdemos.html

If you think that good PC programs need to take up megabytes of hard drive space, download a few of these and see what you can get in under 4K (yes, less than 4096 bytes). You'll never look at bloated application programs the same way.

Hypermedia

Ten years ago, *hypermedia* meant any sort of system that had links in the content, such as automatic jumping from the index to the main text. Multimedia now encompasses hypermedia, much of which doesn't even have graphics or sound.

HypArt Project

http://rzsun01.rrz.uni-hamburg.de/cgi-bin/HypArt.sh

Instead of hypertext, the HypArt project does hyperart, which is art with links to other art. It is a participatory project where many artists contribute and intermingle their works.

Hypertext Discussion on Usenet

news:alt.hypertext

One of the few places where hypertext (as compared to full multimedia) is still discussed. The conversation ranges from hypertext help files for software to the question of whatever happened to Ted Nelson's Project Xanadu, the genesis of hypermedia.

ALSO RECOMMENDED:

Hypermedia Timeline

http://epics.aps.anl.gov/demo/guide/ www.guide.app.a.html

A short chart dealing with the history of hypermedia.

Information About Hypertext

http://www.lawrence.edu/www/ hypertext.html

An index of hypertext documents, with many sites as examples.

Institutes

Berkeley Plateau Multimedia Research Group

http://www-plateau.cs.berkeley.edu/

These folks are studying what they call *continuous media,* which is a fancy term for video and sound (things that you play continuously, as compared to viewing a picture). Some areas they're addressing are video-on-demand and video e-mail.

Composition/New Media Program at CalArts

http://shoko.calarts.edu/
NewMediaProgram.html

On a less technical side, this program is meant for artists with a strong musical bent. The projects look at the aesthetic interaction of music and video, how an artist interacts with the composition tools, and so on.

Research Program on Communications Policy

http://farnsworth.mit.edu/

Another area of study that relates to multimedia is how public policy affects the content you get to see. This includes regulatory decisions, the structure of the companies that deliver multimedia content, and the way that current providers of television will change into multimedia providers in the near future.

Research Program on Communications Policy

Digital Image Center

http://www.lib.virginia.edu/dic/

Libraries at universities usually act as collections of information, and this site is an attempt to collect images for use in multimedia. Instead of just being a bunch of clip art, the collection is aimed at multimedia technologies and concepts.

Digital Image Center

Entertainment Technology Center

http://cwis.usc.edu/dept/etc/

Let's face it, most of multimedia is about entertainment, and this center at USC fully admits that. Being in Los Angeles, it makes sense for the center to study the entertainment aspects of multimedia and to track the progression of various parts of the field.

Pegasus Project

http://www.pegasus.esprit.ec.org/

Recently, some operating systems have been including more support for multimedia but usually just as add-ons which aren't really part of the low level. The Pegasus Project is an academic research project to look at how to include multimedia in a variety of operating systems.

Networked Multimedia Information Services (NMIS)

http://www.nmis.org/

A gang of academics and computer companies who are studying the feasibility for networked multimedia over the Internet. The basic idea is to see how parts of the Internet can be used to deliver multimedia in a way that is similar to how networks deliver television today.

Japan Advanced Institute of Science and Technology

http://mmmc.jaist.ac.jp:8000/

This site shows a Japanese perspective on multimedia and mobile computing.

Center For Digital Multimedia

http://found.cs.nyu.edu/

An artsy-fartsy site that requires the Netscape Web browser and an appreciation for heavy graphics.

MBONE

Multimedia on the Internet is difficult due to technical issues related to TCP/IP, the communications backbone of the Internet. However, many people are working on solutions, the best-known being the MBONE (which stands for *multimedia backbone*).

Videoconferencing and the MBONE

http://www.lbl.gov/ctl/vconf-faq.html

One of the best features of the MBONE is that you can hold real-time, interactive videoconferences with people all over the world. This guide explains the hardware and software you need to set up such videoconferences. It's useful for both techies and executives.

Multicast Channels

http://town.hall.org/radio/live.html

As an experiment in using the MBONE, the Internet Multicasting Service multicasts audio-only information on the Internet. At this site, you can find out how to hear things such as satellite-based radio coverage, U.S. congressional hearings, and other events.

ALSO RECOMMENDED:

Getting Connected to the MBONE

ftp://genome-ftp.stanford.edu/pub/mbone/mbone-connect

A short explanation of what the MBONE is and how to get a connection to it.

WXYC on the Internet

http://sunsite.unc.edu/wxyc/

You can hear WXYC, the radio station at the University of North Carolina, Chapel Hill, live 24 hours a day on the Internet.

Organizations

Interactive Multimedia Association

http://www.ima.org/

Although it appears mostly as a publication, the IMA has many services that can help folks interested in the multimedia field. They have meetings, annual conferences, a bookstore, and of course online discussions.

National Multimedia Association of America

http://nmaa.org/

Another organization for multimedia professionals, this one tends to be a tad more serious and less enamored with the fact that they are talking about multimedia. Their services also seemed a bit more aimed at multimedia professionals.

Pictures

Clip art and background pictures have been around as long as computers have been able to display graphics. People love to put them in their printed work, as backgrounds, and just to stare at on-screen. There are dozens of sites with collections of pictures, some of them well-organized, others haphazard. Of course, you should pay attention to copyrights before using any of the pictures you find at these or other sites.

Herp Pictures

http://gto.ncsa.uiuc.edu/pingleto/lobby.html

Frogs and toads and snakes and lizards and more. Lots of close-up photos from Mike Pingleton's personal collection. One wonders where he found them all and how he got them not to bite him.

Animal Art by Shannon Chase

http://alaskan.com/cgi-bin/vendor?/usr/local/etc/httpd/htdocs/shannon

A commercial site selling these wildlife pictures. They are watercolor portraits of various animals, many from the American Northwest and most rendered in great detail.

ARPA Image Database Browser

http://moralforce.cc.gatech.edu/

An interesting experiment in growing a database of pictures and searching for them by description. You can add your own pictures and descriptions to the database, and of course search for everything already there.

OTIS

http://sunsite.unc.edu/otis/otis.html

What a cute acronym: *Operative Term Is Stimulate.* This is a very large collection of pictures in many formats, cataloged much better than similar sites. It is presented as a gallery, although most of the works are taken from other places.

Automobile Picture Archives

http://dutoc74.io.tudelft.nl/voitures/archive.htm

Not just another site with a bunch of pictures plopped down and ignored. The maintainer has very good descriptions, and there is even a "car of the week." Sounds like someone who really likes his cars.

Ophelia's Mirror

http://www.teleport.com/~mabs/ophelia.html

A very nice collection of pre-Raphaelite art, with many small-size images downloadable. This is a good place to visit if you get tired of all the photos in most of the other picture sites.

NASA Ames Imaging Library System

http://ails.arc.nasa.gov/

This is a very high-quality site of pictures of space, planets, spacecraft, airplanes, and lots of other related topics. You can search by keyword, and the pictures are quite well organized.

HyperDOC

http://www.nlm.nih.gov/

A large collection of medical images as well as viewing software. There are many historical photos, anatomy pictures, and so on. The collection is well-maintained and easy to browse, assuming you like Western medicine's view of the body.

Hawai'i

http://www.hcc.hawaii.edu/hawaii/

Lovely photos of a lovely set of islands. There is quite a variety here, with everything from individual native plants to the typical could-be-a-postcard shots. There are even some basic tourist shots taken in the tourist traps.

Random Portrait Gallery

http://oz.sas.upenn.edu/portraits/portraits.html

Yet another silly site, but one that has class. This is a collection of people's self-portraits, taken from their Web home pages. Click on the random link, and find yourself staring at … someone. Goes to show that there are real people on the Web.

Astronomy Images

http://force.stwing.upenn.edu:8001/~jparker/astronomy/

Not links to other sites, a well-organized collection of pictures of all things astronomical. Great pictures of the local region of space (the planets in our solar system) as well as far-flung nebulae and other clusters.

Declassified Intelligence Satellite Photographs

http://edcwww.cr.usgs.gov/dclass/dclass.html

Want to see what the spies used to think you shouldn't see? This site shows samples of now-unclassified photos and gives a bit of information on how you can get more. Warning: they probably aren't as exciting as you might hope.

Earth Observation Images Database

http://www.clearlake.ibm.com/ERC/SSEOPhomepage.html

A massive database of satellite pictures of Earth. You can search by name and topic and then download from the collection of more than 20,000 images. You can search using fairly narrow location names, which makes it easier to find pictures you want.

Michael's Photo Gallery

http://www.netaxs.com/~mhmyers/image.html

Another personal site, but with very high quality images. Michael has some professional-quality photos of the moon, animal photos taken with telephoto lenses, and some other oddities.

ALSO RECOMMENDED:

ZooNet Image Archives

http://www.mindspring.com/~zoonet/gallery.html

Pictures of more animals than you can imagine, from folks who love zoos.

Image Archive

http://www.comlab.ox.ac.uk/archive/images.html

This uninterestingly named archive also has a great list of links to other sites, particularly those in Europe.

Glenn's List

http://www.cse.unsw.edu.au/
~s2156495/pics/

An Australian collection of pictures and pointers to an incredible variety of other image archive sites.

Virtual Image Archive

http://www.astro.wisc.edu/~casey/
picts/picts.shtml

Another list of pointers, but fairly well organized with an eye towards quality of the pieces.

Aviation Image Archives

http://acro.harvard.edu/GA/
image_archives.html

The name says it all, with hundreds of pictures and pointers to other sites.

Dan's Gallery of the Grotesque

http://zynet.com/~grotesk/

Tread through this one slowly, preferably not immediately after a meal.

Kodak Sample Digital Images

http://www.kodak.com/digitalImages/
samples/samples.shtml

It's more than just film. Kodak offers many images as a way to get you interested in their PhotoCD discs.

G'Day Australia

http://ebweb.tuwien.ac.at/ortner/
australi.html

Dozens of great photos of Australia by an Austrian tourist.

Boats

ftp://tivoli.com/pub/boats

Dozens of pictures contributed by people who read the rec.boats Usenet newsgroup.

Space Images Libraries

http://www.okstate.edu/aesp/
image.html

Good list of links to space-related sites.

Sound

It seems that people are more interested in pictures than in sounds, given the much larger number of picture sites than sound sites. However, there is still plenty of interesting and fun sounds available for your use in multimedia productions.

Multi-Media Music

http://www.wavenet.com/~axgrindr/
quimby.html

This is a fairly extensive music site aimed specifically at multimedia producers. There are full pieces as well as loops, as well as pointers to many different sound tools. Much of the music sounds quite professional.

Best-quality Audio Web Poems

http://www.cs.brown.edu/fun/bawp/

If you like spoken poetry, this is the place for you. Each issue has poems spoken by various not-famous poets, often from poetry nights at local coffee houses. If you're not familiar with spoken poetry, by all means sample a bit of the work here.

Ragtime

http://www.ragtimers.org/~ragtimers/

Ragtime music seems to keep its popularity over the years. This site has dozens of ragtime pieces converted to MIDI files and also has a fair number of sampled pieces of ragtime music usable in multimedia productions.

Sites with Audio Clips

http://www.eecs.nwu.edu/~jmyers/
other-sounds.html

By far the best index to other sites that have audio files. The sound sites are categorized into sounds, music, and spoken word, for a total of over 350 sites. If you can't find it here, it may not exist.

ALSO RECOMMENDED:

RML Sounds

http://www.acm.uiuc.edu/rml/
Sounds/

Hundreds of sounds, sorted both alphabetically and by date.

Aardvark Sounds

http://www.ucsalf.ac.uk/pa/soundp/sphome.htm

A top-notch British site with lots of its own sounds and pointers to other sites (mostly British).

Sounds Archive

http://pmwww.cs.vu.nl/archive/sounds-html/index.html

Another archive with mostly novelty sounds.

Classical MIDI Archive

http://www.hk.net/~prs/midi.html

An astounding number of classical music pieces converted to MIDI.

MIDI from Usenet

http://www.warwick.ac.uk/~phulm/midis.html

A collection of MIDI pieces automatically downloaded from various Usenet newsgroups.

User Groups

Media 100 Worldwide

http://www.callamer.com/~boomer/media100

The site for this user group has many how-to tutorials aimed at all levels of multimedia creators. There are people from all segments of the multimedia universe who contribute to the group, and the content seems quite polished.

ALSO RECOMMENDED:

MMUG Research Triangle Park, NC

http://www.spadion.com/spadion/mmug/

A very local group whose site is mostly about meetings and members' recent projects.

Video

Multimedia's big promise has always been video. Any year now, typical PC and Mac users will be able to view full-screen videos that seem lifelike, or so they promise. But because of the size of video files, downloading video clips from the Internet is still only for those with the fastest connections.

MPEG Archive

http://www.cs.tu-berlin.de/~phade/mpeg.html

An excellent collection of MPEG software and pointers to sites with lots of downloadable movies. You can also download the contents of a very full CD-ROM of MPEG clips and samples.

Space Movies

http://www.univ-rennes1.fr/ASTRO/anim-e.html

A very extensive selection of astronomy movies, including solar eclipses, the Shoemaker-Levy comets hitting Jupiter, Apollo missions, and so on. Just to keep the "space" theme going, there is also a small selection of science fiction movies and a few clips from *Star Trek*.

ALSO RECOMMENDED:

RML MPEGs

http://www.acm.uiuc.edu/rml/Mpeg/

Another extensive MPEG site with dozens of movies and a bit of software.

ClipMedia in Finance

http://www.cob.ohio-state.edu/dept/fin/resources_education/clips.htm

Videos of pithy talks by speakers about the business of business.

International MPEG Bizarre 1st Film Festival (I'M B1FF!)

http://www.best.com/~johnp/film.html

With names like "Raytraced Fruitfly Ovaries" and "The Pinata Incident," how can you go wrong?

Skateboarding Videos

http://www.enternet.com/skate/video.html

Mostly home-shot stuff, but some fun stunts.

Footbag Multimedia

http://www.footbag.org/mpeg.html

About as much fun as, well, watching others play footbag.

Videoconferencing

In the past few years, videoconferencing has garnered much more publicity as a business tool. Although videoconferencing on the Internet is still quite limited, there are many new tools for small-scale videoconferencing between individuals. This may well become The Next Big Thing for multimedia and the Internet.

CU-SeeMe

http://www.wpine.com/cu-seeme.html

One of the most popular low-end videoconferencing systems available, CU-SeeMe exists both as freeware and commercial software. It is flexible, easy to install, and works well over the Internet even during slow times.

DT-5

http://fiddle.ee.vt.edu/succeed/videoconf.html

An excellent overview of desktop videoconferencing (as compared to the dedicated, stand-alone boxes you sometimes see in meeting rooms). There is a long introduction to the field and a discussion of some of the products that are commonly used today.

ALSO RECOMMENDED:

INRIA Videoconferencing System

http://www.inria.fr/rodeo/personnel/Thierry.Turletti/ivs.html

Free software for videoconferencing using industry-standard protocols.

Multimedia Miscellany

Multimedia Information Sources

http://viswiz.gmd.de/MultimediaInfo/

Probably the most complete index for multimedia on the Internet. It is very well organized, with an emphasis on professional multimedia (although there is plenty on entertainment multimedia as well).

MediaWeaver

http://lummi.stanford.edu/Media2/ASD/ASD_Homepage/Multimedia.html

On the more academic side of multimedia, there are many projects for multimedia databases. MediaWeaver is an ongoing project to help multimedia creators work from a large database of objects and to integrate their work with the works of others.

MICE Multimedia Index

http://www.cs.ucl.ac.uk/mice/

A specialized index that covers multimedia conferencing. There are pointers to other Internet sites as well as reports on the state of electronic conferencing.

Digital Currency

http://www.laig.com/dcweb/

This magazine covers topics such as copyrights in multimedia (and how they differ from traditional copyrights), multimedia creation for grassroots organizations, the ownership of multimedia corporations, and so on. Definitely recommended.

ALSO RECOMMENDED:

IEEE Multimedia

http://www.computer.org/pubs/multimed/multimed.htm

A quarterly academic magazine about multimedia, with all the dryness that you might expect from such a venture.

Media.Maniacs

http://www.crawford.com/media.maniacs/media.html

Yet another avant garde magazine that's heavy on graphics and sound.

Networking and Communications

The Internet is but one method for networking computers. There are literally dozens of other types of networking, and even simple modem-to-modem communications can be considered a form of networking. For example, more business PC users are much more familiar with Novell's

NetWare than with the Internet. Thus, the offerings in this section reflect the panoply of non-Internet networking and intercomputer communications.

Archives

High Performance Networks and Distributed Systems

http://hill.lut.ac.uk/DS-Archive/

Instead of just a list, this is a text narrative of all the types of information that pertain to the high end of networks. Within each part of the narrative are links to other Internet sites that have more detail. A novel approach that works well.

Black Box Reference Center

http://www.blackbox.com/bb/refer.html/tigf012

An interesting combination of a reference book and mail-order catalog from a company with a very large variety of networking hardware and software. This is a good place to roam around if you want to learn not only about networking but also about what kind of commercial products are available in each area.

ALSO RECOMMENDED:

Communications Archive

http://sunsite.unc.edu/dbarberi/communications.html

A small site with many links to communications papers and descriptions.

ATM

For the highest speed networking at long distances, most companies are turning to ATM (Asynchronous Transfer Mode), a new standard. ATM is optimized for bandwidth-heavy users such as video and high-quality audio, but it is also useful for regular data transfer as well.

ATM Forum

http://www.atmforum.com/

This is the main group responsible for promoting ATM and creating ATM standards. Essentially everyone in the ATM world is a member, making this site a good place to find links to ATM manufacturers' Web sites and so on.

CANARIE National Test Network

http://www.canarie.ca/ntn/

What good is a new technology if you don't test it? This network, based in Canada, has over 60 switches and 6000 kilometers of cabling and is being quite useful in finding problems and solutions for large ATM networks.

ALSO RECOMMENDED:

Telecommunications Information

http://www.ee.umanitoba.ca/~blight/telecom.html

An excellent index site covering all telecommunications, but with an emphasis on ATM and high-speed networking.

BEATMAN

http://www.cs.colorado.edu/homes/batman/public_html/Home.html

Boulder, Colorado, has its own ATM network, and this is the best place to find out how well it is working.

Cel-Relay Retreat

http://cell-relay.indiana.edu/cell-relay/

A small, good overview site covering ATM and related technologies.

Bulletin Boards

Bulletin Board Systems, more commonly called BBSs, have been popular hangouts for computer users with modems for over a decade. There are tens of thousands of BBSs in the U.S., some of them with regional interest, others topical. A few BBSs are on the Internet, but most have yet to hook up. You can find almost anything you want on a BBS somewhere.

BrintaBBS

http://bromo.ptf.hro.nl/brintabbs.html

This is a great place for students all over the world to chat with each other. The BBS runs on Telnet, so you don't have to dial into a separate modem number for the BBS as long as you have a Telnet client for your computer.

Flying High BBS

http://www.mcs.net/~teleman/flyhibbs.html

This BBS covers all aspects of commercial and hobby flying. Even if you don't join the BBS, the site has a wealth of pointers to other aviation Web sites, including many to airline companies and space organizations.

Threads

http://www2.interpath.net/sbi/Threads/

A Web-based BBS where the topics are picked by the Web administrator, but all the discussion comes from folks wandering the Web. The main groupings, called "chunks," are pretty broad, so the discussion can be pretty free-flowing.

Virtual Gateway

http://www.vgateway.com

An entertainment BBS with many links to other BBSs and the Internet. There are numerous online games that you can play, chat areas, and downloading from CD-ROMs. Of course, there are also lots of basic discussion areas as well.

Anything Goes BBS

http://www.mxi.com/~mooncrow/bbs.html

This Hawaii-based BBS has an emphasis on Anime (Japanese animation), general comics topics, and role-playing games. There is also an active Amiga section, which is quite handy for the remaining Amiga owners of the world.

Channel 1

http://www.channel1.com/

One of the largest BBSs in the United States, Channel 1 was an early pioneer in hooking the Internet to standard BBSs. The site has the best of both worlds, with over 30 gigabytes of downloadable files, as well as conversation, Internet pointers, and so on.

Church Of Unholy Love

http://www.teleport.com/~signe/.CoUL/CoUL.html

A BBS with an emphasis on anonymity. You can say whatever you want here, and you can say it without anyone knowing who you are. Of course, that has both advantages and disadvantages, but if you're a privacy buff, this is the place for you.

Exec-PC

http://www.execpc.com/

Another huge BBS, Exec-PC has been around for over a decade. The dial-in part of the system has more than 300 incoming lines, and the BBS offers gazillions of downloadable files. They have many different plans for Internet users with and without dial-up capabilities.

Pandora's Box

http://ccwf.cc.utexas.edu/~jcbrown/index.html

If you're into hacking (either on the light or dark side), this BBS has lots of resources for you. There are also sections for vampires, goths, cyberpunks, and so on. Considering the topics covered, it's quite a lighthearted site.

Coffee House Connection

http://www.slip.net/~wgregori/

Computers and coffee are a well-know symbiosis. This is a network of San Francisco coffee houses with public-access terminals. The idea is to create a common culture for people with little in common. Others are welcome to drop in and join the caffeine-stimulated chat.

Software Creations

http://www.swcbbs.com/

And yet another huge BBS, this one emphasizing online multiplayer games and chatting. Of course, they also have the requisite gigabytes of downloadable files, but the emphasis is more on human contact than on just getting data from them.

The WELL

http://www.well.com/

The venerable discussion board of the West. The WELL (which stands for Whole Earth 'Lectronic Link), originally affiliated with the magazine *Whole Earth Review* but now independent, has long been regarded as a great place for good talk, interesting folks, and a sense of community.

Telnetable BBS List

http://www.tiac.net/users/cody/bbs/
bbslist.html

A very long list of BBSs that let you connect to them through telnet. Given that long-distance calling to BBSs can eat into your phone bill very quickly if you have Internet access, telnetting to BBSs across the country from you can be a great money-saver.

ALSO RECOMMENDED:

Hour House BBS

http://www.intex.net/hour_house/
hour_house.html

A fairly eclectic BBS with many different topics, ranging from 4x4 cars to crafts.

Starfire

http://www.webb.com/nywebb/
sf.html

This BBS seems to specialize in esoteric belief systems and new age thought. Nice art on the Web site.

WB3FFV Amateur Radio BBS

http://wb3ffv1.sed.csc.com/bbs.html

Ham Radio information and an Internet connection, all in one site.

Amazons Arena

http://www.globalmark.com/
globalmark/amarena.html

An "adult" BBS that specializes in tall and muscular women. How's that for specific?

Burn This Flag BBS

http://www.btf.com/

Lots of very odd stuff here, including many weird stories and pictures from "Crank" magazine. Enter at your own risk.

D2

http://www.site.gmu.edu/~afiyouza/
bbs.html

An interesting, open-access, Internet-accessible BBS with very few rules.

MIDILink

http://www.midilink.com/users/
midilink/

A good place to find all things MIDI, such as sound files, software, and support.

SonicNet

http://www.sonicnet.com/

Lots of sounds, lots of pictures, and an odd sense of place. Definitely have the sound on your computer turned on for this one.

Electronic Mail

E-mail is an almost universal medium for communication between people who use networked computers. There are dozens of different e-mail programs for the Internet and many more for people on non-Internet networks. For many folks, e-mail is the only way to communicate on the Internet, making it all that much more important to them.

Beginner's Guide to Effective Email

http://www.webfoot.com/advice/
email.top.html

This is a top-notch introduction to e-mail for novices. The author has a friendly tone and she covers all the basics without going too far into system-specific details.

Anonymous Remailers

http://electron.rutgers.edu/
~gambino/anon_servers/anon.html

If you are concerned about not letting out your identity when sending e-mail, you should certainly read this. It describes the theory and practice of *anonymous remailers,* systems that strip your name and address from the e-mail you send.

ALSO RECOMMENDED:

UUCP Mail Protocol

http://cs.weber.edu/home/rlove/
HTML/uucp.html

A good reference page about UUCP, a common method for computers with part-time connections to exchange e-mail.

Ethernet

Thank you, Dr. Metcalfe.

Ethernet Primer

http://pclt.cis.yale.edu/pclt/comm/
ether.htm

An excellent introduction to Ethernet.
This document takes you from
nontechnical overview of networking
hardware to the relevant features that
set Ethernet apart from other
networking hardware.

Ethernet page

http://wwwhost.ots.utexas.edu/
ethernet/

Some bits of information on Ethernet,
including a scan of the drawing of the
first Ethernet system design.

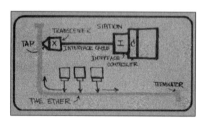

General Information

Client/Server Coffeehouse

http://dgoats.onr.com/clients.html

An ongoing discussion of client/server
issues. The informal coffeehouse
setting is a bit incongruous with the
serious topics discussed, but this site
is much more interesting than many
of the "we-tell-you-what's-what" sites.

Networking Virtual Library

http://src.doc.ic.ac.uk/bySubject/
Networking.html

A top-notch reference to networking
information on the Internet. The site is
sorted by topic, and many topics have
their own lengthy lists of their own.
This is certainly a good place to start
looking for anything network-related.

ALSO RECOMMENDED:

SMDS Overview

http://www.cerf.net/smds.html

A nice little guide to Switched
MultiMegaBit Data Service (SMDS).

Gigabit Networking

A network that runs at a gigabit per
second is fast — like, *really* fast. It is so
fast that lots of unexpected things
happen, things that don't happen on
regular networks. Thus, a fair amount
of research is going on to investigate
how to create and maintain these fast
networks.

Gigabit Testbed Initiative

http://www.cnri.reston.va.us:4000/
public/gigabit.html

This is the best place to start looking
for information on gigabit networks. It
is a well-funded research project that
brings together the information of
universities and hardware vendors
who have been testing real gigabit
systems. There are also links to many
other gigabit sites.

ALSO RECOMMENDED:

Bay Area Gigabit Testbed
(BAGNet)

http://george.lbl.gov/BAGNet.html

Information about the 14-member
network running in the San
Francisco area.

Massachusetts Information
Turnpike Initiative

http://www.umassp.edu/miti/
miti.html

A similar testbed, this one
in Massachusetts.

Institutes

Information Networking Institute

http://www.ini.cmu.edu/

This facility, at Carnegie Mellon
University, looks at more than just
networking hardware and software. Its
focus is how information travels over
the network and how to make
networks more efficient for particular
kinds of information.

Communication Networks
Laboratory

http://networks.ecse.rpi.edu/

The fields of study at this lab, which is
part of Rensselaer Polytechnic
Institute, is more down-to-earth than
similar labs. Some of their areas of
study include using ISDN more
effectively for businesses and
metropolitan-area networks of fiber-
optic cables.

OSI-Protocol Testing Laboratory

http://www.osilab.ch/

Part of the Swiss PTT, this lab tests hardware and software for conformance to the well-established OSI networking protocols. It is also interested in the X.400 and X.500 directory protocols.

ISDN

The next major step up in Internet speed for home and small business users will come from ISDN. Regional and local phone companies are just now stepping up their efforts to make ISDN available at a reasonable price, and the next few years should show a great increase in interest in ISDN networking.

Dan Kegel's ISDN Page

http://www.alumni.caltech.edu/ ~dank/isdn/

An extensive list of pointers to ISDN sites on the Internet. The page is well organized and very up-to-date. The sites referenced are both commercial and educational sites, so you can get a balanced picture of the ISDN world.

ISDN User's Guide

http://www.pacbell.com/isdn/book/ toc.html

Even though it is written partially as an advertisement for PacBell's ISDN service, this guide is probably the best place to get started with ISDN. Most of the concepts are described as non-technically as possible, making it fairly easy to read.

Network Management

One of the more difficult parts of networking is managing networks as they run (or stop running). Network management gets particularly hard when parts of the network are made by different manufacturers or use different protocols. Good network managers are worth their weight in gold.

Netman Development Group

http://www.cs.curtin.edu.au/ ~netman/

This research project at the Curtin University of Technology in Perth, Western Australia, evaluates and creates network management software for a variety of systems. If you manage an Ethernet network, check out their tools and resources.

Network Management Discussion on Usenet

news:comp.dcom.net-management

A great resource for network managers looking for answers to questions that have probably already been answered.

Organizations

International Communications Industries Association

http://www.usa.net/icia/

An association of professionals who deal with all sorts of communications, not just networking. The group has been around for more than 50 years and emphasizes education and training.

International Interactive Communication Society

http://www.intac.com/~virtual/

The "Virtual Chapter" of this group maintains a pretty good Web page with pointers to network-related Web sites.

Networking and Communications Odds and Ends

Communications & Telecommunications Virtual Library

http://www.analysys.co.uk/ commslib.htm

The preeminent site for communications links. These sites are based around communications more than networking and cover fields like telephony, broadcasting, satellites, and so on.

Data Communications and Networking Links

http://www.racal.com/ networking.html

Another good index, this one supported by Racal-Datacom, a networking hardware manufacturer.

Operating Systems

Every computer has an operating system, although some operating systems are more obvious than others. On some computers, the operating system is written and supported by the people who make the computer; on others, most notably Intel-based PCs, the best-known operating systems are written by other companies, most notably Microsoft.

Some of the sites listed here are the "official" sites for the operating system, but many of them have been created by users to help each other.

DOS

Given that MS-DOS is currently the most widely-used (which is not to say the most popular) operating system in the world, there is much less support than you would expect for it. Fortunately, there is still support from Microsoft.

Free-DOS Project

http://sunsite.unc.edu/pub/micro/pc-stuff/freedos/freedos.html

These folks want to create a clone of MS-DOS that can be given away for free, source code and all. The result of this could be more stable Intel-based computers, and faster-running programs, even under Windows 3.1. Stay tuned for more developments.

ALSO RECOMMENDED:

Mark's Candy Store

http://uptown.turnpike.net/M/mlanders/candy.html

The "candy" here are small MS-DOS utilities that help you in your daily work.

RxDOS

http://world.std.com/~mikep

A MS-DOS-compatible operating system from which you can learn about operating system internals.

File Systems

In the Good Old Days, about 15 years ago, most of the visible work of an operating system was making files available to users. File systems have come a long way since then, and are now considered a completely necessary part of the operating system. Still, a few independent file systems exist.

AFS Reference Page

http://www.cs.cmu.edu/afs/andrew.cmu.edu/usr/db74/www/afs.html

AFS, better known as the Andrew File System, lets many networked computers use files from each other with a consistent naming scheme. This makes all the files look local to each user, which is a great boon in helping beginners take advantage of networked computers.

Alex

ftp://alex.sp.cs.cmu.edu/www/alex.html

Because so many files are now available by ftp, there is a need to make them easily available to people in a transparent fashion. The Alex file system does just that, and the software to do it is free and easy to install on most Unix systems.

GEOS

This operating system has undergone more major shifts in the past few years than many go through in their lifetimes. GEOS and Geoworks started off as competitors to MS-DOS for low-end systems, then transmorgified into an OS for hand-held computers. Where they will go next is anyone's guess.

GEOS Index

http://www.cis.ohio-state.edu/~jbearden/geos/

A nonofficial (and fairly opinionated) site covering all versions of GEOS. There are links to other sites, some good discussion and wild rumors, and a solid set of downloadable programs.

ALSO RECOMMENDED:

GEOS 2.X Applications

http://www.ios.com/~mb/geos/

One-stop downloading for some of the best freeware and shareware for GEOS.

Mach

One of the more popular Unix variants in the past few years, Mach came out of a research project at Carnegie Mellon University. Mach is a very small, very portable microkernel that vastly reduces the amount of machine-specific code needed to make an operating system. It has been adopted by both commercial and freeware companies as the center of their Unix development.

Mach Info Central

http://www.cs.cmu.edu/afs/
cs.cmu.edu/project/mach/public/
www/mach.html

This site, maintained at Carnegie Mellon, has the best set of pointers to all known Mach information. Because Mach is free software, you can also download the sources and many related files from this site.

MASIX Project

http://www-masi.ibp.fr/francais/
recherches/sr/masix/masix.html

A distributed operating system with many personalities, built on top of Mach.

OMOS

http://www.cs.utah.edu/projects/
flexmach/

A new module manager for Mach version 4.

OS/2

Although not nearly as popular as MS-DOS or Windows from Microsoft, IBM's OS/2 has a strong following in the PC market. Many users feel that it is more stable and friendly than Windows, although it has the obvious disadvantage of having many fewer programs written for it.

Getting Warped - Installation Guide

http://lwaber.swmed.edu/os2/
index.htm

If you're moving from Windows to OS/2, you should definitely visit this site. It is a step-by-step installation guide for getting OS/2 into users' hands. It includes information IBM wouldn't necessarily approve of, and is thus all the more valuable.

OS/2 Info from IBM

http://www.austin.ibm.com/pspinfo/
os2.html

Here's the place to get it from the horse's mouth. Although there are many different sites within IBM that have bits of OS/2 information, this is considered to be the central location, particularly for OS/2 news and patches.

Device Driver Repository

http://www.europe.ibm.com/getdoc/
psmemea/progserv/device/

An absolutely indispensable site if you have anything other than an out-of-the-box standard PC. You can find the latest versions of drivers for graphics boards, CD-ROMs, and other commonly added hardware.

OS/2 Entertainment Development Council

http://naftalab.bus.utexas.edu/
os2games/

Many people feel that OS/2 is superior to Windows for games and other graphical applications, although only a few games have actually come out in OS/2-specific versions. This group promotes writing games for OS/2 and tries to convince software authors to convert.

OS/2 Internet Apps

http://www.phoenix.net/~vccubed/
os2apps.html

Site lists all known programs for interacting with the Internet through OS/2. Each program has the current version, date, cost, type, size, and requirements listed, and there is also a list of which sites have copies of the program.

OS/2 Shareware BBS

http://www.os2bbs.com/

Some of the best software for OS/2 is shareware, and this site has all of it. The site seems somewhat like a user's group, with a very friendly discussion area and good descriptions of the downloadable files.

Warp Pharmacy

http://godzilla.eecs.berkeley.edu/os2/
pharmacy/WarpPharmacy.html

With mirrors all over the world, this is one of the best places for finding out OS/2 news without going through IBM. The information is often good, and there are places where you can ask questions in the style of a BBS.

ALSO RECOMMENDED:

CyberBlue OS/2 Online Exploration Guide

http://www.cyberblue.com/

An excellent index of Internet resources and source for OS/2 freeware and shareware.

Getting Warped with OS/2

http://www.csv.warwick.ac.uk/ ~phueg/os2/

A great personal site with lots of OS/2 pointers, and even a bunch of OS/2 jokes.

OS/2 Index

http://www.ccsf.caltech.edu/~kasturi/ os2.html

Another personal list of OS/2 resources on the Internet, fairly long and well organized.

MIT OS/2 Users Group

http://www.mit.edu:8001/activities/ os2/os2world.html

Another list-of-lists, but this one emphasizes the home pages of other OS/2 user groups.

OS/2 Information Page

http://www.cen.uiuc.edu/~jt11635/ os2/os2.html

This list emphasizes locations of shareware and freeware OS/2 programs rather than just sites.

DOS Games Settings List

http://eyelab.msu.edu/os2games/

A list of how to get OS/2 to run problematic games.

OS/2 Publications

http://www.austin.ibm.com/pspinfo/ books.html

IBM's list of all known books, magazines, and other writings about OS/2.

UNIX

The UNIX operating system is probably discussed much more on the Internet than anywhere else. You can find dozens of Usenet news groups and thousands of Web sites, which may seem a bit odd, given that the UNIX market is much smaller than, say, the Macintosh market. The reason for this overcoverage on the Internet is history in that the Internet was initially mostly UNIX computers, so it seemed like a good place to talk about UNIX. The sites described here cover most of the UNIX variants.

BSDI

http://www.bsdi.com/

One of the better-known commercial UNIX systems for Intel-based PCs. BSDI's UNIX, called BSD/OS, is a supported, enhanced version of the free BSD UNIX, and is popular among people who want real customer support and updates.

NetBSD Project

http://www.netbsd.org/

A volunteer effort to produce a high-quality, free version of BSD UNIX. NetBSD is being ported to many hardware platforms, not just Intel-based boxes. The system is somewhat supported by the many people who work on it.

AIX Support

http://auk.uwaterloo.ca/

AIX, IBM's version of UNIX, is popular among users of larger IBM systems. This site, at the University of Waterloo, has up-to-date news on AIX for various platforms and a good set of pointers to other support sites on the Internet.

Linux Organization

http://www.linux.org/

Linux is rapidly becoming the most popular version of UNIX running on Intel-based computers. Linux is free, comes with source code, and is being worked on by thousands of volunteers working on various parts of the system. Sounds too good to be true, but it isn't. This site is a good starting location for finding other Linux sites.

Linux Documentation Project

http://sunsite.unc.edu/mdw/linux.html

Everything you wanted to know about Linux, often in excruciating detail. This is the central repository for all the Linux FAQs, how-to guides, and manuals. Fortunately, most of it is searchable, so you can find the parts that relate to a particular question you might have.

UnixWorld Online Magazine

http://www.wcmh.com/uworld/

An online magazine for UNIX users, particularly the technical ones. There are occasional articles, lots of technical tips, and reviews of UNIX software. This is a spin-off of the old *UnixWorld Magazine,* which is now called *Open Computing.*

Unix Security

http://www.alw.nih.gov/Security/security.html

UNIX servers are often the target of attacks both from outside and inside, and there are many ways to thwart such attacks. This list is a fairly comprehensive description of known UNIX security problems and tools to help close the gaps.

SunSoft

http://www.sun.com/sunsoft/index.html

SunSoft, the developers of the Solaris operating system, have a strong presence on the Internet with essentially all their technical and marketing literature online and easily searchable. This is the central site for finding out about Solaris.

Solaris Developer Home Pages

http://www.sun.com/sunsoft/catlink/index.html

This is one of Sun's ways of helping the companies that develop software for Sun systems. You can find URLs for almost any software or hardware developer at all related to Solaris development.

UnixWare

http://unixware.novell.com/

Novell's somewhat popular UNIX variant that runs on PCs. When Novell first bought this software line from AT&T, many people said that it would soon become the only UNIX for PCs, but it has remained only one of many.

Usenix

http://www.usenix.org/

This group has long been the pre-eminent organization for UNIX techies. This is one of the few user's groups that really care about long-range research and development, and its meetings are much less commercial than almost any other in the computer industry.

SAGE

http://sage.xerox.com/sage/

SAGE, the Systems Administrators Guild of Usenix, is one of the few places of refuge for the harried UNIX system administrators. Maintaining a UNIX system is an almost Sisyphusian task, and SAGE helps keep its members apprised of new tools and techniques.

X/Open

http://www.xopen.org/

A standards organization that specializes in UNIX systems, X/Open was one of the first groups to specify how hardware and software makers could create interoperable UNIX systems and software, and is still a force in UNIX development today.

A L S O   R E C O M M E N D E D:

A/UX

http://jagubox.gsfc.nasa.gov/aux/

A personal page devoted to A/UX, Apple's ill-fated UNIX port running on Macintosh computers.

Linux Links

http://www.winternet.com/~chronic/Linux/

A great set of pointers to the unofficial Linux sites around the world.

UNIX Haters Handbook

http://web.kaleida.com/u/hopkins/
unix-haters.html

In case you are less than enamored with UNIX and want emotional support.

Unix Industry Home Page

http://www.nis.com/

Resources for folks who work in the UNIX industry, particularly software manufacturers.

UNIX is a Four Letter Word (and Vi is a Two Letter Abbreviation)

http://tempest.ecn.purdue.edu:8001/
~taylor/4ltrwrd/html/unixman.html

A wonderful introductory text on using UNIX and vi, written in a very light and witty style.

Windowing Systems

This category is dominated by the most popular windowing system today, X Windows. X Windows is used on almost every graphic-based UNIX system sold, mostly because it is free, portable, and there is a huge amount of software written for it. It also runs on other operating systems on systems that are networked to UNIX systems.

Introduction to Motif Application Development

http://www.iftech.com/classes/motif/
motif0.htm

An excellent set of tutorials describing how to create applications in Motif, which is a set of standard graphical components that works with X Windows. These tutorials are based on a book of the same name.

X Consortium

http://www.x.org/

These folks are the primary maintainers and developers of X Windows. They make sure that X Windows systems stay compatible with each other, and move the standard forward with periodic updates to the software.

XFree86 Project

http://www.xfree86.org/

This is a free version of X Windows running on PCs running UNIX. The purpose of the group is to make the X Windows run as well on PCs as it does on other workstations, and to make the product widely available, particularly with other free software such as the Linux operating system.

XPIP

http://cns-web.bu.edu/pub/xpip/
html/xpip.html

If you want to program in X Windows but don't want to spend the money to license Motif, you still have other choices. XPIP has many of Motif's features but is freely available and easily ported to a wide variety of systems.

ALSO RECOMMENDED:

DESQview/X

http://www.qdeck.com/dvx.html

A popular commercial X Windows system for PCs.

LessTif

http://www.cs.uidaho.edu:8000/
hungry/microshaft/lesstif.html

A freely available replacement for Motif.

X Windows/MOTIF Programming Course

http://arachnid.cm.cf.ac.uk/Dave/
X_index.html

The course notes from an extensive programming course in creating X Windows programs.

X Advisor

http://landru.unx.com/DD/advisor/
index.shtml

A new, free, online magazine about X Windows and Motif, mostly about programming.

Windows 3.1

By the time you read this, some of the Intel-based PC world will have moved on to Windows 95, but a significant portion will have chosen to stay with Windows 3.1 (or 3.11, also known as Windows For Workgroups). In fact, some predict that there will still be tens of millions of Windows 3.1 users at the turn of the century.

CICA

http://www.law.indiana.edu/misc/ftp-
cica.html

This is the premiere ftp site for Windows-specific programs. There are many other sites, not at CICA, which have Web-based searching of the CICA archives. If you're looking for almost any shareware or freeware Windows program, it is likely to be here.

Microsoft

http://www.microsoft.com/

Although most of the site is now promoting Windows 95, there is still a wealth of information for Windows 3.1 users. Specifically, the Microsoft Knowledge Base has thousands of articles about bugs, special patches, and workarounds that users might need.

Windows Multimedia Support

http://www.cs.cmu.edu/Web/People/johnmil/pc/win/MM/WinMM.html

An incredibly detailed discussion of how to create multimedia under Windows. This document describes how Windows supports multimedia devices, how to program for multimedia, and where to get more information.

Adding Internet Access to PCs

http://pclt.cis.yale.edu/pclt/winworld/winworld.htm

If you are having problems getting your PC to talk to the Internet, this article may be for you. It is an in-depth review of all the things you need to have to get connected to the Internet, with a fair amount of how-to thrown in as well.

ALSO RECOMMENDED:

Internet Resources for Windows Developers

http://www.csn.net/~rmashlan/windev/windev.html

A great list of sites with programming tools, sample code, and so on.

Windows Rag Magazine

http://www.eskimo.com/~scrufcat/wr.html

A great, pugnacious, online magazine for people who don't want to own the biggest and fastest PCs.

Windows 95

The excitement! The thrills! The operating system! After all the pre-release hype for Windows 95, early users are discovering that, yes, in many ways it is better than Windows 3.1, but no one is writing love sonnets. And, like Windows 3.1, there are plenty of good sites for getting information about Windows 95, with more coming along all the time.

Windows 95 on the Internet

http://www.sccsi.com/dbrewer/

This page leads not only to the best Windows 95 Internet software, but also has many articles about how to hook your PC up to the Internet. Nearly everything you learned in Windows 3.1 is now wrong, and this site has lots of good information about how to use the new capabilities.

Windows 95 Internetworking Headquarters

http://www.mwci.net/win95/

Another excellent site for finding out the latest on using Windows 95 with the Internet. There's a bit of everything here, but the emphasis is on Internet software and how to install it.

ALSO RECOMMENDED:

Cutter's Windows 95 Crossroads

http://www.io.com/~kgk/win95.html

A good personal site run by someone who is enamored with Windows 95.

Dylan's Windows 95 Page

http://cville-srv.wam.umd.edu/~dylan/windows95.html

Talk about cute: all the graphics look like they came from the Windows 95 screen. Many good links to other sites.

Windows NT

Microsoft's more mature 32-bit OS, but outhyped by Windows 95, Windows NT is now getting much more respect for its stability and robustness. Although NT is still too expensive for many people, it works quite well as a server for applications and Internet connectivity.

Windows NT Fax Solutions

http://www.mcs.net/~sculptor/NTFAX-FAQ.HTML

One of NT's early weaknesses was its inability to send and receive faxes, mostly due to device driver incompatibilities. Now there are many competing fax systems for NT, all of them listed here with descriptions of their features.

Windows NT FAQ

http://www.inlink.com/~sangria/winntfaq.html

This FAQ comes from two different Usenet news groups, comp.os.ms-windows.nt.misc and comp.os.ms-windows.nt.setup. The information is mostly about how to deal with installation and regular petty annoyances of the operating system.

Windows NT Administration FAQ

http://www.iftech.com/classes/admin/admin.htm

Because Windows NT can act as a multiuser server, it can become an administration headache just like any multiuser system. This FAQ deals specifically with administration issues, the ones that are rarely discussed in most other places.

Windows NT Resource Center

http://bhs.com/winnt/resources.html

One of the most complete Windows NT sites on the Internet. There are many sections with their own information here and pointers to most of whatever freeware and shareware is available for NT.

ALSO RECOMMENDED:

Network Specialist NT

http://infotech.kumc.edu/

Many good NT links, particularly those about networking.

Miscellaneous Operating Systems Sites

Operating Systems and OS-related Research

http://www.cs.arizona.edu/people/bridges/oses.html

A grand collection of information about lesser-known operating systems, particularly those of the academic variety. More than just a list of OSs, there are descriptions of each operating system and the type of research being done on them.

Amiga OS 3.1 Replacement Project

http://www.telesys-innov.fr/AmigOS/AOS.html

An ambitious project to clone the Amiga's operating system to be platform-independent and freely distributable. Now that the Amiga is pretty much gone (but not quite), these folks want to retain the best parts so that other companies can keep the Amiga flame alive.

IBM's VM Home Page

http://vmdev.gpl.ibm.com/

VM, the crusty but durable operating system for IBM mainframes, lives on. This site has (believe it or not) announcements of new versions of VM, and of VM's many variants and subsystems. This is also a good place to find out about VM-related events.

KA9Q

http://inorganic5.chem.ufl.edu/ka9q/ka9q.html

A network operating system for PCs, even old ones with little RAM. KA9Q is versatile enough to run Internet services like Web servers, and can act as an Internet point of presence server as well.

NextStep Information

http://www.omnigroup.com/Documentation/NEXTSTEP/Guide.html

One of the most spectacularly public failures in the UNIX industry has been NeXT Computers, the company that Steve Jobs started after leaving Apple Computers. All that seems to be left of the company is the operating system, NextStep, which still has many adherents.

OSF Distributed Computing Environment

http://www.osf.org/dce/index.html

Distributed Computing Environment (DCE) is a variant of UNIX that is popular because it is based on open standards, published by the Open Software Foundation. This site lists pointers to DCE information both within the OSF and elsewhere.

Plan 9 Unofficial Home Page

http://www.ecf.toronto.edu/plan9/

Bell Lab's Plan 9 operating system is one of the few commercial OSs to fully support distributed computing and easy hardware portability. This page has links to the research that went into Plan 9 as well as current implementations that use Plan 9 as a core.

OS-9 FAQ

http://www.cs.wisc.edu/~pruyne/os9faq.html

One of the early, popular, real-time operating systems, OS-9 is at the core of many popular devices. It is easily extensible and runs incredibly fast even on old, slow chips, making it a good operating system for inexpensive systems.

QNX Information

http://www.cuug.ab.ca:8001/~zimmerm/qnx/

QNX is one of the most popular, real-time operating systems in the world. It runs on a variety of CPUs, it is incredibly modular, and there are many manufacturers who sell add-on products for it. This site has pointers to dozens of related QNX resources.

VMS

http://www.montagar.com/index_openvms.html

Digital Equipment's minicomputer operating system, VMS, has been in wide use for more than 15 years. In its heyday, the venerable VMS was the commercial operating system of choice for most non-IBM shops. This site has pointers to the archives and commercial sites for VMS software.

Personal Computers

The history of personal computers is littered with models and brands that never made it. Every year, people predict how the whole market will soon be Intel-based, but that never seems to happen. Many types of computers not built around the old IBM PC model are still popular, and new lines that carve out a niche are introduced every few years. Users of the less popular types of computers are particularly reliant on Internet sites that have information and support for their PCs.

Acorn

The Acorn line of computers is much more popular in Britain than in the U.S. There, Acorn is known as a major innovator in both hardware and software, having somewhat of a similar reputation as Apple has here.

Acorn Computers

http://www.acorn.co.uk/

This is the main corporate site for Acorn. It has quite an extensive set of technical specifications and marketing material about Acorn's various lines, as well as an FTP site with quite a variety of software and documentation.

Simon's Acorn Pages

http://www.csc.liv.ac.uk/users/u1smt/Acorn.html

An extensive collection of papers and articles about using Acorn computers, as well as the expected links to other sites. There is a great deal of information for programmers as well as for folks looking for games and entertainment.

AMULET Group

http://www.cs.man.ac.uk/amulet/

A fascinating project to create a completely new kind of CPU based on asynchronous logic. If successful, this could make processors much smaller and less expensive without losing any speed. Their first target is to duplicate the actions of Acorn's ARM processor.

ALSO RECOMMENDED:

Acorn Index

http://www.cs.bham.ac.uk/~amw/acorn/

This is a fairly extensive personal page covering many different kinds of Acorn computers.

Amiga

Video and game buffs have long sung the praises of the Commodore Amiga computer. The hardware and operating system were designed to handle graphics, particularly video, with greater ease than other PCs. Unfortunately, Commodore has stopped producing them, but Amiga users are helping each other maintain the computers.

Amiga Network Applications List

http://www.hut.fi/~puhuri/Amiga/NetAppList.html

A list of essentially all the programs that work with the Amiga on networks. Each program is described in detail, and any that are available on the Internet have links to their respective home pages.

Aminet

http://wuarchive.wustl.edu/pub/
aminet/info/www/home.html

This is the largest collection of Amiga shareware, freeware, and user-written documentation in the world. It is up to date and maintained by Amiga fanatics to help keep the Amiga flame bright.

Amiga Information Resource

http://www.omnipresence.com/
Amiga/

Probably the most extensive Amiga resource on the Web. Plenty of links to other Amiga sites, but also a great deal of local information and archives of various online Amiga discussions.

Amiga Web Directory

http://www.prairienet.org/
community/clubs/cucug/amiga.html

Another very extensive collection, emphasizing news and current events in the ever-changing Amiga market. There is a good listing of commercial hardware and software vendors, even those without links on the Internet.

ALSO RECOMMENDED:

Spock's Logical Amiga Page

http://www.wspice.com/spock/
amiga.html

Lots of pictures of various Amigas, and links to other Amiga sites.

Amiga Power User

http://www.olemiss.edu/~badwf/
homepage.html

Lots of interesting news about the new Escom Amigas, as well as technical information about older, high-end Amigas.

Atari

Atari computers were *the* low-cost game computer of the early 1980s, but they never got much further than that. There are still many Atari users in the U.S. and Europe, however, and they do their best to support each other.

Atari 2600 Information

http://www2.ecst.csuchico.edu/
~gchance/2600Stuff/2600index.html

Personal note: The first computer I owned was an Atari 2600, so I have a soft spot for this site. Given that the machine is long gone, there is an incredible amount of good info here, including a collection of screen shots from some classic games.

CAIN

http://ace.cs.ohiou.edu/personal/
mleair/cain.html

Central Atari Information Network (CAIN) is a user group with lots of information on all of Atari's machines, particularly their later systems. The site

has lots of good information and listings for people buying and selling Atari computers and parts.

ALSO RECOMMENDED:

Atari Links and Info

http://www.algonet.se/~dark/
atari.html

A nice little site with mostly European links.

Commodore 64 and 128

Although it never got as much press as the Apple II, the Commodore 64 was one of the best-selling inexpensive personal computers of the early 1980s. Its successor, the Commodore 128, was also well received, both here and in Europe.

CBM 8-bit Computers

http://garnet.msen.com/~brain/
cbmhome.html

This is a superb collection of information and links for all Commodore 8-bit computers. It is also the home of the FAQs for a couple of the related Usenet news groups, such as comp.sys.cbm and comp.emulators.cbm.

Commodore 8-bit Server

http://www.hut.fi/~msmakela/cbm/

Given how popular the Commodore systems were in Europe, it is not surprising that many of the better Web servers for the system are based there. This has one of the more complete listings of other sites, as well as an impressive amount of old documentation.

Yahoo!

ALSO RECOMMENDED:

C64 Files

ftp://ccnga.uwaterloo.ca/pub/cbm/

An extensive FTP site with many games, text files, and so on.

IBM-Compatible PCs

Who needs to say more?

ExpressNet

http://www.pcxpress.com/xpresnet/xpresnet.html

A very comprehensive site with a great deal of its own information, not just pointers elsewhere. This site has a great list of mailing lists and Usenet news groups that relate to the PC, as well as other good resources for folks just starting on the Internet.

Introduction to PC Hardware

http://pclt.cis.yale.edu/pclt/pchw/platypus.htm

The good folks at PC Lube and Tune describe what makes a PC tick, how to make a good guess at what might not be working correctly, and so on. In a few pages, this article does a better job than many books at giving you the basics of PC hardware.

Platypus Computer Systems

PowerPuss 433C
33Mh 486DX
64K Cache
4M 70 nsec memory
ISA bus
200M IDE HD
SVGA
14" NI Display

The Platypus - a creature of spare parts assembled by a God with a sense of humor

---

PC Professional's Place

http://wl.iglou.com/Jim_Dial/pcprof.html

A list of links for people who work in the PC industry. Most of these are the same as on other sites, but there are also some links unique to career news for PC professionals. There is also a bit of new content on the site, again aimed at folks who work in the PC field.

ALSO RECOMMENDED:

Computer User Groups on the Web

http://www.melbpc.org.au/others/index.htm

A good list of all the PC user groups who also have Web sites.

Macintosh

For more than ten years, the Macintosh has been the hardware platform that PC users loved to hate, or at least loved to ignore. Although Apple holds around 10 percent of the personal computer market, the design choices made by Apple have always exerted a huge influence on the rest of the PC market.

Apple

http://www.info.apple.com/

One of the best company-sponsored Web sites anywhere, Apple provides tons of information about its products here. Everything is searchable, and all Apple-approved news appears here within hours of its being released to the press.

Macintosh Educators Page

http://www.netins.net/showcase/macintosh/

If you use Macintoshes in your classroom, you should certainly check out this page. It covers the Mac world from the teacher's point of view, and is fairly honest about things such as budget restrictions, real educational software (as compared to entertainment), and so on.

Macintosh Street Prices

http://www.interport.net/~joholmes/street_price.html

Great information on how to buy Macintoshes without spending more than you have to. Much more than a price list, this site has up-to-date news on which Apple systems are actually for sale, who's discounting the most, and so on.

PowerMac Page

http://www.books.com/staff/dw2/derrik.htm

Apple's recent additions of PowerMacs have somewhat split the Macintosh market, and this site covers the higher end, namely the PowerMacs. There is lots of news, some lists of manufacturers, and pointers to non-Apple PowerPC sites.

Apple Developer Services and Products

http://www.info.apple.com/dev/

If you are going to do any programming on the Macintosh, you should certainly visit here. Apple's support of its developers is second to none, and Apple freely gives pointers to non-Apple sites that have Macintosh programming resources.

Macintosh Programming Resources

http://www.astro.nwu.edu/lentz/mac/ programming/home-prog.html

An extensive selection of Macintosh programming resources from a non-Apple perspective. This means more emphasis on third-party tools, more honesty about Apple's failings, and even a tad of humor thrown in.

Macintosh Directory

http://pogo.wright.edu/mac/mac.html

A fairly complete list of Mac-related Internet sites. The hardware and software vendor listing is particularly impressive. This is also the home of Newt's Place, a good collection of information about Apple's Newton computer.

Well-Connected Mac

http://www.macfaq.com/

Probably the most complete resource around. The maintainer has meticulously brought together a variety of sources, and has made them all text-searchable. For example, he has many of the Mac-related FAQs locally, making them easier to search than at many sites.

TidBITS

http://www.dartmouth.edu/pages/ TidBITS/TidBITS.html

This is the probably the best source of Macintosh news anywhere on the Internet. It is a weekly newsletter full of great reviews, opinionated discussions of the Mac's failings, and lots of late-breaking news. Highly recommended.

BMUG

http://www.bmug.org/

Probably the best-known Mac users' group in the world, BMUG is in the business of giving away information for free. Its Web site has lots of information generated from its help lines, as well as articles from its award-winning newsletters.

ALSO RECOMMENDED:

Repository of Macintosh Information

http://www.cs.wisc.edu/~tuc/mac/

A great collection of lesser-known pointers and lots of news.

Mac Internet Applications

http://community.net/~csamir/ macapp.html

A very good list of the various kinds of Internet client and server software available for the Macintosh.

PowerBook Army

http://hisurf.aloha.com/PBA/ index.html

Interesting information on Macintosh PowerBooks, as well as on using Macs in both English and Japanese.

TopSoft

http://www.topsoft.org/

A nonprofit group developing various programs for the Mac.

Welcome to Macintosh

http://www.astro.nwu.edu/lentz/mac/ home-mac.html

Some great lesser-known pointers on the Internet, and nice Mac-specific diversions.

Macintosh Users Groups

http://www.apple.com/Documents/ UserGroups.html

Apple's list of all the users groups it knows of that have Web sites.

Other PCs

Apple II Resources

http://www.ugcs.caltech.edu/ ~nathan/apl2.resource.html

Yes, the venerable Apple II is still being used, mostly by educators. Quite a number of other people still support it as well, and most of them are listed here.

MSX Computers

http://www.cs.umd.edu/users/fms/ MSX/

MSX was a short-lived attempt by Microsoft to standardize the hardware used in PCs for game-playing. Only a few MSX computers came out in the U.S. but many were released in Japan and Europe.

Security and Encryption

Privacy and authentication are certainly hot topics on the Internet, but they also affect all parts of our lives. Many businesses need privacy in their communications so that their competitors can't take advantage of them. Authentication is an issue for most of us every day when we pay for anything by check or credit card. All of these topics, and much more, are widely discussed on the Web.

Anonymous Remailers

http://electron.rutgers.edu/ ~gambino/anon_servers/anon.html

An introduction to systems that let you send Internet e-mail anonymously. Essentially, these systems remove information about you and send your letters on without a trace of who originally sent it. This site has a description of how anonymous remailers work and who does it.

Applied Cryptography

http://www.openmarket.com/info/ cryptography/ applied_cryptography.html

A bevy of programs used in cryptography. These are programs shown or described in the book *Applied Cryptography* by Bruce Schneier, which is considered to be one of the best books on the subject.

COAST

http://www.cs.purdue.edu/coast/

The COAST (Computer Operations, Audit, and Security Technology) project links many academic computer security researchers. The topics covered include break-ins, password cracking, and other forms of computer insecurity.

Cryptography Articles

http://www.cs.umbc.edu/~mohan/ Work/crypt.html

An extensive collection of articles and software related to cryptography. There is plenty here for the beginner, as well as some interesting viewpoints for seasoned security professionals. Many of the articles also cover privacy, not just the technical end of things.

Cryptography Export Control Archives

http://www.cygnus.com/~gnu/ export.html

It is illegal for U.S. citizens to export many kinds of cryptography, and most people in the field believe that this has a very negative effect on U.S. commerce. This site has a great deal of information about exactly what is illegal and what the law really says.

Firewalls Tutorial

http://www.greatcircle.com/gca/ tutorial/main.html

One of the most effective ways to thwart many attacks on Internet servers is with firewalls. This tutorial gives you an overview of what firewalls are, what they protect you from, and how to install them. It is presented by a company that consults on and installs firewalls.

Phrack Magazine

http://freeside.com/phrack.html

One of the original magazines for hackers and crackers, *Phrack* is widely read by folks in the security field as a way to know what the hackers are telling each other. Lots of good tips on how to break into things and where to go once you get in.

Computer Security Research at UC Davis

http://seclab.cs.ucdavis.edu/

Another academic security site, mostly describing its own work. Projects include many ways to detect intrusion into systems and auditing system logs to detect hacking. There are also pointers to a few other security labs.

Kerberos Reference Page

http://www.cs.cmu.edu/afs/ andrew.cmu.edu/usr/db74/www/ kerberos.html

One of the more popular methods for securing a network that has many workstations is with Kerberos, a free software system developed at MIT. This page has links to many articles about Kerberos as well as to the software itself.

FIRST

http://csrc.ncsl.nist.gov/first/

A group that helps coordinate other security groups, FIRST (Forum of Incident Response and Security Teams) distributes information about known methods of attack, as well as acting as a center for reporting incidents of security breaches.

CERT

ftp://cert.org

The Computer Emergency Response Team (CERT) is a central place for people to report computer break-ins and to find out about security. In addition, CERT is usually the first to announce vulnerabilities in operating systems and popular hardware.

CIAC

http://ciac.llnl.gov/

Although mostly for the U.S. Department of Energy (the folks who do all the nuclear research), CIAC lets its resources be viewed by everyone in the Internet community. CIAC distributes a variety of security-related software, mostly for Unix systems.

PGP Resources

http://netaccess.on.ca/~rbarclay/pgp.html

PGP is the most popular program for encrypting and authenticating electronic mail and other documents for personal computers. This Canadian site has a good explanation of PGP, where to get it, and how to use it in many different circumstances.

Risks Mailing List

http://catless.ncl.ac.uk/Risks

The Risks mailing list is one of the better-known places to find out about the kinds of things that computers can do to hurt you or hurt others. This site has a Web-based interface for reading old and current issues of the mailing list.

SATAN

http://www.fish.com/dan/satan.html

One of the most misunderstood security tools of the year, SATAN allows site administrators to test some well-known security holes before malicious people do. This site has the latest source for SATAN as well as a bit of information about what it is good for.

Cypherpunks Archive

ftp://ftp.csua.berkeley.edu/pub/cypherpunks/Home.html

This is a pretty good source of privacy software and information. Instead of being pointers to other sites, all of the software and documentation is kept on this site, so you're pretty assured that the links are good. There are also some humorous rants about Big Brother, as well as quite a few scary ones.

Computer Viruses and Security

http://www.einet.net/galaxy/Engineering-and-Technology/Computer-Technology/Security/david-hull/galaxy.htm

One of the better single-source places to find out about viruses on personal computers. There are pointers to the various freeware and commercial virus software sites, good literature telling you what is and isn't a virus, and a fair amount of hand-holding for the frightened.

RSA's Frequently Asked Questions About Today's Cryptography

http://www.rsa.com/rsalabs/faq/

RSA Data Security's introduction to security is one of the better-written introductions around. It is slanted toward the technology for which this company has a patent, but that technology also is among the most widely used in the world.

ALSO RECOMMENDED:

Remailers List

http://www.cs.berkeley.edu/~raph/remailer-list.html

An automatically updated list of anonymous remailer sites.

Bacard's Privacy Site

http://www.well.com/user/abacard/

A good list of pointers to the pro-privacy groups with Web sites.

SAIC Security Library

http://mls.saic.com/mls.security.html

Good set of pointers to some lesser-known security sites.

Macintosh Cryptography

http://uts.cc.utexas.edu/~grgcombs/htmls/crypto.html

Descriptions and pointers for various Mac-specific cryptography programs.

Internet Underground

http://www.engin.umich.edu/~jgotts/underground.html

Some good pointers to hacking resources, with a silly disclaimer about the contents.

Internet Spoofing

http://www.msen.com/~emv/tubed/spoofing.html

Pointers to information on IP address spoofing, one of the more advanced methods people use to break into Internet computers.

Operation Cyber Prometheus

http://www.cam.org/~gagnon/

Many security-related articles and links, with some of the only ones around covering telecommunications security.

Georgia RACF Users' Group

http://www.mindspring.com/~ajc10/garug.html

A users' group with great information about RACF, IBM's mainframe security software.

PGP Index

http://www.mantis.co.uk/pgp/pgp.html

Another great list of information on PGP, with a European slant.

Random Number Conditioning

http://www.clark.net/pub/cme/html/ranno.html

Random numbers are extremely important in cryptography, and this site tells you how to make sure that the numbers you use are sufficiently random.

RIPEM Information Pointers

http://www.cs.indiana.edu/ripem/dir.html

A good source of pointers about RIPEM, one of the many systems for adding security to Internet e-mail.

Steganography

http://www.thur.de/ulf/stegano/

An odd and interesting method for hiding the fact that you are even communicating with someone.

Security Pointers

http://www.cs.cmu.edu/afs/cs.cmu.edu/user/bsy/www/sec.html

An extensive list of pointers, with a good coverage of commercial sites that are sometimes overlooked.

Unix Security Information

http://www.alw.nih.gov/Security/security.html

Very complete, and not only about UNIX.

Software

Talk about a catch-all area! This section covers some of the same topics as others in this chapter, but many topics are covered only here. Note that some of the sections are for all software that runs on certain hardware or operating systems, such as Atari, whereas other sections cover a type of software, such as databases.

Archives

OAK Software Repository

http://www.acs.oakland.edu/oak.html

One of the best-known archives of freeware and shareware for a variety of computer systems. Mostly known for its coverage of Intel-based computers, the repository also houses sites for CP/M computers, amateur radio, Multics, and a few nonspecific computers as well.

SHASE Virtual Shareware Library

http://www.fagg.uni-lj.si/SHASE/

This library is based on the novel idea that they will catalog and categorize software for other libraries. Thus, the result of searching SHASE is not to find a file *there,* but to find pointers to one of the other large software library sites around the world. The searching works quite well.

Atari

The Atari computer still has many users, and the software written for it is often still supported. Although a great deal of Atari software was for entertainment, there is still a fair amount used for home offices.

Calamus Desktop Publishing

http://web.city.ac.uk/~cb170/
CALAMUS/calamus.html

An easy-to-use desktop publishing program.

Emagic

http://www.mcc.ac.uk/~emagic/
emagic_page.html

A user-supported site for the Emagic MIDI sequencer.

Children

Kids' software, like business software, ranges from the great to the abysmal. Parents can't stand spending $50 or more on a package only to find out that it doesn't work right or that it's aimed at the wrong-aged children. Kids' shareware from the Internet is often as good as commercial software, but comes with much less financial risk.

Wierenga Software

http://www.xmission.com/~wwwads/
sharware.html

These folks make a series of MS-DOS software that is meant to get kids using their creative minds. Bert's Coloring Books is a set of programs that kids can use to describe a story, create pictures of that story, and then color them in. The site covers a few similar programs as well.

To-Soft

http://www.teleport.com/~tosoft/

A couple of kid's freeware packages, along with some more adult software (for quitting smoking).

Communication

You would think that by 1995 computer-to-computer communications would be easy, but it is still difficult to get terminal and fax programs that work right the first time. Due to old protocols and arcane rules with modems, users still struggle with simple communications. Maybe next decade.

HylaFAX

http://www.vix.com/hylafax/

Folks on PCs and Macintoshes are used to getting fax software when they buy a modem, but UNIX users aren't so lucky. HylaFAX is a complete fax sending and receiving package for UNIX, and is completely free. There is a surprising amount of documentation, much more than you would expect for a freeware package.

Kermit Communications Software

http://www.cc.columbia.edu/kermit/

Although the Kermit file-transfer protocol is not as popular as ZMODEM, it is nonetheless widely supported. The Kermit software project at Columbia University distributes free software for almost any kind of computer that supports text and file transfer and is usually quite easy to operate.

MUTT

http://www.graphcomp.com/mutt/
mutt.html

If you use Internet MUDs and are on a Windows-based system, MUTT (Multi-User Trivial Terminal) may be the answer. It lets you view many different connections at the same time, supports macros and other common MUDisms, and comes in both free and shareware versions.

Waffle

http://www.spies.com/waffle/

If you're interested in setting up your own BBS, check out this shareware BBS system for PCs. It is well supported and has many users all over the world. With it, you can set up a complete BBS that also exchanges e-mail over the Internet.

EWAN

http://www.lysator.liu.se:7500/users/
zander/ewan.html

A Windows-based terminal emulator with a great acronym: EWAN (Emulator Without A good Name).

Tag BBS

http://metro.turnpike.net/metro/I/
inferno/tagbbs.html

An interesting, full-featured freeware BBS system for PCs.

Compilers

Although most compilers are described in the "Languages" section earlier in this chapter, there are some compilers that are not language specific. These sites describe compilers of general languages.

PRECC

http://www.comlab.ox.ac.uk/archive/redo/precc.html

PRECC, which stands for "PREttier Compiler-Compiler," compiles other languages into ANSI-C, which can then be compiled separately. It is used to research the correctness of other languages, as well as to make creating compilers faster because the definition of the language is enough to create the compiler.

Stanford SUIF Compiler Group

http://suif.stanford.edu/

A research group at Stanford looking specifically at compilers and how they work. The group has created a compiler system that makes researching compiler techniques easier, and is working on many interesting projects such as parallel languages.

Compression

Compressing data can be a huge boon both for saving disk space as well as for getting faster transmissions over phone lines. There are many different ways to compress data, and research in data compression is coming up with more all the time.

PKWARE

http://www.pkware.com/

These folks are the makers of PKZIP, which is by far the most popular file-compression software for PCs. The PKWARE site has the latest versions of their freeware and shareware, as well as information on their commercial products and libraries for programmers.

WinZip

http://www.winzip.com/winzip/

Windows users will find WinZip to be one of the best programs for opening and saving ZIP files. It is simple, fast, and can even open lesser-known formats such as ARJ, LZH, and ARC. It also opens UNIX compressed files in a variety of formats, all with the same easy interface.

ALSO RECOMMENDED:

Info-ZIP

http://quest.jpl.nasa.gov/Info-Zip/Info-Zip.html

A group of folks trying to bring the ZIP format to many other computer platforms, and to do it free of royalties.

Data Formats

Although not really software, many methods of storing data in a structured way are available so that others can read it easily. Using standardized formats can help you make your data more easily transportable to other computers and programs. Some of the formats described here are for binary data, others for text.

Common Internet File Formats

http://www.matisse.net/files/formats.html

A wonderfully complete table describing all the most common file formats that you might encounter when wandering around the Web. There is also a well-written description of which formats are used for what, and where to find software for reading and converting files in those formats.

Common Data Format (CDF)

http://nssdc.gsfc.nasa.gov/cdf/cdf_home.html

Developed by NASA's National Space Science Data Center's (NSSDC), CDF is "a self-describing data abstraction for the storage and manipulation of multidimensional data in a discipline-independent fashion." Whew! What that means is that it describes a super-language that allows databases to describe their own format.

JOT

ftp://hplose.hpl.hp.com/pub/WWW/jot.html

This is the first widespread attempt to standardize how "electronic ink," which consists of handwritten notes, sketches, signatures, and fill-out forms, should be represented and transferred between programs.

Introduction to SGML

http://www.brainlink.com/~ben/sgml.html

Markup languages allow you to specify how the text and pictures appear on your page. SGML is coming on strong as the standardized markup language of choice. The Web's language —

HTML — is in fact a derivative of SGML. If you want to learn a bit about SGML without getting bogged down in the technical aspects, this is the site for you. The tutorial is easy to browse and goes into enough detail for you to determine which parts of SGML are of most interest to you.

SGML Open

http://www.sgmlopen.org/

These are the folks who are taking SGML into the future. It is a vendor-neutral organization with the somewhat daunting task of making a markup language seem important to a world in which most people have trouble programming their VCRs.

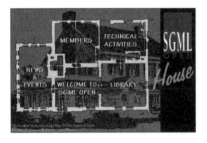

Scientific Data Format Information FAQ

http://fits.cv.nrao.edu/traffic/scidataformats/faq.html

If you use scientific or engineering data, this is a must-have document. It describes dozens of types of data formats used mostly by scientists and engineers and how they relate to each other. There are also numerous links for each format so that you can find software that stores and reads documents in that format.

PNG Format Announcement

http://www.compuserve.com/new/news_rel/png2.html

CompuServe's proposed follow-up to the GIF graphic file format, PNG involves no licensing and has many better features.

Hierarchical Data Format (HDF)

http://www.ncsa.uiuc.edu/SDG/Software/HDF/HDFIntro.html

A proposed standard from NCSA for passing around scientific and other data.

Multimedia File Formats on the Internet

http://ac.dal.ca/~dong/contents.html

Useful information about common file formats, particularly for pictures, sound, and video.

Databases

Long before personal computers became popular, the word *mainframe* was pretty much synonymous with *database*. That's where the data was stored, and that's where you needed to go to get it. Now, database software exists on all kinds of platforms, from older mainframes to the smallest PC. Many of the entries under this heading are for specific brands of databases, such as Ingres and Access.

Transaction Processing Benchmarks

http://www.ideas.com.au/bench/bench.htm

A wonderful collection of results from a variety of database ratings, collected by an Australian publisher. These ratings tell you how many transactions that a database can process per second, a very useful number for busy databases.

Catalog of Free Database Systems

ftp://ftp.idiom.com/pub/free-databases

You can get many database software packages for free (yes, free!). This is an excellent, comprehensive list of close to all the database systems that are available for free. It is updated regularly and gives very detailed information about each database.

FoxPro Yellow Pages

http://www.transformation.com/foxpro/

Microsoft's FoxPro is becoming one of the most popular database systems for mid-range Windows and Macintosh users. This site has a comprehensive list of all sorts of commercial add-ons, free code, consultants, and user groups for FoxPro.

Oracle Magazine

http://www.oracle.com/info/
magazine/magazine.html

On the higher end of the database world is Oracle, a system that runs on the biggest and most powerful computers around. Like FoxPro, there are a handful of useful Oracle sites, but the *Oracle Magazine* site has the official information on Oracle, because it is published by its manufacturer.

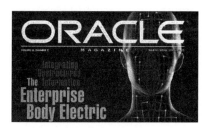

PowerBuilder information

http://web.syr.edu/~eastephe/
pb.html

If you are doing serious client/server database development, you have probably heard of PowerBuilder. If not, then you probably don't care. This site has many good PowerBuilder tools, including demonstration setups.

Information Systems Meta-List

http://www.cait.wustl.edu/cait/
infosys.html

An incredibly detailed list of everything having to do with Information Systems, including databases and client-server program development. This is probably the best place to begin if you are looking into using databases for client/server applications (or just want to find out what all the buzzwords mean).

ALSO RECOMMENDED:

ConceptBase

http://www-i5.informatik.rwth-
aachen.de/CBdoc/cbflyer.html

An interesting multiuser object database that is quite robust.

FlagShip

http://aztec.co.za/users/jckruger/fs/
FlagShip.html

Information about the XBase-compatible database that runs on UNIX systems.

Development Tools

People developing programs need more than just a language. Development tools help programmers create better programs by helping to organize their work, debugging the programs so that they work properly, and integrating the work of many people into a single program.

Configuration Management

http://www.loria.fr/~molli/cm-
index.html

When more than one person is working on a programming project, it is difficult to be sure that each person is working on the newest code without using some sort of configuration management software. This site has pointers to the best documentation on configuration management and its tools.

GNU Concurrent Versions System

http://www.winternet.com/~zoo/cvs/

CVS is a free implementation of many of the ideas embodied in configuration management. It works with other GNU tools to help structure programming groups to be more efficient and less prone to making errors that would wipe out each other's work.

DJGPP

http://www.delorie.com/djgpp/

A complete, free C++ environment for 32-bit PCs. Using this system frees you from having to buy commercial C++ systems, and it includes a host of additional GNU-licensed development tools that work with cross-platform systems.

DejaGNU

http://www.cygnus.com/doc/
dejagnu/dejagnu_toc.html

Testing programs has always been one of the most difficult parts of applications development. DejaGNU makes it easy to create testing scripts that can be run on a wide variety of hardware and software platforms, and it is freely available under the GNU license.

ALSO RECOMMENDED:

Gamesman, Inc.

http://www.kwanza.com/gamesman/

These folks sell a fairly complete set of Visual Basic add-ons.

Visual Voice

http://www.stylus.com/

A commercial system for adding telephone handling to Windows-based programs.

Software Configuration Management

http://www.sei.cmu.edu/tech/cmHomePage.html

Another good list of references on configuration management and the software that you can use to enhance group programming.

Editors

Text editors have always been the mainstay of programmers and writers who don't want to be slowed down with formatting when they write. Almost every operating system comes with its own simple text editor, and there are many more capable text editors available for most systems.

GNU Emacs FAQ

http://scwww.ucs.indiana.edu/FAQ/Emacs/

One of the most popular, high-powered text editors on any system is Emacs. The GNU version of Emacs has been ported to virtually every known operating system, and its users find that it is one of the best editing and working environments available anywhere.

NE, a Nice Editor

http://www.chem.emory.edu/ne/ne.texinfo_toc.html

Much smaller than Emacs, NE runs on almost any UNIX system and has many of the same features for simple and not-so-simple text editing. It includes macros, keyboard remapping, and many other high-end features, but uses far fewer system resources than Emacs.

Electronic Mail

E-mail is by far the most-used Internet technology, but much more attention has been given to the Web and other newer technologies in the past few years. Even people not entirely "on" the Internet can in many instances send and receive Internet e-mail. More and more, e-mail is one of the most important communications tools that people are using in their work. Because of the uncanny usefulness of e-mail, an incredible variety of e-mail software packages have appeared.

E-Mail Web Resources

http://andrew2.andrew.cmu.edu/cyrus/email/

A very complete list of many of the places on the Web that you can find out more about e-mail. This list includes lots of documentation, sources for free client software, and information for e-mail server maintainers.

Engine Mail

http://pharmdec.wustl.edu/juju/E.M./engine_mail.html

This software acts as a gateway between the Web and e-mail. This allows a Web maintainer to create customized mail from a Web form, letting people get e-mail sent to them by users on the Web. The mail is structured and can include the contents of a form that users fill out.

Eudora

http://www.qualcomm.com/quest/QuestMain.html

Eudora is one of the most popular and elegant e-mail packages for Macintoshes and PCs. It is available both as freeware and as an enhanced commercial package. The commercial version works with many different types of mail servers.

Oak

http://www.ee.msstate.edu/~simmons/oak.html

One of the many advanced e-mail clients for the X Windows system, Oak is one of the few that is free. It has support for many features such as PGP, IMAP, and direct connection with Web browsers so that clicking on a URL in a mail message will automatically open your browser.

Pine

http://www.washington.edu:1180/
pine/

Although character-based systems get little press these days, tens of millions of users still rely on them. For those users, Pine is one of the more popular e-mail clients, giving them access to most modern e-mail features with a fairly easy, full-screen interface.

Z-Mail

http://www.ncd.com/Z-Code/
zcode.html

The Z-Mail family of e-mail clients is gaining popularity in multiplatform offices because it works the same on PCs, Macs, and most UNIX systems; in fact, there is even a version for character-based terminals. It is easily customized and can handle many different types of e-mail.

ALSO RECOMMENDED:

Majordomo FAQ

http://www.math.psu.edu/barr/
majordomo-faq.html

Loads of information for people who run mailing lists using the popular Majordomo software.

File Management

When hard disks were 10 megabytes big and cost thousands of dollars, people didn't have that many files to worry about. Now, it is not uncommon for even novice computer users to have many *thousands* of files on their systems. Certain utilities can help you sort through the files and figure out what you have (the *why* is up to you to figure out).

UltraFind

http://www.demon.co.uk/ultratec/
ultrafind.html

A wonderfully handy shareware utility for Macintoshes. It not only finds files by their names and types, it even searches inside the files for particular text, and does it all much faster than similar programs. Another nice feature is that you can specify what to do with the found files as a group.

ALSO RECOMMENDED:

Disk Piecharter

http://www.xs4all.nl/~hanszorn/
zornshare.html

A shareware utility that adds pie charts to the Microsoft Windows 3.1 File Manager.

WebCom File Manager

http://www.webcom.com/help/fmgr/

The first file manager that you can use over the Web. Pretty odd, but useful.

Graphics

Let's face it: Graphics are usually more interesting than numbers or words on the computer screen. Graphics programs range from those that help you create graphics to those that generate graphics without human intervention.

BRL-CAD

http://web.arl.mil/software/brlcad/

A free solid-modeling package for UNIX systems. The software uses Constructive Solid Geometry (CSG) to build up items in a picture, and you

can output the results on a variety of workstation monitors and printers. The site has links to many articles about using BRL-CAD with other applications.

WinViz

http://www.iti.gov.sg/iti_RnD/
infosheet/is/winviz.html

Seeing many bunches of numbers often does not convey the meaning of those numbers; visualization programs can help. WinVis is a visualization tool that works with spreadsheets and databases, and uses many methods to show your data from a variety of perspectives.

Graphics viewers, editors, utilities and info

http://www2.ncsu.edu/bae/people/
faculty/walker/hotlist/graphics.html

An incredible list of programs that can view data and graphics files. Many entries have multiple sites listed for downloading, and there are often references for just the documentation so that you can see what you are getting.

i3D

http://www.crs4.it/~3diadm/

As virtual reality (see the Entertainment chapter) becomes more integrated into the Web, more and more VR viewers will appear. i3D is one such viewer, and it already has ties to Netscape and Mosaic to allow you to view a three-dimensional scene that has Web links integrated into the graphics.

Kai's Power Tips and Tricks for Adobe Photoshop

http://the-tech.mit.edu/KPT/KPT.html

If you use Photoshop, or use the popular Kai's Power Tools line, you'll want to explore this site. There are numerous tips on getting the most from the software, and there is a discussion area where you can chat about ideas and questions that you have.

©1994 Tom Karlo

VisuVoxel

http://www.univ-reims.fr/ Documentation/sciences/leri/IN/ didier/visuvoxel_eng.html

An advanced volume-rendering package for UNIX of interest in many academic fields. The software helps create different kinds of solid models quickly so that researchers and analysts can experiment with different views and data.

ALSO RECOMMENDED:

Fractal Puzzle

http://www.cris.com/~rmac/ puzzle.html
A cute cross between Rubik's cubes and fractal designs.

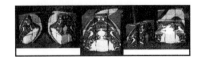

Gnuplot

http://www.cs.dartmouth.edu/ gnuplot_info.html

A free plotting program for equations and data that runs on many platforms.

LASSPTools

http://www.lassp.cornell.edu/ LASSPTools/LASSPTools.html

Interesting UNIX tools for numerical analysis and graphing.

LView Pro

http://mirror.wwa.com/mirror/busdir/ lview/lview.htm

An inexpensive shareware image editor for Windows that can handle many different file formats.

Groupware

People work together, and people who have to share information and documents in their work need software to help manage the process. Groupware has been around for more than a decade but has only recently caught on as a valuable business tool.

Introduction to Groupware

http://fiddle.ee.vt.edu/succeed/ groupware.html

An excellent overview of the many parts of the groupware puzzle. This is a good place to start if you want a noncommercial description of the need for groupware and an idea of what kind of tools are available now, or will be within the next few years.

Lotus Notes FAQ

http://www.turnpike.net/metro/kyee/ NotesFAQ.html

Everything you wanted to know about using Notes in day-to-day work. The FAQ goes into a great deal of detail about programming Notes, which is really the only way to get it to work within your company's organization. Many good Notes sites also are listed in the FAQ.

WWW Collaboration Projects

http://union.ncsa.uiuc.edu/ HyperNews/get/www/ collaboration.html

The folks at NCSA are hot on getting more people on the Web, and this project sees groupware as the way to get that to happen. This list gives many ideas of how to turn the Web into a groupware server, and points to a few of the first attempts at getting Web-based groupware into users' hands.

ALSO RECOMMENDED:

Groupware Yellow Pages

http://www.consensus.com:8300/ GWYP_TOC.html

A great list of books and articles about groupware.

Delta - Designer Team for Lotus Notes Applications

http://www-iwi.unisg.ch/delta/ index.html

A terrific collection of links for Lotus Notes, particularly for companies who have Notes-related products.

Internationalization

Internationalizing software means making a piece of software that is useful in many countries, without rewriting the entire package.

INSOFT-L

http://iquest.com/~btatro/in2.shtml

This site is an archive for an active mailing list covering software internationalization. The list has many aspects, including changing the language used in menus and dialog boxes, possibly using a different character set, and often changing the assumptions that the program makes regarding the user's innate understanding.

ALSO RECOMMENDED:

Win/V

http://www.gol.com/winv/winvhome.html

This add-on to English (U.S.) versions of Windows lets you run Japanese Windows software side-by-side with U.S. software.

Macintosh

Although the Macintosh's hardware has some interesting differences from PC hardware, much of the early interest in the Mac was due to its very different software. Although many other operating systems have adopted some of the Mac's user interface, the "feel" of Mac software is still the Mac's strongest feature.

Info-Mac

gopher://sumex-aim.Stanford.EDU:70/11/info-mac

The largest and most popular Macintosh collection of information, shareware, and freeware. This Gopher archive, which has dozens of mirror sites around the world, is one of the better organized software archives. It also has a more extensive collection of helpful text files than typical PC archives.

UMich Mac Archive

http://www.umich.edu/~archive/mac/

Although not as large as Info-Mac, this archive sometimes has software that's not on Info-Mac. The PowerMac collection is particularly impressive, and some of the other sections are also worth poking around if you're out looking for good freeware and shareware.

MacVersions

http://www.cyserv.com/sam/MacVersions/

This is a wonderful service for Mac users who can't keep up on with all the new versions of software. It lists the current version number for most popular commercial, shareware, and freeware programs. Why hasn't someone done this for the PC?

CodeWarrior

http://www.metrowerks.com/

Serious Macintosh programmers have flocked to Metrowerks' line of programming languages for the Mac. The tools include advanced C and C++ compilers, entire development suites, and development tools that make creating 68K and PowerPC applications from the same code a breeze.

Mac Net Journal

http://www.dgr.com/web_mnj/

This is a wonderful magazine from folks who really care about the Macintosh. They often have write-in sections asking for reader's feedback to recent Mac developments, and their reviews are often more critical than what you find in the print magazines. Well worth reading.

JPEGView

http://www.med.cornell.edu/jpegview.html

If you have many graphics files to look at, you want this program. It reads graphics files in many formats, not just JPEG, and can display them individually or as a slide show. It's almost freeware: If you like the program, you're supposed to send the author a picture postcard.

HyperArchive

http://hyperarchive.lcs.mit.edu/
HyperArchive.html

A searchable mirror of the Info-Mac archive.

Mac Super Game Archive

http://www.rbi.com/~salegui/mike/
archive.html

A nice personal page with lists of this person's favorite games and demo software.

Macintosh TCP/IP Programmer's Guide

http://www.metrowerks.com/tcpip/
index.html

Answers to common questions regarding how to write Macintosh TCP/IP programs.

Grand Unified Socket Interface

http://err.ethz.ch/members/neeri/
macintosh/gusi-qa.html

This is a nice attempt to make programming of Macintosh network software compatible with BSDI-based UNIX programs.

ZipIt

http://www.awa.com/softlock/zipit/
zipit.html

Great little Mac shareware program for reading and creating files compatible with PKZIP on the PC.

Mailing Lists

Most Internet users are well acquainted with mailing lists, although few know of the software that makes them run. Most Internet mailing lists run off of one of three software packages: LISTSERV, listproc, and Majordomo. Of course, there are also many non-Internet packages for local mailing lists.

LISTSERV

http://www.lsoft.com/listserv.html

The first well-known mailing list software package, LISTSERV, is still in use at thousands of sites on the Net. It runs on a variety of hardware, and many of the largest mailing lists in the world are distributed through it. This site is the home of the now-commercial LISTSERV package.

Majordomo FAQ

http://www.math.psu.edu/barr/
majordomo-faq.html

Many sites prefer the freeware Majordomo over the other list servers because of its greater user friendliness and the fact that it is written in Perl, which makes it easier to debug. This FAQ has what you need to get started with Majordomo, and pointers of where to get more information.

ListSTAR

http://www.starnine.com/liststar.html

A commercial mailing list package for the Macintosh that can handle both Internet and non-Internet mailing lists.

LWGate

http://www.netspace.org/users/dwb/
lwgate.html

Software for Web sites that gives users a nice Web interface to mailing list archives.

Mathematics

Computers are great at simple math, but most mathematicians need computers to do much more sophisticated work than what you can get out of typical spreadsheets. Fortunately, most computers can handle complex math as well. Math software also is valuable to many nonmathematicians, such as engineers and research scientists.

Guide to Available Mathematical Software

http://gams.nist.gov/

A comprehensive list of software for mathematicians and others who do heavy math work. The list covers all types of computers as well as both free and commercial software. Each package has a fair amount of contact information listed.

Maple

http://www.maplesoft.com/

One of the best-known math programs for computers ranging from PCs to large workstations. Maple solves symbolic math problems and can generate both numerical and graphical answers. It also is used in teaching algebra and college math.

Mathematica

http://www.wri.com/

Another popular symbolic math package is Mathematica from Wolfram Research. Mathematica was a well-known pioneer in offering modern user interface features in a math package, and there is quite a market of Mathematica users sharing and selling their add-on collections of results and templates.

MATLAB

http://www.mathworks.com/matlab.html

A third popular PC math program, MATLAB emphasizes numeric computation and data visualization by analyzing linear systems of equations. MATLAB is particularly popular in the electrical engineering field.

MicroMath

http://www.micromath.com/~mminfo/

MicroMath's products are used for solving equation systems and fitting experimental data, and are thus more used by folks who work with real data instead of just equations. They have specialized software for various science fields such as chemistry and pharmacology.

ALSO RECOMMENDED:

Logic Software from CSLI

http://www-csli.stanford.edu/hp/

Information about software products that help you learn a few areas of mathematics using your personal computer.

NetLib

http://www.netlib.org/

A well-known collection of math papers, algorithms, and software, fully searchable.

Multimedia

The software that runs multimedia is sometimes almost as important as the multimedia content itself. Multimedia software generally falls into two categories: programs that let you experience multimedia, and programs that let you create it.

Director Web

http://hakatai.mcli.dist.maricopa.edu/director/index.html

This nonofficial page covers many aspects of Macromedia Director, the popular program for creating multimedia on the PC and Macintosh. It has pointers to many different how-to documents, as well as sites with examples of Director output.

ALSO RECOMMENDED:

MPEG Player for XWindows

http://www.geom.umn.edu/docs/mpeg_play/mpeg_play.html

A free video viewer for UNIX folk. The page also has links for MPEG players for PCs and Macs.

Internet UnderWater

http://kbt.com/atlantis/atlantis.html

A small multimedia company with some great design on its Web pages.

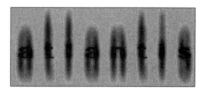

Protocols

This catch-all section collects information about the zillions of standards for data communication that have evolved since two computers were able to talk to each other. Protocols are sets of rules that allow people to get their hardware and software to communicate, and they are often full of arcane descriptions of very low-level abstract gunk. Without them, however, it would be almost impossible to get anything done in the computer world.

DNS Resources Directory

http://www.dns.net/dnsrd/

The Internet's Domain Name System (DNS) is what lets you refer to a host computer by its name (such as www.yahoo.com) instead of by its numerical address. This site has an incredible collection of information on how the DNS protocol works and how to steer around the problems it presents.

IP Next Generation (IPng)

http://playground.sun.com/pub/ipng/
html/ipng-main.html

The next big technical change to happen on the Internet will be the Internet Protocol (the "IP" part of "TCP/IP") being updated to take care of more addresses, better encryption, better routing of information, and so on. You can read all about it, and the many folks working on the changes, at this site.

Introduction to SNA

http://pclt.cis.yale.edu/pclt/comm/
sna.htm

An excellent article introducing SNA and explaining it in both historical and technical contexts. It explains where SNA is today and how other protocols took over the market that IBM owned. Well worth reading for anyone still on an IBM mainframe.

SNMP & CMIP: An Introduction to Network Management

http://
www.undergrad.math.uwaterloo.ca/
~tkvallil/snmp.html

Network management is becoming an increasingly important field as more and more novice users have their computers hooked to LANs. This site gives a good overview of the two most common standard network management protocols and explains each protocol's advantages and disadvantages.

Introduction to TCP/IP

http://pclt.cis.yale.edu/pclt/comm/
tcpip.htm

A quick but complete introduction to TCP/IP and why the typical Internet user would want to know something about it. The text is friendly, and the authors keep the amount of previous technical understanding that you need to a minimum.

Winsock Info

http://sunsite.unc.edu/winsock/

Anyone programming Windows applications using Winsock should visit here. The full specification is available, as well as descriptions of the basics of Winsock programming. There's even a funny section with examples of how *not* to program with Winsock.

Z39.50 Resources

http://ds.internic.net/z3950/
z3950.html

The international standard for database querying and responding. This site has a good list of links to the actual standard, many implementations of it, and the various groups that discuss Z39.50.

A L S O   R E C O M M E N D E D:

APPN Implementers Workshop

http://www.raleigh.ibm.com/app/
aiwhome.htm

One of IBM's last gasps at keeping SNA and its affiliated protocol APPN alive.

IP Over ATM

http://www.com21.com/pages/
ietf.html

Lots of information about how these two protocols are interacting, and the future of sending IP information over ATM lines.

SLIP vs. PPP Performance Comparison

http://www.morningstar.com/
MorningStar/slip-ppp-compare.html

A great technical discussion that I hope will put an end to the debate of which protocol is faster.

NNTP Server Reference Software

http://www.academ.com/academ/
nntp.html

The definitive program for running a Usenet news server under UNIX.

UUCP

http://cs.weber.edu/home/rlove/
HTML/uucp.html

A good, short discussion on the old way to send mail and news between UNIX computers.

Winsock FAQ

http://mars.superlink.net/user/mook/
winfaq.html

Lots of good information for both programmers and users with technical problems due to Winsock failures.

Shareware

The shareware concept, which is that you can try out a program on your machine before you purchase it, has been quite popular for almost as long as the PC has been around. It's impossible to categorize software by whether or not it is shareware, because shareware is a marketing tool, not a software type. Still, many people prefer to buy shareware rather than other commercial software just because it says something about the author of the program — namely, that he or she trusted the user to pay for it after trying it.

MCR Software

http://www.hooked.net/users/mcrsoft/mcr_home.html

Shareware content that isn't just software. These folks have shareware collections of quotations on many subjects, organized and indexed for easy copying or just for fun reading.

RegNet

http://www.xmission.com/~wintrnx/regnet/regnet.htm

Registering shareware can sometimes be a hassle, particularly if the author is in another country or doesn't accept payment in the form that you want to give it. RegNet hopes to alleviate those problems by making it easy for you to pay for your shareware on the Web in one central place.

Aunt Annie's Crafts

http://www.dnaco.net/~dalafara/annie.html

A book of paper crafts that you can make with household items.

Shareware Center

http://netcenter.com/netcentr/bookstor/sharewar/index.html

A selection of interesting shareware from many authors, with reviews and feature overviews.

Software Engineering

This is the academic end of creating software. More than just programming, software engineering includes topics such as reusing software, automated programming, and interpreting source code into human language.

Inter-Language Unification (ILU)

ftp://parcftp.parc.xerox.com/pub/ilu/ilu.html

One of the biggest problems with programming in large organizations is programs that are written in different programming languages. The ILU project aims at making differences between different object-oriented languages become unimportant for multilanguage projects.

Year 2000 Information Center

http://arganet.tenagra.com/year2000/

At the stroke of midnight at the end of 1999, the date will change to 2000. No problem for most people, but what about for computers? A lot of programs have year dates hardwired as two-digit numbers. This site has lots of information about how to avoid what could be massive problems that are just a few years away.

Software Engineering Virtual Library

http://www.erg.abdn.ac.uk/users/brant/sre/soft-eng.html

An incredibly complete list of the software engineering sites throughout the world, particularly in Europe. The list is broken down by general category, and many sites have multiple entries for different subfields in Software Engineering.

Comprehensive Approach to Reusable Defense Software (CARDS)

http://dealer.cards.com/

The Air Force's view of reusable software as a way to reduce costs and make better programs.

Software Engineering Papers

http://www.rai.com/soft_eng/index.html

A commercial vendor of research papers with an extensive catalog of software engineering papers.

Software Engineering Archives

http://www.qucis.queensu.ca/Software-Engineering/

A very complete list of Internet sites with software engineering topics.

Miscellaneous Software Sites

Guide to Japanese Computing

http://www.uwtc.washington.edu/Computing/Japanese/JapaneseResources.html

A list of resources, mostly in English, covering how computers are used in Japan. There are many sites that describe using Japanese software and how the three Japanese character sets are represented in software and hardware.

Software Licensing Issues

http://www.viman.com/license.html

This is an excellent overview of the many issues around software licensing, such as site licensing over networks, managing licenses, enforcing single-computer licenses, and so on.

Introduction to CORBA

http://www.acl.lanl.gov/sunrise/DistComp/Objects/corba.html

If you're interested in object-oriented programming, you should certainly know a bit about CORBA (Common Object Request Broker Architecture), one of the few well-established standards in the industry. This site is an excellent introduction, and has lots of pointers to academic and commercial sites working with the standard.

Screensavers For Windows

http://optimum.optimum.nf.ca/savers/savers.htm

People's intense interest in screen savers has always been somewhat of a mystery. But the demand for fun and exciting screensavers is real, and this site lists dozens of different screensavers for Windows, as well as places to get free modules for commercial screen savers such as After Dark.

ALSO RECOMMENDED:

Alpha NT Tools & Utilities

http://www.garply.com/tech/comp/sw/pc/nt/alpha.html

An archive of Windows NT programs that run on the DEC Alpha series.

IEEE Software

http://www.computer.org/pubs/software/software.html

One of the biggest academic journals covering software and its creation from a computer science viewpoint.

What is Object-Oriented Software?

http://www.soft-design.com/softinfo/objects.html

A great site that answers a really ugly question.

Standards

Keeping up with all the standards in a dynamic industry such as computers is pretty difficult. Standards can exist for everything from hardware interfaces to software structure, and there are dozens of standards being created every day. It is unlikely that anyone can really know all the relevant standards for more than a narrow area of interest, so there are groups of people who do nothing other than track standards.

Accredited Standards Committee X3

http://www.x3.org/

The X3 committee is somewhat of a center for voluntary standards, and the results of their work cover a range of computer fields. They also cover such issues as the interface between standards and patents, and how standards documents should change over time.

ISO

http://www.iso.ch/

The International Standards Organization, ISO, is one of the most significant players in the standards field. The ISO Web site has lots of information about ISO, but not much in the way of actual standards, because they sell their standards documents for a hefty price in order to support themselves.

A L S O   R E C O M M E N D E D:

Information Technology Standards Integrated Web Server

http://www.itsi.disa.mil/

All the military standards that you could possibly want, as well as pointers to the nonmilitary standards used by defense contractors.

Unicode

http://www.stonehand.com/unicode.html

This is the best shot the world has to settling on a single character set that can be used by everyone.

Supercomputing and Parallel Computing

The field of supercomputing has pretty much merged with that of parallel computing in the past few years. Unfortunately, parallel computing is not moving ahead nearly as fast as people predicted five years ago, and some of the early leaders in the field have pulled back or gone out of business. This is not to say that parallel computing isn't going

anywhere; there is still a great deal of room for development of both the hardware and software.

Concurrent Supercomputing Consortium

http://www.ccsf.caltech.edu/cscc.html

A group of supercomputer sites who have banded together to share information and resources. This site described in detail what each member site is doing with their supercomputers and has links to the Web sites for more information.

High Performance Computing and Communications Software Exchange

http://www.netlib.org/nhse/

A great central repository of software and algorithms used on high-performance computers. The software is easily searchable, and there are also links to many papers and other research documents of value to programmers working on parallel computers.

Parallel Tools Consortium

http://www.llnl.gov/ptools/ptools.html

These folks are mostly focused on the tools used in parallel computing, as compared to the topics on which people are using parallel computers. The tools described range from extensions to existing languages all the way to entire new languages that are optimized for parallel computers.

A L S O   R E C O M M E N D E D:

National Consortium for High Performance Computing

http://www.nchpc.lcs.mit.edu/

Another group of supercomputer users.

Supercomputing and Parallel Computing Resources

http://www.cs.cmu.edu/Web/Groups/scandal/www/resources.html

A very detailed list of resources, organized by date.

World Wide Web

Ah, the Web. That everything-to-everybody Internet service that will make us all happy at last. For the past year, you couldn't read an article about the Internet without hearing about how great the Web will be, and now they all say that the Web and cable TV are bound to merge. It's unfortunate that the Web's reputation has been so much based on what it might do in the future, since there are plenty of things in the present that it does just fine.

Announcement Services

If you've created your own Web page, you probably want other people to come look at it. However, letting people know that Web pages exist is not easy. These sites, often searchable, are collections of various kinds of Web pages. Note that many of the sites in this section could just as easily be listed in the section titled "Indices to Web Documents" below.

A1 Index of Free WWW URL Submission & Search Sites

http://www.vir.com/~wyatt/index.html

This meta-list tells you all the other sites that let you submit your home page address, and which ones let you search for other pages. There are also good instructions for how to get the most out of your announcements.

New WWW Servers

http://www.w3.org/hypertext/DataSources/WWW/Geographical_generation/new-servers.html

People often forget that even though there is no geography in the Internet, there is still one in the rest of the world. This list is arranged by geography: one site for each country other than the U.S., and one for each state in the U.S.

NCSA's What's New Page

http://www.ncsa.uiuc.edu/SDG/Software/Mosaic/Docs/whats-new-form.html

This is the first, and possibly largest, page of new Web site announcements. Originally used as a

way for Mosaic users to find something fun to look at, it rapidly became *the* place to look at, and just as quickly fell from many people's attention. Add your site here.

Net-Happenings

http://www.mid.net/NET/input.html

This site lists Internet resources of all types of interest to K-12 educators. Fortunately, the curator has a pretty wide view of what that means, so the list is quite extensive, but has much less of the typical commercial stuff than others. If your site might fall into this range, submit it here.

Netscape's What's New

http://www.netscape.com/escapes/submit_new.html

Not as extensive as other lists, this one is clearly put together by humans who understand a bit about writing and grammar. It seems to have a stronger emphasis on commercial sites than home pages, but the material is at least quite easy to skim through.

Submit It!

http://submit-it.permalink.com/submit-it/

If going from site to site registering your home page seems a bit of a pain, you should visit here first. You can register your site to over a dozen sites by filling out just one form. The sites represent most of the "top" sites and many lesser-known ones, too.

Pointers To Pointers

http://www.homecom.com/global/pointers.html

Another list of which sites let you post your URL. This one is different in that it has much better information about each site, and has the sites classified by what type of URLs they are looking for.

ALSO RECOMMENDED:

AddALink

http://www.i-link.net/cgi-bin/adamlistlinks

A gazillion links, listed in no particular order. Anyone can add a link, it seems.

Hendrik's Reciprocal URL Collection

ftp://islandnet.com/ideas/html/URL_List.html

A nice long list of URLs of people who also list Hendrik's page.

Global On-Line Directory

http://www.gold.net/gold/gold2.html

A little bit of everything, very nicely arranged, but somehow something seems missing....

ALIWEB

http://web.nexor.co.uk/public/aliweb/doc/registering.html

A British site that lets most anyone register their site.

Starting Point

http://www.stpt.com/util/submit.html

A cute idea: the starting point for everyone on the Web.

Webula

http://www.eg.bucknell.edu/cgi-bin/webula/index.html

Although it is smallish, the entries seem pretty high-quality. A nice little niche list.

What's New Too

http://newtoo.manifest.com/WhatsNewToo/submit.html

They cull the other sites and take your own submissions, and the site ends up looking pretty spiffy.

Commercial Sites Index

http://www.directory.net/dir/submit.cgi

None of those personal home pages here. A very business-oriented site that is liberal about who they let register.

WebPromote

http://www.stpt.com/shc/wp.html

Not sure where to start in promoting your Web site? These folks can help, for a price.

Beginner's Guides

Primer For Creating Web Resources

http://www-slis.lib.indiana.edu/Internet/programmer-page.html

This is a great starting place for people who want to create Web pages or run Web servers but don't know where to start. There are many pointers to the better online guides, as well as introductory material about what you will need to get going.

Bare Bones Guide to HTML

http://www.access.digex.net/~werbach/barebone.html

After you've learned HTML, you may still need a quick reference chart. This site has a great chart, available in many formats (HTML, HTML with tables, text-only, and so on). There is also a translation into French, which is a nice touch to combat the English-centric Web.

World Wide Web: Origins and Beyond

http://homepage.seas.upenn.edu/~lzeltser/WWW/

If you're the kind of person who wants to know a bit about what the history of something is before you start using it, you should certainly read this. It is a short, well-written piece that describes

the Web in terms of what came before it and where it fits into the bigger picture of communications.

World Wide Web FAQ

http://sunsite.unc.edu/~boutell/faq/

Short answers to dozens of common questions from novices and not-so-novices about the Web and all the baggage it carries with it. There are useful lists of software, hints, and advice. The FAQ is full of good pointers to other parts of the Web, but it doesn't rely on them.

ALSO RECOMMENDED:

Learning Outcomes

http://www.gactr.uga.edu/exploring/toc.html

Very friendly, gently-paced, and non-intimidating introduction to the Web.

Finding a WWW Host for Your Project

http://www.ucsc.edu/civil-war-letters/host.html

A nice short list of things to think about when you are searching for a place to put your Web pages.

Introduction to HTML

http://www.cwru.edu/help/introHTML/toc.html

There are dozens of them on the Web, but this one stands out as being easy to read and follow by beginners.

Sample Form

http://www.uni.edu/~wells27/samform.html

If you're delving into creating HTML forms, take a look here for a good example of everything.

WWW Authoring Information

http://www.netspace.org/users/dwb/www-authoring.html

Probably the best compact list of pointers for folks who are writing their own Web pages.

Best of the Web

Everyone likes awards, and the Web's newness seems to make them all the more desirable. Given that there is no central government for the Web, all the awards here are pretty much ad hoc, but they do tend to get people to spiff up their pages a bit. The names can be a bit confusing, however.

Best of the Web

http://wings.buffalo.edu/contest/

This was the most publicized of the Web site contests in 1994, and therefore will probably stay that popular over time. The awards are categorized by type of service, and there are also awards for technical merit and design.

Best of the Net

http://gnn.digital.com/gnn/wic/best.toc.html

Most of these are for the Web, but there are some non-Web resources tossed in here. This isn't as much of a contest as it is a list of what the GNN

folks think is best at the moment and over time. Content seems to be worth more than glitz here.

Mirsky's Worst of the Web

http://mirsky.turnpike.net/wow/Worst.html

Things that are the best are important to acknowledge, but so are things that are the worst. Like on America's Funniest Home Videos, some of these sites try to be the worst, but some of them are just inadvertently bad. Mind-numbing fun.

Best of British Web Sites

http://www.vnu.co.uk/vnu/pcw/bob.htm

Enough of this U.S.-centric Web stuff! There are some wonderful sites around the world, but you rarely see them in the "best of" lists. This site has pointers to many very nice pages, some of them much better than their American counterparts.

Useless WWW Pages

http://www.primus.com/staff/paulp/useless.html

Another collection of "not the best", in this case pages that are silly, obscure, or just plain confusing. This is not to say that these pages are "worst", just good examples of things that probably were created more for the medium than the message.

ALSO RECOMMENDED:

Macmillan Winner's Circle

http://www.mcp.com/general/workshop/winner/

A weekly contest for the best-designed pages, mostly by individuals.

Netcenter's Tour of the Internet

http://netcenter.com/yellows/tour.html

Well, with 3000 sites, it isn't really a "best of", but the guided tour idea is nice, and they did pick through the sites.

Browsers

Web browsers (more properly called "Web clients") are obviously a very important part of the Web. The browser market is fairly fickle, and the surveys about who is using which browser come up with different numbers each month. If you go out on the Web much, you should get to know your browser well.

W3 Browsers

http://www.w3.org/hypertext/WWW/Clients.html

Don't let the simple name fool you: this is the most complete list of Web browsers available. Maintained by the W3C, it lists all the browsers by their operating system, and has links to the home pages for the browser's manufacturers. If you are searching for a new browser, start here.

BrowserWatch

http://www.ski.mskcc.org/browserwatch/index.html

You need to have a table-enhanced browser to appreciate this site, but there is much more information here than even the W3C list. There is also a great news list that has announcements and rumors of new versions.

Web Browsers & Privacy

http://www.uiuc.edu/~ejk/WWW-privacy.html

This is a very important note about the kind of information that your Web browser is telling strangers about you. For example, some Web browsers will identify you by your e-mail address to almost any Web server; not too nice, eh? You can also test what your browser is saying about you.

Arena for HTML Version 3

http://www.w3.org/hypertext/WWW/Arena/

If you are trying to stay up with all the latest changes in HTML, you probably have to run Arena, an XWindows browser from W3C. It is kept scrupulously up-to-date as the features in HTML version 3 shift around, and is the best way to track what things will look like in the future.

Emissary

http://www.twg.com/emissary/emiss1.html

This is much more than a Windows Web browser: it's all the Internet applications (including e-mail) in a very integrated package. It ends up feeling like a full Internet desktop, of which the Web is a big part, but so is e-mail. Could be a very popular environment.

I-Comm

http://www.best.com/~icomm/

If you have a character-based Unix or VMS account, you can still use a graphical Web browser if your site runs I-Comm. This system allows sites to treat their users nicely without having to change over to SLIP or PPP accounts.

Lynx

http://www.cc.ukans.edu/lynx_help/Lynx_users_guide.html

There are still tens of millions of users on character-based systems, and Lynx is about the only usable Web browser for them. Although it is pretty unwieldy, it works reasonably well for getting straight text and simple HTML files off the Web.

Mosaic from NCSA

http://www.ncsa.uiuc.edu/SDG/Software/MacMosaic/MacMosaicHome.html

http://www.ncsa.uiuc.edu/SDG/Software/WinMosaic/HomePage.html

http://www.ncsa.uiuc.edu/SDG/Software/XMosaic/

Mosaic gets a great deal of the credit for starting the whole Web revolution, and you can still get the software for free. These three sites provide the software and documentation for the Macintosh, Windows, and XWindows versions of the browser.

WWW Viewer Test Page

http://www-dsed.llnl.gov/documents/WWWtest.html

Want to be sure that the viewers and helper applications for your Web browser work right? This page has a good collection of (mostly small) files for a wide range of file types. Click on one and see what your browser does!

WWW Browsers That Can Display Japanese

http://www.ntt.jp/japan/note-on-JP/browsers.html

The Web still isn't all that friendly to non-Roman character sets, and there are too many different ways to display Japanese and Chinese characters (never mind many Arabic sets). This document can help you navigate through the different Web browsers that can display kanji, hirakana, and katakana characters.

ALSO RECOMMENDED:

Air Mosaic Express

http://www.spry.com/sp_prod/airmos/airmos.html

An inexpensive browser for Windows. You can try a demo of the software for free at this site.

Amiga Mosaic

http://www.omnipresence.com/amosaic/2.0/

Amiga users shouldn't have to suffer without a good Web client. This one is derived from NCSA Mosaic.

City.Net Browser Checkup

http://www.city.net/checkup.cgi

Want to know if you are running the latest version of your browser? Go here and find out instantly.

Charlotte

gopher://p370.bcsc.gov.bc.ca/11/vmtools

Gotta have a browser for every environment, even 3270 terminals running in VM/CMS on mainframes!

W3 for Emacs

http://www.cs.indiana.edu/elisp/w3/docs.html

If you're an Emacs user, you don't have to leave your favorite editor to wander around the Web.

Enhanced Mosaic

http://www.spyglass.com/three/index.html

This is a good place to find out where to get one of the many commercial versions of Mosaic.

HotJava

http://java.sun.com/

A Web browser that understands Java, the new programming language for interactive Web toys.

I-View

http://www.best.com/~icomm/

A great, small, free non-Internet HTML browser with lots of features. Good for putting on diskettes with content.

W3C Line Mode Browser

http://www.w3.org/hypertext/WWW/LineMode/

The worst possible interface for the Web, but it runs on almost any character-based system.

MacWeb and WinWeb

http://www.einet.net/EINet/MacWeb/MacWebHome.html

http://www.einet.net/EINet/WinWeb/WinWebHome.html

A nice, free alternative set of browsers. Not as fancy as Mosaic or Netscape, but simple and small.

Mariner

http://www.ncd.com/IP/mariner.html

Another Windows-based integrated Internet package that uses the File Manager as a user interface model.

Netscape Navigator

http://www.netscape.com/info/how-to-get-it.html

Instructions for downloading the latest versions of the software that seems to have taken over the Web.

Netscape Extensions to HTML

http://www.netscape.com/home/services_docs/html-extensions.html

So far, these HTML extensions only work with Netscape browsers, but it seems likely other browsers will add them soon.

OmniWeb

http://www.omnigroup.com/Software/OmniWeb/

Using the NeXTStep operating system? You probably want to use OmniWeb, a free Web browser just for you.

SlipKnot

http://plaza.interport.net/slipknot/slipknot.html

Shareware Windows browser that does not require a SLIP or PPP account, but does require some help from your character-based host.

tkWWW

http://uu-gna.mit.edu:8001/tk-www/help/overview.html

A nice little Web browser for folks using XWindows and Tk/Tcl. Freeware, of course.

Browser Statistics

http://emporium.turnpike.net/J/jc/public_html/stats.html

Want to know which browser is most popular? These folks keep statistics based on millions of hits.

Public Browsers by Telnet

http://www.w3.org/hypertext/WWW/
FAQ/Bootstrap.html

If you have access to Telnet but not a
Web browser, you can find a public
site that will help you out.

CGI - Common Gateway Interface

If you are setting up your own Web
site, you certainly need to know about
HTML, but you may also need to do
some programming. By far the most
common way to communicate
between your Web server and
programming language is CGI, a very
rudimentary but workable interface.
Also see the "Programming" section
below, which covers much of the
same material.

Learn to Write CGI Forms

http://www.catt.ncsu.edu/~bex/tutor/
index.html

A gentle introduction to using CGI and
forms. It uses Perl as the language for
the scripts, which makes sense
because string handling in Perl is
infinitely easier to understand than in
C or C++. A good beginner's guide,
particularly for people who already
know Perl.

CGI Programmer's Reference

http://www.best.com/~hedlund/cgi-
faq/

A very good FAQ for CGI programmers.
It explains more than the basics,
covering things such as language-
specific issues and smart ways to
handle form input. There are also
many pointers to other CGI resources.

Perl5 CGI Library

http://www-genome.wi.mit.edu/ftp/
pub/software/WWW/cgi_docs.html

Perl 5 programmers will love this one.
It is a library that lets you interact with
CGI in a Perl-like fashion. It also has a
really easy method for creating HTML
forms from Perl calls so that you can
create forms on the fly from within
your scripts.

ALSO RECOMMENDED:

Common Gateway Interface Overview

http://hoohoo.ncsa.uiuc.edu/cgi/
overview.html

The definitive document on the CGI
interface, including CGI 1.1
information.

Simple CGI E-mail Handler

http://siva.cshl.org/email/index.html

A small C program that lets you create
forms that e-mail their results to
anyone you want.

Ada 95 Binding to CGI

http://wuarchive.wustl.edu/
languages/ada/swcomps/cgi/cgi.html

If you want to use Ada (admittedly
odd, no?) for your script programming,
you should certainly look here.

AppleScript and Frontier CGIs

http://cy-mac.welc.cam.ac.uk/cgi.html

A nice collection of CGI programs
written both in AppleScript and
Frontier scripting language for the
Mac.

CGIwrap

ftp://pluto.cc.umr.edu/pub/cgiwrap/

If you are a site administrator, and
your users can write CGI scripts, this is
an important security tool well worth
checking out.

EIT's CGI Library for C

http://wsk.eit.com/wsk/dist/doc/
libcgi/libcgi.html

A bunch of useful functions for C
programmers dealing with writing CGI
scripts. Simple and elegant.

Felipe's AppleScript CGI Examples

http://edb518ea.edb.utexas.edu/
scripts/cgix/cgix.html

A collection of more advanced CGI
scripts written in AppleScript for
Macintosh servers.

CGI Pointers

http://www.cyserv.com/pttong/
cgi.html

A good, compact list of many pointers
to CGI programming resources.

Windows CGI

http://www.city.net/win-httpd/
httpddoc/wincgi.htm

If you use CGI on Windows-based systems, you should know about WCGI, the slight abridgment of CGI for Windows systems.

Communication

While wandering around the Web, you might get the impression that the Web is pretty much a one-way medium where people tell you things, maybe occasionally letting you fill out a form. Generally, that's most of the Web today, but there are pockets of two-way communication, such as Web-style chat and BBSs.

Chat Server

http://www.magmacom.com/
~cbjustus/chatserver.html

An interesting experiment in chatting. The environment is set up as a virtual hotel with a lobby, bar, and many different settings. It is often quite busy, and all sorts of chatting happen in the different rooms.

Futplex

http://gewis.win.tue.nl/applications/
futplex/

Not a chat server, but it could be used as one. This software for UNIX systems lets Web users have multiple update access to a document, such as for group revisions, discussion, and so on. You can also make some of the document read-only, and allow folks to delete messages from each other.

HyperNews

http://union.ncsa.uiuc.edu/
HyperNews/get/hypernews.html

This is an innovative way of making Web sites that have many of the desirable features of current BBS packages, and also take advantage of the Web's unique features. For example, you can enter a message that has links to other messages, or to other sites. Watch for this one to grow soon.

Sociable Web

http://judith.www.media.mit.edu/
SocialWeb/SociableWeb.html

This is a slowly-evolving project to design and test different ways of displaying who is involved in a Web-based chat, and to let the chat in a more natural format. Instead of just a bunch of names, you get visual representations of who is online, and what they are doing.

WebChat

http://www.irsociety.com/
webchat.html

An advanced, commercial chatting system that lets users input more than just text. If the chatters know HTML, they can insert that directly, and if they have audio or video they want to include in the chat, they can do that as well.

Whimsy

http://monet.uwaterloo.ca/john/
whimsy/start.htm

If you like to wander around what appears to be a real town in your chat interactions, check this place out. Not only can you create your own characters, you can create your own spaces within the town as a way to attract chatters.

ALSO RECOMMENDED:

Asynchronous Link Protocol

http://www.theworld.com/alp/
alp.htm

A proprietary chat system for Windows users through a Windows NT server.

Columbus Home Page Chat Server

http://www.ohiocap.com/Chat/

A nice, fairly friendly group of folks in a moderated but open forum.

CyberSight Real-Time Chat

http://cybersight.com/cgi-bin/cs/ch/
chat

Watch and participate in a very random chat.

ParentsPlace

http://www.parentsplace.com/
talking.html

A refreshing change from what passes for "adult" chat: parents talking to each other about parenting issues.

Podium

http://www.proxima.com/podium/

Commercial chat software with an emphasis on the user interface.

Talker

http://www2.infi.net/talker/

A very busy, open chat system that works with simple Web forms.

WebNotes

http://webnotes.ostech.com/

This server software includes everything you need to become a Web chat site, including the HTTP server itself.

WWW Collaboration Projects

http://union.ncsa.uiuc.edu/
HyperNews/get/www/
collaboration.html

An extensive list of pointers for collaborative interaction on the Web, mostly for work-related sites.

Conferences

There are now over a dozen conferences of many sizes that cover the Web. Most are commercial conferences, although a good number are more academic. In addition, it's hard to go to almost any computer conference without finding some discussion of the Web. The following three conferences were the first academic conferences covering the Web. Each site still has lists of the papers given, and some of the papers are available in full as well.

First WWW Conference

http://www.elsevier.nl/cgi-bin/ID/
WWW94

Held in May 1994 in Geneva, Switzerland, this conference was the first Web-specific gathering of any major size.

Second WWW Conference

http://www.ncsa.uiuc.edu/SDG/IT94/
Proceedings/

Held in October 1994 in Chicago, this conference had significant vendor support and happened just as the Web was starting to get more commercial.

Third WWW Conference

http://www.igd.fhg.de/www/www95/
old/www95-old.html

Held in April 1995 in Darmstadt, Germany, with a much more European flavor to it than the second conference.

Databases and Searching

One of the features of the Web that makes it more popular than other Internet services is that it is easy to hook in search mechanisms into Web pages. In this way, a Web site can be an interface to as large of a database as the site wants. In the future, it is likely you will see many more huge, fully-searchable databases appearing on the Web.

Isite

http://vinca.cnidr.org/software/Isite/
Isite.html

Supported by CNIDR (the Clearinghouse for Networked Information Discovery and Retrieval), this free package has everything you need to include searchable databases on Unix-based Web servers. It also includes a gateway to WAIS databases.

Glimpse

http://glimpse.cs.arizona.edu:1994/

This is fast becoming one of the most popular free text databases used with the Web. Instead of indexing just single files, it indexes over entire filesystems, making it useful for Web sites with many users. It has many other advanced features, and is extremely fast and well supported.

Harvest

http://harvest.cs.colorado.edu/

The Harvest index system lets you set up generalized searches and find information in a variety of places on the Internet. As Harvest becomes more popular, more sites are supporting Harvest searching, making all the more useful for indexing world-wide knowledge.

WebLib

http://selsvr.stx.com/~weblib/

If you have many different database systems on a single site, it is incredibly difficult to support them all with a single interface. WebLib solves that problem, and makes it easier to create Web searching programs that might search across different databases.

Zelig

http://fiaker.ncsa.uiuc.edu:8080/
WWW94-2/paper.html

Regardless of the database you use, it is often difficult to take the records returned from a query and turn them into useful HTML documents. The Zelig project hopes to change that, allowing you to simply give an example of how your data looks and have the program be able to correctly generate HTML for it.

WAIS, Inc.

http://www.wais.com/

This company is the best-known supporter of the WAIS protocol, which at one time was thought to become *the* database protocol for the Internet. It turns out that WAIS has been largely ignored, however, and there are relatively few people using the WAIS databases on the Internet.

WWWWAIS

http://www.eit.com/software/
wwwwais/wwwwais.html

If you are using freeWAIS or SWISH as a database, you should certainly check out this utility as well. It automatically creates HTML query forms for your data, and sets up the query code to interact with different databases.

WinWAIS and MacWAIS

http://www.einet.net/EINet/
winWAIS.html

http://www.einet.net/EINet/
MacWAIS.html

Searching using the WAIS protocol is not pretty. Unfortunately, there are very few graphical browsers for WAIS searching. These two, both from EIT, have reasonable interfaces, although their error messages are a bit cryptic and they are by no means bug-free.

ALSO RECOMMENDED:

FFW

http://www.nta.no/produkter/ffw/
ffw.html

Another free text search engine that can be hooked into the Web.

Htgrep

http://iamwww.unibe.ch/~scg/Src/
Doc/htgrep.html

A simple text search system that lets Web users specify the kind of information they want, not just a keyword.

SWISH

http://www.eit.com/software/swish/

A user-friendly text searching system with a terminally cute acronym: Simple Web Indexing System for Humans.

Integrating Structured Databases Into the Web: The MORE System

http://rbse.jsc.nasa.gov/eichmann/
MORE_abstract.html

An interesting paper on using relational multimedia databases on the Web.

Connecting to Sybase SQL Server via WWW

http://www.sybase.com/WWW/

Instructions for Sybase users on how to create CGI scripts to interface to their Web servers.

Oracle Web Database Kit

http://dozer.us.oracle.com:8080/

A set of free utilities that help you link Oracle database queries into Web pages.

PROCGI

http://www.progress.com/webtools/
procgi.htm

Yet another database kit, this one for the Progress database.

freeWAIS

http://cnidr.org/cnidr_projects/
freewais.html

An unsupported but still popular free version of the WAIS database search engine.

Yahoo!

FreeWAIS-sf

http://ls6-www.informatik.uni-dortmund.de/freeWAIS-sf/README-sf

A more up-to-date version of freeWAIS with direct support for CGI connections.

Wais and WWW Pointers

http://www.cs.vu.nl/~anne007/waissearch/pointers.html

A very long, well-organized list of places to look for code for hooking different versions of WAIS into the Web.

Telnet-based WAIS Client

telnet://wais@wais.com/

You can use this free character-based WAIS client to search many WAIS databases throughout the world.

Gateways

The Web doesn't exist in a vacuum. Many Internet users, possibly the majority, have no direct Web access, and there are many Internet services for which there is not direct Web access. For both of these situations, people have created gateways to and from the Web.

WWW to Finger Gateway

http://www.cs.indiana.edu/finger/gateway

A fun way for Web users to get "finger" information through their browsers. This is more than a simple text gateway: the user fingered can also choose to have a picture of themselves included in the response.

Whois++ Gateway

http://union.ncsa.uiuc.edu/whoispp.html

Whois++ is a new Internet protocol useful for distributed directories and databases. This gateway is a simple form for creating whois++ queries to the few experimental databases that are available.

WebMail Service

http://www.best.com/~pierre/web-mail/

A shareware gateway between e-mail and the Web. For e-mail-only users, or people with personal digital assistants that only do e-mail, this is a great way to get Web pages through e-mail. Non-members are limited to the number of pages they can get, but members can get unlimited Web pages.

ALSO RECOMMENDED:

Discuss-WWW Gateway

http://www.mit.edu:8008/

A gateway for reading Discuss mailing lists using a Web browser.

WWW Mail Gateway

http://www-bprc.mps.ohio-state.edu/mailto/mailto_info.html

This is a CGI script that allows Web users to send preformatted mail to any place on the Internet.

geo-gw

http://www-iwi.unisg.ch/~dlincke/geo-gw/index.html

A nice little gateway to a geography server. You can search for locations from a Web form.

Web-to-Notes Gateway

http://www.digicool.com/notes_to_www.html

A still-under-development system for letting Web users access Lotus Notes databases and Notes users access the Web.

WWW Interface to X.500

http://http1.brunel.ac.uk:8080/wlu.html

A very clean gateway program for sites running X.500 directory services.

WWW-to-Z39.50 Gateways

http://is.rice.edu/~riddle/webZ39.50.html

A very nice list of the dozens of programs that let you hook Z39.50 (better known as WAIS) to the Web.

HTML Converters

There are many page layout and formatting programs that are much more advanced and easier to use than HTML. Thus, there is a need for people to be able to convert their information from those applications into HTML to put on the Web. Some programs have their own HTML output, but others require conversion utilities such as these.

Mosaic Hotlist to HTML Converters

http://www.envmed.rochester.edu/wwwrlp/html/winh2htm.htm

It is sort of surprising that the "hot lists" in many Web browsers are not in HTML format. If you have collected interesting sites into a hotlist but want to see that as a regular HTML document, you need a converter. This site has a few nice converters for Mosaic hotlists.

man2html

http://www.oac.uci.edu/indiv/ehood/man2html.doc.html

Lots of documentation exists in Unix "man" pages format. This fairly advanced Perl program converts man pages into HTML files, making things like headings and examples appear as they should with HTML tags.

Mozilla Print Gidget

http://www.netscape.com/people/mtoy/cgi/www-print.cgi

Want to get a PostScript file from an HTML page on the Web? Go to this site, fill out the form (which asks for the URL of the page and your e-mail address), and the PostScript server will read the page and mail you a (hopefully correct) PostScript file.

Archive of HTML Translators

ftp://src.doc.ic.ac.uk/computing/information-systems/www/tools/translators/

A comprehensive collection of various utilities for translating to and from HTML. More than just pointers this site mirrors these utilities from their original homes, and seems very up to date.

CyberLeaf

http://www.ileaf.com/ip.html

This somewhat pricey commercial program can convert files put out by Word, Interleaf, FrameMaker and WordPerfect into HTML files with very little effort. It can handle inline graphics and URLs in your documents as well.

Earl Hood's Tools

http://www.oac.uci.edu/indiv/ehood/

A sizable collection of Perl scripts that convert to and from HTML. For example, he has an Internet mail-to-HTML converter that can convert mailboxes to HTML files, as well as a program that converts FrameMaker documents into HTML.

Excel 5.0 to HTML Table Converter

http://rs712b.gsfc.nasa.gov/704/dgd/xl2html.html

This is a great way to make HTML tables: use Excel, then convert the range of cells to HTML using this Excel macro. It works with both PC and Mac Excel, and it handles many tricky table features in the conversion.

2HTML

http://www.netweb.com/cortex/content/software/2Html.sea.hqx

Word/Mac users will love this one: a Word macro that converts Word documents to HTML with almost no effort. The program is very easy to use, has a very spiffy interface (not

something you see very often on Word macros), and creates surprisingly clean HTML output.

HTML Markup

http://htc.rit.edu/klephacks/markup.html

An incredibly handy program for Mac users to convert plain text files into good first guesses of HTML files. The program puts the correct HTML incantations at the top and bottom of the file, and can intelligently choose to use the first line as the title or a top-level heading. Lots of other neat tricks, too!

HTML to ICADD Transformation Service

http://www.ucla.edu/ICADD/html2icadd-form.html

The ICADD (International Committee for Accessible Document Design) SGML template can create documents that can be "displayed" in Braille, large print, or with voice synthesis. This experimental site allows you to convert an HTML file on the Web to an ICADD document.

ALSO RECOMMENDED:

HTML Converters

http://www.w3.org/hypertext/WWW/Tools/Filters.html

A list of pointers to other programs that convert to and from HTML, as well as pointers to information on how to program your own.

Converters to and from HTML

http://union.ncsa.uiuc.edu/
HyperNews/get/www/html/
converters.html

Another very good list, this one with
more description of each of the
converters and what it runs on.

RosettaMan

http://www.jinr.dubna.su/~gagin/
rman.pl.html

A program that turns Unix "man"
pages into a variety of other formats,
including HTML.

C++ to HTML

http://www.atd.ucar.edu/jva/
c++2html.html

This is a great for people who want to
document their C++ code using HTML
and extract the comments easily.

Dave

http://www.bucknell.edu/bucknellian/
dave/

An AppleScript program that extracts
articles from PageMaker files and
converts them into HTML.

dtd2html

http://www.oac.uci.edu/indiv/ehood/
dtd2html.doc.html

If you're an SGML hacker, you might
want this package, which converts an
SGML DTD into HTML code
explaining it.

LaTeX2HTML

http://cbl.leeds.ac.uk/nikos/tex2html/
doc/latex2html/latex2html.html

Converts your LaTeX files (you'd know
them if you had them) into
nice HTML.

MHonArc

http://www.oac.uci.edu/indiv/ehood/
mhonarc.doc.html

Converts mail files to HTML, including
mail files with MIME enclosures, and
makes a list of the discussion threads.

Quark to HTML Conversion

http://the-tech.mit.edu/~jeremy/
qt2www.html

A discussion of the sorry state of the
Quark-to-HTML conversion utilities,
with pointers to the ones that exist.

txt2html

http://www.cs.wustl.edu/~seth/
txt2html/

Another text-to-HTML converter, this
one for Unix users. It does some very
smart things, like recognizing lists and
quotations.

WP2X

http://www.milkyway.com/People/
Michael_Richardson/wp2x.html

Converts WordPerfect files to HTML,
and a host of other formats. Oddly, it
runs on Unix systems, not MS-DOS.

HTML Editors

Creating HTML files is easy for some
folks, difficult for others. If you don't
think in terms of text formatting
languages, it is usually hard to come
up with correct HTML. There are now
many editing packages that turn out
nice HTML with very little effort, and
even experienced HTML hackers might
find them valuable.

HoTMetaL PRO

http://www.sq.com/products/
hotmetal/hmp-org.htm

One of the darlings of the HTML
editing set, this one seems to have
everything, do everything, and runs on
all the popular platforms. It is full
WYSIWYG, shows your graphics, has a
spelling checker, the whole works.
There is even a freeware version.

WordPerfect Internet Publisher

http://wp.novell.com/elecpub/
intpub.htm

A very nice free system for editing
HTML documents in WordPerfect for
Windows. The add-in integrates nicely
with WordPerfect, has a reasonable
set of HTML templates, and you can
put out documents in WordPerfect's
Envoy format.

Alpha

http://www.cs.umd.edu/~keleher/
alpha.html

A very powerful shareware editor for
the Macintosh that has a strong set of
HTML editing tools. Alpha is not for
the faint of heart: it is definitely a
dweeb's editor, but one that anyone
who does a lot of HTML creation will
love, particularly for its Tcl
scripting extensions.

Information on *Alpha*

Microsoft Internet Assistant for Word

http://www.microsoft.com/Msword/default.map?93,29

This is much more than an HTML editor: it is a Web browser, editor, and toolbox rolled into one. If you have Microsoft Word for Windows, you want this free extension. Not quite as full-featured as some other HTML editors, but if you are already comfortable with Word, you'll be at home with this.

ALSO RECOMMENDED:

Gabriel's HTML Editor List

http://luff.latrobe.edu.au/~medgjw/editors/

A wonderful, very long list of dozens (maybe hundreds by now) HTML editors for various platforms.

HTML Editor Reviews

http://www.interaccess.com/users/cdavis/edit_rev.html

Many in-depth, fairly critical reviews of Windows-based HTML editors. Well worth a peek before you commit to one.

HTML Tools

http://www.w3.org/hypertext/WWW/Tools/

Quite the long list of HTML editors and a few conversion tools thrown in for good measure.

GT_HTML

http://www.gatech.edu/word_html/release.htm

A nice, simple extension to Word for Windows (and maybe the Mac) that lets you put HTML tags into your documents.

Web Weaver for Macintosh

http://www.student.potsdam.edu/web.weaver/about.html

A very sophisticated HTML editor for Mac users. It seems to have just about everything.

HTTP

To many users, the Web is seen through their Web browsers: they forget that everything they see is served by some server somewhere. Every Web server speaks a protocol, HTTP, which was specifically designed to support hypertext and quick connections to documents.

HTTP Specifications

http://www.w3.org/hypertext/WWW/Protocols/

Hey, if you want to talk protocol, you should look at the documents that describe the nitty-gritty details of HTTP. Actually, the protocol documents are not that difficult to read if you understand a bit about data structures and how text is passed around on the Internet.

Performance of Several HTTP Demons on an HP 735 Workstation

http://www.ncsa.uiuc.edu/InformationServers/Performance/V1.4/report.html

This is about the only paper ever written that attempts to compare the performance of different HTTP server software. There are many problems with the paper with respect to representing the real world, but it is an admirable start.

WWW Security References

http://www-ns.rutgers.edu/www-security/reference.html

Many of the changes that the Web will see in the future will come in the area of security. There are currently many different security methods, and a few will come out as standard. Until the situation settles down, it's a good idea to know about all the different methods.

Secure HTTP

http://www.eit.com/projects/s-http/index.html

Probably the most talked-about improvement to HTTP for security will be S-HTTP. At the time of this writing, there is still much debate about the features that will go into it and how it will be licensed, but it seems likely to be the most-used security system for the Web once it is standardized.

NCSA httpd

http://hoohoo.ncsa.uiuc.edu/

This is probably the most popular Web server software in use. It is free, runs on many Unix systems, and is constantly being improved by both NCSA and other groups of programmers. The documentation is quite complete, which is good because many of the setup options are a bit cryptic.

WN

http://hopf.math.nwu.edu/

A free Unix Web server which emphasizes security and ease of administration. WN runs on most any Unix system, and has many advanced features normally found only in commercial servers, such as advanced server-side includes and controlling user directories.

WebSTAR

http://www.starnine.com/webstar/webstar.html

It is indeed possible, and easy, to run a Web server from a Macintosh. WebSTAR exists both as a shareware and commercial server, and it has many of the advanced features of other Web servers. If you like the Mac interface and want to run a Web site, you should certainly check it out.

ALSO RECOMMENDED:

WWW-SPEED

http://sunsite.unc.edu/mdma-release/

A mailing list (and its affiliated archive) discussing some methods for speeding up HTTP.

Web Servers Chart

http://www.proper.com/www/servers-chart.html

A list of all the supported Web server software packages and the features of each.

Log Analyzers

http://union.ncsa.uiuc.edu/HyperNews/get/www/log-analyzers.html

A long list of programs that you can use on your HTTP logs to get summaries and look for patterns of use of your site.

Webmasters Starter Kit

http://wsk.eit.com/

This is a somewhat simple, all-in-one package for Unix system administrators who want to start serving Web documents.

Indices to Web Documents

You've been seeing indices throughout this chapter, but there are some that don't fall into neat categories. Kinda sounds like the Web, huh?

Cool Site of the Day

http://www.infi.net/cool.html

A different Web site every day, mostly ones that are more interesting than the average site. The selection is quite wide, ranging from well put-together personal home pages to interesting corporate sites. Well worth a look if you're wondering what's up on the Web.

What's New in Japan

http://www.ntt.jp/WHATSNEW/index.html

A very good site for finding out how the Web is expanding in Japan. Many Japanese Web sites have both English and Japanese versions, and there is quite a variety of social, political, and cultural sites appearing every week.

Geographical List of Web Servers

http://www.w3.org/hypertext/DataSources/WWW/Servers.html

A very long list (and, fortunately, a summary) of all the Web servers that have registered with the W3C. If you want to know about which Web servers are in a particular area, especially those outside the U.S., this is a good place to go.

ALSO RECOMMENDED:

Random Yahoo! Link

http://www.cen.uiuc.edu/cgi-bin/ryl

Wonder how wide the selection is on Yahoo? Select this site and end up somewhere completely different.

URouLette

http://kuhttp.cc.ukans.edu/cwis/organizations/kucia/uroulette/uroulette.html

Another random link generator, this one with a more fun interface.

Political Site of the Day

http://ross.clendon.com/siteoftheday.html

Another "site of the day," this one with a theme that should find interest with almost anyone.

Boot Hill

http://www.fn.net/business/boothill/

An index to all of the Western and cowboy-related Web sites.

Information and Documentation

Usenet News and Mailing Lists about the Web

http://www.leeds.ac.uk/ucs/WWW/WWW_mailing_lists.html

Instead of reading about the Web in magazines and books, many people stay current by reading the many Usenet news groups and mailing lists about the Web. This list has lots of both of these, with descriptions of what you might find if you subscribe.

Apple Internet Providers

http://abs.apple.com/apple-internet-providers/

If you use a Macintosh to provide Internet services, you should certainly visit this site often. It's Apple's way of promoting the Mac as an Internet

server, and it includes pointers to every known piece of serving software, as well as hints and tips on a variety of issues.

Challenges for Web Information Providers

http://www.rpi.edu/~decemj/cmc/mag/1994/oct/webip.html

A superb article by longtime Internet researcher John December about what needs to happen for the Web to become universal and really useful. It points out many of the weak spots in the Web today and shows how things will have to change in order for the Web to really attract hundreds of millions of people.

ALSO RECOMMENDED:

Western World Wide Web

http://www.warwick.ac.uk:8000/wwww.html

An interesting paper challenging some of the optimistic assumptions about the Web.

Page Design and Layout

Setting up Web pages without thinking about what they will look like is a sure way to end up with ugly pages. There's a good reason that good layout artists get good money for their work, although you can often do at least an OK job on your own.

Advice to Christine

http://www.el-dorado.ca.us/~advice/

A wonderful way of learning about how to set up and design a Web site. The description is a set of letters to someone who was wondering what it

took to set up Web sites, and the information is good, practical, and devoid of hype.

Tips for Writers and Designers

http://www.best.com/~dsiegel/tips/tips_home.html

A very well thought-out list of things you should consider before putting your Web site out in public. There is also a very interesting essay on how the fractioning of the Web browser market is making it almost impossible to create nice looking pages for everyone.

Interface Design for Sun's WWW Site

http://www.sun.com/sun-on-net/www.sun.com/uidesign/

An interesting description of how they design their pages at Sun Microsystems. This is much more than do's and don'ts; for example, they let you see how their design changed over time and the decisions they made along the way.

ALSO RECOMMENDED:

Top Ten Ways To Tell If You Have A Sucky Home Page

http://www.winternet.com/~jmg/topten.html

Dripping with sarcasm, this is actually quite a good list of common mistakes that too many people make on their pages.

HTML Style Guide & Test Suite

http://www.charm.net/~lejeune/styles.html

A combination of examples of what HTML tags do and examples of what they look like on your browser.

WWW Calendar Generator

http://www.intellinet.com/CoolTools/CalendarMaker/

Cool trick: it creates calendars using Netscape table features based on the month and year you give it.

Programming

If you write scripts for the Web, you're probably aware of the many fun things you can do. Many other programmers have already created many great programs using the CGI interface (described above in the "CGI" section), and they love to show off what they've done.

W3C Reference Library

http://www.w3.org/hypertext/WWW/Library/Status.html

This is the C source code used by the W3C as the reference standard for creating both Web servers and browsers. Although the code is free, many people don't use it directly but check it carefully when they create their own Web programs.

WWW Homepage Access Counter

http://www.semcor.com/~muquit/Count.html

It seems like many home pages want to tell you how many times they've been accessed. And, being the Web, they want to do it with graphics. If you want to add such a doohickey to your Web page, check out this site, which has the code and some sample digits you can use.

Imagemap Help Page

http://www.hway.com/ihip/

A common feature of many Web pages are imagemaps, which are pictures you can click on and have the server know where you clicked. The programming needed to interpret the clicks is not that difficult, but many folks still need lots of help in getting imagemaps working. This site has that help, and many useful links as well.

ALSO RECOMMENDED:

libwww-perl

http://www.ics.uci.edu/pub/websoft/libwww-perl/

A library for Perl version 4 that handles all access to and from the Web, useful if you are creating your own fancier programs.

Verify Web Links

http://wsk.eit.com/wsk/dist/doc/admin/webtest/verify_links.html

A nice tool that will make sure that all the links on your Web actually work.

Searching the Web

Yahoo! is not the only service you can use to search the Web, although it is probably still the best one. The Yahoo! folks are nice enough tell you how to get to the dozens of other Web search tools, particularly the ones that are arranged in a different format from Yahoo!

WebCrawler

http://webcrawler.com/

Instead of trying to index the Web, "spiders" roam the Web, going from link to link and indexing the contents of pages. One of the best-known spiders, now part of America Online, is WebCrawler. Its search interface is very simple, and it is rarely too busy to answer a search request.

Lycos

http://www.lycos.com/

Another popular spider is Lycos. In fact, Lycos is so popular it is often hard to get it to respond to queries. The Lycos database is quite different from WebCrawler's in that the responses to queries gives you a great deal of text so you can see the context of the responses.

FunCity Web Search

http://www.funcity.com/search.html

You can use all the best Web search tools from this one site. Better than a bunch of pointers, this form lets you directly search each search site without having to deal with a zillion different forms. A great tool when searching for the obscure.

InfoSeek

http://www.infoseek.com/

This generalized search service has an incredible selection of Web sites, Usenet news groups, and so on. Many of the searches are free, and you can subscribe to get an even wider range of services and more complete search results.

ALSO RECOMMENDED:

World Wide Web Robots, Wanderers, and Spiders

http://web.nexor.co.uk/mak/doc/robots/robots.html

Information about the existing spiders on the Web, as well as an explanation of what they do.

SavvySearch

http://www.cs.colostate.edu/~dreiling/smartform.html

Another site for searching many sites at once. This site actually submits the searches for you, and gives you a single response.

Security

Security on the Web is always a hot issue, and many companies have diverging ideas about how it should be implemented. There are standards and counter-standards, and it will probably be quite some time before you can use the Web securely without having to juggle security keys and protocols.

SSL Information

http://www.netscape.com/info/SSL.html

SSL is the first semi-standard for security on the Web. Developed by Netscape as a protocol that would work on the Web and other Internet services, SSL is built into all Netscape browsers and many servers, and allows you to speak securely to a server even if you've never been there before.

Key Challenge

http://home.netscape.com/newsref/std/key_challenge.html

The export version of SSL uses a weak algorithm and small keys, because that's all the U.S. government will allow (so far). This document is Netscape's very reasoned response to someone who broke one such message, explaining what the break means to consumers and to the cryptography world.

ALSO RECOMMENDED:

Archives of the www-security Mailing List

http://asearch.mccmedia.com/www-security.html

Lots of interesting discussion here about current problems and future solutions.

SSLeay

ftp://ftp.psy.uq.oz.au/pub/Crypto/SSL/

A free implementation of SSL that has almost no restrictions on it.

Electronic Commerce Standards Proposal

http://www.spyglass.com/six/developers_tech_doc2.html

An interesting view of how the Web can be made secure for financial transactions by one of the biggest marketers of Web browsers.

Assorted Web-Related Sites

Harvest Cache and Httpd-Accelerator

http://excalibur.usc.edu/

This is a popular cache system for sites that have many Harvest or Web users. It caches requests in a fairly intelligent fashion, and checks its cache entries when it seems right. They say it can speed up accesses by 10 times.

Yahoo!

GVU's WWW User Survey

http://www.cc.gatech.edu/gvu/
user_surveys/

An interesting poll conducted twice a year covering who uses the Web and why. Although fairly non-scientific (it gets its results from people who volunteer to respond, not a random sample of users), it generates more interesting data than other such surveys.

HTML Writers Guild

http://www.mindspring.com/guild/

An interesting group of folks who hope to improve the craft of writing HTML and help each other create nice Web pages. The group is informal and has both beginners and expert HTML craftpeople. If you have to create HTML all day, you should probably join.

A L S O   R E C O M M E N D E D:

Virtual Reality Center

http://www.newtype.com/NewType/
vr/index.htm

A good place to find out about VRML and other virtual reality add-ons for the Web.

These education sites are not just for educators, mind you. Plenty of opportunities abound for everyone, kids and adults, to learn about diverse topics such as butterfly migration, geometry, Egyptian art, and the laws of probability. In the '90s, it's becoming clear that as long as we're living, we have to keep learning.

One of the numerous great things about the Web is the fact that anyone can become a publisher. New voices for education reform are able to present their points of view to the world and foster interaction with fellow thinkers on this hot issue. In addition, individuals as well as institutions are experimenting with multimedia and interactivity in learning. And it's all right there for you to try, too.

Education

The Internet has deep roots in academia — remember that the first popular Web browser (Mosaic) was developed at the University of Illinois. So education is close to the heart of the Web. And the spirit of sharing information, so vital to Net culture, is found all over Yahoo!'s Education section.

Yahoo! is a terrific place to look for information about universities and schools of all kinds. Many schools have their own Web sites, offering in-depth information about their facilities and courses. The most interesting educational sites often are the elementary schools, where you can see students' own work posted online. There's also a good representation of schools and companies offering courses online, everything from customized electronic tutoring to hypertext independent study documents.

Teachers are a prime audience for the dozens of education sites offering resources on curriculum development. The ERIC (Educational Resources Information Center) database, supported by the Department of Education, is well represented in this area, and components of ERIC are hosted on a number of servers throughout the Web, mainly university and government servers. What better way to locate these resources than in this comprehensive education listing?

And ERIC is not the only resource for teachers. Dozens of sites are designed especially for teachers that point them to scholarly articles or journals or present complete curriculum units that can be instantly adapted to their class-rooms. NASA, for example, is one of the better-represented organizations in this field. Like ERIC, NASA has servers all over the Net, dedicated to different aspects of space education.

Adult Education

Need to brush up your Urdu? How about your Shakespeare? Always wanted to throw pots? Learning is a lifetime proposition, and continuing education programs in your field are out there on the Web available for you, no matter where you live. You can also learn online, teach online — even learn how to teach by going online.

Mindquest: Online High School Education for Adults

http://informns.k12.mn.us/~0271eis/mindquest/

Mindquest is an interactive program that allows busy adults to complete their high school education by interacting with teachers, counselors, and other students on the Internet.

National University

http://www.nu.edu/

Californians might want to check out National University. It operates academic centers all over the state, and offers a curriculum designed specifically for working adults.

Alternative

Education reform is in the air these days, and more families are looking for alternatives to standard public schooling. The Web not only contains information on alternative schooling, it even hosts some virtual schools.

The NETSchool

http://netschool.edu/

This site aims to be the first K-12 school on the Internet, where everyone learns, administers, teaches, and publishes. Message boards and chat areas allow maximum interaction.

Home Education Resources Center (HERC)

http://www.cts.com/~netsales/herc/

HERC is a valuable resource for home schoolers, or for parents wishing to enrich their child's educational life. HERC includes reading lists, links to other Net resources, and home-schooling regulations for all 50 states. And the monthly feature Science Fun from the Backyard Scientist is not to be missed: Hands-on experiments you can try with your kids at home. Not to mention the catalog of home schooling materials, conveniently arranged by subject.

Karl M. Bunday on Education Reform

http://www.bookport.com/welcome/bunday/rxs

Karl Bunday is a proponent of education reform who is very active in online discussions in several languages. His site includes reading lists on home schooling, language development, teaching of reading, and critiques of the educational system.

Alternative Colleges Network

http://hampshire.edu/html/cs/alt-colleges/Home.html

This site is a guide to what's going on at progressive college campuses and online colleges. Get more information via their mailing list discussions.

College Entrance

Applying for college is a nerve-wracking experience for students and their families, and online information can be a huge help.

Internet College Exchange

http://www.usmall.com/college/

Don't know where you want to go to college? Use the ICX Search utility to help narrow down your choice from more than 5000 institutions in the U.S. and its territories. This utility even calculates your tuition costs. ICX resources also show you how to

choose a school, how to apply, and how to pay for it. The bulletin board system is a forum for sharing information about school admissions. The Bookstore allows purchase of merchandise from popular schools, as well as books on college admissions and school ranking.

CollegeNet

http://www.collegenet.com/

Forms-based searching pinpoints undergraduate and graduate programs, and specialized lists provide links to Web servers at hundreds of institutions. Also includes links to databases and search engines on financial aid and scholarships.

Community Colleges

Like universities, community colleges are well represented on the Web. The assortment at Yahoo! is a good starting point to give you an idea of what community colleges offer.

Web U.S. Community Colleges

http://www.utexas.edu/world/comcol.html

This page contains links to central Web servers at more than 100 community colleges across the United States.

Companies

(See also the Business Directory chapter.)

Here you'll find pointers to a wide assortment of education-related products, from individual entrepreneurs to corporations.

EduNet

http://edunet.comcorp.com/

EduNet offers online registration to authorized Microsoft, Novell, and Lotus Education Centers, plus forums on technical education and instruction.

Mind Tools

http://www.demon.co.uk/mindtool/index.html

Mind Tools is a collection of shareware, articles, and tips on optimizing mental performance to help people define and achieve their dreams. An interactive questionnaire even helps define your learning style.

InfoVid

http://branch.com/infovid/infovid.html

Need to learn how to groom a horse, insulate your attic, or do the tango? InfoVid is a source for thousands of educational, instructional, and special-interest videos.

ALSO RECOMMENDED:

Allegro Information Services

http://catalog.com/allegro/

Another source for educational videos.

edu.net

http://www.execpc.com/~jlk/

edu.net is a company formed by professional educators with the mission of helping classrooms, schools, and districts establish e-mail, home pages, Web access, and more. The Site of the Week identifies an

Internet site valuable for educators and includes a lesson plan for teachers to use the site in class.

Four Winds

http://www.nicoh.com/fourwinds

Four Winds presents products and educational items created by Native Americans. Medicine pouches hold your most sacred objects; hand drums are used in rituals. Books and videos inform viewers on customs such as the Sundance and rituals such as sweat lodges. Four Winds can also send teachers, spiritual healers, and dance performers to your location for seminars.

IBM K-12 Education

http://www.solutions.ibm.com/k12/

The Teachers' Corner presents Internet curriculum activities for teachers to use in their classrooms. And by the way, IBM sells products for use in K-12 classrooms.

Knowledge Products

http://www.cassettes.com/

Knowledge Products produces spoken-word audiotapes narrated by well-known actors, journalists, and writers. Topics range from history of science through classics of philosophy, economics, and international politics. And best of all, you can order online.

Pitsco Guide to Technology Education

http://www.usa.net/~pitsco

Pitsco bills itself as a one-stop shop for educators, with links to education sites and descriptions of its top products for technology education.

Scholastic Central

http://www.scholastic.com/

Scholastic, the large educational publisher, presents an Internet Center with three electronic publications: *Electronic Learning,* for educators interested in using technology in schools; *Environmental Express,* with children's writing and artwork about the environment; and *PressReturn,* written by and for students, with a different theme each month. Plus other fun stuff.

Small Planet

http://www.smplanet.com/

Small Planet Communications develops materials for educators. Its home page contains articles, strategies, lesson plans links, and materials for teachers and students.

Talis

http://www.talis.com

The Talis site focuses on the mystical and metaphysical, with a downloadable multimedia demo of the I Ching and a daily Galactic Signature feature, which seems to have something to do with Mayan cosmology and offers a handle on how to handle the day.

SyllabusWeb

http://www.syllabus.com

The publishers of *Syllabus,* a magazine on using technology in the curriculum, present a Web site with searchable archives of the magazine as well as a newsletter about the Internet and the new frontier of Net technologies.

A L S O   R E C O M M E N D E D:

Peterson's Education Center

http://www.petersons.com

Web site for Peterson's, the well-known guidebooks publisher.

Courses

Many universities have started supplying course materials for individual classes on their Web sites. Although these are likely to be of interest only to the students in the classes, many available materials are suitable for independent study.

Project NatureConnect

http://pacificrim.net/~nature

This site tackles the problem of modern humanity's disconnection from nature. Articles about applied ecopsychology lay out the scope of the problem. Take a free class by e-mail to reconnect to nature, the source of wellness and spirit.

Distance Education via the Internet

http://www.dsu.edu/distance-ed/internet.html

The pioneers at Dakota State University are offering classes via the Internet. Courses include tech writing, programming, music composition, and artificial intelligence. Several articles give background on electronic education.

The Text Project

http://uu-gna.mit.edu:8001/uu-gna/text/index.html

This site aims to generate a collection of hypertext textbooks to teach subjects online. The Project already has a number of textbooks: learn about Greek myths, astronomy, or tech writing. Contributors are invited to help create new texts.

The World Lecture Hall

http://www.utexas.edu/world/lecture/

An index to all kinds of home pages relating to courses. Many of them are just supplements to standard classroom courses but often contain glossaries and bibliographies that can be useful.

A L S O   R E C O M M E N D E D:

Accounting on the Internet

http://www.csun.edu/~vcact00g/acct.html

A complete introductory accounting course.

General Psychology Course

http://www.indiana.edu/~iuepsyc/P103Psyc.html

Indiana University offers this introductory class online. A textbook is required, but assignments and evaluations are given over the Net.

Databases

ERIC is a household name in the education field. It stands for Educational Resources Information Center, is supported by the U.S. Department of Education, and is the world's largest educational database. Parts of ERIC are located on servers all around the Net.

ASKEric Home Page

http://ericir.syr.edu/

This site offers pointers to all the components of the ERIC clearinghouse. These include a section of resources on civic education, results of annual surveys on the use of technology in schools, and hotlinks to useful education-related Web sites of all types.

ERIC Clearinghouse on Reading, English and Communication

http://www.indiana.edu/~eric_rec/

Here you'll find reviews of books for parents, teachers, and administrators; lists of bilingual materials; and resources on teaching values and critical thinking. This site also contains a Web Demo with a linked tour to representative and interesting sites around the Net.

ALSO RECOMMENDED:

TASL - Training and Seminar Locators

http://tasl.com/tasl/home.html

Are you a business person needing training? Search this database by topic to find the help you need.

Educational Standards and Testing

Kaplan Educational Centers

http://www.kaplan.com

Kaplan prepares students to take tests such as the SAT and the GRE. Kaplan Online is full of informative areas about the contents of the various tests. There is also a free software download area, with programs that provide practice in typical testing techniques.

The Princeton Review

http://www.review.com

Another major test prep firm offers information about grad schools and financial aid.

Educational Testing Service

http://hub.terc.edu/ra/ets.html

The company that gives the tests the others prepare you for. Here you'll find handy schedules for upcoming test dates for the SAT, the GMAT, the GRE, and TOEFL (Test of English as a Foreign Language).

Environmental Education

Everybody *wants* a better environment. Here are the people who are *doing* something about it, from scientists posting abstracts of their experiments to grass-roots activists.

The Wild Ones

http://www.cc.columbia.edu:80/cu/cerc/WildOnes/

This international club allows kids to participate in environmental projects by posting their reports on local conditions. *Zoo News* gives updates and pictures of events at the Jersey Zoo on the English Channel Island. A contact page allows members to contact scientists working in the field.

The Environmental Education Network

http://envirolink.org/enviroed/

Sponsored by the H.J. Heinz School of Public Policy and Management, the EEN is aiming to be the clearinghouse for all environmental materials and resources on the Internet. It currently features extensive hotlists to interesting, environmentally related sites all over the world.

Financial Aid

With education always under the budget-cutters' axes, the subject of financial aid only becomes more and more important. The cost of a college education can be staggering these days, and students need to plan carefully. Fortunately, a variety of resources are available for searching on the Web.

The Student Guide to Financial Aid

http://www.ed.gov/prog_info/SFA/StudentGuide/

More than 80 percent of student aid comes from federal programs. Here's the guide to applying for these programs and good advice on looking for aid elsewhere. Straight from the U.S. Department of Education.

Financial Aid Information

http://www.cs.cmu.edu/afs/cs/user/mkant/Public/FinAid/finaid.html

This page provides links to dozens of sources of information on obtaining financial aid. It also features fastWEB, Financial Aid Search Through the Web, at no cost. This searchable database contains information on more the 180,000 private sector grants, loans, and scholarships. Try out the financial aid estimation form, which performs an instant need analysis that will give you a general idea of your ability to pay for college.

A L S O   R E C O M M E N D E D:

Minority Scholarships and Fellowships

http://web.fie.com/htbin/cashe.pl

A searchable index helps find cash. A number of private companies promise to help students get cash grants, loans or fellowship, for a research fee. Most require you to mail or e-mail an application.

(Also see Business and Economy: Companies: Education: Financial Aid.)

General Information

Educom

http://www.educom.edu/

Educom is a consortium of colleges and universities that want to transform education through the use of information technology. What's neat about this site is that its bimonthly magazine, *Educom Review,* is archived and available for free. Also, the Edupage, updated three times a week, offers news items on information technology — and is also free on the site.

Engines for Education

http://www.ils.nwu.edu/~e_for_e/

This is a hyperbook created to explore what's wrong with the education system and how to reform it. You can browse through a tour if you like. For example, in the hyperbook, you'll find out why some schools fail to teach, why science is boring when it should be thrilling, and what the top ten mistakes are in education. You can also read Mike Royko's thoughts on cultural awareness.

One World Resource

http://www.nav.com/OWR/oneworld.html

This is a free service that attempts to list all university sites on the planet into an easy-to-use list. It includes hotlinks to the actual sites of these universities. These folks have their heart in the right place.

Government

Most of the government sites seem to be home pages for state departments of education, giving information about what the particular departments are doing and what your tax dollars are accomplishing.

Federal Information Exchange

http://www.fie.com/

FIE aims to be the cyberlink between government and education. In here, you'll find links to government agencies that provide opportunities and activities for education. There's a searchable database to locate programs in any of the many agencies. For example, a search for the word *fossil* yields 39 sites on fossil fuels.

U.S. Department of Education

http://www.ed.gov/

Everything you could possibly want to know about what the U.S. government is doing about education. The department publishes several newsletters that you can receive online or by e-mail, such as *The Community Update,* a monthly letter for parents and educators involved in improving schools. Congressional testimony from the department also is

available. A large collection of documents tells what the department has in store for technology education, as well as giving the party line on the controversial Goals 2000 document.

Grants

Yes, free money! Billions and billions of dollars await the savvy researcher. As if you needed extra incentive to surf the Web. Seek in this section and ye shall find $$$.

Research Funding Opportunities and Administration (TRAM)

http://tram.rice.edu/TRAM/

This contains a library of electronic forms for various government grant-giving agencies, as well as a compendium of federal regulations on government grants. Furthermore, there is a page of links to foundations and other funding sources that you can use in your search for a grant.

National Endowment for the Humanities

http://neh.fed.us

This is the agency that makes grants for projects in history, languages, philosophy, and the humanities. One caveat: This site may be defunct by the time you read this if the Republican Congress succeeds in dismantling the agency.

Yahoo!

The White House Fellows Program

http://www.whitehouse.gov/White_House/WH_Fellows/html/fellows1.html

Hang out with Socks! Order pizza for George Stephanopoulos! But seriously, this site has everything you need to know to become a White House fellow. What is a White House fellow? One of around 20 highly motivated and talented young people appointed to observe the challenging tasks of American government, that's what. In other words, a few smart young people every year get to work in the White House. If you'd like to be one of them, check out this site.

Guidance

Ah, memories of the guidance counselor. Anxiety over a steel gray desk. The aroma of tattered college catalogs. Helping students achieve their ultimate dreams.

The Ideas of a University

http://quarles.unbc.edu/ideas/

This is a multimedia guide to understanding how to make the most of the university experience, no matter which university. Interviews with professors may help students clarify their own goals as the profs explain how they chose their fields and how their disciplines relate to the real world. Further, it gives concrete information on what to expect in the course of studying various disciplines. There's also a hyperdocument on the history of the idea of the university (hint: it started with the Greeks).

Higher Education

The Apple Virtual Campus

http://www.info.apple.com/hed/home.html

Not surprisingly, much of this site boils down to a big ad for the Macintosh, but you'll also find useful sections full of articles on learning technologies and distance learning. Plus links to sites that elaborate on those topics. And because it's Apple, of course, the site is very easy on the eyes.

Internet Resources Newsletter

http://www.hw.ac.uk/libWWW/irn/irn.html

This is aimed at the higher education crowd, but it has news and interesting commentary about the Internet. Presented in its entirety online.

Institutes

This section zeroes in on specialized institutes, some of them independent, others associated with universities and colleges.

The University of Oregon College of Education

http://Interact.uoregon.edu/

This site contains the Media Literacy Online Project, which is a database and gateway to hundreds of Internet sites related to film, TV, magazines, and multimedia of interest to those studying media literacy. Something for everyone: for example, a section on children and online activities and a section on reference tools available on the Internet (such as a dictionary of computing terms and a global currency converter).

The Institute for Study of Distributed Work

http://www.dnai.com/~isdw/

Just think. Instead of cruising cyberspace in your *spare* time, you could be on your computer all day, every day. This site studies the emergence of electronically distributed global workplace (aka telecommuting).

Instructional Technology and Training

Empowering People

http://intele.net/~empower/

Empowering People is a company that wants to share its knowledge about classroom management and parent-child communications. Articles are posted on such topics as bus behavior, stopping the war between parents and children, and parenting tips from A to Z. There's also an opportunity to ask the expert, Dr. Nelsen, individual questions about problem children.

ExCITE

http://www.excite.sfu.ca/

This is a very well-done site by the Exemplary Center for Interactive Technologies in Education, of Canada's Simon Fraser University. It's a demonstration site for educational multimedia. Explore the ocean floor with a safari touch tank. Click on the starfish and get a description, or view an animation. *Science, eh?* is an online, interactive magazine. All are invited to participate in discussions and real-time conferences. There are also hyperlinks to other exciting science sites on the Web. Get kids motivated with the Young Scientists Clubhouse. Kids can submit multimedia files to the online magazine. All in all, a wonderful site for getting kids involved in science.

Using Technology in Education

http://www.algonquinc.on.ca/edtech/index.html

A handy hotlist from Algonquin College of targeted hyperlinks for educators who want to use technologies such as multimedia and distance learning. For those who need to get educated about how to educate about the Web, this site points the way.

Interest Groups

This is a collection of sites devoted to special topics in education, from teaching Arabic to curriculum development to promotion of education in rural China.

The Educational Technology Review Center

http://www.cacs.usl.edu/Departments/ETRC/

A clearinghouse for information on technology and the curriculum. Read the online journal for articles on topics such as multicultural multimedia, interactive language software, and ubiquitous computing.

Educational Technology Review Center

The George Lucas Educational Foundation

http://glef.org

From the creator of *Star Wars* (or his foundation, anyway) comes *Edutopia*, a twice-yearly newsletter on integrating technology with learning.

The Gorbachev Foundation

http://www.clark.net/pub/gorbachev/home.html

The Gorbachev Foundation USA addresses nothing less than the crises of the post-Cold War world. Keep up on Gorby, his foundation, and his State of the World Forum.

Journals

Oskar's

http://www.oskars.de

Send your teenager to Germany! *Oskar's* is "The American-German Student Magazine," with both English and German sections, and is devoted to encouraging prospective exchange students, in the interest of encouraging international friendship and understanding. Oskar's is based on a print magazine distributed in Germany and the U.S., and supported by government ministries and cultural institutes. The magazine includes articles on what it's like to go to a German school, a guide to living and learning in Germany, and a quiz designed to predict a student's compatibility with exchange life.

Chreods

http://s13a.math.aca.mmu.ac.uk/

And now for something more abstruse. *Chreods* is a journal exploring math education. It uses terms like *psychosemiotic* and *transference,* but it also gives sketches of hands-on experience teaching children math concepts. Journal issues from recent years are presented in their entirety.

Chreods

Educational Policy and Analysis

http://info.asu.edu/asu-cwis/epaa/welcome.html

EPAA is a scholarly journal published only electronically. It features articles on such topics as the coordination of school and family, anti-intellectualism in schools, and the irrelevance of much educational research to the teacher's experience. Good luck.

The Journal of Technology Education

http://scholar.lib.vt.edu/ejournals/JITE/jite.html

The *Journal for Industrial Teacher Education* is available here (full text) for those who want to know about vocational education issues. There's also a journal for teaching teachers on this topic.

K-12

In case you aren't aware, K-12 means Kindergarten through 12th grade. That pretty much covers it.

Academy One

http://www.nptn.org/cyber.serv/AOneP/

Academy One is a virtual school that has a wealth of activities for involving both students and teachers online. Students can participate in online projects, post their work, get information on medical and social issues, write to "keypals," and look up reference information. There is even an online tennis college.

Quest: NASA K-12 Internet Initiative

http://quest.arc.nasa.gov/

Quest is supported by NASA. It puts students in touch with NASA scientists and lets them participate in online interactive projects. Other resources help teachers apply for grants, and

find the large number of educational resources that NASA places on the Internet. How about that Space Colony Design Contest or the JPL archive for teachers!

AskERIC

http://ericir.syr.edu/

Here's another component of the ERIC system, supported by the U.S. Department of Education. This time, it's a virtual library with lesson plans, archives, and a searchable database.

Building Blocks to Reading

http://www.NeoSoft.com/~jrpotter/karen.html

Here's some fun activities and ideas for boosting kids' reading readiness. This simple page offers activities, tips, and word search puzzles ready for printing out.

Cisco Educational Archive

http://sunsite.unc.edu/cisco/edu-arch.html

"Educators helping educators" is the tagline here. A searchable archive provides thousands of articles and links on all facets of education. The Virtual Schoolhouse, a metalibrary of K-12 Internet links, has pointers to software archives, teaching resources, museums and online exhibits. Sponsored by Cisco Corporation.

Classroom Connect

http://www.wentworth.com/classroom/

A well-designed image map is the front door to this site, which offers comprehensive resources for educational Internet products. Read sample articles about online activities from K-12 from *Classroom Connect* newsletter.

CNIDR

http://k12.cnidr.org

The Center for Networked Information Discovery and Retrieval hosts several Web servers offering information and activities related to education. See EdWeb, cosponsored by the Corporation for Public Broadcasting, exploring the worlds of educational reform and information technology. Or ArtsEdge, which offers the newsletter *Technology for Learning*.

Microsoft Focus on K-12

http://www.microsoft.com/K-12/

This site rounds up all of Microsoft's educational products, whether for use in the classroom or at home. The Resources section offers activities for parents and children (using Microsoft products, of course), and there are case studies of schools' technology solutions.

ALSO RECOMMENDED:

CTDNet Gallery

http://ctdnet.acns.nwu.edu/supp/creative.html

Here's a gallery of music, art, writings, and video created by talented students for your viewing pleasure.

Educational Software Institute

http://www.bonsai.com/q/edsoftcat/htdocs/esihome.html

ESI Online hosts a large collection of K-12 educational software titles. Search this site for the program you need and order online if you like.

Scottie Cybernews

http://199.79.172.24/pub/scottiecn.html

Elementary school students in Austin, Texas, offer this experiment showcasing their experimentations with Web publishing. For example: Miss Martin's first-grade class home page has contributions from 14 students on the history of Texas, with original artwork of the state map and the flag. Great job, kids!

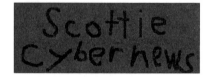

Explorer

http://unite2.tisl.ukans.edu/

Explorer is a database of educational resources for K-12, such as instructional software, lab activities, and lesson plans. Search for what you need or toss the dice with "EduLette" for a random approach.

Destination Everywhere, or The Fuzzy Logic Home Page

http://www.digi-net.com/Fuzzy/Home.html

Follow the story of Mr. Fuzzy Logic as he careens through adventures in space and around the world. The story includes side trips via hotlinks to sites on Mayan astronomy and the search for extraterrestrials.

Geometry Forum

http://forum.swarthmore.edu/

For geometry lovers. Highlights of the forum: Ask Dr. Math, Problem of the Week, MathMagic problem-solving, searchable resources archives, software, and forums discussing recent research.

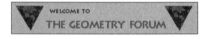

The Weather Unit

http://faldo.atmos.uiuc.edu/WEATHER/weather.html

Here's a complete guide to teaching a weather curriculum to elementary students. Activities relate to all classroom disciplines, and include advice on classroom props and field trips.

Gifted and Talented Resources Home Page

http://www.eskimo.com/~user/kids.html

Here's the place to find out all about special programs for gifted kids, such as summer programs, distance learning, early entrance programs, and scholarships. Other resources listed are publications and organizations, schools with programs for talented students, and a listing of mail order catalogs of special interest.

ALSO RECOMMENDED:

TAG Family Network

http://www.teleport.com/~rkaltwas/tag/

Articles give practical advice for families of talented and gifted students on dealing with schools, teachers, and curriculum issues.

Global SchoolNet Foundation

http://gsn.org

GSN supports educational networking on the Internet and in the classroom, and created the concept of the Global Schoolhouse, where students work together online. There are opportunities for interaction with scientists and researchers in astronomy or geology, and cooperative games and puzzles. Students write articles and post them in the Newsday section.

GNN Education Center

http://gnn.com/gnn/meta/edu/index.html

A resource that provides educators with teaching tools and connections to their peers. Groups are formed to develop curriculum units online, articles discuss the value of networking in education, and links lead to relevant internet projects. Post an ad in the teacher classifieds to find collaborators. Keep track of events with the calendar.

Cyber High School

http://www.webcom.com/~cyberhi/

Through this high school operating completely on the Internet, students can work independently to prepare for college. Lessons and tests are delivered by e-mail or online in real time, and students get the chance to interact in online class discussions or via mailing lists. They also work together on projects via e-mail. There is no virtual prom or online homecoming game. Yet.

Cyberspace Middle School

http://www.scri.fsu.edu/~dennisl/CMS.html

Not a complete middle school online but designed to intrigue middle school-age students. The bimonthly electronic magazine, *MidLink*, is open to participation by readers.

Reinventing Schools: The Technology is Now

http://www.nas.edu/nap/online/techgap/welcome.html

Well-designed site sponsored by the National Academy of Sciences, addressing issues of technology in children's lives and in schools. Beyond the hoopla of computers and networks, what technology is appropriate for children's education?

ALSO RECOMMENDED:

TeacherTalk

http://www.mightymedia.com/talk/working.htm

Here's a conferencing system for K-12 educators. Share ideas or simply get to know new people.

Vocal Point

http://bvsd.k12.co.us/cent/Newspaper/Newspaper.html

This is a fine example of a school paper online, produced by students at the Centennial Middle School in Boulder, Colorado. Each monthly issue has a theme.

The Renaissance Online

http://www.scsn.net/biz/dfork/

Another good school newspaper, from Dutch Fork, South Carolina.

SLUMMIT Home Page

http://spider.netropolis.net/slummit/

Literary magazine, by and for teachers and students. Material may be browsed or downloaded.

Web 66

http://web66.coled.umn.edu

A project aimed at creating a nationwide infobahn for K-12 schools.

Busy Teacher's Website, K-12

http://www.gatech.edu/lcc/idt/Students/Cole/Proj/K-12/TOC.html

An illustrated list of pointers to resources, organized by subject area.

Languages

This is a good area to find out where to study languages and where to learn how to teach languages. Not only are schools listed, but so are private companies offering language instruction. Plenty of links to English as a Second Language resources as well.

The Pen Pals Page

http://www.xs4all.nl:80/~jwbos/floris/ppe.htm

Here you can place a request for a penpal/keypal. Using a form, you place your personal information on the page. Then wait by the e-mailbox for the letters to flood in from all over the world!

Libraries

The Library of Congress

http://www.loc.gov/

The Library of Congess is the biggest and grandest of all contemporary libraries, and it operates a huge and interesting site. It really should be

called The Library of the United States. One of the archival sections presents Civil War photographs, thumbnail sized with descriptions, which can be blown up to full size with a click. Incredibly detailed, fascinating photos. Another section, THOMAS, allows access to up-to-date information on what Congress is up to. The exhibits section gives access to the documents and images on current display at the library.

Math and Science Education

AIMS Education Foundation

http://204.161.33.100/

AIMS stands for Activities Integrating Math and Science, and that's just what this site offers for teachers around the world. Discussion areas allow interaction, a Puzzle of the Month tests the brain, and a library of downloadable files makes available its database of activities.

Computer as Learning Partner

http://www.clp.berkeley.edu/CLP.html

Researchers at the University of California at Berkeley have spent years working with experts in education, science, and technology to develop a semester-long middle-school curriculum on thermodynamics, light, and sound. The site describes their conceptual framework as well as presents the curriculum and research papers to back up the theories.

Bugs in the News

http://falcon.cc.ukans.edu/~jbrown/bugs.html

A series of articles about bacteria, viruses, genes, and other microscopic doohickeys that affect health is presented out of the Internet spirit of the free sharing of information. There are pictures of biological molecules and recent updates from the CDC and WHO.

The Franklin Institute Science Museum

http://sln.fi.edu/

As in *Ben* Franklin, formerly of Philadelphia. The Franklin Institute brings exhibits and resources from the museum to the desktop with online exhibits and a publications library. It also provides curriculum units on science topics for use in schools. Very well-organized and well-executed site.

The Exploratorium Learning Studio

http://isaac.exploratorium.edu/learning_studio/

The famous "hands-on" science museum brings its unique approach to exhibits online. Multimedia files illustrate and demonstrate the process of scientific inquiry. Plus, they make cool sounds. *The Science Snackbook* explains how to build your own versions of experiments at home.

Monarch Watch

http://129.237.246.134

Monarch butterflies are beautiful and mysterious, and this site invites students and adults to cooperate in studying migration patterns. Working together around the world, volunteers can identify threats to the monarch and promote conservation.

NASA Aerospace Education Services Program

http://www.okstate.edu/aesp/AESP.html

A free program for teachers, students, and the general public to increase understanding of science and technology. Put in a request by e-mail, and a professional educator will give a lecture-demonstration at your school. Also, hotlinks to related NASA education sites.

ALSO RECOMMENDED:

Science on the Web

http://www.cs.brown.edu/people/art035/Bin/science.html

If your browser has the right multimedia extensions, you can see animations of DNA, closeups of skeletons, and virtual-reality human cells.

Math Teaching Assistant

http://www.csun.edu/~vcact00g/math.html

Teachers can download shareware for math learning at all levels.

News

Chronicle of Higher Education

http://www.chronicle.merit.edu/

A summary of the highlights of this weekly publication, with additional special sections. Includes a searchable jobs listing.

On-line Teaching and Learning

With the interactive and multimedia innovations offered by the Web, education at a distance can become much more rich and meaningful. No more waiting at the mailbox for the next installment of the correspondence course! Check the extensive listings in this section for your area of interest.

National Teachers Enhancement Network

http://www.montana.edu/~wwwxs/

Graduate-level courses for teachers in science and math, taught by university scientists, offered online. Teachers can participate by dial-up modem or by Internet access.

CyberEd at UMass Dartmouth

http://www.umassd.edu/cybered/distlearninghome.html

A branch of the University of Massachusetts is currently offering college classes that can be completed online. Most materials are presented online, but it may be necessary to purchase textbooks. Tuition per credit is reasonable, and on-campus fees are waived.

Hewlett-Packard E-mail Mentor Program

http://mentor.external.hp.com/

HP is sponsoring this program to match up employees with 5th – 12th grade students, or K-12 teachers. The goals are to motivate students to pursue their interests, assist students and teachers in locating information on the Internet, and to encourage students to take responsibility for their education. The site contains full instructions on how to participate.

KIDLINK

http://www.kidlink.org/

KIDLINK runs this project to get children 10 – 15 years old involved in online dialogs with other kids around the world. Participants introduce themselves, and then are free to take part in "Cafe" discussions in a number of languages.

The Chance Database

http://www.geom.umn.edu/docs/ snell/chance/welcome.html

A group of universities has gotten together to create a quantitative literacy course that uses probability and statistics items as reported in newspapers and magazines. Suitable for self-study or use in a classroom.

A L S O   R E C O M M E N D E D:

The Learning Path

http://www.biddeford.com:80/ learningpath

Private tutoring and advice via the Internet.

Spectrum Virtual University

http://horizons.org/campus/

Low-cost classes via the Internet.

Ultimate Children's Internet Sites

http://www.vividus.com/ucis.html

A list of links to sites that are fun and educational for children, from preschool to teenagers.

Programs

In this section, specific programs offered by schools and university groups are described. There are also sites and programs that anyone anywhere can participate in.

Fishnet

http://www.jayi.com

This cool site for students is like an electronic magazine, with tons of articles on topics such as "Money for College," "Tunes for the Brain," "Stop the Violence," and "The Amazing Folding Boat." Full of fun facts and features relevant to teens. The site includes monitored discussion boards and links to other education sites.

The ITTI Gravigs Project

http://info.mcc.ac.uk/CGU/ITTI/ gravigs.html

This group is developing training materials on computer graphics and visualization, consisting of handouts, workbooks, visual aids, demonstration programs, and sample code. The stuff is available free from the Web site, and bound, printed versions are available for purchase, with discounts for universities.

National Registration Center for Study Abroad

http://www.execpc.com/~nrcsa/

Here's where to find out about foreign language centers around the world, the best programs for foreign visitors of all ages, and how to get information about the region you'd like to study in. NRCSA keeps track of thousands of programs and selects the best. Preregistration is by e-mail or fax, and interested students can receive updates by e-mail.

Youth for Understanding

http://csbh.mhv.net/~yfu/ welcome.html

This private, nonprofit organization promotes international understanding by arranging exchange programs for high school students. Its site offers information on being an exchange student, hosting a student, and what it's like to study in different countries. A Q&A form allows the user to ask questions that will be answered by former students or host families.

Social Studies

Social Studies Sources

http://www.halcyon.com/howlevin/ social.studies

This index-style site provides links to Web resources on history, government, geography, current events, and social studies education. Extremely handy for teachers or parents, or anyone interested in this broad subject area.

ALSO RECOMMENDED:

Institute of Egyptian Art and Archaeology

http://www.memst.edu/egypt/main.html

Includes a tour of the artifacts residing at the Institute and a color tour of Egypt.

The Age of Enlightenment

http://dmf.culture.fr/files/imaginary_exhibition.html/

This site combines historical background on France with a tour of French painting in French national museums.

Special Education

University of Kansas Department of Special Education

http://www.sped.ukans.edu/welcome

Although most of this site is directly concerned with the university's program, there is a good section on Internet Resources on Disabilities. This list of lists contains scads of starting points to research topics relating to disabilities and education.

ALSO RECOMMENDED:

Deaf Resources

http://darwin.clas.virginia.edu/~tms4s/deaf.html

A brief collection of links to resources for and about the deaf.

Teaching

Educational Resources for Teachers

http://www.educ.kent.edu/ed/teachers/teachers.html

A usable guide, an index to other indexes that points to resources on teacher training, specialized topics, and instructional materials. A good place to start.

ALSO RECOMMENDED:

ConnectEd

http://www.mindspring.com/~fordp/pasha/

A resource for English teachers to find literature and tools and ideas on the Web.

Television

Discovery Channel Online

http://www.discovery.com/

This place is great! Well designed, with a good concept. Just as it promises up front, there are originally produced interactive stories with film, music, photography, and illustration. It works more like a CD-ROM than a typical Web site. The coolest thing is the Knapsack, which promises to be a personal researcher. It goes out and searches the Web for everything that matches your interest … *even when you're not online.* It even sends you an e-mail later to let you know when it's found something. A must see.

Universities

http://www.yahoo.com/Education/Universities/

The end of the baby boom has caused a crunch in the higher ed biz, and a lot of those colleges and universities have latched onto the Net as a new way to hawk their hallowed halls to the dwindling pool of students.

From Argentina to Zambia, check out the home pages of more than 1,000 universities in 65 countries throughout the world. Great for somebody checking into where to go to school. Find out all you need to know: admissions info, how to apply, campus maps, costs, computing resources, sports facilities, even academics! Also a great way to track down alumni.

For an example of a good college site, not surprisingly, check out Marc Andreessen's alma mater: the University of Illinois at Urbana/Champaign (http://www.uiuc.edu/), if for no other reason than to see the photo at the top of the home page, which changes with the local weather.

If you have a souped-up machine, the University of Massachusetts at Amherst (http://home.oit.umass.edu/) offers a multimedia tour of the campus.

U.S. Universities

Yahoo! - U.S. Universities

http://www.yahoo.com/Education/
Universities/United_States/

This is an extensive list of U.S. universities indexed by state (there's a clickable alphanumeric index for those whose first semester courseload includes remedial reading).

Vocational Colleges

A brief, handy guide to various vocational institutions, mostly in the United States.

French Culinary Institute

http://plaza.interport.net/fci/

Hungry? Check out the French Culinary Institute's recipe of the month. Mmmm.

Indices

Distance Learning List

http://www.dacc.cc.il.us/~ramage/
disted.html

Distance learning may include taking classes by satellite, by videoconferencing, by mail, or by e-mail. It may involve occasional trips to a campus or complete independent learning. Check out the multitude of opportunities.

NASA Educational Resources

http://www.nas.nasa.gov/HPCC/K12/
edures.html

A complete guide to educational resources, on NASA's servers and elsewhere.

The amazing diversity catalogued in Yahoo!'s Entertainment section illustrates perfectly the constant, cultural clash that is the Web. You can enjoy (or not) the in-your-face bravado of the punk music pages and, with just a click or two, suddenly experience the profoundly moving prose of a new author or poet. Then, with just one more click, you can catch up with Madonna or the latest celebrity scandal.

Now, *that's* entertainment.

Advice

From advice to the lovelorn to oracular pronouncements, there's someone on the Web who wants to help you make the most of your life. Just remember that the advice you get on the Internet is pretty much worth what you paid to get it.

$tarving $hirley's $avings

http://www.mindspring.com/ ~kmims/ss.html

$tarving $hirley provides penny-pinching pointers for parsimonious people. $hirley's tips range from saving money on food to recycling clothes for fun and profit.

EZ-Survival Guide

http://www.woodradio.com/ guide.html

Every morning, EZ-105.7 FM in Grand Rapids, Michigan, broadcasts five bite-sized tips for survival in the modern world — some thoughtful, some mundane, all useful. Two recent examples: "Five Tactics When Your Spouse Always Interrupts" and " Five Tips to Save Big Bucks on Airlines."

Entertainment

In this section you'll find some of the most interesting places on the entire World Wide Web. Also some of the most numbingly self-indulgent. So it's fair to say that under Entertainment lurks the best and worst the Web has to offer. Sometimes they're even on the same site.

You can be sure that pretty much no matter what you find entertaining — from gossip to travel, books to food, comics to contests, radio to roller coasters — somebody has already set up some Web pages devoted to your interests.

If you love music, then this *really* is the place you've been looking for. Artists, composers, instruments, even marching bands — they all have a spot here. There are probably more sites than you can ever see. Major artists usually have an official site, plus many Web pages put up by fans. But it's even better to browse through and find an artist that you've never heard of, download a sample of their work, and discover worthwhile new music. Several Web music archives are devoted to new, unsigned artists from virtually every musical genre. Because virtually any band can put up a music page, it's rather like panning for gold: You're likely to reject a lot of artists before you find some that shine.

Many of the most experimental pages on the Web are devoted to music, film, and especially online magazines (called *e-zines,* or just *zines*). Pay special attention to the Cool Links section; those sites are the ones creating the buzz, the ones that make the Web a new medium worth exploring.

Go Ask Alice!

http://www.columbia.edu/cu/healthwise/

The counselors and medical professionals at the Health Education and Wellness program of Columbia University Health Service provide well-written, serious answers to your questions about health, sex, and psychology. The site maintains a good selection of archived questions that give up-to-date info on many health-related subjects.

ALSO RECOMMENDED:

Magic 8-ball

http://www.resort.com/~banshee/Misc/8ball/index.html

Is a Web version of a childhood toy fun and useful or a complete waste of bandwidth? Reply hazy — ask again later.

Regarding Sex - Ask the Expert: Kim Martyn

http://www.interlog.com/~peer/ate.html

Sexual health expert (and apparently unshockable) Kim Martyn candidly answers questions about human sexuality and relationships. Ms. Martyn recently assured one reader that his sex fantasies about Amazon cannibal women were just fine. Um, *OK*.

Usenet - Miss Manners

news:clari.feature.miss_manners

Netiquette, schmetiquette. Miss Manners gives you the lowdown on preventing rudeness in the *real* world.

Amusement/Theme Parks

Every summer, hordes of people troop out to the amusement parks of America, looking for fun, thrills, and various forms of cuisine-on-a-stick. They usually return happy, exhausted, and with sticky fingers from all that cotton candy. And broke. That's OK; they'll be back for more next year.

Walt Disney World Home Page

http://www.travelweb.com/thisco/wdw/wdwhome/wdw.html

Hey! We're goin' to Disney World! The official WDW site gives you the lowdown on virtually every aspect of the "Jewel of Orlando." Ticket prices (make sure you're sitting down), lodging, transportation, plus lots of information about the three park areas: Magic Kingdom, EPCOT, and Disney/MGM Studios.

World of Coasters

http://tmb.extern.ucsd.edu/woc/

Everything you always wanted to know about roller coasters. And probably lots of stuff you never even thought of. Tip: For extra realism, raise your arms and scream as this page loads in your Web browser.

ALSO RECOMMENDED:

Coney Island Circus Sideshow

http://dockmaster.phantom.com/coney/pages/sideshow.html

Freaks, Wonders, and Human Curiosities. They're still performing for you on the Coney Island Boardwalk. The last authentic Circus Sideshow

promises to show you astonishments such as Electra, The High Voltage Lady; Demonica, The Snake Enchantress; and of course Kiva, The Fire Eater and Human Volcano. Step right up! The Freaks are waiting for you! (Note: If you're considering a career change, the purveyors of this page are always looking for new and unusual performers.)

Audio-Visual Equipment

If your idea of nirvana involves the dulcet sounds of Nirvana, then you'll find all of the equipment you need for pure fidelity right here. Links point you to the best-sounding recordings in virtually all genres. Videophiles are well served, too: numerous pages are devoted to laserdiscs, movies, satellite dishes, and the best in video gear.

Lucasfilm's THX Home Page

http://www.thx.com/thx/thx.html

Learn everything about how to create earth-shaking sound in your living room (and how to really annoy your neighbors) with Lucasfilm's home theatre sound system. Complete information about THX for the home, including where to get it and how to set it up.

Secrets of Home Theater & High Fidelity Magazine

http://www.sdinfo.com/

This site calls itself "A Scholarly Journal Dedicated to the Enjoyment of Audio and Video Experiences," and it lives up to its billing. You'll find interesting equipment and technology reviews, skewed toward the serious audiophile and videophile.

Books

Books Online

Ahh, there's nothing like the feel of a book in your hands, right? The heft, the smell, the feel of the pages under your fingers. The Internet has loads of electronic pages devoted to the love of paper pages. Plus, although your neck may start to hurt before too long, you can access the full text of thousands of books online (due to those pesky copyright laws, these selections are mostly classics that are in the public domain).

Banned Books On-line

http://www.cs.cmu.edu/Web/People/spok/banned-books.html

Strike up the banned! Here's a compendium of books available on the Internet that have been banned by bluenoses around the world, including Joyce's *Ulysses* and Voltaire's *Candide*. This site is a subset of the On-line Books Page.

The Great Books of Western Civilization

http://roger.vet.uga.edu/~lnoles/grtbks.html

Routinely derided in the '90s as the work of "a bunch of dead white guys," the books here (usually with links to the full text) are nevertheless the works of the seminal thinkers of Western civilization. Writers such as Euripides, Descartes, Keats, Dickens, Shakespeare, and Whitman. Where else will you find a compendium of 2,500 years of deep thoughts?

The On-line Books Page

http://www.cs.cmu.edu/Web/books.html

Thousands of books are already available on the Internet with more coming every day, and this page points you to them. Full searching capabilities and good pointers to other book resources make this site an indispensable resource.

Project Gutenberg Home Page

http://jg.cso.uiuc.edu/PG/welcome.html

Project Gutenberg is perhaps the oldest of the many efforts to put public-domain books and literature on the Internet. Now publishing 16 new electronic texts every month, the project's goal is to have 10,000 titles available by the year 2001.

PROJECT GUTENBERG
"Fine Literature Digitally Re-Published" ©

The Bob Book

http://www.gigaplex.com/wow/books/bob/index.htm

Chances are, if you know somebody named Bob, he's just a swell fellow. For some reason, that's what Bobs are, and *The Bob Book* is a celebration of the ultimate OK guy. Famous Bobs in fact and fiction get their due, along with a look at such fascinating topics as "What is Bobness?" and a scintillating look at "Bob's Weekend."

Mysteries

The Mystery Zone

http://www.mindspring.com/~walter/mystzone.html

When I woke up I was slumped over my keyboard. My head felt like it was filled with a team of hyperactive midgets. Mean ones, and they wanted out. What had happened? I squinted at my computer's screen through bloodshot eyes, and there was the culprit. I'd been knocked out by a mystery site that packed all the wallop of a cheap palooka with a taste for brass knuckles. The first punch was mystery news and fiction excerpts; the followup was a fistful of reviews. But it was the bleeding bullet hole graphics that had finished me off. I pulled my hat down over my eyes, and moved on into the foggy night.

The Mysterious Homepage

http://www.db.dk/dbaa/jbs/homepage.htm

If you love a mystery, you'll find lots of good pointers here to mystery fiction and related resources on the Internet. It's an excellent jumping-off place when "the game's afoot!"

ALSO RECOMMENDED:

The Elements of Style

http://www.cc.columbia.edu/acis/bartleby/strunk/

The definitive, pithy guide to written English style, in a well-done hypertext format. "Omit needless words! Omit needless words!" Listed here in the hope that more Usenet posters will read it one day.

BookWeb Home Page

http://ambook.org/bookweb/

Sponsored by the American Booksellers Association, you'll find up-to-date, national info on new releases, author tours, and bookstores.

Comics

Looking through the comics resources available on the Web, it quickly becomes clear that comics aren't just for kids. Sure, you'll still be able to find cute, fuzzy bunnies on these pages, but you're also likely to be blown away by some very sophisticated artwork and solid storytelling. There are lots of political and satirical comics around, too.

Anime and Manga Resources List

http://csclub.uwaterloo.ca/u/mlvanbie/anime-list/

The home of cartoon characters with big eyes and giant hair. An encyclopedic list of links to *manga* and *anime* (Japanese comics and

animation) on the Web. And yes, you'll find Speed Racer's home page here.

The Inkwell

http://www.unitedmedia.com/inkwell/

A collection of editorial cartoons by syndicated newspaper artists, with trenchant insights into today's political scene, life in America, and world events.

The Non-stick Looney Toons Page

http://www.tncnet.com/~jmccarthy/

Be vewy quiet! I'm hunting wabbit! … Here's the unofficial Looney Toons page, with links to other sites about the classic Warner Bros. animation series.

The Animaniacs Page!

http://www-cgi.cs.cmu.edu/afs/cs.cmu.edu/user/clamen/misc/tv/Animaniacs/Animaniacs.html

Hello, Nurse! Obsessively complete, this page has pointers to more info about Yakko, Wakko, and Dot than you can shake the Wheel of Morality at. And of course, Slappy Squirrel and Pinky and The Brain are well represented, too.

Comics Online

http://www.eden.com/comics/comics.html

Two classics of "alternative" comics reside here: "Too Much Coffee Man" and "The Eden Matrix." This site also has pointers to some cool horror comics.

Yeeeoww!!! Digital Cartoons

http://www.smartlink.net/~yeeeoww

This animation studio in Pasadena, California, has a fun site that's definitely worth a look. There's even an interview with the head of the studio that supposedly ran in *Backyard Computing and Landscaping Magazine.* Yeah — sure it did.

Contests, Surveys, Polls

Test your wits against your fellow net.denizens, take a survey, and sound off on the issues of the day.

Brain of the Internet

http://www.zynet.co.uk:8001/amb/

Weekly brainteasers from the UK, done in a multiple-round, elimination-style contest. The winner gets bragging rights to the "Brain of the Internet" title, and even gets a fabulous $10 prize. (Note: If you can't rattle off the names of five or six of the world's largest islands right now, you probably aren't Brain material.)

Gallup Organization, Latest Surveys

http://www.gallup.com/index.html

Find out what the American public thinks, according to Gallup, one of the best-known public polling companies. You'll find the results of the latest surveys, along with archives of past months' polls.

GVU WWW User Surveys

http://www.cc.gatech.edu/gvu/
user_surveys/User_Survey_Home.html

An exhaustively researched survey of users on the Web. Data from more than 13,000 users, classified by age, income level, geographic location, and many other criteria.

Jury Talk

http://www.computek.net:80/jurytalk/

It's your chance to participate in a survey regarding the day's high-profile jury trials. In the spirit of the Roman coliseum (and/or Siskel and Ebert), give your thumbs-up/thumbs-down opinion on the defendants that catch the country's imagination.

Ralph's Sweepstakes Page

http://www4.ncsu.edu/eos/users/r/
rrcraig/www/sweeps/index.html

All sorts of information about sweepstakes, including sweeps that you can enter via the Web or toll-free 800 numbers. Lists of links to other sweepstakes resources are included.

Student Space Awareness Petition

http://seds.lpl.arizona.edu/ssa/
petition.html

Who says the youth of America are apathetic? These high-school and college students are working to save the U.S. space program from more cuts by congressional budget-slashers. You can help by filling out their petition and contacting your congressperson.

Survey - Net

http://www.wisdom.com/sv/

There are usually several concurrent surveys running here regarding issues of the day. Your answers to a survey are tallied and added to the results immediately, so you can see how your opinions compare to other survey participants.

The Asylum Poll

http://www.galcit.caltech.edu/~ta/cgi-bin/poll

An ever-changing series of wacky — and usually geeky — polls on such topics as "Signs Your System Manager Might Be Crazy," and "Ways to Identify a Newbie." (Example: If a newbie pesters you with too many questions and complaints, just tell him to contact the people who run the Internet. That should keep him busy for awhile.)

You Make The Call

http://phobos.kiss.de/~donald/lists/
u_pickit.html

Tired of self-styled Internet gurus who think they have the best guide to Web sites? Why, you've probably looked at other people's hot lists and thought "Hey! I can do that!" Well, here's your chance to add to a constantly growing collection of hot sites from every corner of the Web. Where else could your stumble upon sites such as "Sad Mr. Wu's Send-a-Pickle Service"?

VALS Interactive Server

http://future.sri.com/vals/
valshome.html

The VALS (Values And Lifestyles Survey) page lets you answer a short questionnaire and then categorizes you according to several personality types. (This writer found out that he is an "Actualizer/Fufilled," with a propensity for reading the *New Yorker,* drinking espresso, and eating bagels. They got the bagel part right.)

ThreadTreader's Web Contests Guide

http://www.4cyte.com/
ThreadTreader/

The most comprehensive guide to all of the contests and sweepstakes being run by companies with Web sites.

Cool Links

Cool is in the eye of the beholder, of course, and a cottage industry in picking cool Web sites has sprung up. Your best bet is to use these sites as a jumping-off point for your own explorations; after a while you'll warm to the task, decide what's cool for yourself, and build your own hotlists.

Capt. James T. Kirk Sing-a-long Page

http://www.ama.caltech.edu/~mrm/
kirk.html

Some say he can't act. This page is proof that he can't sing, either. We're talking about William Shatner. Sound snippets from his late-'60s album, including his immortal rendition of "Mr. Tambourine Man." The horror! The horror! What next — Scotty's bagpipe album?

Cool Site of the Day

http://www.infi.net/new/esotd.html

The original link to the cool site of the day. It changes every evening at midnight EST, and stays up for 24 hours. Chosen by Glenn Davis, the Webmaster of infi.net, more than 20,000 people visit this page every day.

Coolest Hostnames on the Net

http://homepage.seas.upenn.edu/ ~mengwong/coolhosts.html

People can — and do — give their host computers and domains the most bizarre names. We like net-free-or-die.org, but there's also mayo.nais.com, dijon.nais.com, multiple.org, tragically.hip.berkeley.edu, and, for you *Star Trek* fans, locutus@of.The-B.org.

Explore the Universe with NASA's Astro-2

http://shuttle.nasa.gov/

Links to shuttle pages and all other things NASA. This site offers lots of information on space shuttle missions, including live "Ask the Astronauts" sessions when a mission is in progress. Great for students and other space fans.

The FBI's current "Ten Most Wanted Fugitives"

http://www.fbi.gov/toplist.htm

Look at it this way: This is one way to get the government to make *you* a home page.

INTELLiCast Home Page

http://www.intellicast.com/

Weather, skiing, and ocean conditions around the world. Essential for those net.geeks who would rather find out the current weather conditions on their computer than stick their heads outside to look.

Internet Travel Network - Online Booking and Travel Information

http://www.itn.net/cgi/get?itn/index/

The Internet travel information resource that lets you book your travel arrangements through an agency near you. But first, you can get complete info on flights through an easy-to-use, forms-based set of pages. Netscape is the browser of choice for this site, as it makes extensive use of tables. This is a very useful site for travelers; it's easier to use than similar online travel services.

Letter R.I.P.

http://www.dtd.com/rip/letter.cgi

Backwards hangman. The onscreen zombie loses a limb when you guess an incorrect letter. Tasteless? You bet! Funny? You know it!

Mirsky's Worst of the Web

http://mirsky.turnpike.net/wow/ Worst.html

The dark side of PEZ dispensers. Safety tips for those who enjoy shooting home appliances. Mirsky has done humanity a great favor by compiling a list of links to some of the worst Web sites ever created. What can you say besides that people vie to be listed here?

Preview The Heart

http://sln.fi.edu/tfi/preview/ heartpreview.html

A full-color tour of your heart. Get to know the part of you that never rests.

WWW TV Themes Home Page

http://www.tvrecords.com/tvbytes/

It's About Time that someone compiled a page like this. The Name of the Game is nostalgia. Never in My So Called Life have I seen a site that is so Absolutely Fabulous; but here it is, In Living Color. Cheers to sitemeister Patrick Kenny for this page that reminds us couch potatoes of our Wonder Years. Get Smart and see What's Happening here. After all, you only have One Life To Live. Cheers!

The Body Space

http://www.surgery.com/body/topics/ body.html

Plastic surgery over the Web. You can get info on that tummy tuck you've been thinking about, with before-and-after pictures of several procedures. There's even estimated cost information, and they can refer you to a plastic surgeon near you.

The Postcard Store

http://postcards.www.media.mit.edu/ Postcards/

Not only can you take a virtual vacation by visiting Web sites around the world, but now you can send a postcard to show folks where you've been! They have cards from Boston, Tokyo, and New York, as well as many fine art cards with works by Monet, Van Gogh, da Vinci, and others.

The Spot

http://www.thespot.com/

The first episodic Web site. Think of it as the *Melrose Place* of the Net, and you won't be too far off. The Spot is a beach house in Santa Monica, California, with a 40-year history of revelry, mystery, and possibly murder. Join the current five (sometimes more) attractive, twentysomething Spotmates as they post their daily journal entries. Oh, and Spotnik, the Cyberian Husky (and Spot mascot) that's been with The Spot since the beginning, occasionally weighs in with the canine perspective. The story is fascinating, plus this is one of the most attractive sites around. (And we're not just talking about the hunks and hunkettes at the beach house, either.)

the ultimate band list

http://american.recordings.com/wwwofmusic/ubl/ubl.shtml

Links to every music-related page in the universe.

ALSO RECOMMENDED:

Who's Cool In America Project

http://www.getcool.com/~getcool/

The folks who officially decide who and what is cool in America. You can apply to be included in the Who's Cool Registry. But if you were really cool, you wouldn't have to beg, now would you?

Autopilot

http://www.netgen.com/~mkgray/autopilot.html

Automatically throws you to a new URL every 12 seconds. Wheee!

Freeways by Alamo Rent-A-Car

http://www.freeways.com/

Enough with the "Information Superhighway" already! What if you're one of those old-fashioned souls who likes to travel on real, honest-to-goodness asphalt? This site offers useful info for travelers, including detailed directions between locations.

NYNEX Interactive Yellow Pages — Home Page

http://www.niyp.com/

Allows you to add links to your home pages from its Yellow Pages listing. You can search by name or business category.

Drinks and Drinking

From soft drinks to the hard stuff, there's a page for virtually every pause that refreshes. Bottoms up!

Bruce's Wine Page

http://www.pcix.com/wine/index.html

Whether you're an occasional wine taster, or a serious oenophile, this page should satisfy you.

Boat drinks!

http://tigger.cc.uic.edu/~toby-g/boat.html#pd-wdwgdas

Longing for that trip to the Caribbean? It's the middle of winter and you could really use some tropical warmth? Slap in a Jimmy Buffett CD, mix up a boat drink, and you'll soon get that island spirit. Have two or three boat drinks, and you can even simulate that queasy, hurling-over-the-rail feeling.

Over The Coffee

http://www.cappuccino.com

This site will give you a jolt. Take a break from the daily grind. Lots of info about coffee, and links to pages from other caffeine addicts worldwide. You can even leave your own ode to coffee on the Wall of Java. Now, talk amongst yourselves.

The Land of Snapple

http://www.snapple.com/snapple/main/sn.main1.html

The place to go to find out about The Best Stuff on Earth. Want to know more about Wendy, the Snapple Lady? Of course you do. Care to know how much the Snapple Mascot's costume weighs? Of course you do. It's all here.

You can even win a case of Snapple if you're the winner in the Snapple Flavor Poll.

Internet Bartender's Guide

http://www.public.iastate.edu/~evers/adam/guide/contents.html

Can't remember how to make that Afterburner or mix that Fuzzy Navel? You'll find 'em here, along with virtually every other drink known to man or beast.

Food and Eating

Warning: this section could be hazardous to your waistline. Scientific studies have conclusively proven that uncontrolled snacking behavior occurred in 83.8 percent of test readers of this section. You have been warned.

The Bovril Shrine

http://medianet.nbnet.nb.ca/medianet/curioso/bovril/bovril.HTM

"Bovril, in essence, is liquid cow." It's thick. It's brown. It's incredibly salty. It's British. 'Nuff said.

Spam

http://www.yahoo.com/Entertainment/Food_and_Eating/Spam/

Links to the Church of Spam, the shrine to Spam and the Spam Haiku

Archive, among others. You're invited to submit your own Spam haiku. Here's a sample to inspire you:

*agglutinous gop
slithers through my dreaming mind
pork product nightmare*

— WhaarfRat@aol.com

Chocolate

I Need My Chocolate!

http://www.qrc.com/~sholubek/choco/start.htm

For people with a serious chocolate habit, this site has the scoop on the perfect food.

Recipes

Bread

http://www.vuw.ac.nz/who/Amy.Gale/recipes/bread/bread.html

More recipes for breads, rolls, biscuits, scones, and so on than you can shake a breadstick at.

Virtual Health

http://health.net/Virtual/index.html

Recipes and more from Virtual Health, the interactive health store. Good food that's good for you, too.

Mama's Cookbook

http://www.eat.com/cookbook/index.html

The Ragu people have put together a site that's interesting and fun, with some good Italian recipes. *Mangia!*

Welcome To Eleanor's Kitchen

http://www.columbia.edu/~js322/eleanor/eleanor.html

A collection of yummy Czechoslovakian recipes. Czech it out!

Cooking Mushrooms

http://www.igc.apc.org/mushroom/cook.html

Fun with fungus! Marvelous for mycophiles. A constantly-changing selection of recipes with mushrooms.

Pit Cooking

http://www.cco.caltech.edu/~salmon/pit.html

Team Mumu Pit Cooking Page: Or, how to tell dinner from a hole in the ground. This crack team of Caltech engineers shares the results of its research into the proper methods of pit cooking, including the crucial secret tool for cleaning stray dirt off your roast pig after it's been dug up.

The Recipe Archive

http://www.arion.com/info/recipes.html

For people who just can't get enough recipes, links to lots of other recipe pages.

Vegetarian Pages

http://catless.ncl.ac.uk/Vegetarian/

Links to numerous other veggie sites. The recipes, like the URL, are presumably catless (note hostname).

The Foodplex!

http://www.gigaplex.com/wow/food/index.htm

Los Angeles food critic Merrill Shindler gives us a food page that revels in eating, for people who live to eat. Snappily written, you'll find such oxymoronic topics as "The Joy of Rice Cakes," the distribution of animals in a box of animal crackers (one lion, two tigers, five bears, oh my!), and where to get the best steak in America.

This Page Stinks! (The Garlic Page)

http://broadcast.com/garlic/garlic.htm

Ah, the stinking rose by any other name would still be that wonderful herb, garlic. Like its namesake, this page will linger with you, long after it has left your screen.

J.B.'s Jelly Donut Home Page

http://www.moscow.com/homepages/KLEINR@UWPLATT.EDU.html

Mmmmmm. Jelly Donuts! OK. We admit it. This is a completely useless page that really doesn't deserve to be in this book, but it made us laugh, and it appears that we've fallen under the Evil Jelly Donut Spell, and now after reading this page, we've learned about where to meet a nice Jelly Donut, and the key role Jelly Donuts are playing in law enforcement, and the Ode to A Jelly Donut, and —

Welcome to the CHILI-HEADS home page

http://www.netimages.com/~chile/

Giving a new meaning to the term *hot list,* you'll find a wealth of info about chili peppers, with recipes, pictures of more than 50 varieties, and a discussion of the hottest pepper (it's the habañero). There are several hot sauce vendors on the Net, and this page points you to them. Excuse us, we need some ice water.

Dining Out on the Web

http://www.ird.net/diningout.html

Hungry? You'll find a list of the best places to eat in your town, provided you live in a major city. This site is really a list-of-lists; it'll take you to your local restaurant guide. *Bon appetit!*

Julie's Low & Fat-Free Resources List

http://www.eskimo.com/~baubo/lowfat.html

Hey, you! Yes, we're talking to you! Put down that slice of pizza and that Yoo-Hoo (no relation to Yahoo!) and check out this page immediately. You'll thank us later. So will your arteries.

Straining credulity, these pages are only a few of the really odd pages available on the Web. If the whole range of human experience is on the Net, that's an awful lot of pages you just might not want to see.

House of Socks

http://www.caprica.com/~jmares/house_of_socks.html

This site asks, "What happened to that one missing sock?" Then you can look for it in the dryer, the washer, or find out what other dastardly fate has befallen your wayward hosiery.

News of the Weird — Chuck Shepherd

http://www.realworks.com/~mbrandes/notw.htm

Pretty weird stuff, and all true. Here's a recent favorite: "Eric P. Wilson, 40, was convicted of burglarizing a home in Roanoke, VA in March. He was done in by his obsession with shining his shoes, which he does several times a day with the polish and personalized cloth he carries with him. Wilson had paused during the burglary to polish his shoes and accidentally left the rag and fingerprinted can of polish behind."

Prayers Heavenbound

http://www.primenet.com/~prayers/

Hi-tech has finally caught up with mankind's spiritual needs. Here is a nondenominational, publicly accessible direct link to Heaven that can beam prayers, hopes, and dreams into space, into time, into forever. All for the low cost of $9.95!

Humor, Jokes, and Fun

Despite the grave concern and manic hype about the Internet, there are a lot of plain old laughs along the Infobahn. Here are some of the funniest rest stops.

Mind Reading Markup Language (MRML)

http://www.oxy.edu/~ashes/mrml.html

The Mind Reading Markup Language (MRML) is a proprietary extension of the HyperText Markup Language (HTML). Current technology enables very primitive mind control using MRML tags. The so-called Brainwashing tags are delimited by the the special pair of tags <!—HYPNOTIZE><HYPNOTIZE—>.

An Anagram Generator on the WWW

http://csugrad.cs.vt.edu/~eburke/anagrams.html

Generate your own anagrams.

Yahoo!-Archives

http://www.yahoo.com/Entertainment/Humor__Jokes__and_Fun/Archives

So many jokes, it's not even funny.

The Tao of Programming

http://www.acm.usl.edu/~dxh0844/other/tao.html

Geek humor at its finest. How to find your Higher Power through coding.

Confuse Your Roommate

http://www.mps.org/~rainbow/Words/ConfuseRoommate.html

One hundred ways to drive your roommate crazy. A sample: "Buy a Jack-In-The-Box. Every day, turn the handle until the clown pops out. Scream continuously for 20 minutes." Yep, that'll do it.

Dead People Server

http://web.syr.edu/~rsholmes/dead/index.html

Remember whatshisname? He played the guy in that dumb movie with whoziss. What ever happened to him? Specifically, is he dead yet? Here's where to find out. The Dead People Server is simply a list of interesting celebrities who are, or might plausibly be, dead, with information as to who has really Rung Down the Curtain and Joined the Choir Invisible, and who's Just Resting.

Fidel For President

http://www.slugs.com/imagesmith/fidel

With the slogan, "This time, send a real revolution to Washington," this page kicks off the Fidel Castro for President '96 campaign. Just think of the cigars we'd have.

Shakespearean Insult

http://www.nova.edu/Inter-Links/cgi-bin/bard.pl

Creates a new insult every time you reload the page. Here's one: "Thou fawning tickle-brained strumpet."

Jay's Comedy Club

http://paul.spu.edu/~zylstra/comedy/index.html

A very good list of humor sites.

Canonical List of Lawyer Jokes

http://www.infi.net/~cashman/humor/canonical/lawyer.html

If a lawyer and an IRS agent were both drowning, and you could only save one of them, would you go to lunch or read the paper?

Mr. Edible Starchy Tuber Head Home Page

http://winnie.acsu.buffalo.edu/potatoe

You say potato, I say Edible Starchy Tuber.

Magazines

There are two main types of magazines here: the Web version of traditional paper magazines and e-zines, which exist only in electronic form. Of the two, the e-zines tend to be more adventurous because they don't have to provide a familiar format to the reader. There are many cool magazine sites, and more are popping up everyday. You should revisit this area of Yahoo! on a regular basis to browse the new magazines that are sure to appear.

c|net

http://www.cnet.com

More than an e-zine, more than a television network, c|net is an integrated information souce devoted to computers and the digital revolution.

Automobiles

PM Automotive

http://popularmechanics.com/
popmech/auto/1HOMEAUTO.html

Popular Mechanics' car pages deliver solid, timely data on auto manufacturers' rebate programs, new car and truck profiles, and owner reports on dozens of models.

AAOW - African Americans On Wheels

http://www.ip.net/cbo/aaow/

Here's a tidbit: African Americans spend over $13 billion of their $339 billion annual income on new automobiles. The money spent is more than the gross national products (in U.S. dollars) of Ethiopia, Ghana, Kenya, Uganda, or Zaire. This magazine provides automobile information targeted to the African-American audience.

America's 4x4 4U Video Magazine WWW

http://www.4x44u.com/pub/k2/
am4x44u/4x4.html

Let's hit the road in our big four-wheelers! Four-wheel-drive enthusiasts should downshift to this site for road tests, event listings, and more. There's even the obligatory pictorial of large-breasted women posing with trucks.

ALSO RECOMMENDED:

Mobilia Magazine

http://www.mobilia.com/

Devoted to automobile collectibles, from classic license plates, to toy cars, to radiator ornaments.

Special Car Journal Homepage

http://www.specialcar.com/

This online magazine for classic, exotic, and sportscar enthusiasts includes pointers to exotic car auctions, classified ads, and car clubs around the world.

Entertainment

Camden Lock - Delphi Internet's UK Home Page

http://www.delphi.co.uk/

A very attractive site, with excellent graphics and interesting content. The games section had an interactive ferret race when we checked it out. Really.

The Tyrtle Times

http://www.dfw.net/~soulmate/
btt.html

Weird and funny musings about life. Plus features like "The Galactic Web Empress Handbook," and "Shrink Wrap," transcripts from really stupid callers to a psychologist's radio show.

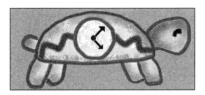

bOING bOING

http://www.zeitgeist.net/Public/
Boing-boing/

The tirelessly hip and hilarious cyberzine hits the Web at last. Look for the *Happy Mutant Handbook,* coming to you soon.

Cyber Babble

http://www.kernel.com/usr/rich/
CyberBabble.html

A well done e-zine about cult movies, cyberpunk, and book and music reviews, of special interest to Macintosh users. Reviews of Mac CD-ROM games and other Mac products.

Welcome to ENTERTAINMENT WEEKLY

http://www.timeinc.com/ew/

A slick Web version of the popular entertainment magazine.

Firehorse

http://www.peg.apc.org/~firehorse/
welcome.html

A very interesting e-zine from Down Under. Mostly about the Web, but you'll find some fascinating opinion pieces too.

Games Domain Review

http://wcl-rs.bham.ac.uk/gdreview/

This games e-zine from the UK has opinions, reviews, news, and rumors about what's happening in the world of electronic gaming. It's especially good that GDR isn't limited to only one or two hardware platforms; all electronic gaming, from GameBoys to PC and Mac games, is represented, although most reviews are of the PC versions.

NewType Gaming

http://Web.Actwin.Com/NewType/

Another games magazine, with departments about the gaming culture, and some very up-to-date info about virtual reality efforts happening on the Web.

THE GIGAPLEX!

http://www.gigaplex.com/wow/

The Gigaplex is a huge entertainment site, with areas on food, yoga, film, music, theater, golf, books, and lots more. Well worth the time it takes to load the big graphics.

MELVIN Magazine

http://www.melvin.com/

Among all the dross of alleged humor magazines on the Net created by dorky college sophomores, Melvin shines with genuine humor. Done like a newspaper, the recent page 1 headline: "Parents Abandon Baby Touched By The Hand of God — 'It doesn't smell like us anymore,' reports mother." Now *that's* funny.

The Texas Chainsaw Magazine

http://ccwf.cc.utexas.edu/~heretic/tcmag.html

Refreshingly nasty, mean-sprited, and just plain fed-up sarcasm, rants, and satire from a guy who doesn't suffer idiots at all. A sample nugget: "To all you braindead, cyberpunk wannabe preteens who get sweaty palms by starting Web sites filled with JPEGS of famous women superimposed on bodies that are obviously not their own — I wouldn't even mourn if all of you were to die a nasty painful death involving your CD-ROM, a cordless drill, and a large Vlasic pickle."

Sam Johnson's Electronic Revenge

http://pobox.com/slt/sam.home.html

Yes, Virginia, there is lively, intelligent, literary writing on the World Wide Web. You'll find it here, along with other stuff from the folks at Silly Little

Troll Publications. Some really good prose resides here, and they're publishing new writers with abandon.

TikiZine

http://www.students.uiuc.edu/~cricket/tikizine/

Billed as a "bi-weekly survey of what's cool," TikiZine is a melange of movie, TV, and music reviews, with a touch of opinion and "weird things happening in the staffers' lives" thrown in.

Tum Yeto Digiverse

http://tumyeto.com/

Cool e-zine written by a crew of 20-ish writers and artists, with some excellent departments. There's a snowboarding section, "Foxy," an "e-zine for chicks," and the obligatory music section. This one rocks.

ALSO RECOMMENDED:

Teleparc

http://teleparc.infoweb.or.jp/en/index.htm

A Japanese e-zine about technology, entertainment, and the Web, with some interesting cross-cultural insights.

dimFLASH e-zine

http://turnpike.net/metro/futrelle/
index.html

Weird commentary, funny writing, and some medium-to-OK graphics. Worth a look.

Vanguard Station

http://www.cybervanguard.com

A decent science fiction e-zine, though it was a little sparse at press time. The site shows real potential; if they build it up, it could become a must-see for science fiction fans.

General Interest

Pathfinder

http://www.pathfinder.com

This is the gateway to all of the online magazines published by Time Warner. *Time, Entertainment Weekly, Money, People, Sports Illustrated,* and more. But it's not just magazines; they're trying to give you access to the whole Time-Warner empire. So you'll see stuff from Warner Bros. (the movie studio), HBO, Elektra Records, and Time Warner Interactive, the CD-ROM group. Can you say "corporate synergy," kids?

Planet Texas

http://www.planet-texas.com/home

You've landed at Planet Texas, the place where they show you what makes Texas so, well, Texas-y. The wide open spaces here host a passle o' information about Texas events, Texas people, Texas music, and the Planet Texas Town square, where Texas merchants pitch their wares.

They're even setting up "homesteads," your own home page on their site. So git along and become an honorary Texan, Web-style.

People Magazine

http://www.pathfinder.com/people

The Web version of Time Warner's celeb-o-thon. Most of the text of the magazine is available here; most of the pictures aren't.

Raging Smolder

http://www.comet.chv.va.us/rag/
index.html

An interesting e-zine, made up of news, commentary, events, and humor, compiled from other sources on the Net. The best part of this 'zine is that it includes a widely disparate collection of info; the overall effect is to keep you pleasantly surprised.

The New American Magazine

http://www.primenet.com/~tevans/
newamericanindex.html

Far-right opinions from the John Birch Society's magazine. Recent issues tell why the United Nations is a threat to America, how Rush Limbaugh is too liberal, and why President Clinton is a fascist.

The Smithsonian Magazine

http://www.si.edu/resource/simag/
start.htm

A wonderful introduction not just to the magazine, but to the 16 museums and the National Zoo that make up the Smithsonian Institution. The magazine portion of the site has abstracts of the articles in *Smithsonian Magazine* (if only it would post the full text, at least for the older articles!), and the site changes daily.

Word

http://www.word.com/index.html

Attractively done and intelligently written, *Word* is devoted to, well, all kinds of things. *Diversity,* that's the word we were looking for.

t@p online

http://www.taponline.com

Aimed at college students, t@p online is a large site that has lots of pages about schools, sports, fashion, music, and news. As former students, we were especially amused by three of the products listed on their sponsors page: Advil, Hershey's chocolate, and Vivarin. Sounds like educational essentials to us.

The Freehand

http://vvv.com/adsint/freehand

A network of weirdness and independent magazines, with links to other alternative and interesting sites. The Unusual or Deep Site of the Day is here; so is a link to "Sexy Beach Babes and the Luxury Cars They Want You to Drive." No kidding.

Zine Net

http://www.zine.net

A listing of printed zines, billed as a "guide to the chaotic world of independent publishing." It's not yet a very comprehensive guide, but we were able to find out about some interesting printed zines that don't have their own Web sites yet.

Magical Blend Magazine Online

http://www.eden.com/~magical/main.html

A long-running magazine about raising and extending human conciousness, and other New Age issues. Recent issues include interviews with Bob Weir, Jaron Lanier, and Whitley Strieber.

Intrrr Nrrrd

http://www.etext.org/Zines/Intrrr.Nrrrd/intrrr.html

The motto on the title page says, "Saving souls with Punk Rawwwwk Since August 1994." Combined with a pseudo-religious style and some funny pieces such as "Opening Bands are People Too!", *Intrrr Nrrrd* is for punk fanatics.

Shift Online

http://www.e-commerce.com/Shift.home

A teaser version (only part of the paper magazine's contents are presented online) of another magazine about popular culture. This one, however, is notable because it hires good writers, and they lack that hipper-than-thou attitude.

Strobe Magazine

http://www.iuma.com/strobe

Yet another music-and-culture magazine; this one based in Los Angeles. Good stuff. Has that L.A. feel. Whatever that is.

Virus

http://198.147.111.1/Virus

There's some really weird sh … uh … stuff here. Stuff that could corrupt Middle America if it becomes known. Stuff that should be seen if you have a warped sense of humor.

Indices

Electronic Magazines

http://www.abc.hu/unix/magazines.html

An alphabetically sorted listing of many of the magazines available on the Web, with links and brief descriptions, when necessary. A good resource to add to your bookmarks or hotlist.

Electronic Newsstand Homepage

http://www.enews.com

A mostly Gopher-based browsing service that offers text excerpts from many traditional magazines from every walk of life. The magazines offer the table of contents and a few articles from their current issues as a taste of what's available. You can then subscribe to the magazine via e-mail or snail mail. Another good choice for your Web browser's hotlist.

John Labovitz's E-zine List

http://www.meer.net/~johnl/e-zine-list

The guide to the e-zines. Listings, with short descriptions, of more than 400 e-zines, with more than a dozen being added every month. If you have the slightest appreciation for the wide variety of human interests, it will be further broadened by an hour's browsing here.

Music

Acoustic Musician

http://www.netinterior.com/acoustic

A nice adjunct to the paper version of this magazine for acoustic music. Includes a monthly Instruction segment with a song that illustrates a particular playing technique. The cover story about an acoustic artist often has a detailed rundown about that artist's instrument and gear choices.

Addicted To Noise

http://www.addict.com/ATN

An excellent magazine about contemporary music and popular culture, with a great stable of writers. Absolutely recommended.

Alternative Music Notes

http://www.club.net/MusicNotes

A weekly tip sheet with news about bands such as R.E.M., Depeche Mode, Smashing Pumpkins, and other staples of alternative radio.

Audible Evolution

http://www.mw3.com/electro/audevo.htm

Get those alpha waves in sync with the music described in these pages. Ambient, trance, dubs, break beat, and dub music for that blissed-out feeling. There's also something called "electro organic," whatever that is.

Big O

http://www.asia-online.com/bigo

One of the terrific things about the Net is that it gives you the chance to see things that you might never get to see otherwise. *Big O* is an Asian rock magazine that is definitely worth the trip. The magazine covers a wide range of rock topics and does a decent job of being all things to all rock fans. Recent feature stories on the return of Patty Smith, Foo Fighters, Warren Zevon, and Radiohead, plus coverage of Asian rock.

Guitar World Online

http://www.evolution.com/~ignition/gwo/contents/cn.page1.html

A slick Web-ized version of the printed magazine. Worth a look for both the hard-core and amateur guitarist.

InterDance Web mEgaZINE

http://www.idw.be/idw

If you like to go to clubs and shake it, this Belgian page gives you the lowdown on every type of danceable music. Techno, rave, hip-hop, house, eurodance, trance — you name it. If it moves you, it's here.

The Lighthouse

http://www.netcentral.net/lighthouse

A lively, very well-done site about the world of Contemporary Christian Music (CCM). Unless you're a Christian, you may not know that there's a huge Christian pop-music industry, and this magazine covers it well, with feature articles, reviews, and news.

Mister Lucky

http://www.wco.com/~coconutg

Good music — mostly jazz, Latin, and vocals in this case — and good booze. Essential elements in Mister Lucky's world. Good music reviews and excellent drink recipes. A fine combination.

Muse Magazine

http://www.val.net/VillageSounds/Muse/index.html

A journal of women in music, *Muse* covers music made by women (not just so-called "women's music") in virtually every musical genre, with a focus on popular music. There were some interesting interviews with Sarah McLachlan, Lisa Germano, Lydia Lunch, and Joan Osborne in recent issues. A bit light from the critical standpoint on the CD and concert reviews, which tend to the gushy.

Music Week

http://www.dotmusic.com/MWhome.html

News, record charts, and A&R reports for the music business in the United Kingdom. Check this one out for the scoop on the biz in Britain.

POP-i

http://criticalmass.com/popi

An all-digital music magazine. Of special interest because of its wide use of the RealAudio system to feed you audio clips of artist interviews and music reviews. Just starting up at press time, so it will be interesting to see how it matures. There's a CD-ROM version available by subscription, too.

Progression

http://www.gold.net/users/ex14/index.html

Monthly music, arts, and culture magazine with a guitar slant. Practical articles for the working (and working-at-it) musician.

West Coast Music Review Homepage

http://www.cyberstore.ca/WCMR

Finally! A zine that covers music other than punk, hip-hop, or alternative. This one features country, roots music (jazz, blues, folk), rock, and pop music (the mainstream stuff!), New Age, and music for kids.

A L S O   R E C O M M E N D E D:

The FolkBook Index - Periodicals

http://www.cgrg.ohio-state.edu/ folkbook/resources/periodical.html

A good listing of folk music resources available on the Internet.

Computer Music Journal

http://www-mitpress.mit.edu/ Computer-Music-Journal

MIT Press's online journal for the seriously technical electronic musician. Archives of source code for music manipulation programs, and abstracts of articles published in the paper version of the journal.

Electronic Urban Report (EUR)

http://www.trib.com/bbs/eur.html

Not a Web magazine per se, this page is a subscription interface to the free, daily e-mail publication dealing with Urban/Black entertainment.

Travel

Condé Nast Traveler

http://www.cntraveler.com

For travelers, this is simply a terrific site. A ton of information, beautifully and clearly presented. There's a wonderful Beach and Island Finder that lets you enter your perfect criteria for a coastal vacation and then suggests appropriate choices. In 1996, it'll add European and American destinations.

Shoestring Travel E-zine

http://metro.turnpike.net/eadler/ index.html

If you like to ramble around the world but are on a budget, Shoestring Travel has the goods on inexpensive travel worldwide. Even if you just want to save a few bucks, this is a good resource.

TravelASSIST MAGAZINE

http://travelassist.com/mag/ mag_home.html

A good selection of travel information, with a section of paid advertising for bed and breakfast establishments, inns, and small hotels.

Web Travel Review

http://webtravel.org/webtravel

Personal travel accounts are on this site, including Phillip Greenspun's "Travels with Samantha," which was picked as a Best of the Web '94. It's a travel journal covering Greenspun's journey from Boston to Alaska and back. Funny, moving, and insightful. Don't miss this one.

Miscellaneous

Yahoo! couldn't manage to put these sites into any of its usual categories, and after you take a look at them, you'll understand why. Some of these are thoughtful, some are silly, and some are just plain weird.

Cauldron — A Labyrinth of Ideas

http://www.bluemarble.net/~bcs/ cauldron/calhome.html

The old Zork computer game had a place in it described as "You are in a maze of twisty passages, all alike." The Cauldron is a maze of twisty passages for your mind, all different. Zen-esque, surreal writing and images fill many, many pages that lead to one another. Is there a goal? You'll have to experience it to find out.

G.O.D. Bros Travelling Circus

http://godbros-circus.com

This odd site is about as "miscellaneous" as it gets. If you can figure it out, you're one up on us.

The Excuse Generator

http://islandnet.com/~brokers/ excuse/excus1.htm

More of an Excuse Bank, there are excuses here ranging from the riduculous to the preposterous.

Do It Yourself: The Virtual Support Hotline

http://xavier.tangent.com/.z/vsh

Yes, you too can whine with the best of them, thanks to this forms-based page that lets you pick technical support problems even sillier than the ones you really make. This may be a useless page, but it's funny.

Find Your Name in Hawaiian

http://hisurf.aloha.com/Find.html

This page translates your name into Hawaiian, but it may be broken. This writer understands that his name translates into a Hawaiian name that means "Klutz who will never learn to surf." Mahalo.

Fun with Grapes — A Case Study

http://www.sci.tamucc.edu/ ~pmichaud/grape

"Ordinary grapes, when properly prepared and microwaved, spark impressively in an extremely entertaining manner." So begins this tale of grape depravity, wherein perfectly nice grapes are tortured until they explode. Kids, don't try this at home. Or if you do, don't tell us about it. We're not responsible. In the same spirit as this page, check out http://ghg.ecn.purdue.edu/, which describes how a bunch of misguided engineers in Indiana light a barbeque grill with liquid oxygen. They have pictures to prove it.

PhoNETic

http://www.soc.qc.edu/phonetic

Converts phone numbers into letters, or vice versa. Even has dictionary checking, so that you only get results that contain real words.

Movies and Films

Let's go out to the lobby ... and while we're there, we'll check out the links to the silver screen. From the Oscars to cult movies, from panting actress fan pages to serious film criticism, you'll find it here.

AMPAS

http://www.oscars.org/ampas

The official Oscar page, from the Academy of Motion Picture Arts and Sciences.

Cyber Film School

http://www.io.org/~cincan/cfs.htm

An interesting site that includes some of the information you'd find if you went to a real film school. Lectures, interactive workshops, and more. And here, there's no problem in checking out that light meter from the equipment room — there isn't one.

The Web Wide World of Film Music

http://web.syr.edu:80/~ebedgert/ wwwfm.html

A good listing of links about the music in films, slanted more at the dramatic underscoring kind of music, rather than hit pop songs from film soundtracks.

The Hollyweb Online Film Guide

http://www.ingress.com/users/ spease/hw/hollyweb.html

A cut above the run-of-the-mill film site. Inside studio information, box office reports, and links to reviews galore.

Hollywood Online

http://www.hollywood.com

Very lavish, very slick, beautifully done. Lots of Hollywood puffery, but useful if you want to find out the background on current and upcoming movies. Not the place to look for hard-hitting film criticism.

Fade In: ONLINE

http://www.best.com/~market/fadein

The online magazine for screenwriters. Think that's too specialized? You don't live in Los Angeles.

The Movie Clichés List

http://www.well.com/user/vertigo/ cliches.html

Thanks to bad movies with poor writing for bringing us this list of terrible movie clichés, sorted and categorized. Two of my favorites: "Medieval peasants always have filthy faces, tangled hair, ragged clothing — and perfect, gleaming white teeth" and "Complex computer calculations and loading of huge amounts of data will be accomplished in under three seconds. Movie modems usually appear to transmit data at the speed of two gigabytes per second."

MovieLink 777FILM Online

http://www.777film.com/

Browse the latest movie information by film or by theatre. Each film has background information, where it's playing, the times, and some even have trailers. And once you decide on what, where, and when, you can purchase your tickets online!

Yahoo! — Reviews

http://www.yahoo.com/
Entertainment/Movies_and_Films/
Reviews

There are too many good movie reviews pages to single out just one or two. You're better off browsing them right from Yahoo!.

Ronnie Cramer's Cult Film Page

http://sepnet.com/rcramer/index.htm

A listing of cult classics, categorized by genre, such as horror, science fiction, drive-in classics, etc. Only one of my two fave bad movies is listed here: *Brain From Planet Arous,* but not *Monster From The Surf.* Other classics: *Reefer Madness,* the Ed Wood catalog, and many Corman stinkers. You can also buy the listed films on this site on VHS via mail order.

Screenwriters On Line

http://screenwriter.com/insider/
news.html

News for screenwriters, with interviews with successful writers, industry gossip, and info on writers' workshops.

Yahoo! — Studios

http://www.yahoo.com/
Entertainment/Movies_and_Films/
Studios

Find the direct links to movie studio pages via this Yahoo! page.

Yahoo! — The Internet Movie Database

http://www.yahoo.com/
Entertainment/Movies_and_Films/
The_Internet_Movie_Database

This is simply the best database on movie and TV information available on the Internet, with info on thousands of films and TV programs. The main database is located in the United Kingdom; we've chosen to list the Yahoo! address because it shows the main worldwide mirror sites. Use the one nearest to you.

Actors and Actresses, Directors, Festivals

Yahoo! — Actors and Actresses

http://www.yahoo.com/
Entertainment/Movies_and_Films/
Actors_and_Actresses

Yahoo! — Directors

http://www.yahoo.com/
Entertainment/Movies_and_Films/
Directors

Yahoo! — Festivals

http://www.yahoo.com/
Entertainment/Movies_and_Films/
Festivals

There are thousands of sites listed under Actors and Actresses, Festivals, and Directors. You're best off using

Yahoo!'s Search form to find the site you're interested in, or just browsing through the pages until you find something that catches your eye.

Indices

Cinema Sites

http://www.webcom.com/
~davidaug/Movie_Sites.html

A comprehensive guide to movie sites around the Web. Updated daily.

ALSO RECOMMENDED:

The Entertain-Net

http://userwww.sfsu.edu/~jkafer/
welcome.html

Mostly links to other entertainment resources on the Web, but nicely presented and edited.

Music

The Music section is one of Yahoo!'s largest, with thousands of entries, though most of those are in the Artists section. It would be impossible to give a comprehensive "best of" in this category, since there are so many musical genres and tastes. We've tried to provide a flavor of the interesting sites, and places that can serve as a jumping-off point for your own musical journey.

Yahoo! — Artists

http://www.yahoo.com/
Entertainment/Music/Artists

The way to get to the thousands of music artist's pages on the Web. Searchable by name.

Hype! One-Hit Wonder Compilation

http://www.hype.com/nostalgia/onehit/onehitin.htm

If you've been wondering what happened to Blue Swede or Argent, they ended up listed here in the One-Hit Wonder department.

Harmony Central Main Menu

http://harmony-central.mit.edu

A site for musicians and other music makers. Info on MIDI, recording, and music software, as well as instruments.

On-Line Guitar Archive

http://www.umn.edu/nlhome/m161/schn0170/olga.html

A WWW front end to OLGA, the On-Line Guitar Archive. Guitar tablature for songs from all over the world.

Les Miserables Home Page

http://www.ot.com/lesmis

An unofficial home page for the long-running Broadway musical.

Rock & Roll Hall of Fame and Museum

http://www.rockhall.com

The pride of Cleveland, the Rock and Roll Hall of Fame's site has the "500 Songs That Shaped Rock and Roll" list, plus lots of info about the museum

and the Hall of Fame inductees. But how did Sam the Sham and the Pharoahs' "Wooly Bully" get onto the "500 Songs" list?

Global Electronic Music Marketplace

http://192.215.9.13/Flirt/GEMM/gemm2.html

GEMM helps you find fan clubs, Usenet groups, listservs, downloadables, lyrics, and other Internet resources related to your favorite artists or types of music. It also provides you with sources where you can purchase that music.

Harmony Music List

http://orpheus.ucsd.edu/harmony

About a zillion links to artists, instruments, and virtually any other music resource on the Internet.

Addicted To Sounds

http://www.mindspring.com/~labrams/a2sound.htm

Features Bands With Names That Make You Want To Go Back To Bed (some favorites: Giant Testosterone Explosion and Big Fat Pet Clams from Outer Space). Also has little-known links to other audio and music resources.

Archives

Internet Underground Music Archive

http://www.iuma.com/IUMA/index_graphic.html

An excellent guide to independent bands, record companies, and

publications. IUMA provides MPEG audio excerpts of the artists' music, a description, and contact information. This site is chock full o' graphics, so be patient.

Paranormal Phenomena

You are getting very sleepy … no, you are leaving your body — wait, no, the stars have pointed you to this area, with pages galore for astrologers, numerologists, the occult, and New Age religions. Alien abductors, Nostradamus, and psychics rub shoulders here. There's even a healthy dose of skepticism.

Astral Projection Home Page

http://www.lava.net/~goodin/astral.html

A guide to *really* getting away from it all, this page features basics on the Out Of Body Experience (OOBE) the "Astral Projection Tip of the Month," plus links to other OOBE resources on the Net.

Dark Side of the Net Home Page

http://www.cascade.net/dark.html

A listing of gothic, vampiric, wiccan, pagan, occult, and other dark resources on the Web and other places on the Net. It's creepy. It's spooky. It's altogether ooky.

I-Ching

http://cad.ucla.edu/repository/useful/iching.html

Performs an I-Ching reading for you, with interpretations. The interpretations are inscrutable, but that's just part of the fun.

Internet UFO Group

http://erau.db.erau.edu/~elston/IUFOG/

Have you seen the Roswell alien autopsy film yet? If there are no UFOs, why all the secrecy? You might be able to find out with this comprehensive digest of UFO material. Lots of links, lots of stories, lots of conspiracy theories, lots of GIFs and JPEGs.

Tarot

http://cad.ucla.edu/repository/useful/tarot.html

From the same guy as the I-Ching page, but the interpretations here are quite good. Go figure! This page can cast the traditional short three-card reading, or the extra-keen Full Celtic Spread.

The Zodiacal Zephyr

http://metro.turnpike.net/S/SRozhon/index.html

Very comprehensive site; includes basic info on astrology, conference announcements, ephemerides, where to find books and astrology software, and lots more.

Chinese Zodiac

http://falcon.cc.ukans.edu/~mothball/mystik/Chinese%20Zodiac

This page describes the 12-year Chinese Zodiac, with each year named after a different animal. This writer discovered that I was born in the Year of the Monkey and have these characteristics: "You are very intelligent and are able to influence people." Clearly, this is the most accurate of all astrology systems.

ALSO RECOMMENDED:

Internet Horoscopes

http://www.ws.pipex.com/tis/horoscop/horo5.htm

Nice graphics, plus links to other astrology pages.

Today's Humorscope

http://www.teleport.com/~ronl/horo.html

Sure to offend the true astrology believers, a typical daily missive is: Libra — "Excellent day to adopt an obviously fake French accent and to use typically French put-downs, such as 'Your mother was a hamster, and your father smelt of elderberries.'"

The WWW Virtual Library: Archive X, Paranormal Phenomena

http://www.crown.net/X

Another list of lists, this time to other strange sites on the Web. Broken into categories such as Ghost Encounters, Channeling Submissions, and Angel Encounters.

Yahoo! People

http://www.yahoo.com/Entertainment/People

The People section is where you'll find individuals' home pages.

The original broadcast medium is going strong on the Internet, with hundreds of sites from which to choose. Get receptive and tune in to the following Web sites for the best of the radio genre. In fact, there's such an embarassment of riches here, we can only provide a taste.

Amateur Radio

http://www.mcc.ac.uk/OtherPages/AmateurRadio.html

The best of the many directories of amateur radio (ham radio) pages. Links to amateur radio clubs around the world, plus pointers to the many radio newsgroups.

AMSAT

http://www.amsat.org/amsat/Amsat.html

AMSAT is a worldwide group of Amateur Radio Operators who share an active interest in building, launching, and communicating with each other through noncommercial, Amateur Radio satellites. They've launched more than 30 satellites into Earth orbit.

Digital Radio: The Sound of the Future!

http://www.magi.com/~moted/dr

From Canada, an explanation of digital radio, which promises CD-quality radio with no interference. An interesting look at the possibilities for this not-yet-standard system.

Brentwood

http://www.hallucinet.com:80/brentwood

An online soap opera, presented as RealAudio sound clips. Just starting at press tirne.

NPR Online

http://www.npr.org

National Public Radio's site is the online home of programs such as *All Things Considered* and *Morning Edition*. It carries complete rundowns of each day's shows, and now you can even find out who does the music it plays between segments (one of its most frequently asked questions).

Television

As with the radio section, there are thousands of TV sites, many devoted to shows that left the air long ago but that live on in the hearts and Web servers of their fans.

Welcome to PBS

http://www.pbs.org

The Public Broadcasting Service's site has the inside scoop on PBS programming, local affilliates, and educational services.

Usenet: alt.tv.commercials

news:alt.tv.commercials

Commercials. Bane or blessing? Debate the merits — if any — of TV commercials on this newsgroup.

Newton's Apple

http://ericir.syr.edu/Newton/welcome.html

The premier science program for kids, Newton's Apple is now in its 12th season of scientific discovery. You'll find additional info here for each of the season's shows, plus similar pages for the past three seasons. Now, where's Bill Nye the Science Guy's Web page?

Nye Labs

http://www.seanet.com/Vendors/billnye/nyelabs.html

Oh, here it is. Looks like we complained a bit too soon in the last entry. Here at Nye Labs lives the requisite episode guide, plus lots of cool science info (including home experiments), presented in that wacky Nye fashion.

The Satellite TV Page

http://itre.uncecs.edu/misc/sat.html

If you're interested in receiving TV via satellite dish, this is the place to go. It's a comprehensive list to satellite links, including manufacturers, FAQs, programming, and lots more.

What's On Tonite!

http://www.tv1.com/wot

TV listings for the U.S. Quite complete for the 40 channels it covers, but several second-tier cable channels, such as C-SPAN 2, HBO2, and The Movie Channel, aren't listed.

Yahoo! — Television Shows

http://www.yahoo.com/Entertainment/Television/Shows

There are too many shows to list individual ones here. Find your favorite with Yahoo!'s Search feature.

Videomaker's Camcorder & Desktop Video Site

http://www.videomaker.com

Lots of good info about shooting and editing your own video. Discussion forums help with your questions, and there is a breaking-news section with info on the latest innovations in camcorders.

Usenet: alt.video.laserdisc

news:alt.video.laserdisc

All about laser discs and laser disc players.

Usenet: rec.video

news:rec.video

Everything you wanted to know about miscellaneous video topics. Plus lots of passionately felt opinions from people you probably wouldn't talk to in real life.

Tardis TV Archive

http://src.doc.ic.ac.uk/public/media/tv/collections/tardis/index.html

This archive contains episode guides and miscellaneous files related to television programs of all kinds. Very extensive, and covers shows from the U.S., UK, Canada, Japan, and Sweden.

Trivia

Facts that aren't very important are the business of this section, and you can be sure that there are people cataloging the most niggling of details for your enjoyment.

The Internet Index

http://www.openmarket.com/info/internet-index

An occasionally updated collection of facts and statistics about the Internet and related activities. Inspired by the *Harper's* Index, it has odd bits of info about the Internet. As an example:

Estimated number of different users searching the Yahoo! database between May 1 and May 7, 1995: 1,400,000.

Estimated number of different users visiting the Smithsonian Institution between May 1 and May 7, 1995: 10,000.

The Straight Dope Archive

http://www.mcs.net/~krikket/html/tsd.html

Answers to trivial and not-so-trivial questions by Cecil Adams. *The Straight Dope* (TSD) is a column published by the *Chicago Reader* that answers questions on virtually any subject. People write in to Cecil and pose questions to which he digs up the answers. For example: Why do Wintergreen-flavored Life Savers spark when you bite them in a dark room?

Today in History

http://www.unison.com/wantinfo/today

The name pretty much says it all. Who was born and what happened on this day.

World Wide Trivia

http://www.mindspring.com/~kmims/wwt1.html

A quiz that you can take if your browser supports forms. Hard questions, too.

Useless Pages

In the anarchic world of the Internet, there are some sites that just seem to serve no purpose except to be fun. All of the Useless pages qualify.

Body Music!

http://www.wbm.ca/users/kgreggai/html/bodymus.html

Embarassing Body Noises — Coming to terms with the facts of human nature and our digestive tracts. "Our goal is to help people understand and not make fun of body functions beyond our control." Good luck, guys. If you're looking for audio files of burps and farts, you're at the right page. Yeesh!

Centre for the Easily Amused

http://www.islandnet.com/~cwalker/homepage.html

We spent way too much time at this site. Guess you know what that makes us.

Ground Zero

http://www.primenet.com/~moshman/index.html

Not really that useless. There's a whole bunch of links here under the blanket title "Links That Don't Suck." That's what this book is for.

Mediocre Site of the Day

http://pantheon.cis.yale.edu/~jharris/
mediocre.html

From the page's description: "The Web is overpopulated by Cool Sites and 'Worst of the Web' sites — in other words, pages lauding only the top and bottom 1 percent of all Web sites. This page was created to pay homage to the middle 98 percent — the mediocre, the unremarkable, the so-so, average sites that we encounter on a daily basis." How nice.

Useless WWW Pages

http://www.primus.com/staff/paulp/
useless.html

One of the original compendiums of the truly useless. Let's just hope your personal home page doesn't show up there one day.

Virtual Reality

Tired of that boring, workaday world? Resolutely refuse to get a life? Well then, build your own little world inside of a computer.

The Dockingbay

http://www.csd.uu.se/~johnn

Interesting site that takes you to a virtual space station. Acts like an adventure game in the way you travel through the station.

Nowwwhere

http://imagiware.com/nowhere.cgi

This virtual world lets you interact with other people who are accessing the site at the same time. You have to solve some puzzles as you explore Nowwwhere, and you eventually discover your goal.

Meta Virtual Environments

http://www.cc.gatech.edu/gvu/
people/Masters/Rob.Kooper/
Meta.VR.html

A good listing of virtual reality sites.

3DSite: vrml-links

http://www.lightside.com/3dsite/cgi/
VRML-index.html

Links to sites that can tell you all about the next step on the Web, 3-D worlds, being driven by Virtual Reality Modeling Language (VRML).

Hot Virtual Reality Sites

http://nemo.ncsl.nist.gov/~sressler/
hotvr.html

Just what the name says.

Government

A Libertarian's nightmare: Rules, regulations, and documents from U.S. federal and state government sites add up to billions of bytes of bureaucratese. On the other hand, this section offers some surprisingly fun and intensely interesting material. One could spend days on the U.S. Census Bureau's site alone. Overall, the Government section of Yahoo! is pretty heavily U.S.-centered.

U.S. government agencies were among the first users of the Internet, in fact (see the Introduction to the Internet chapter). So it's not surprising that they have a strong presence even now on the Net. Want to know your rights and privileges as an American citizen living abroad? Check out the Citizenship area. Interested in changing the tax structure? Check out Commissions. Have a plan for paying off the national debt? Submit your own federal budget with the National Budget Simulator. You'll also find information on conferences, various government institutes, legal policies, research organizations, and branches of the military.

Agencies

More than 300 sites listed, and growing. Here you'll find a wide variety of agencies that deal with everything from fishing rights to aviation regulations.

U.S. Census Bureau

http://www.census.gov

Statistics, we got 'em. Back up any argument, win any bet, advance any political position, here are all the statistics you'll need to convince anybody that *your* view of America's socioeconomic situation is correct. If you have a question, the Ask the Experts section even lets you send e-mail to authorities on housing, income, poverty, health, education, and other subjects. A great site.

FedWorld

http://www.fedworld.gov/

In its own words: "The goal of NTIS FedWorld is to provide a one-stop location for the public to locate, order, and have delivered to them U.S. Government information." Just a guess, but if you printed out every document FedWorld links to, you could probably wallpaper the Pentagon a hundred times over.

ALSO RECOMMENDED:

CIA

http://www.odci.gov/

All you conspiracy theorists out there will just love to add the audio welcome from the Director to your multimedia Christmas cards. More usefully, the *CIA World Factbook* is online, as well as samples from newly declassified satellite photographs. If you need facts at your fingertips, this site has statistics on hundreds of countries and regions.

Tiger Mapping Service

http://tiger.census.gov/

A godsend to teachers of geography and others who need mapping information, this site's create-your-own-map software also suggests a new game: Enter a longitude and latitude at random, and see whether or not you end up in the sea.

Citizenship

Information on taxation, medical insurance, and whether or not foreign-born children are American citizens. (If you think the answer is an unqualified yes, then you'd better check out American Citizens Abroad.)

American Citizens Abroad

http://iprolink.ch/aca/

ACA has been working since 1978 to improve U.S. laws and regulations that discriminate against Americans who live abroad.

Conferences

Yahoo! - Government Conferences

http://www.yahoo.com/Government/Conferences/

The conferences listed here cover public policy issues and conferences sponsored by government agencies. At press time, topics included a conference on the 1992 Los Angeles riots and a Canadian forum on technology in government.

Countries

Official information from and about governments from Argentina to Zimbabwe, including Australia's http://www.wombat.com.au. Most sites are either written in English or provide English translations; however, there's still plenty to keep your Maori or Finnish up to snuff. View them, and send *kommentteja ylläpitäjälle,* (that's Finnish for "comments to webmaster"). It's from sites like these that the Net's reputation for information overkill derives. Still, if you need information on, say, the Luxembourg Ministry of Education or elections in Slovakia, you'll find it here.

Warning: Connections from the U.S. can often be excruciatingly slow, especially if you are accessing a site at prime business hours in its home country.

African National Congress

http://www.anc.org.za/

The ANC home page contains news, links to related sites, and a form that lets you send e-mail to President Nelson Mandela. And this stunning

quote: "Nelson Mandela's greatest pleasure, his most private moment, is watching the sun set with the music of Handel or Tchaikovsky playing. Locked up in his cell during daylight hours, deprived of music, both these simple pleasures were denied him for decades."

ALSO RECOMMENDED:

Sound from Stortinget (Norwegian Parliament) On the Internet

http://sauce.uio.no/Stortinget/English.html

Norway is one of the most wired countries in the world. Log on in the middle of the night in America, and you can usually hook up with a lot of engineering students surfing the Net when they should be paying attention in their morning classes. Norway is so wired, they broadcast their parliamentary speeches over the MBONE. This site has audio clips of Norwegian legislators, perfect for befuddling unsuspecting friends.

Documents

From the Federalist Papers to the Federal Register, with stops at the Magna Carta and the Constitution. Because so many public documents can be obtained through several sites, you should always double-check if the document you want appears only in excerpted form, or with a charge. It's probably available in its entirety somewhere, and most likely for free.

Yahoo!

GPO Access on the Web

http://thorplus.lib.purdue.edu/gpo/

A searchable WAIS database of document collections including GAO "blue book" reports, the Congressional Record, Federal Register, Congressional bills, United States Code, and more.

Embassies

Information on embassies in several countries. You'll also find information on embassies if you look under specific country names in the Countries category.

The Electronic Embassy

http://www.embassy.org/

If there's any place for *Nightline*'s researchers to hang out on the Web, this is it. This site includes a marvelous Help and Resource Center with links to, for example, State Department Travel Advisories. Without their help we never would have known to watch out for Homicidal Danish Bicyclists who have the right of way over, and we do mean *over,* pedestrians. The Electronic Embassy is sponsored by TeleDiplomacy, Inc., which has also provided the resources for the Women for Women in Bosnia Web site.

ALSO RECOMMENDED:

The Embassy Page

http://www.globescope.com/web/gsis/embpage.html

A similar site to the Electronic Embassy, this one has an easy, alphabetical index of embassies and consulates in the United States and a growing list of other embassies in other countries (for example, the Royal Danish Embassy in Tokyo.)

Executive Branch

Sites brought to you by the people who gave us the term *Information Superhighway.*

The White House

http://www.whitehouse.gov

Includes everything from audio files of Socks meowing to a virtual walking tour of the First Ladies' Garden to links to every department in the Cabinet, 28 federal agencies, and the complete texts of conferences. Good place to get stuff with titles such as "White House Forum on the Role of Science and Technology in Promoting National Security and Global Stability." You don't have to be a Democrat to appreciate this site, but you might want to note that Socks doesn't sound too happy.

Federal Employees

Yahoo! - Federal Employees

http://www.yahoo.com/Government/Federal_Employees/

Lots of information for federal employees, including a festively presented news digest called Club Fed, where you'll learn about the new security clearance policies, retirement funds, and other fed employee-related info. Great site if you listed your Civil Service rank in your wedding announcement.

Institutes

Policy Wonk heaven.

Harvard - JFK School of Government

http://shango.harvard.edu/

Abstracts of cases considered by the school. Full text may be ordered by e-mail. An excellent online resource for journalists and others studying the impacts of public-policy decisions.

International Organizations

Checkpoints on the Information Superhighway, including NATO, the European Union, the UN, and the World Bank.

United Nations Scholars' Workstation at Yale University

http://www.library.yale.edu/un/unhome.htm

Subjects include disarmament, economic and social development, environment, human rights, international relations, international trade, peacekeeping, and population and demography.

Judicial Branch

Yes, there is more to the United States legal system than the O.J. Simpson trial. Here you'll find oodles of information on state and federal courts.

The Federal Judicial Center

http://www.fjc.gov/

The Federal Judicial Center is the federal courts' agency for research and continuing education. Among its many useful links is a searchable database (by topic and keyword) of Supreme Court decisions. Essential and fascinating.

Law

The Yahoo! legal index includes sites for legal professionals, along with a selection for the do-it-yourselfer. Please sign and return three notarized copies of our disclaimer before proceeding further.

In all seriousness, *caveat surfer.* Remember, there's no telling what'll get put on the Internet. If it's legal background you're seeking, the resources are generally excellent, but if it's legal *advice,* it might be very good or it might be you're getting what you paid for.

Note: Steve Arbuss, a partner in the Los Angeles law firm of Pircher, Nichols & Meeks, maintains a hotlist of legal sites at http://www.paranoia.com/~ebola/hotlaw.html.

Arbitration and Mediation

For firms, please see Business and Economy: Companies: Law: Arbitration and Mediation.

Arbitration and Mediation, Brief History

http://www.gama.com/his2.htm

A quick overview background on arbitration and mediation both in the U.S. and abroad.

GAMA: The Global Arbitration Meditation Association, Inc.

http://www.gama.com/

Includes convenient boilerplate legal forms. Naturally, there's a disclaimer regarding their use.

Cases

http://www.yahoo.com/Government/Law/Cases

From the inevitable Microsoft to the ubiquitous O.J.

This area also includes a chilling assortment of "it can't happen here" cases. Read the details of trials where investigative incompetence meets prosecutorial ego, and you have to wonder how much we've really advanced. More cases are added on a regular basis.

Defense Funds

The Phil Zimmerman Legal Defense Fund

http://www.netresponse.com/zldf/appeal.html

The Phil Zimmerman PGP case is currently the Internet's most important legal battle. The U.S. government says that Mr. Zimmerman may have broken export control laws when he released his encryption program PGP (Pretty Good Privacy) to the Internet. Many in the industry beg to differ. The implications of the case range far and wide. Do you want Big Brother (or other undesirables) reading your e-mail? It's not just civil libertarians who are following the case, either. Encryption software firms say that the U.S. government's restriction on exporting strong encryption beyond U.S. borders harms their software sales abroad.

As the saying goes: When encryption is outlawed, 8%gT3 >:eJ[-0 koo22@sP)*Jl, jm~"|+k lOPJS* 3jnh"(.

Commercial

Uniform Commercial Code

http://www.law.cornell.edu/ucc/ucc.table.html

Articles 1-9, General Provisions with hypertext definitions and a search engine.

Arent Fox Advertising Law Site

http://www.webcom.com/~lewrose/home.html

An excellent example of practicing what you preach, or perhaps that should be preaching what you practice.

Constitutional

Arguing Constitutional Law is something of a parlor game on Usenet. Be the first on your newsgroup to get your facts straight. (For censorship information, see Government: Politics: Censorship.)

First Amendment Cyber-Tribune

http://w3.trib.com/FACT/

Edited by Charles Levendosky, editorial page editor and award-winning columnist for the *Casper Star-Tribune.* The first stop for First Amendment issues on the Net, this site includes background, links to organizations and legal sites, weekly alerts on legislation or regulations that encroach on First Amendment provisions, and a Q&A where you can mail in your First Amendment queries.

Civil Liberties and Civil Rights

http://www.pls.com:8001/d2/kelli/httpd/htdocs/his/93.GBM

From the collection of the House of Representatives Internet Law Library. Varied selections on civil liberties topics in the United States and worldwide. Includes pointers to all holdings within the library.

ALSO RECOMMENDED:

Constitutions

World Constitutions

gopher://wiretap.spies.com/11/Gov/World

A diverse collection of historic and contemporary constitutional documents, from the Magna Carta to the 1992 Draft Constitution of the Estonian Republic.

Consumer

Sites for the both the professional and the layperson.

Alexander Law Firm

http://www.seamless.com/talf/

The Consumer Law Page presented by the Alexander law firm, specialists in consumer product liability, links to Netwide consumer interest resources, contains more than 100 consumer information brochures and articles on such topics of interest as product liability and toxic torts. An excellent and generous commercial site.

Bankruptcy

U.S. Bankruptcy Code

http://www.law.cornell.edu/uscode/11/

Bankruptcy Code; hypertext version of the code.

U.S. Supreme Court Bankruptcy Decisions

http://www.law.cornell.edu/syllabi?bankruptcy

Searchable database of Supreme Court bankruptcy cases

http://tsw.ingress.com/tsw/talf/txt/intro.html

ALSO RECOMMENDED:

Tenant Net

http://tenant.blythe.org/TenantNet/

Mainly focused on New York City with some links to other places, Tenant Net is nonetheless a comprehensive

resource for tenant activists. It also offers "On the Lower East Side: Observations of Life in Lower Manhattan at the Turn of the Century." This series of monographs, developed by St. Mary's College, Minnesota, is a superb background resource for those in the field of urban studies.

Corporate and Securities

Most of the information listed is legislation and background for the field.

University of Cincinnati College of Law - The Center for Corporate Law

http://www.law.uc.edu/CCL/

A growing database of the federal securities laws and their accompanying rules and forms.

Countries

A selection of legal documents and resources from around the world.

Canada

Canadian Legal and Government Resources

http://www.io.org/~agahtan/master.htm

Comprehensive listings of Canadian resources.

Mexico

Documents on Mexican Politics

http://daisy.uwaterloo.ca/~alopez-o/polind.html

Provocative assortment of articles dealing with Mexican legal and political issues. Some documents are only in English, others only in Spanish.

Russia

Russian Legal Server

http://solar.rtd.utk.edu/~nikforov/main.html

Information about Russian legislation and legal practice. Some of this site is in Cyrillic characters.

Employment Law

Most of the information in this section is geared toward professionals in the legal, benefits, and human resources fields.

Benefits Link

http://www.magicnet.net/benefits/index.html

Statutes and resources related to ERISA. This comprehensive site also includes yellow and white pages directory listings for firms and benefits administrators and help-wanted/position-sought postings. It also offers a large selection of commercial and downloadable shareware software. An excellent resource for benefits professionals.

Bureau of Labor Statistics (BLS)

http://stats.bls.gov/

Includes statistics, government publications, and private research papers among other resouces. Much of the information is searchable.

Employment Discrimination Law Materials

http://www.law.cornell.edu/topics/employment_discrimination.html

From the Legal Information Institute at Cornell Law School. Includes both overviews and links to complete regulations.

Entertainment

So, babe, it's this fabulous Web site, it's SGI meets GNN with a little CMP, you see where I'm going with this, I mean, we're talking hit city. I'll have my people e-mail your people. Historically chock-full of entertainment lawyers, Los Angeles is now a hotbed of multimedia, so it's not surprising that three L.A. firms have put up exceptional sites with generous resources.

Entertainment Law CyberCenter

http://www.hollywoodnetwork.com/Law/

Tons of tips for screenwriters, producers, and directors. Along with legal and financing information, includes the Internet Crimewriting Network.

Entertainment Law Resources

http://www.laig.com/law/entlaw/

Essential tips (plus a few horror stories) from attorney/writer Mark Litwak (author of *Reel Power: The Struggle for Influence and Success in the New Hollywood*).

International Entertainment & Multimedia Law & Business Network

http://www.laig.com/law/intnet/

From attorney and UCLA lecturer Harris Tulchin. The site has numerous legal and film links and the complete lecture notes from Mr. Tulchin's UCLA classes on copyright and other issues for multimedia producers.

Federal

Code of Federal Regulations

gopher://gopher.counterpoint.com:2001/

If you're into it, your heart must be pounding.

The following are presented by the Legal Information Institute of Cornell University Law School. Essential for practitioners and for laypeople, these sites might help those episodes of *Law & Order* make more sense.

U.S. Supreme Court Rules

http://www.law.cornell.edu/rules/supct/overview.html

Federal Rules of Civil Procedure

http://www.law.cornell.edu/rules/frcp/overview.htm

United States Code

http://www.law.cornell.edu/uscode/

Federal Rules of Evidence

http://www.law.cornell.edu/rules/fre/overview.html

General Information

CyberLaw & CyberLex

http://www.portal.com/~cyberlaw/cylw_home.html

According to this site: "CyberLaw is an educational service focusing on legal issues concerning computer technology. CyberLex reports legal developments touching the computer industry." Steve Arbuss rates it "the best site for developments in online and computer law."

Law Employment Center

http://www.lawjobs.com/

About the most straight-to-the-point URL you're ever gonna see. Updated daily, hundreds of searchable legal employment listings from the *National Law Journal,* and *New York Law Journal.* The site promises listings from *Law Technology Product News* in the near future.

LawInfo

http://www.lawinfo.com/

Information on how to find, whom to find, and how to do it yourself.

Legal Information Institute

http://www.law.cornell.edu/

An excellent resource containing information about court decisions, codes, regulations, and more.

Translink

http://www.webcom.com/~pjones/

A Web site dealing with legal issues arising from use of EDI (Electronic Data Interchange) in international transport. Undoubtedly a growth field.

Immigration

Sites range from government offices to many law firms announcing their services.

FAQ - Dual Citizenship and U.S. Law

http://www.mks.com/~richw/dualcit.html

A FAQ on dual citizenship prepared by an American/Canadian citizen.

Institutes

Law schools and public policy institutions worldwide.

Chicago-Kent's Guide to Legal Resources

http://www.kentlaw.edu/lawnet/lawlinks.html

Searchable netwide resources on law.

Norwegian Research Center for Computers and Law.

http://www.jus.uio.no/iri/nrccl.html

Has an excellent hotlist of telecommunications-related sites.

University of Massachusetts at Amherst

http://www.umassp.edu/legal/home.html

U Mass offers what it calls an Internet law "hypercourse" with the full texts of related books and articles online.

Intellectual Property

Forget all that pornography nonsense—this one's the real hot-button issue. The distribution of information has never been easier in all of human history. In the same way that extending the frontiers of medicine has left professionals and laypeople alike dealing with heretofore unimagined issues, intellectual property is going to be a growth field. To sum up the issue: Information may be free, but rent isn't. Or to update a Net axiom: Information wants to be free, but writers and programmers want to be paid.

Copyrights

FAQ - USENET Copyright Myths

http://www.clari.net/brad/copymyths.html

Brad Templeton, publisher of ClariNet News, has prepared this definitive FAQ. Read it before you post an opinion about copyright, and before you flame someone else's.

Technology

EFF Intellectual Property Issues & Policy Archive

http://www.eff.org/pub/Intellectual_property/

The Intellectual Property page of the highly regarded Electronic Frontier Foundation.

Technology Law Resources [Jeffrey R. Kuester]

http://www.kuesterlaw.com/

This site contains an excellent online primer and links to other resources.

Legislative Branch

Several sites are dedicated solely to Newt Gingrich. Look for him under Government: House of Representatives: Representatives. Not every representative or senator is on the Net — yet — but we have no doubt it's only a matter of time.

By the way, if you're ever looking for visitors' info for a particular state, a representative's page is generally a great place to start.

THOMAS: Legislative Information on the Internet

http://thomas.loc.gov/

Total Heuristic Organization of Managed Archive Servers. Or something like that. We just can't believe that THOMAS isn't an acronym. No, actually the THOMAS server is named for the man who was our 3rd and arguably our most literate president. Essential for any browser's bookmark list.

ALSO RECOMMENDED:

The Electronic Activist

http://www.crocker.com/~ifas/activist/

Push-button democracy is here! Now that you've read all the bills on THOMAS, send your opinions by way of The Electronic Activist, which provides e-mail addresses and pop-up mail-to forms for both politicians and the media.

Military

The Army, Air Force, Coast Guard, Marines, and Navy are represented here, as well as information on ballistic-missile simulators, explosives ordnance disposal, and pretty pictures of airplanes. The ultimate in the Law of Unintended Consequences may be the military origins of the Net.

Air Force

United States Air Force Museum

http://www.am.wpafb.af.mil/museum/usaf_museum.html

A virtual tour of the Air Force museum, with great photos of planes and text on the history of flight.

News

Breaking news from the U.S. Information Service.

U.S. Information Service Gopher Server

gopher://hk.net/11/.usishk

A daily compendium of news, official statements, and information transmitted electronically from the U.S. Information Agency in Washington, D.C.

Politics

Ultimately, the "killer app" of the Internet may turn out to be not home shopping but democracy. And whether you find that exhilarating or terrifying is entirely dependent on your view of

human nature. If you're politically active, this is the place to find a wealth of resources. Even if you're politically passive, you can learn a lot by browsing this section. Wide-ranging topics include activism, censorship (on the Internet and elsewhere), information on past and upcoming elections in the U.S. and other countries, nuclear testing, religious freedom, and much more.

Yahoo! - Current Politics Headlines

http://www.yahoo.com/Government/Politics/Current_Politics_Headlines/

Start your day with Yahoo!'s listing of Reuter's top stories from the day's political news.

Activism

From rugged American individualists ("ranting conspiracy freaks") to long-established Washington organizations ("fat-cat lobbyists"), left, right, center, and off the edge, there's something for everyone on the Internet. Many times, even if you find a page's point-of-view antithetical, you may find the supporting links extremely useful.

Calyx Internet Access: Other Places

http://www.calyx.com/activist_links.html

Listings are from a Progressive/ Libertarian perspective. In addition, several excellent resource links, including the searchable Government Manual Gopher site at the University of Michigan.

Yahoo!

Censorship

Trying to control what others may read, say, hear, and think is an age-old human endeavor. It usually doesn't end up working too well. And the ease with which the Internet crosses political, geographic, and cultural boundaries makes censorship that much more difficult. As Mike Godwin of EFF said: "The Internet interprets censorship as damage and routes around it."

Nevertheless, the struggle to control the information flying around the Net is growing more heated as more people discover the consensual anarchy of cyberspace, and if that doesn't scare you silly, then you're a [CENSORED].

Censorship and the Internet

http://dis.strath.ac.uk/people/paul/Control.html

A list of links on the subject of controlling and regulating the Internet. There's enough source material, including many international cases, to create a graduate class. The one we all wish Martin Rimm had taken.

Project Censored

http://zippy. sonoma.edu/ProjectCensored/

Project Censored's Top Ten List of stories (going back to 1989) that were overlooked or underplayed by a general media obsessed with O.J. and cyberporn. Fascinating and terrifying.

We Will Not Be CENSORED

PROJECT CENSORED
Sonoma State University
Rohnert Park, CA 94928
707/664-2500 FAX 707/664-0597

Clinton Administration

Topics such as Clinton Administration Woes and Rush is Right! It is recommended that Democrats do not read these listings before bedtime.

Countries

Yahoo! - Countries

http://www.yahoo.com/Government/Politics/Countries/

Under Government: Countries you will find listings of what governments are doing for their citizens. Under Government: Politics: Countries, tragically, you will find listings of what countries are doing *to* their citizens.

Crisis in Rwanda

Several sites giving updates to this huge tragedy and providing ways to contribute.

Volunteers in Technical Assistance: Rwanda Emergency Situation

gopher://vita.org/11/disaster/rwanda

Provides a Gopher menu of detailed updates on the Rwandan crisis.

Volunteers in Technical Assistance: Main Page

gopher://gopher.vita.org/

Frequently updated reports on natural and human-rights disasters around the world and in the United States. A superb resource.

Elections

Yahoo! - Elections

http://www.yahoo.com/Government/Politics/Elections/

U.S. national, U.S. local, and international elections. Take a break from the Perpetual Campaign in America and see how it's going out there in the rest of the world.

Forums

Democracy Direct

http://www.cais.com/infoplaza/vote.html

After reading so many other people's opinions, here's a chance to express your own. An interesting suggestion of what electronic democracy might be like.

Votelink

http://www.votelink.com

Similar in concept to Democracy Direct but divided by country as well as issue.

Humor

Sites to amuse and offend all sides of the political spectrum.

FIDEL '96 — The Ultimate Washington Outsider

http://www.slugs.com/imagesmith/fidel/

Desperate times call for desperate measures, and so Adam Reith has appointed himself coordinator of the Fidel for President '96 campaign: "In this era when EVERY candidate rhetorically claims to be outside the American political machine, here's a guy that is thoroughly loathed in a completely bipartisan way. Following this 'outsider' logic, he must be THE SINGLE BEST HOPE WE HAVE."

Magazines

Would it surprise you to find there are four anarchist magazines listed, and another that bills itself as "A zine for people who quit being anarchists because there were too many rules"? Plenty of offerings from those who actually still believe in governments, too.

The Congressional Quarterly

gopher://gopher.cqalert.com/

The *Congressional Quarterly* was founded in 1945, "in the belief that only an informed public could forge a true democracy." Among the information accessible through the *CQ* Gopher: Lead stories of the current *CQ Weekly Report*; Current weekly news brief from *The CQ Researcher*; Status of appropriation bills and other major legislation.

The New Republic

http://www.enews.com/magazines/tnr/

Presented by the Electronic Newsstand in Gopher format, this text-only archive is useful, if not colorful. Its self-promotion asks, "Have you ever wondered how people like Barry Diller, Alan Greenspan, Ted Koppel, Ruth Bader Ginsburg, David Geffen, Barbra Streisand … develop their opinions and nurture their thinking?" Ahh … so it was the *New Republic* that convinced Barbra Streisand that she could play a callgirl at 40-something.

Parties and Groups

From the Big Two to fringe groups and anarchists, you'll find platforms, manifestos, and miscellaneous information on political parties. The Net doesn't seem to have quite caught on as a campaign tool yet; at press time, only two Democratic candidates had sites listed under the 1996 Presidential Election category: Bill Clinton and Pat Paulsen. The Republicans were doing much better, with eight candidates listed.

Alaskan Independence Party

http://www.polarnet.fnsb.ak.us/End_of_Road/soapbox.dir/aip.dir/

Along with the party's platform, varied links to information about the landmass some consider a state, and others, a colony. Including *Mushing* magazine with its helpful cover story on "How to compost Dog Manure."

Anarchy

The usual range of discourse, from ranting, antigovernment blather to reasoned, enlightened argument.

Spunk Press

http://www.cwi.nl/cwi/people/Jack.Jansen/spunk/Spunk_Home.html

Informative and written in a tone that shouldn't put off those with less radical viewpoints. Spunk has this to say about the infamous *Anarchist Cookbook*: "The general consensus among anarchists seems to be that the book is very badly written, and full of factual errors. These go so far that you will probably blow yourself up if you try one of the bomb recipes, or poison yourself if you try a drug from the book. The rumor is often heard that the book was compiled by a CIA agent for exactly this reason. Believe this or not to your own liking."

Conservative

The Right Side of the Web

http://www.clark.net/pub/jeffd/index.html

In its words: "The Right Side of the Web exists to counter all the socialism and moral anarchy you'll find on the Net." They've certainly got their work cut out for them.

Yahoo!

Conspiracy

Yahoo! - Conspiracy

http://www.yahoo.com/Government/
Politics/Parties_and_Groups/
Conspiracy/

Paranoid whackos or canaries in a coal mine? In this section you'll find "news and events that the national and international media would never be allowed to print." Why would IDG Books let us point you to it then? Well, maybe that's just part of the conspiracy.

Democratic

The Democrats are the greatest party in history, and if you will only keep electing them, everything will be all right. For why everything is screwed up, see Republicans.

Democrat's Source Page

http://www.wp.com/lookn2it/
home.html

A good jumping-off point for information on the Democratic Party, with information on contacting members of Congress, as well as lots of links to other resources.

United States Senate Democratic Policy Committee

ftp://ftp.senate.gov/committee/Dem-
Policy/general/dpc.html

"Provides information on legislation and promotes the Senate Democratic Agenda." Needless to say, not the most objective analysis of the issues. However, the site has convenient links to current legislation, including the complete text of recent bills, and information on the week's Senate schedule, upcoming bills, committee hearings, and other Senate activity.

Fringe Groups

Yahoo! - Fringe Groups

http://www.yahoo.com/Government/
Politics/Parties_and_Groups/
Fringe_Groups/

And you thought the worst thing on the Internet was cyberporn.

A-Z of Cults

http://www.observer.co.uk/a-z-cults/
index.html

A dryly humorous rundown of cults worldwide. Apparently starting one's own religion is an international growth industry. (Note: This is a British site. Members of certain established American denominations would no doubt take offense at their inclusion.)

Green Party

Yahoo! - Green Party

http://www.yahoo.com/Government/
Politics/Parties_and_Groups/
Green_Party/

Save trees and learn German at the same time.

Liberal

Yahoo! - Politics: Parties and Groups: Liberal

http://www.yahoo.com/Government/
Politics/Parties_and_Groups/Liberal/

Proof that they exist outside of their native habitat in Massachusetts.

Jeff's Progressive Pages

http://www.crl.com/~jeffj/home.html

Simple and serious, an excellent rundown of liberal/progressive resources and links.

Libertarian

The closest thing the Internet has to a state religion.

The Cato Institute

http://w3.ag.uiuc.edu/liberty/cato/
index.html

The Cato Institute is named for *Cato's Letters,* libertarian pamphlets that helped lay the philosophical foundation for the American Revolution. From P.J. O'Rourke's address to the Cato Institute: "We are part of a huge invisible picket line that circles the White House twenty-four hours a day. We are participants in an enormous non-march on Washington — millions and millions of Americans not descending upon the nation's capital in order to demand nothing from the United States government. To demand nothing, that is, except the one thing which no government in history has been able to do — leave us alone."

Militia

Yahoo! - Militia

http://www.yahoo.com/Government/
Politics/Parties_and_Groups/Militia/

Your one-stop info source for info on paramilitary groups.

Natural Law

Yahoo! - Natural Law

http://www.yahoo.com/Government/
Politics/Parties_and_Groups/
Natural_Law/

Apparently, these folks propose to combat crime in America by teaching inmates Transcendental Meditation. Well, it's probably worth a try.

Republican

The Republicans are the greatest party in history, and if you will only keep electing them, everything will be all right. For why everything is screwed up, see Democrats.

Information Headquarters for the Republican Primary

http://www.umr.edu/~sears/primary/
main.html

Includes links to all the major Republican candidates. A good place to keep an eye on as the U.S. primary elections approach.

ALSO RECOMMENDED:

The Right Side of the Web: The Speaker's Corner

http://www.clark.net/pub/jeffd/
mr_newt.html

Numerous Newt-related tidbits, including speeches, remarks, book excerpts, and even a photo essay. A veritable love-fest for fans of Newt (in contrast to some of the less-charitable sites in the "Gingrich, Newt" section).

Socialists

Yahoo! - Socialists

http://www.yahoo.com/Government/
Politics/Parties_and_Groups/Liberal/

Sites for American and Canadian socialists young and old. Couldn't have made this up if we tried: The American Socialist party has an AOL address.

United We Stand America

Yahoo! - United We Stand America

http://www.yahoo.com/Government/
Politics/Parties_and_Groups/
United_We_Stand_America/

Mr. Perot's followers air their views on the Web.

We The People

Yahoo! - We the People

http://www.yahoo.com/Government/
Politics/Parties_and_Groups/
We_the_People/

Just when you thought 1992 was over. A national organization formed by those involved in Jerry Brown's presidential campaign.

Petitions

You could stand in a parking lot in the pouring rain with a clipboard full of soggy papers, asking, "Are you a registered voter?" and watching everyone scurry past mumbling "no."

Or you could put up a Web site.

Save Paradise Reef

HTTP://synapse-group.com/
save.the.reef/petition.cgi

This international petition drive sponsored by Jean-Michel Cousteau asks the world to protest a cruise ship pier the government of Mexico wants to construct in the middle of Paradise Reef in the Cozumel National Underwater Refuge.

Political Science

Welcome to Moscow Libertarium!

http://www.fe.msk.ru/libertarium/
ehomepage.html

What a wacky bunch of political scientists. This Russian site features political speeches, articles, primers on liberalism, and FAQs in English and Russian. Plus, of course, this great graphic.

Institutes

Political science institutes in the U.S. and abroad.

The National Election Studies at the University of Michigan

http://www.umich.edu/~nes/

Contains the complete 1994 National Election Study and information on The Comparative Study of Electoral Systems (CSES), "a collaborative program of cross-national research among election studies conducted in forty-seven consolidated and emerging democracies." Fascinating for specialists.

PoliticsUSA

http://PoliticsUSA.com/

Get the latest information about the U.S. political scene. Includes information about upcoming elections, Campaign '96, a daily user poll, and much more.

ALSO RECOMMENDED:

Political Campaigning Graduate Program - University of Florida

http://www.clas.ufl.edu/CLAS/Departments/Polisci/Campaign.html

Just felt it was only fair to warn you: The University of Florida now offers degrees in political campaigning.

Reengineering

Even the government has to try and remake its image every so often.

Budget Payroll and Personnel System (BPPS) Project

http://www.uth.tmc.edu/ut_general/special_interest/committees/bop/index.html

This site at the University of Texas-Houston provides links to Quality Management resources all over the Net, including the quality.org site, which — not surprisingly — is "under continuous improvement." We could've guessed that.

Research Labs

Not for the crowd who needed to be told Apollo 13 actually happened. From Ames and Los Alamos to Lawrence Livermore and Sandia Labs, hundreds of sites created for and by the people who do research.

Cool NASA Site of the Week

http://www.jsc.nasa.gov/nasa/Cool.html

A happy reminder that even Nobel prizewinners were once little kids shooting off rockets in the backyard, this is NASA's *own* cool sites index. You may still need an advanced knowledge of computers, not to mention a UNIX machine, to understand some of their ideas of fun, but many links have the gee-whiz stuff that appeals to everyone.

ALSO RECOMMENDED:

NASA SpaceLink

http://spacelink.msfc.nasa.gov/

The site is geared toward professional educators, but could certainly be used by parents whose kids have already passed through the dinosaur phase. Teachers may apply for SpaceLink accounts, which allow kids to initiate telnet sessions with NASA scientists.

States

Included here is mostly official information from state agencies. Additional travel information may be found under Regional Information. Which agencies and what type of information is listed varies from state to state.

State of Alaska - North to the Future

http://www.state.ak.us/

An assortment of administrative links, plus a gorgeous photo gallery (http://ccl.alaska.edu/local/adfg/gallery/galhome.html) that lives up to all of our *Northern Exposure* fantasies. Who knew halibut grew that big?

Indices

From now on, whenever we hear of the foresight of our nation's founders, we will think gratefully of the choice of Red, White, & Blue for our flag. How impossible it would have been to look at all the sites in this section, had our national color scheme been, say, chartreuse, orange, and hot pink.

INFOMINE

http://lib-www.ucr.edu/govpub/

Never was a site better named. You can dig for information by subject, keyword, and title, and make use of lots of well-organized government and academic links.

Internet Corruption Ranking

http://www.gwdg.de/~uwww/ intro.htm

No, it's not about how the Internet corrupts children or even how hackers corrupt the Internet. It's actually a ranking of political corruption ("improper practices") worldwide, and it's fascinating. Test your cynicism by guessing where the U.S. ranks before you check.

Health

This Yahoo! category is a good example of Yahoo!'s ease-of-use. The main point of a good index is to help you find what you want. In the Yahoo! scheme, a large measure of redundancy is built into the system. Suppose you're looking for a supplier of vitamins, for example. Should you try Commercial Health Products? Companies? Alternative Medicine? Well, it turns out that any of those will probably work. The names of some suppliers with catalogs of vitamins are often stashed in five or six different places within Yahoo!. In other words, you don't have to guess right the first time to find what you want.

Another point about Health is that this category is absolutely stuffed to the eyebrows. Thousands of newsgroups and mailing lists on Health topics were around even before the Web became popular. These groups and lists got converted into Web sites at lightning speed, and thus Health makes up one of the biggest information exchanges on the Web.

Alternative Medicine

Most of these sites carry disclaimers of one kind or another, but in the interests of Yahoo! I might as well add one more. Some of the treatments currently listed as alternative medicine may one day be accepted by the medical establishment. Some of them will fall out of favor even as a form of wild-eyed quackery. You just can't tell. A healthy skepticism about alternative medicine (and for that matter, skepticism about mainstream medicine) is a sound policy — when it comes to health care, you should be prepared to do lots of reading and lots of thinking.

Acupuncture

Acupuncture.com

http://www.acupuncture.com/acupuncture/

This is not only a very complete acupuncture resource, it's rapidly developing links to all sorts of alternative-medicine sites. You can download your own map of all these little places you are supposed to stick needles for particular results, and for that matter you can order your own set of needles.

Chiropractors

This classification has all sorts of topics that aren't really chiropractic but more along the lines of "New Age bodywork," so to speak.

Alexander Technique

http://none.coolware.com/health/alex_tech/FlyerBody.html

The Alexander Technique is a form of bodywork that dates to early in this century, and has been much in favor with actors and other performers. It amounts to a re-education of your habitual patterns of muscle tension.

Companies

There's another category for Companies at the first directory level. These companies in this section are, as you would expect, all in the alternative medicine business, but many of them are also found in a variety of different categories.

Health and Healing from ConsciousNet

http://www.consciousnet.com/hlth$hl.htm

This is a very big resource for all kinds of stuff, including directories of online stores and so forth. If you are looking for hypnotists or aromatherapy consultants, you can find them here.

Feldenkrais Method

http://www.cbima.com/Gabriel/feldenkrais.html

This is a bodywork method developed in Israel that bears remarkable resemblances to the Alexander Technique (see above). Maybe it turns out there are actually just a few ways to get the same kinds of body results after all.

Nature's Medicines

http://www.halcyon.com/jerryga/welcome.html

This site is a big catalog of all types of services and products, from fairly mundane nutritional items to very, very weird stuff.

Present Moment

http://www.presentmoment.com/

So, probably what I should do is order lots of books from this gigantic informational site, so I can figure out the stuff in the previous site. It is almost odd that the warp-speed world of the Internet is becoming a resource for meditation and philosophy, but maybe Web-heads can use some help appreciating the "present moment."

Quantum Medicines

http://www.usa.net/qmed/

Quantum medicine is fairly difficult to describe, but its implementation seems to deal with electro-physiological reactivity and acupuncture-plus-electric-current. For the intellectually curious, this is a good place to explore a frontier area of alternative medicine.

Walker's Dynamic Herbs and Botanicals

http://www.txdirect.net/kombucha/

Kombucha is an Asian fungus/mushroom that will grow from a starter culture in a pot of tea with sugar. You then drink what's left, and devotees of this stuff claim that it has many amazing medical properties. It has many adherents among people for whom standard medical practice has failed to produce results. Generally, people just pass around the starter cultures for free, but if you don't know anyone doing this, you can get some from the company at this site.

Commercial Health Products

Allergy Supply Company

http://aaabiz.com/AL/alhp.html

This is perhaps the definitive collection of hard-to-find asthma medications, and a collection of allergy-related remedies. It's an interesting example of an Internet-based store — the Internet is probably the only place you could locate this collection of items and sell them at a profit, unless you found a big city with severe allergy problems.

Cybershrink

http://www.gate.net/~cyshrink/

Hey, why not? This is one of many e-mail psychological counseling services. The evidence isn't necessarily in yet of the efficacy of this system, but it's hard to believe that it will be much worse than the efficacy of standard, office-based "talking cure" practice. Maybe people are more willing to go into more depth with someone they can't see.

Diabetes

Sugarbusters

http://www.iquest.net/sugarbusters/
sugarbusters.html

Besides a catalog for ordering insulin and syringes and testing equipment, this site has an information service. Here, in fact, you may find some recent good news: Testing for blood sugar may not require actual blood samples in a few years, and alternatives to insulin injection are developing.

DocTalk

http://www.indirect.com/user/
cnewhall/

This service provides online medical advice, and it's pretty good advice at that. The developer, Clark Newhall, is also an attorney, so it's a good bet he's thought through the legal implications of handing out this kind of advice to strangers online. One interesting feature of this service is called SkinFlix, which offers QuickTime movies and JPEG stills. Not, however, what you might think from the name — these are X-rays and MRI scans.

Fitness and Exercise

cybercise

http://www.cybercise.com/

If you have started to slump over permanently from working day and night at a keyboard, you might want to order yourself some exercise equipment from these people.

Good Health Web

http://www.social.com/health/

Good Health Web is a sort of directory-within-a-directory. From this site, you can find almost everything in the Yahoo! health listing.

Health Technologies Network

http://www.ieway.com/business/
max/welcome.html

Connoisseurs of late-20th century American business practices will want to check out this site — it's more or less an Amway-type business. Will this work on the Web, or does the whole premise of so-called "multilevel-marketing" depend on face-to-face contact with friends and relatives you can guilt-trip into buying things? Stay tuned as we all find out.

The Lead Tester

http://branch.com/epa/

If you live in a building that's more than 20 years old, you should consider ordering a lead-testing kit from these people. The problem is that you have no way of getting rid of lead (or other heavy metals) once you ingest it, so the whole point is not ingesting it in the first place.

MuscleZine

http://internet-designs.com/ultimate/
bodies.htm

It's Jock Central, right here on the Web. This site has lots of links outward — you can probably send an e-mail to Arnold Schwarzenegger if you follow them far enough.

Nutritional Products

This is a huge category, with more than 60 entries. If you are convinced that you don't have enough blue-green algae, protein powder, barley juice, or megavitamins in your diet, this section of Yahoo! will fill your every need.

Shrink-Link

http://www.westnet.com/shrink/
shrink.html

This is yet another e-mail psychologist thing. This time, however, the advice costs $20 per message.

Windy Hill Professional Labs

http://perry.gulfnet.com/advertisers/
drug_testing/drug1.htm

Now here's a delicate little issue. You are about to start a new job where they do mandatory drug testing. You've cleaned up your act but might be worried that traces of strange substances might still be floating around in your system. You may be concerned about the possibility of a false positive — not a negligible consideration, either. So you contact these people, they send you a kit, you send it back, and you get an answer by e-mail for $65.

Companies

You just can't get lost on Yahoo! If you missed the alternative medicine category the first time 'round, here's another category of alternative medicine companies. Anyway, look for this particular category to explode during 1996, as companies flood onto the Net.

Bassett Aromatherapy

http://www.eskimo.com/~joanne/

This site has a very nice catalog of scents, and it's conveniently located near Microsoft Corporation. Send Bill Gates a mellow birthday present and see what happens.

Biomedical

This big section is the hangout for an assortment of high-tech firms.

BIO Online

http://cns.bio.com/bio.html

This site is a serious research-data exchange center. It includes an employment center with dozens of major sponsors, all kinds of industry investment and regulatory information, and online journals.

Biosupply Net

http://www.biosupplynet.com/bsn/

If you ever had an impulse to become a mad scientist, this site deserves your attention. It has links to the online catalogs of 1,400 suppliers of biotechnology supplies and equipment. With a good credit card and some quick online effort, you can start cloning yourself.

Genentech

http://www.gene.com/

The whole story on this pioneer biotech company, including annual reports, research papers, and directions for upcoming research.

Physician's GenRx

http://www.icsi.net/GenRx.html

This site is good for finding any sort of drug equivalents — you will be amazed at the impenetrable welter of trade names that exist for even the simplest pharmaceuticals. The service used to be open to anyone. For security reasons mostly, you now have to sign up for the service.

Insurance

Insurance Research Network

http://mmink.cts.com/mmink/dossiers/irn.html

We'll be seeing more of this. This company can find you a quote on different types of insurance. Since the Web is an ideal place to collect a risk pool, insurance is a natural service. Also, the insurers offering term life insurance should be happy because the average Web user is roughly 28 and won't die for decades.

MedLink

http://www.medlink.com/

This service matches up doctors with jobs worldwide. The interesting implication from reading the notices here is that doctors may become as mobile as software programmers within a decade, instead of staying in practice at a single office or hospital forever.

Modern Body Design

http://www.ipworld.com/market/fitness/modbody/homepage.htm

This company sells an exercise "sling" in the price range of $50 – $100. Has to be seen to be believed — that's why we put the address here.

Nursing

This category contains information about professional associations, and also resumes of individual health service people.

Telephone Triage

http://innet.com/~kathiw/triage.html

This fascinating site discusses training and seminars in *triage* for nurses. If you're not familiar with the term, triage means sorting people out according to degree of medical need. The course teaches you to determine who gets put on hold and who gets rushed to the emergency room.

Yahoo!

Optometry

Yahoo! - Optometry

http://www.yahoo.com/
Business_and_Economy/Companies/
Health_and_Fitness/Optometry/

Dozens of local purveyors of laser eye surgery are listed here, along with piles of companies that sell discount contact lenses online.

Pharmaceuticals

The drugs are in other categories. Here you'll find information on individual pharmaceutical companies.

Eli Lilly

http://www.lilly.com/

Lilly posts QuickTime movies, research reports, ads, employment bulletins, and all sorts of public relations material.

Physician Finder Online

http://msa2.medsearch.com/pfo/

This site offers a keyword search for finding a doctor, by specialty or region or language or six other criteria. So far, it still needs a larger assortment, but it's filling in fast.

Relax the Back

http://www.relaxtheback.com/

According to recent research, back ailments are second only to colds and flu as a reason people miss work. Here's a big catalog of ergonomic products, and a little online 60-second exercise drill.

Death and Dying

In the words of the notorious t-shirt, "Eat right, exercise, die anyway." So we need a Death category under the Health classification.

Christ Church Parish

http://www.seanet.com/Users/jbrian/
memorial.html

This service lets you post Web memorials to people who have recently died. It's very nicely done, too.

Death Net

http://www.islandnet.com/
~deathnet/open.html

It's your one stop — your one *last* stop — for online memorials, information about right-to-die legislation, funerals, survivors' rights, and any other death-related topic. There's a valuable hospice directory.

Disabilities

This is a real hot spot on the Web. If you think about it for a moment, you will see that putting the world online is potentially a revolutionary development for both access and employment for people with disabilities. On the Web, no one can see your wheelchair or tell if you're deaf, so it's a much more egalitarian place than the glass-and-brick universe.

Archimedes Project

http://kanpai.stanford.edu/arch/
arch.html

We assume that the title here is a reference to a supposed quote by Archimedes ("Give me a place to stand, and I will move the earth."), pronounced after he had figured out the principle of the lever. This site has a collection of design ideas and arguments for making the physical world more accessible to everyone.

Autism Resources

http://web.syr.edu/~jmwobus/
autism/

Long lists of information resources on this baffling disorder. If you want to convince yourself that cognitive psychology doesn't have all the answers yet, check out some of these FAQs.

Deafness

Deafness is a large category, probably because the Net developed deaf resources very early and, of course, because being deaf basically isn't a disability in the online world.

Deaf World Web

http://deafworldweb.org/deafworld/

This is a single, unified, well-organized site that has everything for deaf people online, and it's available in four languages besides.

Disabilities Access Online

http://www.pavilion.co.uk/
CommonRoom/DisabilitiesAccess/

Like Deaf World Web, this is a central directory for all sorts of disability issues, medical, physical, and legal.

Gallaudet

http://www.gallaudet.edu/

Gallaudet College is a great institution, the only university specifically for deaf people. The site includes an online catalog, information and forms for admissions, financial aid data, and college background.

General Info

http://weber.u.washington.edu/ ~britell/

This is a very complete index site, mostly concerned with physical rehabilitation issues, maintained by a professor at the University of Washington Medical School.

Hyperlexia

http://www.iac.net/~whaley/ gordy.html

Hyperlexia refers to really superior early ability to read combined with some autism-like traits. This site was assembled by parents of a hyperlexic kid and is really interesting reading.

Mental Health

This is a huge section. It would appear that every psychiatrist and psychologist in America is online now.

Ask Siggy

http://www.psychology.com/ asksiggy.htm

What, *another* online shrink?! Yes indeed. The site offers free answers to some questions and includes a directory of therapists.

Attacking Anxiety

http://www.sover.net/~schwcof/

You can order a video on anxiety problems here and get FAQs on anxiety disorders.

cyber-psych

http://www.charm.net/~pandora/ psych.html

The dysfunctional Mother of All Directories. A huge list with pointers to everything else on mental health issues from addiction and depression to work issues.

Madness

http://www.io.org/~madness/

Another page that leads everywhere, with mailing lists and Gophers. There's an emphasis on patients' rights in much of this material.

THRIVEnet

http://www.webcom.com/ ~odyssey1/thrive/

This link features "survivor stories" — much of it inspirational material about overcoming adverse situations and getting out of victimhood.

Index Mental Health Pages

http://www.sover.net/~schwcof/ links.html

And everything indexed at the other mental health sites is recapitulated here. This site is exceptionally well maintained.

Diseases and Conditions

The disease category is an excellent place to look for a second opinion or for background if you have been diagnosed as having a condition. If you are feeling all right, it's a great place to drive yourself into fits of hypochondria — at some sites you can type in a few vague keywords and get a scary prognosis. In time, there's reason to believe that online interactive diagnosis will produce results of the same accuracy as a visit to a live physician.

AIDS

Index-Aids Resource List

http://www.teleport.com/~celinec/ aids.shtml

This one stop has all the information on AIDS that's available online, which in fact is virtually all the information on AIDS. The HIV-positive community has been connected by bulletin boards for a decade, and all that material migrated to the Web.

Asthma

Asthma FAQ

http://www.cco.caltech.edu/~wrean/ asthma-gen.html

Here's the main FAQ on asthma, with links to subtopic pages.

Cancer

There are about 100 topics here, with significantly better information than you are likely to find at a public library. The latest research now appears here before it appears in print medical journals.

Cancer Net

gopher://gopher.nih.gov/11/clin/cancernet

If you click on the Cancer Net link, you get connected to this site, which will let you keyword-search on cancer topics.

Medicine Online

http://www.meds.com/

If you are going to get any kind of medical services, you should check this site. The information quality is higher than you'll usually get in the photocopied handouts from a hospital or doctor.

OncoLink

http://www.oncolink.upenn.edu/

This is especially worthwhile in having lots of good explanations in laymen's language, rather than medical jargon.

ChronicIllnet

http://www.calypte.com/

Abstracts on groundbreaking research, research bulletin boards, events calendars, guest lectures, news articles and more. Dedicated to chronic illnesses including AIDS, cancer, Persian Gulf War Syndrome, autoimmune diseases, Chronic Fatigue Syndrome, heart disease, and neurological diseases.

Diabetes

Because diabetes is a very widespread condition, it's well represented on the Web. Look here for the latest encouraging research — diabetes management is making real progress.

Diabetes homepage

http://www.nd.edu/~hhowisen/diabetes.html

Lavish use of graphics and searching over other diabetes resources make this an award-winning site. It's even better with a very fast connection, though.

Diabetes knowledgebase

http://www.biostat.wisc.edu/diaknow/index.htm

A searchable database on all diabetes topics.

Environmental Health

Hazardous Substances Database

http://atsdr1.atsdr.cdc.gov:8080/hazdat.html

The fact is, it's pretty much up to you to protect yourself from dangerous substances in the workplace. Wouldn't hurt to read a few labels and then check this site for good advice.

Toxic Hotspots

http://www.econet.apc.org/hotspots/

Look up your own community on this map. Or better yet, pray it's not there.

These maps identify documented problem areas. Research suggests you can cut your cancer risk in half just by avoiding certain substances and places.

Fitness

Flashtrends

http://neuroscape.com/neuroscape/flash/flashtrends.html

This site is a sort of Buzzword Central for health and fitness matters. Sometimes, it's enough to make you wonder how there can possibly *be* new health fads every few years or so. This site offers a bit of perspective.

Ultramarathon World

http://Fox.NSTN.Ca/~dblaikie/

If you're a Yahoo! fan, you're probably bored with regular old marathons. Check this site for the latest on 100-mile runs through Death Valley. Feats that used to be confined to Tarahumara Indian couriers are now being attempted by desk-bound yuppies every other weekend, apparently.

Abdominal training FAQ

http://www.dstc.edu.au/RDU/staff/nigel-ward/abfaq/abdominal-training.html

So you sit there Web surfing, night after night. You order out for pizza, drink lots of Jolt Cola, stare at the screen, and make up pages of hotlists. After six months of this, you find that you have increased a couple of inches in pants size. Hit this site and do what they say!

General Health

This block of topics is a good place to start a health search, because most of these lead back into more specialized stuff in other sections.

First Aid

http://www.symnet.net/Users/afoster/safety/

In most communities, unless you can prove you have been attacked by a Gila Monster, you can wait a long time on hold calling for help. You might want to visit this site, download an FAQ or two, and print them out for reference. It is amazingly well organized for emergency use, though.

General Health

gopher://adp.wisc.edu

A shockingly well-organized Gopher reference for every conceivable health topic. Speaking of conceivable, that includes reproductive issues, presented here with authoritative neutrality.

RuralNet

http://ruralnet.mu.wvnet.edu/

If you have ever spent much time more than 50 miles from a big city, you have probably noticed that health care resources can become a problem. This site has several directories of services and advice on organizing rural health-care facilities.

Magazines

There are about 20 magazines here at press time, and there will soon be more. Check the Magazines section every few weeks if you are actively interested in health topics.

Electronic Gourmet

http://www.deltanet.com/2way/egg/

So, ya wanna eat tofu forever? This online magazine has piles of interesting recipes and discussions. Some of the recipes may start you dreaming about a steak, but in fact a short sampling will convince you this site is pretty useful.

International Health News

http://vv.com/healthnews/

Some things online are worth buying. This is one of them. You have to pay for this abstracting service, but the information covers many important journals and is easy to follow.

Practical Psychology

http://www.well.com/user/selfhelp/

A free e-mail journal, with more and better advice than you would find in a number of magazines readily available at a newsstand. Of course, for in-depth advice you should probably always consult *Cosmopolitan* first, but a second opinion is always useful.

Medicine

Medicine is a giant section that leads back to all the others, following the Yahoo! philosophy that you should never be allowed to miss anything. When you get there, you should find more than 1000 items under this heading: sports medicine, space medicine, pediatrics, and other things you may or may not need to know about are present in great profusion.

HyperDoc

http://www.nlm.nih.gov/

Your health-care tax dollars at work. This gigantic enterprise, probably more useful to professionals than to laypeople, is like a bulletin board for the National Institutes of Health. There's a searchable database with probably more than you ever wanted to know about everything you never wanted to have.

Medical Imaging

http://www-sci.lib.uci.edu/HSG/MedicalImage.html

Be warned that this is a big project with a big home page — about 150K. But if you are interested in medical imaging (far, far beyond X-rays), this is the site for you. You can admire your own innards here for hours. This site also links outward to every health resource imaginable.

Aqua Thought

http://www.access.digex.net/~sunilg/

This site (under Neurosciences) is devoted to human-dolphin communication. After all this heavy-duty depressing stuff on diseases, you might want to cruise by and say hi to Flipper.

Yahoo!

Shuffle Brain

http://www.indiana.edu/~pietsch/
home.html

No, it's not a unique sport for retirement cruises but a fascinating neuroscience resource. All sorts of papers may be found here on the still-unresolved question: What does the brain have to do with the mind?

News

The Web is probably a better source for health news than any medium ever invented. The average citizen will do better here than with the *New England Journal of Medicine.*

Harvard Health Publications

http://www.med.harvard.edu/
publications/Health_Publications/

Now this, folks, is a bargain. Actually, it's free — the whole spectrum of health publications from Harvard, online, pictures and all, for free. This may be one of the most worthwhile resources on the Web, especially if you are already in reasonable health.

MedWire

http://www.callamer.com/itc/
medwire/

This is a hotline where companies post their press releases about new medical products of all kinds. It's updated monthly and worth a look. One reason to check this site is that it shows you how much of the material that you read in newspapers is just a straight copy of a press release.

Nutrition

Nutrition Pages

http://deja-vu.oldiron.cornell.edu/
~jabbo/index.html

This is one of the most objective (it's not company sponsored) sites for nutrition information. It's like a mini-Yahoo! on this topic and has its own directories on different aspects of nutrition.

Pharmacology

It's all here, from the latest on aspirin and heart attacks through recent experiments and clinical trials, to a page from Amsterdam (where marijuana is basically legal) with an advanced perspective, at least by American standards.

WWW Drug Information Server

http://www.paranoia.com/drugs/

This page mostly has recreational drug content — the more scholarly material on individual pharmaceuticals usually turns up as a resource under individual disease categories (asthma drugs under asthma, and so on).

Index of Internet Accessible Drug Resources

http://kiwi.uwaterloo.ca/
drug_info.html

More material with a recreational emphasis. This page has links to absolutely everything else on drugs.

Sexuality

And tucked away down here, with a title that is designed to make you think of the social-hygiene movies you had to watch in high school, is where Yahoo! has stashed everything remotely controversial about sex. Absolutely X-rated sites (most require a credit card or some other proof you're over 18), discussion groups for gay/lesbian/bisexuality issues, health matters, contacts with people who have probably forgotten what the missionary position is — this is it. You may want to (ahem) explore this topic on your own rather than see a listing of greatest hits posted here. After all, your tastes may be different.

Also, be prepared for a lot of *File not found* messages in this area, which seems to be much more volatile than, say, Women's Health.

Women's Health

In most communities, you are probably more likely to find a much wider variety of perpectives on women's health issues on the Web than in your hometown.

Women's Health Hot Line

http://www.soft-design.com/softinfo/
womens-health.html

This is an e-zine with well-considered articles and is the source of much of the info you will find in other places (magazines, newspapers). Check for monthly updates.

News

This is news like you've never seen it before — news that can be as little as seconds old. Yahoo! organizes News into numerous sections.

In the Business section, stock and mutual-fund information is available from a number of sources.

Daily News is one of the most diverse parts of Yahoo!, where you can get newspapers, business briefs, and even cartoons over the Internet each day.

There's also a Current Events section with links to great NASA information and updates on hot Web sites.

The Government News section is a gateway to the largest Department of Defense and military information sites, where you can find up-to-date DOD news and information bulletins.

The International section features up-to-the minute Reuters newswire reports on current international headlines; here you'll also find newspapers and information sources for specific countries.

If you want to find out more about the nature of the news business, check out the Journalism section, where you'll encounter links to journalism schools, sites devoted to helping reporters use the Internet, and even personal home pages of working journalists. Schools producing newspapers for the Internet range from universities to grade schools; the latter shows what up-and-coming journalists can do for themselves, and features some interesting student material.

Sports fans need not feel left out. The sites in this section are filled with schedules, player information and interviews, and even interactive Sports Chat zones.

The Newswires section features news stories from agencies such as the Associated Press and Reuters.

For an alternate take on the news (often one of the faster information sources you can find), check out the Usenet section. The sites listed there help to make sense of the immense number of Internet newsgroups and their message flow, and contain search tools and menus that will help you be truly productive.

Finish up with the Indices section, a series of virtual newsstands that link you to varied news sources on the Web.

Current Top Headlines

Top Story Headlines

http://www.yahoo.com/headlines/current/news/

Yahoo! hosts a news feed from Reuters NewMedia that is updated every hour. Come scan the headlines, peruse the summary pages, or wade through the full-text stories.

Business

Current Business Headlines

http://www.yahoo.com/headlines/current/business

Business headline news, hosted by Yahoo! from Reuters. You can browse the headlines directly or story summary pages, or you can read the full-text stories. The headlines are updated every hour.

Asia Business Daily

http://infomanage.com/~icr/abd/

Capsule news on business and political issues in several Asian countries. You can search back issues by keyword. This site also features links to Asian stock market closings and bank information.

In, Around, and Online

http://www.clark.net/pub/robert/home.html

Weekly information about the online community. Past articles have focused on the Microsoft Network and an America Online class-action suit. There's also a tasty rumor mill.

Technology Transfer Business

http://canam.dgsys.com/ttbiz

A quarterly focusing on technology-to-business transfer. Past issues have included articles such as "Corporate Tech Scouts" and sections on the top 500 tech transfer businesses.

Wall Street Journal Money & Investing Update

http://update.wsj.com/

Impressively formatted Web version of *The Wall Street Journal* update. You can jump to various sections by using the top button bar, or go directly to special reports from front-page articles. There's also an online glossary

and help system, as well as an events calendar. You'll need a browser that supports authentication (Quarterdeck Mosaic, for example, which is included on the CD-ROM in the back of this book) to register and use this service.

WSGR Interactive New Media Weekly Recap

http://www.ensemble.com/wsgr/recap/recap.html

Capsule reports on multimedia industry news from Wilson Sonsini Goodrich & Rosati, a Palo Alto entertainment law firm. You can also browse back issues and request copies by e-mail from this site.

Current Events

1996 Presidential Elections

http://www.yahoo.com/Government/Politics/Elections/1996_U_S_Elections/Presidential_Election/

A collection of sites from all over the Web following the '96 campaign trail. All the parties, all the candidates, all the dirt...

Current Mission of NASA's Space Shuttle

http://shuttle.nasa.gov/

A great site where you can find out about the latest shuttle flights, including crew information, mission

objectives, and current orbital status. There are lots of good pictures and links to interactive shuttle pages.

Music Events Calendar

http://www.automatrix.com/concerts/

Musi-Cal is an online database you can search to find out about upcoming live-music events. You can look by performer or band, location, or type of music. Enter your own music event into Musi-Cal by using the Concert Itinerary Slicer Dicer. There's also information via e-mail.

FAQ - misc.news.bosnia

http://www.cis.ohio-state.edu/hypertext/faq/usenet/bosnia-news-faq/faq.html

Frequently asked questions from the Usenet newsgroup devoted to Bosnia. This document also contains lists of other Internet sites you can access for more information.

Daily

Major breaking news for business, entertainment, and national/international affairs. Here you'll find newspapers and other information sources, as well as editorials and comics. There are also sites with current CNN and ABC News Radio clips.

Business

Interactive Media Business [Netscape]

http://www.netscape.com/newsref/news/index.html

Brief summaries of topics of interest in interactive media, as collected by the Netscape people. Each summary is linked directly to its source, so you can get the full report.

internetMCI

http://www.fyionline.com/infoMCI/update/BUSINESS-MCI.html

MCI's business news summaries from Reuters NewMedia, in a basic text format.

AMEX Market Summary

http://www.amex.com/summary/summary.htm

Up-to-date market summaries, including equity and options, total volume of transactions, and overall changes. The most active, percent gainers, and percent decliners information is presented in a highly readable table format.

Money Magazine Money Watch

http://www.pathfinder.com/money/moneydaily/1995/latest.html

Updates in the finance field from *Money* magazine, including capsule summaries of news and events. A recent entry outlined a nuclear power plant's family tour offerings and U.S. unemployment statistics. There are also links to previous daily summaries and the *Money* Personal Finance Center.

Nando Times Business Section

http://www.nando.net/nt/biz

Interesting daily business news updates from the *News and Observer,* including brief summaries linked to full stories. You can also review the entire day's list of newswire stories and select the ones that interest you.

San Jose Mercury News - Business

http://www.sjmercury.com/biz.htm

Subscription-based business news stories, columns, and features. You can read article summaries directly, but you have to register (for a nominal fee) to access the full stories.

WWW WorldNews Today - Business

http://www.fyi.com/wnt/wntbus.html

This site features newswire business stories and briefs, and financial market summaries.

Comics

Borderline Daily Cartoon

http://www.cts.com/~borderln/todays.html

Gabe Martin's *Far Side*-esque cartoon, in a nice gray scale format. There's also contest information and a link to the Borderline home page.

Dilbert

http://www.unitedmedia.com/comics/dilbert/todays_dilbert.gif

The world's favorite cube-dweller. See Dilbert, Dogbert, Ratbert, and the whole office crew take on the rigors of modern working life here daily.

Kev's World

http://www.cris.com:80/~Mppa/s2f/kevin.shtml

Kevin Nichols' daily color cartoon, focusing on current topics such as the grunge look, tropical hurricanes, and weight-loss injections. There's an archive of back cartoons in GIF or Adobe Acrobat formats.

Today's Computer Cartoon

http://zeb.nysaes.cornell.edu/CGI/ctoons.cgi

Daily cartoons with a computer or technology twist from John M. Zakour. There's also a link to an FAQ for more information.

Editorial

San Francisco Chronicle

http://www.sfgate.com/cgi-bin/chronicle/article-list.cgi?Editorial:ED:/chronicle/today

The *San Francisco Chronicle* Editorial page features commentaries on local, national, and foreign events. You'll also find political and humor columns and a "Letters To The Editor" section.

San Jose Mercury News - Editorial

http://www.sjmercury.com/edit.htm

The online version of the *San Jose Mercury News* is a subscription-based service. Here you can read capsule summaries of current editorials and letters to the editor.

WWW WorldNews Today

http://www.fyi.com/wnt/wnted.html

A current editorial on national and international news subjects, plus a "Letters" section and e-mail links you can use to post your own comments.

Entertainment

Secret Agent X9

http://mmnewsstand.com/AgentX/

A professionally presented strip from Hearst Co.'s Multimedia Newsstand. Watch X9 outwit the Bad Guys.

Index - Web Comics Daily

http://www.cyberzine.com/webcomics/comics.html

A nicely presented list of links to lots of comics across the Net. There are also some comics presented on the pages here. You can go to a What's New page to check out new listings, or access an e-mail link to send comments.

Quote Of The Day: Frank Zappa

http://www.fwi.uva.nl/~heederik/zappa/quote/

An interactive daily Frank Zappa random quote generator. Not unlike the Delphic Oracle. (Examples:

"Politics is the entertainment branch of industry" and "Jazz is not dead, it just smells funny.") You can also submit your own Zappa line to the database (is "Green beans for Utah! That's right!" in there yet?) or download or view all of them.

The Cyber Sleaze Report

http://metaverse.com/vibe/sleaze/00latest.html

Tasty news summaries on stars in the music/entertainment industries and entertainment events, from Adam Curry's MetaVerse site.

Today - Daily Calendar

http://www.uta.fi/~blarku/today.html

Truly useful information from this Finnish site includes a list of historical events and birthdays for the particular date, Hebraic and Islamic calendars, and global sunrise/sunset times. There's also a set of links to other daily information on the Net.

What's On Tonite! at HollyNet

http://tv1.com/

TV listings on the Web. Choose your region from an interactive map, and then select from several formats to view listings by day. Formats include a classic grid, a time schedule, program categories, or channel lineup. You can also search the site to locate a program directly, and request "lite" listings via e-mail.

WWW WorldNews Today

http://www.fyi.com/wnt/wntinsty.html

Lifestyle and entertainment industry news stories.

Government

White House Press Releases

http://www1.ai.mit.edu/search/white-house-publications?everything+%3eyesterday+%3d200+@www.whitehouse.gov%2fwhite_house%2fpublications%2fhtml%2fpunblications.html

Daily press briefings and presidential statements from the White House, arranged by date and title. You can select an entry and read the full text online.

International

African National Congress Newswire (South Africa)

http://minerva.cis.yale.edu/~jadwat/anc/

News briefings collected by the ANC from several sources on local goings-on in South Africa. These are sorted by headline and article length.

CET On-line

gopher://gopher.eunet.cz:70/11/Journals/cet-online/tm

This Gopher site features text news summaries on Central European topics. The site also includes an archive of back issues.

CNN World News

http://www.cnn.com/World/
index.html

Who better to bring you international news than CNN? You don't get to see or hear Wolf Blitzer, but it's a good site, nonetheless. Up-to-the-hour stories accompanied by photos.

FutureNet World News

http://www.futurenet.co.uk/News/
today/index.html

World news summaries and U.K. news stories, including sports information. There's also a separate section featuring stories in the information technology field.

The Electronic Telegraph

http://www.telegraph.com

Beautiful electronic version of the U.K. *Daily Telegraph,* including major World and Home news sections with color photographs, editorials, sports columns, and features. Registration is free via an online form.

News

CNN Interactive

http://www.cnn.com/

Ted Turner's worldwide vision comes to the Web in fine fashion. Launched in August '95, this site offers a good combination of graphics and content, as it offers news stories and photos updated hourly.

Interactive Age Daily

http://techweb.cmp.com/ia/current/

Interactive media daily news, including industry perspectives, linked story summaries, and a hotlist of companies mentioned.

internetMCI

http://www.fyionline.com/infoMCI/
update/NEWS-MCI.html

Reuters news summaries from MCI, in a brief digest format.

Nando Times - U.S. Report

http://www.nando.net/nt/nation/

National news from the *News and Observer,* including news summaries with links to longer articles (requires authorization).

San Francisco Chronicle - News

http://www.sfgate.com/chronicle/
index.shtml

News from San Francisco and the world beyond, in a good format. Choose from a list of headlines to go directly to a story or browse departments and features.

San Francisco Examiner - News

http://www.sfgate.com/examiner/
index.html

Browse the *Electric Examiner* by topic (News, Business, Sports, or Style sections) to reach articles on world, national, and San Francisco Bay Area subjects.

San Jose Mercury News - Latest Headlines

http://www.sjmercury.com/
whatsnew.htm

Breaking international, national, and local news story summaries. You'll need to register to access the full text. Also see the Today's Newspaper section linked here.

The Independent

http://www.bnt.com/~hermit/

In this interesting experiment, readers are invited to join the staff and write their own news stories on world and regional issues. Participation is encouraged, and you can sign up by filling out a form.

The News Page - The Social Cafe

http://www.social.com/social/
news.html

Voice Of America news stories from around the world are presented here, as well as a link to a daily report on the computer industry.

Time Daily - News

http://www.timeinc.com/time/daily/
time/1995/latest.html

Short clips from *Time,* with pictures, maps, and links to related articles. You can also search directly for other articles on the same topic.

USA Today

http://www.usatoday.com/

This site is recognizable at first site. Unlike most other newspapers, *USA Today* did not have to make a transition to color graphics when moving to the Web. The site is laid out in sections identical to the paper's. But the Web site has some extra features that the paper doesn't, including news updated on the weekends and sports scores that are updated every two minutes.

WWW WorldNews Today

http://www.in.net/sfics/wwwwnt/wnt.html

The WWW WorldNews features full-text stories in a number of areas, including international and national news.

Sources

ABC News [RealAudio]

http://www.realaudio.com/contentp/abc.html

ABC News site, featuring up-to-date RealAudio clips on News, Sports, and Commentary. You'll have to add RealAudio (provided at this site) to your Web browser to listen in. The clips are long, but start playing almost immediately under RealAudio after you click on them.

Internet CNN Newsroom

http://www.nmis.org/NewsInteractive/CNN/Newsroom/contents.html

CNN daily news stories, in MPEG format (huge files, averaging 20 to 30 megabytes). If you've got the bandwith, you can view 3- to 4-minute Top News Stories, In The Headlines, and Editor's Desk news coverage video clips right here. There's also a closed-caption text breakdown for mere mortals.

The Nando Times

http://www2.nando.net/newsroom/nt/nando.html

News and Observer daily news stories, including international, national, and local coverage, in a good visual format. AP news stories at this site require authorization to access.

Sports

19th Hole Golf News

http://www.sport.net/golf/news.html

Golf news, including schedules, tournament progress, articles on hot golfers, and tips from the pros.

internetMCI Sports Summary

http://www.fyionline.com/infoMCI/update/SPORTS-MCI.html

Reuters news clips on sports topics, in digest format.

Technology

Popular Mechanics Tech Update

http://popularmechanics.com/popmech/tech/1HOMETECH.html

Nice-looking daily technology update from *PM,* including a feature article with pictures and a searchable archive of back issues.

Weather

Weather World

http://www.atmos.uiuc.edu/wxworld/html/general.html

Get a daily view of what's over your head. This University of Illinois at Urbana-Champaign site features daily satellite weather photos and charts from several different agencies.

X Of The Day

Your daily information source. Find new jargon, words you never thought of, unusual questions, and phrases that will make you *kewl.*

Cool Jargon of the Day

http://www.bitech.com/jargon/cool

A daily dose of jargon, with pronunciation guide, definition, and examples. There's also a link to the *New Hacker's Dictionary* site, where you can browse at will. Paradoxically, you're going to need this dictionary just to figure out how to access it: "You can unpack this file with the gunzip command, also available on prep (uncompressed!) in source as gzip-1.0.7.shar. If your request is for jarg300.txt, the MIT server will run gunzip and give you an uncompressed copy." Yikes!

Cool Word/Phrase of the Day

http://www.dsu.edu/projects/word_of_day/word.html

This site features a link to a definition page, and also to a list of past cool words. You can also submit your own (we added *bloviate,* one of our favorites). Was it pure chance our random daily word was *schizophrenia?* Who knows?

Yahoo!

Question of the Day

http://www.ptown.com/qod/

Random daily questions (example: "What is the best possible hand that you can get in the game of poker?") from the Internet at large. Test your knowledge by using the answer form, or submit your own question. There's also a report generator that will tell you the number of correct answers, so you'll know how you measure up.

Word of the Day

http://www.wordsmith.org/words/today.html

A word a day, plus definitions, and an audio pronunciation clip. You can also reach an archive of past words. If you crave epexegesis, you'll have to check out the site itself.

Indices

Index - Daily News @ Fun City

http://www.funcity.com/news/daily/

A good collection of links to news sources across the Internet, including *The New York Times, The Wall Street Journal, Time,* and regional newspapers. There's also a set of links to international news sources, TV news, comics, and weather.

Index - News: the Daily News-Omnivore

http://ukanaix.cc.ukans.edu/carrie/news_main.html

Comprehensive links to news sources on the Net, in areas such as Weather, Global Regions, Finance, Entertainment, and Sports. There's also a QuickNews section for fast access to up-to-date information.

Index - The Newsroom

http://www.auburn.edu/~vestmon/news.html

Links to major news sources and top headlines, including sections on U.S. and World News, Current Affairs, Business and Finance, Features, and Resources. There's also a morgue of past articles you can browse directly.

Events

Events of all types can be found in this section, from sports to computers, business and industry, and film. Check the listings for specific events, and go to the referenced sites for up-to-date information, including registration dates and event times. Recent listings have included city and country arts festivals, robot competitions, bike tours, architectural conferences, defense management symposiums, and conferences on women. There's also specific information for events such as the Daytona Air Show, Lollapalooza, Macworld, the San Francisco AIDS Walk, Saint Patrick's Day celebrations, Renaissance Faires, and the National Black College Showcase.

EXPOguide

http://www.expoguide.com/

A computer industry trade show, events, and exhibitions database. You can search by alphabetical index, date, place or keyword. Listings include show dates and contact information.

Indices

Index - EventsLink

http://www.events2000.com/itshappening/index.html

Events listed by topic and state. Topics include art and antique shows, computer events, music/dance festivals, outdoor fun, sports shows, and specialty events. You can also link your event's site here.

Index - World Wide Events Database

http://www.ipworld.com/HOMEPAGE.HTM

Search for event listings in this database by type of event, time, and place. Categories: agriculture and farm shows; art, craft, and hobby fairs; conferences; and performing arts events.

Government

DefenseLink - OSD Public Affairs

http://www.dtic.dla.mil/defenselink/

A visually impressive site from the Office of the Secretary of Defense, with links to major Defense Department agencies, including the Pentagon, the White House, individual Armed Forces branches, and the Joint Chiefs of Staff. You'll also find online publications and informational resources, including a search engine that allows you to query a federal documents database.

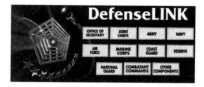

NavyOnLine

http://www.navy.mil

Hey, sailor! A wide range of naval information available online, laid out in an alphabetical subject index, including ship and station operations, schools, and support/logistics branches. There's also a search panel you can use to look for specific information.

U.S. Information Service (USIS)

gopher://hk.net/11/.usishk

A Gopher site with daily USIS Washington, D.C., reports transmitted to USIS agencies abroad as advisories. Topics include daily main news, U.S. regional relations, Presidential administration information, and U.S. Consular releases.

United Nations Daily Highlights

gopher://gopher.undp.org/11/uncurr/DH

A Gopher site with daily news updates from the UN Central News service. A good way to keep up to date with current events involving the UN and the global community.

International

Current International Headlines

http://www.yahoo.com/headlines/current/international

International headline news, hosted at Yahoo! from Reuters NewMedia. You can browse the headlines directly, or use an informative international summary, also linked to full-text articles.

The Baltics Online

http://www.viabalt.ee/

News from the Estonian News Agency covering the Baltic Republics, in a nice table format, with reports listed by time and day.

Jornal do Brazil

http://www.ibase.br/~jb/

Brazilian native language daily. The site includes news stories, an index, and an FAQ list.

Canadian News Digest

http://xenon.xe.com/canpress/hlines.htm

Daily news stories from the Canadian Press (CP). There are also links to Canadian newswire information and picture services.

CBC News Briefs

http://radioworks.cbc.ca/radio/programs/news/headline-news/

Text of hourly Canadian Broadcasting Company headline news reports. You can browse by date and time, and select a link to view the entire file.

CBC News Experiment (cmu.edu)

http://www.cs.cmu.edu/afs/cs.cmu.edu/user/clamen/misc/Canadiana/CBC-News.html

The Carnegie-Mellon University site features daily audio newscasts from the CBC, in standard computer audio (AU) and RealAudio formats.

Chinese News Digest

http://www.cnd.org

A nonprofit information resource about China and Chinese affairs. This site leads to online news magazines, electronic mailing gateways, and the CND InfoBase (where you can find information on the Tiananmen Square uprising, scenic pictures of China, and classic Chinese literature).

Global Chinese Electronic Daily News

http://www.infocom.net/~gedn/

Chinese language daily news, in sections such as Mainland and Taiwan news, and U.S. and International reports. There's also a Reader's Mail Box. You'll need to set up special software for your browser to be able to display Chinese fonts; information on downloading it is here as well.

Lyon Capitale

http://www.dtr.fr/lyoncap/

News from Lyon, in a good visual format, including political updates, festival information, sports, and society news (in French).

Consultation of the French newsgroups

http://prof.inria.fr/~pierre/news.html

Good index of the French Usenet newsgroups, arranged by categories such as announcements, business, science, and jobs.

Der Spiegel

http://www.hamburg.pop.de/nda/spiegel/

This site features full-text articles in German from this widely read magazine, and also includes English summaries.

Die Welt

http://www.welt.de/

This German-language daily newspaper site has easy navigation icons to sections for world and local news and market information.

Germany Alert

http://www.chantry.com/ga/

English-language publication centering on issues such as nationalism and racism in Germany and Europe.

Projekt TAZ im WWW

http://www.prz.tu-berlin.de/taz/

The online edition of *Die Tageszeitung,* Germany's leading left-wing newspaper, in German.

The Irish Times

http://www.irish-times.ie/

Daily news from Ireland, including national and world coverage, features, and commentary. There's also an archive of past issues.

Daily News from Israel

Gopher://israel-info.gov.il/11/new

Gopher server with text-based daily reports, including a survey of the Israeli press, policy statements by political leaders, and news flashes.

Windows On Italy

http://www.ansa.it/

News from ANSA, the Italian National Press Association, includes daily press updates on political, economic, and financial news, as well as entertainment, sports, and cultural stories. Back issues are also available.

Tokyo Kaleidoscope

http://www.smn.co.jp/

Alternative news source for Japan, published weekly. Articles include news stories, editorials, U.S.-Japan forum reports, and conference bulletins. In English and Shift-kanji.

Mexican News (in Spanish)

http://www.infosel.com.mx/

Spanish-language news from *El Norte* and *Reforma* newspapers, plus an online database to Mexican magazines and other publications.

Latest Russian News

http://sunsite.sut.ac.jp/asia/russia

Links to Russian sites and a daily electronic mailing list digest on Russian affairs, including up-to-date news and information.

The St. Petersburg Press

http://www.spb.su/sppress/

The weekly English-language version of this Russian newspaper includes news and features stories in a good digest format, with pictures and links to longer articles. You can also go to the Prospects St. Petersburg Culture and Lifestyle guide from here, and browse online classifieds.

Taiwan Headline News

http://sinanet.com/bay/news/

Major Chinese stories in business, domestic and international news are readable directly from this Web site without having to install a separate Chinese operating system. There's also an English-language version available from here. Published everyday except Sunday.

Indices

Index - Daily News Service

gopher://gopher.nstn.ca/11/Cybrary/News/news

A Gopher server with a lot of links to worldwide news sources, including native-language text information, Web site addresses, and multimedia files.

Index - Gerben's news page

http://www.cs.vu.nl/~gerben/news.html

Daily news links by country. There's a jump index that gets you to the area of your choice quickly, and a top-level current-events section with links to breaking news.

Journalism

Sites for working journalists and the interested public, including places you can go to learn how to use the Web as an information source, as well as home pages for professional organizations and societies, journalism schools, and media watch groups.

A Reporter's Internet Survival Guide

http://www.qns.com/~casey/

Quick links to specific-incident sites, government sources, and reference materials. You can branch out to a lot of informative sites from here.

Journalism List Redux

http://www.clark.net/pub/journalism

Billed as the connection between the Cyberspace Frontier, the Information Superhighway, and the Electronic Marketplace, this site features links to collections of information sources, news sites, and a wide range of resources.

Institutes

Here you'll find information on journalism schools at several U.S. and international colleges and universities. Most sites offer course information, faculty contact lists, and admission information.

American University School of Communication

http://www.soc.american.edu

This site features a virtual tour of the school in pictures, information on academic programs, and Virtual Journalist guides to press information on the Internet for a variety of subjects.

SF State Journalism Online

http://www.journalism.sfsu.edu/

Links to online publications, student projects, and Internet tools and resources for journalists.

Syracuse Newhouse School of Public Communications

http://newhouse.syr.edu/

Information on the school's programs, plus a photographic portfolio, a student humor magazine, and links to Internet media sites.

UC Berkeley Journalism School

http://ng-118-1.news.berkeley.edu/

The visually impressive Graduate School of Journalism site features information on school programs, new media technologies, Internet publications, and online California government report sources. There's also a basic guide to getting started with the Internet, and lists of Internet and journalistic resource links.

Journalists

Sites for professional and amateur journalists, including magazine and newspaper columnists and computer-industry specialists.

Gleick, James

http://www.around.com

Columns from the *New York Times Magazine* on science and technology and related information. Gleick is the author of *Chaos: Making a New Science* and *Genius: The Life and Science of Richard Feynman.*

Soloway, Colin

http://www.vmedia.com/colin/index.htm

Reports from *Newsday, Time,* and *The Toronto Star* on the war in the former Yugoslavia. The articles are listed by magazine/newspaper and also by country dateline. You can also read Soloway's CV and work he has done for *The Nation* and the *News and Observer.*

Vernon Stone

http://www.missouri.edu/~jourvs/

Findings from national surveys in the field of radio and television, including reports on station operations, salaries, staff benefits, and minority/women hiring practices. There's also advice for aspiring TV/radio journalists.

Wall Street Journal Personal Technology

http://ptech.wsj.com/html3/

Nice-looking *WSJ* site for Walt Mossberg's Personal Technology column. You can read the current installment, browse back issues, and read background information. There's also an online suggestion box.

Yahoo!

Media Watch

Media watchdog groups: the watchers watching the watchers.

EXTRA!

http://www.igc.org/fair/

The site for FAIR (Fairness and Accuracy In Reporting) includes selected articles from *EXTRA!*, the media critique magazine, and information on the CounterSpin radio show. There are also links to special FAIR publications available online.

Media Watch at MIT

http://theory.lcs.mit.edu:80/~mernst/media/

MIT's Media Watchdog is a collection of media-watch sites, arranged into categories such as time-sensitive information and action alerts, media criticism organizations, and censorship resources. There's also a monthly "what's new" list to help you keep track of current issues.

MediaFilter

http://MediaFilter.org/MFF/mfhome

Political information and an alternative take on the news are highlighted at this site. Find out about domestic/foreign covert operations, police abuse, and activism issues.

Organizations

National Press Club

http://town.hall.org/places/npc/

This site features an online Information Center and Newsroom, with online resources for journalists and links to hot news sources for breaking stories. There's also information on the NPC's facilities, programs, and services.

The Wire Service Guild

http://www.interport.net/~wsg/222.html

The home page for this union organization features information on current contracts, labor relations updates (with links to related sites), and Guild policies/bylaws.

Indices

Lists of journalism resources on the Internet from a variety of sources, arranged by subject and locations covered.

Journalism - WWW Virtual Library

http://www.cais.com/makulow/vlj.html

A comprehensive site for journalism information, presented in a good outline format. Categories include associations and organizations, awards and prizes, colleges and universities, news bureaus, and related fields.

Journalism and Communications WWW sites

http://www.jou.ufl.edu/commres/jouwww.htm

Regional listings of academic journalism sites by country, including international and national colleges and universities.

WebOvision Presents The Media Page

http://www.catalog.com/media/sd/web'o'vision.html

Media information at this colorful site includes journalism and news sources, TV and radio information, film and theater links, and software resources. You can also get to online magazines, newspapers, and e-mail lists from here, and there's a handy search page.

K-12 Newspapers

Newspapers from schools around the world, including professional-looking high-school productions and class reports.

Green Raider High School Newspaper

http://www.ridleysd.k12.pa.us/green/greenraider.html

This Pennsylvania high-school production has a good look, and features sections for editorial opinion, class news, sports information, and cool stuff. There are also links to other high-school newspapers on the Net.

ISN KidNews

http://www.umassd.edu/
SpecialPrograms/ISN/KidNews.html

The International Student Newswire is a place where students can post and read stories from across the globe. Sections include news, features, and profile stories, how-to guides, reviews, poetry/fiction, and sports. There are also teacher/student discussion areas.

Newswires

PR Newswire

http://www.prnewswire.com/

PR news from public and private corporations, government agencies, and trade associations. There's also a special section on finance and the Web, including PR Newswire rate information.

Search of AP Wire

http://www1.trib.com/NEWS/
APwire.html

The Associated Press newswire archive, with current reports available by topic (including General and World reports). You have to register via an online form to use the service. Be sure to remember your password!

VOA News and English Broadcasts Wire Service

gopher://gopher.voa.gov/11/
newswire

Transcripts of Voice Of America correspondent broadcast reports for the past seven days, available in text format on this Gopher server.

Sports

We could make jokes about tennis servers on the Net, but we won't.

ESPNet Sportszone

http://espnet.sportszone.com/

Top sports headline news from ESPN. There's also a baseball scoreboard and a special features section. You can also jump to news indexed by a particular sport.

Global Network News Sports Page

http://gnn.com/gnn/meta/sports/
index.html

GNN Sports is your link to sports sites across the Internet, including sections on auto racing, baseball, football, soccer, and tennis. There are also news and interview pages for specific sports such as baseball and football.

NandoX - Football Server/NBA Server

http://www.nando.net/SportServer/
basketball/

http://www2.nando.net/Sport Server/
basketball/

The *News and Observer*'s comprehensive sites for football and basketball news, including professional and college ball. There's a search engine to help you look up teams and players, and you can also hang out in the Nando Sports Chat section and shoot the breeze with other fans online.

U.S. Ski Reports

http://garnet.msen.com:70/1/vendor/
aminews/ski-reports

Up-to-date ski reports from AMI News, arranged by U.S. region. Information includes new snowfall, snow depth, and operational lifts for selected ski areas.

Technology

internetMCI - Science and Technology

http://www.fyionline.com/infoMCI/
newsletter/SCIENCE-MCI.html

Technology-industry and scientific-community news briefs, linked to longer articles. These are from news and PR wires and are updated frequently.

University Newspapers

Don't pass these up. This section is where some of the more interesting experiments in online newspapers are taking place. You can use local college and university newspaper sites to access information specific to your area, including crime reports, sports and entertainment calendars, and event listings.

Boston University - NETCOMTALK-College of Communication

http://web.bu.edu/COM/
communication.html

The COM site has daily updates from the communications world, selected student multimedia projects, and information on awards ceremonies.

Brown Daily Herald

http://www.netspace.org/herald/

HeraldSphere features current issues of the *Daily Herald* and *Good Clean Fun* (a weekly entertainment guide). There's also an archive to back issues. You can look into the Treasure Chest to find a collection of top articles, and access a set of links to local area information.

Duke University - Chronicle Online

http://www.chronicle.duke.edu/

An impressive student newspaper for the Duke community. Features include an easy-to-use button interface, linked lists of articles by headline, and an integrated search engine. The articles are well-written and comprehensive. There's also a local Data Bank with sports and entertainment information and campus issues reports.

Johns Hopkins News-Letter

http://www.jhu.edu/~newslett

Student news about the university and the Baltimore area. Some stories are in HTML format, with photos, and others are available from a linked Gopher server.

MIT: The Tech

http://the-tech.mit.edu

News from the MIT community, published weekly during the school year and monthly during the summer. There are local-interest stories, world and national reports, and arts/sports sections. You can search the article archives (for issues going back to 1881!). There are also links to interesting resources such as a Kai's Power Tools tips site, a literary classics archive (with 184 volumes online), and a digital images gallery.

The Daily Bruin

http://www-
paradigm.asucla.ucla.edu/

UCLA's student newspaper, published weekly during the summer, daily during the school year. Online articles include well-formatted local news and entertainment stories. There are also special sections (such as "Shrouded In Secrecy," which deals with gender crimes) and a photo gallery.

The South End

http://www.southend.wayne.edu/

Wayne State University's weekly newspaper, focusing on campus and Detroit-area news. The online edition has a good look and feel, and stories include numerous links to related information sources on the Internet.

Vanderbilt Hustler

http://www.vanderbilt.edu/Students/
Publications/hustler/

News, perspectives, and sports for the Vanderbilt campus and community, including articles with pictures and links to related Internet sites.

ALSO RECOMMENDED:

Index - Campus Newspapers on the Internet

http://beacon-www.asa.utk.edu/
resources/papers.html

Lists of campus papers by daily, weekly, and monthly circulation. There's also a section on experimental and prototype Internet college newspapers, as well as a form you can use to register your site.

Index - Campus Newspapers on the Web

http://www.spub.ksu.edu/other/
journ.html

This index is arranged by daily, weekly, and monthly circulation, and includes international publications.

Usenet

Anchorman, a Hierachical Newsreader

http://www.ph.tn.tudelft.nl/People/
pierre/anchorman/Amn..html

Newsgroups by hierarchy. This site is easy to navigate, and includes a search panel that will quickly take you to a specific newsgroup.

Binary News Archive

http://pmwww.cs.vu.nl/usenet/
.news.html

Computer programs and pictures from clean Usenet newsgroups, converted to binary files and displayed here for downloading. If you've had trouble with encoded files in alt.binary newsgroups, come here instead.

DejaNews Research Service

http://www.dejanews.com/

A fast-search gateway to the Usenet newsgroups. There's also online help, and you can create special query filters to limit searches to particular groups, dates, or authors. It's really useful and works well.

Find Newsgroups

http://www.cen.uiuc.edu/cgi-bin/find-news

A simple search engine that looks for newsgroup names (and words in their descriptions), and returns an unrestricted list of Usenet news links.

GRN USENET multi-part article decoding daemon

http://www.cs.ubc.ca/grn/
newsgroups

This site features binary and (clean) picture postings from newsgroups in a decoded format that you can download directly. You can also read the text descriptions that accompany the postings.

Semi-Automatic News HREFs

http://www.cs.cmu.edu/afs/
cs.cmu.edu/user/bsy/www/
auto_news/auto_news.html

This Carnegie Mellon site features hyperlinks to Web addresses mentioned in Usenet newsgroup postings, along with surrounding context information. You can look at links for up to five days past, and easily move to the related sites.

Stanford Netnews Filtering Service

http://woodstock.stanford.edu:2000/

The SIFT server allows you to set up a Net news profile based on your interests, and have the related newsgroup postings go directly to your e-mail address. There's registration information and a service outline available here as well.

Usenet Info Center Launch Pad

http://sunsite.unc.edu/usenet-b/
home.html

Here's where you go to find out about Net news centrally. You can also browse and search annotated newsgroup lists and access a FAQ page for more information.

Zippo's News Service

http://www.zippo.com/

Good graphical interface to newsgroups in several categories, including politics, sports, computer information, and classified ads. There are also links to newsreader/decoder software, decoded picture binary files, and a full news feed you can browse.

The Daily News

Final Edition
50 Cents

Zippo's News Service

Friday
June 1, 2001

A L S O   R E C O M M E N D E D:

Index - mg's House of News Knowledge

http://www.duke.edu/~mg/usenet/

Information on Usenet news and related links, including sections on how to create newsgroups, pending group proposals, Net news documentation and maps, and news articles about News.

InterNotes News Gateway

http://www.notes.net/

Information on how to link your office Notes setup to the greater world, from Lotus.

So You Want to Create an Alt Newsgroup

http://www.math.psu.edu/barr/alt-creation-guide.html

Plenty of information on how to start an unmoderated Alt newsgroup of your very own, with links to related information sites.

Index - Public Access News Servers on the Net

http://www.phoenix.net/config/
news.html

A list of public-access news server addresses you can plug into your newsreader or Web browser. Information is also included on whether you can post to the server, or if access is read-only.

Yahoo!

Weekly

internetMCI Net Editors

http://www.internetMCI.com/whats-new/editors/index.html

Weekly commentary from MCI editors on issues such as digital-privacy rights, Internet etiquette, and life online. There's also an archive of past articles.

Weekly Celebrity Hotlist

http://gnn.com/gnn/wic/hot.toc.html

Celebrity Webmasters describe their own favorite sites here, with a new guest hotlist appearing weekly. You can also view past celebrity lists. It's a good way to see what experts consider interesting on the Web.

Indices

Arne's Media Index

http://www.oslonett.no/home/arnehk/eng.html

Comprehensive media list, including journals, magazines, newspapers, and related news sources and organizations.

Ecola's Newsstand — Newspapers

http://www.ecola.com/ez/newspapr.htm

Online newspapers listed by U.S. state (very helpful), and a collection of links to interesting publications worldwide. This is a good summary of what's available.

HomeTown Free-Press Globe

http://www.well.com/www/niche/globe.htm

Links to worldwide news sources on the Internet, arranged by country in an annotated list.

Editor & Publisher

http://www.mediainfo.com/edpub/

The Planetary News Online Newspaper Resource Directory has a good annotated list of links to interesting developments in the online newspaper industry, including top sites, research papers, conferences and workshops, and even job offerings.

News Resources on the WWW

http://www.phlab.missouri.edu/~wlspif/news.html

A list of newspapers, magazines, and news services on the Net. Categories include major news sources, news providers, national, regional, and local papers, and college news.

Taxi newsstand

http://www.deltanet.com/users/taxicat/newsstand.html

A good collection of international online newspaper and journal links, in a nice table format (click on the flag of your choice to view a list of sites in that country).

Taxi International News

The Yankee News Desk

http://www.tiac.net/users/macgyver/news.html

A good list of U.S. newsfeeds, online papers and magazines, and reference information for writers and journalists (including Strunk's *The Elements of Style* online, just in time!).

Recreation

There are few things we take as seriously as leisure, and the vast category of Recreation reveals just how serious we are. Couch potatoes and marathoners, global jet-setters and down-home trekkers have managed to mark their territory on the Web.

Warning: Browsing these pages will make you want to escape your mundane routine, risk a twisted ankle, gamble your hard-earned cash, or otherwise prove your recreational prowess. Not to mention its impact on your productivity. We cannot be held responsible.

Amusement / Theme Parks

Karen's Disneyland Home Page

http://www.wdc.net/~sdewan/disney/dispage.htm

Serious homage to the 40-year-old park, including links to a Disney timeline and a trivia page, a Disneyland FAQ, and Karen's collection of snaps taken on site. Don't miss obscure gems such as the Jungleland Cruise spiel script and the Hidden Mickey List.

Yesterland

http://www.mcs.net/~werner/yester.html

Curator Werner Weiss has created a "theme park on the Web" based on his photos and lovingly detailed prose about many exhibits, now departed, that he has taken in at Disneyland since 1957.

Carousel!

http://www.access.digex.net/~rburgess/

A virtual center for the appreciation of historic carousels and old amusement parks. Preserve your favorite menagerie by joining the National Carousel Association, and, for authentic simulation, order the commemorative stamps and download the band organ audio files.

(See also the Entertainment chapter.)

Animals, Insects, and Pets

Whether your idea of a pet is a sheep, a slug, or a hedgehog, you better believe there's a Web page from a devoted pet owner or two. Lots of info on caring for, breeding, and even memorializing our departed multi-legged friends.

Quadralay's Armadillo Home Page

http://www.quadralay.com/www/Austin/Dillo/index.html

They're quite fond of *Roadkillibus Texanis* in Austin, and here are the jokes, facts, and hot links (to yet more armadilloania) to prove it.

The Armadillo

(Roadkillibus Texanis)

Homer's Home Page

http://www.hu.mtu.edu/~asveenst/homer/

Homer was named for a character in John Irving's *The Cider House Rules,* and not after Homer Simpson, which his behavior might not indicate at first blush. Get to know him and his habitat as constructed by Michigander Aaron Veenstra. Homer's favorite links include a budgies page, Amazing Parrot Cam, and *La Cage aux Folles* (really).

Cats on the Internet

http://http2.sils.umich.edu/~dtorres/cats/cats.html

This is an excellent place to browse for cat monikers, if you need one. Check out Mr. Puddy's home page (and advice column), or stop in at the White House for the First Cat's own meow.

Fathers Cattery

http://www.cam.org/~bobrob/

"Purrfection in God's Loving Care" is the motto of this monastic order in Montreal. They breed and raise Persian and exotic shorthairs to give to senior citizens who have been neglected or abandoned by their families. (True story.) One-stop shopping here: link to meta-cat info, as well as pages on Montreal and on Catholicism, courtesy of Father Bob Roberts.

Cows Caught in the Web

http://www.brandonu.ca/~ennsnr/Cows/

"When a cow laughs, does milk come out its nose?" Inquiring minds want to know not only this, but what cows cost, what they sound like, and how to find the alt.cows.moo.moo.moo newsgroup.

Canine Web

http://snapple.cs.washington.edu:600/canine/canine.html

Whether you're looking for an Akbash, a Leonberger, or a Borzoi, this is the place to learn more about dog breeds, dog products and organizations, vets, police and service dogs, or a multitude of sled dog races. Mush!

The Hamster Page

http://www.tela.bc.ca/hamster/

Hamstery resources that are useful, useless, and not really hamster-related at all can be found here. But don't look for "the mean things that people supposedly do to unconsenting hamsters," as that is verboten on this page.

The Salmon Page

http://www.riverdale.k12.or.us/salmon.htm

Not exactly pets, perhaps, but they are animals, in a meta-sense. Travel upstream from the daily fish passage report to advice on how to catch them and how to save them to a crucial link: How to Order Smoked Salmon on the Internet.

ALSO RECOMMENDED:

Virtual Pet Cemetery

http://www.lavamind.com/pet.html

For those pets we have loved and lost. Even the hardest-hearted will tear up reading these e-mail obits.

ZooNet Image Archives

http://www.mindspring.com/~zoonet/gallery.html

Did you say you wanted a picture of a Chinese alligator lurking under a log? A flamingo standing in grass? A white peacock? Here you go.

Automobiles

Feeling velocity-shy? Wheels not snappy enough? Browse here to get a dose of auto-mania. At least cruising automotive pages doesn't contribute to global warming or loss of the ozone layer.

About Car/Puter

http://ocean.winnet.net/c/gsn/ABOUTCP.HTM

"When you step into an auto showroom without the answers to some key questions, you are at the mercy of the salesperson." Car/Puter urges you to take charge of the situation by ordering its new and used car-pricing reports for cars from 1980.

DealerNet - The Source for New Car Information

http://www.dealernet.com/index.htm

Here's a "virtual showroom" with a searchable database of car makes, prices, and styles. There's also a pre-owned page, one catering to specialty cars, and online insurance quotes.

Team.Net British Cars

http://www.team.net:80/sol/

Offshoot of a hardy newsgroup, the Scions of Lucas host all of the British car info you might want, even a British-American dictionary of car terms.

Carshow and Cruise Night Home Page

http://www.tiac.net/users/cody/carshow/welcome.html

If you are enamored of all things automotive, schedule your year according to the calendar of U.S. and Canadian car events here, or enter your own confab on the schedule. The place to go if being called a motorhead makes you smile.

The Car Place

http://www.cftnet.com/members/rcbowden/

Robert Bowden, aka Redneck Without a Cause, is a former auto editor and author of *Boss Wheels.* Go straight to his thumbs-up or -down take on every new model and then some. Here's Robert on the 1995 Chevy Cavalier: "First marketed in 1982, this thing had only one virtue: It was cheap. Now it's (relatively) cheap and has a few more virtues, like up-to-date safety equipment. But it's still flawed and probably always will be. How come Detroit can't make a first-rate small car? Huh? How come?"

Reasonable Drivers Unanimous Home Page

http://www.clark.net/pub/kevina/sl/

Operating on the belief that "many traffic laws are unreasonable, therefore broken," Kevin Atkinson makes a case for upping the speed limit, mandating slowpokes to pull over, and why Americans might just have "a god-given right to drive." It's unanimous, isn't it?

Discount Tire Direct

http://www.tires.com/

Of course you can order tires online. Wheels, too. Weekly specials and queries by e-mail.

ALSO RECOMMENDED:

Vehicle Disposal Service for CHARITY

http://www.vector.ca/aadco/

"Any vehicle, any condition, any location" — and you can get a tax receipt. Call 1-800-463-5681.

Aviation

Icarus was only the first in a long line of folks who just had to get their feet off the ground. The technical, the goofy, and the practical aspects of those incredible flying machines are all available on the Web.

AirPage

http://trex.smoky.ccsd.k12.co.us/~dlevin/air/air.html

By his own admission, 11th-grader Dimitri Levin has been an aircraft maniac since age 6. Here is exacting documentation, history, and technical data on more than 240 historical, commercial transport planes and helicopters. "I also collect the aircraft themselves (well, okay, scale models of aircraft)," reports the honest-to-a-fault Mr. Levin.

Ballooning Online!

http://sunsite.unc.edu/ballooning/

For the lighter-than-air crowd, here are announcements and news from the balloon front, a directory of clubs and events, weather links, mailing lists, a glossary, safety info, classifieds — oh, yes, and prayers for ballooning. Yikes!

Hang Gliding WWW Server Home Page

http://cougar.stanford.edu:7878/ HGMPSHomePage.html

And for the foot-launched flying community, this meta-page of photos, discussion list digests, QuickTime and MPEG movies, photo gallery, pilot services, FAQs, and weather info, lots of it. And comics.

Guide to Bush Flying

http://www.fepco.com/ Bush_Flying.html

F.E. Potts is a real bush pilot living in Alaska, which makes him an excellent source for info on necessary equipment, flying techniques, and the environment that bush pilots must face. Long narrative passages and pilot skill-building texts, including my favorites, "Optical Illusions" and "Swing Low (But Not Too Low)."

Nels Anderson's Home Page

http://www.ultranet.com/~nels/

If you're into flight simulation, Nels Anderson has uncovered a host of links to FS pages. There are "Flight Sim Oriented Businesses" and general aviation resources here, too.

Airpower Journal

http://www.cdsar.af.mil/apje.html

The professional journal of the U.S. Air Force, *AP* is a forum for discussion about strategy and tactics, military doctrine, and readiness. Downloadable articles and subscription info.

Dance

If, like Gene Kelly, you "gotta dance," you'll find it admirably represented here, from belly to samba to tap. Go on, now, emulate the pros: left, two, three, right, two, three.

Welcome to the New York City Ballet

http://www.nycballet.com/

Gracefully presented, the NYCB page has repertory performance notes, the current season schedule, ticket ordering, and a trivia contest. Naturally, the *Nutcracker* gets its own hot button.

The Clogging Page

http://www.hahnemann.edu/tap/ clogging.htm

Plain-text information galore on clogging, a descendant of Celtic and Scottish step-dancing. Nice integration of e-mail discussion, pointers to newsgroups, and where-to-buy and where-to-dance info.

Middle Eastern Dance

http://www.lpl.arizona.edu/ ~kimberly/medance/medance.html

This meta-page takes you the world over to absorb all elements of dance orientale: history, supplies, studios, GIFs, song lyrics, and media covering the subject. How about browsing a list of Arabic names for your nom de performance? (We're fond of *Nouna*, "dimple in the chin.") Don't miss the link to Arabic Naming Practices.

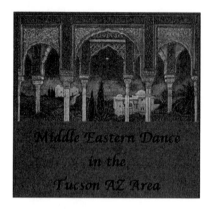

Dance for the Fiberoptic Planes

http://www.cgrg.ohio-state.edu/ ~rshaw/home.html

Now here's a compelling argument for ISDN: a selection of large video clips (15–30 minutes each, using a 14.4-Kbps modem) by Robbie Shaw and the Ohio State University dance department, which you are free to arrange in a collage of your design. Even having created this, the dancers remind us that "nothing can match the magic of live dance!"

Fashion

Clothes make the person, and pages about clothes make us wonder what is de rigeur to wear when cruising the Web.

The Fashion Page

http://www.charm.net/~jakec/

Lots of articles and links geared to the style-conscious among us. At least the page isn't a slave to (current) fashion; there is info on last season, next season, and timeless fashion, for example, Underwear Through the Ages. Bibliographies, movie reviews, and video clips of Todd Oldham and John Galliano's runway extravaganzas.

Is Fashion Silly?

http://www.softeam.it/pittimmagine/

Italian fashion students have compiled a 'zine to explore the culture of fashion in society. In English or Italian, and multihued. Where else could you get a JPEG of the latest Italian knit stitch?

What Do You Expect for Free, Vogue?

http://www.sils.umich.edu/~sooty/fashion.html

Chatty, down-to-earth page, sans supermodel GIFs, because today, "anyone with a PPP connection can be a fashion victim." And head on down to the Urban Runway, uptown to MCI's @fashion, or over to the alt.sex.fetish.fashion FAQ.

FashionNet

http://www.fashion.net/

Created by the Fashion Industry Network, this understated page links you to a groovy selection of magazines covering the F-world (Vibe, Word, HotWired); Salonline; browsing sites from Paris to Planet Reebok, and, of course, online shopping opportunities. A Dutch wedding dress? A Nicole Miller vest? Levis? Come on down.

Charlie's Sneaker Pages

http://www.neosoft.com/~sneakers/

A loving tribute to everyone's fashion favorite, no matter what couture. Charlie waxes nostalgic over past sneakers, logo placement, and this factoid: A Converse Chuck Taylor All-Stars box is the perfect size for storing data-processing supplies, including CD-ROMs and QIC-80 tapes.

Games

Playing to win or just killing time, the games category is bound to have a little something for you. More than 350 Internet games alone — but please, would you go outside to play paintball?

American Poolplayers' Association Cool Pool Links

http://www.bigmagic.com/pages/apa/apa_link.htm

Pool, billiards, and snooker aficionados need look no further. Tournament news from Europe and the U.S., player bios, history, and FAQs.

The WWW Backgammon Page

http://www.statslab.cam.ac.uk/~sret1/backgammon/main.html

Here's the place to pick up Postscript or plain-text annotated matches, and telnet to an Internet backgammon server. Or, read books about backgammon or check out related games.

Internet Chess Library

http://caissa.onenet.net/chess/

Chess memorabilia, online game databases, ratings for the 1,000 best — and worst — players, and an art gallery homage to chessboards. Ever heard the word *chessic* before? Now you have, courtesy of one Karl Schwamb.

Chess Space

http://www.redweb.com/chess/

A proverbial mini-Yahoo! of chess data: database games, classes, events, players, organizations, publications. Wow — who would have thought of chess audio clips? T.S. Eliot does a reading of "A Game of Chess" from *The Wasteland* and HAL says, "Would you like to play a game   of chess?"

DominoNet

http://neon.ingenia.com/dominet/

Bet you didn't know that the cafeteria at Lisgar Collegiate Institute is "practically the domino capital of eastern Ontario!" The Lisgarians have constructed a detailed page of essayettes on the rules and variants of the black tile game, to wit: "It is very bad form to cheat at Dominoes, since it's so easy. I can only think of two ways that anyone could cheat: by looking at somebody else's hand, and by rigging the initial mixing so you get the 6/6, say. This is truly, truly low. If this is the only way you can win, go play chess or go rob old people."

Introduction to Go

http://www.well.com/user/mmcadams/gointro.html

Here's the history of one of the oldest games in the world, with its asymmetrical board and black-and-white stones. "The white stones invade a black-bordered area; the black stones creep in under the edge of a white-bordered area; and vice versa. The stones at game's end touch one another's edges, illustrating the battles won and lost, forming a map of the contest of two minds."

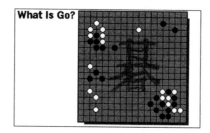

What Is Go?

Go Page Index

http://ltiwww.epfl.ch/~warkent/go/golinks.html

A long and helpful international meta-page from Ken Warkentyne on Go Web sites, commercial products, explanations of rules, Go news, Internet Go servers and game collections, clubs, players — even Postscript files to print Go diagrams.

Squizz's Cryptic Crosswords

http://www.cs.curtin.edu.au/~squizz/cryptics.html

A collection of mind-contorting crosswords to challenge the most intrepid crosswordian. David Squire, aka Squizz, provides Postscript and HTML forms of some 20 games, their solutions (much farther down the page!), and a guestbook for those who can hold their heads high.

The Game Cabinet

http://web.kaleida.com/u/tidwell/GameCabinet.html

Lots of reviews, rules, and info on "family, beer and pretzel, and strategy games" from around the world, and around the Net. Includes links to game magazines, clubs, manufacturers for games such as Duel der Schamanen: "shamen duke it out in a mystic game of Tic Tac Toe"; or, try A.R.E.N.A., "mayhem for mayhem's sake."

San Jose Scrabble Club No. 21

http://www.yak.net/kablooey/scrabble.html

If you're a Scrabble player, this humble plain-text site alone is worth the price of the book. Yes, it contains hot links to lists of two-letter, three-letter, vowel-heavy (70 percent or more!), J, Q, X, and Z words — even words with no vowels (brr, psst, crwth). Bonus: There are some seven-letter bingo study lists attached, too.

Card Games

You've seen the movie, read the book, heard the soundtrack — now, play the card game. But please, keep the stakes low.

Bridge on the Web

http://www.cs.vu.nl:80/~sater/bridge/bridge-on-the-web.html

Results and news from tournaments and federations around the world, Usenet links, and pointers to two live-on-the-Net bridge games.

Bridge

http://abacus.bates.edu:80/~rshepard/bridge.html

Randy Shepard's downloadable bridge game for Windows, with "numerous cosmetic improvements" over the previous version, and some context-sensitive help. Load and save hands, and custom-build your own.

Magic: The Gathering

http://marvin.macc.wisc.edu/
deckmaster/wotc.html

Many pages to this Dungeons and Dragons card game are played with collectible cards. Its many fans have created a host of pages available here on the rules and variants, card lists, and card databases.

An IRC Poker Dealing Program

http://www.cs.cmu.edu/afs/cs/user/
mummert/public/www/ircbot.html

If you're a poker regular in the analog world, how about upping the ante with a digital game using Internet Relay Chat? The program manages the action and "understands" a number of games. This page gives quite detailed instructions for how to join or leave a game, perform status-of-game commands, and allowable game actions. Then there's tournament level IRC poker. ...

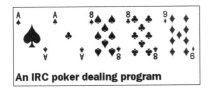

An IRC poker dealing program

Poker Dictionary

http://www.universe.digex.net/
~kimberg/pokerdict.html

"I had to re-buy after the second hand when I had quads shot down." If this is not readily decipherable, stroll through the Poker Dictionary. Exhaustive cross-referenced hotlinks courtesy of Dan Kimberg. You can hardly play the game without the lingo.

Some Poker Variants

http://www.wolfe.net/~peter/
poker.html#Mitsubishi

Feeling stuck in a five card-stud rut? Here are numerous variations of draw, stud, shared-card and miscellaneous games, with detailed descriptions of the deal, the plays, and the standard variations for each. Link to poker terms and hand rankings info.

Star Trek: The Next Generation Customizable Card Game

http://129.21.204.63/HTML/
STCCG_Home.HTML

If your manias run to both *Star Trek* and cardplaying, this is your page. Bonus points if you like simulations, as the point of this game is to play through an episode that you and your partner create with some 60 cards you have collected from the total deck. Pictured here is Chalnoth, from the "Dilemma" cards. Yep.

SimCity: The Card Game

http://weber.u.washington.edu/
~starfish/simcity/simcity.html

You've played the game, now collect the cards, read the rules, and play the game again. Link to SimClassifieds and solitaire puzzle decks.

Computer Games

Computer games are surely what keep us going during a long day of spreadsheets and report writing. Just wait till the boss has made the rounds before you refresh the screen.

Milkman's Air Warrior Page

http://www.bby.com.au/~gnb/AW/

If you must ask, "Air Warrior is just about the best use of a computer and modem ever invented." Having said that, ace fan Milkman displays a page of info and downloadable game files of WWII or Korean War-era flying battle games with up to 100 human pilots. "You will never be satisfied with computer opponents in any game after playing against scheeming (sic), devious, unpredictable people." Thus spake Milkman.

U of C Bolo Page

http://student-www.uchicago.edu/
users/vboguta/bolo/bolo.html

Author Stuart Cheshire: "Bolo is a 16-player graphical networked real-time multi-player tank battle game. It has elements of arcade-style shoot-em-up action, but for the serious players who play 12 hour games with 16 players working in teams, it becomes more of a strategy game." In other words, it's a big production and will require you to skip work or school to play it.

Braintainment Center

http://world.brain.com/index.cgi/UN/
Index.html

Software, books, tapes, games for your brain! Compare your brainpower to others by country, profession, domain. Take three-minute Personal Insight Query tests for thinking-style analysis. Visit an online oracle (the traditional kind)! Believe me, this is a busy site. The mind is a marvelous thing.

Complete Gaming Headquarters

http://world.brain.com/index.cgi/UN/
iq/hsc.cgi

Multilinks to scores of game files, multiple sites for Doom, Descent, Terminal Velocity, R.O.T.T., Duke Nukem 3D. You may never get out.

Digital Nostalgia

http://www.umich.edu/~sloane/
games.html

Mark Sakey fondly remembers the "old" days and has provided downloadable old PC games (some of which run really fast on today's machines), all of which are between 25K and 500K. If you didn't have them before, get 'em now: Kerboom, Scorched Earth, Viper, Here They Come, lots more.

Colin's DOOM, DOOM II and Heretic Levels

http://www.islandnet.com/~ccaird/
doom/

A fix for the tireless Doom gamer. Find a player in your area code (international); check out different sound cards for best effect; post to newsgroups; and, of course, link to pix and info on levels for Doom , Doom II, Ultimate Doom, and Heretic.

DoomGate

http://doomgate.cs.buffalo.edu/
doomgate/

A meta-DoomWeb, covering the many incarnations and variations of Doom; add-on programs and utilities to enhance Doomism at all levels; technical info; discussion groups and mailing lists; ftp sites of yet more Doom shareware releases (DOS, NeXT, Linux, Sun); spoilers; cheat codes; WAD-ever else you need.

Hank Leukart's Homepage

http://www.portal.com/~hleukart/

Just who is Hank Leukart? He's the official DOOM FAQmeister and author of a DOOM Hacker's Guide. His page links you to that definitive FAQ, lots of Internet shareware game news and rumors, a slew of reviews and previews of games, and downloads of same.

Games Domain

http://wcl-rs.bham.ac.uk/
GamesDomain/

This vast page houses thousands of game, patch and demo files, FAQs, ftp sites, game 'zines, and commercial and personal home pages on games, from MUDs to Mortal Kombat, DOOM to Darts. Games programming, competition news, and GD Review, updated daily, with its reviews, news and opinions by gamers for gamers.

Hyper@ctive

http://hyperactive.com/games/
index2.html

This handsome Australian PC game 'zine covers the rumors, previews, reviews, and other stuff that make the gamer froth with excitement. There's an archive of more than 2,400 cheats and hints for 632 games on all major platforms. (No wonder they're hyperactive!)

Internet Modem Players Listing

http://www.xmission.com/
~morrison/IMPL/home.html

Phone bill too high? Try this searchable database of players (U.S. and selected other countries) wanting to play the same networkable games that you do. "Enjoy the challenges of a human opponent instead of a stale computer opponent."

The Myst Hints Web Page

http://www.stack.urc.tue.nl/~remya/myst/myst.html

General hints for navigating and figuring out clues to the enigmatic best-selling CD-ROM game; a guide through the different Ages of Myst, and, as a last resort for the Myst-impaired, Actual Answers.

Internet PC Games Charts

http://www.xs4all.nl/~jojo/

Jojo Appelo of the Netherlands has an elaborate e-mail voting system that ranks the Top 100 commercial PC games and the top 40 downloaded shareware games weekly. He also keeps smaller lists of the top five in various categories, along with detailed voting instructions, if you want to take a stand. Savvy game developers watch this list closely.

Techno Weenie

http://www.rubyslippers.com/spaceweenie/text/weenie1.html

This "Toybox to the 21st Century" contains game reviews, graphics add-ons, and graphics-intensive pages out the wazoo. Each product is Robert-Rated from the low end (Weenie Roast) to highest accolade

(Hot Dog!). Note to designers: Blue and yellow text on black screen may be hazardous to our future game-playing ability.

The Gamer's Ledge

http://www.medio.net/users/mgodsey/games.html

Mike Godsey reviews the latest PC and CD games such as Burn Cycle, Full Throttle, and The Riddler, and has built some nice links to download files, reviews and demos, online game mags, vendor/developer pages, modem play, and non-PC platform sites.

Cyber/Darts Home Page

http://www.infohwy.com:80/darts/CYBERDTSHM.HTML

Darts fanatics unite! Affectionate articles preaching to the converted, weird team names, shirt designs — and also tournament news and schedules, not to mention directories of pubs providing either steel-point or soft-tip darts.

UnOfficial Guide to Drinking Games

http://silver.ucs.indiana.edu/~bquick/drgames.html

Undoubtedly, designated drivers are best suited to absorb the action as drinking parties or barflies attempt

Beeramid, Drop the Dime, Fuzzy Duck, Robo-Slam. Games described and rated for their alcohol intake requirement (low to deadly — "don't do it, you idiot!")

Gambling

"If I didn't have bad luck, I wouldn't have no luck at all," goes the old blues song. Hope your luck holds as you negotiate lots of Web opportunities to double your money.

Blackjack Server

http://www.ua.com/blackjack/bj.html

The rules are simple: start with $1,000 of virtual money, blackjack beats drawing to 21. Sit down and play a hand or two. Save time by preloading the playing card bitmaps. Between games, browse the week's top 25 players.

Rec.Gambling

http://www.conjelco.com/r_g/las_vegas/r.g.html

If you've got a yen to gamble, click on the map to see where the nearest U.S. casino is (and even get weather reports for Las Vegas, Reno, and Atlantic City). Link to lots of info on blackjack, poker, craps — and double your fun by finding the gambling-related movies page.

The Pool

http://www.xmission.com/~winner/pool.html

Accept no substitutes: This is a sports betting service. Pay $100 up front to play against an average of 500 other risk-loving sports hounds. Send your picks two days before the Big Game via snail mail and then wait: You can win up to $10,000 per game.

Interactive Fiction

Destination: Cyberspace

http://www.blvl.igs.net/~vanburen/

It's 2095 on the Internet, and you've just entered unauthorized cyberspace. What do you do? What do you do? 1) Turn tail. 2) Reply, "Out of my way, or IÆll ftp you to a Commodore VIC 20!" or 3) Engage the software that you got from pre-arrest Kevin Mitnick. Each response branches several ways. Your fate is truly in your hands.

Letters from ABroad

http://www.ftech.net/~arc/abroad/abroad.htm

The world's first "tawdry, interactive soap opera on the Web," and you can play a part by sending e-mail directly to the major characters, Birdie or Doreen, gal-friends and secretaries at the New York multinational ad agency, Way Cool. The monthly archives of letters are quite a piece of work; see if you don't agree.

XYZZYnews Home Page

http://www.users.interport.net/~eileen/design/xyzzynews.html

If you have a weakness for MUDs or the old Infocom games, or you go for the new text adventure games, check out bimonthly XYZZYnews, with news and sneak previews of games, interviews with Infocom programmers, reviews, a spoiler page, and more. Download it in ASCII or PDF forms, or read it on the Web.

Internet Games

Something tells me it wasn't all work and no play in the old ARPAnet days. How else to explain this absolutely immense storehouse of games to be played on, or downloaded via, or facilitated by, the Net?

The ISearch Home Page

http://www.cris.com/~is/isearch/isearch.shtml

Matt Alberts posts a biweekly Internet hunt game featuring 4–8 questions of varying difficulty, a few hints, and links to Net search tools. Play alone or on teams, and then e-mail your answers by the deadline. The correct URLs are hot-linked on the answer page. There is a prize — though Matt's not forthcoming in the FAQ as to what it is — and he reminds us that ISearch is supposed to be fun, though it may lead to time loss and hair loss.

Welcome to MUDdom

http://www.shef.ac.uk/uni/academic/I-M/is/studwork/groupe/home.html

Surely the most complete FAQ ever, complete with lots of graphics, navigation buttons, and detailed

history on the many variations of the immensely popular Net text-based role-playing games. (On Yahoo! alone, there are 200+ Web pages of MUDs, MOOs, MUCKs, MUSHs, and MUGs.) An excellent starting point for MUDder wannabes.

Netrek Home Page — Front Page

http://factoryx.factoryx.com/

Yet another manifestation of our devotion to *Star Trek*, Netrek is a multiplayer, graphical, real-time battle simulation using ST themes. Dogfights and planet conquering prevail. Would Gene Roddenbery approve? Would Mr. Spock? Seems likely.

Pinball Links

http://www.webcom.com/~cgould/pinlink.html

Wizard Tommy himself would be pleased with how many Web sites there are dedicated to his game. Includes links to pinball manufacturers, collectors, tournaments, and some cool photos.

Puzzles

They seem innocuous enough at first, but they can reduce us to babbling, cursing fools in a few short minutes. There are all kinds of crazy-making routines here — try to stay away. Dare you.

Yahoo!

John's Word Search Puzzles

http://www.NeoSoft.com/~jrpotter/puzzles.html

Take a break from that spreadsheet and try to find the words — backwards, forwards, up, or down — in the jumble of letters that John's placed inside the box. Yeah, you'll feel relaxed real soon ;-).

Jumble and Crossword Solver

http://odin.chemistry.uakron.edu/cbower/jumble.html

Chuck Bower offers a real insanity-prevention device: a searchable database to resolve those scrambled words or incomplete crosswords that you just can't figure out. Just type the letters that you do know from the crossword, or the entire scrambled word, and the server jumps into action.

Riddle du Jour

http://www.new3.com/riddle/

"While I was walking down the lane, From the dead the living came, Six there were, seven to be, Solve this riddle and I'll set you free." If you like untangling this kind of puzzler, you're bound to win the daily prize and join The Sphinx's Hall of Fame.

Video Games

Seems like only yesterday that PacMan was gobbling up the screen. Now they make feature films based on video games. Witness the avid state of gamers' fanaticism and learn about the games that inspire them.

coNsOle.wORlD

http://www.cm.cf.ac.uk/Games/

Multilayer video-game page includes lots of info on Sega, Nintendo, Amiga, Atari, 3DO, and other 32X and CD-i titles. Graphics, sound clips, archives, magazines, newsgroup lists, and other video game-ana.

Classic Video Games Homepage

http://www2.ecst.csuchico.edu/~gchance/

This page is awash in nostalgia for seemingly ancient game systems such as the Atari 2600, Mattel Intellivision, Vectrex, Bally Astrocode, and lots more. Greg Case even includes his diary of video games past, and trades that he's willing to make. 1982–83, Top 10 lists of games, too.

Game Zero

http://www.gamezero.com/team-0/

Rumor control, video clips, features, and reviews, presented complete with manga-style comics on "Your Detonation Point for Video Gaming Information." Fire away, and may the best controller win.

Video Game Console Hotlist

http://www.cyberspace.com/ellisd/vidgames.html

Pick your platform: Ultra 64, Playstation, Sega Genesis, Atari Jaguar or Lynx, 3DO, Super SNES, or Game Boy, to link to fan pages and those from the manufacturers themselves.

Hobbies

SalvoWeb

http://www.scotborders.co.uk/salvo/

This cheerful hodgepodge of a page from Ireland has lots of bits on architectural antiques and salvage, public sale of antique goods (Scottish police boxes c. 1930, say, or dismantled barns). Classifieds, magazines, and a U.K. antique dealer list too.

Antiques and Arts Monthly

http://www.connix.com/thebee/aweb/aa.htm

The Web page for a Connecticut-based weekly paper featuring an auction calendar, antique show calendar, links to the Antiques Council, and an index of other sites.

Aunt Annie's Craft Page

http://mineral.galleries.com/annie/auntannie.htm

Auntie prepares a different project weekly: stencils, homemade stamps, puzzles. You can download Annie's shareware for paper crafts, or order the Windows disk. Good for kids and family fun — just watch out for paper cuts. Tissue paper painting coming right up.

Birds and Birding

Bird Watching and Related Information on Birds

http://www.gorp.com/gorp/activity/birding.htm

A veritable meta-page about birds, whether they be penguins, eagles, or

budgies: bird art, a song archive, waterfowl migration, rare birds. Many international links and U.S. Fish and Wildlife Service info, too.

Up At Six

http://www.upatsix.com/upatsix/

The commercial aviary with a descriptive name offers a customizable bird database for professional and hobbyist bird breeders, and Q&A with experts on bird care, debate (for example, raising hybrid Macaws), and lots of links to newsgroups, mail lists, and many bird sites (parrots on IRC).

Collectors

The Web attracts the sort of folks who are obsessed with something, and the Collectors area puts their obsessions in their best light. Whether it's trading cards, candy bar wrappers, paperweights, or Hot Wheels, it shouldn't surprise you to learn that a collector has staked a claim here.

The Plastic Princess Collectors Page

http://deepthought.armory.com/ ~zenugirl/barbie.html

Barbie turned 30 recently, and her fans are going strong. This page has a strong Barbie component (magazines, books, videos, vendors) but also reviews and discussions of other doll-collecting aspects: price guides, restoration, even "doll-related tourist spots" for your next vacation.

Coin Universe

http://www.coin-universe.com/ index.html

That old Mercury dime or Lincoln penny you've been hanging onto might be worth something. Here's the place to check. Then there's the *Coin Dealer Newsletter*, rare coin graphics, teletrade auctions, and directories of dealers and shows.

Collectors' Index

http://www.bdt.com/home/k55k/ collect.html

Connect here with others who share your fascination via a searchable database (e-mail form to send your own entry), or visit the Hall of Homes, Web sites about many collectibles. There's a calendar of estate sales, trade shows, fairs, and auctions.

Juggling Information Service

http://www.hal.com/services/juggle/

Need to brush up your technique? Check out the MPEG clips of Five-Ball Cascade. Where to buy the right clubs or balls with which to grow deft? Get started at the JIS. Even Ren and Stimpy expound on the topic in a sound clip.

All Magic Guide to the World Wide Web

http://www.uelectric.com/ allmagicguide.html

Conjure up this page for lots of links to individual magic and magicians' sites, e-zines, calendars, and Houdini-ania. Brought to us by Robinson Wizard — how did he do that?

Puppetry Home Page

http://www-leland.stanford.edu/ ~rosesage/puppetry/puppetry.html

Shrine to tireless creators and stars: Kukla, Ollie, Rowlf, Punch, Judy, along with puppet building, performance, and puppeteers. Catch the debate: "Is puppetry anachronistic?" Heaven forfend.

The Fireworks Page

http://bronze.ucs.indiana.edu/ ~wwarf/firework.html

Now this is an elaborate hobby. The National Fireworks Association and the Pyrotechnics Guild have pages, and there are JPEGs of memorable displays, including ones at Disneyland, the yearly convention, and Fourth of July at the U.S. Capitol. rec.pyrotechnics attracted too many "mad bomber" types to maintain it, but the pyrotechnics crowd still publishes a detailed FAQ.

Home and Garden

Fixer-uppers and the green-thumbed have converged on the Web to inspire — or tantalize — you with their notions of what is possible to improve in house and home.

Bonsai Home Page

http://www.pass.wayne.edu/~dan/bonsai.html

The tiny trees hold their own on this page. There's a six-part FAQ, many tips from bonsai aficionados, Gopher files, and a bibliography.

Windowsill Orchid Picture Gallery

http://www.umich.edu/~nplummer/orchid.html

Nick Plummer has done his homework on the flowering plant that appears everywhere in the world but Antarctica. He claims that orchids take little more work than "a really good philodendron." OK, if you say so, Nick.

The Garden Gate

http://www.prairienet.org/ag/garden/homepage.htm

Lots of Internet resources on gardening, including glossaries, FAQs, plant lists. Reviews of gardening and

landscaping software and products, books, catalogs. No green thumb? Visit The Sun Room: "Whether you call them houseplants, indoor, or greenhouse plants, you can learn how to stop killing them." I feel better already.

The Tree Doctor

http://www.1stresource.com/t/treedoc/

Jim Cortese is a certified arborist "nurturing the urban forest via the Internet." Visit his page or give him a call about root problems, diseases, or referrals: 800-827-0532.

Time Life Complete Gardener Encyclopedia

http://www.pathfinder.com/vg/TimeLife/CG/vg-search.html

The Virtual Garden is a really cool searchable database that aims to house info on some 2,000 species of North American plants, trees, and shrubs. You can also search by amount of light, soil type, drainage, height, color, and blooming season. Then, read all about what you've found, and view a pretty good image of each plant you seek.

WoodWeb Home Page

http://www.woodweb.com

The online e-zine for woodworking products and tools, with news on shows, manufacturers, and seminars. E-mail discussion forum and articles on topics such as clamping pressures, the new glues, lumber grades, and woodworkers' contracts.

Motorcycles

Internet BMW Riders — Mailing List

http://world.std.com/~ibmwr

Web home of all things about BMW bikes: dealers, directories, how-to articles, patches, T-shirts, and, of course, a FAQ.

Denizens of Doom

http://www.ssc.upenn.edu/~awhite/Interests/Motorcycle/DoD/DoD.html

Rules, regulations and bylaws of DoD: Rule #1: There are no rules. Rule #2: Go ride. Blue highways road lists that make you wanna head out on the highway. Is that Steppenwolf I hear?

World Wide Glide

http://www.halcyon.com/zipgun/wwg/wwg.html

Excellent Harley links: designations, performance books engine GIFs, toolkit info, plugs and pipes, and the *Harley Digest*. Check out "And you think bikers are scum?" — a Canter and Siegel Web flame. (Canter and Siegel were the infamous "green-card lawyers" who learned the hard way about abusing the Net.) Live to ride. Ride to live.

Motorcycle Links

http://jupiter.lfbs.rwth-aachen.de/~markolf/Moto_Links.html

Meta-list of international sites by country; also, organizations and clubs, products, manufacturers, e-mail lists. If you were looking for The Iron Butt Association, your search is over (http://world.std.com/~ironbutt/).

The Motor Scooter Index

http://weber.u.washington.edu/~shortwav/scootcontents.html

Clubs, rallies, restoration info, and racing sites for the cute little cousin of the motorcycle.

Outdoors

You may think outdoors types eschew the Web, but they do get home between treks, and then they sit down at the computer and put up Web pages about their trips, with lots of dos and don'ts and friendly advice.

The Backcountry Home Page

http://io.datasys.swri.edu/Overview.html#pages

Feel like heading out beyond the reach of a T-1 line? Stop by this page for lots of pointers to books, newsgroups, places of interest, recipes, trip reports, and weather info.

Hiking and Walking Homepage

http://www.teleport.com/~walking/hiking.html

Take a hike! Here is trail info for many international spots from Kilimanjaro to Pinnacles to Newfoundland. Link to hiking organizations and newsgroups, treks and tours, and info on hiking gear and books.

Hiking and Walking Homepage

Bungee Jumping Home Page

http://www.geopages.com/siliconvalley/1414/

Yikes! Catch big air at this huge store of bungee data. International bungee sites including contact info and price. Bottoms up! Er, no, wait, not that way!

Princeton Outdoor Action Program: Planning a Safe River Trip

http://www.princeton.edu/~rcurtis/rivplan.html

Long, detailed article and good check list by Rick Curtis on all aspects of planning a group rafting trip.

Watersports Resources!

http://www.halcyon.com/wtr/Watersports_Resources.html

All manner of sea kayaking and whitewater paddling info is here, including clubs, outfitters, articles, trip reports, and an alpha list of suppliers by state.

Big Wall Climbing Home Page

http://www.primenet.com/~midds/

Has your routine gotten humdrum? Try spending multiple days and nights climbing the largest rock faces in the world. John Middendorf tells you how on this page, which includes equipment info, pictures, and ratings of big walls. Don't miss the photo of a vertically challenged tent with fearless climber resting inside.

GORP — Great Outdoor Recreation Pages

http://www.gorp.com/default.htm

Whatever you seek in nature probably has a home at GORP. Worldwide locations, activities from hiking and biking to caving and windsurfing, books and maps, trips and treks, gear, travelers' tales, food (including GORP, do you think?), and even cartoons that reflect the unique sense of humor that one needs to cultivate in the great outdoors.

Outdoor Home Page

http://www.wsa.com/ool/ool1home.html

Outdoors Online Inc. offers many hunting, fishing, and shooting links; guides, outfitters and equipment; regional info and news.

NetWoods Virtual Campsite

http://www.wsa.com/ool/
ool1home.html

A meta-page for adult Scout leaders and for Scouts, too. Created by Steve Tobin, scoutmaster of BSA Troop 39 in Cannon Falls, Minnesota. Scouting resources on the Net, home pages of various Scout units, and many outdoor and recreation sites.

The NetWoods Virtual Campsite

Telemarque Home Page

http://www.telemarque.com/

All you free-heel skiers out there have a friend in Telemarque, a comprehensive U.S., Canadian, and European resource page. Articles on routes, equipment reviews, and links to many Telemark and Nordic ski sites. Searchable database of ski info submitted by readers.

Cyberboarder Magazine

http://www.cyberboarder.com/

In case you didn't know it, snowboarding has taken off, and here's a 'zine to prove it. Good first-person essays on trips taken, scenes made (don't miss Grrrl Talk for the female boarder's perspective), chatty letters to the editor, and equipment pages. Extensive links to overlapping interests in cyberpunk, surfing, and alternative music.

Sports

This huge category is topped by Reuters hourly sports headline news and a vast (hot link) subdirectory of all the sports sites listed in Yahoo!. No sport too small or too odd; if it requires a coordinated mind and body competing with others, chances are it's here.

Auto Racing

American Racing Scene

http://www.racecar.com/

Get your Indy Car and NASCAR results and detailed reports in this racing car fan's e-zine. Readers frequent Shop Talk via e-mail to compare notes and races.

The Racer Archive

p://www.eng.hawaii.edu/Contribs/
carina/ra.home.page.html

Handsome page on Formula 1, Indy Car, and NASCAR races where you'll find championship results, stats, and directories of clubs, teams, and tracks. Also, pointers to digital sites including newsgroups, and a photo gallery of cars.

Motorsport News International

http://www.motorsport.com/
Index.html

Links to articles on many types of racing: endurance, open wheel, rallies, off-road, plus areas on sprint cars, stock cars, touring cars. The page is based on the info at the rec.autos.sport.info newsgroup. Stories are indexed alphabetically and chronologically.

Baseball

The national pastime.

ESPNet SportsZone: Major League Baseball

http://espnet.sportszone.com/mlb/

A large and efficient commercial site, ESPNet offers free access to live scoreboards and box scores, headline news, stats and previews, chat areas and product areas; the columnists, clubhouse, and player access are by subscription only. Stop here for any of the major sports and a number of minor ones.

Fantasy Baseball Home Page

http://www.usatoday.com/sports/
baseball/newwebpg.htm

Created in 1980, Fantasy Baseball is yet another way to immerse yourself in the sport by creating and managing your own teams, using actual stats from the players during the season. Sometimes called Rotisserie League ball, it has a growing following. Here are player ratings, NL and AL games, and home pages from Fantasy League hobbyists.

Instant Baseball

http://www.InstantSports.com/
baseball.html

Up-to-the-minute scores for National and American League via Instant Sports, Inc.'s computer system in Austin, Texas, which receives live feeds from reporters covering games. Box scores, player stats, and division standings updated regularly, too.

Subscribe to get e-mail notifying you of your favorite team's standing, and Hideo Nomo fans can also get inning-by-inning updates via e-mail by sending mail to nomo@instant sports.com.

Welcome to the Digital Dugout

http://www.gatech.edu/lcc/idt/ Students/donturn/donturnbb.html

Don Turnbull's meta-page with links to many of the standard league resources plus info on the Negro Leagues, newsgroup listings, "Today in Baseball History," and even an interview with Ken Burns.

Basketball

Big Ten Basketball News

http://www.princeton.edu/~mcelrath/ BigTen/

Ryan McElrath provides the Big 10 conference standings, scores, game summaries, info pages for each team, and more. Links to the top recruits for the Big 10, and to other NCAA sites.

College Basketball Page

http://www.cs.cmu.edu/afs/ cs.cmu.edu/user/wsr/Web/bball/ bball.html

Playing schedules, recruiters' top lists, and men's and women's scoreboards are featured here. Conference Web pages and newsgroup info, too.

Women's College Basketball

http://espnet.sportszone.com/ncw/

Good overview page for the top-ranked women's teams, game recaps, box scores, and chat from ESPNet Sportszone.

Bowling

Bowling Home Page

http://www.pitt.edu/~pktst/ bowling.html

Loyal bowler Michael Thompson dedicates this meta-page to "the best sport in the world." Besides bowling organizations and tournament info, bowling tips and a survey about the balls that bowlers prefer, there's a glossary — and a striking file of bowling GIFs.

College sports

College Nicknames

http://grove.ufl.edu/~recycler/ sports.html

If you're not totally up to speed on college team names, this list can help. Schools around the U.S. from any athletic division that offer degrees and have sports programs are included. Nine schools have teams called the Aggies; 8 are Bearcats; 14 are Rams. Here you'll learn that Lincoln Memorial U. houses the Railsplitters, Wichita State is home to the Shockers, and Georgia's Oglethorpe U., well, its team is the Stormy Petrels.

College Athletics WWW Pages

http://www.intellinet.com/~bryan/ colleges.html

Hats off to Bryan Fritchie, who has created a meta-page organized by conference for every college program he can find (and he accepts new entries). Everything from Big East and Colonial League to Pacific 10. Hot links to Division II and III and NAIA schools, too. Go from here to virtually every team sport that he has found on the Web.

Croquet

The Digital Croquet Lawn

http://www.medio.net/nwnews/ affiliates/croquet/

"Never mind the physical dangers of balls flying through the air. Croquet will enslave you and your world will never be the same." If you're feeling up to the challenge, check out John Soltys' homage to the sport that he claims is his master.

Cycling

VeloNet: The Global Cycling Network

http://www.cycling.org/

An "electronic information desk" for cyclists, with scads of links: to worldwide biking organizations, e-mail lists, and a Reading Room with articles on unicycling, racing, safety, and multisport events, among many others. Created by "High Speed Digital Commuter" Patrick Goebel.

International Human Powered Vehicle Association

http://www.ihpva.org/

"Promoting improvement, innovation, and creativity in the design and development of human powered transportation," the IHPVA has links to championship races and cycle fests for "recumbent" bikes, the kind you lie back and pedal. Bike geeks, check out the software library for gear-inches and spoke-length calculators. And, of course, The Recumbent FAQ.

WOMBATS on the WEB

http://www.wombats.org/

Women's Mountain Bike and Tea Society, founded by Jackie Phelan, is a rich resource for women bikers. Articles ("Zen and the Art of Crashing Gracefully"), upcoming events and chapter notes, and WOMBAT art.

The WWW Bicycle Lane

http://www.cs.purdue.edu/homes/dole/bike.html

Thanks to Bryn Dole, here are nicely organized links to magazines and articles on commuting, rides and tours, races, safety info, and the U.S. Cycling Federation.

EquiLinQ

http://www.wsmith.com/equilinq/mainmenu/main.html

A wide-ranging horse enthusiast's page, from dressage to the rodeo. Top news stories from the horse world; publications, products, and organizations.

Sonja's Fencing Page

http://www.brad.ac.uk/~tglaniad/Sonja/fencing.html

Sonja invites us to "saber the moment" with her fanaticism about fencing. Detailed info on rules, equipment, terms — and don't miss why fencing is better than sex. En garde!

Ultimate Frisbee Sites

http://www.contrib.andrew.cmu.edu/usr/mj1g/all-frisbee.html

Chucky's compilation page on the flying disc and its many permutations: Ultimate, Frisbee Golf, pickup Frisbee. What, no homage to dogs and Frisbees? It's bound to be in the works.

Football

College Football World Wide Web Site

http://www.math.ufl.edu/~mitgardt/rsfc.html

The digital gridiron with cool graphics and even a Mozart MIDI clip. Summaries, scores, stats, teams, conferences — college ball, you get it all from rec.sports.football.college.

College Sports Channel Network — Football

http://www.xcscx.com/colsport/

Links to Web sites of schools in the NCAA Division 1 football conference, also alphabetically and by state via map.

Team NFL

http://nflhome.com/

A good-looking home page for the National Football League, complete with contests, newswire, rule book, and much, much more. There's a kids' area, too.

Pro and Fantasy Football

http://www.best.com/~football/football.html

The ideal fan solution: get your pro ball info via this page, and if you don't like what's happening, jump into fantasy football, where you create your own team (based on actual players and their performance). Cast your vote in a weekly contest with questions such as: Which city has the best fans?

AllSports.Com Football Hotlist

http://allsports.questtech.com/nfl/
football.html

Here's a handy page of annotated links to lots of teams, standings and stats, and even Two Minute Warning, the NFL trivia game.

Golf

GolfDataWeb

http://www.golf.com:80/index.html

This is a one-stop clubhouse: a pro shop, tourney info, clubs and associations, publications, golf vacations. Check out the Course Locator to find the nearest green.

GolfWeb

http://www.golfweb.com/

From *Golf Digest*, lots of golf news organized by week. The OnCourse database has 14,000 courses to pick from, and you can search by area code, groundskeeper, distance in yards, weekend fees, and more.

World Wide Hole in One Club

http://interchange.idc.uvic.ca/~golf/
holein1.html

Register your hole-in-one on the Web! Tell the world the glorious details via e-mail form, and enjoy your 15 minutes of golfing glory.

Hockey

Hockey Links on the Web

http://www.eskimo.com/~dstrauss/
hockey.html

A yeo-person's job done by Dave Strauss. The definitive starting point with links to all leagues (NHL, AHL, European, and more), scores, fantasy hockey, roller hockey, PC hockey games, and even hockey IRC.

The Goaltender Page

http://www.wwu.edu/~n9143349/
goalie.html

Doug Norris' homage to the guy who daily risks permanent damage from a vulcanized rubber puck hurtling toward him at high velocity. Bios of past and present goalies, trivia, goalie of the day, and miscellany by and about these foolhardy souls.

Martial Arts

Aikido Information

http://www-cse.ucsd.edu/users/
paloma/Aikido/

Archives, a calendar, Web pages, and Gopher files, as well as dojo listings by state or country.

CyberDojo

http://cswww2.essex.ac.uk/Web/
karate/CyberDojo/

Don't leave home without this meta-page on traditional Japanese or Okinawan karate, complete with a kata list, dojo directory, glossary, and a bibliography. You can join by completing a membership form and agreeing to Dojo Kun, the precepts of

karate training. In cyberspace, this means no flames or offensive posts, and respect for your fellow students. Arigato to Patrice Tarabbia.

The Martial Arts as I've Learned Them

http://student-www.uchicago.edu/
users/fun5/martial.html

Kent from Chicago has concocted an informative page of short essays differentiating the various practices, and has helpful and provocative links elsewhere, including the Martial Arts Doublespeak Guide.

Dave's Rugby and Sailing Page

http://info.census.gov/~dsliom/

Fortunately for us, Dave likes these two sports enough to provide overview links and good photo images of both.

Rick's Delphi Scuba Sig's Page

http://www.evansville.net/~mmd/
rscuba.html

Technical diving, ecology and marine science, travel and charters, underwater photography links and ftp sites, not to mention links to Rick's own books on diving.

Soccer

Soccer Cybertour

http://www.cts.com/browse/jsent/soccer.html

The world has become mad for soccer, and this page, packed with links to international and pro soccer teams, leagues, and championships proves just how mad. There's a kids' area inviting participation from young players.

SportsWorld.Line.Com

http://sportsworld.line.com/

An umbrella page that offers scores, live chat, and a discussion area customized for your favorites: football, baseball, tennis, racing, hockey, and golf. Free subscription upon registration.

WebSwim

http://alf2.tcd.ie/~smftzger/swim/header.html

Donncha Redmond provides world records and other scores, but also information on workouts, teaching swimming, products, a bibliography, and nutritional advice for the competitive swimmer. Practical topics such as "Goggles with prescription lenses."

Tennis Country

http://www.tenniscountry.com/cgi-bin/signon

Latest scores from various tourneys, newswire, playing and fitness tips. Send a welcome-back message to Monica Seles. Kids' area, too.

Volleyball Worldwide

http://www.volleyball.org/

In 1995, volleyball marks its centennial! Celebrate by heading to this definitive source. Besides the usual team and league info, VW features the history of beach volleyball, info on Wallyball, and pointers to the American Deaf Volleyball Association and the National Gay Volleyball league, among many others.

Windsurfer.com

http://www.windsurfer.com/

Postings on places to surf and places to stay when facing those wild and windy waves. There are weather links and articles filled with tips and technical info. Check out the Windsurfing calculator — convert wind speeds, weights, and lengths to get multiple equivalent values in various measuring systems.

Wrestleweb

http://www.missouri.edu/~c621097/wrestleweb.html

Steven Black and a host of wrestling fans have outlined the wrestling organization and league info, and also provide ringside reports and a list of champions and hall of famers. A wrestling encyclopedia is en route, according to Steven. And, by the way, try saying Wrestleweb five times really fast.

Toys

Not a large category on its own, but wily Web cruisers will also search under headings of particular interest, such as sports, antiques, and hobbies to find much, much more.

The Action Figure Web Page

http://www.aloha.com/~randym/action_figures/

Fan Randy Matthews' catalog of little plastic painted dolls derived from different comics and TV shows. Get the industry news on what new models are being released when, for your collecting pleasure. Classifieds and how to reach Kenner, Mattel, and the other big guns in the action figure biz. Be sure to go to Other Toy Pages, especially for *Star Wars* toys.

LEGO Information

http://legowww.homepages.com/

These little Danish plastic bricks engender serious fans such as engineers and architects, and serious building projects for robots, fighter planes, and elaborate cities. Factoid: Lego means "play well" in Danish and "put together" in Latin. They warrant two newsgroups, too.

Nerf: Foam Weapons Arsenal

http://www.halcyon.com/wrd/nerf/nerf.html

Written in the style of a munitions manual, this guide details Nerf guns (sidearms, heavy weapons, and holdout guns) and ammo (foam balls, suction cup darts, and fin-stabilized darts). Why, pray tell? "To aid you in selecting the appropriate arms for improving your chances in household skirmishes."

View-Master Information

http://www.teleport.com/~shojo/View/vm.html

If you know what View-Master is, come here to brim with nostalgia. If you don't know, you'll be incredulous at the trouble someone went to for you to be able to view postcard images in miniature slide form with a hand-held projector gadget.

Travel

Got an itch to split? There is a wealth of travel info on the Web. Savvy travelers will know to search under the name of their wished-for destination, as well as under resorts, books, and sports, too.

Air Travel

Air Traveler's Handbook Home Page

http://www.cs.cmu.edu/afs/cs/user/mkant/Public/Travel/airfare.html

The meta-page of the rec.travel.air newsgroup, this is a very comprehensive annotated list of air travel and general travel information. Currency, packing, insurance, charters, mailing lists — an excellent starting point.

800 Airline Phone Numbers

http://www.xmission.com/~aoi/f103.html

Save this text alpha list of toll-free numbers on your hard drive.

Monthly Courier Travel Newsletter

http://www.dgsys.com/~jlantos/index.html

No-frills global travel tips and guide to flying on the cheap as a courier with time-sensitive business cargo. Free excerpts of the newsletter online; subscription fee to the full edition.

Universal Currency Converter

http://www.xe.com/xenon/currency.htm

Enter the amount of currency that you want to change from one currency to another and get the present rate from the Royal Bank of Canada, which is now developing a real-time data feed, so stop back later for that added feature.

Travel Logs (Travelogues)

http://www.yahoo.com/Recreation/Travel/Travel_Logs__Travelogues_/

Armchair travelers and folks actually planning trips should check out this long list of personal accounts listed geographically, sporting titles such as "Ed's Excellent European Adventure" and "Wandering Through The Yucatan." Some of them, such as Philip Greenspun's award-winning "Travels with Samantha," link you to related side excursions along the way.

Travel Weekly's Home Page

http://www.novalink.com/travel/

Make this your first stop en route to any trip. It's a vast and good-humored collection of well-organized pages on U.S. and world destinations, adventure travel, hotels, planes and trains, news from the print edition of *Travel Weekly*, and much more.

TravelGram

http://www.csn.net/~johnhart/tfb.html

A weekly newsletter on bargain fares, hotel specials, resort deals and more. (You can subscribe via e-mail.) Link to related news at SkiGram and Travel Hotlinks. Looking for a villa or timeshare to rent? Stop on by and then pack your bag.

Reference

Yahoo!'s Reference section is where you can do things like look up unfamiliar words and acronyms in online dictionaries and access experimental translation services. You can also view Morse codes and browse through all kinds of Web encyclopedias.

There's also a useful FAQ section (Frequently Asked Questions, the help system of the Internet), with search tools and browsable indices for a large number of subjects, and not just computer-related ones.

Look at the Interesting section to find a site listing Castles on the Web, a good collection of weird information from various sources. And don't miss the Wiretap guide to alternative texts.

The Library area has a lot of resource listings, for public and university library systems. Some of these include online reading rooms and librarian-staffed Reference Desks.

Look to the Man Pages for that UNIX fix you need. Interactive sites you can use to look up commands may be helpful if you're trying to keep a server up and running.

Phone number indices and postal information can help keep you connected. You can check area codes and address information with interactive query tools at these sites.

Scan the Quotes section to grow your personal knowledge database. Warning: many of these sites can be addictive and will almost certainly increase your Net surfing time!

The White Pages section lists sites that can help you find someone with an Internet (Web or e-mail) address. You can also register and use free directory services.

Listing of acronyms, abbreviations, and definitions

http://www.umiacs.umd.edu/staff/amato/AC/main.html

Lists of abbreviations and acronyms found in e-mail messages and Usenet newsgroups, in a simple list format. These can be helpful when you're navigating the Internet and you come across a term you're unfamiliar with.

Calendars

Ecclesiastical Calendar

http://cssa.stanford.edu/~marcos/eccal.html

Use this form to find the dates of Easter Sunday and the moveable celebrations around it for a particular year — any after 1582.

Codes

Morse Code and the Phonetic Alphabets

http://www.soton.ac.uk/~scp93ch/refer/alphabet.html

A table of Morse code letters with the associated dot and dash patterns, plus the English, American, International, and NATO phonetic equivalents. Yankee Alfa Hotel Oscar Oscar!

Dictionaries

In the jargon-choked world of the Internet, you're gonna need these sooner or later.

ECHO - EuroDicautom

http://www.uni-frankfurt.de/~felix/eurodictautom.html

Experimental interface for translating technical and computing terms between several languages, including English, French, German, Italian, Spanish, Dutch, and Portuguese. You can submit a query in any of these and specify results in any other.

English-Estonian Dictionary

http://www.ibs.ee/dict/

Estonian translation engine with more than 17,000 entries. You can enter queries in either language using a simple form interface.

English-Slovene Dictionary

http://www.fer.uni-lj.si/dictionary/a2s.html

70,000-word two-way Slovene translation engine, via a form interface. This site also has a link to a Slovene alphabet and character set.

English-Slovene Dictionary

English-to-Spanish Dictionary

http://www.willamette.edu/~tjones/forms/spanish.html

Small Spanish translation index (1300 items). You can search for words and word combinations in English.

Finnish-English-Finnish dictionary

http://mofile.fi/-db.htm

You can look up Finnish words and their English equivalents here. There's also an online version of *Roget's Thesaurus* in English.

Norwegian and English dictionaries

http://www.nr.no/ordbok

Norwegian-language dictionary engine. Here's where you can look up *lutefisk* and get the complete rundown, in Norwegian.

The Devil's Dictionary

http://www.vestnett.no/cgi-bin/devil

A smashing form interface to Ambrose Bierce's famed cynical dictionary, well-suited to the online world. Find out what words really mean (e.g., Liberty: One of imagination's most prized possessions).

Computing Dictionaries

Free On-line Dictionary of Computing

http://wombat.doc.ic.ac.uk/

Good search interface to a hyperlinked computer dictionary. Your comprehensive definition will contain many other links to related information.

Jargon File Resources

http://www.ccil.org/jargon/
jargon.html

Links to resources for the Jargon File, a large collection of hacker definitions and explanations. You can browse the online edition and download copies from this site.

The New Hacker's Dictionary

http://www.eps.mcgill.ca/~steeve/
tnhd.html

Information on the book version of the Jargon File, including ordering instructions and reviews. Sometimes hard copy is good!

English

Casey's Snow Day Reverse Dictionary (and Guru)

http://www.c3.lanl.gov:8075/cgi/
casey/revdict

A dictionary where you enter the definition first, and it provides you with the associated word. You can also tap the Guru for clues to life. Answers are provided via a hypertext list of words with related definitions.

Hypertext Webster Interface

http://c.gp.cs.cmu.edu:5103/prog/
webster

Good interface to Webster's, with definitions provided from other hyperlinked words (meaning you could eventually look up every word in the definition itself!). Very comprehensive and useful.

French-English

English-French Dictionary

http://mlab-power3.uiah.fi/
EnglishFrench/avenues.html

A nice-looking translation dictionary site, with two search engines. You can perform a general keyword search, as with other language dictionary sites, or use a browseable topic tree. There are also online vocabulary tests you can use to improve your language skills, and you can use either a French or English version of the main interface.

French-English Dictionary Form

http://tuna.uchicago.edu/
forms_unrest/FR-ENG.html

A University of Chicago dictionary, using a simple forms interface to a database with 75,000 entries. There are also instructions on how to compose searches for accented words using easy keyboard equivalents.

German-English

German-English and English-German

http://calamity.rz-berlin.mpg.de/
eg.html

Easy form-based translation dictionary, with instructions for entering special German characters in your word searches.

Index-Dictionaries

http://www.uni-passau.de/forwiss/
mitarbeiter/freie/ramsch/
englisch.html

A German index to other dictionary sites, featuring German to English dictionaries, other European language translators, hacker jargon sites, thesaurii, and alternative word lists.

Thesauri

ARTFL Project: ROGET Form

http://tuna.uchicago.edu/
forms_unrest/ROGET.html

A University of Chicago search interface to an online version of the famed thesaurus. You can search the full text of the book or headword entries, or browse a hypertext list of headwords. It's fast and comprehensive.

Roget's Thesaurus (nih.gov)

gopher://odie.niad.nih.gov/77/
.thesaurus/index

Gopher forms interface to the *Roget's Thesaurus,* with mixed results. Your search will only take you near your term and its related words, and you'll have to scan the text documents returned for relevancy.

Encyclopedia

Encyclopedia Mystica

http://www.bart.nl/~micha/mystica.html

A nice-looking encyclopedia centering on things magical. You can browse a list of all available articles or go to a subsection by letter. Visual feedback lets you keep track of how many articles are in a section, and you can also post your own definitions and explanations. We found a beautiful piece on unicorns, and there's much more here.

Global Encyclopedia

http://www.halcyon.com/jensen/encyclopedia/welcome.html

A free encyclopedia with articles written by volunteers (like yourself). You can search by article title, jump to an alphabetical section, or view a list of all articles. There's also a section of most recent additions you can use to see new articles at a glance.

Internet Encyclopedia

http://www.cs.uh.edu/~clifton/encyclopedia.html

An index to information available on the Internet, by an alphabetical topic list of site names. Subjects include books, chemistry, demographics, education, film, TV, geography, reference, history, the intelligence community, Judaism, kids, law, linguistics, money, museums, Native Americans, news, physics, reference material, sleep disorders, tourism, the U.S. government, Yuletide Celebrations, and a whole lot of zines.

Don't miss this one; it leads to a lot of good information.

FAQs

A Frequently Asked Questions document is your best way to find information on a lot of subjects covered on the Internet. Use them to see if your question has already been answered, so you don't get the special appellation of *newbie* by asking questions that have been getting answered for about five years.

List of USENET FAQs

http://www.cis.ohio-state.edu/hypertext/faq/usenet/

An alphabetical hypertext list of FAQs available from Usenet news on a number of subjects. You can also jump to an alphabetical section by letter or view the list by newsgroup. There's a search engine you can use to look up a FAQ by subject. Results often include a link to a full Web version of the FAQ that's easier to use in your browser than plain text.

rtfm.mit.edu USENET FAQ list

ftp://rtfm.mit.edu/pub/usenet

A large FTP site of FAQ text files in directories arranged by various newsgroups, listed alphabetically.

Usenet Newsgroup Hierarchy with Searchable FAQ Archive

http://www.lib.ox.ac.uk/internet/news/

Newsgroups and their related FAQs in an outline format, by group subclass. You can also view FAQs by category and newsgroup directly and search a FAQ archive for particular information.

Interesting

These are not boring.

Castles on the Web

http://fox.nstn.ca/~tmonk/castle/castle.html

Links to castle sites around the globe, with pictures and descriptions. These range from English sites like Buckingham Palace and Windsor Castle to America's Hearst Castle. There's also a link to a Gopher server with more castle pictures.

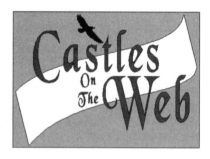

Computer Almanac - Numbers About Computers

http://www.cs.cmu.edu/afs/cs.cmu.edu/user/bam/www/numbers.html

Numbers for trends in computer use and the Internet compiled from various sources. There are also links to more comprehensive information sources.

Data Powers of Ten

http://www.ccsf.caltech.edu/~roy/dataquan/

A list of data sizes, ranging from 0.1 byte (a binary decision) up beyond terabytes (1,000,000,000,000 bytes, a mass storage system), with hyperlinked pictures or descriptions for most of the described quantities.

Yahoo!

Guide to Lock Picking

http://www.lysator.liu.se:7500/mit-guide/mit-guide.html

A hypertext guide to entering without breaking. Sections cover the basics of different lock mechanisms and techniques, and there are also illustrations to help you along. Pay close attention to the hacking community's opinion linked at the beginning, and realize that it's not as easy as it looks! There's also a PostScript version of the guide for downloading.

Questionables (Wiretap)

gopher://wiretap.spies.com/11/Library/Untech

Gopher site filled with documents on questionable technology, including secret ATM codes, cellular phone hacking, pyromania, home built rocket engines, moonshining, and hobbyist nuclear weapons.

The Weird Zone

http://mistral.enst.fr/~pioch/weird/

Miscellaneous weirdness from online sources, arranged by month in text files. Dip in, but expect to spend some time here. Topics include frivolous lawsuits (three Idaho inmates filed a $10.7 million lawsuit against their county prison because jail guards failed to give them late-night snacks) and random Internet weirdness.

The WEIRD Zone

World Population

http://sunsite.unc.edu/lunarbin/worldpop

A big counter of the current estimated world population. You can also go to an animated version (under Netscape 1.1) and watch an animated display. There are links to other population-related sites and information on the data used to calculate the counter rate.

Libraries

Bill's Library

http://www.io.org/~jgcom/library.htm

A well-organized set of links to books and magazines across the Web, arranged in a magazine rack, a poetry corner, and a public/legal section. Each section has a clear title to the works linked, and a colorful use of bullets keeps the entries separated well. This is a great gateway to literature available on the Internet.

Committee on East Asian Libraries

http://darkwing.uoregon.edu/~felsing/ceal/welcome.html

CEAL's site includes links to East Asian resource sites (arranged by country), and also features lists of related libraries and general information.

GSFC Homer E. Newell Memorial Library

http://www-library.gsfc.nasa.gov/

A NASA library located at Goddard Space Flight Center. You can look up new books, travel around the library floors, and access circulation information/help desks and an Interlibrary Loan section.

Internet Public Library (IPL)

http://ipl.sils.umich.edu/

A great online library site, this one offers an interactive Lobby map leading to divisions like Reference, Youth, and Librarian Services. You can also visit classrooms, exhibit halls, and reading rooms with online books, demos, and tutorials. Also check out the information on the IPL MOO, a multi-user environment you can use to interact with other users in real time.

Kaapelisolmu - the Knot at the Cable

http://www.kaapeli.fi/knot-at-cable.html

Alternative Finnish site with electronic texts, NetComics, Hyper-Kalevala (the National Epic), artwork, and other library resources.

Karen's Kitchen: The Librarians' Menu

http://www.intac.com/~kgs/libpalate.html

This site includes library subject guide information, a Freedom Page with links to related sites and lists of banned books, and a great collection of Internet reference success stories, showing how well the Web can perform as an information resource.

National Archives and Records Administration

http://www.nara.gov/

Links to large amounts of information on American historical documents of importance at NARA's Gopher servers. There are also online exhibits (like the *Declaration of Independence*), sample publications, and links to related sites.

The Public-Access Computer Systems Review

gopher://info.lib.uh.edu/11/articles/e-journals/uhlibrary/pacsreview

A Gopher-based electronic journal with articles on online libraries and end-user access issues.

Digital Libraries

University libraries with pilot projects to place more materials from their collections online. Most are still in a development phase, but a few working prototypes are listed.

UC Berkeley Environmental Library Project

http://elib.cs.berkeley.edu/

Environmental information, including online documents and interactive picture databases you can search using a form. There's also an interactive map of Sacramento County linked to aerial pictures of the related terrain.

Information Science

Conservation OnLine - Stanford University Library Preservation Department

http://palimpsest.stanford.edu/

The CoOL site has information on document preservation for libraries, including hyperlinked topics like disaster planning, ethics, education and training, and electronic media issues.

Library Schools on the Net

http://www.itcs.com/topten/libschools.html

A bulk list of Library Information School Web sites from around the globe, listed alphabetically.

Information Retrieval

University of Massachusetts at Amherst - Center for Intelligent Information Retrieval /CIIR

http://ciir.cs.umass.edu/

Information retrieval documents and experimental real-time IR databases you can try out. There's also information on case-based reasoning and natural language processing systems.

Institutes

Syracuse - School of Information Studies

http://istweb.syr.edu/

This interesting site for the IS school at Syracuse includes a range of button icons leading to program information, faculty, staff and student directories,

research updates, and event listings. There are also maps of the Syracuse area.

UC Berkeley's School of Library and Information Studies

http://info.berkeley.edu

General school information on degree programs, as well as research and class projects, some with interactive demos.

University Libraries and Scholarly Communication

http://www.lib.virginia.edu/mellon/mellon.html

An online copy of a study prepared for the Mellon Foundation on historical trends in university library collecting and the impact of new technologies.

Index - Information Science Resources Worldwide

http://www.inf.fu-berlin.de/~weisshuh/infwiss/otherdepts.html

IS department Web sites in Europe, North America, Australia, and Asia. You can jump directly to sites listed by continent, and there's also a list of related links of interest.

Organizations

American Library Association

http://www.ala.org/

Information on ALA programs in publishing, public awareness and education, intellectual freedom, library outreach, conferences, and awards.

CLASS - Cooperative Library Agency for Systems and Services

http://www.class.org

A nonprofit cooperative organization that provides goods and services to member libraries. This site includes private services pages, information on member benefits and services available, and links to member library home pages.

International Federation of Library Associations and Institutions

http://www.nlc-bnc.ca/ifla/

IFLA's site contains information on programs, services, and upcoming conferences. There's also a Virtual Library with interesting links to Internet guides, IS policy statements, and electronic documents, and it's searchable as well.

PALS

The Project for Automated Library Systems public access catalog is designed to make member libraries' information interactively accessible. Web and Gopher versions exist.

HyperPals - HyperText Interface to PALS

http://bingen.cs.csbsju.edu/pals/hyperpals.html

A search engine using forms to the PALS database. You can query the database by author, subject, or year, and restrict your search to a particular library system.

Presidential Libraries

Library archives of U.S. presidents from Roosevelt to Reagan.

Eisenhower Center

http://history.cc.ukans.edu/heritage/abilene/ikectr.html

Ike's site has a chronological list of main events during his presidency, a transcription of his farewell address, and favorite quotes from various sources. There's also general historical information on D-Day and World War II.

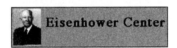

Franklin D. Roosevelt Presidential Library Gopher

gopher://musicb.marist.edu/1-gop/fdrg:gopherd.menu

This Gopher server features lists of the FDR Institute's collections, bibliographies, and researcher information.

Lyndon B. Johnson Presidential Library Gopher

gopher://ftp.cc.utexas.edu:3003/11/pub/lbj-library

An interesting LBJ Gopher site at the University of Texas that includes declassified national security papers (some in WordPerfect format), information on Democratic National Committee activities during the 1960s, and a great annotated picture archive.

Public Libraries

Libraries from across the country with general area information, and collections that are just starting to become available online.

Connecticut Library

http://www.scsu-cs.ctstateu.edu/lib/ct_library.html

A clickable Connecticut information source you can browse by region (text or graphics) or subject. The site also includes an online tourism guide and a local search engine you can use as a shortcut.

Houston Public Library

http://sparc.hpl.lib.tx.us/

This site includes a graphical history of the Library, a list of frequently-asked reference desk questions, and information on how to connect to the online catalog system using telnet.

New York Metropolitan Reference and Research Library Agency

http://metro.org/

MetroWeb features online copies of the *For Reference* library newsletter, a hyperlinked handbook, and links to regional resources.

New York Public Library

http://gopher.nypl.org/

NYPL's site includes a historical introduction and overview, lists of upcoming events, and a section on the Library's publications. There's also a multimedia sampler featuring photography exhibits and hypertext subject guides, and a link to a telnet gateway for their online catalog system.

Provo City Library

http://www.provo.lib.ut.us/

Interesting online library with good pointers to information across the Web. You can look up subjects by Dewey Decimal classification, browse the stacks, and delve into children's sections and periodicals.

Tampa Bay Library Consortium

http://snoopy2.tblc.lib.fl.us/

Another good library to information across the Web, this site includes a main section with links to online libraries, virtual reference desks, and librarian resources. There's also a Reading Room with links to online books, magazines, and periodicals, and a large set of Florida-related links by subject under "Floridiana."

Index - Public Libraries With Internet Services

http://sjcpl.lib.in.us/homepage/
PublicLibraries/
PublicLibraryServers.html

A good set of links to libraries with Internet-accessible sites. These are arranged by Gopher, Web server, or telnet sites, so you can restrict yourself to full Web-browser library sites if you choose. You can also search for a particular library or register one via an online form.

University Libraries

Libraries for colleges and universities. These site contains some of the more interesting online library uses of Web technology.

BYU Libraries Information Network

http://library.byu.edu/

The Brigham Young University site features a hypertext online catalog that returns call numbers and circulation information. There's also a link to a more conventional telnet catalog interface, and sections for Library news and information. Check out the Special Projects area for multimedia exhibits.

Cornell University - Mann Library

http://www.mannlib.cornell.edu/

A gateway to a large number of databases available via telnet, arranged by subject. There's also an Electronic Reserve with online courseware and related Web links.

INFOMINE - UC Riverside Libraries

http://lib-www.ucr.edu/

A good selection of forms-based databases you can search directly highlight this site. Topics include biological, agricultural and medical resources, physical and social science information, government sections, and Internet enabling technologies and instructions.

MIT Libraries

http://web.mit.edu/afs/athena/dept/
libdata/applications/www/top.html

Information on collections and services in the library system at MIT, including departments with online sections. There's also an Internet Resource Collection with links to related sites of interest on the Web.

MIT Libraries

Scripps Institution of Oceanography Library

http://orpheus.ucsd.edu/sio/

A lot of informational links to oceanographic and earth science sites across the Web, listed by library resources, electronic periodicals, institutions, data services, and Internet guides. There's also information on local ocean conditions in the San Diego area.

Stanford Libraries & IR

http://www-sul.stanford.edu/

Information on the library system and the Academic Information Resources at Stanford. Information online includes sample texts (mostly PostScript) and related links in areas like patents, newspapers, theses, and electronic books.

UC Berkeley - Library

http://infolib.berkeley.edu/

A good use of layout helps this library site to be really useful. Look for information on library resources and related Internet links, a large interactive map of library buildings, and connection points to the online catalog system (via telnet).

Yahoo!

University of Arizona Library

http://dizzy.library.arizona.edu/

Highlights of this site include WWW exhibits, including picture galleries, as well as general library information and a collection of Internet resources. You can also ask a question at the online reference desk and browse a hypertext list of frequently-asked-questions.

THE UNIVERSITY OF ARIZONA. LIBRARY

University of Toledo Libraries

http://www.cl.utoledo.edu/

Reference material here includes interactive library guides and maps as well as special exhibits such as "19th Century Medicine." There are also links to the UTMOST online catalog (via telnet) and to Internet resource tools.

Yale University Library

http://www.library.yale.edu/

This site features well-formatted pages with links to various information resource databases available here (via telnet), and selected Web guides. There's also information on the Yale library system and related publications.

Indices

Index - Libraries

http://www.umd.umich.edu/~nhughes/links/lib.html

A basic list of various online libraries available via your Web browser.

Index - Library Technician

http://www.eskimo.com/~rainbird/

A good set of links to online library and librarian information on the Internet, arranged well.

Index - Library WWW Servers

http://www.lib.washington.edu/~tdowling/libweb.html

Washington University's LibWeb is a set of links to libraries and library associations on the Web, arranged by country. There are also links to library-related companies and Information Science schools.

Index - ZWeb Library Search Gateway

http://zweb.cl.msu.edu/

An interactive gateway to online libraries and information resources across the Internet. You can pick a particular library to search from a scrolling list, and go to it directly. You can also search the entire site from a simple form.

Man Pages

These are instruction manual entries for computer operating systems, mostly UNIX-based. The sites usually contain search engines that make the online references very easy to use.

BSDI Hypertext Man Pages

http://www.bsdi.com/bsdi-man/

A simple form interface to the Berkeley UNIX man pages.

CSUWEB: RTFM, Web Style

http://csugrad.cs.vt.edu/manuals/

Read The Friendly Manuals, a hyperlinked guide to information on public-domain UNIX programs.

HP/UX Manual Pages

http://www.cis.ohio-state.edu/man/hpux.top.html

An online manual to HP UNIX, searchable by keyword or browsable via hypertext section entries.

Man Pages (Ohio State)

http://www.cis.ohio-state.edu/hypertext/man_pages.html

A set of links to various interactive UNIX system man pages, with a search engine that can look through all of them at once.

Pyramid Manual Pages

http://www.cis.ohio-state.edu/man/pyramid.top.html

A search engine to Pyramid UNIX — you can also browse via an alphabetical subject index.

SGI Man Page Index

http://reality.sgi.com/cgi-bin/getman/

An interface to SGI UNIX you can search by keyword.

Solaris 2.1 manual pages

http://www.cs.ubc.ca/man/solaris2.1

A search interface to the man pages for the newer version of Sun UNIX.

SunOS 4.1.3 Manual Pages

http://www.fh-wolfenbuettel.de/cgi-bin/man2html

Man pages for the SunOS still in use at many sites, searchable via keyword.

Yoav's Manual Pages

http://www.mit.edu:8001/people/yoav/mym.html

An index to searchable man pages, including UNIX operating systems, X11R5, and VMS.

Measurements

Conversion Table

http://sol.acs.uwosh.edu/~wallinp/convert.html

A standard-metric conversion table in a long text file. There are also temperature conversion formula tables and an online help section.

Local Times Around the World

http://www.hilink.com.au/times/

Current times around the world, arranged by major continents and regions. You can use a comprehensive hypertext list to find the exact city or area you're looking for.

Niel's Timelines and Scales of Measurement List

http://xalph.ast.cam.ac.uk/public/niel/scales.html

This site features a collection of scientific ASCII files, including timelines for evolutionary/geological and cosmological events and a measurement scale.

Phone Numbers

AmeriCom Long Distance AREA DECODER

http://www.xmission.com/~americom/aclookup.html

An interactive form you can use to look up area codes by city, state, and country.

Health Information Resources: Toll-Free Numbers for Health Information

http://nhic-nt.health.org/htmlgen/htmlgen.exe/Tollfree?Descriptor='800'

An annotated list of health resources arranged alphabetically, including contact information and program descriptions.

NTC U.S. Phone Number Lookup

http://www.natltele.com/form.html

A U.S. area code search page that lets you look up entries by state name, area code, city codes, prefix, and telephone number.

PhoNETic

http://www.soc.qc.edu/phonetic/

A phone number-to-keypad letter converter. Enter a number, and see the letter combinations that can be made from it. There's also online help and explanations.

WWW Phone Dialing

Internet Speed Dialer

http://www.thesphere.com/Sphere/ttone.html

A touch-tone generator. Enter your number, and you'll get back the dialing tones needed to connect. Just hold the phone handset mouthpiece up to your computer's speaker. You can also enter text phone numbers like 1-800 CALL YOU.

WWW Dial Service

http://pluto.ulcc.ac.uk/Sound/dial.html

Bring an end to endless hours of phone-button-pushing misery with the ULCC PersonalFoneMate, another phone dialer-tone generator form. This one includes a list of predefined numbers for the University of London Computer Center.

WWW Phone Dialing Services

http://maxwell.phys.csufresno.edu:8001/phone/phone.html

Yet another phone dialer form. This one features a graphical keypad as well, which reproduces individual tones.

Postal Information

Post office information, including rates, areas of service, and interactive ZIP code forms.

Geographic NameServer

http://www.mit.edu:8001/geo

A search engine you can use to look up cities across the world. Information returned includes postal codes and geographic locations.

Postal Abbreviations

gopher://gopher.princeton.edu/00/.files/university/postal

A list of correct state abbreviations for addressing mail, in a simple text format.

USPS ZIP+4 Lookup Form

http://www.usps.gov/ncsc/aq-zip.html

Several forms for ZIP code lookup by address, city, and state are available here. There are also lists of postal abbreviations and a USPS service area map.

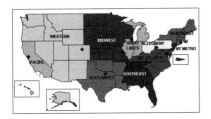

ZIP code 4 Address Database

http://www.cedar.buffalo.edu/adserv.html

This site features an intelligent address database that can correct mistakes and give proper addresses with ZIP codes. You can also download a printable PostScript file of a successful address match that includes a barcode.

USPS Postal Rates

Postal Rates (Pitney-Bowes)

http://www.pitneybowes.com/rates/rates.htm

Postal rates from the Pitney-Bowes metering company, including different mail classes and priority/express charges.

USPS Postal Rates

http://www.usps.gov/consumer/rates.htm

Comprehensive hypertext tables of current domestic and international postage rates. This page also includes a synopsis of current postal rates.

Quotations

Bartlett's Familiar Quotations, 9th Ed.

http://www.columbia.edu/~svl2/bartlett/

Nice site for *Bartlett's*, where you can enter words into a form to find quotes that include those words. There's also an alphabetical list of authors linked to their entries.

Humorous Quotes

http://www.cs.virginia.edu/~robins/quotes.html

Great quotes from famous personages, nicely arranged. "It is better to have a permanent income than to be fascinating" — Oscar Wilde.

Internet Movie Database - Quote Search

http://www.cm.cf.ac.uk/M/search_quotes.pl

A search page you can use to look up movie quotes containing words of your choice. It's up-to-date, and results also include actors and films related to them.

LOQTUS - quotations server

http://pubweb.ucdavis.edu/Documents/Quotations/homepage.html

A large set of links to quotation sites on the Internet and related quote collection files you can download.

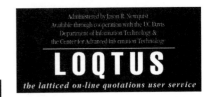

Some Quotes I Like

http://pen.k12.va.us/~cfifer/quotes.shtml

More than 300 humanities and entertainment quotes arranged by subject. There's also a short set of links to other quote servers.

Speaking words of wisdom

http://www.sils.umich.edu/~sooty/thoughts.html

Out of the mouths of babes comes the true source of wisdom. Supermodels tell all here, in hilarious category groupings. Remember, "Everyone should have enough money to get plastic surgery."

Scientific Constants

Standard Atmosphere Computation

http://aero.stanford.edu/StdAtm.script

Enter altitude in feet in the search form here and you'll get results for pressure, temperature, sound speed, and density.

Weights and Measures [CIA Factbook]

http://www.ic.gov/94fact/appendf/appendf.html

A list of standard measurement tables from the CIA World Factbook, in a large format.

FAQ - NASA Constants and Equations

http://www.ksc.nasa.gov/facts/faq04.html

Space math from NASA, with equations and explanations. There are also direct links to planetary information here.

Standards

American National Standards Institute

http://www.ansi.org/

The ANSI standards body site features information on the federation and a catalog of published standards, as well as a calendar of upcoming events and an online reference library.

Standards Documentation

http://www-atp.llnl.gov/standards.html

Indexed lists of computer and communication standards sites across the Web are featured here.

Department of Commerce's atomic clock timeserver

http://www.bldrdoc.gov/doc-tour/atomic_clock.html

The real time, from the Department of Commerce. Time to set your clocks and watches.

Index - Standards and Standardization Bodies - WWW Virtual Library

http://www.iso.ch/VL/Standards.html

National and international standards bodies in a comprehensive hypertext list format.

White Pages

How to find people. Look for regional, state, and college directories, as well as specialty indices and email address lists.

Four 11 Directory Services (SLED)

http://www.four11.com/

A free Internet directory with more than 1,000,000 listings and 100,000 users, searchable by name, and supporting PGP encryption.

FOUR 11

Free Phone

http://www.procd.com/sr/freesrch.htm

An AT&T toll-free 800 number directory you can search by name, city, and state.

InterNIC Directory Services

http://www.internic.net/ds/dspgwp.html

An interface to WHOIS and Netfind Internet locator services. You can reach a Gopher search index here and look up registered Internet users. There's also online information about the particular services.

LookUP! Directory Service

http://www.lookup.com/

Member-based e-mail directory you can search by name. There's also information on e-mail programs integrated with the LookUP! Directory Service.

NetPages

http://www.aldea.com

A directory of Internet names and addresses, in sections for reference, business, and personal listings. You can use the online Web version or download an electronic book version for use locally.

Yahoo!

OKRA – net.citizen Directory Service

http://okra.ucr.edu/okra/

A service from University of California at Riverside that will help you find e-mail addresses of your friends, enemies, organizations, and anyone else who is wired. The database is not complete but it's growing constantly, and you can add to it.

PH: A More Advanced User Interface

http://fiaker.ncsa.uiuc.edu:8080/cgi-bin/phfd

A good forms-based Internet phone directory utility. You can scroll through the names of several sites to restrict your searches, and sort the results by name, phone number, or e-mail address.

Index - Hunting for E-Mail Addresses

http://twod.med.harvard.edu/labgc/roth/Emailsearch.html

Links to various local and international Internet search tools that will help you find e-mail addresses, including WHOIS, Finger, and NetFind clients.

Indices

On-line Reference Works

http://www.cs.cmu.edu/Web/references.html

A small but well-balanced collection of links to online reference works from Carnegie-Mellon University, including dictionaries, encyclopedias, Internet resources, and geographical information.

The Wiretap Gopher Site

gopher://wiretap.spies.com/

This site features an index to the great Wiretap Online Library of alternative information and also includes information on various electronic text archives.

Index - City.Net United States

http://www.city.net/countries/united_states/

City.Net's U.S. States page features a good alphabetical list of state names with related lists of sites linked directly. There are also links to education, culture, government, travel, and map sites related to the U.S. States.

Index - English Servers' Reference

http://english-server.hss.cmu.edu/Reference.html

An alphabetical hypertext list of reference works across the Web, featuring humanities, business, and scientific information sites.

Index - The Virtual Reference Desk

http://thorplus.lib.purdue.edu/reference/index.html

A large set of reference links is at this site, grouped around categories like dictionaries and thesauri, information technology, maps and travel, phone books, ZIP codes, and scientific measurement. There is also an annotated list of selected U.S. federal government documents available over the Web.

REFERENCE

Regional

A vast amount of regional information is available via Yahoo!. More than 10,000 different sites are listed. This section is broken up into categories for 150 countries, each listed separately. Under those sections, you'll find tourist information, international universities, cities around the globe, and travelogues.

The individual states of the United States of America account for a great deal of the regional sites (more than 7,000 of them — 2,000 for California alone). You'll find the same kind of information for the 50 states that you will for countries, including travel and tourism guides, schools and governmental institutions, and local sites for major cities.

In each country's (or U.S. state's) section, be sure to check out the Cities listings for more specific information about major cities.

You can use the CIA World Factbook sites as a way to get a fix on geographical information for the entire world, or you can just go into the Countries and U.S. States sections and do your own exploring. You're bound to find something interesting, either in your own backyard, or coming to you from the far corners from the globe. Enjoy yourself!

CIA World Factbook

Gopher sites for versions of the CIA World Factbook date back to 1990. Now there are Web sites where you can do interactive searches of recent editions. The Factbook is a large selection of country reports and maps collected worldwide by the U.S. Central Intelligence Agency (your tax dollars at work). Is it the most useful thing the CIA has ever done? We could tell you, but then we'd have to kill you.

CIA World Factbook 1992 at Wiretap

gopher://wiretap.spies.com/00/Library/Classic/world92.txt

A large text version of the Factbook available from Wiretap. You can search it using the Edit/Find command available in most Web browsers.

CIA World Factbook Search

http://www.research.att.com/cgi-wald/dbaccess/411

An interactive database for the 1993 edition of the Factbook. You can search by country and organization, or by general terms.

The World Factbook 1995

http://www.odci.gov/cia/publications/95fact/

A good Web interface to the 1995 Factbook, with hyperlinked country sections you can browse directly and jump to by letter. There are also lists of reference maps, publication information, and common definitions, notes, and abbreviations.

Countries

More than 150 countries are listed at Yahoo!, and the number is growing daily. Here is a selection of interesting sites from a subset of the larger international locations.

Australia

G'Day Australia

http://ebweb.tuwien.ac.at/ortner/australi.html

This site contains many photos of Australia divided by territory. There's also a Virtual Guided Tour, maps, satellite pictures, and links to other relevant sites with Australian information.

Guide to (Over 1,000) Australian Webs

http://gwb.com.au/gwb/

A large set of links arranged around a good image map. Interactive buttons lead to categories like community and corporate webs, business sites, and event information. You can also browse a private gems collection and a section on global heroes.

Guide to Australia

http://www.csu.edu.au/education/australia.html

Encyclopedic information about the country from various governmental and private institutions. Categories include geography, communications, travel, and governmental history.

Index - Annotated Australian Address Book

http://www.aussie.com.au/

A large guide to interesting Australian sites, including government, business, and personal pages. Check out the Cookie Jar section for some eclectic site picks.

Outdoors

Australian National Parks

http://www.odyssey.com.au/uspecies/parks/

A visual guide to selected Australian parks, with strong graphics, pictures, and interactive maps.

South Australian Climbing

http://audrey.levels.unisa.edu.au/itr-users/paul/SA-climb/home.html

Grab your carabiner and head out. This site has lots of information on the climbing world down there, including online guide books, news and gossip sections, classifieds, and pictures.

Brazil

Brasil Web

http://www.escape.com/~jvgkny/Brasil.Web.html

The site for Brazilians and lovers of Brazil. Sections include country information, culture links, and news. Most links lead to sites in Portuguese.

Brazilian Mall

http://www.BrazilianMall.com/brazil

A commercial Web directory for Brazil. Sections include an art gallery, a business center, a music emporium, and a travel agency, with links to interesting Brazilian information and resources.

Brazilian WWW Resources

http://www.cs.ucl.ac.uk/staff/swarrick/brazil.html

Links to country information, including guides, university sites, newspapers and electronic mailing lists, and travel resources.

Meu Brasil

http://darkwing.uoregon.edu/~sergiok/brasil.html

A good introduction to Brazilian information on the Web. Sections include tourist attractions, news, economic development, culture, history, sports, entertainment, and the environment. You can also access detailed area maps here.

Web Central Brasil

http://www.magics.com/bus/brazil/brasil.html

A site in Portuguese with information on the arts, country reference guides, university listings, and news links for Brazil.

Index - Brazil's Web Directories

http://www.embratel.net.br/dirweb.html

Portuguese-English directory of Brazilian Web directories. There's a Web Index service with many categories available via a button map, and a separate business section.

Yahoo!

Index - Brazilian Links

http://sensemedia.net/sprawl/
21826#Links

A list of Brazilian links on various subjects. There are also festival and events listings and contact information.

Canada

Atlas of Canadian Communities

http://ellesmere.ccm.emr.ca/
ourhome/

An atlas of communities across Canada created by students from over 100 schools. Good interactive maps lead to interesting regional sites with pictures.

Canada Net Pages

http://www.visions.com/netpages/

A commercial Net site for Canadian businesses offering goods and services, listed in areas like real estate, tourism, and finance (stocks and funds). There's also an online White Pages section and a business directory.

Canadian WWW Master Index

http://nereid.sal.phys.yorku.ca/
services/w3_can/www_index.html

A large list of Canada-related links, presented by province, city, and scope (subjects covered). There's also an online FAQ help section and a searchable archive of past lists.

Canadiana — The Canadian Resource Page

http://www.cs.cmu.edu/Web/
Unofficial/Canadiana/README.html

A comprehensive information resource from Carnegie-Mellon University. Links are grouped under topics like news and information, government services, politics and history, technology and commerce, and cultural heritage.

Geography

National Atlas Information Service - Canada

http://www.nais.ccm.emr.ca

An interesting cartographic site. You can browse thematic country maps (on subjects like ethnic diversity, exploration, and seismicity) or search for a particular area by name. The site also features a geographic quiz, and a section where you can create your own maps by selecting terrain features from lists and menus.

China

China (Haiwang Yuen)

http://bronze.ucs.indiana.edu/
~hyvan/

China facts, culture, art, travel, language, health and business links, presented in a good ideogrammatic visual layout, with annotations. There's also a set of related home page links about China and Chinese culture.

China Business and Commerce

http://www.worldtel.com/enercana/
china.html

Information on doing business in China, the world's third largest economy. Sections include an overview of the China market and lists of business opportunities and capital goods market segments.

China Home Page [ihep.ac.cn]

http://www.ihep.ac.cn/china.html

A Beijing site with links to public scientific, technical, and business information on China. There are also links to Chinese art sites, personal home pages, and a list of Web servers based in China.

China Information [sut.ac.jp]

http://sunsite.sut.ac.jp/asia/china/
china.html

Resources at this site include links to general information, maps, economic policy and business reports, a Chinese music archive, and a good list of related Web sites.

NetChina

http://www.netchina.com/

Chinese cultural, business, and art information links, in Chinese. Most pages require you to have a special Chinese terminal system installed to view them properly, but you can also access copies of the *China News Digest* (Hua Xia Wen Zhai, HXWZ) in graphic mode without it.

Pictures

Scenery Pictures of China

http://www.cnd.org/Scenery/
index.html

Beautiful pictures of China, arranged
by scenic sites, ancient buildings, and
natural landscapes.

Index - Chinese Culture Page

http://www.ceas.rochester.edu:8080/
ee/users/yeung/china.html

Strong graphics lead to linked sections
covering people, news, businesses,
languages, education, culture, and
entertainment in China. There are also
travel and regional information areas.

Egypt

Egypt Interactive

http://www.channel1.com/users/
mansoorm/index.html

This site includes an annotated index
to Egyptian Internet resources,
focusing on travel, history, culture,
religion, and Egyptology. There's also
information on how to subscribe to
CyberScribe, an e-mail magazine that
covers topics on Egypt and
the Internet.

Guide to Ancient Egypt on the Internet

http://www-oi.uchicago.edu/OI/
DEPT/RA/ABZU/
ABZU_REGINDX_EGYPT.HTML

An index of resources for studying
Ancient Egypt, this site includes links
to archaeological information, site
reconstruction (imaging), museums
and collection, papyrology, philology,
and travel. You can also browse the list
of resources alphabetically by author.

The Egyptian Gallery

http://www.mordor.com/hany/egypt/
egypt.html

Picture and sound areas at this gallery
include halls for the Flag and National
Anthem, Ancient Egypt and Cultural
Pictures, Old and Modern Songs,
Music, and Sound Clips.

France

France - WWW sites

http://web.urec.fr/docs/
www_list_fr.html

An annotated list of France-based Web
server links, presented in French. You
can jump to different areas and the
index using a button menu.

France [hall.org]

http://town.hall.org/travel/france/
france.html

An interactive tour of France from the
French Embassy in Washington, D.C.
and the Internet Multicasting Service.
You can pick city and region
destinations to visit, view an online
painting exhibition, or learn French

from Radio France International's
online lessons.

Les serveurs W3 en France (sensitive map)

http://web.urec.fr/france/france.html

An interactive area map of France.
Click on a specific region to go to a
submap with town names linked to a
list of Web servers based there. It's an
interesting way to look for information
on a particular place, or to just explore
French geography.

Webfoot's Guide to France

http://www.webfoot.com/travel/
guides/france/france.html?Yahoo

A good set of Web links to sites with
French information, including travel
tips, embassy information, city/
regional sites, online travelogues,
transportation, food, lodging,
museums, history, and culture.

Paris

Paris

http://www.paris.org/

A great site with lots of information on
the City of Light, including over a
thousand pages grouped under
museums (check out the interactive
maps here), tourist attractions, event
calendars, culinary journals, and
shopping indices. There's also a Paris
directory, a Metro guide, and an
online glossary.

![Yahoo!]

Travel

French Travel Gallery

http://www.webcom.com/~wta/

Good graphics highlight this interactive travel site. Choose between a free hotel booking form (for France and Monaco), a Travel Mall where you can order items delivered directly to your hotel, and a section with useful country information, event listings, and "Survival Guides."

Germany

Germany

http://www.chemie.fu-berlin.de/adressen/brd.html

Lots of information on Germany, including lists of sites with economic, government, and geographic information, maps, and a good summary of general country statistics.

Germany Map

http://www.leo.org/demap/

LEO, the Link Everything Online map of Germany, features a good graphical map of the country and related cities. Click on a city name to get a detailed Web site list with more information. You can also go directly to a city-area list.

Netbox

http://www.netbox.de/

The German infostop on the Internet. NetBox features a strong layout and good visuals for their German-language Internet information site.

Webfoot's Virtual Germany

http://www.webfoot.com/travel/guides/germany/germany.html?Yahoo

The Webfoot guide to things German, including general information and area maps, city and site links, online travelogues, transportation resources, museum and culture guides, and tourist tips.

Index - German Resources - WWW Virtual Library

http://www.rz.uni-karlsruhe.de/Outerspace/VirtualLibrary/

Web site resources for German information arranged under subject headings, including philology and cultural studies, law and economics, the physical sciences, agriculture, engineering, and art.

Berlin

http://www.chemie.fu-berlin.de/adressen/berlin.html

A page with general Berlin information, including a city map, historical information, and lists of tourist sites.

Berlin Bear

http://www.berlin-bear.de

Follow the Bear (the English language one is standing in front of the U.S. flag) to information on Berlin arts and music events and exhibitions, city businesses, news sources, school and organization lists, and tourist information.

The Berlin Bear
Your One-Stop Source For Information About Berlin & Brandenburg
Please choose a language:

Greece

Greece

http://www.ntua.gr/local/greece.html

An interactive map of Greece with Web servers marked by location. Clicking on a name will take you to the Web site associated with it.

Greek Connection

http://www.algonet.se/~nikos/greek.html

A collection of Greek information sites, including universities, general WWW servers, weather information, interactive tours, and Greek societies.

HELLAS List

http://velox.stanford.edu/hellas/

Hellenism information and an online discussion list highlight this page. There's a good set of links to Greek information across the globe, including general information, special events, audio news reports, Hellenic student societies, and FTP sites with pictures, music, and fonts you can download.

HELLAS MAP (sensitive map)

http://www.forthnet.gr/hellas/hellas.html

Interactive metamap of Greece, with lots of informational links to city and regional information, Web servers, and online libraries.

The Hellenic Page

http://www.nchgr.nih.gov/~gjp/hellenic.html

Cool site with Greek information arranged in categories like Classical, Hellenistic, and Byzantine studies (art, architecture, literature and more), and information on the modern Greek Diaspora. There's also a form you can use to add your own page, and a good "What's New" section.

Arts

Historical Museum of Crete

http://www.knossos.gr/~hmuseum/index.html

An interesting site here at the Cretan museum. It features information on collections, as well as a selection of online exhibits (including a smashing El Greco painting and historical frescoes).

Travel

Brief Virtual Tours in Greece

http://www.lance.colostate.edu/optical/Leo/Greece/

A small collection of tours of architectural sites and universities in Greece, as well as an online biography and a brief chronicle of 20th century Greek currency.

Hong Kong

Hong Kong

http://www.hongkong.org/

The official Hong Kong home page, with government information, historical background resources, and news, business, and tourism links. You can also read a hypertext version of the joint Sino-British agreement documents that will end British governmental control in Hong Kong in 1997.

Hong Kong People around the World

http://sfbox.vt.edu:10021/T/tlai/person.html

Personal home page links from Hong Kong people worldwide, listed by country. You can search the list using the Edit/Find command under most Web browsers.

Hong Kong WWW Starting Point

http://csclub.uwaterloo.ca/u/nckwan/hk/hongkong.html

Good HK links for organizations, fact sheets, entertainment information, business resources, power networking, news sources, and miscellaneous sites (including online *I Ching* and *Tao Te Ching* services). This is a great place to start getting to know Hong Kong inside-out.

Hong Kong Starting Point

WWW servers in Hong Kong

http://www.cuhk.hk/hkwww.html

A good list of Web servers located in Hong Kong, arranged by University and school departments, commercial business sites, entertainment links, online maps, and other information resources.

Pictures

Hong Kong Picture Archive

http://sunsite.unc.edu/hkpa/

Pictures from Hong Kong, divided in Pop Star, Scenery, Comics, and Miscellaneous sections. There's also an online FAQ (under development).

India

Gateway to India

http://www.isc.tamu.edu/~msr/msr.html

A site with information on India in Tamil and English, including electronic texts on yoga, politics, and economy.

India

http://scam.acs.nmu.edu/~bobby/india.html

Information in a good table format, focusing on regions, states, and cities, as well as languages, religions, and music. There's also an image archive.

India - WWW Virtual Library

http://metro.turnpike.net/S/spaoli/index.html

This site contains links to general India information, including city, state, and regional home pages, and a section on Indian newsgroups and electronic mailing lists.

India [temple.edu]

http://www.temple.edu/~betul/iu/

A great guide from Temple University, with much useful information, including lists of newsgroups and FAQs, hotels, holidays, languages, currency exchange rates, recipes, travel agent surveys and travel tips, and more. You can also download Indian fonts and pictures. Don't miss the India Humor page!

India Information [SunSITE Japan]

http://SunSITE.sut.ac.jp/asia/india/

Economic and business overviews, country reports, maps and images can be found at this site. There are also links to JITNET, the Japan-India Technology Network, and related sites.

India Network and Research Foundation

http://india.bgsu.edu/

Bowling Green State University's site features information on a free, member-based virtual community on India. You can access a page with information on the various electronic digests available, and instructions on how to subscribe. There are links to the Embassy of India home page and to related sites for research, culture, business, and travel.

India Page [B. G. Mahesh]

http://www.jagunet.com/~mahesh/india.html

Good India home page with lots of informational links in areas like news, business, travel, and culture. There's also a table explaining the various Usenet newsgroups dealing with India, and downloadable picture and fonts sections.

INDOlink

http://www.genius.net/indolink/

Links to Indian information, available from a large button grid, in areas like news, analysis, law, film and book reviews, poetry, and humor. There are also sections on travel, astrology, and Indian recipes. Check out the Quiz Time section to see how your knowledge stands up.

Information on India

http://spiderman.bu.edu/misc/india/

Categories include Indian states, maps, wildlife, social services, images, sounds, and sports. There's also tourism information and a set of related links with more information.

Virtual Tour of India

http://www.tiac.net/users/whb/India.html

A good graphical tour to interesting places in India, including historical monuments and archaeological sites.

Ireland

Active Maps of Ireland

http://slarti.ucd.ie/maps/ireland.html

This site features an interactive map to Web server locations and regional sites across Ireland. You can also go directly to site listings under art, archaeology, film, festivals, museum, opera, politics, and radio headings.

Ireland: The Internet Collection

http://itdsrv1.ul.ie/Information/Ireland.html

Miscellaneous Ireland sites, annotated here with direct links. Here's where you can find out about Irish radio, Gaelic Football, genealogical research, peace declarations, and related information collections.

Irish Information Servers

http://www.ieunet.ie/ieunet/launch/irish/

Links to information resources relating to Ireland, including commercial services, academic institutions, and tourist/leisure sites (including a Celtic Music section).

National Archives of Ireland

http://147.252.133.152/nat-arch/

A gateway to general historical information at the National Archives of Ireland. The site contains general information on library policies and collections, and more specific information in areas like genealogy (including how to commission a search of available records).

Index - All Things Irish

http://www.rmii.com/mckinley/irish.html

A bed of clover is home to a large collection of links to Irish information, including online newspapers, music archives, bank and telecommunications sites, and University contact points.

All Things Irish

Israel

Israel - Country Study

gopher://umslvma.umsl.edu/11/LIBRARY/GOVDOCS/ARMYAHBS/AAHB6

A Gopher server featuring the U.S. Army Area Handbook for Israel, a series of text files arranged in chapters on history, politics, geography, social structure, education, national defense, and foreign relations.

Israel Information Service (IIS)

http://www.israel.org/

A comprehensive, visually effective site from the Israeli Foreign Ministry, featuring a menu-based keyword search page you can use to look up current information, and an interactive illustrated guidebook with sections on history, culture, and Israeli economics. Also look for the Jerusalem 3000 illustrated exhibition, with areas focusing on the peace process and archaeological treasures.

SABRA of Israel

http://www.csun.edu/~hfffl001/israel/sabra.html

A good guide to sites in Israel on the arts, business, governmental agencies, institutions, computer companies, and more. Some sites require you to install a Hebrew font to view them properly (downloading instructions are here to help you out).

The (almost) Complete Guide to WWW in Israel

http://gauss.technicon.ac.il/~nyh/israel/

An annotated list of country sites, including universities, businesses, and governmental organizations. There's also a section of interesting site links covering Israel and its cities, art, and celebrities, and an online Israeli Yellow Pages.

The (Presumably) Complete List of Israeli WWW Servers

http://www.cs.huji.ac.il/misc/ilwww

A good set of multiple site listings, grouped under headings for academic institutions, commercial businesses, museums, and miscellaneous subjects.

Tour of Israel

http://dapsas.weizmann.ac.il/bcd/bcd_parent/tour/tour.html

A virtual tour of Israel and its related areas. There are sections on the Western Galilee and the Carmel, Jerusalem, and the Negev Desert, each with interactive maps linked to more detailed information and pictures.

World Wide Web Server for Israel

http://www.ac.il/

Hebrew and English-language site with an interactive map to certain academic sites, and an annotated hypertext list of site links arranged by academic departments, information servers, and commercial businesses.

Italy

GARR-NIR (sensitive map)

http://www.mi.cnr.it/NIR-IT/NIR-map.html

Good overall country map of Italian Web servers for cities and geographic areas, coupled with buttons linked to University and commercial site lists, a general subject tree, a Windows On Italy guide, and a What's New section.

Government

Rome - S.P.Q.R.

http://www.comune.roma.it

A guide to sites about Rome, in Italian. You can find city and municipal agency links, tourist information, and cultural listings.

La Piazza

http://lapiazza.it.net/

ITnet's Piazza site features links to information in Italian on Web resources for commercial services, nonprofit organizations and public agencies, tourist information, and volunteer organizations.

Italy

http://www.mi.cnr.it/NIR-IT/Italy.html

Information collected from the CIA World Factbook on Italian geography, government, communications, and defense.

Travel Info Italy

http://www.travel.it

Current information (with pages in English and Italian) on hotel accommodations, tours, and transportation. There's also specific information on touring in Rome and thermal sites (hot springs).

Webfoot's Guide to Italy

http://www.webfoot.com/travel/guides/italy/italy.html

A great list of Italian links, including State Department reports, an interactive Lira currency converter, satellite images, weather information, and tourist offices. There's also a set of links by subject area, including cities and regions, online travelogues, transportation, lodging, museums, sports, and culture.

Japan

Clickable W3 Map for Japan (sensitive map)

http://www.ntt.jp/japan/map/

A map of servers with specific area sites listed. You can go directly to any of them by clicking on their name. There's also another interactive map available for exploring Japan by region and city.

Cyberspace Japan

http://www.csj.co.jp/index.html

A "Yahoo-like guide to Japanese Web servers" — the sincerest form of flattery. Classifications include art, business, education, entertainment, government, personal pages, and shopping.

Inforum Project

http://www.glocom.ac.jp/inforum/ifrm.hp.itg.html

Select the graphical page to view a selection map with links to Japanese information on social sciences, policy matters, history, business, communications, economics, sociology, culture, and international relations.

Internet Guide to Japan Information Resources (Experimental)

http://fuji.stanford.edu/japan_information/japan_information_guide.html

A Stanford University guide to Japan, with areas covering science and technology, business and economics, law, international relations, and

politics. There's also information on working, studying, traveling, and living in Japan, and a section on history and culture.

Japan - Country Study

gopher://umslvma.umsl.edu/11/LIBRARY/GOVDOCS/ARMYAHBS/ARMANTOC

A Gopher site for the U.S. Army Area Handbook on Japan. Text-based chapters include comprehensive historical overviews, population and social organization statistics, and political information. There are also sections on special interest groups, mass media, and the culture of Japanese management.

Japan Information [sut.ac.jp]

http://sunsite.sut.ac.jp/asia/japan/jpn.html

Information on Japan, including nice images, maps, business guides, and technology information. There's also a good list of related site links.

Japan Information Resource Center

http://futures.wharton.upenn.edu/~hernbl08/jp.html

A good selection of links to information on business, culture, news, upcoming events, history, sports, and travel can be found here. There are also sections on moving to Japan, current living conditions, and job opportunities.

Japan Window

http://jw.stanford.edu/

A nicely-laid-out site with links to government, tourism, business and technology sites. There's also an event calendar, a map of Japan, and a special Kids' Window section for U.S. and Japanese kids (with online language and origami lessons).

Mexico

Luis' Mexico Information Page

http://gaia.ecs.csus.edu/~arellano/index.html

This site has a good collection of links to Mexican sites on art and museums (including a Freida Kahlo page), Spanish newspapers, general information, and travel.

Mexico [MexWeb]

http://www.mty.itesm.mx/MexWeb/Info2/

General information links, including maps and consular offices, as well as sections on Mexican society and culture, newspapers, and tourism. There's also a helpful list of links to information on Mexican cities by state.

Mexico [udg.mx]

http://mexico.udg.mx/

The University of Guadalajara has a vivid site here, with historical, geographic, arts and folklore sections, tourism information, and coverage of Mexican sports. Most of the site is in Spanish, but selected areas (History, Geography, Art, and Mexican Cuisine) have English equivalents.

WWW Servers in Mexico (sensitive map)

http://www.mty.itesm.mx/MexWeb/Mapa2/

A large, interactive map of Mexican Web server locations, with particular sites for Mexico City listed, and a new server section.

Mexico TravelNet

http://www.forthrt.com/mextnet.com

Travel information, including hotels and destination sites, and a map of Mexico.

Russia

All Regions of Russia by Pictures

http://www.cs.toronto.edu/~mes/russia/photo.html

A well-indexed photographic track of Russian places, including Moscow, St. Petersburg, the Urals, Siberia, and the Far East. There's also a good selection of Russia-related links.

Library of Congress Soviet Archives Exhibit

http://www.ncsa.uiuc.edu/SDG/Experimental/soviet.exhibit/soviet.archive.html

A museum tour focusing on the Soviet era of Russia and U.S.-U.S.S.R. relations. Exhibits include political background information, translated documents, and pictures.

Map of Russian WWW Servers

http://www.ac.msk.su/map.html

A big interactive map of Russian server locations. You can zoom down to larger views and go to sites by name. There's also an alphabetical list of sites here.

Pekkel's Russian Page

http://mars.uthscsa.edu/Russia/

Little Russia has links to Russian-related sites and information, including country reports (CIA World Factbook), major attractions (architecture and museums), music pages (audio and video clips), a How To page (information on traveling and Russian-U.S. culture), an interactive bulletin board, computer programs and Cyrillic fonts, a newsstand (with translated articles), and even a joke section!

Russia - Friends and Partners

http://solar.rtd.utk.edu/friends/home.html

A joint Russian-American information service, with information on history, art, geography, language, and tourism. You can also view information on exchange programs and funding, health and medicine issues, news reports, and weather updates.

Russia Information [SunSITE Japan]

http://SunSITE.sut.ac.jp/asia/russia/

General information, including country reports, maps, and lists of Web servers. There's also a link to a Russian Studies Archive with more information in text format.

Russia-NIS Home Page

http://www.clark.net/pub/global/russia.html

A good Web guide to information on Russian and the Newly Independent States. Check here for sites with data files on the fifteen republics of the ex-U.S.S.R., Russian and East European home pages, and country studies.

Switzerland

Information about Switzerland

http://www.ethz.ch/swiss/Switzerland_Info.html

A large area map highlights this site, where you can find links to information on population, geography, government divisions, and history.

SwissInfo: Everything about Switzerland

http://www.swissinfo.ch/

Virtual Switzerland, where you can find information like city guides, business and electronic market services, shopping sites, and lists of Swiss firms. There's also a Swiss Political Forum area and a What's New section.

Switzerland - Home

http://heiwww.unige.ch/switzerland/

The Graduate Institute of International Studies site has a good interactive map you can use to zoom into more specific Swiss information. Icon categories include cities, universities, and organizations. There's also an event list, a collection of related links of general interest, and a directory to more Swiss information on the Net.

Geneva International Guide

http://www.isoft.ch/GenevaGuide/

The Geneva International Guide has lists of organizations based here, as well as information on culture and tourism, a business section, and area maps. There's also a Virtual Art Gallery.

Aerial Views of Switzerland

http://www.eunet.ch/Customers/multimedia/index.html

Information on a CD-ROM with aerial views of Swiss sights from Swissair and the National Tourist Office, including background information and sample pictures.

Taiwan

Taiwan Information

http://peacock.tnjc.edu.tw/ROC_info.html

General information in a hypertext list, including sections on geography, travel and tourism, business, weather, and population. There's also information on current exchange rates, and links to Taiwan World Factbook reports and the Republic of China Yearbook.

Taiwan, ROC OnLine

http://www.roc.com/

A good site with a large number of links to Taiwanese sites, arranged in sections including a trade directory (businesses), industry associations, and current events. There's also an online Trade Talk area, where you can participate in a forum on Taiwan trade issues using Web forms.

Hotel Guide Taiwan

http://tradepoint.anjes.com.tw/~hotel/

A useful hotel information site, where you can find out about accommodations in specific regions. Hotels are rated by International, Business, and Budget class, and you can also use a link to current exchange rates from here to find out what you'll have to spend.

United Kingdom

Britnet

http://www.britnet.co.uk/

The best of British Web sites, arranged in sections for business, finance and legal, travel and tourism, news and sport, games and entertainment, and jobs. There's also an alphabetical index you can browse, or jump to a section by letter.

Hmmmmmmm

http://www-pnp.physics.ox.ac.uk/~page/home.html

Information on the Oxford (U.K.) music scene, plus film and audio reviews, pub crawl reports, and a set of mildly amusing jokes and anecdotes. There are also links to collected useless sites, interactive pages, and a random lottery number generator.

Map - Our U.K. Sensitive Map

http://scitsc.wlv.ac.uk/ukinfo/uk.map.html

A large sensitive map of Web sites in the U.K. This allows you to go to regions directly by clicking on their names. The map also includes a list of London and Southeast England sites. The site features a link to a classified U.K. Web page search engine you can query directly or browse by category (Dewey Decimal).

U.K. Page

http://www.neosoft.com/~dlgates/uk/ukindex.html

A comprehensive guide to U.K. sites, listed in major categories, including academic institutions, cities, government, culture, travel, and employment. There are also links to maps (of the U.K. in Europe, fun places, and the country as a whole), and downloadable pictures (of the Royal Family and those ubiquitous thatched cottages).

U.K. Guide

http://www.cs.ucl.ac.uk/misc/uk/intro.html

An interactive site map and a guided tour are featured at this site. The tour also includes links to more interactive maps, travel information, and entertainment sites.

U.K. directory

http://www.ukdirectory.com/

More than 1,000 U.K. Web sites are listed here, in alphabetical order. There are group listings under business and finance, community service, education, employment, entertainment, government, news, sports, shopping, and travel.

London Hotels and Tourist Information

http://www.demon.co.uk/hotel-net/

A guide to London hotels and self-catering flats (sublets). There's also a guide to attractions and sights, a theater directory, a map of the Underground, and an Events Diary.

state51 - Knowhere List of U.K. Towns

http://www.state51.co.uk/state51/knowhere/

Knowhere promises no kilts and not a thatched roof in sight. An unconventional guide to areas and cities in England, Ireland, Scotland, and Wales, concentrating on food, pubs, skateboard shops, places to buy records, and general impressions.

The Better Accommodation Guide

http://Alpha.Solutions.Net/rec-travel/europe/uk/baguk95b.html

An annotated guide to good places to stay. Listings include interesting descriptions of accommodations, prices, and addresses/telephone numbers.

United States

Geographic NameServer

http://www.mit.edu:8001/geo

A search page you can use to look up information on U.S. cities and states. Results include geographic information and ZIP codes.

National Economic, Social, and Environmental Data Bank

http://www.stat-usa.gov/BEN/Services/nesehome.html

Information on a low-cost subscriber database service with a large amount of U.S. statistical data. You can also test drive a sample database to see how the query service works.

United States of America

http://white.nosc.mil/states.html

Planet Earth's Home Page for the U.S.A. includes lists of United States servers, collections of state links, related U.S.A. topics of interest, and specific search engines for more information.

Around the United States by Train

http://gold.interlog.com/~lavender/hometra.html

An interesting account of a trip by rail across the U.S., with links to more information for cities and places mentioned. There are also links to railroad-related resources.

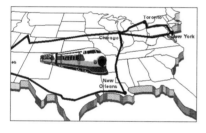

Travel - An American Adventure

http://xray.chm.bristol.ac.uk:8000/holiday/Mainpage.html

An illustrated tour of selected parts of Arizona, New Mexico, and Texas. There's also a collection of links to U.S.-related travel sites.

Traveler's USA Notebook

http://www.interactive.line.com/travelers/cover.html

A guide to upcoming events in the U.S., including attraction descriptions, locations, dates, and contact information.

U.S. States

Sometimes the Internet feels very U.S.-centric. This is one of those times.

Alabama

State Of Alabama

http://alaweb.asc.edu

AlaWeb features online tours of the renovated Capitol, state campgrounds and beaches, and tourist hot spots. There's also information on doing business with local government and links to Alabama news media and universities.

Alabama Government Information Service

http://sgisrvr.asc.edu/archives/agis.html

The ADAH (Alabama Department of Archives and History) site has a well laid out button map with links to general information, museum tours, reference services, and online publications. There's also a state agency directory and sections on Alabama history and genealogy.

Index - Alabama Clickable Image Map

http://www.eng.auburn.edu/alabama/map.html

A large interactive area map of Web sites in the Alabama area. You can go directly to specific sites by clicking on a region.

Alaska

Alaska Information Cache

http://www.neptune.com/alaska/alaska.html

Beautiful Alaskan site, presented in a good visual format. Learn about history and places to visit. Sections covered include areas like the Far North, the Interior, Southcentral, Southwest and the Inside Passage. There's also tourism information.

Information About Alaska

http://info.alaska.edu:70/1s/Alaska

History and related information links covering the 49th state. You can find out about local politics and government, literature, sports and recreation, and related Web sites. There's also a search page you can use to look up Alaskan place names (Flapjack Island?).

Travels With Samantha

http://webtravel.org/samantha/

Philip Greenspun's vivid account of his travels in North America includes a trip across Alaska's Inside Passage (Chapter VIII), with good coverage of local people and scenery and great photographs.

Arizona

Arizona Home Page

http://arizonaweb.rtd.com/index.html

ArizonaWeb features good graphics, including an interactive state map of city and local area Web servers. Click on the cacti for more information and gateways to remote sites.

Arizona's WebHub

http://www.Emerald.NET/webhub/

Subject index to lots of state information, including sections on government and politics, universities and schools, libraries, art and entertainment, tourism, real estate, and employment. There are also personal pages for Arizona residents, a What's New section, and a list of Arizona WebHub choice sites.

Arizona Destinations

http://www.amdest.com

This site includes the Arizona Yellow Pages (a guide to businesses and services), free maps (with online ordering instructions), and links to interesting Web pages and sites (including Arizona Kids Net, The Pat Paulsen Presidential Campaign, sports information, photo galleries, and museums).

Arkansas

Central Arkansas

http://161.31.2.29/BCProjects/CentArk/title.html

An interactive tour of state parks and Little Rock area landmarks and attractions is located at this site. There's also information on dining, hotels, and live music.

Arkansas Department of Computer Services

http://w3dcs.state.ar.us/

Information on Arkansas, including a fact sheet and links to the Governor's office. There's also an online Visitor's Center with links to related Web sites.

Arkansas Educational Television Network

http://www.aetn.org

You'll find a good list of educational resources here, including the Arkansas Public School Computer Network. There's also a link to a site with a good interactive map of Arkansas Internet sites by city.

California

California (white.nosc.mil)

http://white.nosc.mil/california.html

Planet Earth's California page has a comprehensive list of California Web servers and a list of related information resources, including sites for pictures, libraries, weather, attractions and events, geographical information, and more.

California - Virtual Tourist

http://www.research.digital.com/SRC/virtual-tourist/California.html

You can find tourist information and event listings at this site, including entertainment, sports and recreation sections, and a large list of tourist attraction Web sites. There are also sections with online California resources (maps and pictures), government and educational information, and a state Yellow Pages of goods and services.

California World-Wide Web Servers

http://www.llnl.gov/ptools/california.servers.html

This site features a good search index you can use to look up information directly (or by city name), and sensitive maps of California and the Bay Area. You can also find general state information here, such as information on federal, state, and local government, as well as commercial and academic organizations.

ALSO RECOMMENDED:

Yahoo has more than 2,000 sites listed under California. Dive into a huge amount of information on Northern California (sections for the Bay Area, Berkeley, Cupertino, Hayward, Marin, Napa, Oakland, San Francisco, San Jose and Palo Alto) and

Southern California (sections for Anaheim, Beverly Hills, Hollywood, Long Beach, Los Angeles, Orange County, and Pasadena). There are also many more small town coastal and inland regional sections listed.

Colorado

Colorado Information and Links

http://phoebe.cair.du.edu/~bcole/colorado.html

This site features good links to state information, statistics, and business sites. There are also links to city and regional information and area maps.

Colorado Travel Guide [rec.travel library]

http://www.digimark.net/rec-travel/north_america/usa/colorado/colorado

A text file from the rec.travel newsgroup, with travel-related information for selected cities and state parks, as well as a Colorado travelogue.

Southwest Colorado Access Network (SCAN)

http://www.scan.org

Information on businesses and community organizations, as well as educational and governmental resources. There's also a collection of links to related Colorado sites, travel and entertainment information, and weather reports.

Connecticut

Connecticut (std.com)

http://www.std.com/NE/conn.html

Annotated links to city and state sites, including libraries, universities, media services, agricultural fairs, government organizations, tourist information, and sports teams.

Connecticut Guide

http://www.atlantic.com/ctguide/

This site features state information resources, including tourism, census, and interesting facts. There's also a section featuring news from the Hartford Courant, and lists of related Web servers.

Connecticut, USA

http://www.connecticut.com/

Information you can find at this site includes government and city sections, information on events, tourism and the state park system, and Connecticut maps. You can also find out about virtual tours in development.

State of Connecticut

http://www.ctstateu.edu/state.html

A joint project of the State Library and university systems, this site provides information on Connecticut life and recreation, economics, government, libraries and services, natural resources, and transportation.

Delaware

Delaware State Data Center

http://www.state.de.us/govern/agencies/dedo/dsdc/dsdc.htm

State information, including quick facts, statistics and census information, school and farm reports, and economic data. There are also links to related state sites and regional data centers.

Delaware Web Servers

http://www.dtcc.edu/delaware.html

A great site for links to Delaware information, including weather info, interactive maps, colleges and grade schools, government information, transportation services, tourist guides and accommodations, and local organizations. There's also a section on how to have a good time in Delaware (trips to Philadelphia don't count), including dining information, hobbies, music, and sports.

Delaware WWW map

http://www.udel.edu/delaware/map.html

An interactive map of Delaware cities, linked to server lists for each location. You can also browse a subject list of the related servers directly.

Florida

FloridaNet

http://www.florida.net

Check here for the Florida Marketplace, a list of shops and services, as well online magazines like the *South Florida Dive Journal* and *XSO,* featuring news and entertainment stories.

Hit The Beach!

http://www.hitthebeach.com/

Here you can find Florida resources for travel and accommodations, shopping, and event listings. There are also special features and contests, a dining and nightlife guide, and online personals.

Florida Fun in the Sun

http://Florida.com/attract1.htm

You can find Florida attractions described here for North, Central, and South regions. By checking a box next to each description and filling out an online form, you can have more information mailed to you.

Tour Florida

http://www.florida.com

The Florida Internet Commerce Center features good information in a nice layout, with buttons leading to areas for state attractions and shopping, RV camping, and tour information. There's also a Hurricane Information Center.

Georgia

Georgia Web Servers

http://www.cc.emory.edu/GaCern/GA.html

An extensive hyperlinked list of Georgia Web servers, arranged alphabetically with annotations. You can search the list using the Edit/Find command in your Web browser.

Index - Georgia Web Guide

http://www.ajc.com/atl/gaweb.htm

Access Atlanta's site is a great guide to Georgia, including general information (maps, oral histories, and genealogical reports), city and regional links (online city/neighborhood guides and 1996 Olympics information), and entertainment/music links. There are also lists of local online publications, media services, organizations and groups, and government services.

Georgia Roadmap

http://www.america.net/com/gem/gamap.html

A big view of Georgia's roadways can be found here, with state roads and cities clearly marked.

Hawaii

Hawai'i

http://www.hawaii.net/

A central resource site, you'll find information arranged by businesses, organizations, education, and government. There's also an online Vistors Center with links to vacation bureaus, museums, picture galleries, and Polynesian culture sites. Use the Hawai'i Connections link to search for information directly.

Hawaii Overview

http://www2.hawaii.edu/visitors/overview.html

A brief look at the Island State, featuring a map of the area, geographic information, and a section on state emblems and insignia.

HUKILAU ! (Gateway to Polynesia)

http://www.maui.net/~hukilau/

Information on the island culture, including links to some of the more complete Web sources for Hawaiian information. You can also view the annual homecoming of the Polynesian voyaging canoes at the Virtual Village, with great pictures.

Virtually Hawaii

http://www.satlab.hawaii.edu/space/hawaii/

Space and aircraft images of the Island State abound here. You can also find current weather information, including satellite images, and virtual field trips to places like Maui, Molokai, Oahu, and the Kilauea volcano.

Idaho

Idaho's Weather Station

http://www.mrc.uidaho.edu/weather/weather.html

Good Idaho weather information, including satellite radar images and movies of the Pacific Northwest. There are also specific city weather reports here.

State of Idaho

http://www.state.id.us/

The State site features Web-linked information under headings for business, city and county listings, recreation and tourism, events, and government. You can also search the site directly using a form, or browse an alphabetical topic index.

Unofficial Idaho

http://www.cs.uidaho.edu/~beers/Idaho/

This site has a good list of Idaho facts, government and technology resources, academic site lists, and links to city information. There are also sections on recreation and travel, and links to microbrewery and vegetarianism info.

Illinois

Chicago Mosaic

http://www.ci.chi.il/

The official city site features an electronic tour guide, a directory of city services, and information on a community policing project. There's also a What's New section, and a statement from the Mayor's Office.

The Web Wanderer's Chicago Guide

http://www.xnet.com/~blatura/chicago.shtml

Links for Chicago and the surrounding neighborhoods, grouped in sections for general information, entertainment, sightseeing, towns and suburbs, sports, organizations, and media.

State Of Illinois

http://www.state.il.us/

Official information, including lists of state agencies, educational institutions, libraries and museums, and government bureaus. There's also a section on Illinois tourism, and a search engine you can use to look up information directly.

Indiana

Bloomington [HoosierNet]

http://www.bloomington.in.us

HoosierNet provides community information for the Bloomington and Monroe Country districts of Indiana. Here you'll find links to information in sections on arts and leisure, events, business, education, and social services. There's also employment guides, weather information, and links to news sources.

CICA Virtual Tourist Map Indiana

http://www.cica.indiana.edu/news/servers/tourist/index.html

The Center for Innovative Computer Applications' site features an interactive map you can use to select lists of Web sites for cities and areas in Indiana. It's a good way to get an overall perspective of the state. You can also view the hyperlinked list of servers directly.

IDEAnet

http://ideanet.doe.state.in.us/

The Indiana Department of Education Access Network site features links to selected educational sites for Indiana and elsewhere. There are also links for community institutions and services, news organizations, libraries, and state agencies.

Iowa

Iowa Database

http://www.iptv.org/iowa_database/

Information on state agencies and professional organizations. You can also search selected databases using the Matchmaker query engine.

Iowa Virtual Tourist

http://www.jeonet.com/tourist/

A good interactive map leads to lists of Web server sites for a wide range of Iowa locations. You can also choose them from a hypertext menu. Also check out the information on the Amana Colonies listed here, a prime Iowan historical attraction.

Iowa City Online

http://www.wcci.com/i-mart/icmag/icmaghome.html

A magazine covering the Iowa City-Coralville area (Where's that? Check out the map below!). Sections include city directories, editorials, restaurant and hotel guides, and a Best of Iowa City list.

Kansas

Kansas Sights

http://falcon.cc.ukans.edu/~nsween/europa.html

Things to do and see in Kansas. This site has a lot of good photographs and annotated links to information on tourism, government, and sports. There are also links to local libraries and universities, and historical information (did you know that basketball was first played here?).

Virtual Old West Lawrence

http://falcon.cc.ukans.edu/~kdayton/vowl.html

A developing guide to an eclectic neighborhood in Lawrence, you can also find links to more Kansas information, including the University of Kansas' KU Info site and the related Internet Guide To Kansas. Two of our favorite characters from Lawrence: author William S. Burroughs and Yahoo!'s Srinija Srinivasan.

Wichita

http://www.southwind.net/ict/

Information on this site includes an overview of Kansas' largest city, the Peerless Princess of the Plains, and links to business information, community organizations, and government sites. There's also historical information and an events calendar.

WICHITA, KANSAS

Kentucky

Kentucky Atlas & Gazetteer

http://www.uky.edu/KentuckyAtlas/kentucky-atlas.html

A good series of interactive state maps from the University of Kentucky, linked to city and county maps and information. You can also find county border, relief and physiognomic maps versions here (the relief map has clearer city and county markers). Kentucky counties are also presented in a separate list for browsing.

Kentucky Network Services

http://www.uky.edu/kentucky-network-services.html

An interactive map of state Web sites, with a related alphabetical hyperlinked list. There are also links to Kentucky-related gopher information servers.

WWW Servers in Kentucky

http://www.uky.edu/www-us-ky.html

An annotated alphabetical list of Web sites for the Commonwealth of Kentucky. You can search the list using the Edit/Find command of your Web browser.

Louisiana

Gumbo Home Page

http://www.webcom.com/~gumbo/

A good guide to Southern Louisiana, including New Orleans and Acadiana. Here you can find out about area music, culture and food, read Creole and Cajun recipes, and check out a guide to Acadiana (Cajun Country).

Louisiana

http://www.accesscom.net/la/la1.htm

The Louisiana home page has sections for tourism, selected sights of interest, an event calendar, and business/government listings. You can also find out about regional food, nightclubs, recreation areas, shopping, and music.

New Orleans Connection

http://www.noconnect.com/

Cultural, shopping, and entertainment information can be found here. There's also local information, including area weather reports and a convention calendar.

The Official New Orleans Mardi Gras Web Site

http://www.neosoft.com/citylink/mardigr/default.html

Information on the great event, including online press releases, parade schedules, sound samples, and a dictionary. You can also check out local tour information and accommodations, and shop virtual Bourbon Street for souvenirs (get some King Cake!).

Maine

Maine (std.com)

http://www.std.com/NE/maine.html

An annotated list of interesting Web sites for the Pine Tree State, including Arcadia National Park, local businesses, State government, and historical associations.

Maine Information (thomas.edu)

http://www.thomas.edu/www/maine.html

Thomas College's site includes links to general information (tourism and Maine WWW server lists), local business and economic sites, Federal and State government information, and statistics.

Maine Map of WWW Resources

http://www.destek.net/Maps/ME.html

A good interactive map with an associated hyperlinked list of many state Web resources. You can search the list using the Edit/Find command in your Web browser.

Maine Resource Guide

http://www.maineguide.com/

"The Way Life Should Be." Check here for virtual tours, an online Travel Center, and a CyberMall you can visit to shop local vendors.

Index - The Maine Index

http://www.mbeacon.com/ndx/ndx1.html

This site features a well-laid-out set of buttons leading to Web sites for universities and colleges, commercial businesses, the Maine community, state and local government, and publications. There are also local Yellow Pages and Cool Sites sections.

Maryland

List of Servers (USA - Maryland)

http://www.fie.com/www/maryland.htm

A large annotated list of all kinds of Web sites coming from Maryland, presented alphabetically. Search the list using the Edit/Find command in your Web browser.

MarylandNet

http://www.marylandnet.com

A guide to the Free State. Information here includes a brief state overview, regional guides, and reference materials. You can also search the MarylandNet Database directly using an online form.

Sailor - Maryland's Information Network

http://sailor.lib.md.us/

The Sailor Network has links to state government, local cities, counties, and communities, libraries and education resources, and miscellaneous Maryland information. There's also a topical list that leads to information on

technology, culture, entertainment, employment, and news.

Massachusetts

Massachusetts (std.com)

http://www.std.com/NE/mass.html

A good list of state resources, including an alphabetical list of city and area home pages, and information on sites for agriculture, sports and recreation, employment, local government, and history. There are also links to maps, travel resources, and a quiz (where you can see how much of a Massachusettes native you are!).

Massachusetts Map of WWW Resources

http://donald.phast.umass.edu/misc/mass.html

You'll find a large interactive map to Massachusettes Web sites here, with town and city sites clearly marked by number, and inset maps for Amherst and Boston area sites. The site also features a subject list of online resources, in categories for universities, commercial sites, cities and town, museums, non-profit organizations, and event listings.

Massachusettes Office of Travel and Tourism

http://www.magnet.state.ma.us/travel/travel.html

Information on sights, neighborhoods, and historic locations (including Boston and Cambridge, The North Shore, and Cape Cod) can be found at this site. There's also travel and tourism contact information.

Michigan

Northern Michigan Connection

http://www.iquest.com/michweb/

Information on events, local businesses and communities, and tourism can be found here. There are also lists of Michigan wineries and golfing locations, and local weather reports.

RING!OnLine - Michigan Magazine

http://www.ring.com

This site features sections for local news and events, sightseeing and travel, non-profit organizations, and business. There's also a collection of State resource links and online classified ads.

West Michigan Interests

http://www.iserv.net/wmich/

Find information on entertainment, businesses, education, sports, and government sites for Grand Rapids and Western Michigan here, arranged in hyperlinked subject indices.

Minnesota

The State of Minnesota Gopher Server

gopher://gopher.state.mn.us/

Text information from this server includes sections on the State Legislature and the Department of Transportation (featuring daily weather reports for selected cities).

Index - Minnesota Web Listings

http://www.primenet.com/~kennyb/mnhome.htm

An alphabetic list of well-maintained sites of all kinds, including eclectic personal pages with state and regional information.

Index - MNdex

http://www.skypoint.com/members/lmerry/mndex/

This site features sections for Minnesota arts and leisure (including tourism information), business and employment, and news in a nicely-laid-out index format. There's also a community section with information on state, city and personal Web resources.

Mississippi

Jackson Area Information

gopher://gopher.millsaps.edu/11GOPHER_ROOT_CWIS:[JACKSON]

This Gopher site features a visitor and travel directory (including information from the Mississippi State Tourism

Office), as well as sections for area restaurants, cultural events and art listings, and weather reports.

Misnet Topology Map

http://www.mcsr.olemiss.edu/misnet/

A comprehensive interactive map of Mississippi sites, including cities and regional areas. You can also browse sections for cities, communities, and towns, businesses and educational institutions, and state government agencies.

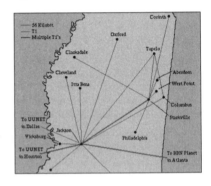

WWW Servers in Mississippi

http://www.msstate.edu/MS/www-list.html

This site has lists of sites arranged in areas for universities and colleges, kindergarten and high schools, communities, state government, commercial organizations, and online publications.

Missouri

University of Missouri System

http://www.system.missouri.edu

This site features information and area maps for the State University, and links to more Missouri information (including the State of Missouri home page).

Kansas City ONLINE

http://www.SafariBeach.com/
KansasCity/

Look to this site for a virtual Visitor's Center, an online business directory, and a personal section for KC residents' information. You can also browse information on selected communities in the Kansas City Metro Area.

St. Louis

http://www.st-louis.mo.us/

A view from the top of the Gateway Arch leads off this official city page. Here you can find information on local tours, news, weather, business, schools, arts, and sports. There's also a special kids' section and community info.

Montana

Maps of Montana

http://nris.msl.mt.gov/gis/
mtmaps.html

Vivid maps of Montana are located here, including views of counties, forests, lakes and streams, highways, railroads, population density, land use, Indian reservations, and legislative districts.

MontanaWeb!

http://montanaweb.com/
montanaweb/

Links for the last, best place include sections for artists and galleries, businesses, entertainment, government information, recreation, lodging and travel, and outdoor recreation. There are also a good selection of Montana images from Glacier Falls and Yellowstone Park.

Peaks Magazine

http://www.cyberport.net/peaks/

This online magazine has features on Montana lifestyles, photo exhibits, and virtual tours of selected sights (try the Flathead Valley Click Tour). There's also a section with links to Montana Web resources and a General Store for local products and services.

Index - Montana WWW Resources Page

http://www.ism.net/montana/
index.html

You can find city and government listings here, as well as educational institutions and miscellaneous Montana sites.

Nebraska

Nebraska: A Journey to the Good Life

http://esu3.esu3.k12.ne.us/nebraska/
nebraska_studies/
Home_Nebraska_Page.html

This site features information on Nebraska schools, lifestyles and recreation activities, local communities, and state government.

There are also links to information on Nebraska natural systems, including virtual tours of selected sights and attractions.

Game and Parks Commission

http://ngp.ngpc.state.ne.us

This site has a virtual tour of state recreation resources, including parks and wildlife areas, and information on fishing and boating. There's also a land database you can search by county name (or learn the counties by using the interactive map).

Nebraska Travel and Tourism

http://www.ded.state.ne.us/
tourism.html

The State Tourism Board's electronic guide to attractions, events, and accommodations is located here. You can also find also general information about Nebraska and a set of related site links.

Nevada

Nevada Sites

http://www.unlv.edu/nevada-
map.html

An interactive map leading to Reno or Las Vegas Web site listings. You can also browse a list of sites arranged alphabetically, with annotations.

WWW Servers in Nevada

http://www.unlv.edu/www-nevada.html

An alphabetical list of Nevada site links, with descriptions. You can search this page using the Edit/Find command in your Web browser.

About Las Vegas

http://www.vegas.com/vegas/aboutlv/

Vegas.COM's colorful site features sections on local attractions, history, Vegas celebrities and heroes, outdoor activities and (of course) the gambling industry.

Las Vegas On-Line

http://www.intermind.net/im/lasvegas.html

Follow the Strip sign to information on hotels, restaurants, scenic attractions, the Las Vegas Convention Center, and local news.

New Hampshire

Access NH/NH Access Internet

http://www.nh.com/

Colorful buttons lead to a lot of information on the Granite State's offerings. Sections include economic development, state government, real estate, technology, tourism, history, education, and culture. There's also a Facts and Fun section and an events calendar.

Seacoast NH

http://www.star.net/people/~marshall/summer95.htm

A guide to current concerts, plays, and happenings for the Hampton Beach area. There's also a link to another Seacoast home page with picture and sound files of the beach area.

New Hampshire [std.com]

http://ftp.std.com/NE/nh.html

An alphabetical list of annotated state links is found here. You can go directly to selected city and county sites, museums, and pages for local weather information.

Vermont/New Hampshire Map of WWW Resources

http://www.destek.net/Maps/VT-NH.html

An interactive area map of Web resources, featuring schools, university departments, and businesses. There's also a list of various New Hampshire links below the map.

New Jersey

The Center Of The Universe

http://www.cnj.digex.net/~lars/center.html

Recent reports show the Center of the Universe is in New Jersey! Find out what the Galactic Garden State has in store for you here. There's a good collection of NJ hot spots, business links, and local interest information.

IN Jersey

http://www.injersey.com/

This site features a nicely laid out digital information network for the Garden State. Sections include business, education, entertainment, lifestyles, and sports. There are also online message forums you can participate in, a What's New section, and an area focusing on local issues.

NJ WWW map page

http://www.stevens-tech.edu/nj.html

A sensitive map of the Jersey area and related Web resources. There's also an alphabetical list of site links you can search using the Edit/Find command in your Web browser.

Of New Jersey Interest (WOI)

http://woi.com/woi/indexnj.html

You can find good regional news and weather information at this site (with maps and images), as well as Atlantic City listings (casino information, including a link to online Blackjack). There are also lists of related NJ sites of interest, education and sports team home pages, and lottery results.

New Mexico

New Mexico Album

http://www-swiss.ai.mit.edu/philg/new-mexico/album.html

A "strange photo essay" from Philip Greenspun, with vivid photographs of the New Mexico desert area.

NMSU Library

http://lib.nmsu.edu/

The New Mexico State University site has local information for the Las Cruces, Southern New Mexico, and El Paso/Juarez area, including general regional information, city services directories, movie listings, and tourism links.

VIVA New Mexico!

http://www.viva.com/viva/nm/nmhome.html

This site features a lot of state information in sections for art, events, science and technology, restaurants and food, and culture. There's also a What's New area for updated information, an online guidebook, and a regional almanac.

WWW Servers in New Mexico

http://www.unm.edu/servers.html

An alphabetical list of Web site links for New Mexico, with descriptions. Search the list for topics of interest with the Edit/Find command in your Web browser.

New York

NYC Online Information

http://www.mediabridge.com/nyc/

A great site for lots of Manhattan information. The How section includes pages on history and facts, general info, transportation guides, and survival tips (!). The Wow section has dining, shopping and hotel information, as well as lists of museums and places to sightsee. The Now section is for current news and event listings, and sports information. There's also an online marketplace of local goods and services.

Online Guide to Upstate New York

http://www.roundthebend.com/

A good guide to the Upstate area, listed by geographic regions and by activities you can do there (including camping, golfing, and museums to visit). There's also a tidbits page with area facts and information.

WWW Servers in New York

http://wings.buffalo.edu/world/nywww.html

The Virtual Tourist's interactive New York Site map has clear locations for statewide Web resources (and for the states surrounding it). You can zoom in to Net locations for specific cities and regions, as well as university and corporate Web sites.

North Carolina

North Carolina [unc.edu]

http://sunsite.unc.edu/nc/nchome.html

Information at this site includes a list of college and university web sites, state and government links, and a list of nifty NC Web resources (including online museum exhibits, local weather info, and state statistics).

North Carolina Encyclopedia

http://hal.dcr.state.nc.us/nc/cover.htm

A great online information resource for the state. Sections include county overviews and profiles of the education system, geography, historic sites, state government information, and a page of state symbols.

WWW Servers in North Carolina

http://www.persimmon.com/lists/nc.html

An alphabetic list of North Carolina Web sites, arranged in sections for the Triangle area and elsewhere in NC, with descriptions. You can search this page using the Edit/Find command under your Web browser. There's also a link to interactive maps you can use to reach area servers by location.

North Dakota

North Dakota University System

http://www.nodak.edu

This site includes links to State educational institutions, as well as a Gopher information server for the campuswide system (and beyond). There's also a link to the official State of North Dakota Web server.

See more information on businesses and city Web sites under sections for Fargo and Hillsboro.

Ohio

Guide to Cincinnati

http://www.cinci.com

A well-designed guide to the best in Cincinnati, this site has sections for visitor and general area information, entertainment, business, recreation, real estate, and dining. There's also a What's New section and links to electronic mailing lists on area topics.

Cleve.net: A Guided Tour Of The North Coast

http://www.en.com/cleve.net

This site features information on arts and entertainment, commerce, education, government agencies, and business organizations for the North Coast area.

Columbus

http://www.ohiocap.com/columbus/

The Columbus Home Page features sections on local area activities, arts and entertainment, business, news, and weather. There are also TV listings and a comics page, and information for visitors from out-of-state (maps included).

Information on the State of Ohio

http://www.commerce.digital.com/oetc/state/info01.html

This site has sections on tourism, small business, commerce, economic development, regional information, and more. Remember: "If money's your problem, you have no problem in Ohio." Not sure what that means, but what the heck.

Oklahoma

Lodges, Resorts and State Parks of Oklahoma

http://www.oklaosf.state.ok.us/osfdocs/tour-cab.html

Links to the above information can be found here, including descriptions and contact information. There's also a link to the Oklahoma State Government Master Homepage for more information.

Virtual Oklahoma

http://www.icon.net/commercial/commerce/index.html

This site features sections on regional information, event listings, museums and attractions, accommodations, and meeting facilities. There are also areas that cover Oklahoma restaurants and nightclubs, entertainment and recreation resources, and shopping.

Index - Oklahoma WWW Servers

http://www.cpb.uokhsc.edu/okwww.html

A map of Oklahoma Web sites, with a related subject list for University departments, news and media sites, and a miscellaneous unclassified section. Also see information on the tragic Oklahoma City bombing here, most of it posted at the time the incident occurred in April 1995.

Oregon

Carrie's Crazy Quilt from Central Oregon

http://www.mtjeff.com/~bodenst/page1.html

Eclectic Oregonian information can be found at this site, including the Central Oregon Cultural Diversity Page, and collected links to city and county sites, state parks, local weather reports, and general state information resources.

Central Oregon

http://www.bendnet.com/co.htm

This site features good information on the various communities of the Central Oregon area, including area descriptions and maps. There are also links to local news reports and tourism information, including event calendars and a bed and breakfast guide.

Oregon Traveler

http://www.teleport.com/~mindseye/

A good travel and entertainment guide, with regional reports and remote site links for various parts of Oregon (including 101-The Coast, the I-5 Corridor, Central Oregon - Cascades, and Eastern Oregon - Desert). There's also a map you can use to see how the regions fit together, an online mileage guide (with road maps), and an events calendar.

Oregon Web Resource Map

http://www.willamette.edu/~tjones/Oregonmap.html

Oregon Web sites arranged alphabetically by county, including community pages, school sites, and business locations. You can search this page using the Edit/Find command in your Web browser.

Pennsylvania

N.E. Pennsylvania

http://mtmis1.mis.semi.harris.com/pa.html

This site features local weather, news, and maps of the Northeast corner area. There are also links to regional information centers (including Pennsylvania libraries and more geographical data), city and county Web servers, and local universities.

LibertyNet

http://www.libertynet.org/

The Philadelphia Region's Home Page is a great site, with information on local attractions (also look for the Virtual History tour), business and commerce sites, community organizations and health services, educational institutions (including area schools), and local government. There are also a number of regional event calendars and an alphabetical directory of Philadelphia-area Web sites. It's all here!

City of Pittsburgh Online!

http://www.pittsburgh.net

PittsburghNet features sections on local lifestyles, area history, and commerce. There's also a business Yellow Pages for local goods and services. Use the search panel at the bottom of the home page to look for information directly.

Pittsburgh Links

http://www.maya.com/Local/mazur/daBurgh.html

Not the Pittsburgh Yahoo!, this site features links to area information in subject headings for food and drink, music, sports, news media, local organizations and communities, general fun, and miscellaneous Pittsburghian Web resources.

Rhode Island

Rhode Island [ids.net]

http://www.ids.net/ri/ri.html

This site features local information in sections for current weather, business news, recreation and tourism, government archives and State House links. Also check out the local attractions (featuring an electronic museum tour).

Rhode Island [std.com]

http://www.std.com/NE/ri.html

Here you can find listings for art, brewpubs, education, gay and lesbian RI info, historical information (WPA oral histories), and a Brown University gopher with lots of good local information.

South Carolina

SCENIC

http://scenic.ricommunity.com/

The South Carolina Entertainment & News Internet Community site features sections on local tours, general state information, entertainment, news, and shopping. There's also an online SCENIC guide, with help on navigating the Web site, an index of all available information, and links to other South Carolina Web resources.

The South Carolina Extravaganza!

http://www.sunbelt.net/cni/statesc/schome.htm

A good guide to the Palmetto State, featuring a visual State tour, historical material, a museum guide, and a list of local African American cultural resources. There are also sections on educational and state government sites and an event calendar.

Who's in South Carolina? (clickable map)

http://www2.persimmon.com/scmap.html

An interactive map to SC Web resources. You can go to a server by clicking on a blue square next to its name, or browse an alphabetic subject list directly.

South Dakota

South Dakota Parks and Recreation Areas

http://www.state.sd.us/state/execut~1/tourism/sdparks/sdparks.htm

Information on the park system, including lists with descriptions. There's also an online calendar of events, cabin reservation instructions, and a section on winter activities.

State of South Dakota

http://www.state.sd.us

The official State site features tourism information, SD Internet resource links, and information on local government, city areas, and educational institutions. You can also search the page directly for items of interest.

South Dakota Group Tour Planning Guide

http://www.state.sd.us/state/executive/tourism/grptour/grptour.htm

You can find maps and mileage charts here, as well as major attractions and event information, and sections on cities to visit and Native American culture to appreciate.

Tennessee

Virtual Chattanooga

http://www.chattanooga.net/

This site features sections with visitor information (local sights), area statistics , community sites, and a list of related links of interest. There's also an online business directory.

Nashville.Net

http://www.Nashville.Net

A good image map leads to information on music and entertainment, local government and business, educational institutions, and shopping. There's also a link to a page with RealAudio sound samples (including Metro police calls from downtown Nashville, and local music).

Tennessee! [Edge.Net]

http://www.edge.net/tennessee/

This site features a link to the Official Tennessee Vacation Guide, interactive maps you can use to look for local Web resources (or use a subject guide), lists of electronic shopping malls, and local weather reports.

Texas

Dallas - Fort Worth Information Servers

http://www.utdallas.edu/DFW/dfw-infoservers.html

A list of Internet resources for the Metroplex area, arranged by type (FTP, gopher, and WWW). You can go to a list of Web server pages arranged by headings for commercial, educational, government, non-profit organizations, and regional information sites. There are also area maps available from here.

Index - The Dallas Page

http://www.master.net/dallas

This site features local information in sections for community information, suburban area descriptions, education, music, and sports. There's also a list of miscellaneous Dallas and Greater Texas links.

Texas Travel Information

http://volvo.gslis.utexas.edu/~texas/texas.html

An interactive map of five Texas regions leads to area reports and city descriptions. You can also find links here to sites with Texas maps, local weather reports, and historical information.

Texas Information Servers

http://www.quadralay.com/www/Misc/TexasInfoServers.html

Internet resources for Texas, listed by counties, and further broken down by Web, Gopher, or FTP site. You can browse for regional information sites here.

Utah

Network Services in Utah

http://wings.buffalo.edu/world/utahwww.html

A good interactive state map is at this site, with direct links to corporate and university Web servers, city and area sites, and tourist attractions. There's also a closeup map of sites located in Wasatch Front (Salt Lake City area), and links to online travel guides, and the official Utah State home page.

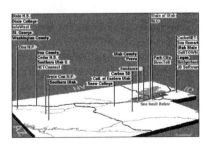

Discover Utah!

http://www.infowest.com/Utah/

A colorful map leads to regional information for Utah attractions, including maps, descriptions, and mileage tables. Check out Dinosaur National Monument or Starvation National Park.

Utah Travel Guide Online

http://www.netpub.com/utah/

This site features descriptions of Utah travel regions, a Travel Council event calendar, and an interactive, form-based campground locator. There's also a link to the Ski Utah home page.

Vermont

Scenes of Vermont

http://www.pbpub.com/vermont/

Good visual guide to Vermont's pretty scenery, bed and breakfast locations, and local attractions. There are also online tours available here.

Vermont (std.com)

http://www.std.com/NE/vt.html

This site features subject links to state Web resources, including a brewpub guide and information on federal education resource sites. There are also links to state government offices and information on local sports, museums, news, and weather.

Vermont/New Hampshire Map of WWW Resources

http://www.destek.net/Maps/VT-NH.html

An interactive map of Vermont Web resources, including university and business sites. There's also an alphabetical list of links you can browse directly.

Vermont: The Green Mountain State

http://mole.uvm.edu/Vermont/

This University of Vermont site features a brief overview of the state, with sections focusing on local history, government, and geography, official state treasures, natural and recreational resources, and business.

Index - State of Vermont

http://www.cit.state.vt.us/

The official state site features information on Vermont-related WWW sites, educational resources, and local government departments. There are also links to *Vermont Life,* an online travel and tourism magazine, and a calendar of upcoming events.

Virginia

The Battlefield Web

http://www.ahoynet.com/

AhoyNet's site features information for the Woodbridge, Fredericksburg, Stafford, Quantico, Spotsylvania and surrounding historic Virginia communities. You can take a virtual tour of Civil War battle sites, check out local businesses, and view a collection of local user home pages. There are also lists of related Virginia site links.

Virgina Tourism Information

http://www.nomious.com/~va/virginia.htm

Tourism information and State facts can be found at this site, including an overview of the state economy. There's also a link to a list of tourism offices.

Williamsburg Online Tourism Guide

http://www.williamsburg.com/wol/tour/tour.html

A pictorial overview of the Historic Triangle area, including Colonial Williamsburg, Jamestown, and Yorktown. There's also information on local attractions, and a section on how to get there (with maps).

Washington

EmeraldWeb

http://www.cyberspace.com/bobk/

This site features a directory to Internet resources for Seattle and the Puget Sound area, listed under headings for general information, businesses, area people, and local government.

SeattleWeb

http://www.seattle.net/

A vivid site for information on the Puget Sound area, including sections on the local scene, city info, businesses, dining, education, and the great outdoors. There's also a search engine you can use to find information quickly, and online maps.

U/Seattle - Seattle's Online Entertainment Guide

http://useattle.uspan.com/

A great site from the University of Seattle, with sections on local movies, music and nightlife, dining and restaurants, hotels and motels, sports and fitness, and that shopping thang. You can also read local news and weather reports here.

Washington State's Olympic Peninsula

http://www.olympus.net/olympic-peninsula.html

This site features sections on local arts and entertainment, business, and government. There are also lists of community events, recreational opportunities, and area places to stay, as well as a section on Peninsula towns.

Washington, D.C.

Area Map

http://www.whitehouse.gov/White_House/EOP/html/DC_map.html

This White House site has great maps of the D.C. area. You can zoom in on specific regions, and click on selected buildings for more information.

District of Columbia [Planet Earth]

http://white.nosc.mil/washington.html

A good list of D.C. information is available at this site, arranged in sections for government branches and servers, archive and document collections, universities and colleges, and local information.

Visitors' Guide [Julia Ridgely]

http://ftp.clark.net/pub/jridgely/dc/dcguide.html

A guide to D.C. area local attractions, museums, and memorial sites. There's also a dining out section, transportation information, and a list of selected virtual tour links (including Library of Congress and Smithsonian exhibits).

Washington Web

http://www.washweb.net/

This site offers information for the Greater D.C. area, arranged in sections covering art, business and finance, community and culture, education, government and politics, news and current events, and travel. There's also an online reference section.

West Virginia

West Virgina Tourism Information

http://www.nomius.com/~wv/westva.htm

State information, including local facts and an economic overview, and contact information for the State Tourism Offices.

West Virginia

http://www.hsc.wvu.edu/wv.html

This site features information on local government, recreational activities, and educational institutions. There are also links to a list of W. Va. Web resources and a related Web site map.

Index - West Virginia Information Servers

http://www.marshall.edu/www/wv-map.html

Marshall University's site provides a good interactive map of W. Va. Web resources, arranged by city. You can go directly to a list of area Web servers for the cities listed here.

West Virginia

Wisconsin

Travel Information

http://badger.state.wi.us/agencies/tourism/places/Cover.html

The Wisconsin Tourism Division site features an interactive map of 15 travel destinations in the State. You can select an area to find out more about cities located there.

Wisconsin Visitor Information

http://execpc.com/~whospweb

The Visitor's Web provides information on top events in cities and regions across the state. You can go directly to specific city and regional pages from here. There's also information on Wisconsin State Tourism associations.

Index - Wisconsin Information and Web Sites

http://infomad.com/wisconsin/

This site lists state Web resources in sections for educational institutions, state and local government, entertainment and culture, commercial sites, and media organizations. There's also a list of Internet-based Wisconsin information sources.

Wyoming

WAVE Communications - Wyoming Links

http://wave.sheridan.wy.us/index.html

This site features information on hunting and fishing, sports activities, and travel destinations. There are also links to Wyoming weather reports, local newspapers, and university sites.

Windy Wyoming Web

http://math.uwyo.edu/State_Links.html

A great topological map leads to a lot of information on Wyoming, arranged in Yahoo-like categories for art, business, cities and counties, education, entertainment, government, recreation, society and culture, and weather. Follow the category links to good lists of sites in subject outline format.

Indices

City.Net United States

http://www.city.net/countries/
united_states/

City.Net features an alphabetical list of
U.S. States at this site, linked to Web
resource listings under categories like
city and regional areas, education,
food and drink, government, and
general state information.

USA CityLink

http://www.NeoSoft.com/citylink/

CityLink is a comprehensive list of city
and state information. City
descriptions include sightseeing
opportunities, accommodations,
places to eat, and shopping locations.

Science

Scientists built the Web and were its first inhabitants. It's not surprising: Science is an enterprise with a unique need for exchanging large chunks of information among sites all over the globe. People in Kuala Lumpur could always read the Asian *Wall Street Journal* for stock market information. But Malaysian scientists used to have to wait months for U.S. chemistry and physics journals and make contacts at annual meetings. The Web has changed all that and made the world one big laboratory.

Here's one way to gauge the importance of science on the Web: This category is bigger than Entertainment!

Note that, as elsewhere in this book, a few subcategories under Science have been skipped here. That's because they are extensively covered in other main categories, such as Health or Business and Economy. Not to worry: Yahoo! doesn't let you miss anything, and sites often appear in several places.

Acoustics

Auditory phenomena

http://www.music.mcgill.ca/~welch/auditory/Auditory.html

This site gives you a multimedia guide to all sorts of interesting psychoacoustic phenomena. Scientists still have a lot to learn about the way the brain processes sounds.

Technical University of Delft

http://wwwak.tn.tudelft.nl/index.html

Seismics plus acoustics plus sonic imaging. It's strange to think that the same basic phenomena underlie human hearing and the detection of underground oil deposits. How far away is that truck? Where's the shale oil layer? They're nearly the same question, physically.

Agriculture

Once you consider the simple logic that we all have to eat but we don't all have to Web surf, this category understandably turns out to be one of the largest sections, dwarfing even most computing topics.

Agriculture Online

http://www.agriculture.com/

This is *the* source for commercial ag information. There's an old joke: "How do you make a small fortune in farming? Start with a large fortune and keep farming till it's nearly gone." Those days are over for the most part, and besides that, they're now wired down on the farm. Even if the next house is a half-mile away, remember, we're all neighbors on the Web.

SCORE

http://www.rr.ualberta.ca/~dpuurvee/score/scorintr.html

This Canadian project looks at sustainable cropping in the plains of Alberta. Have you ever wondered exactly how many years you can raise wheat on the same plot of land before it conks out utterly? It's nice to know someone's thinking about it.

Alternative

Alternative in the context of science can come close to meaning *not*. Nevertheless, this is a great collection of resources that might be tactfully described as speculative. And some of it no doubt will turn out to be true.

Centre for Alternative Technology

http://www.foe.co.uk/CAT/

These people in Wales are interested in green technology.

Weird Science

http://www.eskimo.com/~billb/weird.html

Your one-stop shopping center and link-farm for everything, from Tesla coil experiments to UFOs to ESP and everything in between. When you're bored with *X-Files* reruns, stop here and make up your own show.

Anthropology and Archaeology

More than 60 sites about people who are mostly nonurban. To qualify for anthropological study, the unifying link between these groups seems to be that none of them is likely to have any VISA cards.

Aboriginal Studies Database

http://coombs.anu.edu.au/SpecialProj/ASEDA/ASEDA.html

The Australian aborigines have graduated from being hunted like kangaroos, to being urban outcasts, to being at least recognized as a "problem" by the Australian government — and now at last they have their own Web site.

Aquatic Ape Theory

http://www.brad.ac.uk/~dmorgan/aat.html

Face the facts. Unlike every other primate, you're practically hairless, you have big paddle-shaped feet you can't type with, and you have ungodly amounts of body fat — all characteristics more associated with a sea lion than a chimp. Some people speculate that this is because humans went through a period of evolutionary aquatic adaptation. Check this interesting site for the theories.

Palaeolithic Figurines

http://www.cmcc.muse.digital.ca/cmc/cmceng/pal00eng.html

A nice, online museum displaying some of the oldest sculptures ever discovered. Check out these 25,000 – 35,000-year-old "Venus" figurines depicting the female body.

DNA to Dinosaurs

http://www.bvis.uic.edu/museum/Dna_To_Dinosaurs.html

This is an online museum organized by The Field Museum in Chicago, and it's an example of how an online museum should be done. There are links to other collections as well. (If you get to Chicago, be sure to visit the real thing.)

The Perseus Project

http://www.perseus.tufts.edu/

This fantastic resource has online texts of the Greek classics but also a guide to the entire archaeology of the Eastern Mediterranean. You can track down individual artifacts in museums! Extra Yahoo! points for you if you know why *Perseus Project* is an appropriate name.

Artificial Life

The next time someone tells you to get a life, say you have one but it's artificial. It seems that computer programs sometimes exhibit behavior that is curiously similar to biological life. Called artificial life (or a-life), this is a small but expanding category at the fascinating frontiers of computation.

Live Alife

http://www.fusebox.com/cb/alife.html

If you need to show a friend what's cool about the Web, try this. It displays running simulations of the key artificial life programs, demonstrating why this subject is so fascinating. "Boids," a bird flock simulation, is irresistible, as is its progeny, "Swarm."

Marco's Maddening A-Life Page

http://www.wi.LeidenUniv.nl/home/
mvdweg/alife.html

Some of the best stuff on the Web is
the work of one dedicated (or
demented) individual. This site has
links to all major a-life papers and
other resources.

Astronomy

This giant category has multiple paths
to every significant photograph ever
taken of space and to every current
astrophysical theory. As this is written,
the age of the universe itself is a top
source of controversy (it seems to be
younger than some of the objects in it,
for example). After all these years of
watching the skies, still more
questions abound than answers.

Astronomy Cafe

http://www2.ari.net/home/
odenwald/cafe.html

"For the astronomically
disadvantaged." This site has all sorts
of friendly materials. An ideal place to
point a young person for a
science project.

AstroVR

http://brando.ipac.caltech.edu:8888/

Although this is really for
professionals, it gives you a glimpse
into how the Web is changing things
in science. It's a collaborative,
interactive, "virtual astronomy
laboratory," with access to main
research databases and sky catalogs.

Earth and Universe

http://www.eia.brad.ac.uk/btl/

A dazzling, spectacular, multimedia
astro-extravaganza. Really a very cool
collection of astronomical topics is to
be found here, with amazing photos
and animations.

SkyMap

http://www.execpc.com/~skymap/

This is a great online planetarium,
essentially the equivalent of the
commercial product of the same
name on CD-ROM. See what the sky
looked like the day you were born.

Star*s Family

http://cdsweb.u-strasbg.fr/~heck/
sf.htm

This contains a directory of
astronomers, resources, pictures, and
organizations. Better yet, this site
appears to work all the time (some
individuals' Web sites in astronomy
seem to suffer periodic eclipses).

Aviation and Aeronautics

AirPage

http://trex.smoky.org/~dlevin/air/
air.html

This site leads to a huge catalog of all
planes, from the Wright brothers and
World War I to experimental aircraft
today. A great resource if you're at all
interested in flying.

Hubble Space Telescope

http://newproducts.jpl.nasa.gov/sl9/
hst.html

Because it looks like we're not getting
off this planet any time soon, the next
most exciting adventure is finally
getting (after lots of trouble) a decent
telescope that works outside of our
own blurry atmosphere. Check here
for the latest and greatest from HST.

NASA Spacelink

http://spacelink.msfc.nasa.gov/

The people who run NASA have quite
correctly figured that the general
public is bored with routine
commercial-satellite launching runs
and telescope-repair bungling. But
they have high hopes that Webheads
will be more sympathetic to their
cause, so they have put together a
Web site that's as good or better than
a movie. This one is a must-see, even
if only as an example of HTML design.

Biology

Molecular biology and the Web were made for each other. One is a giant spewing stream of information; the other is the only organizational distribution scheme with the power to make sense of this exploding mess of data.

BioBox

http://www.csc.fi/cgi-bin/topbio

Wow! Biologists post their favorite URLs here, and the duds are gradually weeded out by Darwinian selection. This site leads outward to every important resource in modern biology.

BioSci

http://www.bio.net/

A professional resource that connects all the online literature in biology to databases. Formerly government-sponsored, BioSci now has commercial backers as well. (As a Yahoo! fun fact, one of the site's sponsors [Molecular Dynamics] is a down-the-road neighbor of the Yahoo! offices.)

The Froggy Page

http://www.cs.yale.edu/homes/sjl/froggy.html

It's junior high school. You have a scalpel in your hand. Today's the day. You have a dissection to do. For years, biology will mean frog guts to you. We can't all be DNA scientists. This page is everything a frog lover could want, including a sound collection.

Visualization for Science

http://www.cs.brown.edu/people/art035/Bin/science.html

This is an online classroom of phenomenally good animation on topics in biology. A very nice place to spend an afternoon. It gives you hope that the Web will still be an educational resource after all the businesses sign on.

WWW VL

http://golgi.harvard.edu/biopages/edures.html

If you don't know RNA from the NFL, port yourself to this site and look at the instructional material. This is a particularly worthwhile resource for teachers.

Chaos

Chaos is still a hot topic in science, and everyone knows that fractals are fun to watch. What some people don't know is that fractals are a pain to compute, taking days in some cases to get an interesting picture. So just download someone else's pictures!

Fractal Movie Archive

http://www.cnam.fr/fractals/anim.html

This is a premier archive for cool fractal MPEGs (movie files). You get access to mind-boggling displays whether you know any math or not.

Institute for Nonlinear Science

http://inls.ucsd.edu/

If you want a professional resource with access to papers in chaos and related topics, this is it. The site leads to software archives and lots of special collections as well.

Chemistry

Every day you put the products of the chemical industry in your mouth, on your head, into your car, into the air, and into the trash. And if you're like most people, you can't identify most of the ingredients on the back of a shampoo bottle. Get with the Industrial Age and learn a little chemistry. Yahoo! is here to help.

Index of Biochemical Resources

http://biores.com/

This page leads out to all the companies that produce chemicals, biochemicals, and equipment. Not much fun, but it's very useful.

Nanoworld

http://www.uq.oz.au/nanoworld/nanohome.html

One quick way to learn something about molecules is to see what they look like. This site has tons of atomic-scale pictures of chemicals in action, surfaces, crystals, and so forth.

The Alchemist's Den

http://gpu.srv.ualberta.ca/~psgarbi/psgarbi.html

The American Chemical Society and other resources are indexed here. This site is like a special Yahoo! for chemists. Much of this concerns organic chemistry specifically.

Web Elements

http://www.cchem.berkeley.edu/Table/index.html

This is a searchable online periodic table. For best results, you will need to view it in Netscape or another browser that can handle HTML tables.

Complex Systems

Quite frankly, nobody really knows whether the study of complex systems will yield incredible insights or whether the field will consist of the same hundred people talking endlessly to each other at the same round of conferences. It's interesting, though, to follow this field and see what develops.

Complex Systems

http://life.anu.edu.au/complex_systems/complex.html

This truly great site not only has the best professional sources, it contains beginner's tutorials in the core areas of complexity (cellular automata, fractals, fuzzy logic, and so on). A real Web treasure for the intellectually curious.

Self-Organizing Systems

http://www.ezone.com/sos/

At the interface between computing and ecology, scientists are trying to figure out how large, complex systems assemble themselves.

The Santa Fe Institute

http://www.santafe.edu/

And if it turns out that this whole complex systems subject only produces a bunch of conferences, most of them are here. This site is the main U.S. resource in complexity theory, apart from Dr. Stephen Wolfram himself.

Computer Science

As you might expect, every university computer science department on earth is hooked up to the Web. Their interests might be slightly different from yours in computing, but you can get answers to all higher-level questions at least.

Concurrent Supercomputing Consortium

http://www.ccsf.caltech.edu/cscc.html

Computers are being designed right now that will make today's hot systems look like a left-handed abacus. If you want to see how fast computers can be, and what we'll do with them, look here.

3D Animation

http://www.intellinet.com/~aclight/kim/3d_ani.html

Advice on doing animation, as well as a collection of animations themselves.

3-D animation is the next commercial frontier in computing — after all, nobody needs 300 MHz, 4-processor parallel computers for word processing.

Monte Carlo and the Juggernauts

http://www.umich.edu/~umsoais/isweb/people/dcm/

Every now and then, it is permissible for you to have some fun, leaving aside for a moment the rigorously educational pursuits favored there. This site is a riot.

Creatures Born in Cyberspace

http://www.demon.co.uk/trash/Art/Liz_Dalton.html

Check out this site for interesting pictures and information on *morphing*. You will see some amazing things in this area in the near future.

Atlas of the World Wide Web

http://ua1vm.ua.edu/~crispen/atlas.html

You have this book, so you may as well consult this online resource too. Yahoo! gets you the best stuff the fastest, but this site is worth a look too.

Global Village Tour of the Internet

http://www.globalcenter.net/gcweb/tour.html

Mostly for beginners, this site gives you a tour of all the rest of the Internet besides the Web.

Personal IP

http://www.charm.net/pip.html

If you are going to access the Web with Netscape, you need a SLIP or PPP account. You can get a line on the details, which are sometimes confusing, from this well-designed resource.

WWW Associates

http://www.wwwa.com/index-x.html

And if you want to put a business on the Web, you might want to consult with these people, who will take care of all of the details. It's a lot easier than figuring it all out for yourself.

Earth Science

The pace of research is slower here than in molecular biology (you can expect walk-in DNA sequencing before accurate earthquake prediction, for example) but interesting earth science work is done all the time. Also, much of it is easy for ordinary people to follow.

Geo Exchange

http://giant.mindlink.net/geo_exchange/index.html

This is a good resource for people who have an amateur interest (in gems or volcanoes, for example) and also for Web links to professional info. Besides, here you can see the cartoon Unreal Estate, which is one of the best on the Web.

Northern Lights Planetarium

http://www.uit.no/npt/homepage-npt.en.html

In Norway, they know a lot about fjords, herring, and the Aurora Borealis (Northern Lights). This online Norwegian planetarium gives you a nice computer display, in case you live too far south to see the Lights.

Current Weather Maps/Movies

http://clunix.cl.msu.edu/weather/

You may not be able to predict it, but it's fun to watch. This comprehensive collection lets you show a movie of the weather over your town, anytime you like.

OCEANIC

http://diu.cms.udel.edu/

A pretty good guide to all sorts of oceanographic data, most particularly the large-scale oceanic circulation experiment.

Ecology

This is a rather undernourished area of the Web, especially considering the amount of interest in ecology worldwide. Perhaps the reason is that no one has figured out how to make more money by saving the planet than by paving it. Yet.

EcoNews Africa

http://www.web.apc.org/~econews/

If you're interested in ecology, you may as well be interested in an area that has the worst, fastest-developing problems. A good site for monitoring the proximal demise of the black rhino, for example.

Rainforest Action Network

http://www.ran.org/ran/

If anything, the rainforests are under more direct assault by humans than the savannahs of East Africa. Check here for the latest on rainforest conservation.

Energy

Energy is business, and many of the sites here cross-reference to the business part of the index. The sites themselves have a little more scientific focus.

Alternative Energy

http://www.nando.net/prof/eco/aee.html

This index site shows you how to find information on generating your own power. It's more useful perhaps for noncity folks, but it can be interesting reading even for Manhattan apartment dwellers.

DIII-D Fusion Home Page

http://FusionEd.gat.com/

It's remarkable that cold fusion was denounced so vehemently as a scam, given the billions of dollars pumped into hot fusion so far with little positive result. This page details the current state of the art in government-sponsored fusion research, as seen by General Atomics in San Diego.

International Association for Solar Energy Education

http://www.hrz.uni-oldenburg.de/
~kblum/iasee.html

One source of fusion energy that works right now is, of course, the sun. Incremental improvements in solar cells will probably make them appear on a roof near you within a decade. You can follow the process at this site.

Engineering

You could argue that Engineering should be its own main category and get its own chapter, like Science. Or you could be happy with it tucked away here as a subcategory.

Biomedical Visualization

http://www.bvis.uic.edu/

This is a central resource for the design of biomedical equipment that will actually be used in or on people.

EE Circuits Archive

http://weber.u.washington.edu/
~pfloyd/ee/index.html

No point in reinventing the wheel, and no point redesigning a circuit. This big library covers hundreds of circuits, all tested and practical.

Plastics

http://www.io.tudelft.nl/research/
lmb/degrade/

The Material Science section under Engineering has all sorts of professional archives. This site answers the question: How come my plastic lawn furniture disintegrates if I leave it outside? Turns out, plastics and ultraviolet light more or less don't mix.

Studies in Engineering Design

http://class1.ee.virginia.edu/~tmo9d/
Fall94/home.html

A very nice, online review of things that work (Panama Canal) and things that don't (Space Shuttle *Challenger*) and the reasons why. It's enough to make you wait a year or so before trying out new aircraft or bridges.

Rapid Prototyping

http://cadserv.cadlab.vt.edu/bohn/
RP.html

You may not realize it, but rapid prototyping is one of the few manufacturing advantages of advanced, computer-loaded countries. This engineering site links to all design centers in this evolving activity.

Mathematics

It's the so-called Queen of the Sciences, and it's a big deal on the Web. You can find a whole undergraduate curriculum here, or just answers to easy questions, or the latest research at the frontiers. You will probably be amazed, actually, at how little impact computers have had on mathematics overall.

American Mathematical Society

http://e-math.ams.org/

The Godzilla of math sites. It leads everywhere, but everything is already here anyway. Journals, jobs, papers, you name it. And most major university programs are cataloged here as well.

Wolfram Research

http://www.wri.com/

These people produce Mathematica, probably the most influential piece of math software in the world. This site links to collections of Mathematica notebooks, which are now a standard medium of research exchange.

CHANCE

http://www.geom.umn.edu/docs/
snell/chance/welcome.html

The CHANCE project is a statistics course, freely distributed, that explains the stats behind the headlines in today's news. Your appreciation of the nonsense-level of TV news will be greatly enhanced thereby. A Web all-star site.

Introduction to Wavelets

http://www.best.com/~agraps/
IEEEwave/IEEEwavelet.html

You may not hear much about wavelets just yet, but you will. Wavelets are extremely useful in a big range of math/engineering problems that can be analyzed by computer, which means the important ones.

Paleontology

Very old stuff on the Web? Why not? The dinosaur stuff here needs work, but some sites stand out for design excellence.

Prehistoric Shark Museum

http://turnpike.net/emporium/C/celestial/epsm.htm

The shark is nature's best example of the principle of "if it ain't broke, don't fix it." Prehistoric sharks look a lot like current sharks, except the ancient ones sometimes had bigger teeth. Comforting thought, eh?

Rad World

http://mindlink.net/fabrice_cordey/rad.htm

Radiolarians are microscopic creatures that are used to establish the date of ancient sea sediments. You can learn a lot from tiny things, and this is a particularly attractive, museum-style site.

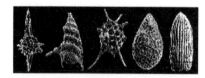

Physics

Always remember, the Web is a gift from the world physics community to you … although the Web's designers, the staff at the European Center for Nuclear Research in Geneva, probably didn't anticipate that every teen-aged kid in the U.S. would some day put up a home page with a picture of his or her dog. The physics category tends toward the serious, but there are some amusing cruising sites as well.

Buckyball Home Page

http://buckminster.physics.sunysb.edu/

Buckyballs are whimsically named carbon structures that resemble little soccer balls or geodesic domes. (*Bucky* refers to Buckminster Fuller, father of the dome.) Nobody knows quite what to do with them yet, but all sorts of industrial uses have been proposed, as soon as enough material becomes available.

Physics for Poets

http://seidel.ncsa.uiuc.edu/Phys150/

A remarkable course taught at the University of Illinois, and all of the material, including slide shows associated with the lectures, is available here. If you would like to take a dry run at a good, basic physics course before doing the real thing for a grade, this would be your best bet.

Web Advanced Research Project

http://www.hia.com/hia/pcr/

Way cool site for all sorts of interesting topics in the New Physics and other amazing things. Almost impossible to describe. You must visit this page yourself.

The Holography Page

http://www.hmt.com/holography/index.html

This is an index page for commercial and experimental holography. Order holograms, get them made from your photos, or learn to do it yourself.

Laser Programs

http://www-lasers.llnl.gov/

At the cutting edge of laser research — mainly because it has lots of your tax dollars to play with — is Lawrence Livermore Laboratory. This site tells you what it's doing with the biggest collection of lasers on earth.

Physics News

http://www.het.brown.edu/news/index.html

This is a bulletin board with links to all major physics research sites. Mostly for researchers.

Relativity

http://www.hia.com/hia/pcr/st1.html

This is a self-pace multimedia course, advertised as "for trekkies." You can't do much about relativity, but everyone nonetheless finds it fascinating compared to agriculture.

Psychology

There doesn't appear to be a clear boundary between psychology and mental health, at least in terms of Web classification categories. Most of the sites here, however, are concerned with academic research.

Behavior Analysis

http://www.coedu.usf.edu/behavior/
behavior.html

Tests, e-journals, research reports, and just plain gossip among the pros are featured at this University of South Florida resource. You might want to read the material on programmed instruction, because the Web is ideally suited to developing material for that endeavor.

Bjorn's Philosophy Page

http://www-und.ida.liu.se/
~y92bjoch/

The Web version of a nice undergraduate course in philosophy. It's just splendid that someone has gone to the trouble of doing this, so sign the guest register and tell Bjorn he's cool.

Human Languages

http://www.willamette.edu/~tjones/
Language-Page.html

This is a central source for information on languages past and present. You can tell these people are serious, as the introduction to the site is posted in such languages as Finnish, Afrikaans, and Basque — besides English and the other familiar ones.

Zoology

Electronic Zoo

http://netvet.wustl.edu/e-zoo.htm

Washington University has always been an Internet hotspot, and this zoo is a great, sophisticated attraction. Stop by some afternoon. In fact, drop in while you're at work!

Eurosquid

http://www.abdn.ac.uk/~nhi104/

There's just no way, after a long day of touring and reviewing index sites, we could pass up one called Eurosquid. Did you even know squid live in the North Atlantic?

Herp Pictures

http://gto.ncsa.uiuc.edu/pingleto/
lobby.html

OK, it's a bunch of pictures of snakes and amphibians. But they're very good pictures, and there seems to be vast interest in this topic among Netheads. Hmm.

Social Science

There has been considerable debate about what happens when you try to quantify the Humanities into a science. Some of the results of this approach have been important insights into human nature, the rediscovery of minority history, and the reexamination of canonical texts.

On the other hand, some of it has resulted in doctoral dissertations on Madonna.

And it seems like *all* of it has found its way to the Internet.

African Studies

(Note: For further information on African Studies, check the Society and Culture chapter, under Cultures: African.)

Black/African Related Resources (Art McGee's List)

http://www.sas.upenn.edu/
African_Studies/Home_Page/
mcgee.html

Art McGee's famous list of FTP sites, Gopher sites and other sources covering African- and African-American related studies and activism resources.

African Studies at U. Penn

http://www.sas.upenn.edu/
African_Studies/AS.html

This site has been called "definitive" and to the extent that anything on the ever-changing Net *can* be, it certainly lives up to that appellation. Among its many resources are information on the African Studies Association and a K-12 Africa teaching guide. It also has a search engine for UPenn servers.

Index - African Studies - WWW Virtual Library

http://www.w3.org/hypertext/
DataSources/bySubject/
AfricanStudies/africanWWW.html

Includes links to historically black colleges and universities, nationwide African Studies programs, organizations and historical and cultural sites.

African-American Studies

(Note: For further information on African-American Studies, check the Society and Culture chapter, under Cultures: African American.)

The Faces of Science: African-Americans in the Sciences

http://www.lib.lsu.edu/lib/chem/
display/faces.html

Profiles of African-American scientists. Also includes bibliography of sources for Technology and the role of African-Americans in education and scientific exploration.

AFROAM-L Griot Online [Afrinet]

http://www.afrinet.net/~griot/

Fascinating site with the complete online archives of the AFROAM-L mailing list (AFROAM-L@harvarda.harvard.edu), which averages nearly 6.5MB a month. Other offerings range from academic essays to African folktales that are fablelike and wonderful for children.

American Studies

Academia used to be a place where scholars appeared to compete to research the most arcane and esoteric subjects in all of human history, arcane and esoteric, of course, being merely the insider's terms for trivial and obscure. It was thought at the time that the situation couldn't possibly get worse. Then it did. With the emergence of Pop Culture as an academic discipline, some graduate students now strive for Ph.D.s in the self-evident and, to the hysterical wonder of laypeople, dedicate years of their lives to dissertations on such topics as, "Sex, Drugs and Rock 'n Roll: The Discourse of the American Imagination, 1955-1970."

Laypeople too have terms for such things — they call it self-parody.

American Studies Web

http://pantheon.cis.yale.edu/~davidp/amstud.html

Maintained by David Phillips, a doctoral candidate in American Studies at Yale. One of those sites that leaves you reeling with its comprehensiveness. Immerse yourself in subject-organized hypertext lists to more than 350 sites covering all aspects of American culture and archival documents.

ALSO RECOMMENDED:

Center For the Study of Southern Culture (at the University of Mississippi)

http://imp.cssc.olemiss.edu/

Featuring "The 1995 International Conference on Elvis Presley" and posters of William Faulkner. Shouldn't that be a conference on William Faulkner and posters of Elvis?

Anthropology and Archaeology

(Note: Please see the Science chapter, under Anthropology and Archaeology.)

Armenian Studies

(Note: For further information, check the Society and Culture chapter, under Cultures: Armenian.)

Armenian Research Center (at the University of Michigan)

http://www.umd.umich.edu/dept/armenian/

Information about programs at the center and general information about Armenia, including fact sheets on the Armenian Genocide and the current conflicts in Nagorno-Karabagh. As of this writing, the center is planning to include a searchable database.

Asian Studies

UCI Southeast Asian Archive

http://www.lib.uci.edu/sea/seahome.html

From the site: "Since the end of the Vietnam Conflict in 1975 a large number of refugees and immigrants from Cambodia, Laos, and Vietnam have come to the United States, and especially to California. In order to document their experiences in a new culture, the University of California, Irvine Library established the Southeast Asian Archive in 1987."

Index - Asian Studies - WWW Virtual Library

http://coombs.anu.edu.au/WWWVL-AsianStudies.html

Definitive and exhaustive.

Asian-American Studies

(Note: For further information on Asian-American Studies, check the Society and Culture chapter, under Cultures: Asian American.)

Asian American Resources

http://www.mit.edu:8001/afs/athena.mit.edu/user/i/r/irie/www/aar.html

Comprehensive links covering everything from professional events and cultural activities to academic journals and popular media.

ALSO RECOMMENDED:

Who Killed Vincent Chin?

http://bronze.ucs.indiana.edu/~tanaka/vincent/vincent.html

The answer is two white assailants who beat him to death two days before his wedding. They were given three years' probation and a $3,000 fine.

Communications Studies

Semiotics. Give generously. Perhaps they can find a cure.

(Note: For Journalism, please see the News chapter, under Journalism.)

American Communication Association

http://www.uark.edu/depts/comminfo/www/ACA.html

Surfer's delight — a truly *amazing* cornucopia of links. Perhaps even more amazingly, and what makes this a bookmark essential, is the well-ordered menu. Go from Telecommunications: Law, Policy, and Society with its up-to-the-minute menu of Internet legal controversies to links for Classical, Medieval, and Renaissance Rhetoric and the Oxford Arthurian Society to The Barbie Page (under Communication and Gender) to the 1901 edition of *Bartlett's Familiar Quotations* (under Study, Research, and Writing Skills).

Index - History of Communication Media Technologies

http://spot.colorado.edu/~rossk/history/histhome.html

Created by Kristina Ross, a doctoral candidate at the University of Colorado at Boulder, and featured in an article in *The Chronicle of Higher Education*, this site covers everything "from petroglyphs to pixels." It has bright, fresh graphics and an excellent organization. Impressive.

A L S O   R E C O M M E N D E D :

Propaganda Analysis

http://carmen.artsci.washington.edu/propaganda/home.htm

If some of the insights on this site seem obvious, it's because the Institute for Propaganda Analysis's *The Fine Art of Propaganda* was the source for them — in 1939. A good

review of terms is here, especially with another presidential campaign season already under way.

Data Collections

Imagine government agencies, private research centers and university graduate schools producing statistical studies that fill boxes, file cabinets, bookshelves, buildings, subterranean archives that catacomb across state borders. Now aren't you glad they invented networked computers?

(Note: For further information, check also the Government chapter, under Agencies: Census Bureau.)

Economics

(Note: Please see the Business and Economy chapter, under Economics.)

European Studies

In some quarters at least, the Europeans still think that Shakespeare and Joyce are more worthy of study than the Beatles and U2.

EuroDocs: Primary Historical Documents From Western Europe

http://library.byu.edu/~rdh/eurodocs/

A fascinating set of links that connect to Western Europe (mainly primary) historical documents that are transcribed, reproduced in facsimile, or translated.

Mannheim Centre for European Social Research

http://www.sowi.uni-mannheim.de/

The Mannheim Centre for European Social Research (MZES), at the University of Mannheim, was founded with a mandate to study "The Developed Industrial Societies and Western Europe in Transition." Sounds like fun, eh? The site contains a library (including a large statistics library) that can be searched online and links to academic and government sites in the field of European studies. In English and German.

Genealogy

(Note: Please see the Social Science chapter, under History: Genealogy.)

History

In a time of shrinking library budgets, the Internet has become a godsend to the study and reading of history. Many universities and museums have been munificent, giving generously of their Internet server space to host reams of public domain documents. In addition, many have shared resources from their own funded research. Now when the local library is only open three days a week, or the university library closes at 8, remember that you can still find a copy of *Beowulf* at 4 a.m. — in translation or facsimile. And the online copy of *Beowulf* is searchable to boot.

Eighteenth-Century Resources on the Net

http://www.english.upenn.edu/~jlynch/18th.html

Comprehensive eighteenth-century listings including literature, philosophy — even landscape gardening — by Jack Lynch, Ph.D. candidate in English literature at the University of Pennsylvania. One of those definitive sites that is excellent for scholars and students and intimidating as hell for laypeople. One has to wonder: When did he find time to read all this, let alone to compile it? Link to Jack Lynch's home page for a link to his superb page on Grammar and Style notes: http://www.english.upenn.edu/~jlynch/grammar.html. It's a substantial asset to the Web, gratefullywise.

History of Medicine Division, National Library of Medicine

http://www.nlm.nih.gov/hmd.dir/oli.dir/index.html

The library has included the complete text from its exhibitions, and "Online Images from the History of Medicine" — a searchable database of nearly 60,000 images from the prints and photographs collection (however, it seems to require some prior knowledge of its holdings).

Ancient History

Dead Sea Scrolls Exhibit

http://sunsite.unc.edu/expo/deadsea.scrolls.exhibit/intro.html

Descriptions and facsimiles from the Library of Congress exhibit.

Classics and Mediterranean Archaeology

http://rome.classics.lsa.umich.edu/welcome.html

Searchable database that appears to be definitive for Internet resources.

ALSO RECOMMENDED:

The Seven Wonders of the Ancient World

http://ce.ecn.purdue.edu/~ashmawy/7WW/

A very pretty site created by Alaa Ashmawy, a doctoral candidate in geotechnical engineering at Purdue, with well thought-out links that starts with that most frequent Seven Wonders FAQ, "What were they?" and goes on to provide a great deal of interesting history: The Great Pyramid of Giza was "the tallest structure on Earth for more than 43 centuries, only to be surpassed in height in the nineteenth century AD."

Egyptian Civilization: Papyrology

Papyrology

http://www.umich.edu/~jmucci/papyrology/home.html

"Welcome to the papyrology homepage." Could anything stand as a better statement of the confluence of old and new? An excellent site for scholars.

American History

American Memory from the Library of Congress

http://rs6.loc.gov/amhome.html

This is the start of the Library of Congress's contributions to the National Digital Library. At the moment, there seems to be no organizing principle other than showing off the variety of the holdings — and they are vast and wonderful. Among the items currently featured is the WPA oral history project, an absolute must for history teachers and their students and for anyone interested in "living" history. Most remarkably, in the sense of a medium coming full circle, there are downloadable copies of some of the earliest motion pictures (1897–1916) ever made.

La Belle

http://129.109.57.188/index.htm

The site follows the investigation of a recently discovered shipwreck, which may be La Belle, given as a gift by Louis XIV of France to the French explorer René Robert Cavelier, sieur de La Salle, the European discoverer of the Mississippi. "La Belle was lost in Matagorda Bay in 1686 during the explorer's final, disastrous expedition. If this preliminary identification proves correct, the shipwreck would be one of the most historically important shipwrecks ever identified in North America." The site includes background and links on maritime history, seventeenth century French and American history. A fascinating site.

U.S. Historical Documents

gopher://wiretap.spies.com/11/Gov/US-History

A miscellany of digitized documents from the Revolutionary War to World War II. For additional sources, see sites under Government.

Index - History Research Links

http://134.129.87.200/jrhome.htm

Created by James Ross, an Assistant Professor of Economic History and the History of Technology at State University in Fargo, North Dakota, this site and its links reflect his taste and specialty. Of special interest is a message board on the site, where people have taken to posting notification of their own history web sites — it should continue to be useful for updates in the field.

People

Papers of George Washington

http://poe.acc.Virginia.EDU/~gwpapers/GWhome.html

Excerpts and commentary from the ongoing curatorial project on the papers of George Washington. You think you send a lot of e-mail? When completely published, the collection of letters written to and by George Washington are projected to fill 85 volumes.

Benjamin Franklin: Glimpses of the Man

http://sln.fi.edu/franklin/rotten.html

Glimpses is an accurate description. Unlike the preceding scholarly Washington site, this site is geared more toward schoolchildren. (Parents — you may want to read up to get a jump on the kids!)

ALSO RECOMMENDED:

Shadows of the Past

http://d.armory.com/~zenugirl/sotp.html

For those who never outgrew their first cowboy movie. Perhaps you've been spending too much time on the computer, and your friends and family are telling you to get a life. Well, here's a place where you *can,* even though you may be about a century out of date. Shadows of the Past is an Old West reenactment group; its site gives background information, historical clothing resources, and links to other groups with names such as Bad Company, Gunslingers of the MotherLode, and the Sierra Outlaws. We could find no information on buckskin laptop cases.

(Note: If you're into this sort of thing, you might want to check Shauna Orr's 18th Century Seamstress page, where you can even order period clothing: http://www.inasec.ca/pers/jembree/shauna.htm (listed in Yahoo! under Business and Economy: Products and Services: Arts and Crafts).

Genealogy

Yahoo! lists 66 sites as of this writing, covering meta-sites, software, personal pages, and local genealogical societies. You'll also find museums, churches, and other online repositories.

Genealogy Home Page

http://ftp.cac.psu.edu/~saw/genealogy.html

A meta-site with links to resources across the Internet, including Usenet newsgroups.

Holocaust

Yad Vashem

http://yvs.shani.net/

"Normal human language is inadequate to describe an event like the Holocaust."

Journals

History Reviews On-Line

http://www.uc.edu/www/history/reviews.html

An excellent and useful site for both educator and layperson, this journal includes reviews of new scholarly works and biographies and other studies — and recommendations for their suitability within a college curriculum. The reviews often suggest companion volumes and provide much-needed contexts for the author's thesis.

Latin America

Latin America

http://history.cc.ukans.edu/history/reading_rooms/latin_america.html

Comprehensive hypertext list of sources in the field of Latin American history.

Maritime History

R.M.S. Titanic 83 Years Later

http://www.lib.virginia.edu/cataloging/vnp/titanic/titanic1.html

A superb site of analysis and primary source material from newspapers from the time. It also makes one thankful for Netscape's background tag.

The text appears over an image of the ocean on a foreboding, overcast day. A sense of doom, of falling beneath the waves pervades as you read.

Medieval Studies

Guide to Early Church Documents

http://www.iclnet.org/pub/resources/christian-history.html

A bookmark site for medievalists, it's truly catholic in its comprehensiveness, including not only writings of the Apolistic Fathers and later patristics, but contemporary Greek and Roman writings, timelines, and other sources.

(Note: Please see the Society and Culture chapter, under Religion: Christianity: Early Church Documents.)

Organizations

The organizations listed under this category are a mixture of scholarly societies and "Forward into the Past!"* re-enactors.

(Note: For further information on the Society for Creative Anachronism, see the Society and Culture chapter, under Alternative: Society for Creative Anachronism. *For information about Firesign Theatre, see the Firesign Theatre WWW Home Page http://mtritter.jpl.nasa.gov/firesign.html).

Labyrinth - Medieval Studies

http://www.georgetown.edu/labyrinth/labyrinth-home.html

"The Labyrinth project on the World Wide Web is designed to allow you to make your own Ariadne's thread through the maze of (medieval/

classical) information available on the Internet." *Mirabile Dictu!* Not only a marvelous site, a whole new metaphor for the Web.

(See also http://www.princeton.edu/~rhwebb/myth.html, a link on Myths & Legends. And don't miss http://www.mit.edu:8001/people/mouser/myth.html), in the Arts section of Yahoo!, under Literature: Mythology.)

Military History

(Note: For Veterans Information, see the Society And Culture chapter, under Veterans Affairs. The National Department of Veterans Affairs (VA) is listed on Yahoo! under Government: Agencies: Executive Branch: Department of Veterans.)

American Revolutionary War (Home Page for Re-enactment Organizations)

http://www.ccs.neu.edu/home/bcortez/revwar/revwar.html

Have a real problem with the way the American Revolutionary War turned out? Here's your chance to get in there and do your bit for His Majesty King George.

Redstone Arsenal

http://www.redstone.army.mil/history/home.html

A great starting point for students of American military history, this site has detailed essays about the Redstone Arsenal Complex in Huntsville, Alabama. Topics covered include the Gulf War, the space program, the WWII origins of the arsenal, and "Women at War," with quotes from primary sources from the period. This site should be on the bookmark list of

anyone interested in Women's Studies and African-American history: "Arsenal records noted that no demand was made for large numbers of black female employees until the local labor market was exhausted of white females. The lack of 'toilet facilities to take care of race distinctions peculiar to the South' was the reason given for this decision."

Mil-Hist

http://kuhttp.cc.ukans.edu/history/milhst/m_index.html

Well-organized site including text and graphical resources for what seems like every war since the dawn of time.

Civil War

The American Civil War is just far enough in the past to have obtained a romantic glow, yet still close enough for families to pass down first-hand stories and diaries of great-great-grandparents. You can feel all of that as you read through the holdings on the Internet, which vary from scholarly studies to dedicated reenactors to families who have made their ancestors' private correspondence available to the public.

The United States Civil War Center Louisiana State University

http://www.cwc.lsu.edu/

Facilitating the creation of a database with all private and institutional holdings of Civil War materials in the U.S. Already a great number of links to Civil War resources.

Civil War: Documents

Letters Home from a Soldier in the U. S. Civil War

http://www.ucsc.edu/civil-war-letters/home.html

There are several moving collections of letters from Civil War soldiers on the Web, all of which are worth reading. These are especially striking because they are presented by the descendants of the correspondents, and they tell of a love triangle interwoven with the story of the War.

Selected Civil War Photographs

http://rs6.loc.gov/cwphome.html

From the Library of Congress's collection of Civil War photographs (which includes most of the images made under the supervision of Matthew Brady, and others from private collections.) The site has a cross-indexed search on the photographs, which is a superb asset for researchers because it permits a search on images as well as subject. In other words, type *horse*, and the search engine retrieves any photograph containing a picture of a horse.

National Civil War Association

http://ncwa.org/

One of the premier "living history" organizations, recreating both sides of the Civil War. Contains links to other Civil War historical sites, and other reenactment organizations. If you think all you need to do to join is watch *Gone with the Wind* 20 times, check out the NCWA trivia test found on the Civil War Documents and Books site: http://www.access.digex.net/~bdboyle/docs.html

D-Day

D-Day

http://192.253.114.31/D-Day/Table_of_contents.html

A moving site from a very interesting source: "Patch American High School, located at Patch Barracks, Headquarters for US EUCOM, the United States European Command, in Vaihingen, a small section of Stuttgart, Germany. Built in 1979, Patch is a testbed site for technology insertion programs in the Department of Defense Dependents Schools system." Contains a link to an equally moving project on the fall of the Berlin Wall at http://192.253.114.31/Berlin/Introduction/Berlin.html.

Philippine-American War of 1899-1902

The War from a Parlor: Stereoscopic Images of the Philippine-American War and Soldiers' Letters Home

http://www.maxwell.syr.edu/unofficial/fjzwick/centennial/stereo/

This site is the ideal Internet museum-style exhibit — the stereoscopic images are small enough that they can appear "life-size" on a computer screen, and one can immediately read the accompanying text from the letters of American soldiers, which are ironically juxtaposed against the "happy natives" tourist images.

Vietnam War

Vietnam-era U.S. Government Documents

gopher://wiretap.spies.com/11/Gov/US-History/Vietnam

A rich collection of crucial documents from the Vietnam era. From President Eisenhower's letter to Ngo Dinh Diem to President Johnson's Tonkin Gulf Resolution to Senator John Kerry's "Vietnam Veterans Against the War Statement to the Senate Committee of Foreign Relations on April 23, 1971."

Images of My War

http://www.ionet.net/~uheller/vnbktoc.shtml

The private memoir of Ulf R. Heller, RVN. An excerpt: "We got on a plane at Binh Hoa and began the long flight home … The next thing I knew I was in San Francisco Airport … My mother had sent a green uniform to the airport Holiday Inn so I wouldn't freeze in my khakis. I changed and went to the restaurant to eat a good steak. I automatically reached into my back pocket and snapped open my Buck knife with one hand to cut my steak. The sound of the knife opening echoed through the room and everyone looked at me with my knife in the air."

World War II

World War II - "50 Years Ago"

http://www.webcom.com/~jbd/ww2.html

This site offers a day-by-day history of events during World War II and numerous historical links. But the most special parts of the site are the numerous anecdotes from veterans and survivors. Place a box of tissues next to your computer before you start to read these stories.

Voice of Hibakusha: Eye-witness accounts of the bombing of Hiroshima

http://129.171.129.67/mf/hibakusha/index.html

This site will more than use up the rest of the tissues from the last site. These are graphic, indelible accounts, and parents should judge whether or not their children are old enough to handle them.

Enola Gay Perspectives

http://www.glue.umd.edu/~enola/welcome.html

This site discusses the Smithsonian's controversial exhibit on the Enola Gay. It gives a complete, annotated chronology of the controversy that led to the resignation of the Director of the National Air and Space Museum. It also includes background on the war in the Pacific.

Memorial Hall of the Nanjing Massacre (1937-38)

http://www.arts.cuhk.hk/NanjingMassacre/NM.html

"In December 1937, Nanjing (China) fell to the Japanese imperial army. The Japanese army launched a massacre for six weeks. According to the records of several welfare organizations which buried the dead bodies after the massacre, around three hundred thousand people, mostly civilians and POWs, were brutally murdered … It is just one of the "wan ren keng" (pit of ten thousand corpses) which can be found in many Japanese occupied areas during the war."

Museums

The Firehouse Museum

http://www.globalinfo.com/noncomm/firehouse/Exhibit.HTML

Marvelous JPG graphic files of antique fire-fighting equipment. Excellent for students and photo researchers.

The International Museum of the Horse

http://www.horseworld.com/imhmain.html

Horsies! Actually, this superlative site is an encyclopedic resource on the history of the horse, starting with the Eohippus of 58 million years ago. "It is commonly believed that the great war-horses, also called destriers, were developed during the Middle Ages to support the great weight of the armored knight. Actually, a good suit of armor was not over 70 pounds in weight; and therefore, the horse would only be expected to carry some 250 to 300 pounds. The real reason large horses were useful was because their weight gave greater force to the impact of the knight's lance, both in warfare and in the tournament." An essential resource for anyone interested in the history of the horse, or needing images of horses.

Organizations

Organization of American Historians

http://www.indiana.edu:80/~oah/

This site at Indiana University includes other history links plus an online job bank.

Renaissance

Project Aldus

http://www.jhu.edu/~english/aldus/aldus.main.html

An archive for primary source and secondary materials related to the study of the English Renaissance/Early Modern Period.

Roman History

Index - Rome Project, The

http://www.nltl.columbia.edu/groups2/rome/rome.html

Comprehensive links on an extremely attractive, well-designed site including Internet resources on Roman subjects covering literature, philosophy, military issues, books and book reviews, and more. Includes an imagemap that actually *is* a map, with links to further resources on each of the Roman Provinces.

Science

History of the Light Microscope

http://www.duke.edu/~tj/hist/hist_mic.html

An extensive history of the Light Microscope beginning with early uses of the lens, until around 1900. Corrective lens-wearing historical reenactors will be grateful for this tidbit: "The modern reinvention of spectacles occurred around 1280-1285 in Florence, Italy."

If you're a collector of any kind of scientific or medical antiques, make sure to link over to the Sci/Med Antique Collecting System home page at Duke University for some excellent pointers on how to avoid getting ripped off by dealers (http://www.duke.edu/~tj/beware.html).

Indices

Several general indexes are listed here, and each one is excellent and certainly beats waiting two weeks for that InterLibrary loan.

ALSO RECOMMENDED:

Alternate History

http://thule.mt.cs.cmu.edu:8001/sf-clearing-house/bibliographies/alternate-histories/

Whew. Had your fill of the real stuff? Have some fun with The Usenet Alternate History List, an annotated bibliography of "what if" fictional histories maintained by R.B. Schmunk. A favorite example: "What if: After defeat by Cromwell at Worcester, Charles II accepted the invitation to place his throne in Virginia and took control of British N. America. Story: Charles would have been a more kingly figure on his return to London, and the neglect of the colonies which provoked the Revolution would not happen." Posted quarterly (January, April, July, October) to the Usenet newsgroups rec.arts.sf.written, alt.history.what-if, rec.answers, alt.answers and news.answers.

Today in History

http://www.unison.com/wantinfo/today

Trivia-buff and editorial writer heaven. Presented as a free service by Unison Software. Didja you know that on September 8, 1157, King Richard "the Lion Hearted" I of England was born and on September 8, 1966, *Star Trek* debuted?

Latin American Studies

Latin American Economic Data Bank

http://milkman.cac.psu.edu/~rlg7/hist/proj/garner.html

Economic data from the fifteenth through the nineteenth centuries for Latin America. (Hint: Definitely read the READ.ME files to make sense of it all.)

Index - Latin American Studies - WWW Virtual Library

http://lanic.utexas.edu/las.html

A good collection of pointers to institutes and schools dealing with Latin American history.

Linguistics and Human Languages

The Human-Languages Page

http://www.willamette.edu/~tjones/Language-Page.html

Actually, that's human and other languages (four sites list Klingon). A growing site that is attempting to be a comprehensive index to all the human language resources on the Net. Includes many "English to Other" dictionaries and links to software for non-Roman alphabets. It will include a search engine.

Indices

Yamada WWW Language Guides

http://babel.uoregon.edu/yamada/guides.html

The Yamada WWW Language Guides claim to be the definitive guide to language resources on the World Wide Web, and there certainly doesn't seem to be any reason to doubt them. *Incredible.* "The guides contain information about 103 languages. There are 112 fonts in our archives, for 40 languages." Check out the name of their server!

Linguistics Resources

http://www.sil.org/linguistics/linguistics.html

The Summer Institute of Linguistics had missionary origins — which gives it tremendous resources on obscure, indigenous languages.

Applied Linguistics WWW Virtual Library

http://www.bbk.ac.uk/Departments/AppliedLinguistics/VirtualLibrary.html

Still another definitive site on language and linguistics.

ALSO RECOMMENDED:

Bibliography of Planned Languages

http://www.io.com/~hmiller/biblio.html

Apparently Esperanto has cousins. Absolutely fascinating in an incredibly arcane sort of way. To people who are annoying you: "Sorry, I don't understand. I only speak Volapük."

Names That Sound Like or are Verbs

http://fas-www.harvard.edu/
~jsbloom/name_verb.html

Yes, really. That's all this site is, a hypertext, alphabetized list of "Names That Sound Like or are Verbs." You give your kid a computer for Christmas. He might learn enough to get into Harvard at 15. He might try to break into the Pentagon. Or he might come up with something like this. You know, maybe giving the kid a calligraphy set wouldn't be such a bad idea. (On the other hand — these kids apparently *did* get into Harvard!)

The Darmok Dictionary

http://www.wavefront.com/~raphael/
darmok/darmok.html

A site that asks the why-didn't-anybody-think-of-it-before-*Star Trek* question about the Enterprise's ongoing mission: "Doesn't it seem a little odd that … a ship that's going to encounter unknown aliens doesn't include some sort of professional linguist?"

Languages

An extensive section with many varied offerings ranging from software for non-Roman alphabets to audio files of pronunciation for tourists.

(Note: For more information, see also the Society and Culture chapter, under Cultures.)

English

Please see also: *Grammar and Style Guide* by Jack Lynch, previously listed, at http://www.english.upenn.edu/
~jlynch/grammar.html.

English Usage Page

http://www.webcom.com/~kcivey/
engusage/

H.W. Fowler might be overjoyed — or might weep. Links to many resources including Strunk's *Elements of Style* (without White, this is the now public-domain 1918 original). A special favorite: Henry Churchyard's "Singular 'Their' in Jane Austen: Anti-Pedantry Page" (http://uts.cc.utexas.edu/
~churchh/austheir.html). So, like, hopefully, you're gonna learn something.

Writers' Resources on the Web (INDEX)

http://www.interlog.com/~ohi/www/
writesource.html

From the World Wide Web Virtual Library, superb and comprehensive, one of its best sections.

Middle East Studies

(Note: For more information, please see also the Society and Culture chapter, under Cultures: Arabic, Palestine, Turkish, et.al.)

Middle East Studies Association Bulletin

http://www.cua.edu/www/mesabul/

This journal is a service of the Catholic University of America. Contains links, books, articles, online resources, and information about conferences.

The Middle East-North Africa Internet Resource Guide

http://www.alquds.org/middle-east-guide/contents.html

From the University of Utah. An excellent, detailed hypertext index to Gopher sites, mailing lists, Web sites, and telnet sites of Middle Eastern resources.

Philosophy

"Philosophy is nothing more than an unusually obstinate attempt to bring all of our ideas into a consistent and harmonious relationship."
— William James

Philosophers

Arisbe: A Home for Charles S. Peirce Studies on the Internet

http://www.peirce.org/peirce/

Hypertext editions of all the works of the seminal American philosopher, along with links to other philosophy resources.

The Jacques Maritain Center at Notre Dame

http://www.nd.edu/Departments/
Maritain/ndjmc.htm

The Notre Dame archives of the great Catholic philosopher. The site also includes many other philosophy-related links, including the works of Aristotle and both a Latin Wordlist and Grammar Aid and a French Dictionary and Grammar Aid.

Chinese

Chinese Philosophy

http://www.monash.edu.au/cc/staff/sas/sab/WWW/index.html

Comprehensive Chinese philosophy site with tons of information and links to other similar sites on the Net.

Ethics

MacLean Center for Clinical Medical Ethics at the University of Chicago

http://ccme-mac4.bsd.uchicago.edu/CCMEHomePage.html

The kind of philosophical questions more and more people are likely to encounter.

ALSO RECOMMENDED:

Objectivism

Objectivism on the WWW

http://avocado.wustl.edu/~diana/objectivism/hsieh/apodrink.html

A comprehensive list of Objectivist sites on the Net, of which there are many. Along with the serious stuff, it links to Paul Hsieh's "a.p.o. Drinking Game" at http://avocado.wustl.edu/~diana/objectivism/hsieh/apodrink.html. Much of the scoring is peculiar to a.p.o. (alt.philosophy.objectivism), but a great deal of it is all too familiar to anyone who's been on Usenet for awhile. Examples: "Someone threatens to put someone else in a *kill file* — 1 shot — Someone actually admits that they were wrong — 5 shots."

Recreation and Leisure Studies

A field whose very name is an oxymoron.

Index - Recreation and Leisure Studies

http://www.geog.ualberta.ca/als/rlsres.html

Links to academic departments and programs in the field and related sites.

Academy of Leisure Sciences

http://www.geog.ualberta.ca/als/als1.html

Although its name sounds like a *Saturday Night Live* routine (and from its logo, the academy's members do get the joke), the site actually presents several very provocative essays on the subject of leisure and society's priorities.

Russian and East European Studies

(Note: For further information on Russia and Eastern Europe, see the Society and Culture chapter, under Cultures: Polish, Russian, Tuva, Ukraine.)

Russian and East European Network Information Center

http://reenic.utexas.edu/reenic.html

The University of Texas at Austin Russian and East European Network Information Center includes a Country Directory for Eastern Europe and the former Soviet Union (FSU) with full cultural, economic, and historic info for each nation.

Index - Russian and East European Studies

http://www.pitt.edu/~cjp/rshist.html

Annotated hypertext list of Russian and East European Internet resources.

Sociology

(Note: For further information on sociology, check the Government and Society and Culture chapters.)

Research Engines for the Social Sciences

http://www.carleton.ca/~cmckie/research.html

Universal Codex for the Social Sciences. Never did a site name itself better. Impressive.

Criminal Justice

Criminal Justice Links

http://www.stpt.usf.edu/~greek/cj.html

Compiled by Dr. Cecil Greek, Associate Professor of Criminology at the University of South Florida. Extremely comprehensive, very well-organized, and astoundingly eclectic hypertext lists of Internet resources, presented under a distressingly attractive picture of Alcatraz.

Institutes

ANU Demographic Archive

http://coombs.anu.edu.au/ResFacilities/ANUDemogPage.html

Includes dissertation abstracts and the searchable archives of the Demographic-List international e-mail forum.

Urban Studies

Varied resources for students and professionals, ranging from conservative to progressive approaches.

Planning Commissioners Journal: Citizen Planners Resource Center

http://www.webcom.com/~pcj/welcome.html

A quarterly publication designed for people who serve on local planning and zoning boards. Includes links to planning resources.

Planning and Architecture Internet Resource Center

http://arch.buffalo.edu:8001/internet/h_pa_resources.html

This is a superlative site collecting just about all the stuff on the Net for professionals in architecture and urban planning with annotated descriptions.

Women's Studies

A newly hired female scientist at a nationally renowned research institute phones the institute's female office administrator.

Scientist: "What are the library's hours?"

Administrator: "Secretaries can't use the library."

Scientist: "I'm not a secretary."

Administrator: "Then what are you?"

Similar true stories are at http://www.ai.mit.edu/people/ellens/Gender/humor.html

Women's Wire

http://www.women.com/

Well, they got the domain name right, for sure. They've also put up a darned good magazine, strikingly designed and a great read. And they've got Nicole Hollander's *Sylvia*!

Organizations

International Network of Women in Technology

http://www.witi.com/

"A professional association of women representing a tremendous diversity of backgrounds, positions and disciplines working in and for technology organizations, academia and governmental agencies." An important, growing, and exciting organization with the best acronym in the business (WITI).

Publications

Women in Higher Education

http://www.itis.com/wihe/

A monthly newsletter subscribed to by women administrators, staff, and faculty in universities in the U.S. and Canada. Includes online job listings.

Institutes

University of Colorado - Women's Resource Center

http://ucsu.colorado.edu/~coult/wrc/wrc.html

Excellent links to Net resources and a searchable database of Net listings and holdings from its collection.

Indices

Feminist Activist Resources on the Net

http://www.igc.apc.org/women/feminist.html

Organized by subject and geared toward activism, with an excellent overview annotation of the listed resources.

E-shirtz! Project your cyber-side

http://turnpike.net/emporium/N/networth/index.htm

E-shirtz are fun, quality t-shirts that sport your e-mail address or URL. For those who don't mind being somewhat, uh, geeky in public. Each shirt also comes with a matching bumper sticker. This is a funny site.

Net Sweats and Tees

http://www.icw.com/netsweat/netsweat.html

Sweatshirts for net surfers, online. The site also offers a number of sweatshirts and long-sleeved tees from famous alpine ski resorts throughout the world, along with weather links, resort background info, and phone numbers.

Route 66

http://www.route-66.com/jeans.html

Looking for used Levis? I thought so. You'll want to check this site out for its extensive selection of Levis and other clothing. Remember: They're not just the clothes you wear, they're how you live your life. Or something.

Architecture

Glance up from your computer screen next time you're on the Web and ask yourself if your home is as airy, attractive, and comfortable as you'd like. If not, perhaps some time spent with an architect who appreciates the unique needs of a cyberjockey like you might be an appropriate step to take.

Beezley Designs & Production

http://www.so-cal.com/bdp/

Small, efficient building design firm specializing in small to large, detail-oriented, custom home and addition designs.

George Thomas Howard Associates

http://emporium.turnpike.net/G/GTHA/index.htm

For the actor in you: an internationally known, full-service theatre consulting firm with offices and an online presence based in glamorous Hollywood, California.

Holmes & Narver, Inc.

http://www.csn.net/~faulhabe/hn.htm

A full service architecture, engineering, communications, and technology company providing fully integrated solutions for companies and individuals.

InterCAD Company, Inc.

http://www.village.com/intercad/welcome.html

Computer-assisted design (CAD) conversion services for companies wanting to save money when converting engineering drawings to computer databases.

Lord, Aeck & Sargent, Inc.

http://ideanet1.ideanet.com/~las/

An architectural firm recognized for design innovation, advanced computer technology, and effective project leadership.

Arts & Crafts

Whether you're looking for works by great masters or pop-art posters, Yahoo! is a great place to start your searching.

Christies International

http://www.christies.com/

World renowned art auctioneers with global selling offices. Site includes upcoming sales listings arranged by location and type, a story on a spotlighted object of the month, and contact information for potential buyers and sellers.

Parallax Gallery

http://www.colossus.net/rwsa/parallax_gallery.html

An unusual collection of outstanding art objects, fine art, jewelry, mineral specimens, sculpture, blown glass, and even espresso to assuage your thirst.

Gallery of The Proletariat

http://www.insync.net/~agitfoto/proletar.html

Fine art work by local Texas artists. Features items available for sale direct from the artists.

Jon Keegan Illustration

http://web.syr.edu/~jmkeegan/Default.html

Freelance illustrator Jon Keegan's Web page offers a fun online sampling of his portfolio, resume, and miscellaneous goodies. Also of interest to artists, publishers, and other prospective clients in need of a Net-savvy illustrator.

Lone Star Gallery

http://www.pic.net/uniloc/lonestar/

Classic artwork, Dallas Cowboy photography, and Hubble Space telescope photographs. How eclectic can you get?

Number 9 - The Artist's Resource

http://www.tesser.com/number9/

Marketing and business services to artists offering their works for sale and encouraging smart business practices among artists on the Internet. A valuable online resource for anyone engaged in creative endeavors.

Automotive

Yes, you can actually buy a car on the Web. See the Products section (later in this chapter). But if you're in the auto manufacturing business, is the Net still for you? Absolutely.

AutoGroup, Inc.

http://www.tpoint.net/autogroup/

This group desires to facilitate electronic automotive commerce between consumers, dealers, vendors, and manufacturers.

Alamo Rent A Car - Freeways

http://www.freeways.com/

A fast and easy way to reserve a car — online. But that's not all — you'll also find travel tips, scenic drives in popular destinations, and even some travel games to keep the kids entertained.

Aviation

Learn how to fly a plane — even commercially. Or buy new parts for your existing flyer.

Aviation On-Line Network

http://www.airparts.com/airparts/

This site contains the most current, up-to-date aviation material ever assembled in a single electronic library.

Comair Aviation Academy

http://www.mindspring.com/~beets/comair.html

Airline training for all experience levels and an outstanding airline pilot placement program!

Biomedical

The biomedical field definitely qualifies as high-tech, so it's no surprise to find a variety of biomedical firms with a presence on the Internet.

Cambridge Healthtech Institute

http://www.xensei.com/conferences

Established to facilitate the discussion and exchange of technical/commercial information through the organization and sponsorship of biomedical conferences.

Life Technologies

http://www.lifetech.com

Producer of Gibco BRL products, now offers Custom Primer ordering and information on the Internet. This site also contains Life Technologies' Training Center Schedule and information about the company.

Nanothinc

http://www.nanothinc.com/

Fascinating information services about nanotechnology (extremely small machines) and related enabling technologies, which include supramolecular chemistry, protein engineering, molecular design and modelling software.

Books

Where to get more of what you're reading right now. Publishers and booksellers have been some of the first to use the Web to enhance their businesses. Books are all over the Web.

Battle Street Books

http://netshop.net/BSB/

An Internet catalog of works by author and playwright Ernest Langford, featuring the novel *Kingdom of Chombuk* and others, plus short stories and dramas.

Dutton's Brentwood Bookstore

http://www.earthlink.net/~duttons/

Dutton's is the largest independent bookstore in Southern California with over 100,000 titles and an extensive selection of compact discs, laser discs, and CD-ROMs.

InfoBook Electronic Bookstore

gopher://gopher.interlink.net/11s/services/mc3

InfoBook is the electronic version of MC3 Computer Books, a bookstore specializing in technical and reference books. Its selection of more than 10,000 titles is intended to offer useful works to people ranging from the introductory level to seasoned professionals.

M.E. Sharpe

http://usa.net/mesharpe/mesh.html

M.E. Sharpe prides itself on producing timely books and journals in the fields of Asian Studies, Economics, European & Russian Area Studies, History, and Political Science, and its online Web site offers a glimpse of many of its most popular titles.

Northtown Books

.http://www.northcoast.com/unlimited/product_directory/ntb/ntb.html

Features a stock of more than 27,000 titles and 300 periodicals with an emphasis on literary fiction, politics, environmental studies, women's issues, gay and Native American issues, travel guides, and children's books.

The Space Between

http://www.tagsys.com/Ads/SpaceBetween/

Bookstore with info on UFOs, secret societies, conspiracy theories, fringe science, lost worlds, survival issues, western esoterica, world origin theories, and more other weird things than you can shake a stick at!

Chemicals

Manufacturing companies are discovering the Web, and there are already many sites put up by chemical manufacturers.

Aspen Technology, Inc.

http://www.aspentec.com/

This company produces a variety of products serving the simulation and modeling needs of the chemical process industries.

AVEX Electronics

http://www.huber.com/Avex/AVEXHome.html

With manufacturing facilities throughout the United States, Europe, and the Pacific Rim, AVEX is one of the largest contract providers of integrated manufacturing and engineering services.

ChemSOLVE

http://www.eden.com/~chemsolv/

Site offers a virtual environmental analytical laboratory, specializing in analytical services and providing reference software for the environmental professional.

Lanxide Coated Products

http://www.ravenet.com/lanxcoat/

Titanium carbide coated graphite components with exceptional wear, corrosion and temperature resistance, for the chemical, electronic, glass, fiber, paper and metallurgical industries. Could be a good replacement for your current trackball or mouse too.

Collectibles

Coins or stamps, bottle caps or silver spoons, everyone collects *something*.

Apple Basket Antiques and Gifts!

http://wmi.cais.com/abasket/index.html

Hand-crafted wrought iron gifts from Amish craftsmen of Lancaster County Pennsylvania, with a catalog online.

Antique Networking, Inc.

http://www.smartpages.com/antique/

An online database designed to network buyers and sellers of high-end antiques locally, nationally, and internationally. It is utilized by antique dealers and their customers, brokers, collectors, trade show organizers, and repair/restoration shops.

Antiques Oronoco

http://www.ic.mankato.mn.us/antiques/AOronoco.html

Specializing in quality furniture (original, refinished, and "in the rough") and glassware, Antiques Oronoco carries hundreds of unique items in many categories.

Coin Universe

http://www.coin-universe.com/collectors/coins/

The starting point for numismatics and anyone interested in coins and coin collecting. The site contains pointers to directories of coin dealers, Internet sites that have to do with coin collecting, and coin shows.

Reyne Hogan Antiques

http://www.tias.com/RHA/

Reyne Hogan Antiques buys and sells American and European art glass, depression and carnival glass, estate and costume jewelry, and fine porcelain and pottery, with a fine online gallery explaining each of these types of antiques.

Communications and Media Services

Great designs, works of art, and online spots don't just happen — they're created by teams of creative folks who supplement the knowledge and experience of their clients. That's what communications and media services focus on: fine-tuning your message and turning you into a major player.

Caribou Visual Presentations

http://www.maine.com/caribou/

A 35mm slide service bureau and information resource that produces slides, overhead transparencies, and associated hardcopy for use in business, scientific, medical, and educational presentations.

CircumStance Design Studio

http://www.circumstance.com/enter/

An innovator among interactive studios. CircumStance transforms interactive technologies into media as compelling and memorable as the best of television, film, and graphic arts.

Hart Consulting

http://www.hartcons.com

Quality Web page design and construction. This site also offers writing and editing for online and paper distribution.

Haywood + Sullivan, Inc.

http://www.hsdesign.com/

Graphic design firm specializing in packaging, user interface design, multimedia development, and identity systems.

Intuitive Systems

http://www.intuitive.com/

Interface design company focused on building easily understood systems both for software applications and online presences. This site also includes some excellent articles and tutorials discussing online page design and the Internet.

Metzger Associates

http://usa.net/metzger/

Boulder, Colorado-based firm provides media relations, writing services, investor relations, and online communications for clients across the country.

Computers

A category in which it's difficult to imagine businesses that aren't already on the Internet, at some level or other. Also, see the Computers and Internet chapter.

Apple Computer, Inc.

http://www.apple.com/

A great resource for anyone using or looking to buy an Apple product or find out what's coming down the pipeline. If you're not a Mac user, the "Apple History" timeline alone is worth the visit.

ARSoftware

http://www.clark.net/pub/arsoftwa/

ARSoftware, a wholly-owned subsidiary of Applied Research Corporation, is an international electronic publisher of scientific and technical software applications.

Arztec Computer Resources

http://www.Arztec.COM/Arztec/

Primary focus is the import and the export of computer components and supplies. Through international contacts, Arztec provides customers with siginificant savings.

Avaika Networks Corporation

http://www.io.com/~webpub/avaika/index.html

High-speed network products that enable users to run distributed, time-critical applications effectively.

Changing Technologies

http://www.mindspring.com/~cti/home.html

Network and personal computing management tools to help reduce support costs.

Compression Technologies, Inc.

http://compression.com/

Offering a family of data link optimization products that deliver, on average, two to five times the throughput normally available on existing data links.

Computer Solutions

gopher://ftp.std.com/11/vendors/compsol

A full-service computer store that provides hardware, software, training, and networking solutions to businesses, educational institutions, and individuals.

CyberStar

http://www.vistech.net/users/cstar/

Buyer and seller of used and refurbished data communications and networking equipment, including routers, terminal servers, CSU/DSUs, modems, ISDN, multiplexors, transceivers, and bridges.

Data Exchange Corporation

http://www.dex.com/

A leader in providing contract manufacturing, end-of-life product support, computer peripheral depot repair, and worldwide inventory management systems for OEM, resellers, and end users in the minicomputer and microcomputer markets.

WORLD LEADER · DEPOT REPAIR — Data Exchange Corp

Eagle Nest Intelligence

http://kaleidoscope.bga.com/eaglenest/eaglenest.html

A comprehensive line of SPARC-compatible workstations — specializing in custom software installation and configuration.

Electronic Systems, Inc.

http://www.esr.com/

This site features information about Banyan, an online GSA schedule for Federal buyers of networking products.

Ensemble Information Systems, Inc.

http://www.ensemble.com/

Software that automatically delivers the full text of *The Wall Street Journal* via DowVision and the *New York Times* News Service directly to your desktop.

Future Computer Industries, Inc.

http://futureci.isdn.inch.com/

One of the largest providers of interactive media solutions for high-end multimedia and the World Wide Web.

GE Rental

http://www.ge.com/gec/pcrental.html

Need a Mac or PC for a few weeks, or a Unix machine for the weekend? Check out GE Rental, the largest renter of computer equipment in the United States for more than 20 years.

IBM

http://www.ibm.com/

No business directory would be complete without an IBM listing. As you would expect, IBM offers a comprehensive site detailing their gazillion product offerings. The site also contains a list of their trademarked names that rivals a phone book in length.

InfoSouth

http://fly.hiwaay.net/~beangl/infosouth.html

A full-service factory and authorized technical repair facility servicing the complete line of consumer electronic goods.

InterActive Computing

http://www.mind.net/ic/

Used Macintosh and IBM-compatible computer reseller for both notebook and desktop systems. They buy, sell, and trade used notebook computers and have listings online.

ISIS International

ftp://ftp.netcom.com/pub/is/isis/home.html

ISIS International specializes in Macintosh business and connectivity solutions. Its products include System 7 Pack, ISIS Notes, and Flash-Data.

LAN Performance Labs

http://www.ftel.com/t100/lpl_home.html

State-of-the-art 100 megabit/second, high-speed fast Ethernet LAN adapter solutions, perfect for the overworked Internet server site.

Meyer Consulting

http://www.phone.net/

Unix consulting, document writing and editing, World Wide Web services, and extensive Amiga expertise.

Microlytics

http://www.microlytics.com/

White and yellow pages telephone directories, multimedia, and natural language interfaces.

Microplex Systems Ltd.

http://www.microplex.com/

Designer and manufacturer of local and wide-area network communications equipment since October 1978, located in Burnaby, a borough of beautiful Vancouver, British Columbia, Canada.

Mind Logic

http://www.crl.com/~jdulaney/logic.html

Deep discount CD-ROM discs, hardware, and multistandard video gear. Freebie shareware, images, and icons are all available at this site.

Mount Baker Software

http://www.mount-baker.com/~bminor/MtBaker.html

Easy to use, high-quality OS/2 apps. A new personal financial package for OS/2 called Easy Finances is featured on this Web page.

NECX Direct

http://necxdirect.necx.com/docroot/index.html

NECX was one of the first companies to utilize Web advertising on a large scale. It is a large online computer product store that offers almost anything. It is well organized and simple to use.

NuTek

http://nutek.sj.scruznet.com/

A California-based computer company that offers useful utility products for Macintoshes and PCs running Windows.

PC Heidens

http://www.teleport.com/~pcheiden/

Computer hardware and CD-ROM software at discount prices. Choose from more than 900 CD-ROM titles.

Silicon Graphics

http://www.sgi.com/

The kings of 3-D show their stuff. If you have a fast connection to the Net, this is a highly entertaining site. If you have a 14.4 modem (or less), click cautiously. (And, of course, all the company product information is here as well.)

Software Factory

http://www.softfact.com

A wide range of services offered, from simple diskette duplication to complete turnkey solutions, including package design and fulfillment services.

SolTech Systems Corporation

http://www.soltech.com/

Value-Added Reseller of products and services for Sun Microsystems Computer Corporation, Cisco Systems, Inc., Cray Communications, Inc., and Xylogics, Inc. Reseller of SunBelt.Net Internet services; Preferred Systems Integrator for Oracle Corporation software products.

Sun Microsystems, Inc.

http://www.sun.com/

A great resource for anyone using or looking to buy a Sun product, hardware or software. In addition to product info and customer service resources, the site also contains interesting feature stories.

Technetix, Inc.

http://teknetix.com/

A value-added reseller of Sun Microsystems and Hewlett Packard workstations in southeastern Wisconsin. Its primary focus is systems integration of Unix workstations and servers with X-stations, Novell networks, personal computers, minicomputers, and mainframes.

Total Systems Inc.

http://www.lynqs.com/TSI/

Focusing on networking and networking accessories, from Novell software to Network Interface Cards. It also features PC-server motherboards.

United Computer Exchange Corp. (UCE)

http://www.uce.com./uce.html

A great place to get used price guides and to list used equipment for sale (and, of course, to look for used equipment to buy).

Webalog, Inc.

http://figment.fastman.com/vweb/html/vidmain.html

An information source for the exciting and fast-paced world of desktop video.

Wilson WindowWare, Inc.

http://oneworld.wa.com/wilson/pages/

Wilson WindowWare develops, recommends, and sells software that runs in the Microsoft Windows and Windows NT environments.

X Communications Multimedia

http://www.webcom.com/~xcomm/

This is an online multimedia firm with a hip site that includes interviews and multimedia presentations featuring alternative music soundtracks.

Zocalo

http://www.zocalo.com/

Site features networking and interface design for Macintosh, Microsoft Windows, and NeXT computers.

Construction

Build we must, even in cyberspace.

HPC Holland bv

http://support.nl/HPC/

Design and engineering of superstructures for industrial buildings, asbestos removal, and placement of hydraulic 13-person elevators to existing flats.

Kajima Corporation

http://www.kajima.co.jp/

Kajima is one of the most famous general construction companies in Japan. Online it introduces you to its latest technologies and provides lots of information about civil engineering and architecture.

Shilstone Companies

http://rampages.onramp.net/~shilston/shilstone.html

Concrete consulting firm specializing in architectural concrete, concrete mixture proportioning, and concrete quality control.

Consulting

When it's time to expand your company, an excellent alternative to hiring more people is to bring in a team of consultants, specializing in just what you need.

Asset Partnership

http://www.rednet.co.uk/homepages/whitlam/whitlam.html

Management development, organizational change, learning, and the achievement of human potential are all part of what this firm offers.

Andersen Consulting

http://www.ac.com/

An international management and technology consulting organization whose mission is to help its clients change in order to become more successful. The organization helps its clients link technology, strategy, processes, and people.

D.L. Boone & Company, Inc.

http://www.digex.net/boone.html

Site dedicated to creating a world-class professional services organization using the existing infrastructure of small (usually one-person, home-office) firms and talented and experienced individuals on the Net.

Formula Group

http://www.netaxs.com/people/formula/

Providing goal management, business strategy design and planning, operational analysis, quality management, and training services.

Marketing Services International

http://africa.com/pages/msi/page1.htm

A well-established international business development company, MSI has the rare ability to provide practical and effective solutions to companies ready to find, develop, or expand their markets.

Prism Performance Systems

http://argus-inc.com/prism/index.html

Site talks about this full-service training and consulting organization providing services that assist clients in achieving performance systems which result in maximum productivity and competitiveness.

Performance Enhancement Group, Ltd.

http://mfginfo.com/service/peg/peg.htm

A development consulting firm specializing in teambuilding, benchmarking, customer and employee surveys, and continuous improvement technologies.

SAIC Los Altos

http://losaltos.saic.com/

A leader in the development of risk, reliability, and safety methodology.

SAIC applies those techniques on actual processing plants, aircraft, and other large engineering systems. An interesting Web site.

Conventions and Conferences

Does it seem like you always hear about the coolest conferences the day after they end? Wish you could attend some of the biggest ones but don't have the time? Then you're not using your online resources. Tsk tsk.

Conference Copy Inc.

http://www.confcopy.com/TAPES

Firm specializes in the on-site recording of major educational events and the production of audio and video cassettes for immediate availability to the attendees.

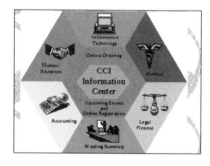

A Day At The Consumer Electronics Show (CES)

http://www.halcyon.com/ces/welcome.html

A Day At The Consumer Electronics Show allows users to experience the thrill of one of Las Vegas's largest shows. CES visitors experience a myriad of consumer electronic products — from games to peripherals to software. Now you can see some of them yourself through this fun virtual photo tour.

Corporate Services

Companies offering services to larger businesses.

Background Verification Service

http://www.mountain.net/hp/marcom/hitec.htm

Employers use the services of this firm to conduct criminal history, credit report, and prior employer checks on potential or current employees.

Creative-Leadership Consultants, Inc.

http://www.cts.com/~clc/

Creative-Leadership Consultants is a human resources and management consulting organization specializing in the selection and development of people.

Grant & Associates: Safety Program Consultants

http://www.northcoast.com/unlimited/services_listing/grant/grant.html

Provides effective safety programs by interacting with employers to meet their needs. Each program is customized to fit the specific needs of individual employers based on industry standards and regulations.

Countries

Geographically-based business is alive and well online.

Contraste Canada Inc.

http://www.contraste.com/

Firm specializes in large WAN network implementation, networked banking, and Internet application development with a comprehensive Web site.

Delta Computers Oy

http://www.jsp.fi/delta/

Finnish firm providing solutions for the electronic publishing market. It offers consulting and analysis and installation, and has its own software department which is actively involved with the latest products and releases, and which writes solutions specifically tailored for customer needs.

Digital Island

http://www.isn.net/di/

An Internet sanity, systems consulting, dance and poetry marketing, and nifty ideas company based in Kingston, Prince Edward Island, Canada — right next door to a field of dairy cows, who also make an appearance on its Web page.

Duine Adviesburo Netherlands

http://www.zeelandnet.nl/duine/

Independent brokerage firm specializing in insurance, retirement plans, employee benefits, mortgages, tax-friendly investments, and savings and loans in Holland. A good presence online.

European Consultancy Services

http://mkn.co.uk/help/extra/people/EUGRANTS/

A comprehensive European Union grants-identification, submission, advice, and lobbying service for all types of organizations both within the European Union and outside its political boundaries.

MediaNet Berlin - Brandenburg / Germany

http://www.Contrib.Net/MediaNet/MediaNet.html

Media-related information system with a local Berlin and Brandenburg media-address database and lots of information for movie professionals.

Page de France

http://gplc.u-bourgogne.fr:8080/pdf/

The first French bookstore on Web. Buy all the French books at the same price as if you were in France, no matter where you live on the planet.

Paideia

http://www.nl.net/~paideia/

Paideia provides the resources for earning a global masters degree on the Internet. The program of study is based on the creation of a portfolio, participation in peer dialogue groups, interaction with peers and mentors for critique, and the taking of an examination in Amsterdam.

Shopping City Austria

http://www.sca.co.at/eabin/pwrap/sca/

Shopping City Austria is a virtual city where you can buy products from all over Austria. Find out about the latest tourist attraction, watch art galleries, visit some great Austrian hotels, and shop at a wide variety of online stores.

Sony Corporation

http://www.sony.com/

This is a media junkie's dream. It's all here: Sony Music, Sony Pictures, Sony Electronics, Sony Interactive… you get the picture.

Taskon A/S

http://www.oslonett.no/html/adv/TASKON/TASKON.html

A Norwegian firm supporting various categories of end users with individually tailored information systems through object-oriented technology. The company builds on technology developed during the past 15 years at the Center for Industrial Research.

Education

The Net is always a learning experience, but it can also be specifically educational too, and for the whole family.

The Fourth R

http://www.cristine.com/cannon/welcome.htm

Information on child and adult computer literacy is featured at this site.

The Big Picture

http://www.bigpicture.com/abc

A program designed to help students integrate life experiences with school experiences and thereby promote a more effective learning environment.

InfoVid Outlet: The Educational & How-To Video Warehouse

http://branch.com/infovid/infovid.html

An informative guide to the best educational, instructional, and informative videos from around the world. More than 3,500 hard-to-find titles on a wide variety of subjects. Everything from auto repair to aerobics, boating to business, crafts to computers, and many more.

Peterson's Education Center

http://www.petersons.com:8080/

A gateway to extensive information and services related to researching educational and career opportunities and applying online.

Electronics

More things to plug into the wall and other modern technological artifacts.

Cermetek Corp.

http://www.isi.net/ebs/cermetek/index.html

Site features a broad line of modem components and telephone-line interfaces for the data communications industry.

Corax Specialty Home Electronics

http://daffy.cadvision.com/corax/corax.html

A selection of home electronics, including telephone call monitoring systems (caller ID) and a full selection of home theatre products.

Motorola ISG

http://www.mot.com/MIMS/ISG/

Information about modems, integrated services digital network (ISDN) terminal adapters, frame relay devices, and networking products.

Employment Services

Recruitment online is one use of the Net that's proven a great fit and quite popular both with potential employees and employers. Ranging from executive placement services to temporary agencies, there are dozens of ways to find a job without leaving your computer.

DP Jobs

http://www.intex.net/jobbs/
dpjobb.html

This page is for technical computer people looking for work in the Dallas, Texas area. Interesting Texan information available.

E*SPAN

http://www.espan.com/

A fascinating Web site that features an entire online career area in addition to thousands of available jobs.

J. Robert Scott - Executive Search

http://j-robert-scott.com/

Retainer-based executive search firm specializing in the recruitment of senior-level professionals and managers.

Job Search

http://www.adnetsol.com/jsearch/
jshome1.html

An exclusive database of 40,000 companies. Provides access to the "hidden" job market for anyone seeking employment in Southern California.

NationJob Network

http://www.nationjob.com/

Thousands of current detailed jobs, company profiles. Seems to be mostly in the Midwest region.

Computer Professional Staffing

http://www.opennet.com/cps/

Positions in Tampa Bay and the state of Florida in computer-related industries, particularly telecommunications.

Energy

A network of firms ensuring that the lights never go out.

Ridge & Associates, Inc

http://www.xmission.com/~gastown/
ridgeco/index.html

Consulting engineers run this full-service engineering company which specializes in petroleum and flammable liquid handling and loading and airport fueling facilities.

Engineering

Engineering and technological design have inspired the imagination for centuries, and the emergence of online access has compelled engineers to create interesting and informative Web sites.

Anderson & Associates, Inc.

http://www.bnt.com/~anderson/

Site is focused on civil, environmental and transportation engineering, planning, landscape architecture, and surveying.

Ansys Inc.

http://www.ansys.com/

Develops and markets design optimization software. A leader in the field of computer-aided engineering.

HyperMedia Corporation

http://www.hypermedia.com/

Geoscience and engineering information experts focus on organizing and integrating a corporation's data assets.

Vaughan Engineering Associates

http://ba.hypercomp.ns.ca/
vaughan.html

Concentration in the fields of engineering, geomatics, computer graphics, and environmental and management consulting.

Entertainment

Starwave Corporation

http://www.starwave.com/

Starwave is one of the pioneering entertainment companies on the Web. It has done a number of great sites: ESPN Sportzone, Outside Online, Mr. Showbiz and Ticketmaster Online. All of them are reachable via Starwave's homepage.

Time Warner

http://www.yahoo.com/
Business_Economy/Companies/
Entertainment/Time Warner/

An entertainment media company so big it needs its own category. In this category you'll find many recognizable names, including HBO, Sports Illustrated, People Magazine, and Life Magazine.

Walt Disney Studios

http://www.disney.com/

The cast of characters are all here in this informative entertainment site. Mickey, Minnie, and Tinker Bell mingle with characters from Disney's recent acquisitions. This is not so much a family oriented site as it is a glimpse into the size of the Disney Empire.

The Interactive Fantasy Network

http://www.ifnet.com

A gorgeous site. A must see. If their fantasies come true, this could be a prototype for the future of the Web.

Environment

It's the air we breathe, the water we drink, the land we live on. And online environmental businesses are here.

Air Conditioning Contractors of America

http://www.acca.org/

Provides information and services to HVACR contractors, including load calculation and system design procedures.

Global Recycling Network Inc

http://grn.com/grn/

A cool information service set up to help businesses around the world recycle resources, especially surplus manufactured goods and outdated or used machinery.

Recycler's Exchange

http://www.recycle.net/recycle/RNet/
RE_fp.html

This site offers a free interactive, online listing service for those interested in buying, selling, or trading recyclable material and used items.

Financial Services

Computers and calculators have always been an essential part of the financial world, from the first abacus to the large mainframe computers and international commerce systems that characterize today's business environment.

Alliance Credit Corporation

http://www.tq.com/alliance/
alliance_home.html

Nationwide equipment leasing service for vendors of equipment and commercial end users, via the Web.

Australian Accountants and Auditors

http://www.ozemail.com.au/~glillicr/

This site for Australian accountants and auditors offers information about centers of excellence, conferences, selected publications, and new accounting and financial products.

BankNet

http://mkn.co.uk/bank

The first bank to allow accounts to be opened online, and yes, you can even access your balance via the Web. They use public-key authentication for electronic payments, so you don't have to worry about someone else tapping into your account.

Bank of Boston

http://www.llnl.gov/fstc/
bank_of_boston.html

Founded in 1784, the Bank of Boston is the oldest chartered bank in the United States. A variety of information about the bank is available at this Web site.

BDO Spencer Steward

http://bdo.co.za/~bdonatal/

Crossing the globe, this site is for South Africa's national association of accounting firms, and is a part of BDO, the seventh largest accounting and consulting firm in the world.

Business Clearinghouse

http://www.indirect.com/user/equity/index.html

A very useful online site where companies and individuals can find business and financial solutions that aren't readily available through traditional channels — and lots more.

Canada Life

http://www.canadalife.com/

An international mutual life insurance company offering a broad range of financial services and products for individuals and groups, with comparative information online.

Digital Ink

http://giant.mindlink.net/financial/

This site features financial information on public companies, additional related information, and pointers to other Web sites of a similar nature.

Fannie Mae

http://www.fanniemae.com/

America's largest supplier of conventional home mortgages funds, the nation's sixth largest corporation in terms of assets, and, generally, the largest issuer of debt in the United States. An interesting and surprising site about a little-known business.

Insurance Information Institute

gopher://infx.infor.com:4200/

The purpose of this site is to help improve public understanding of insurance — what it does and how it works. The Insurance Information Institute (III) is recognized by the media, governments, regulatory organizations, universities, and the public as a primary source of information, analysis, and referral concerning the property/casualty insurance industry.

Insurance News Network

http://www.insure.com/

An online information service about auto, home, and life insurance. Includes explanations, consumer tips and pricing help, state-by-state insurance facts and phone numbers, and insurance ratings from Standard & Poor's.

Investor Access

http://www.money.com/ssnhome.html

Online database of investment research, sell side data, stock prices, real-time stock graph generation. Packed with the info an individual investor needs.

The Leasing Game

http://www.inforamp.net/~mreid/leasing.html

Online information resource on leasing both for lessees and lessors. The Web version of a widely used financing tool in Canada.

MoneyLine Corporation

http://www.moneyline.com/

Realtime financial market data, news, and analytics, specializing in the fixed income and bond markets.

PMC Capital, Inc.

http://www.marketnet.com/mktnet/pmc

Offering Small Business Administration and conventional loans for small businesses throughout the United States.

Richman Associates, Valuations, Litigation Support Services

http://www.websys.com/richman/home.html

Firm offers financial services for litigation support, business valuations, and fraud examination, with much interesting information online.

Southern Life

http://southernlife.co.za/

Information on a range of innovative products and services and access to a wealth of actuarial resources available in South Africa, and to a broad spectrum of corporate publications.

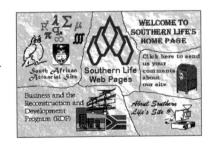

Synergy Worldwide Funding Group

http://www.cfonline.com/cli/consult/synergy/synergy.htm

Accounts receivable financing and factoring solutions to businesses needing working capital and business loans.

Wells Fargo

http://wellsfargo.com/

One of the first to offer online banking on the Web.

Flowers

The flower industry is much more computerized than you may have realized, with international networks of independent florists. So it's not surprising to find also that many of these firms have taken to the Net like kids to candy.

Blooming Candy Bouquetzzz

http://www.marketnet.com/mktnet/bloom/

The floral-like arrangements featured at this fun Web site are made from individually wrapped confection products, including delicious, imported hard candies and chocolates. They look terrific. Too bad the Web doesn't have an interface for the taste buds.

FTD Internet

http://www.novator.com/FTD-Catalog/

Here you'll find an official Florists' Transworld Delivery (FTD) catalog online, with over 80 floral arrangements and gift baskets with delivery available worldwide.

Pennsylvania Dutch Marketplace

http://www.padutch.com/Welcome.html

Source for unique food, crafts, and gifts from the Pensylvania Dutch heartland. The online shops offer items such as Amish quilts, hex signs, clothing, cookies, candy, chips, and pretzels.

National Flora

http://www.mind.net/flora/home.html

One of the better flower sites on the Web. This site makes it easy-as-pie to get those last minute gifts — choose the occasion, choose the arrangement, put in your credit card and you're done.

Food

The Net is a wonderful thing; it's four in the morning, and you can still surf and shop for treats without even leaving your office. Some of these Web sites are just amazingly fun, too.

Ben & Jerry's Vermont's Finest Ice Cream & Frozen Yogurt

http://www.benjerry.com/

Hip and trendy ice cream, including information on the many Ben & Jerry's flavors and products, scoop shop listings, company info, and a schedule of coming events and company-sponsored festivals.

Beer Masters Tasting Society

http://BeerMasters.com/BeerMasters/

This site is dedicated to fun, fellowship, relaxation, tall tales, and tasting experiences shared by beer enthusists around the world. Bottoms up!

Ragu - Mama's Cucina

http://www.eat.com/

This is a site you can't miss. There aren't too many food companies on the Web, and even fewer food sites that are as funny and well done as this.

Rhebokskloof Estate Wines

http://www.os2.iaccess.za/rhebok/index.htm

One of the most prestigious and beautiful estates in the Cape (South Africa) with all the facilities to produce top-quality wine and food. A cool Web spot to visit.

Summer Isles Foods

http://www.highlandtrail.co.uk/highlandtrail/fish1.html

Smoked salmon, a traditional Scottish and Glen Moray whisky cure. Also check out Achiltibuie kippers and smoked trout, all available direct from the United Kingdom.

Games

Not only are there lots of games to play online, but also there is a space for companies selling unusual and collector's games to come online and show off their wares — and a small number of companies have done just that.

BoneGames

http://www.3i.com/bonegames/
bonegames.html

You can download strategic and intellectual games for free from this fun site. Game boards and pieces are also available for printing on your own system.

Ivory Tower Trading Card Co.

http://fohnix.metronet.com/~tower/

Collectible cards and games including Magic, Jyhad, Illuminati, _Star Trek: The Next Generation_, _The Lion King,_ and more.

Gifts

Did you remember to buy a birthday present for your Aunt Edna this year? No? Better start surfing then.

Dancing Dragon Designs

http://www.northcoast.com/
unlimited/product_directory/
dancing_dragon/dancing_dragon.html

Encounter rare and mysterious dragons in every form from gold to silk, in collectibles, books, posters, puzzles, masks, sculptures, jewelry, t-shirts, artifacts, personal and household items, and more. A great Web site.

Flags by Claudia

http://deskshop.lm.com/
Flags_by_Claudia/

This site offers high-quality, beautiful, machine-stitched and hand-trimmed decorative flags and banners for all occasions.

Tech Museum Store

http://www.thetech.org/
techstore.html

The Tech Museum Store is a place where you can find the unexpected: gifts, gadgets, and clever devices, as well as books, software, and special publications that are hard to get and wonderful to find.

Government

Companies and corporations aiming at Federal and other government business.

BTG Technology Systems GSA Schedule

http://www.btg.com/techsys/

BTG provides a comprehensive online catalog of more than 15,000 computer products for Federal and other authorized organizations.

Foresight Science and Technology

http://www.foresnt.com/

Provides services and products to companies, universities, government agencies, nonprofit institutions, and school districts active in science, engineering, and technology development.

Podesta Associates

http://www.dc-online.com/dc-online/
podesta/

A full-service policy and public affairs firm, Podesta Associates provides a broad range of strategic and advocacy services through its interactive Web site.

Health and Fitness

Too much Net surfing and not enough physical activity getting you down? No worries — you can learn more about health and fitness online.

Access Learning Systems

http://www.zondlo.com/access/

Site features information about ACL, a performance consulting company specializing in leadership effectiveness and human resource development (HRD) with health care organizations.

Gerson Institute

http://www.homepage.com/mall/
gerson/gerson.html

The Gerson Institute is an intensive, nutrition-based, detoxifying medical treatment facility for cancer, diabetes, lupus, and other chronic diseases. Explained and illustrated online at this Web site.

SpinMaster Vin

http://www.ipworld.com/market/
fitness/spinmast/homepage.htm

Professionally mixed exercise tapes for aerobic instruction and home-fitness programs are available from The SpinMaster.

Sydney Refractive Surgery Centre

http://www.ozemail.com.au/~cvision/
excimer/index.html

Although this site is an advertisement for Excimer Laser Surgery to correct short-sightedness at a clinic in Sydney, Australia, it also features a very interesting book about optical surgery online, written by a patient at the clinic.

Hobbies

Whether you like to collect stamps, baffle your friends with magic tricks, examine the small print on coins, or engage in just about any other hobby, you'll find something to learn on the Net. And almost certainly, companies catering to your interests are already online.

Atlas Model Railroad Company

http://www.atlasrr.com/

This fun site features information about Atlas trains, high quality model railroad equipment at HO, N and O scales, all available through distributors or directly via mail order.

Hobby Centre Interactive

http://www.comprez.com/hobby/

Model trains, cars, boats, comics old and new, non-sports cards, pogs, Magic the Gathering, and remote-control vehicles are all featured at Hobby Centre Interactive. Very cool toys — check 'em out!

Stevens Magic Emporium

http://www.southwind.net/IMS/
magic/

Selling the finest magical apparatus for more than 50 years, with a customer list that includes noted magic celebrities, semiprofessional magicians, and, of course, lots of amateurs. A site for the *prestidigitatious*.

Toy Train Company

http://www.mountain.net/ttc/

Site aimed at collectors, with online value-guide listings for American Flyer, Lionel, K-Line, MARX, IVES, and a great FAQ (frequently asked questions) section on toy trains going back to the year 1900.

Tower Hobbies

http://www.prairienet.org/business/
tower/tower.html

Tower Hobbies is a direct-mail company specializing in radio-controlled models — airplanes, cars, boats, helicopters, and more.

Home and Garden

Stuff for around the house, inside or out. And believe it or not, the Web is bigger than any hardware superstore.

Electrolux

http://mmm.wwa.com/elux/
index.html

Electrolux is a producer of household appliances. In white goods, the group is the European market leader and, as owner of Frigidaire Company, is the third largest producer in the United States. This Web site contains information on Electrolux's environmental policy and some interesting company history, as well as product descriptions.

Graf & Sons, Inc.

http://www.smartpages.com/grafso

Overhead door and Genie brand garage door opening systems and other door-related products. The store is located in the Columbus, Ohio area.

Hortus Gardening Journal

http://www.kc3ltd.co.uk/business/
hortus.html

Hortus Gardening Journal is a privately published quarterly journal which addresses itself to intelligent and lively minded gardeners throughout the English-speaking world. A very nice Web site, it features some of the magazine's best articles, too.

LifeTime Electrostatic Filters

http://www.sccsi.com/LifeTime/lifetime_welcome.html

Site explains the products from this leading manufacturer of electrostatic filters, which are being used more and more to create a clean and healthy working environment for both humans and computers.

Imaging

Whether you need to translate your documents into digital format or seek a better way to manage all your virtual paper, companies are online that can help.

Document Works

http://www.shadow.net/~peter/document.html

A full-service document solutions bureau, The Document Works offers document imaging, scanning, indexing, and format conversion services, as well as custom, paper-based, data-conversion services, right from its Web site.

Perceptics Corporation

http://www.usit.net/hp/perceptics/home.html

This company offers development, design, manufacture, integration, and support of specialized information systems for applications in document management and imaging.

Industrial Supplies

Things for the factory you run or otherwise products and services of value to manufacturing facilities are now available online. What next? Factory machines directly controllable through Web pages?

Control Technology Corporation

http://cthulhu.control.com/

Control Technology Corporation designs and manufactures advanced machine automation controllers, applying them in a diverse range of industries, including consumer products manufacturers, the computer industry, biotechnology, environmental protection, and semiconductor fabrication.

Electronics Diversified, Inc. (EDI)

http://www.esta.org/homepages/edi/edihome.html

Manufacturer of lighting controls and dimmers for theaters, museums, restaurants, and theme parks, this site reveals more than you probably realized about the nuances of lighting.

W. W. Grainger

http://www.grainger.com/

A leading business-to-business distributor of equipment, components, and supplies to more than one million commercial, industrial, contractor, and institutional customers around the world. Its services are featured at this informative Web site.

Information

The name of the game. There's a ton of it on the Net, of course, but *finding useful* information can be a challenge, to say the least. That's where these information providers and brokers can prove invaluable.

Custom Standards Services

http://www.well.com/user/css/

Through its Web site, CSS guarantees lowest prices on hardcopy documents, test methods, and regulations. CSS offers a free updating service to make sure that you always have the most current editions of the documents you need.

Genealogy SF

http://www.sfo.com/~genealogysf/

Genealogy software (shareware and commercial), genealogy research tips, research CD-ROMs, and genealogy data. Bi-weekly *Ask Glenda* genealogy tutorials, all online at a site your parents would also enjoy.

Information Handling Services (IHS)

http://www.ihs.com/

IHS is a publisher of technical information products, divided into seven major groups: military specifications and standards, worldwide industry standards, vendor catalogs, government personnel and procurement information, electronic component databases, safety and regulatory data, and parts and logistics data.

Information Engineering Group

http://www.pic.net/~infoengr/

This Web spot explains the use of Value-Quest information engineering methodology for defining and creating valuable business information systems.

Knowledge One

http://knowone_www.sonoma.edu/

Knowledge One is a joint service of Pacific Knowledge Systems, one of the leading consulting firms in the electronic information industry and a prestigious California academic library. Knowledge One's team of Knowledge Navigators have access to millions of sources of information, and can provide you with fast, accurate information on a wide range of subjects, usually within an hour.

Whether the topic is corporate earnings or toxoplasmosis, Knowledge One has the information you need to stay ahead.

LCM Research

http://www.icon-stl.net/~lmrazek/

Helps companies develop the systems and skills needed to navigate through databases and info sources on the Internet, commercial online services, and traditional media sources.

Lineages, Inc.

http://www.cybermart.com/lineages/

Looking for your ancestors? Lineages is a full-service genealogical research firm dedicated to assisting researchers with innovative and comprehensive genealogical services.

Questel/Orbit

http://www.questel.orbit.com/patents/

An international online information company specializing in patent, trademark, scientific, chemical, business, and news information.

Internet Consulting

Ready to plug in but think you might need some assistance along the way? Getting set up online is the perfect opportunity to work with one of the many Internet consulting firms available throughout the world.

Arlington Courseware

http://www.crl.com/~gorgon/

A distance-learning consulting firm specializing in teaching using electronic media with an emphasis on education via the Internet.

Center for the Application of Information Technology

http://www.cait.wustl.edu/cait/

This useful site explains about this nonprofit training consortium, providing leading edge training and leadership programs for Information Systems professionals.

Conjungi

http://www.conjungi.com/

A Seattle, Washington-based company that provides network infrastructure design consulting, Conjungi addresses issues of wide-area connectivity to Internet service providers as well as deployment of services and access within the local area network (LAN).

Lucas Internet

http://www.mbnet.mb.ca/lucas/

Lucas Internet can help you set up a Web service to publicize your company and offer your products and services to anyone on the internet. It also offers hands-on, on-site Internet training, as explained on this home page.

McQueen & Associates Internet Training

http://www.mcq.com

On-site instructor courseware that's already been delivered to over 3,000 students with excellent results. PowerPoint slides and Word documents for attendee workbooks, and the courseware is frequently customized for specific audiences.

Internet Presence Providers

Ready to sign up your firm to join the veritable hordes on the Internet? Then you'll need to choose from the hundreds — if not thousands — of Internet Presence Providers out there eager to help you do just that. Here's a small sampling.

AcadiaNet

http://www.acadia.net/

High-speed connections in Downeast Maine: Bangor, Ellsworth, Bar Harbor, Rockland, and Camden. This company provides a full line of Web publishing services including page design, production, and space on its servers.

Bizarre Bazaar

http://www.camtech.com.au/~virtart/clients/bb/

Site features an eclectic virtual market where individuals and small traders can rent stalls on a month-by-month basis for a small set-up fee plus monthly site rental. Bizarre Bazaar

encourages small traders to populate this market space in order that they may all benefit from the popularity of the site as a whole.

Bulldog Beach Interactive

http://www.halcyon.com/duwamish/bulldogbeach/

Provocative design, take-no-prisoners writing, and expert technical knowledge are the watchwords of this funky firm and online site. They promise a design that will get you the international audience your Web page deserves.

CommercePark

http://www.commercepark.com/

This site was designed by communications professionals and developed for the purpose of helping advertising and communications agencies deliver the benefits of Internet marketing to their clients.

CyberPages International Inc.

http://www.cyberpages.com/

An online database of advertisements to the general public. Additionally, CyberPages International maintains a few other, miscellaneous services of public interest.

Digital Planet

http://www.digiplanet.com/DP/

Consults, creates and produces all forms of interactive media. They specialize in creating sites for Hollywood studios and entertainment-related companies on the Internet, the Web, and commercial online services.

Great Connections

http://www.interconnect.com/greatconnect/

Great Connections develops and manages Internet Web sites for professionals, small businesses, and larger organizations. This site features info on business consulting, Web content design and production, process redesign, technical support, marketing, seminars, workshops, and training.

Incline

http://www.infocom.net/~incline/htdocs/companies/Incline/InclineHomepage.html

Training, consulting, and software design services to aid in the accelerated expansion of the Web into Pearland, Texas and the Greater Houston-Galveston Metropolitan Area.

Media Connection of New York

http://www.mcny.com/

This firm helps businesses establish themselves on the Internet with Web site design as well as online marketing. All explained on its Web page.

MelaNet

http://www.melanet.com/melanet/

MelaNet provides a central location for African-American-owned businesses to market their goods and services to one another, and to the huge and rapidly growing online consumer base.

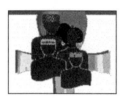

Millennium Communications

http://www.webcom.com/~milcom/welcome.html

A wide array of digital production services; from desktop video, animation, and CD-ROM production to electronic speaker support, interactive multimedia, and Internet home page development.

NSTN

http://www.nstn.ca/

Developers of sustainable networking products, services, and applications. Clients are furnished with cost-effective solutions in response to individual interconnection requirements. This commitment to customized solutions and an extensive range of networking services has uniquely identified NSTN Inc. as one of Canada's foremost networking companies.

Oneworld

http://oneworld.wa.com/

Oneworld Information Services provides value-added information services to companies and individuals who wish to make their marketing and public relations messages available to the Internet.

Phoenix Systems Internet Publishing

http://www.biddeford.com/phoenix/

Internet publishing firm specializing in application development and Internet and World Wide Web resources development, publication, and management.

RealWorks Appraiser Forum

http://www.realworks.com/rw/homepage.htm

A collection of real-estate appraisal firms with useful text and geographic search interfaces online.

TelTECH Computer Consulting

http://bb.iu.net/teltech/

With expertise in Internet related consulting, the most popular service TelTECH is currently offering is that of both turnkey and custom Web and Gopher server development, installation, and support.

Investigative Services

Suspicious about the new neighbor? Wondering whatever happened to your old buddy who skipped town owing you a few thousand bucks? It's good to know that you can now find a virtual Sam Spade through the Net. A number of investigative services have joined the Internet community. Trouble is their business.

Paragon Investigations and Polygraph Services

http://www.tecs.com/invest

One of the many investigative services available at this interesting Web site,

Paragon specializes in coming to your facility and administering polygraph tests. No lie! All explained online.

InPhoto Surveillance

http://www.interaccess.com/inphotowww/

A nationwide investigative company with full-time, properly trained, licensed, and equipped investigators located within a three hour drive of 85 percent of the United States.

Languages

Whether it's German, Italian, Swahili, Dutch, Mandarin, or Tagalog, you can find someone to help you read and write your marketing materials and literature through the power of the Web.

The Intra Group

http://www.internet.com.mx/empresas/intra/index.html

A translation company that provides a completely reliable, single source for all your translating requirements, with extensive knowledge of dozens of languages.

Translation Solutions

http://www.pacifier.com/market/1atransl/tranmain.html

English translation and interpretation services for over 50 languages worldwide. Full foreign language production service.

Law

Given the confusing nuances of online copyright, freedom of speech issues, and the risks inherent in doing business in a litigious society, rest assured that *plenty* of work is available for the online law firms listed in Yahoo!.

Arent Fox Kintner Plotkin & Kahn

http://www.arentfox.com/

The Web site for this firm is divided into five departments; EEH (employment, ERISA and health), Federal Practice, General Business, International, and Litigation.

Brobeck, Phleger & Harrison

http://www.brobeck.com/

Provides links to more than 200 business and law sites on the Internet, plus e-mail links to its attorneys and legal researchers. A good starting point for online legal exploration.

BROBECK
PHLEGER &
HARRISON
ATTORNEYS AT LAW

Cooley Godward Home Page

http://www.cgc.com/

A full-service law firm with a distinguished history of legal service across a wide range of specialties. Its growth and success have paralleled the development of its high-technology clients and those clients who finance hi-tech companies. From this base, Cooley Godward's attorneys have become recognized counselors

to successful, growing companies and their financing sources across the United States.

Decision Strategies International

http://www.tmn.com/dsi/index.html

Foreign and domestic law firms, corporations, financial institutions, insurance companies and private and government clients depend on Decision Strategies for timely, critical, reliable information and advice.

Heller Ehram White & McAuliffe

http://www.digital.com/gnn/bus/hewm/index.html

One of the 50 largest law firms in the United States, with a diverse group of clients involved in such industries as biotechnology, medical and health care, computers, software, telecommunications, consumer products, investment banking, international business, and venture capital.

Law Offices of C. Matthew Schulz

http://www.dnai.com/~mschulz

This firm focuses on immigration matters and works with various government agencies to obtain temporary and permanent authorization to live and work in the United States and selected other countries — all explained online at this Web site.

Roger H. Madon, P.C.

http://www.nar.com/rhm/home.html

Law firm concentrating in Russian-American business transactions, joint ventures, distribution agreements, licensing, and trade. An interesting Web page.

Skornia Law Firm

http://www.internet-is.com/skornia/index.html

A complete range of transactional legal services appropriate for all types of business operations, from startup through the initial public offering. Merger, acquisition, sale or liquidation, and numerous other transactions are all expertly handled by this full-service law firm.

SchoolMatch

http://ppshost.schoolmatch.com/

Research and database services firm that collects, audits, integrates, processes, and manages information. School research, data and consulting services are all featured on its home page.

Magazines

Whether you opt to print the pages out or read them online, hundreds of magazines are available for perusing on the Internet today, ranging from tiny upstarts to large publications that have a significant and thorough online presence. The following group of Web sites helps build and produce these online publications.

d.Comm

http://www.d-comm.com/

Producers of a cool magazine that covers all types of information technology issues, from the desktop PC to networking issues to communications.

LINX Publications

http://www.sims.net/organizations/linx/linxhome.html

LINX (Linux users group Information News eXchange) is the only national provider of monthly information directed to DECUS LUG members. If you're involved with the Linux community, you'll want to find out more online at this Web site.

OverSight Magazine

http://www.earthlink.net/~oversight

OverSight is an online journal of community and alternative art in Los Angeles. Special interests include nonprofit organizations, artist-run spaces, photography, a virtual gallery, Art On Illness, a cartoon strip, art rags, and more.

Manufacturing

Making things is out, and making information is in, right? Well, somebody forgot to tell these firms, manufacturers who now have a presence in cyberspace. If you are involved in manufacturing, quite a few sources and solutions are available online to explore.

James River Corporation

http://www.jrc.com/

A world leader in packaging technology, the James River Corp. home page talks about the firm and its innovative packaging technology.

MarketMatch

gopher://mdagopher.tc.cornell.edu

Information about companies that buy and sell manufacturing processes, services, and raw materials for manufacturing companies in New York State, all available through Gopher.

Optimum Air Corp.

http://netheaven.com/~horizon/optimum/oac.htm

The Optimum Hydrid Source Capture Air Filtration and Rapid Dry System is designed to capture and dry waterborne industrial paints and other coatings without heat and provides consistent production dry times regardless of ambient conditions. Pop over to this site to learn more.

Wahoo's CNC Machining

http://www.neca.com/~wahoo/cncindx.html

This informative site features a guide to CNC machining, dealing with mostly milling applications. Covers history, G code programming, and CNC control operations.

Maps

When it's time to figure out where you are on the planet (as opposed to where you are in cyberspace), it's time to look for a map manufacturing corporation.

World of Maps

http://www.magi.com/~maps/

Wherever you live, wherever you're travelling, you can find a map of the area at the World of Maps Web site. Features include reviews of map and travel books and a list of bestselling maps and guides.

Marketing

Take that better mousetrap and make sure people are interested in buying it. The market must be there and must be willing to give the mousetrap a chance. Same goes for any other product or service.

Allen Marketing Group

http://www.trinet.com/allen.html

This site explains how the group provides a full range of marketing services to help companies improve the effectiveness of their marketing and sales activites.

CC Communications

http://www.webcom.com/~cccomm/welcome.html

A full-service, experienced Internet program consultant. This is a media design, production, and programming company that offers the latest interactive Internet project features, professional management, and program administration at very affordable rates.

Direct Marketing Managers of Hawaii by Paul Klink

http://www.pixi.com/milici/dmmh.html

Paul Klink provides initial free information from Direct Marketing Managers of Hawaii, a division of Milici Valenti Ng Pack Advertising, a DDB Needham Worldwide Associate Agency.

Imagine if...

http://www.imagine-if.be/retail/

This fun site in Belgium features the Imagine If... team, specializing in improving the profitability of point of sales. Imagine If... analyzes consumer behavior and develops retail solutions for chains of stores.

ProActive Marketing

http://www.demon.co.uk/proact/prohome.html

A marketing consultancy that specializes in the application of leading-edge technology for the achievement of marketing goals. Specialist areas for this United Kingdom firm include the Internet, multimedia desktop conferencing, and database marketing.

Media

(See also the News chapter.)

Newspapers, newswires, and other publications with a network presence.

eye Weekly

http://www.interlog.com/eye/

eye Weekly is Toronto's arts newspaper — music, movies, theatre, and so on, along with a large helping of "alternative" news and views. A wonderful Web site and a good example of a hip online news service.

Mining and Mineral Exploration

Gold mines in the Klondike or diamond mines in South Africa? Mining and mineral exploration are an important part of today's global economy, and these sites give a good idea of how this industry is doing on the Web.

Info-Mine

http://www.info-mine.com/

Fun Web spot features comprehensive, worldwide mining and mineral exploration information including details on companies, mineral properties, and more.

Kenrich Mining Corporation

http://www.internet-investor.com/kenrich/

A Canadian mineral exploration company focused on the discovery of gold and silver deposits in the Eskay Creek area of northwestern British Columbia.

Quinto Mining Corporation

http://www.internet-investor.com/quinto/

Quinto's deposit is a rare naturally-occurring combo of extremely fine graphite and sericite. This composite mineral is named Schillerite.

Music

Whether you're into industrial or ska, whiffle or punk, classical or jazz — there's something for every musical taste on the Internet.

i? music/media

http://www.icw.com/cd/imm1.html

This slick site carries more than 100,000 CDs, cassettes, Mini-Discs, and digital compact cassettes (DCCs). Browse these Web pages and you can download samples of featured artists and new or even unsigned artists.

Resonance Records

http://www.netcreations.com/resonance/

This site specializes in — and attempts to explain — Jungle, Ambient, and Hard Trance music. Beyond those genres, this site has quite a varied selection of other types of music, too.

Nanotechnology

Think small. Really small. *Smaller.* Think about computers that are smaller than the head of a pin. Think about building something out of single atoms, one at a time. Think about a technology developed under extremely powerful microscopes and you'll start to get a glimpse of the amazing new field of nanotechnology.

Nanothinc

http://nanothinc.com/

Nanothinc is a San Francisco-based company providing information about nanotechnology and the related enabling technologies, which include supramolecular chemistry, protein engineering, molecular design and modelling software, STM/AFM/etc. (nanoscopy), and even progress in the top-down approach (which includes nanolithography and micromachines).

Networks

The really exciting aspect of the Internet, the reason for its remarkable growth, is the fact that it's not a single network but a massive network of networks. The Net is a collection of interconnected systems. Therefore, when you're ready to plug your own network into the Internet, you'll want to learn about networking and how different networks interrelate.

FUNET Information Services

http://www.funet.fi/

FUNET is a nonprofit organization providing communication services to its members. Besides different network connections (Internet, NORDUnet, and BITNET/EARN),

FUNET also maintains X.500 directory services. It also provides access to different information services (Gopher, WAIS, World Wide Web) and mail gateways (X.400, Elisa, Mailnet, IBM X.400, and others).

New England Community Internet

http://www.pn.com/neci/neci.html

New England Community Internet is a civic organization dedicated to making the Internet accessible to the public without barriers of economics or technical expertise, as explained on this Web site.

Pixel Internacional S.A. de C.V.

http://pixelnet.pixel.com.mx/index.html

PixelNet is the first Internet access provider in Mexico. It offers the usual services such as e-mail, Gopher, World Wide Web access, Usenet news, and local news. The PixelNet headquarters are in Monterrey, Mexico, and it has two other points of presence in Mexico City and Guadalajara. Future plans are to extend these services to other cities of Mexico.

Prodigy Services AstraNet

http://www.astranet.com/

In case you didn't know, Prodigy is a popular, nationwide online service in the United States. Prodigy's Internet unit has assembled a broad collection of what it considers to be among the best publicly available Internet content in categories such as Sports, Finance, News, and Government. A terrific site to bookmark!

Radio-MSU

http://www.radio-msu.net/

The goal of this fascinating project is to develop a high-speed computer network providing access for Russian scientific, research, and educational institutes to the worldwide information resources of the Internet.

Skagit On-Line Services

http://www.sos.net/

Skagit On-line Services is committed to providing convenient, cost-effective access to the emerging information superhighway via the Internet. For businesses and individuals in the Skagit Valley and surrounding communities. As part of Skagit On-Line's mission, it seeks to educate prospective users on the benefits and techniques of Internet access.

Winserve - Windows Internet Server

http://www.winserve.com/

Bridging remote offices and connecting mobile employees to the central office, Winserve uses Microsoft Windows NT Server version 3.5 to provide virtual disk space and an Microsoft Mail postoffice. A good resource for PC-based offices.

News

(See also the News chapter.)

From sports scores and stock quotes to the latest breaking news off the newswire, you can read all the news that's fit to distribute electronically without leaving your workstation on the Internet.

Usenet - clari.matrix_news

news:clari.matrix_news

This service offers a variety of online publications, including *Matrix News* (a monthly networking newsletter), *Newsbytes* (the computer industry's daily news service), discussion and announcements about ClariNet and ClariNews, general news and United States news, sports news and *Techwire* (technical and scientific news). Note: you must be subscribed to ClariNet through your news provider to read this collection of resources.

Office Supplies

Run out of staples again? Why not reorder via the Web? Now you don't *have* to run down to the stationery store to restock on business essentials.

Coast Business Systems, Inc.

http://teletron.com/cbs.html

An office equipment supplier specializing in the sale of copiers, fax machines, and quality service and supplies. The friendly staff, timely followup, and excellent service make Coast Business Systems, Inc. a leader in the industry. Free copier program for Southern California.

Dymo Online

http://www.dymo.com/

Manufacturer of a diverse range of labeling equipment and materials, including the popular Dymo 6000 and Dymo1000 electronic labeling tools.

Esselte Online

http://www.esselte.com/

One of the three largest suppliers of office products in the world. This Web site incorporates Letraset, Dymo, ITC, and Esselte office product companies. See Letraset's Catch of the Month for a free font!

Photography

Weddings, Bar Mitzvahs, corporate functions — or just some new shots for your Web page. Quite a few professional photographers are now advertising their services and showing off their photographs online.

Digital Zone

http://www2.uplex.net/dzone/

This site features information on its photo CD-ROMs from internationally acclaimed stock and commercial photographers Cliff Hollenbeck, Wolfgang Kaehler, Kevin Morris, and Christopher Roberts.

John Rechin

http://www.zdepth.com/rechin/

Silver gelatin prints produced in forty signed and numbered editions. The photographer also accepts editorial and commerial assignments and commissioned portraits. Nice sampling of work online.

Twilight Productions

http://www.commerce.com/twilight/

Twilight Productions is a commercial photography studio that places primary emphasis on advertising and stock photography. Established in 1981, Twilight continues to service commercial accounts nationally and lease reproduction rights for stock photographs internationally.

Wedding Photographer Harold Summers

http://www.village.com/business/summers.html

Preserve those special moments with Harold Summers, an expert wedding photographer who will travel worldwide from his New England studio to provide you with high quality, exciting bridal photos.

Printing

There are many times when moving around information online just doesn't quite work and nothing will do except a printed, hard copy. So it's great to see that some high-quality printing firms are plugging into the Net and are offering fast-turnaround printing without your having to drive across the city to drop off a floppy disk.

Lithocraft, Inc.

http://www.netpress.com/lithocraft/

Geared to service top-quality, color imaging and print production in the San Francisco Bay Area, from high-end disc imagesetting, scanning, and Scitex to four-, five-, and six-color Heidelberg plus aqueous presses and complete bindery.

Photobooks Inc.

http://photobooks.atdc.gatech.edu/

Producers of printed pictorial and text directories for educational institutions, companies, associations, and health care organizations.

Publishing

Printing is only the tip of the iceberg, and if you have printed material to distribute, publishers often prove a better alternative.

Association of American University Presses (AAUP) Online Catalog/Bookstore

http://aaup.pupress.princeton.edu/

The Association of American University Presses is a cooperative, nonprofit organization of university presses.

Formally established in 1937, the AAUP promotes the work and influence of university presses, provides cooperative marketing efforts, and helps its presses respond to the changing economy and environment. Lots of information is available at this Web site.

Academic International Press

http://www.amaranth.com/aipress

Academic International Press is a commercial, scholarly press that publishes reference works including encyclopedias, annuals, statistical collections, and other documents. Complete catalog online.

IDG Books Worldwide

http://www.idgbooks.com/

Well, well, well! It's IDG Books' site on the Web. You'll find the home page for this book here, as well as lots of fun info, sample text, tips, cartoons, downloadable software, and the latest information on the best books covering computers and software. And we're not just saying that.

SuperLibrary Newsletter

http://www.mcp.com/newsletter/

This monthly online newsletter is written by the team at Macmillan publishing and contains articles, columns, and information on new and upcoming books.

PTR Prentice Hall Catalogs

gopher://gopher.prenhall.com/11/
PTR%20Prentice%20Hall%20Catalogs

PTR Prentice Hall has a cool online catalog of the many books in their Networking and Communications, Object-Oriented technology, and C Programming series.

Tom Mulhern & Associates

http://www.mulhern.com/

This site offers information services to the music/audio-equipment industries, including *The Bottom Line* product reviews, users' manuals, newsletters, press and advance product releases, data sheets, and Web pages.

United Brothers & United Sisters Communications Systems

http://www.melanet.com/melanet/
ubus/home.html

This site features examples and information about their published literature by, for, and about African and African-American people.

University of Texas Press

http://www.utexas.edu/depts/
utpress/

The University of Texas Press, founded in 1950 as an integral part of the Texas system of higher education, exists to disseminate to scholars and the general public new information on and interpretations of many subjects of importance.

W. W. Norton & Company, Inc.

http://www.wwnorton.com/

Trade titles and college textbooks. Complete online catalog, info on new publications and author appearances, and news of interest to booksellers.

W. W. Norton & Company
New York • London

Real Estate

Whether you're relocating to another city or state, are interested in selling your existing house and trading up, or even just curious about another locale, the best of these online real estate pages offer a wealth of information about houses and property for sale and the general area served.

Duck's Real Estate / Stan White Realty

http://wmi.cais.com/white/index.html

Two offices to serve your vacation needs. This is a company with more than 20 years experience in property management, vacation rentals, sales, and home building on the Outer Banks. For homes in every price range from Corolla to South Nags Head, all shown online.

Prudential / Lutz Snyder Realtor

http://www.pacifier.com/market/3aekreal/estate.html

Serving the Vancouver, Washington and Portland, Oregon areas of the Pacific Northwest area of the United States. Buyer/seller services for residential, commercial, or investment properties, and online listings too.

This New House

http://www.thisnewhouse.com/tnh/

This great site is brought to you by the producers of the new, nationally distributed educational cable TV program *This New House.* Information includes tips on obtaining mortgages, what cities and cable companies currently broadcast the show, and other information useful to first-time home buyers or long-time home owners.

Research

When your firm isn't finding the innovations you hoped it would, it might be time to call in some independent research agencies to help, and a number of top international firms are on the Internet.

Foresight Science and Technology

http://www.foresnt.com/

Site features services and products available to companies, universities, government agencies, nonprofit institutions, and school districts active in science, engineering, and technology development.

Industrial Research Limited (NZ)

http://www.irl.cri.nz/

This New Zealand firm conducts viable world-class research that leads New Zealanders to internationally competitive added-value opportunities.

IIT Research Institute

http://www.iitri.com/

A not-for-profit organization that performs research and develops technology applications on a contract basis for industry and government. See this Web page for more information.

Teleos Research

http://teleos.com/

This team carries out research and technology development in advanced vision technology, focusing on intelligent perception and control techniques. This is a fascinating Web page to explore.

Scientific

Keep up on the latest scientific and technological marvels from the comfort of your desk chair.

LMSoft

http://geoserver.lmsoft.ca/

Geoscope Network can consult and analyze info about geography, ecology, ocean, atmosphere, and its Hyperpage environment allows it to create multimedia presentations with sounds, texts, images, animations, and programs.

Phase Separations

http://www.phasesep.co.uk/phasesep/

Phase Separations is one of the world's leading manufacturers of spherical silica specifically designed for use in chromatography. This site explains much of what that means.

Semiconductors

Perhaps not the soul of the new machine, semiconductors are definitely the brain and nervous system. Not surprisingly, you'll find lots of Semiconductor info online.

Altera

http://www.altera.com/index.html

This Web site offers information about Altera's programmable logic devices (PLDs) and programmable logic development tools, along with company information and updates.

Teradyne

http://www.teradyne.com/

Teradyne is a manufacturer of automated test equipment, serving the semiconductor, printed circuit board, and telecommunications industries worldwide.

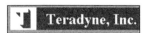

Zilog

http://www.zilog.com/zilog/

Zilog designs, manufactures, and markets application-specific standard products (ASSPs) for the consumer electronics, computer peripherals, and data communications markets.

Shipping

Hard as it may be to admit, the best way to get a product from point A to point B isn't always a modem, after all.

Apex Maritime Co., Inc.

http://cyber.cclims.com/comp/apex/apex.html

International inbound transportation for air and ocean, warehousing and distribution, domestic transport by surface and air, as well as air and ocean exports throughout the world.

Federal Express

http://www.fedex.com/

Tracking your package has never been easier. Type in a tracking number and find out where your package is.

Safa Shipping

http://www.usis.com/~safa/

International freight-forwarding company that provides worldwide air and ocean freight. Safa is especially experienced in shipping to Africa, the Middle East, and the Far East. Cool page.

YONDAR Consulting Group

http://www.magi.com/~yondar/ycg.html

Providing Department of Transportation Pre-Audit Inspections,

Employment Equity, and Employment Services for the Canadian trucking industry.

Shopping Centers

Sometimes it's a lot easier to pop over to a central place with lots of shops rather than poking around one at a time, looking for exactly what you seek. In cyberspace, thousands of shopping centers have sprung up, ranging from the corner strip mall with a half-dozen stores to massive sites with hundreds or even thousands of stores listed.

Downtown Anywhere

http://www.awa.com/index.html

Downtown Anywhere is a great place to browse, learn, share, and trade. Everything you can think of is available. The site offers choice real estate and all the amenities to anyone seeking a virtual office, a virtual showroom, or a virtual laboratory in the heart of the new marketplace of ideas — the Net.

B-To-B Online

http://www.btb.com/

Online resource enabling companies to source, evaluate, inquire about, and purchase a wide variety of products, services, and solutions.

Alpha - Internet Fashion Mall

http://www.fashionmall.com/

This surprising spot features "How To" and "Buying Guides" in addition to deals on a variety of current fashions. The central location on the Internet for better men's and women's fashion lifestyle.

Internet Mall

http://www.iw.com/imall/

The premier spot for shopping on the Internet, the Internet Mall features listings for more than 3500 shops, all organized into a friendly and easily understood shopping mall metaphor with eight floors.

Internet Shopkeeper

http://www.shopkeeper.com/shops/

A place in cyberspace where people from around the world can set up and manage their own shops. The Internet ShopKeeper provides a dynamic global marketplace that brings the power of the Internet and its commercial use to the masses.

Moola Mall

http://www2.interpath.net/sbi/moola/

Books, travel, outdoor gear, learn-on-your-own programs, and other assorted odds and ends that run the gamut from useful to useless. Space for independent vendors online.

Speakers

Spice up your next stockholder meeting or symposium with a professional speaker from the online community, or from one of the many speaking agencies on the Net.

Progressive Development Group, Inc.

http://www.tiac.net/users/pdginc/index.html

PDG provides keynote speakers, in-house training, and public seminars to business and industry. Resumes of speakers are available on this Web site.

Speakers Online

http://speakers.com/

This fascinating site lists a wide variety of different speakers available for talks on a diverse set of topics. Includes resumes and biographical information of speakers.

Sports

From boating to bicycles, climbing to karate, as many companies are focused on sports on the Net, it seems, as there are sports available to play. Here's a small sampling of some of the more unusual sporting firms listed in Yahoo!.

BoatWorks Marine Marketplace

http://www.boatworks.com/index.html

A place where boating enthusiasts come to buy and sell boats, yachts, and other marine stuff. In addition, you can get information on charters and boating events without leaving your computer.

Cyber Cyclery

http://cyclery.com/

A useful resource for information regarding bicycle product lines, after-market bicycle components and accessories, and bicycling-related tour operations.

Shotokan Karate of America

http://www.hmt.com/martialArts/ska/ska.html

Web site explains all about this nonprofit organization that is devoted to teaching karate on its highest level — as a martial art.

Technology Sports

http://www.moran.com/htmld/techspt.html

Developing and marketing high-technology training equipment for amateur swimming events. Cool site.

Telecommunications

In the past few years, telephone service has expanded far beyond being merely a way to call someone else by pressing a few buttons. And hundreds of firms have popped up to help you exploit the full potential of your telecommunications devices.

AT&T

http://www.att.com/

AT&T is a global company that provides communications services and products as well as network equipment and computer systems to businesses, consumers, telecommunications service providers, and government agencies. Its worldwide intelligent network carries more than 140 million voice, data, video, and facsimile messages every business day.

ATU Telecommunications

http://www.atu.com/

The home page for Alaska's largest local telephone company includes an extensive "Community" section, featuring numerous photos and an interactive walking tour of Anchorage, Alaska.

Dash Open Phone System

http://www.dashops.com/

The Dash OPS is a 16 to 128-port computerized phone branch exchange system (PBX) with built-in voice mail, automated attendant, and multiparty conferencing. It's all explained and shown on this informative Web page.

Emulex Europe

http://www.europe.emulex.com/emulex.html

Site contains marketing info and technical support for Emulex Printer servers, Terminal servers, WAN cards, and fibre channel products.

Global Cellular Rental, Ltd

http://www.panix.com/~cellular/cellular.html

Provides cellphones to individuals to remain in touch when abroad. You can book a cell phone before departure and pick it up at any location upon your arrival.

GTE Education Launch Pad

http://www.realm.net/~gte/ei_gte.html

Information about GTE California"s Education Initiative of education grants and services and a valuable K-12 Web site directory.

Inmarsat, The International Mobile Satellite Organization

http://www.inmarsat.org/inmarsat/

A intergovernmental organization with 79 member countries, owned by the private and public telephone companies of the respective countries, who market the Inmarsat space segment.

MCI Telecommunications, Inc.

http://www.mci.com/

You can finally see what all those TV commercials were talking about. MCI has a well laid out site that offers a lot, including a marketplace and an entertainment area. But it is still unclear where Grammercy Press fits in all of this.

NYNEX Interactive Yellow Pages

http://www.nyip.com/

Nynex is the first telco to put its yellow pages on the Web, but it won't be the last. By the time this book hits the shelves, there will certainly be a few more.

SLONET

gopher://gopher.slonet.org/

SLONET is a nonprofit membership organization dedicated to establishing and developing a public access, computerized information and communication service for the general public in San Luis Obispo County in California.

Transportation

How to get from here to there.

Circle International

http://www.circleintl.com/

Circle International, an operating subsidiary of the Harper Group, is a global transportation and logistics solution. They provide air and ocean freight forwarding, customs brokerage, warehousing and distribution, insurance, and inland transportation.

Travel

Time for a vacation? Thought so. Hawaii sound inviting? Or perhaps seeing a few shows in London and popping into a corner pub? Whether your idea of a holiday is roughing it in the wilderness or being surrounded by the luxury of a first class cruise ship, there are travel agents online who can help you turn your dream into reality.

Arctic Adventours, Inc.

http://www.oslonett.no/html/adv/AA/
AA.html

Arctic Adventours is a Norwegian company that specializes in creating exciting expeditions and explorations in the Arctic, including Northern Norway, Jan Mayen, Spitzbergen (Svalbard), Franz Josefs Land, and Siberia. Lots of lovely pictures are featured at this Web site, too.

Cruise Control

http://www.sccsi.com/Star/
cruises.html

Star Travel offers a one-stop resource for cruises, with complete information about all of the major cruise lines, and even an online reservation form.

Getaways of British Columbia

http://interchange.idc.uvic.ca/
~getaways/

This site features more than a thousand listings of bed-and-breakfasts, country inns, and other distinct accommodations in British Columbia.

Guides of Alaska

http://www.alaska.net/~guidesak/

Winter outdoor adventures, with a guide. Tours include snomachine, snowmobile, winter mountain bike treks, viewing the Northern Lights, and much more.

Island Holidays

http://www.diver.com/

Discount diving and accommodation packages to the Caribbean, the Pacific, and the Red Sea. The Island Holidays Web page is liberally sprinkled with terrific underwater and diving information as well.

MIR Travel

http://www.kiss.com/fr/mir.html

Experts in providing travel services for individuals and groups, including business travelers to Russia, Ukraine, Uzbekistan, Kazakhstan, the Baltics, Poland, Czech Republic, and Hungary.

Pelican Airways

http://www.pwr.com/FLYHIGH/
DEFAULT.html

Vintage Air Tours DC-3s can be chartered on an exclusive basis to any desired location, but normally operates within the state of Florida, from Naples, Fort Myers to Key West.

Rocky Mountain Getaways

http://www.fortnet.org/RMGetaways/
rmg.html

Specializing in travel and adventure vacations in the Rocky Mountain West — destinations such as Moab, Yellowstone, and the Grand Canyon. Read about the 1996 packages and begin your booking process online.

Samvinn Travel - Your Partner in Iceland

http://www.arctic.is/Travel/Samvinn/

A great destination calls for a quality travel service. Samvinn Travel is the largest tour operator and travel agency in Iceland, offering both incoming and outgoing travel services.

Small Luxury Hotels of the World

http://www.ibmpcug.co.uk/~ecs/
hotel/slh/slh.htm

Small Luxury Hotels of the World has brought together some of the finest quality hotels around Scotland, embracing the sophistication of city centres, the glamour and charm of resorts, historic chateaux, and country houses throughout the world.

Products and Services

If there's one area of the World Wide Web and Yahoo! which has exploded and proven fabulously popular, it's *business.* Every company and subsidiary, every franchise and its licensees, and every home business has realized that the Internet is a happenin' place to market and advertise products — and occassionaly even to sell a few. Not only is Business by far the largest single category in the Yahoo! database, it's also growing the fastest. From get-rich-quick schemes to the Fortune 100, if it's out there in the real world, it's probably also now on the Web (or on its way).

Ready to actually buy something? Then you'll be interested in finding out about the wide range of services and products that are either directly available through the Net or have a billboard of some type online.

Advertising

Build a better mousetrap and people will come, right? Well, not exactly, and businesses large and small have discovered the importance of having a good advertising agency and public relations campaign. Even if it's for something simple, like a sign ….

ESSL Systems

http://www.lainet.com/color-system

ESSL Systems print giant posters in full color from your graphic design (Mac or PC), or photo, as it makes abundantly clear on its giant-sized Web site. The posters, by the way, are ideal for display ads, show displays, court exhibits, or even just as a memorable way to tell that special someone how you feel.

Animals

Pets are a great addition to just about any life, and a quick visit to the Web will reveal that lots of home pages include pictures of dogs and cats. Yes, there are even home pages entirely devoted to specific animals. If all these online folks have pets, you can bet they'll be needing pet-related products, too, and there are plenty to be found in Yahoo!.

Electronic ID, Inc.

http://www.dfw.net/~tqg/electronicid/

One problem faced by people with show dogs or purebred dogs is the fear of someone stealing the animals. Various strategies to defend against dognapping have been proposed, and one of the more high-tech solutions is the Destron-Fearing ID injectable *chip* and reader. You can learn more about this novel solution on this Web site.

Everlasting Stone Products

http://plainfield.bypass.com/stone/

Quality markers, memorials, monuments, caskets and urns for dogs, cats, horses, and other beloved pets. It may sound a bit macabre, but it's sort of nice to know that if you need a remembrance of your pet after it has passed away, you can now arrange for something right from your desk.

Lassie Dog Training System

http://voyager.bei.net/iquest/products/lassie/lassie.html

With the secrets used to train Lassie, train your dog to be the awe of your family and friends. A boy named Timmy not included.

Apparel

Too busy surfing the Net to go shopping? No worries — buy your clothes online and avoid traffic and parking hassles.

Bladewears

http://www.expanse.com/ep/biz/ads/bladewears

Sometimes you may get the urge to wear fashion that makes people uncomfortable and surprised, and that's when you'll want to visit Bladewears, with its line of smooth skeletonic designs guaranteed to make jaws gape. We don't make this stuff up — go and see these weird designs for yourself!

ColorTech

http://www.fla.net/color.html

So what do you do if you want to start dyeing things yourself? Rather than buying 50,000 boxes of RIT dye at the local store, you'll want to stop in at ColorTech, which features a cool pigment dye system that combines pigments and chemicals for the highest quality results. The system features excellent economy per pounds of textile dyed, too.

Comfort Zone Thermal Footwear System

http://www.pete.com/comfort/

Battery-operated shoe insert for casual wear, sports, health, work, indoors, outdoors, ice, snow, police work, hunting, and skiing. Also a health aid for the elderly and for cold feet patients.

BUSINESS DIRECTORY: COMPUTERS

Country Wears

http://www.xmission.com/~arts/cwears/cwears.html

Creative, comfortable, country jumpers are now available on the Internet from Country Wears of Bucks County, Pennsylvania.

Graphiti

http://libertynet.org/~graphiti/link06.html

Graphiti lets you create your own designs and have them turned into t-shirts, sweatshirts, tote-bags, caps, jackets, mugs, or aprons. Currently, items must be ordered in quantity (usually at least a dozen) but soon enough Graphiti will offer single items, which will be the perfect way to replace your e-mail addressed clothes when you change servers.

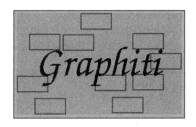

International Male

http://www.intmale.com/intmale/intmale.htm

Lots of great looking guys in pretty nice clothes, International Male offers a slick place to shop online, including shirts, pants, shoes, and more.

Karen's Tie Dye Shop

http://www.tie-dye.com/

Tie-dye via modem, if you can believe it. Karen lets you create your personal tie-dye online by choosing from a variety of clothing styles, patterns, and colors. A groovy site, man.

Mighty Dog Designs

http://sashimi.wwa.com/~notime/mdd/

These pups are the makers of the original WWW Shirt, the coolest Netsurfing shirt on the web, and the new line of NetNation wear, all at this hype-free site.

Namark Cap & Emblem

http://www.accessnv.com/namark/

Looking for custom hats, t-shirts, mugs, or any other clothing items? Namark has you covered, with customized business or personal apparel. You'll probably be amazed at the choices. Visit the site to preview the range of possibilities.

No Nonsense & More Legwear

http://www.vnet.net/nononsense/

Now you can pop over and buy No Nonsense, Easy Spirit, Burlington, Hue & Fashion Accents Pantyhose & Legwear at unbeatable prices.

Palookaville Hats

http://www.primenet.com/~hanibal/hat.html

Not everything is serious online, but you already knew that. If you feel like the cybervillage idiot or — worse — the *global* village idiot, you'll want to pop over to this site and see what it has for you. After all, as you know, life is too short to be serious.

Prism Magic Tie-Dye

http://www.aztech-cs.com/tie-dye/y-home.html

The sixties never died, and even now you can still get custom tie-dye apparel, through the futuristic online ordering system of Prism Magic Tie-Die. Prism Magic specializes in 100-percent cotton, tie-dyed clothing, team t-shirts and sportswear, and you can choose clothing style, color, and patterns all online.

Zeffa - 70's Clothing

http://www.u-net.com/~gaeia/zeffa.htm

Always wanted a biker jacket, a long-collared silk Oxford, or some other classic piece of 70s clothing but kinda missed out? Now Zeffa, from Manchester Englands' Affleck's Palace, can fufill all your material fantasies with its huge range of clothes.

Arts and Crafts

With its emphasis on graphics and design, it's no wonder that artists of all sorts have found the Web to be a fun place to visit. Even amateurs are finding arts and crafts a fun addition to their portfolio. Whether you're looking for supplies to help with your own projects or the product of other craftsfolk, the Web's a jumpin' place for arts and crafts.

The Bolt People

http://earthnews.com/bolt/

You've probably seen them before: Appels Bolt People, metal sculptures made out of everyday nuts and bolts. Included here are fun pictures of the artist's most popular pieces. Look for the Net surfer coming soon.

Ceremonial Robe Blankets

http://WWW.AbInfoHwy.CA/
abinfohwy/abobus/kermode/
robeblkt.html

The traditions of the Navajo and Hopi American Indian tribes are expressed in the four unique blanket designs offered at this site, each in two different color combinations.

Charm Woven Labels

http://www.europa.com/
charmwoven/

Add the finishing touch to your sewing, knitting, quilting, clothing, handiwork, and craft creations with personalized woven labels. Lots of attractive designs online.

Civil War Photographic Gallery

http://www.magibox.net/~civilwar

Compelling and dramatic photographs of the Civil War, all of which are available for viewing online or purchase. They make great decorations in an office and are a dramatic reminder of the pivotal American war.

Civil War Photographic Gallery

Discovery Direct

http://www.blvd.com/browse/
theblvd/discover.htm

Fine art from all over the world. Discovery Direct imports porcelain, crystal, and fine China and then presents and discusses each piece at its online Web site. An interesting place to visit in cyberspace.

Earth Essence

http://www.cfcl.com/cfcl/essence/

Earth Essence is all about gourd art, both contemporary and Native American, with a comprehensive history of gourds, art galleries, and biographies of the artists, all online.

Grampa's Woodworking Workshop

http://www.awinc.com/Cybermall/
shops/great/jd/

We always figured he was building another birdhouse in the basement, but it turns out that Grampa was making a remarkable number of unique lawn and garden ornaments and kitchen gadgets — all out of wood. This is a fun site full of neat things.

Mythopoeia: The Making of Myths

http://www.myth.com/

Mythopoeia, a new work in four parts by photographer Suza Scalora, puts a modern face on many familiar mythological and historical figures and also introduces you to several new creatures. Don't myth it.

National Congress of Art & Design

http://amsquare.com/ncad

ArtReach 95 is a contest that gives you a chance to have your work seen by more than 2000 gallery and museum directors, curators, private and corporate art collectors, art editors and publishers, dealers, designers, and architects throughout the United States. Pop over to the National Congress for more details and an ongoing exhibit of work.

Prints & Posters

ftp://ftp.netcom.com/pub/co/
collector/pat_lithos.html

Liven up those blank walls in your office with a selection of prints and posters available from this online shop. Unique and rare collectibles and limited editions are featured here, but a lot of low-priced, open stock selections are available as well.

Santa Fe Marketspace

http://www.artsantafe.com/
sfmhome.html

The premier collective of fine artists, craftspersons, and alternative healers from Northern New Mexico. The site also lists upcoming art events as well as seminars and workshops being held in the Santa Fe/Taos areas. If there's a spot for harmonic convergence on the Web, this may be it.

Print-Net

http://www.ottawa.net/~helpnet/
printnet.htm

Photographic-quality color prints produced from any graphics file you send to their site. Prints are returned by express courier. Instant hardcopy, in a weird sort of way.

Audio

You probably have a tinny little speaker in your PC, but having a real sound system is much more fun, and you can browse some of the finest audio equipment online.

High Definition Audio

http://www.Village.com/HDA/

Enhance your listening pleasure with this patented audio product for your home stereo, TV, or computer games. If you're on the go, you can also plug this into your car stereo to enhance your listening pleasure.

Wescott Audio-Net

http://starbase.ingress.com/~tonyb/audio/

Wescott Audio-Net has a slick site featuring an interactive, high-end audio home theater component matching system just perfect for audiophiles and videophiles. Why go to the theater when you can rebuild your home and enjoy everything but the sticky cola spills on the carpet?

Automotive

When you're ready to pick up a new set of wheels, the best weapon in your arsenal for dealing with salespeople is information, and that's the real forte of the Internet.

Dealernet

http://www.dealernet.com/

A complete listing of all automotive manufaturers and their respective dealers near you. Other services include all pricing of automobiles, parts, and service repairs and related automotive products organized in an easy-to-find manner. A great site for any car enthusiast.

Edmund's Automobile Buyer's Guides

gopher://gopher.enews.com/11/showroom/edmunds

Information on how to work with car dealers and other tips for buying a car, all available through Gopher, which you can access via your Web browser.

Books

One thing most net.citizens have in common is an enthusiasm for books. All kinds of books — technical, scientific, fiction, and so on — thousands of books are published each year. And it seems that just as many bookstores are around, too. Online, the variety of books is even larger, with bookstores, publishing houses, and a liberal sprinkling of individual authors all promoting their books.

50 Greatest Conspiracies of All Time

http://www.webcom.com/~conspire

Worried about the Illuminati or the grey aliens? How about the Knights Templar or the Bilderbergers? And what about the Man In Black who just "happened" to pop up at the bookstore when you bought this very book, eyeing your purchase and muttering to himself? Then you're a prime candidate for this new, definitive conspiracy book by Jonathan Vankin and John Whalen. Sample chapter and lots of information online.

Annie Sunshine and the White Owl of the Cedars

http://apollo.co.uk/a/asunshine/

Annette Martin audio tape and coloring book can help children learn to trust their feelings and dreams by listening. A relaxing and informative site.

Bookhouse

http://www.winternet.com/~ogrosman/BOOKHOUSE/

Bookhouse features a wide variety of children's literature. This site includes a comprehensive bibliography of titles that feature girls and women as strong characters.

Creating Cool Web Pages with HTML

http://www.mecklerweb.com/~taylor/coolweb/coolweb.html

If you're looking for a fun and non-techie introduction to HTML (hypertext markup language), the language of the Web, then the book *Creating Cool Web Pages with HTML* is a good choice, and you can check out the table of contents and even read a sample chapter on the Web.

The Goddess Within

http://www.primenet.com/~goddess/

This site offers a complete online metaphysical bookstore featuring books, audio/video, and gift items, all focused on the Goddess within each of us.

The Greatest Adventure

http://airspacemag.com/ASE/ASE_Home.html

If you've ever dreamed of being an astronaut, you'll want to zip over to this site where they feature illustrated exerpts from *The Greatest Adventure*, a book written and published by the Association of Space Explorers.

How Does Your Garden Grow

http://www.webdzine.com/eden.html

Green your life! Use the cycles of nature to reduce stress and balance your living. Read the introduction to Marilyn Barrett's book, *Creating Eden: The Garden as a Healing Space* and find out how to get in touch with nature in your own backyard.

I Live on a Raft, by Jerzy Harasymowicz

http://www.digimark.net/iatech/books/intro.htm

Illustrated poetry online. A collection of short, haiku-like verse for children. Harasymowicz, one of the leading poets in Poland, is noted for his unique personal mythology and the spontaneous fantasy of his works. Fun for all.

Internet How-To Book

http://www.demon.co.uk/objective/pkway.html

For beginning to intermediate users of the Internet. You can pop over and read excerpts of this how-to format book for useful and reliable information about using the Net.

Internet Business Guide, 2nd Edition

http://www.mecklerweb.com/~taylor#books

One of the most popular Internet business books, updated to reflect not only the latest events online but the latest predictions for the future of online commerce. Online information includes an extensive, nicely illustrated answer to the eternal question, "Is anyone making money on the Net?"

Legal Care for Your Software

http://www.island.com/LegalCare/

A step-by-step legal guide for computer software writers, programmers, and publishers, written by a lawyer and computer expert. The site includes many useful and important tips.

Lexikon Services Publishing

http://www.apollo.co.uk/a/Lexikon/

Site features excerpts of the fasinating book *A History of Computing: An Encyclopaedia of the People and Machines that Made Computing History.* Gives lots of background information on the computers and networks that comprise the Net.

Life's Great Questions

http://www.primenet.com/~farfan/

Who runs the Internet? Surely that's one of the greatest questions in life. Well, this site offers information about the science of self-questioning to help you find your own answers to important questions in your life. After all, cookie cutter answers to your problems probably don't exist.

Love, Sex and Marriage

http://intertain.com/store/new-browse/Love_Sex_and_Marriage.html

Marriage is a serious topic, and the selection of books at this site offers insight into the more serious side of love, sex, and marriage, with extensive information and online ordering.

Married! The Game of Marriage and Money

http://www.usit.net/harmon

You've read the books about love, sex, and marriage, so now what? Well, now it's time to get some board games from Jim Harmon and group to enjoy the lighter side of marriage — and find out if you're compatible at the same time. A fun preview online.

Multimedia and Hypertext: The Internet and Beyond

http://www.sun.com/columns/jakob/mmhtbook.html

Interface design is an important but unfortunately unheralded aspect of software and systems design. The textbook featured at this site offers information on hypertext, especially that found on the World Wide Web, with an emphasis on user interface design.

Music Book Store

http://www.scinet.com/~musicbk/

Thousands of books, songbooks and sheet music on all types of music, including an extensive catalog of jazz, blues, classical, world, opera, pop, folk, rock, country, and new age. A great place to browse, this site also features some interesting graphics.

Roth Publishing's Poetry Library for Librarians

http://www.rothpoem.com/

Info for libraries and librarians. Background info on some poets who were librarians, on Asian-American poets, and full text of seven poems about libraries (honest!) by poets such as John Greenleaf Whittier.

Tough Times

http://www.caprica.com/ ~amjohnson/tough.html

Tough Times, Tough Tactics is a guide written specifically for tenants who lease office, retail, or restaurant space. If that describes you, you will find the information offered at this site — including excerpts of the guide — to be of value.

Trial of the Century

http://www.mindspring.com/~dpwill/ojbook.html

No book published in 1995 is complete without at least one reference to the O.J. Simpson trial, and (thankfully) we found this site that features an interactive trial guide and description of the trial from the eyes of a juror.

Utah Travel Guide

http://www.netpub.com/utah/

If you're planning to visit this dynamic and exciting state — perhaps for the upcoming Olympics or a ski holiday — you'll be delighted to find the *Utah Travel Guide* online, from the Utah Travel Council and Network Publishing.

Wordplay

http://www.wordplay.com

Wordplay gives you lots of options in your online book browse. You can search for book titles on its online catalog, visit the James Baird Gallery featuring a multitude of Newfoundland artists, browse the CD collection, or take a virtual trip to North America's oldest city, the most easterly point on the continent.

Xplora

http://www.primenet.com/~xplora/

Xplora offers a variety of products, guides, and useful information for new users of the Internet and World Wide Web.

Business Opportunities

Ready to break out of the 9 to 5 rut and make your millions? Here's your chance to sample some of the more compelling business opportunities awaiting you in cyberspace.

Automatic MLM Downline Building

http://catalog.com/netpro/automatic/index.htm

You can now easily sponsor and build a huge, endless downline of productive, self-motivated recruits without selling, meetings, or training. Not sure what a *downline* is? Pop over to this site and read all about the intricacies of multilevel marketing.

Become a Travel Agent!

http://www.cabletv.com/travel.html

Check out One World Travel Center's "Affiliate" program and find out how you can become a travel agent, earning big bucks and seeing the world for free.

Dreams to Reality

http://www.pacifier.com/market/3bdreams/dream1.html

Enjoy an earning potential of $50 to $500 a day while receiving the lowest possible costs for your own long-distance calls through this telecommunications business opportunity.

Genesis International

http://www.village.com/genesis

Manufacturer of unique window treatments offers business opportunity in licensing and franchising for entrepreneur or investor interested in innovative interior decorating product: vertical blinds in stained glass.

High Commission Homeowners Financial Services

http://cyberzine.org/html/Sunde/sunde.html

The concept makes sense: take a job that other people do, but do it better and charge a higher commission. Check it out. This organization is interested in real estate, insurance, mortgage and loan brokers, tax planners, CPAs, and any other motivated entrepreneur.

Income Opportunities

http://www.incomeops.com/online/

This site is tied to the magazine of the same name and is just full of information about starting and maintaining a home-based business. The magazine's editorial content is available to Internet users a few weeks before it hits the streets each month.

Index - Commerce Business Daily (Community of Science)

http://cos.gdb.org/repos/cbd/cbd-intro.html

Commerce Business Daily lists notices of proposed government procurement actions, contract awards, sales of government property, and other procurement information. A new edition of the CBD is issued every business day. Each edition contains approximately 500 – 1,000 notices.

Internet Business Opportunity Showcase

http://www.ibos.com/pub/ibos/

This site is a showcase for small business opportunities, franchise offerings, network marketing opportunities, and business services. Includes lots of ways to make money that you've never thought of, including some that we're not even sure are legal in the United States.

MotoPhoto, Inc.

http://www.ibos.com/pub/ibos/moto/home.html

Drive-thru photo booths are a ubiquitous part of the American landscape and now you can find out about obtaining a franchise to join the rapidly growing, 450-store MotoPhoto network. The site includes background information on MotoPhoto and information how to obtain a franchise information package.

My Life is a Movie

http://www.lainet.com/~kcprods/

First it was the kidnapping, then the brush with fame. Your house burned down, but you were busy winning the lottery. Meanwhile, your spouse stole the car and left you all the dirty dishes. Let's face it: Some lives would make a great film, and the folks at this amusing site are on the lookout for true stories that could be made into movies. Did we mention the poodle incident?

National Center for Sports Medicine

http://www.maf.mobile.al.us/business/b_dir/ncsm

Wondering about your true biological age? Not the number of months since you were born, silly, but the physical condition of your body. Check it out at this site, which explains LIFE tests and shows how they use the results to determine your biological age.

Petro-Net

http://ias.rio.com/larry/gas/index.html

Why fill up at the corner gas station when you could start your own gas/diesel dealership? Find out more at the Petro-Net MLM information center online.

Professional Mobile Car Service

http://www.charm.net/~ibc/ibc2/prof-mob.html

Everyone needs his or her car washed, and this site explains how you can purchase an all-steel, professionally built, fully equipped mobile unit to wash and detail cars at your customer's home or business and make lots of money.

Video Billboard

http://palmbeach.net/ video_billboard/

You can run a video billboard out of your own home and earn top dollar. What's a Video Billboard? Relax — everything you need to know will be sent for your review, as detailed at this very enthusiastic site.

Business Supplies

Man cannot live on bread alone, and businesses — even online businesses — can't live without some occasional supplies, whether it be printer paper, business cards, or briefcases. Fortunately, you can find those products and more on the Net.

CCSR International Business Cards

http://www.terraport.net/CCSR/ homepage.html

Interested in doing business with clients or customers overseas? Then you'll want to visit this site to learn more about translating your business cards into Chinese, Japanese, Korean, Russian, Greek, or, if you're *already* overseas, English.

CEO Agenda

http://global3.breeders.org/c/ceo/ ceo.htm

This very well done Web site specializes in executive accessories: pens, pencils, writing instruments,

Italian leather briefcases, attaches, portfolios, gifts, day planners, electronic address books, specialized administrative supplies, organizers, and more. Well worth a visit for any businessperson.

Forms Solutions

http://www.imageserve.com/ FSHome.html

Predesigned business forms and checks for hundreds of accounting software packages, including Quicken, Peachtree, and many more. In addition, a Paper Direct dealer stocking three- and four-color predesigned papers and products, with all products shown and explained online.

Calendars

If you're not so glued to your computer that you have an online calendar, you might well be interested in a printed one that you can hang on the wall.

Hawaii Calendars

http://www.aloha.com/~petemart/ HwnResources/ HawaiianResources.html

This site offers information on a variety of 1996 calendars available now with lovely photographs from the Hawaiian Islands. It's a beautiful gift and sure to become a collector's item.

New York City Subways Calendar (trains, subway, railroad)

http://www.netstuff.com/subway.htm

This calendar, as you'll learn if you pop over to this site, features the rarely seen, color photography of New York's celebrated transit historian, Don Harold.

Catalogs

Sure, you get these in the mail all the time, but now instead of just piling them up on the table, you can get them electronically, too. A great boon to online shopping, and all these are also reputable, well established firms, too, which is a good thing.

Mac Zone Internet SuperStore

http://www.maczone.com/maczone/

Macintosh users are already familiar with Mac Zone, a popular and competitively priced Macintosh hardware and software vendor. Now you can browse and shop its catalog online, anytime, and pick from the hottest Macintosh hardware, software, and peripheral products.

Scotty Firefighter

http://www.islandnet.com/~scotty/fire1.html

All your childhood firefighter fantasies come true online at the Scotty Firefighter site. Well, maybe — if you were more interested in the equipment on a firetruck than in the fighters themselves. This cool site features nozzles, inductors, back packs, pumps, and portable foam systems for fighting residential, commercial, and forest fires.

Speak To Me

http://clickshop.com/speak/

All products featured in this online catalog actually talk, and they make practical and helpful gifts and novelties. The swearing keychain is especially charming.

Stevens Magic Emporium

http://www.southwind.net/IMS/magic/

This firm has sold the finest magical apparatus for more than 50 years to noted magic celebrities, semi-professional magicians, and amateurs. Included on this fun site are a series of videos that can take the mystery out of magic, and a series of professional catalogs that offer a glimpse into what your favorite prestidigitator is busy purchasing for next week's show.

Children

You probably had no idea you could buy children through the Internet, did you? But seriously, a number of safety and learning products are available on the Net for children and their parents.

Safe Hygiene For Children

http://netmar.com/~back2nat/TTOKidsCare.html

Now the children can take care of their everyday hygiene with these products that have Australian Tea Tree Oil in them. Visit this site to learn more, and check out their Fruity Fun Stuff shampoo, too.

Computer-Ed High-Tech Camp

http://www.servtech.com/public/comped/

This summer camp specializes in computer activities such as building a PC, R/C cars, model rocketry, programming languages, telecommunications, video production, camp radio, drama, photography, breaking into banks, and disrupting worldwide

communications. Well, no, the last two aren't part of the *official* curriculum, but we have our suspicions. Computer-Ed is a fun place for a kid to spend a summer, even if they don't have the hacker instinct.

Clubs

The Internet is one of the easiest places in the world to find information about other people with similar interests, and it's no surprise that a number of clubs are starting to expand into the online frontier.

Abundant Love Institute

http://www.wp.com/lovemore/

The Abundant Love Institute is an organization and resource for people who believe in having more than one intimate partner responsibly and ethically. Abundant Love supports polyamory, extended family, polyfidelity, responsible nonmongamy, and other new relationship forms and publish *Loving More* magazine, with excerpts online.

Hogs Head Beer Cellars

http://www.greensboro.nc.us/frontier/business/hog/

What could be better than two different six-packs of hard-to-find, hand-crafted beer delivered to your doorstep every month? Maybe some peanuts to go with it? A quick visit to this site confirms that it offers lots of great beers but no peanuts. Yet.

Spa Treatment of the Month Club

http://www.mudbath.com/spa/

Take some time out for yourself and enjoy a monthly spa treatment. Each month you will receive some of the world's most luxurious treatments for you to experience, as explained at this relaxing Web site.

Collectibles

Whether its coins or stamps, bottle caps or bits of yarn, everyone seems to have some sort of collection. And when you're on the Internet, you can find others who not only share your private obsession but who are selling precisely the pieces you need.

Absolut Collectibles

http://www.webstreetmall.com/mall/absolut/absolut.html

Absolut Vodka has had a popular series of print advertisements over the last few years — you've seen them. If you're a fan of the ad series, you'll want to visit Absolut Collectibles and find out more about the many advertisements Absolut has run and perhaps purchase something directly from these collectors.

Artoons!

http://www.getnet.com/artoons

Framed sericel/serigraph's of famous cartoons. A serigraph is a painting on a transparent sheet of celluloid. Each color is applied separately, one screen at a time, and the end result is an original, Limited Edition work of art.

CyberCinema

http://www.ibag.com/cinema

Movie fans will be delighted to visit this site which not only features information on the top ten movies in the United States, but also offers a wide range of movie posters and some movie-related memorabilia.

The New England Collectors Society

http://shopping2000.com/shopping2000/the_new_en/the_new_en.html

The New England Collectors Society focuses on creating high-quality, affordable, and attractive collectible products. Don't miss the "dash for the timber" Remington print.

Computers

If you're on the Net, you gotta have some sort of computer, so it's not a surprise that this most common of interests is one of the most popular areas for products and services on Yahoo! There are literally thousands of entries offering software, hardware, peripherals, and much more. Also see the Computers and Internet chapter.

American Computer Exchange

http://www.crl.com/~amcoex

If you haven't been lulled into a false sense of anxiety about the need for the latest and greatest computers, you know that used computers can be a terrific bargain. Six months old and it might be half the price it was originally. The American Computer Exchange publishes the industry standard AmCoEx Index of Used Computer Prices, a valuable spot to check prior to any purchase.

Bighorn Memory

http://www.accessnv.com/bighorn/

If your journeys on the Internet have convinced you that more memory wouldn't sit unused, you've found the solution you seek at Bighorn Memory. It specializes in computer memory with competitive prices, quality products, and terrific customer service. Helpful charts explain SIMM memory and cache memory, too.

Chartwell-Bratt

http://www.studli.se/chartwell.html

This Web site offers computing, engineering, and science books and related mathematics software. They're specialists in computer algebra software and supporting books, perfect for the student in your family.

Chief Legal Officer

http://rampages.onramp.net/~chief/

Chief Legal Officer is a multi-user Windows-based software product designed to meet the needs of the corporate legal department: case tracking, report writing, calendar/tickler, outside counsel fees/expense, budgeting. Lots more information at this, the official Web site.

Christie Communications Ltd

http://www.sas.ab.ca/biz/christie/

Christie Communications has been developing customized training materials and other communication products for 17 years, and this Canadian firm can help you with your training needs, large or small.

DiskIndex

http://www.ior.com/~mikeh/

Ever tried to find a file that's on a 3.5-inch disk but realized that your labelling system leaves something to be desired? Well, now there's a cool, high-tech solution with DiskIndex, a floppy catalog program. More about DiskIndex on this Web site.

Erasable Disk & VHS Label System

http://cyteria.com/vhs.htm

Speaking of floppy disks, one of the reasons that they often get out of date is because you always have to find new labels to slap atop the current one. If you had erasable labels, however, you'd simply wipe off the old info and scribble on the new, quickly and easily. Even better, you can get these erasable labels for videotapes, too.

Face Recognition by Miros

http://www.miros.com/biz/miros/

It's like having a prop from a spy thriller at home: Miros offers a sophisticated face recognition system that can be used to verify identity for secure access to rooms, buildings, and computer networks. TrueFace compares a live face image to a stored image to determine if a user is who he or she claims to be, with remarkable accuracy. This site explains the technology in greater detail.

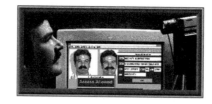

Illinois Network Systems

http://miso.wwa.com/~insnet/

Since not every computer user or network site has a large training budget, the Illinois Network Systems site offers a wide variety of low-cost training materials, ranging from CD-ROMs to videos, hardware and software solutions, and a number of different training manuals. And all can be purchased online.

Index - Softinfo

http://www.icp.com/softinfo/

Softinfo is a database of software products and suppliers, with details on more than 4,500 software suppliers and 16,500 software products. An invaluable site to check prior to any major software purchase decision.

Internet Shopping Network

http://www.internet.net/

From the convenience of your desk, you can easily shop for more than 20,000 different computer hardware and software products at this well-organized site. The prices are good, the interface is slick, and lots of additional information and reading material is available, too.

Magic World of ABC's

http://www.widdl.com/MediaPro/magic.html

Hop aboard the magic carpet with Sam to learn all about this new children's learning game on CD-ROM, with lively sound and colorful animation. You can't download a demo from this site, but you can preview the fun graphics and request a thirty-day evaluation disk.

Memory World Catalog

http://www.memorywld.com/~memory/index.html

Whether it's for your laptop, laser printer, workstation, or any other type of computer product, Memory World has you covered with its product line. Visit this site to see the latest pricing in SIMM Modules, CPUs, motherboards, hard drives, and proprietary memory.

Parham Technologies, Inc.

http://www.jcic.org/GateKeeper/
gate.htm

GateKeeper is a hardware device that operates in pairs, located in-line and in front of your modem or PBX. It silently answers incoming calls and checks for a programmable key prior to passing call to the modem/PBX. A secure solution to your networking needs that minimizes the chance of delinquents visiting your LAN.

Peripheral Systems Group

http://lovedog.com/pub/psg/

One of the first things you realize after spending any time on the Net is that you could have quite a good time downloading all the goodies from all the different sites online. The problem is, where would you put it? Fortunately, a solution has presented itself: a bigger hard drive. Peripheral Systems Groups offers a full line of hard drives, mice, tablets, and wireless communications devices, with prices updated daily.

Puffer

http://execpc.com/~kbriggs/

Puffer is a shareware encryption software program for electronic mail and file transfer that runs on any Windows machine. It features the Blowfish encryption algorithm, as explained in detail at this Web site.

Road Warrior Outpost

http://warrior.com/

If you are a road warrior (carry your portable PC on the road), you'll be glad to find this comprehensive site

which features a wide variety of software and hardware resource for portable computer users. It also includes information on notebook and laptop computer products, services, and news.

RusVocab

http://www.imagi.net/~whitbear/
wbrvshar.html

Ready to learn Russian? You might be surprised how quickly you can learn with the help of RusVocab, a simple Windows shareware program available from this Web site.

Synergy Solutions

http://www.synergysol.com/www/
synergy/

This site features information on Modem Assist, an easy way to share modems on a network, and the Synergy Solutions four-port modem card for PCs.

The Training Registry

http://www.tregistry.com/ttr/

Looking for a training course for yourself or your company but unsure where to turn? The Training Registery is a great first stop, with an online searchable catalog of training courses offered by a number of different companies on a wide variety of subjects.

Construction

Here is a site that you'll probably find very constructive.

Building Industry Exchange

http://www.building.com/bix/

If you're in the construction field and plugged into the global network, you'll definitely want to stop by the Building Industry Exchange, with its resource and communications areas specifically for architects, engineers, real estate developers, government agencies, environment protection services, health and safety services, manufacturers, and construction workers. Information on this site includes education, career planning, news, a library, chat forum, and a virtual industrial park.

Contests

You can win something amazing simply by visiting one of these sites. In fact, a number of different Web sites feature raffles and other promotional giveaways, and it's a good idea to pop into this area of Yahoo! occasionally to see what's brewin'.

American Dream Contest

http://inetads.com/dream/

Here's the gig for this one: They're giving away a $400,000 house in Idaho, but to enter you have to write and mail in a 100-word essay explaining why you want to win, and enclose a $50.00 entry fee. Check it out, and perhaps you'll win the American Dream Contest.

Awesome Video Contest

http://www.worldramp.net/redlion/

Do you have embarassing video clips of friends or families? Submit them through this online site to enter a contest with a $10,000 grand prize.

Hyde Park Suites Promotional Raffle

http://cyber.cclims.com/comp/hps/raffle.html

Hyde Park is one of the lovelier hotels in the San Francisco area and it's offering you the chance to win a one-night hotel stay just for filling out an online survey. Couldn't hurt!

Internet Marketing Questionnaire

http://www.cybersight.com/cgi-bin/cs/s?bazaar.gmml

Voice your concerns on the future commercial development of the Internet and possibly win a prize (can you say *irony*?).

Multimedia Newsstand Interactive Trivia Contest

http://mmnewsstand.com/Trivia/

Win a Harper's Bazaar t-shirt and the 1995 Spring Fashion Video with tips from the runways of Paris, Milan, and New York for your knowledge of literary trivia. Recent questions include "What year was *Dracula* first

published?" and "What author first published short stories under the pseudonym Stephen Daedelus?"

Pro CD - Win Select Phone

http://www.procd.com/contest1.htm

If you've ever despaired of having enough phone books available to obviate the need to ever dial 411, you'll be most interested in Select Phone, a CD-ROM that contains thousands of phone books, online. Better yet, visit this site and you can possibly win a free copy of Select Phone on CD-ROM.

Top Ten Promises Contest

http://turnpike.net/emporium/N/networth/promise4.htm

If you're looking for a good giggle and perhaps even the chance to win a cool bumper sticker, swing by the Top Ten Promises Contest site and learn the ten most common (false) promises heard by the judges. On the list are "Honey, I'll log off in two minutes," "You won't need the receipt," and "I'll behave myself this time."

Two Minute Warning, the NFL Trivia Game

http://www.dtd.com/tmw

This fun and visually attractive Web site allows football fans and trivia enthusiasts to participate in a challenging and fun trivia game for prizes. A typical hard question: Who was the first quarterback to throw 20 touchdown passes in a season?

Win $2,500 Word Puzzle Contests

http://iquest.com/~pinnacle/contests.html

Word puzzles for fun and profit. (In fact, if you know the answer to 25-across, give us a call.) Seriously, this site features a $2,500 shareware registration incentive contest involving some pretty thorny word puzzles.

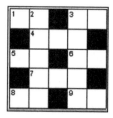

Drinks

All this typing and clicking has made you awfully thirsty, no? Whether your favorite beverage is a cold beer or a steaming mug of caffeine-laced coffee, some companies on the Net offer refreshing libations plus plenty of information.

Cheap Beer Server

http://jaka.nn.com/~tinsel/beer/

There are plenty of places to learn about snooty and limited-run beers, but most folks drink simple beers that quench the thirst without depleting the pocketbook. Here's a happening spot to talk about your favorite brewski.

Diedrich Coffee

http://www.diedrich.com/

The Deidrich family has been roasting coffee since 1921, and this site offers lots of java-related information, including some helpful tips on brewing your own coffee and the ever-popular coffee news (did you know that beans lose more than half their flavor two weeks after being roasted?). The site also offers a variety of custom roasts from the finest quality arabica coffees, imported from around the world.

Demanovka Herbal Liquor

http://www.nomius.com/ ~demanovka/liquor.htm

Fourteen species of secret forest herbs are combined to make this unique herbal liquor from the heart of Europe. Ready for export worldwide, it's similar to Jaegermeister. No free samples online, unfortunately.

The Tea And Coffee Plant (London)

http://www.demon.co.uk/london-calling/coffront.html

When you want a cultured break from the liquor-swilling gang, pop over to this site and learn about its 17 varieties of fresh-roasted coffee and wide selection of teas, straight from London, England. This site also features information about the company's custom tea blend and bags.

Education

Although many sites on the Net offer pointers to educational resources, the number of commercial education products is still rather small. Yahoo! lists the best ones, but for the most part, if you're interested in education,

we still recommend you start with the vast amount of free Web documents and materials online and then move to commercial products and services as needed.

Pimsleur Language Learning

http://www.pimsleur.com/

Pop over to this site and you can download audio files which let you preview the first lesson of beginning courses in Italian, French, German, Spanish, Russian, and Japanese. They also have an extensive list of multi-language software applications and utilities available.

Memory Power Course

http://www.direct.ca/winning/

Imagine remembering the name and face of everyone you meet. appointments and important dates, to-do lists, complex numbers, and even higher grades at school. The home course highlighted at this site gives you a way to improve your memory and an online workbook containing exercises to help you hone your skills.

Electronics

Needless to say, the Net has its share of engineers — amateur and professional — and as a result, a number of firms offer electronic components for the do-it-yourselfer online.

Electronics Distribution

http://www.rell.com

Richardson Electronics is a worldwide distributor of electronic component

parts: electron tubes, power semiconductors, cathode-ray tubes, and security systems. This information-rich Web site explains who the folks at Richardson Electronics are, lists their many products, and offers lots of additional information, including a calendar that lists trade shows and seminars.

Halfin SA Comset Division

http://www.wp.com/Halfin/ home.html

This site highlights the products available from Halfin SA, an independant distributor of semiconductors based in Belgium. Their extensive stock also includes ICs, diodes, transistors, data books, and they work with subcontractors in the United States, Europe, and Asia.

Entertainment

One of the reasons that the Internet is so amazingly popular across a wide variety of different people is very simply because *it's fun*. A sense of play emanates from all over the Net and Web, and the Yahoo! service maintains listings of hundreds of entertainers and entertainment sites, of which these are but a few.

Astrologer's Directory

http://www.astrologer.com/

Wondering if today is a good day to leave the house? You can visit professional astrologers by popping over to the Astrologer's Directory on the Web. In addition, you'll find tons of astrological information at this site.

Horse Racing Handicapping

http://www.netrunner.net/~owl1/

If the sound of the trumpets and the eager chatter of race fans piques your interest, if the sheen of sweat on a horse excites your gambling instincts, then you're going to be thrilled by Cyber Horse Challenge, a Web site dedicated to offering you accurate tip selections and jockey/trainer past performance information. Mostly focused on race tracks in Florida.

New Age Directory

http://www.wholarts.com/psychic/newage.html

This is the most comprehensive listing of New Age resources on the Internet. Here you can easily find information on your favorite New Age topic, from astrology to UFOs.

Outland Chess

http://www.outland.com/OutlandChess.html

Play chess in real-time against others on the Internet at Outland, a new destination where you can play real-time graphical games through the Internet. You get to rate your skill level before playing, but don't overestimate yourself — there are some excellent chess players in cyberspace.

Richard's Golf Jokes

http://www.cerius.com/richard/

Jokes and observations on The Game collected at public, private, and resort course fairways, locker rooms, and bars over the last twenty years. The product for sale on this site is a book of golf jokes, but there are a couple of cute ones you can read for free.

Sound Photosynthesis Psychedelics

http://www.photosynthesis.com/home.html

This wild Web site contains thousands of hours of unique audio and video material documenting some of the great minds of our era. Sound Photosynthesis also maintians large audiovisual libaries of information on psychedelics, shamanism, religion, and related topics. A *must* for Terence McKenna fans. Log in, turn on, and drop out.

Winning Ways (Blackjack secrets)

http://www.paonline.com/winning/

Why work for a living when you can learn the secret of blackjack professionals and nip over to Vegas or Atlantic City to earn millions? You think we're kidding? Pop over to this site and learn all about how casinos stack the game against the player. The blackjack 101 material at this site can teach you how to win anyway. It makes for interesting reading, even if you're not the gambling type.

Environment

Whether you think we're on Starship Earth or figure that Gaia can rejuvenate herself as needed, you'll be impressed by the range of environmental products available on the Internet. Yahoo! maintains a huge listing of environmental sites. Here are but a few.

Genesis II

http://www.gate.net/~genesis/

This site describes a mixed solid-waste composting system that is ecologically benign, economical, and a good choice for governments and businesses that want to process mixed solid waste. Tip: Don't bother visiting unless your Web browser supports graphics.

Touchstone Natural Products Marketing

http://monsterbit.com/touch/touch.html

This innovative site offers its information in English, French, and Spanish, which vastly expands its appeal to millions of Net surfers worldwide. Explore the dozens of different companies and natural products represented at this site. From aquamassage to garlic pills, you'll discover a wide variety of different things to learn about.

Weather Watcher Pager Service

http://www.ns.doe.ca/aeb/commercial/pager.html

If you need to always be on top of the weather, want to be notified of any changes from the National Weather Service, and have a standard alphanumeric pager, then hurry up and zoom over to this site to check out the Weather Watcher Pager Service.

Financial Services

Now that you're making money — and spending it online — you'll no doubt need an accountant or financial advisor to help you manage your funds. Fortunately, quite a few financial services are already online.

Cool Country Credit Cards

http://www.coolcountry.com/cards/

Country music fans will want to have a Cool Country Visa for those visits to Nashville. Visit this site learn how you can choose between Brooks & Dunn, Travis Tritt, Tracy Lawrence, Reba McEntire, or Alan Jackson cards. Now, about that Elvis card ….

FinanCenter

http://www.financenter.com/resources/

This terrific site offers a wide variety of personal finance resources, including information on home, auto, and educational loans, plus info on credit cards and financial institutions. And lots more. FinanCenter also maintains a useful directory of financial professionals and their services.

Galleria Investor's Services

http://www.webcom.com/~galleria/

Lots of financial products, services, and supplies, including weekly Dow Jones stock history since 1910. And don't miss the list of trading and investment portfolio management software hosted at this Web site.

Index: Online Banking and Financial Services

http://www.orcc.com/orcc/banking.htm

Looking for a bank, credit union, investment service, or financial service online? Stop by this comprehensive index of online banking to find information on more than 100 different financial institutions that have a presence on the Web.

Morgan Commercial

http://www.cybercom.com/~aig/morgan.html

If you're looking for a way to save some money on your house, perhaps through a refinancing or second mortgage, you'll be interested in visiting the Morgan Commercial Web site. MC is a 10-year-old mortgage company offering the lowest-rate mortgages for its clients.

Mortgage Strategies

http://www.ais.net/netmall/mortgage/

You may not realize it, but by switching your mortgage to a biweekly schedule, you could save up to 30 percent on the lifetime cost of your house. Intrigued? Pop over to this site and you'll be able to calculate the savings directly and learn how to swtich your existing mortgage, too.

QuickQuote

http://www.quickquote.com/

QuickQuote provides online comparison shopping for annuities and term life insurance in an interesting and informative manner.

Flowers

For some reason, the one product available through the Internet which has garnered the most press in the last year has been flowers from online florists. It seems like every florist in the nation has plugged into the online community, hoping for orders from thousands of Internet denizens. Here's a sampling.

Absolutely Fresh Flowers

http://www.cts.com/~flowers/

Absolutely Fresh Flowers specializes in growing supreme quality miniature carnations in greenhouses and then distributing eye-catching bouquets of hundreds of flowers, all with overnight delivery. A humble site.

Flower Link

http://go.flowerlink.com/html/menu1.html

Your link to flowers, plants, and gifts. Flower Link is the Web site for a national association of florists offering local and FTD arrangements with the option of same-day delivery. The site features useful information on cut flowers and houseplants, too.

FTD Internet

http://www.novator.com/FTD-Catalog/

Many of the florists online are part of the FTD (Florists' Transworld Delivery) system, but this site actually offers the official FTD catalog, which contains more than 80 floral arrangements and gift baskets with delivery worldwide. You can pick a florist to work with quite easily.

Forever Yours Keepsakes, Ltd

http://www.westnet.com/fyk/

Preserve your floral arrangements from weddings and other special occasions instead of tossing them. A neat online poster highlights this site.

Grower Connection

http://www.silcom.com/growerconnection/

Blooming potted plants for you or as gifts to friends, family, and business associates. Also, for Christmas, Grower Connection offers unique wreaths and swags. Instead of buying from a florist, you can now buy your flowers direct from the grower.

Mango Rose Airport Lei Greeting Service

http://www.maui.net/~reman/greet.html

Start your Hawaiian vacation off with the "Aloha" of a special lei greeting at the airport, simply by visiting this site. It can be an amusing surprise for the rest of the travelers in your party, too.

Nature's Rose Floral Services

http://www.intnet.net/Floral/

It's 2 p.m., and today is your Mom's birthday. Think quick! No reason to panic — connect to this site and you can browse through dozens of different floral arrangements, order, and have it delivered, all online.

Tropical Flowers by Charles

http://hoohana.aloha.net/~charles/

Brilliant arrays of tropical flowers and foliage, attractively gift boxed, are shipped anywhere from Kauai, Hawaii. Lots of pictures and information on the exotic flowers and island itself.

Food

Everyone's got to eat, and if you're plugged into the Internet today, you have access to a remarkable — even overwhelming — array of treats and snacks. Unfortunately, no one has yet figured out how to wash dishes in cyberspace.

Captain Morgan Original Spiced Rum

http://sportsworld.line.com/captain_morgan/

Cybership is a virtual vessel of cool things to click on, including a treasure-hunt contest, a sports trivia challenge, recipes, and other info.

Frito-Lay

http://www.fritolay.com/

Your virtual snack counter on the Internet from the makers of Cheetos, Lays Potato Chips, Doritos, and other munchies. Fun, games, and everyone's favorite foods, even recipies — but no free samples.

Indian River Gift Fruit

http://www.awa.com/fruit/

Fresh and delicious oranges, grapefruits, and gift baskets from the Indian River Region of Florida shipped direct, with some mouthwatering graphics.

Irish/English Breakfast

http://www.iol.ie/resource/imi/breakfast/

Attention Irish , English, Scots, and Welsh in the United States: It is now possible to order and receive within 72 hours Irish Rashers and sausages and black and white pudding. Better yet, pop over and actually hear the sound of bacon sizzling on the pan!

Rattlesnake Ranch Gourmet Foods

http://www.wimsey.com/PacificaBlue/ranch/

Don't mess with bland foods ever again. A quick visit to this exciting Web site and you'll be ready to blow off the top of your skull with any of its hot, tasty additions to your kitchen. Try the Salsa Diablo and the Snakebite Salsa.

Vinaigretta

http://www.infop.com/etta/
index.html

This low-key site offers information on farm-grown foods and condiments which offer an explosion of taste, texture, color, and aroma to delight all the senses.

Furniture

Old doors on file cabinets are definitely *tres chic* for a startup office, and cinderblock and pine boards can work for home, but sooner or later everyone wants to upgrade to nice seating, beds, and perhaps even an antique or two.

Atrium Furniture Mall

http://theatrium.com/furniture/

Offering furniture for the living room, dining room, bedroom, office, and even the kids' room, this site is a central online listing for almost 40 different retail stores, all with substantial discounts for their online customers.

Habitech

http://www.habitech.com/

Tough crowds at your office? Have emotional meetings ended with furniture flying? In addition to first-aid equipment — which you can find online (see the Health chapter) — you'll also be interested in the virtually indestructible computer furniture offered by this firm.

Nastalgia

http://www.dnai.com/~mgroll/

Hand-carved replicas of museum quality antiques from the past few centuries are featured here, divided into four main categories: chairs, tables, bookcases, and armoires. Perfect for the new CEO.

Woodcase

http://www.gate.net/~woodcase/

Woodcase offers information on its well-designed home office computer workstation desk that can help you be more efficient and comfortable while working. Even better, it's much safer for your equipment than is a table or floor.

General Merchandise

From the grab bag of Yahoo information, here are some shops that offer general merchandise and more.

Horizon Sales - A World of Products

http://www.ip.net/shops/
Horizon_Sales_Merchandise_Mart/

This site offers a wide variety of products, including giftware, jewelry, tools, kitchenware, business accessories, and more. You'll also want to check out their selection of CDs and music.

O'Shea

http://www.designstein.com/
project900/

If you've ever wondered what happens to old and obsolete equipment that's still in good working order but is no longer the latest fashion or technology, it's time to visit O'Shea. You'll find such amazing things as a crate of Atari 2600 video games, cookie cutters, amplifier phones, and more. Always a bargain.

Project 900, Inc.

http://www.designstein.com/
project900/

A liquidation firm that deals only in first-quality, new, never opened goods. Its attractive pages offer a wide array of products, from housewares to leather coats, toys, and books.

Get Rich Quick

Imagine: Two weeks from today you could be sitting in the lap of luxury with thousands in your bank account and more arriving each day. Are schemes that makes such promises real? One thing's for certain: They're nice dreams. Just be careful.

Passport to Adventure

http://garnet.acns.fsu.edu/~jrioux/

This is, ostensibly, a unique multilevel marketing program that can theoretically help you in achieving the American dream of lots of money for no work.

A Smarter Way To Play Lotto

http://www.interaccess.com/trc/bl_lotto.html

200 chances to win each week through the new Group Powerball Lotto. If you're lucky, you could share in jackpots that average $20 million.

How To Publish a Book and Sell a Million Copies

http://supermall.com/ndi/publish.html

Ted Nicholas, the best-selling author, reveals his secrets to becoming a millionaire at this Web site. Let's see, now first you need to have a Web page ....

Lottery for PC peripherals

http://ebs.support.nl/ebs/lottery.html

Here's a fun idea: Looking for a new peripheral for your PC? Why not buy an electronic lottery ticket for a monthly peripheral drawing? Prizes include remote power devices, modems, remote car controls, and more.

Option II

http://www.sundaypaper.com/www/mlment.htm

The idea here is that you can save money by working with this firm to create gift and endowment programs. It's a multilevel marketing business that's supposed to help you avoid needing collateral for loans.

Voice Bulletin Board Systems

ftp://www.cts.com/pub/rfarrell/infinix.html

Set up your own voice bulletin board system for entertainment, automated support desks, chat lines, voice messaging, and more. Details on the costs and reasonable expectations of profits at this Web site are a bit sketchy, but you may find it intriguing nonetheless.

Gifts

Birthday coming up, holidays approaching, or just want to share your happiness and success with those around you? Why not purchase unique and fun gifts by pointing and clicking? Yahoo! makes it easy to peruse a wide selection of unusual options without leaving your desk.

800 SPIRITS Gift

http://owl.net/OWLspace/spirits/

This site features information about the 800 SPIRITS corporate gift catalog. If you're looking for a different way to thank your employees or partners for a job well done, or just want to get your company name better known, these gifts offer some fun solutions.

Cybermugs!

http://www.webscope.com/cybermugs/homepage.html

Cybermugs are quality 11 oz. mugs that proudly and humorously display Internet-related messages. An example: *caffeine@internet.mug.* It probably wouldn't work as a mailing address.

Dancing Dragon Designs

http://www.northcoast.com/unlimited/product_directory/dancing_dragon/dancing_dragon.html

Encounter rare and mysterious dragons in every form, from gold to silk, in collectibles, books, posters, puzzles, masks, sculptures, jewelry, t-shirts, artifacts, personal and household items, and more, all online.

Flux Productions

http://www.peak.org/~flux/flux/leather.html

Looking for custom-tooled, handcrafted leather for you or as a gift for a friend? This firm offers a variety of leather-related services. You can almost smell the rawhide.

Ghost in a Bottle

http://www.shopkeeper.com/shops/GHOST_IN_A_BOTTLE/

Simply uncork the bottle and prepare yourself for those special pleasures that only a ghost can bring. It's not as scary as you might think.

Harmon & Company

http://www.bnt.com/~harmon/

Harmon & Company offers a wide variety of figurines, miniatures, collectibles, jewelry, and seasonal gifts at this low-key Web site.

Studio Eyebeam

http://www.chataqua.com/SE/

Share the irreverent humor of cartoonist Sam Hurt, creator of the nationally known "Eyebeam" and "Queen of the Universe" strips with unique post cards, t-shirts, books, and other great gifts, all featured at this site.

Xanadu

http://www.sbusiness.com/xanadu/

Everyday and seasonal greeting cards and gifts for all occasions. Don't forget to check out Department 56 when you visit this site.

Government

(See also the Government chapter.)

The government has a reputation for being a bunch of stodgy folk that don't really think much of this newfangled technology, but in fact the U.S. government created the Internet, and many U.S. government agencies — county, state, and federal — are excited about the chance to share their research and information with the general public. Could it be that if they're on the Web, they appear to be more cutting-edge and valuable and may therefore avoid the budget-cutters' axes? Maybe. Third parties also are getting into the act, offering products and services aimed at government employees.

FedCenter: Technology Information for Government into the 21st Century

http://www.fedcenter.com

This free service exists to benefit government end-users, high-tech suppliers, and solution providers to enhance the exchange of value-added information and improve communication and partnerships between the government and industry.

Health and Fitness

Too many hours sitting in front of a screen tapping on a keyboard and pushing a mouse around can definitely prove unhealthy, but what can you do about it now that you're a serious Internet surfer? You can check out some of the many products available in the area of health and fitness. Online, of course.

Audiological Engineering Corp.

http://hermes-op.com/aec/aechompg.html

Research and development of communication aids for deaf and people who hard of hearing. Current products include: TACTAID vibrotactile aids for profoundly deaf people and the CHORUS Universal Receiver.

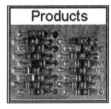

Products

Cybershrink

http://www.gate.net/~cyshrink/

Life got you down? Can't figure out why your boyfriend is always mad at you, or why your girlfriend looks on in horror when you talk with your parents on the phone? Maybe you need some professional help. Some online professional help. That's where Cybershrink comes in. It's a psychological advice service staffed by highly trained mental health professionals online.

Den-Tel-Net

http://www.onramp.net/Den-Tel-Net/

The Dental Telecommunications Network offers lots of information about dentistry for the 21st Century. If you think things aren't changing quickly, you just haven't visited this site.

It Smells SO Good - Aromatherapy Products

http://www.los-gatos.scruznet.com/los_gatos/businesses/smells_so_good/storefront.html

Aromatherapy explores the therapeutic possibilities of aromas. One of many sites where having more than just visuals and audio would be terrific.

MindWorks Press

http://www.interconnect.com/mindworks/

This site explains their various programs for optimizing relationships, health, success, and mind. Including: Attention Deficit Disorder, parenting skills, teaching children values, and overcoming self-defeating behaviors.

Scotlens - Innovative contact lenses

http://www.route-one.co.uk/route-one/scotlens/

Scotlens offer a free global consultancy for their contact lens service. The lenses are made of innovative new materials, and there is a facility for calculating toric lenses online. Great fun for contact lens wearers.

Self Breast Examination and Mammography

http://www.net-advisor.com/
mammog/

Serious insights in breast cancer and tips on breast self-examination. Also provides information from the American Cancer Society, and all within a nicely done Web site.

Ultra Violet Sensometer

http://www.maui.net/~southsky/
uvcard2.html

A simple, credit-card sized device for measuring ultraviolet light intensity. Check UV levels, test sunscreen, sunglasses, more. Help protect yourself from the effects of overexposure to the sun. Quite handy.

Hobbies

These are things you do when you're not working on your computer. Remember your ant farm?

Butterfingers Juggling Equipment

http://www.hub.co.uk/intercafe/
butterfingers/index.html

Just about everything to do with juggling and a huge range of books on juggling and circus skills, all from this UK-based comapny. Pointers to juggling information online, too.

Yarn & Stitches, Inc.

http://www.shoponline.com/SHOP/
YandS/YandS_home.html

This rather slow but attractive Web site offers information about their retail store that sells kits, yarn, needles, hooks, accessories, and patterns, and also serves up lots of information about online crafts and craft information.

Home and Garden

It can be fun and rewarding to fix up your home through painting, decorating, new furniture, and whatnot. And few things produce as peaceful a state of mind as gardening.

Rock Spray Nursery

http://www.capecod.net/LPines/
rspray/rspray.htm

This firm specializes in growing and selling hardy heath and heather ground coverings. The site offers a wealth of lovely photographs and information about the plants, including where they grow best.

Southern Perennials & Herbs

http://mirror.wwa.com/mirror/busdir/
gard/sph/sph_home.htm

If you're ready to change your backyard or outdoor environment, this is a great place to visit, with a complete catalog of perennials, herbs, grasses, gingers, woody plants, and vines online. You can also order a free catalog.

WireNet, Inc.

http://www.deltanet.com/wirenet/
wire-net.htm

Much of modern life, including the Net, depends the electricity in the walls, and when you're ready to add outlets or need to purchase some extension cords to expand your reach, this Web site offers some helpful products.

Industrial Supplies

Big firms are plugging into the Internet as part of their business, and even large manufacturing facilities are now coming online. If you're ready to expand your plant, you'll need supplies, so why not shop online?

RapidTec

http://www.mindspring.com/
~rapidtec/rapidtec.html

Manufacturer of offset printing blankets, lithographic rollers, and printing chemicals for large-scale printing establishments. One of the few places online where you can learn all about compressible duplicator blankets.

XREF Publishing Co.

http://www.daka.com/xref/
xrefhome.htm

This valuable site offers an online version of the XREF Encyclopedia, a cross-reference of parts, supplies, and equipment for the heating, air conditioning, and appliance industry. Lots of surprisingly interesting information for the layperson.

International Trade

Although most of the communication on the Internet is presently conducted in English, the Net is global, and an area that no doubt will experience dramatic growth in the next few years is online international trade. Buyers in distant countries now connect with sellers around the globe, merely by clicking a mouse button.

KEYMEXX - The KEY to MEXican eXports

http://jsasoc.com/keymexx.html

Exporting your product to the Mexican market? You'll need to find out about what's involved with gaining Mexico's safety approval. This site offers a source for what's covered, what's required, how long it will take to get things cleared, and how much it will cost for that all-important government OK for your products.

Internet

Products to help you plug your computer or workgroup or corporation into the Internet.

Cisco Systems

http://www.cisco.com/

Whether you want to build a backbone for your corporation or better network for your workgroup, or even learn about ATM switches, you'll want to visit this well done Web site offering lots of information on networks, networking, and the Cisco product line.

LAN to Internet Gateways

http://www.tic.net/

A full complement of plug-and-play LAN gateways for the Internet. LANlink gateways connect your LAN to the Net with dialup or dedicated access at speeds from 28.8 Kbps to 1.544 Mbps.

Inventions

OK, you've built a better mousetrap. Now what?

4 Tomorrow Inventions Directory

http://www.pacifier.com/market/4tomorrow/4menu.html

A directory of investment products, distributorships, import, and export items. If you have or know of a new invention, find out how to list it for the world to see.

Jewelry

Jewelry stores offer lots of jewelry, but often you see the same old things at store after store. On the Internet, however, you'll find dozens, if not hundreds, of independent jewelers and craftspeople.

Etienne Perret

http://media1.hypernet.com/perret.html

Etienne Perret is an internationally known jewelry designer, famous for innovative use of precious metals and diamonds. This Web site really shows off his beautiful creations.

Lewallen and Lewallen Jewelry

http://www.artsantafe.com/sfm/lewallen/lewallen.html

Original silver jewelry designs for men and women by Ross and Laura Lewallen of Santa Fe, New Mexico. Works are based on travel experiences, with ethnic and shamanistic themes. An interesting spot to visit.

Solitaires

http://www.cts.com/browse/alerner/

A collection of new and old jewelry from around the world, designed and created by master craftsmen, and reasonably priced.

Elaine Coyne Galleries

http://www.mindspring.com/~ecg/ecg.html

Handcast, handforged Art Wear Fashion Accessories; Jewelry and belts. Exotic Patina finishes and limited edition semiprecious stones. Nice graphics!

Rhinestones R Us

http://www.netfactory.com/sparkle/pins.html

Rhinestones aren't just shards of glass, you know, and this site highlights products made from Swarovski Austrian crystal. You can order online from a large selection of in stock themes, custom designs.

Ray Gabriel

http://www.wweb.com/gems/

A source of gemstones for jewelry designers and the jewelry programs at major universities since 1975. An informative site for learning more about gems and gem cuts.

Kitchen Appliances

From dishwashers to washing machines, blenders, and fridge magnets — all can be found somewhere in the wild electronic place we call the Internet.

Philips Domestic Appliances and Personal Care

http://www.dap.philips.com/

Philips is a giant in the household market, with a range of small appliances and personal care products for more than 60 countries.

Magazines

You can read online for hours, but when it comes time to relax and curl up with a cup of coffee, nothing beats a good old paper mag. Several magazines now offer the best of both worlds, a combination of print and online information. The Web is also a great way to preview a magazine, read a few articles, and see if you want to pay for a subscription.

Apple Directions

http://www.info.apple.com/dev/appledirections.html

This online magazine reports Apple's strategic, business, and technical directions every month to help you maximize your development dollar.

Career Magazine

http://www.careermag.com/careermag/

This site offers a comprehensive, interactive career resource, designed to meet the individual needs of job seekers, human resource managers, and career-minded professionals working in the networked nineties.

Computing Canada

http://www.globalx.net/plesman/cc

Canadian biweekly national newspaper serving professionals in the information systems/data processing and telecommunications departments of corporations, governments, and educational institutions. Good general online information source, too.

Computer Magazine Article Database from CMP

http://techweb.cmp.com/techweb/programs/registered/search/cmp-wais-index.html

Search articles from: *Windows Magazine, Home PC, Communications Week, Comm Week International, Computer Reseller News, Computer Retail Week, Electronic Buyers News, Electronic Engineering Times, Information Week, Interactive Age Internet Business Report, Netguide, Network Computing, OEM Magazine, Open Systems Today,* and *VAR Business,* and read them online.

Computer News Middle East

http://gpg.com/cnme/

A monthly computer magazine covering software, hardware, and information technology in the Middle East, in particular Saudi Arabia, GCC states, and the wider Arab world, with articles and references online.

Digital Directions

http://iglou.com/eblawler/directions/directions.html

New electronic magazine is your guide to new design technology. Read how computers have changed the way art directors work and get tips in Photoshop and QuarkXPress, with lots of illustrations.

EXTRA!

http://www.igc.org/fair/

EXTRA! and *EXTRA!Update* are the magazine and newsletter of FAIR (Fairness and Accuracy In Reporting), the national media watchdog group. The publications offer well-documented, objective criticism in an effort to correct media bias and imbalance. Find out how biased things are (or aren't) by visiting.

Future Music

http://www.futurenet.co.uk/music/futuremusic.html

Future Music is the UK's best-selling magazine dedicated to hi-tech music and equipment and offers information of interest to all musicians and music fans.

The Information Center

http://www.greatinfo.com/infocenter

The Information Center is an online business opportunity, resource, and information magazine, devoted to helping people succeed in business. A great place for business people to find up-to-date business articles, topics, financial information, news, and job-search resources.

MacWEEK

http://www.zdnet.com/~macweek/

A terrific Web site that features news and trendy stories from current and past issues of this influential Macintosh newsweekly. "PC Labs Online" offers the industry's most extensive product reviews, and the "INet Highway" column features top Web sites.

MacUser (Europe)

http://www.atlas.co.uk/macuser/macuser.htm

Europe's biggest Mac magazine, aimed at the high-end specialist user, with articles on graphics and video for corporate users. A good Macintosh information source on the Net.

MAC Format

http://www.futurenet.co.uk/computing/macformat.html

This site features news, reviews of affordable and interesting new products, and tips and techniques to help you get more out of your Mac.

Mountain Astrologer Magazine

http://www.jadesun.com/tma/

Mountain Astrologer is probably the best modern astrology magazine on the newsstands today. The magazine and Web information is accessible to beginning students and anyone with an interest in astrology.

Popular Mechanics

http://popularmechanics.com/

Pictures and specs on more than 200 cars and trucks, a searchable archive of illustrated technology news with updates every weekday, neat QuickTime movies, software links, home computing forums, old magazine covers going back 93 years, and more. This is a cool site.

Professional Boatbuilder Magazine

http://media1.hypernet.com/proboat.html

Focused on materials, design, and construction techniques and repair solutions chosen by marine professionals.

Upside

http://www.upside.com/

A hip magazine dedicated to providing technology executives with provocative, insightful analyses of the individuals and companies leading the digital revolution. Subscription based, but worth visiting.

Marketing

You can't sell something unless people know about it. Along with its twin sister advertising, marketing is an important part of any successful business.

Global Internet News Agency

http://www.gina.com/gina

Ready to spread the word about your new Web site or online business, or just interested in publishing your press release online? GINA is a great first stop, and their Web site offers a good overview of recent Intenet news, too.

Optimum Group

http://www.optimum.com/

Strategic planning, implementation and execution of marketing programs and promotional campaigns, graphic design, and visual communications, advertising, and lots more, all explained online.

Miscellaneous

Even at a place as elegantly organized as Yahoo!, some things just don't quite fit in elsewhere.

Balarama Enterprises

http://www.sino.net/thai/commerce/sdcoincs.html

Looking for a lot of incense? This firm specializes in supplying shops with more than 50 different fragrances. (Another site illustrating the need for an aroma interface.)

BASICircuits

http://www.infohaus.com/access/by-seller/BASICircuits

A grab bag of a Web site, seemingly with anything and everything: from electronic plans to recipes, WAV files, JPGs, GIFs, TIFFs, and financial and stock info.

Celtic Cultures

http://sover.net/~celtic/

Musical instruments, clothing, books, jewelry, and information about Celtic Festivals., all at this well-designed site.

Lieber's Luggage

http://www.cyspacemalls.com/lieber/

A complete online luggage and travel store, specializing in fine quality famous-maker luggage collections, and top quality business and travel accessories.

PSINet - The Occult Superstore

http://www.psinet.co.uk/

Magickal materials and equipment, tarot, crystal balls, oils, incenses, candles, books, and more. Trade ads, psychic consultants, and even space for free personal ads. Lots of occult information, hints, tips, and competitions.

RSPI Freethought

http://www.execpc.com/~rspi/bumper.html

Need a "Religion Stops a Thinking Mind" bumper sticker? Blasphemous? Either way, your bumper may need a message. See these to believe, online.

SkyHook

http://www.micron.net/~skyhook/

Made of corrosion-proof, supertough polypropylene, the SkyHook attaches to almost any surface in minutes. You could even hang your laptop from the wall when you aren't using it.

Vacation Rental Source

http://www.vrsource.com/

This interesting Web site offers nationwide vacation rental condo listings divided by geographical area, along with information about different vacation spots throughout the United States.

Music

The presence of audio on the Web is explored ingeniously at the many music-related sites. Two major categories are represented: sheet music and instruction.

AcuTab Publications

http://www.digi-net.com/acutab/Home.html

Books of bluegrass banjo tablature. Product descriptions, sample page GIFs, and ordering info available online, along with a photo gallery of popular banjo players.

Molly-Ann Leikin

http://www.earthlink.com/~songmd/

She's a songwriting consultant based in Los Angeles and can help you take your songs and make hits out of them. An interesting site to visit — check out her songwriting credits.

Newsletters

They're smaller and cheaper to produce than magazines and often have the best information in the industry. Better yet, with an online presence, many newsletters now have space to include longer versions of the articles they print each issue.

Gene Lees' Jazzletter

http://pms.com/pink/jazzlet/

Since 1981, this unique publication has chronicled jazz and the musicians who make it. The site contains lots of information from and about the Jazzletter and articles on various aspects of jazz.

The Internet Letter

http://www.infohaus.com/access/by-seller/Internet_Letter

A monthly newsletter aimed at business use of the Internet, it publishes articles about Internet advertising, electronic shopping, deals, marketing trends and Internet growth. A valuable online site, too.

Netsurfer Digest

http://www.netsurf.com/nsd/

This site features a fun and informative online-only electronic newsletter that highlights the latest trends and activities in business, commerce, and electronic currency from the online world.

Travel Unlimited

http://www.dgsys.com/~jlantos/index.html

A monthly newsletter mentioned by many on the net and elsewhere as a valuable resource for info on discount air fares and travel stories. Good links to other travel sites online.

Outdoors

When the indoor environment of an office becomes too much, or you just need to get away from your house for a few hours, go ahead and explore and enjoy the great outdoors. But first, get all the necessary equipment and information on the Internet.

Above the Clouds

http://www.rscomm.com/adsports/atc/atc_main.html

Worldwide adventure for the discerning traveler, mountain trekking and climbing in Europe, the Himalayas, and the Americas are all detailed.

American Military

http://www.tach.net/public/tradezone/ammil/ammil.html

Interested in survival and outdoor outfitting? Then pop over to American Military, a supplier of military and police equipment. Where else could you buy a NATO uniform online?

Bushy Ridge - The Hunter's Choice

http://www.tbe.com/tech-pubs/products/bushy/bushy.html

Teledyne Brown Engineering is a major supplier of camouflage screens to the United States Army. Now the same high technology used for military camouflage is available through the Bushy Ridge online store.

Charlotte Fishing Expeditions

http://www.terranet.ab.ca/~comm/fishing/homepage.html

Charlotte Fishing Expeditions can take you to the Queen Charlotte Islands of the rugged western coast of Canada to catch salmon, coho, halibut, and red snapper. A great vacation possibility to explore.

Labrador Sportfish Limited

http://www.nfld.com/nfld/clients/jburton/index.html

Atlantic salmon, speckled trout, arctic char fishing, outfitting and caribou

hunting safaris in the Labrador wilderness, all detailed online.

Northern Lite Enterprises Catalog

http://www.eskimo.com/~cplasch/skydive/nl-index.html

Before you make your next jump out of a plane, visit this site to learn about the Infinity harness/container system for sport parachuting. Site also contains info on full rigging services for other skydiving gear, as well as for pilot emergency rigs.

Stroller Pack

http://www.parentsplace.com/shopping/strollpak/index.html

The perfect childcarrier for an imperfect world: Sometimes you need a stroller, sometimes only a backpack will do. Visit this site and learn about a product that offers the best of both worlds.

Personal Care

Even Internet users need to take care of themselves, and an occasional pampering also is a good idea.

don Michael Bannon's Virtual Salon

http://www.southwind.net/~degraff/goodserv/don/dindex.html

An online option for people seeking quality salon products for hair care, including TIGI, Sorbie, and Framesi.

462

Mt. Clemens Mineral Internet Spa

http://www.cris.com/~minerals/home.shtml

The delight and relaxation of a spa visit online. Well, not quite, but it's a fun place to visit and learn about their products.

Personals

Some of the most popular spots on the Internet resemble virtual singles bars, where from the safety and anonymity of your computer you can check out other people and perhaps make a connection with the perfect partner. Rather than wade through the confusion of amateur forums, you can opt for one of these professional services in your quest for a new significant other.

American Singles Non-Profit Dating Service

http://www.as.org/as/

Thousands of personals online from around the world, and you can instantly find your perfect match with a matching system based on astrology. Check it out.

Cupid's Network, Inc.

http://www.cupidnet.com/cupid/

This site is the central spot for a national network of singles organizations. Services online include thousands of personals, an events calendar, and even a singles bookstore.

Exchange Magazine

http://www.public.com/personals/exchange/

An extension of the print magazine, this site offers sample issues — with personal advertisements from women only, including their photos — and explains how the direct no-blind-box mail system works.

P.S. I Love You International

http://www.psiloveyou.com/

A fun introduction and singles matchmaking service offering photos of beautiful, highly educated women from all over the world who are looking to meet men for friendship or marriage.

Single's Choice Introductions

http://206.15.28.19/SinglesChoice/

This Asian-American introduction service is available through cyberspace at this Web site that features listings of more than 100 Asian ladies who are interested in companionship and romance.

Virtual MeetMarket

http://wwa.com:1111/

The place to find that special someone, a new best friend on the Internet, or just someone to talk to. A fun site to visit.

Real Estate

Whether you're relocating to a new city or just want to move up to a larger abode, there are dozens, if not hundreds, of realtors now available on the Internet.

Bay Area Century 21 Realtor Online Directory

http://www.webplaza.com/pages/realestate/century21/Century21.html

A directory of San Francisco Bay Area Century 21 realtors, listed by name and office.

Buying and Selling Real Estate on the Web

http://www.baynet.com/harper/index.html

A comprehensive and useful step-by-step guide to real estate transactions on the Web for both the consumer and real estate professional.

Chesapeake Ads Online

http://www.cybersoft.com/pub/cybersoft/home.html

Homes and properties for sale in the mid-Atlantic region. Mostly for the central Maryland and Chesapeake Bay areas.

Holiday Resales

http://www.halcyon.com/golfer/

A listing of more than 7500 different holiday rental spots throughout the world.

Yahoo!

Long Island Online

http://www.longisland.com/realty/realty.htm

Real estate listings in New York's Long Island. Houses, commercial properties, rentals, and more.

Mercedes Company

http://jstart.com/mercedes/mercedes.html

Private brokerage services to clients seeking to purchase or sell real estate on Manhattan's Upper East Side.

Nunnink & Associates, Inc.

http://www.realworks.com/nunnink.html

A nationwide real estate appraisal and consulting firm with offices in Chicago and Kansas City, Kansas.

Philadelphia New Homes Guide

http://www.homefair.com/homefair/nhphil/phil.html

New homes for metropolitan Philadelphia, including Delaware and New Jersey suburbs.

Ruby Powers Realtors

http://www.fc.net/~david/ruby.html

Residential sales and property management in Austin, Texas and surrounding areas.

Virginia Real Net

http://www.curbet.com/realnet.html

Virginia properties organized by city.

Walter Seago

http://www.getnet.com/cent21/

Full-service land and residential real estate broker serving the Phoenix metropolitan area.

Win Straube

http://www.lava.net/~wstraube/

Operation of intelligent office buildings and office support systems in an interactive multimedia environment.

Religion

And on the eighth day, God created the Internet, and saw that, lo, it was good.

Mystic Fire Video

http://www.echonyc.com/~mysticfire

Browse through a wide variety of videos on subjects ranging from Tibetan Buddhism and the great cultures of the East to poetry, the Beat generation, avant garde cinema, Native American, and much more.

The World, The Word and You!

http://www.isl.net/wwyweb.html

A Christian resource for current events, happenings, Biblical expositions, apologetics, and evangelism.

U.S. Judaica Web Catalog

http://www.tig.com/USJ/index.html

America's Jewish bookstore offers an interesting online catalog of Judaica at this well-designed Web site.

Science

It's a cornerstone of the Internet. Science topics abound on the Net, and Yahoo! has pointers to the best.

Giant Leap: The Apollo Chronicles

http://www.NeoSoft.com/~imagine/gl/giantleap.html

A CD-ROM history of mankind's greatest adventure of the 20th Century. The site itself offers a good preview with interesting information about astronauts, timelines, and spacecraft.

Global Heritage Center

http://www.mindspring.com/~sledet/genealogy/ghc.html

A complete line of CD-ROMs, including extensive U.S. Census records, marriage records, land grant information, Social Security information, and lots more.

Perspective Scientific - Radiation Instruments

http://www.demon.co.uk/radiation-instruments/

Hand-held instruments for detecting and measuring ionizing and non-ionizing electromagnetic radiation. Cool pictures.

Security

Now you can obtain safety and peace of mind without leaving your desk.

APEX Security Systems

http://www.hometeam.com/apex.shtml

Voice response security system controllers and components that handle lights, appliances, entertainment, HVAC systems, and other devices. Online ordering available.

D&S Technologies

http://www.tiac.net/users/dstech/

Alarm annunciators, enclosures, and other system components to the commercial security, fire, and control industry. Cool security map systems.

Safety Products International

http://mainsail.com/safety/safety.htm

A range of safety products, including home alarm systems, motion detectors, and car alarms.

Spy Depot

http://www.canadamalls.com/provider/horvath.html

High-tech surveillance, security, and countermeasures equipment for the James Bond types in your life.

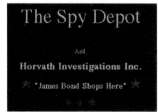

Shopping Centers

Thousands of stores are already online, so it's no surprise to find that thousands of shopping centers and shopping malls are online, too.

DigiMall

http://digimall.com/

Picnic baskets, golf products, shoes and more, all featured at this online shopping spot.

The Highland Trail Company

http://www.highlandtrail.co.uk/highlandtrail/

Scottish food, drink and gifts covering a range of fish, meat, clothing, and crafts.

Hollywood Shopping Network

http://hollywoodshopping.com/hn/shopping/index.html

Entertainment-related services and products.

Internet Fashion Mall

http://www.fashionmall.com/

The central location on the Internet for men's and women's fashion lifestyle.

The Internet Mall

http://www.mecklerweb.com/imall

The central directory of all shops on the Internet, with more than 4000 stores organized into categories ranging from clothes to food, automotive to legal. An invaluable Web reference.

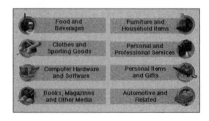

Internet Shopkeeper

http://www.shopkeeper.com/shops/

Dozens of stores offering Tupperware, Alaskan jewelry, auto electronics, wallpaper, movie posters, model trains, and much more.

Internet Shopping Network

http://www.internet.net/index.html?source=DYHB

More than 20,000 different products at this speedy online center, including flowers, gifts, food products, and computer software and hardware.

Speakers

Looking for an inspirational keynoter for that next meeting? You can find one in cyberspace.

Human Awareness Institute

http://www.hai.org/

Creating a world where people live together in dignity, respect, understanding, trust, kindness, honesty, compassion, and love.

The Option Institute and Fellowship

http://www.human.com/mkt/option/index.html

Programs for individuals, couples, families, and groups seeking to improve their quality of life by becoming happier, more effective, and more successful, and by finding a deep place of communion with themselves and others.

Sports

(See also the Recreation chapter.)

From tee-ball to fishing to skating, sports are happening on the Internet, and commercial entities are there to sell the products.

Arvon Cycles

http://www.afternet.com/~arvon/

Site features bicycles custom fitted to the rider, high quality bicycle components, cycling stories, and more.

She Sails Catalog

http://www.aztec.com/pub/aztec/shesails/

Sailing products for women, including small boats, wetsuits, clothing, gloves, training aids, and books.

Tony Entwistle's Fly Fishing Company

http://central.co.nz/~peterlow/tony.htm

Guided fly fishing tours throughout the Nelson Region of New Zealand.

Windspeed Designs

http://media1.hypernet.com/windspeed.html

Quickreefing spinnakers for kayaks and canoes. These sails provide great control. Spinnakers are easy to reef and stow away neatly.

Telecommunications

In the 90s, you gotta be reachable and in touch all the time. Here are products that can help make it pleasant.

Econo-Comm Pager Repair Service

http://www.gate.net/~pagers/

Econo-Comm pager repair offers the best service, at the lowest prices, with the fastest turnaround time.

Interpage Network Services

http://interpage.net/

E-mail delivery to pagers. A complete Internet pager, fax, cell phone, e-mail forwarding service for individuals, ISPs, businesses, and other groups that find it hard to log out.

Marketing Services Group

http://www.websrus.com/msgwatch/

Info on watch-sized pagers with monthly service including weather forecast, Dow Jones closing, New York gold closing, daily prime interest rate, local ski conditions, daily three, and more.

TalkingPower

http://www.att.com/TALKINGPOWER/

Explore the power system at all levels through text and colorful graphics. You can try out, online, an AT&T course that includes animations, videos, and audio.

Television

It looks like a computer screen, but it's a bit harder to interact with: it's your TV! Perhaps the most popular appliance and entertainment device in the world, televisions and related products are, naturally, available online.

Digital Satellite Systems, DirecTV & USSB information

http://www.wco.com/~chuckc/directv.html

All the information you could want on digital satellite systems, including a listing of channels offered and pricing. A terrific Web site.

Prime Time 24 Satellite Programming

http://www.wcs-online.com/pt24/

Satellite programming service from Prime Time 24 Satellite Programming for the home dish user, all detailed online.

VideoTape Copies

http://www.viscomm.com/~videoage/vtc.html

Top quality videotape duplications at affordable prices, and lots of links to video-related spots on the Internet.

Theater

The perfect antidote to computer screen overload is live theater. But, of course, the business of theater can be conducted online.

Karen TenEyck's Scenic Design Studio

http://www.inch.com/user/kteneyck

Pop over to this cool Web site and you'll be able to visit the virtual scenic studio of Karen TenEyck in New York.

Virtual Headbook

http://www.xmission.com/~wintrnx/virtual.html

Attention actors! Put your head shots and resumes online and make them available for viewing by casting agents, agents, and directors of film and stage.

Toys

Stuff for the kids and the adults in your life that act like kids.

MaxBlaster

http://www.inmind.com/newmax

It's the most amazing water pistol you've ever seen. It's like the popular super soaker, except you don't have to pump it to refill. Great for cooling off steamed cybernauts. Just keep the stream away from the keyboard.

Travel

When it's time to take a break and visit someplace, you can explore your travel options on the Net.

Travel Store

http://www.travelsource.com/travelstore/

Merchandise from travel gear manufacturers, including luggage,

backpacks, camera bags, and more. Pointers to other travel info in cyberspace.

Wacky Products

What can we say? These are just wacky products, weird, peculiar, and fun.

Jammin-Johns: Guitar Body Toilet Seats

http://www.iglou.com/Jammin-Johns/Jammin-Johns.html

Made from solid, hand-rubbed Appalachian oak, Jammin-Johns come in six, classic body styles with round or oval seat designs. You'd definitely be the first on your block.

Hominid Skulls

http://www.iea.com/~waltersm/skull.htm

Quality plaster reproductions of Hominid fossil skulls, for educational demonstrations, personal novelty gifts, and bad productions of *Hamlet*.

Wedding Supplies

The stereotype of the online fanatic is that he or she doesn't have much of a personal life. But we know that's just not true, and for online buffs who are ready to jump the broom, you can find wedding apparel and more, all without leaving the comfort of your favorite Web browser.

Engeman Productions

http://www.sisna.com/bill/home.htm

Site offers details on how to set up a beautiful wedding with only butcher paper and still achieve a romantic and beautiful setting.

Sposabella - La Sposa Veil

http://www.hydra.com/sposa/
sposa.html

Sposabella - La Sposa Veil produces custom bridal headpieces, veils, and other interesting accessories. Brides of all ages will find Sposabella an interesting store to visit.

Yahoo!

Index

C

(continued)

(continued)

Polynesian culture, 385
pornographic pictures, 14
postal information, 317
preservation of environment and
    nature, 391
presidential libraries, 313
printing business directory, 430
prison issues, 378
privatizing Internet, 26
products and services, 435–467
  advertising, 436
  animals, 436
  apparel, 436–437
  arts and crafts, 437–438
  audio, 438,–39
  automotive, 439
  books, 439–441
  business opportunities, 441–443
  business supplies, 443
  calendars, 443
  catalogs, 443–444
  children, 444
  clubs, 444–445
  collectibles, 445
  computers, 445–447
  construction, 447
  contests, 447–448
  drinks, 448–449
  education, 449
  electronics, 449
  entertainment, 449–450
  environment, 450
  financial services, 451
  flowers, 451–452
  food, 452–453
  furniture, 453
  general merchandise, 453
  get rich quick, 453–454
  gifts, 454–455
  government, 455
  health and fitness, 455–456
  hobbies, 456
  home and garden, 456
  industrial supplies, 456
  international trade, 457
  Internet, 457
  inventions, 457

jewelry, 457–458
kitchen appliances, 458
magazines, 458–459
marketing, 459
miscellaneous, 459–460
music, 460
newsletters, 460–461
outdoors, 461
personal care, 461–462
personals, 462
real estate, 462–463
religion, 463
science, 463–464
security, 464
shopping centers, 464
speakers, 465
sports, 465
telecommunications, 465
television, 465–466
theater, 466
toys, 466
travel, 466
wacky products, 466
wedding supplies, 467
professional groups, 109
programming and World Wide
    Web (WWW), 201
programs
  AIR Mosaic, 34
  ClarisWorks, 52, 61
  education, 218
  environment and nature, 391
  GrabNet, 60
  MacWeb, 53
  Microsoft Word, 52
  NCSA Mosaic, 33–34
  Netscape Navigator, 34, 40
  Quarterdeck Mosaic, 34
  Spry Mosaic, 34
  Spyglass Mosaic, 34
  winWeb, 53
  WordPerfect, 52
protocols and software, 181–182
psychology, 358–359
public interest groups, 109
public libraries, 313–314

publications
  arts section, 74
  environment and nature, 391
  women's studies, 372
publishing business directory, 430
punctuation in Uniform Resource
    Locator (URL), 35
puzzles, 294–295

Q

Quarterdeck Mosaic, 2–3, 34
  questions about, 6
quick keyword searches, 52–53
quotations, 317–318

R

radio, 240–241
rape, 378
rare objects, finding, 24
real estate, 112–113
  business directory, 431
  organizations, 113
  products and services, 462–463
recipes, 228–229
recreation, 285–305
  amusement/theme parks, 285
  animals, insects, and
      pets, 285–286
  automobiles, 287
  aviation, 287–288
  card games, 290–291
  computer games, 291–293
  dance, 288
  fashion, 289
  gambling, 293–294
  games, 289–290
  hobbies, 295–296
  home and garden, 297
  interactive fiction, 294
  Internet games, 294
  motorcycles, 297–298
  outdoors, 298–299

(continued)

S

Yahoo!

(continued)

T

Yahoo!

Notes

Yahoo!

Notes

Yahoo!

Notes

Notes

Yahoo!

Notes

Notes

Your Quarterdeck software comes with three months of Prepaid VIP Technical Support, including access to our CompuServe and other electronic support forums, support by fax, mail, and our telephone hotline. Your Prepaid VIP Support starts on your first technical contact with our Care and Support Center.

To be eligible for continued support beyond your first contact, please send us your product registration card, which is proof of ownership for a current version of a Quarterdeck product.

Support Online

CompuServe

For the fastest possible support, our Quarterdeck CompuServe forum maintains a complete library of technical bulletins, compatibility updates, and enhancement utilities for Quarterdeck products. In addition, the extensive public discussion area is full of great tips and tricks from power users, as well as our Senior Technical Specialists. It is the best way to get the answers you need 24 hours a day. Just type **GO QUARTERDECK** at the CompuServe prompt.

Internet

E-mail

Private e-mail:
support@qdeck.com

Product information
info@qdeck.com

Public messages:
comp.os.msdos.desqview

See our Technical Note (INTERNET.TEC) for more information. Please note that the **comp.os.msdos.desqview** newsgroup is not run by Quarterdeck, but we do have senior technicians monitoring these messages.

FTP site

Quarterdeck maintains an anonymous FTP site: **qdeck.com**. Our technical bulletins, development tools and additional public domain software are available for download, as follows:

Host Name:
qdeck.com (149.17.8.10)

Login:
anonymous

Password:
type your e-mail address here

Notes:
obtain the README file from ~/pub for file availability.

Q/World: Quarterdeck's World Wide Web site

Be sure to visit our home page at **http://www.qdeck.com/** on a regular basis to find out the latest on some of the hottest software around. Our Web site includes information about Quarterdeck and its products, links to cool places on the Web, search engines to make it easy to find things on the Internet, and prerelease versions of our Internet software products.

1-800-ROBOTECH
Free automated support

For fast, free support, simply try our toll-free, 24-hour automated technical support information system, 1-800-ROBOTECH. Get the most out of Quarterdeck products, gain more memory and get hot tips and tricks.

1-800-ROBOTECH is an automated technical support hotline accessible by a touch-tone phone. Navigation is easy: simply press the corresponding numbers on your phone's keypad.

1-800-ROBOTECH never sleeps! 1-800-ROBOTECH is online 24 hours a day, 7 days a week including holidays.

Using 1-800-ROBOTECH

Dial 1-800-ROBOTECH (1-800-762-6832) or (310) 314-3278 from a touch-tone phone. Once connected, you will be given the option of selecting a topic, varying from Installation Questions, General Troubleshooting, New Products, to Networking Questions.

For a list of the most current 1-800-ROBOTECH menu items, call our Q/FAX system (see next page) and request Technical Note #272.

1-800-ROBOTECH shortcut keys

Menu Commands

Press *P to go to the Previous menu.

Press *T to go to the Top system menu.

Press *C to hear the Current level.

Press *J and the four-digit level number to jump to that menu level.

Message Commands

Press N to hear the Next part of a message.

Press P to hear the Previous part of a message.

Press A to hear the message Again.

Press T to go to the Top or beginning of a message.

Press # to pause a message and # again to resume.

REMEMBER 1-800-ROBOTECH (1-800-762-6832)

Other ways to get answers

In addition to the previously mentioned support options, we also offer many other ways in which you can receive support for your Quarterdeck product.

Take a look at our White Papers and Technotes When you have a technical question that is beyond the scope of your Quarterdeck product's help system, documentation, or READ.ME files, check the **Technotes**, available on your product disk (in the "Technote" subdirectory in the main directory of your Quarterdeck product); or download our more extensive **White Papers**, available from Q/FAX and all our supported electronic forums (see below).

White Papers and Technotes contain complete, written discussions of many hardware and software compatibility issues, as well as helpful explanations to the most commonly asked questions.

Try Q/FAX Quarterdeck's free, 24-hour outbound automated fax is at your service! Using Q/FAX, you can receive technical bulletins, product information, and upgrade notices

directly from your fax machine. To use Q/FAX, **call (310) 314-3214** or **1-800-354-3202** from the phone attached to your fax. Once connected, follow the voice menu. We suggest you request #100, a regularly updated master list. (Quarterdeck was the first software company to offer this service. Give it a try!)

Use the Quarterdeck Bulletin Board System (BBS), designed for fast, personalized technical support. **Call 310-314-3BBS (3227).**

The Quarterdeck Bulletin Board System is available 24 hours a day, 7 days a week. The BBS features open forums to discuss technical issues with both Quarterdeck personnel and other customers with similar interests, private e-mail, and user-download sections. All technical notes, product and upgrade bulletins, patch files, and user-uploaded utility programs relating to our products are available.

Set your modem (14,400 bps or slower) for **8-bit word length, No Parity, and 1 Stop Bit**. Our BBS is also a worldwide SmartNet node to enable local dial-up access.

Use Online Services and Public Message Forums In addition to our telephone, fax, and U.S. mail support channels, Quarterdeck offers electronic technical support through your modem using a variety of online services. Note: Even though many of these forums have PRIVATE e-mail capabilities as well as public message centers, it is usually faster and better to use PUBLIC messages for technical support. Such messages can be read by anyone, serving as a vast database of information 24 hours a day. Here are the forums we support and how to contact us:

CompuServe
Public messages: **GO QUARTERDECK**

BIX (Byte Information exchange)
Public messages: JOIN DESQview

Private e-mail: QOS.REP2

See our Technical Note (BIX.TEC) for more information.

Fidonet
Public messages: DESQview

MCI Mail
Private e-mail: QUARTERDECK

SmartNet
Public messages: DESQview conference

In the rare event your SmartNet provider does not have access to the DESQview conference, request that the provider carry it. See our Technical Note (SNET.TEC) for more information.

Send us a fax Fax Quarterdeck Technical Support by dialing **310-314-3217.**

You can send us a fax 24 hours a day. we will respond as quickly as possible upon receipt of your fax message during normal business hours. Please include your fax number and your Quarterdeck customer VIP number, or product serial number.

If you own Quarterdeck Manifest, we recommend including a printout of the file TECHSUP.MFT created by running the "TECHSUP.BAT" batch file in your QEMM subdirectory. More information on this feature can be found in the Manifest manual.

Write a letter Our mailing address is:

Quarterdeck Corporation
Technical Support Team
150 Pico Boulevard
Santa Monica, CA 90405 USA

Please include your voice phone number, your Quarterdeck customer VIP number or product serial number.

Yahoo!

We will respond as quickly as possible. If possible, include the TECHSUP.MFT printout mentioned earlier.

Still Confused? Call us at (310) 392-9701. Please have your Quarterdeck customer VIP number or product serial number available. We strongly recommend a working knowledge of DOS and a text editor to help expedite your call, but that is not necessary to receive our award-winning technical support.

EXPLORE THE WEB.

Quarterdeck InternetSuite™ has been called "the best overall package" by a Wall Street Journal columnist. It includes the Quarter-deck Mosaic Web browser and Quarterdeck Message Center™ for e-mail, newsgroup and ftp access. This is the easy-to-install, easy-to-use, most complete solution for Internet access.

CREATE A WEB PAGE THERE.

Quarterdeck WebAuthor™ lets you design your own Web pages without having to learn a single command in HTML. It takes your Microsoft® Word for Windows® documents and lets you convert them with a few mouse clicks into bright, compelling home pages for an Internet audience of millions.

PUT IT UP ON YOUR OWN WEB SITE.

Quarterdeck WebServer™ is the easiest way to set up your own site on the World Wide Web – or an internal Web site for your company. You don't need expensive UNIX servers or programming help. Use an existing 486 or better PC and a few minutes to make your presence felt on the Internet.

CALL YOUR MOTHER.
(She'll be glad to hear you turned out all right.)

Quarterdeck WebPhone™ turns your PC into a phone to let you talk with your friends or relatives over the Internet. Hold high-quality voice conversations without having to pay a cent more than what you're already paying for Internet access. You'll make up the cost in a matter of days.

Experience the full breadth of the Internet with Quarterdeck's top-rated line of Internet products. To find out more, call us, or visit http://www.quarterdeck.com.
Call for current pricing. **1-800-683-6696**

QUARTERDECK LICENSE AGREEMENT

License

United States: This License is your proof of license. Please treat it as valuable property.

QUARTERDECK END USER LICENSE AGREEMENT (THE "AGREEMENT")

NOTICE TO END USER: CAREFULLY READ THE FOLLOWING LEGAL AGREEMENT. USE OF THE SOFTWARE (THE "SOFTWARE") PROVIDED WITH THIS AGREEMENT CONSTITUTES YOUR ACCEPTANCE OF THESE TERMS. IF YOU DO NOT AGREE TO THE TERMS OF THIS AGREEMENT, PROMPTLY RETURN THE SOFTWARE AND THE ACCOMPANYING ITEMS (INCLUDING WRITTEN MATERIALS, BINDERS AND CONTAINERS) TO THE LOCATION WHERE YOU OBTAINED THEM FOR A FULL REFUND.

1. License Grant. Quarterdeck Corporation ("Quarterdeck") grants to you (either as an individual or entity) a nonexclusive sublicense subject to the provisions hereof: (a) to use the SOFTWARE solely for your own internal personal or business purposes on a single computer (whether a standard computer or a workstation component of a multi-user network).

You may make and maintain up to three backup copies of the software, provided they are used only for backup purposes or by you personally on another workstation (such as at home) so long as the Software is not used on more than one machine at a time, and you keep possession of the backups. In addition, all the information appearing on the original disk labels (including the copyright notice) must be copied onto the backup labels.

2. Proprietary Rights. You acknowledge that the SOFTWARE is proprietary to Quarterdeck and its suppliers. You agree to hold the SOFTWARE in confidence, disclosing the SOFTWARE only to authorized employees having a need to use the SOFTWARE as permitted by this Agreement and to take all reasonable precautions to prevent disclosure to other parties.

3. Other Copies, except as otherwise provided herein. You will not make or have made, or permit to be made, any copies of the SOFTWARE or portions thereof, except as necessary for its use with a single licensed computer system under the terms and conditions of this Agreement. You agree that any such copies shall contain the same proprietary notices which appear on or in the SOFTWARE.

4. Ownership. Except as stated above, this Agreement does not grant you any rights to patents, copyrights, trade secrets, trade names, trademarks (whether registered or unregistered), or any other rights, franchises, or licenses in respect of the SOFTWARE. Title to and ownership of the SOFTWARE, any reproductions and any documentation shall remain with Quarterdeck and its suppliers. You will not adapt or use any trademark or trade name which is likely to be similar to or confusing with that of Quarterdeck or any of its suppliers or take any other action which impairs or reduces the trademark rights of Quarterdeck or its suppliers.

5. Other Restrictions. This Agreement is your proof of license to use the SOFTWARE in accordance with these terms and must be retained by you. You may not rent or lease the

SOFTWARE, but you may assign your rights under this Agreement on a permanent basis to an assignee of all of your rights, title and interest to such SOFTWARE provided you transfer this Agreement, all copies of the SOFTWARE and all accompanying written materials, and such assignee agrees to be bound by all the terms and conditions of this Agreement. YOU MAY NOT ALTER, MODIFY, REVERSE ENGINEER, DECRYPT, DECOMPILE, OR DISASSEMBLE THE SOFTWARE.

6. Limited Warranty. Quarterdeck warrants that the SOFTWARE will perform substantially in accordance with the accompanying written materials and that the printed materials and diskettes are free from any physical defects for a period of ninety (90) days from the date of purchase. Any warranties on the SOFTWARE, printed materials or diskettes as herein explicitly granted are limited to ninety (90) days.

7. Customer Remedies. Quarterdeck's entire liability and your sole and exclusive remedy shall be, at Quarterdeck's option, either to (a) correct the error, (b) help the end user work around or avoid the error or (c) authorize a refund, so long as the SOFTWARE, printed materials or diskettes are returned to Quarterdeck with a copy of your receipt. This Limited Warranty is void if failure of the SOFTWARE has resulted from accident, abuse, or misapplication. Any replacement SOFTWARE will be warranted for the remainder of the original warranty period.

8. No Other Warranties. QUARTERDECK DOES NOT WARRANT THAT THE QUARTERDECK SOFTWARE IS ERROR FREE. EXCEPT FOR PARAGRAPH SIX ABOVE, QUARTERDECK DISCLAIMS ALL WARRANTIES, EITHER EXPRESS OR IMPLIED, INCLUDING BUT NOT LIMITED TO IMPLIED WARRANTIES OF MERCHANTABILITY, FITNESS FOR A PARTICULAR PURPOSE AND NONINFRINGEMENT OF THIRD PARTY RIGHTS WITH RESPECT TO THE SOFTWARE, THE ACCOMPANYING WRITTEN MATERIALS OR DISKETTES. AS ALLOWED BY APPLICABLE LAW. SOME JURISDICTIONS DO NOT ALLOW THE EXCLUSION OF IMPLIED WARRANTIES OR LIMITATIONS ON HOW LONG AN IMPLIED WARRANTY MAY LAST, OR THE EXCLUSION OR LIMITATION OF INCIDENTAL OR CONSEQUENTIAL DAMAGES, SO THE ABOVE LIMITATIONS OR EXCLUSIONS MAY NOT APPLY TO YOU. THIS WARRANTY GIVES YOU SPECIFIC LEGAL RIGHTS AND YOU MAY ALSO HAVE OTHER RIGHTS WHICH VARY FROM JURISDICTION TO JURISDICTION.

9. Export. You acknowledge that the laws and regulations of the United States restrict the export and re-export of commodities and technical data of United States origin, including the SOFTWARE. You agree that you will not export or re-export the SOFTWARE in any form without the appropriate United States and foreign government licenses and permission from Quarterdeck. You agree that its obligations pursuant to this section shall survive and continue after any termination or expiration of rights under this Agreement.

10. Severability. In the event of invalidity of any provision of this Agreement, the parties agree that such invalidity shall not affect the validity of the remaining portions of this Agreement. The United Nations Convention on Contracts for the International Sale of Goods is specifically disclaimed.

11. No Liability for Consequential Damages. IN NO EVENT SHALL QUARTERDECK BE LIABLE TO YOU FOR ANY CONSEQUENTIAL, SPECIAL, INCIDENTAL OR INDIRECT DAMAGES OF ANY KIND ARISING OUT OF THE USE OF THE SOFTWARE, EVEN IF QUARTERDECK HAS BEEN ADVISED OF THE POSSIBILITY OF SUCH DAMAGES. IN NO EVENT WILL QUARTERDECK'S LIABILITY FOR ANY CLAIM, WHETHER IN CONTRACT, TORT OR ANY OTHER THEORY OF LIABILITY, EXCEED THE LICENSE FEE PAID BY YOU.

12. U.S. GOVERNMENT RESTRICTED RIGHTS.

If this product is acquired under the terms of a: DoD contract: Use, duplication or disclosure by the Government is subject to restrictions as set forth in subparagraph (c)(1)(ii) of 252.227-7013. Civilian agency contract: Use, reproduction or disclosure is subject to 52.227-19 (a) through (d) and restrictions set forth in the accompanying end user agreement. Unpublished-rights reserved under the copyright laws of the United States. Quarterdeck Corporation, 13160 Mindanao Way FL 3 Marina Del Rey, CA 90292-9959.

13. Governing Law. This Agreement is governed by the laws of the State of California.

14. Entire Agreement. This is the entire agreement between you and Quarterdeck which supersedes any prior agreement, whether written or oral, relating to the subject matter of this Agreement.

Should you have any questions concerning this Agreement, or if you desire to contact Quarterdeck for any reason, please write: Quarterdeck Corporation, 13160 Mindanao Way FL 3 Marina Del Rey, CA 90292-9959.

– Important –

Read carefully before opening the software packet. This is a legal agreement between you (either an individual or an entity) and IDG Books Worldwide, Inc. (IDG). By opening the accompanying sealed packet containing the software disc, you acknowledge that you have read and accept the following IDG License Agreement. If you do not agree and do not want to be bound by the terms of this Agreement, promptly return the book and the unopened software packet(s) to the place you obtained them for a full refund.

1. License. This License Agreement (Agreement) permits you to use one copy of the enclosed Software program(s) on a single computer. The Software is in "use" on a computer when it is loaded into temporary memory (i.e., RAM) or installed into permanent memory (e.g., hard disk, CD-ROM, or other storage device) of that computer.

2. Copyright. The entire contents of this disc and the compilation of the Software are copyrighted and protected by both United States copyright laws and international treaty provisions. You may only (a) make one copy of the Software for backup or archival purposes, or (b) transfer the Software to a single hard disk, provided that you keep the original for backup or archival purposes. The individual programs on the disc are copyrighted by the authors of each program respectively. Each program has its own use permissions and limitations. To use each program, you must follow the individual requirements and restrictions detailed for each in "Installing and Using the CD-ROM" located in the back of this Book. Do not use a program if you do not want to follow its Licensing Agreement. None of the material on this disc or listed in this Book may ever be distributed, in original or modified form, for commercial purposes.

3. Other Restrictions. You may not rent or lease the Software. You may transfer the Software and user documentation on a permanent basis provided you retain no copies and the recipient agrees to the terms of this Agreement. You may not reverse engineer, decompile, or disassemble the Software except to the extent that the foregoing restriction is expressly prohibited by applicable law. If the Software is an update or has been updated, any transfer must include the most recent update and all prior versions. Each shareware program has its own use permissions and limitations. These limitations are contained in the individual license agreements that are on the software discs. The restrictions include a requirement that after using the program for a period of time specified in its text, the user must pay a registration fee or discontinue use. By opening the package which contains the software disc, you will be agreeing to abide by the licenses and restrictions for these programs. Do not open the software package unless you agree to be bound by the license agreements.

4. Limited Warranty. IDG Warrants that the Software and disc are free from defects in materials and workmanship for a period of sixty (60) days from the date of purchase of this Book. If IDG receives notification within the warranty period of defects in material or workmanship, IDG will replace the defective disc. IDG's entire liability and your exclusive remedy shall be limited to replacement of the Software, which is returned to IDG with a copy of your receipt. This Limited Warranty is void if failure of the Software has resulted from accident, abuse, or misapplication. Any replacement Software will be warranted for the remainder of the original warranty period or thirty (30) days, whichever is longer.

5. No Other Warranties. To the maximum extent permitted by applicable law, IDG and the author disclaim all other warranties, express or implied, including but not limited to implied warranties of merchantability and fitness for a particular purpose, with respect to the Software, the programs, the source code contained therein and/or the techniques described in this Book. This limited warranty gives you specific legal rights. You may have others which vary from state/jurisdiction to state/jurisdiction.

6. No Liability For Consequential Damages. To the extent permitted by applicable law, in no event shall IDG or the author be liable for any damages whatsoever (including without limitation, damages for loss of business profits, business interruption, loss of business information, or any other pecuniary loss) arising out of the use of or inability to use the Book or the Software, even if IDG has been advised of the possibility of such damages. Because some states/ jurisdictions do not allow the exclusion or limitation of liability for consequential or incidental damages, the above limitation may not apply to you.

7. U.S. Government Restricted Rights.
Use, duplication, or disclosure of the Software by the U.S. Government is subject to restrictions stated in paragraph (c) (1) (ii) of the Rights in Technical Data and Computer Software clause of DFARS 252.227-7013, and in subparagraphs (a) through (d) of the Commercial Computer—Restricted Rights clause at FAR 52.227-19, and in similar clauses in the NASA FAR supplement, when applicable.

The Internet For Macs® For Dummies® 2nd Edition	by Charles Seiter	ISBN: 1-56884-371-2	$19.99 USA/$26.99 Canada
The Internet For Macs® For Dummies® Starter Kit	by Charles Seiter	ISBN: 1-56884-244-9	$29.99 USA/$39.99 Canada
The Internet For Macs® For Dummies® Starter Kit Bestseller Edition	by Charles Seiter	ISBN: 1-56884-245-7	$39.99 USA/$54.99 Canada
The Internet For Windows® For Dummies® Starter Kit	by John R. Levine & Margaret Levine Young	ISBN: 1-56884-237-6	$34.99 USA/$44.99 Canada
The Internet For Windows® For Dummies® Starter Kit, Bestseller Edition	by John R. Levine & Margaret Levine Young	ISBN: 1-56884-246-5	$39.99 USA/$54.99 Canada

MACINTOSH

Mac® Programming For Dummies®	by Dan Parks Sydow	ISBN: 1-56884-173-6	$19.95 USA/$26.95 Canada
Macintosh® System 7.5 For Dummies®	by Bob LeVitus	ISBN: 1-56884-197-3	$19.95 USA/$26.95 Canada
MORE Macs® For Dummies®	by David Pogue	ISBN: 1-56884-087-X	$19.95 USA/$26.95 Canada
PageMaker 5 For Macs® For Dummies®	by Galen Gruman & Deke McClelland	ISBN: 1-56884-178-7	$19.95 USA/$26.95 Canada
QuarkXPress 3.3 For Dummies®	by Galen Gruman & Barbara Assadi	ISBN: 1-56884-217-1	$19.99 USA/$26.99 Canada
Upgrading and Fixing Macs® For Dummies®	by Kearney Rietmann & Frank Higgins	ISBN: 1-56884-189-2	$19.95 USA/$26.95 Canada

MULTIMEDIA

Multimedia & CD-ROMs For Dummies® 2nd Edition	by Andy Rathbone	ISBN: 1-56884-907-9	$19.99 USA/$26.99 Canada
Multimedia & CD-ROMs For Dummies® Interactive Multimedia Value Pack, 2nd Edition	by Andy Rathbone	ISBN: 1-56884-909-5	$29.99 USA/$39.99 Canada

OPERATING SYSTEMS:

DOS

MORE DOS For Dummies®	by Dan Gookin	ISBN: 1-56884-046-2	$19.95 USA/$26.95 Canada
OS/2® Warp For Dummies® 2nd Edition	by Andy Rathbone	ISBN: 1-56884-205-8	$19.99 USA/$26.99 Canada

UNIX

MORE UNIX® For Dummies®	by John R. Levine & Margaret Levine Young	ISBN: 1-56884-361-5	$19.99 USA/$26.99 Canada
UNIX® For Dummies®	by John R. Levine & Margaret Levine Young	ISBN: 1-878058-58-4	$19.95 USA/$26.95 Canada

WINDOWS

MORE Windows® For Dummies® 2nd Edition	by Andy Rathbone	ISBN: 1-56884-048-9	$19.95 USA/$26.95 Canada
Windows® 95 For Dummies®	by Andy Rathbone	ISBN: 1-56884-240-6	$19.99 USA/$26.95 Canada

PCS/HARDWARE

Illustrated Computer Dictionary For Dummies® 2nd Edition	by Dan Gookin & Wallace Wang	ISBN: 1-56884-218-X	$12.95 USA/$16.95 Canada
Upgrading and Fixing PCs For Dummies® 2nd Edition	by Andy Rathbone	ISBN: 1-56884-903-6	$19.99 USA/$26.99 Canada

PRESENTATION/AUTOCAD

AutoCAD For Dummies®	by Bud Smith	ISBN: 1-56884-191-4	$19.95 USA/$26.95 Canada
PowerPoint 4 For Windows® For Dummies®	by Doug Lowe	ISBN: 1-56884-161-2	$16.99 USA/$22.99 Canada

PROGRAMMING

Borland C++ For Dummies®	by Michael Hyman	ISBN: 1-56884-162-0	$19.95 USA/$26.95 Canada
C For Dummies® Volume 1	by Dan Gookin	ISBN: 1-878058-78-9	$19.95 USA/$26.95 Canada
C++ For Dummies®	by Stephen R. Davis	ISBN: 1-56884-163-9	$19.95 USA/$26.95 Canada
Delphi Programming For Dummies®	by Neil Rubenking	ISBN: 1-56884-200-7	$19.99 USA/$26.99 Canada
Mac® Programming For Dummies®	by Dan Parks Sydow	ISBN: 1-56884-173-6	$19.95 USA/$26.95 Canada
PowerBuilder 4 Programming For Dummies®	by Ted Coombs & Jason Coombs	ISBN: 1-56884-325-9	$19.99 USA/$26.99 Canada
QBasic Programming For Dummies®	by Douglas Hergert	ISBN: 1-56884-093-4	$19.95 USA/$26.95 Canada
Visual Basic 3 For Dummies®	by Wallace Wang	ISBN: 1-56884-076-4	$19.95 USA/$26.95 Canada
Visual Basic "X" For Dummies®	by Wallace Wang	ISBN: 1-56884-230-9	$19.99 USA/$26.99 Canada
Visual C++ 2 For Dummies®	by Michael Hyman & Bob Arnson	ISBN: 1-56884-328-3	$19.99 USA/$26.99 Canada
Windows® 95 Programming For Dummies®	by S. Randy Davis	ISBN: 1-56884-327-5	$19.99 USA/$26.99 Canada

SPREADSHEET

1-2-3 For Dummies®	by Greg Harvey	ISBN: 1-878058-60-6	$16.95 USA/$22.95 Canada
1-2-3 For Windows® 5 For Dummies® 2nd Edition	by John Walkenbach	ISBN: 1-56884-216-3	$16.95 USA/$22.95 Canada
Excel 5 For Macs® For Dummies®	by Greg Harvey	ISBN: 1-56884-186-8	$19.95 USA/$26.95 Canada
Excel For Dummies® 2nd Edition	by Greg Harvey	ISBN: 1-56884-050-0	$16.95 USA/$22.95 Canada
MORE 1-2-3 For DOS For Dummies®	by John Weingarten	ISBN: 1-56884-224-4	$19.99 USA/$26.99 Canada
MORE Excel 5 For Windows® For Dummies®	by Greg Harvey	ISBN: 1-56884-207-4	$19.95 USA/$26.95 Canada
Quattro Pro 6 For Windows® For Dummies®	by John Walkenbach	ISBN: 1-56884-174-4	$19.95 USA/$26.95 Canada
Quattro Pro For DOS For Dummies®	by John Walkenbach	ISBN: 1-56884-023-3	$16.95 USA/$22.95 Canada

UTILITIES

Norton Utilities 8 For Dummies®	by Beth Slick	ISBN: 1-56884-166-3	$19.95 USA/$26.95 Canada

VCRS/CAMCORDERS

VCRs & Camcorders For Dummies™	by Gordon McComb & Andy Rathbone	ISBN: 1-56884-229-5	$14.99 USA/$20.99 Canada

WORD PROCESSING

Ami Pro For Dummies®	by Jim Meade	ISBN: 1-56884-049-7	$19.95 USA/$26.95 Canada
MORE Word For Windows® 6 For Dummies®	by Doug Lowe	ISBN: 1-56884-165-5	$19.95 USA/$26.95 Canada
MORE WordPerfect® 6 For Windows® For Dummies®	by Margaret Levine Young & David C. Kay	ISBN: 1-56884-206-6	$19.95 USA/$26.95 Canada
MORE WordPerfect® 6 For DOS For Dummies®	by Wallace Wang, edited by Dan Gookin	ISBN: 1-56884-047-0	$19.95 USA/$26.95 Canada
Word 6 For Macs® For Dummies®	by Dan Gookin	ISBN: 1-56884-190-6	$19.95 USA/$26.95 Canada
Word For Windows® 6 For Dummies®	by Dan Gookin	ISBN: 1-56884-075-6	$16.95 USA/$22.95 Canada
Word For Windows® For Dummies®	by Dan Gookin & Ray Werner	ISBN: 1-878058-86-X	$16.95 USA/$22.95 Canada
WordPerfect® 6 For DOS For Dummies®	by Dan Gookin	ISBN: 1-878058-77-0	$16.95 USA/$22.95 Canada
WordPerfect® 6.1 For Windows® For Dummies® 2nd Edition	by Margaret Levine Young & David Kay	ISBN: 1-56884-243-0	$16.95 USA/$22.95 Canada
WordPerfect® For Dummies®	by Dan Gookin	ISBN: 1-878058-52-5	$16.95 USA/$22.95 Canada

Fun, Fast, & Cheap!™

10/02/95

The Internet For Macs® For Dummies® Quick Reference
by Charles Seiter

ISBN:1-56884-967-2
$9.99 USA/$12.99 Canada

Windows® 95 For Dummies® Quick Reference
by Greg Harvey

ISBN: 1-56884-964-8
$9.99 USA/$12.99 Canada

Photoshop 3 For Macs® For Dummies® Quick Reference
by Deke McClelland

ISBN: 1-56884-968-0
$9.99 USA/$12.99 Canada

WordPerfect® For DOS For Dummies® Quick Reference
by Greg Harvey

ISBN: 1-56884-009-8
$8.95 USA/$12.95 Canada

Title	Author	ISBN	Price
DATABASE			
Access 2 For Dummies® Quick Reference	by Stuart J. Stuple	ISBN: 1-56884-167-1	$8.95 USA/$11.95 Canada
dBASE 5 For DOS For Dummies® Quick Reference	by Barrie Sosinsky	ISBN: 1-56884-954-0	$9.99 USA/$12.99 Canada
dBASE 5 For Windows® For Dummies® Quick Reference	by Stuart J. Stuple	ISBN: 1-56884-953-2	$9.99 USA/$12.99 Canada
Paradox 5 For Windows® For Dummies® Quick Reference	by Scott Palmer	ISBN: 1-56884-960-5	$9.99 USA/$12.99 Canada
DESKTOP PUBLISHING/ILLUSTRATION/GRAPHICS			
CorelDRAW! 5 For Dummies® Quick Reference	by Raymond E. Werner	ISBN: 1-56884-952-4	$9.99 USA/$12.99 Canada
Harvard Graphics For Windows® For Dummies® Quick Reference	by Raymond E. Werner	ISBN: 1-56884-962-1	$9.99 USA/$12.99 Canada
Photoshop 3 For Macs® For Dummies® Quick Reference	by Deke McClelland	ISBN: 1-56884-968-0	$9.99 USA/$12.99 Canada
FINANCE/PERSONAL FINANCE			
Quicken 4 For Windows® For Dummies® Quick Reference	by Stephen L. Nelson	ISBN: 1-56884-950-8	$9.95 USA/$12.95 Canada
GROUPWARE/INTEGRATED			
Microsoft® Office 4 For Windows® For Dummies® Quick Reference	by Doug Lowe	ISBN: 1-56884-958-3	$9.99 USA/$12.99 Canada
Microsoft® Works 3 For Windows® For Dummies® Quick Reference	by Michael Partington	ISBN: 1-56884-959-1	$9.99 USA/$12.99 Canada
INTERNET/COMMUNICATIONS/NETWORKING			
The Internet For Dummies® Quick Reference	by John R. Levine & Margaret Levine Young	ISBN: 1-56884-168-X	$8.95 USA/$11.95 Canada
MACINTOSH			
Macintosh® System 7.5 For Dummies® Quick Reference	by Stuart J. Stuple	ISBN: 1-56884-956-7	$9.99 USA/$12.99 Canada
OPERATING SYSTEMS:			
DOS			
DOS For Dummies® Quick Reference	by Greg Harvey	ISBN: 1-56884-007-1	$8.95 USA/$11.95 Canada
UNIX			
UNIX® For Dummies® Quick Reference	by John R. Levine & Margaret Levine Young	ISBN: 1-56884-094-2	$8.95 USA/$11.95 Canada
WINDOWS			
Windows® 3.1 For Dummies® Quick Reference, 2nd Edition	by Greg Harvey	ISBN: 1-56884-951-6	$8.95 USA/$11.95 Canada
PCs/HARDWARE			
Memory Management For Dummies® Quick Reference	by Doug Lowe	ISBN: 1-56884-362-3	$9.99 USA/$12.99 Canada
PRESENTATION/AUTOCAD			
AutoCAD For Dummies® Quick Reference	by Ellen Finkelstein	ISBN: 1-56884-198-1	$9.95 USA/$12.95 Canada
SPREADSHEET			
1-2-3 For Dummies® Quick Reference	by John Walkenbach	ISBN: 1-56884-027-6	$8.95 USA/$11.95 Canada
1-2-3 For Windows® 5 For Dummies® Quick Reference	by John Walkenbach	ISBN: 1-56884-957-5	$9.95 USA/$12.95 Canada
Excel For Windows® For Dummies® Quick Reference, 2nd Edition	by John Walkenbach	ISBN: 1-56884-096-9	$8.95 USA/$11.95 Canada
Quattro Pro 6 For Windows® For Dummies® Quick Reference	by Stuart J. Stuple	ISBN: 1-56884-172-8	$9.95 USA/$12.95 Canada
WORD PROCESSING			
Word For Windows® 6 For Dummies® Quick Reference	by George Lynch	ISBN: 1-56884-095-0	$8.95 USA/$11.95 Canada
Word For Windows® For Dummies® Quick Reference	by George Lynch	ISBN: 1-56884-029-2	$8.95 USA/$11.95 Canada
WordPerfect® 6.1 For Windows® For Dummies® Quick Reference, 2nd Edition	by Greg Harvey	ISBN: 1-56884-966-4	$9.99 USA/$12.99/Canada

Macworld® Mac® & Power Mac SECRETS, 2nd Edition
by David Pogue & Joseph Schorr

HOT!

This is the definitive Mac reference for those who want to become power users! Includes three disks with 9MB of software!

WINNERS 1994-95
TECHNICAL PUBLICATIONS AND ART COMPETITIONS OF THE SOCIETY FOR TECHNICAL COMMUNICATION

ISBN: 1-56884-175-2
$39.95 USA/$54.95 Canada

Includes 3 disks chock full of software.

NEWBRIDGE BOOK CLUB SELECTION

Macworld® Mac® FAQs
by David Pogue

HOT!

Written by the hottest Macintosh author around, David Pogue, *Macworld Mac FAQs* gives users the ultimate Mac reference. Hundreds of Mac questions and answers side-by-side, right at your fingertips, and organized into six easy-to-reference sections with lots of sidebars and diagrams.

ISBN: 1-56884-480-8
$19.99 USA/$26.99 Canada

Macworld® System 7.5 Bible, 3rd Edition
by Lon Poole

ISBN: 1-56884-098-5
$29.95 USA/$39.95 Canada

NATIONAL BESTSELLER!

Macworld® ClarisWorks 3.0 Companion, 3rd Edition
by Steven A. Schwartz

ISBN: 1-56884-481-6
$24.99 USA/$34.99 Canada

NATIONAL BESTSELLER!

Macworld® Complete Mac® Handbook Plus Interactive CD, 3rd Edition
by Jim Heid

BMUG SPRING 1995 CHOICE PRODUCT

ISBN: 1-56884-192-2
$39.95 USA/$54.95 Canada

Includes an interactive CD-ROM.

NEWBRIDGE BOOK CLUB SELECTION

Macworld® Ultimate Mac® CD-ROM
by Jim Heid

ISBN: 1-56884-477-8
$19.99 USA/$26.99 Canada

CD-ROM includes version 2.0 of QuickTime, and over 65 MB of the best shareware, freeware, fonts, sounds, and more!

Macworld® Networking Bible, 2nd Edition
by Dave Kosiur & Joel M. Snyder

ISBN: 1-56884-194-9
$29.95 USA/$39.95 Canada

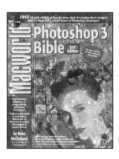

Macworld® Photoshop 3 Bible, 2nd Edition
by Deke McClelland

ISBN: 1-56884-158-2
$39.95 USA/$54.95 Canada

Includes stunning CD-ROM with add-ons, digitized photos and more.

WINNERS 1994-95
TECHNICAL PUBLICATIONS AND ART COMPETITIONS OF THE SOCIETY FOR TECHNICAL COMMUNICATION

NEW!

Macworld® Photoshop 2.5 Bible
by Deke McClelland

ISBN: 1-56884-022-5
$29.95 USA/$39.95 Canada

NATIONAL BESTSELLER!

Macworld® FreeHand 4 Bible
by Deke McClelland

ISBN: 1-56884-170-1
$29.95 USA/$39.95 Canada

Macworld® Illustrator 5.0/5.5 Bible
by Ted Alspach

ISBN: 1-56884-097-7
$39.95 USA/$54.95 Canada

Includes CD-ROM with QuickTime tutorials.

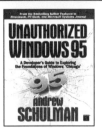

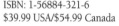

Official Hayes Modem Communications Companion
by Caroline M. Halliday

ISBN: 1-56884-072-1
$29.95 USA/$39.95 Canada
Includes software.

1,001 Komputer Answers from Kim Komando
by Kim Komando

ISBN: 1-56884-460-3
$29.99 USA/$39.99 Canada
Includes software.

PC World Excel 5 For Windows® Handbook, 2nd Edition
by John Walkenbach & Dave Maguiness

ISBN: 1-56884-056-X
$34.95 USA/$44.95 Canada
Includes software

PC World WordPerfect® 6 Handbook
by Greg Harvey

ISBN: 1-878058-80-0
$34.95 USA/$44.95 Canada
Includes software.

PC World DOS 6 Command Reference and Problem Solver
by John Socha & Devra Hall

NATIONAL BESTSELLER

ISBN: 1-56884-055-1
$24.95 USA/$32.95 Canada

Client/Server Strategies™: A Survival Guide for Corporate Reengineers
by David Vaskevitch

SUPER STAR

ISBN: 1-56884-064-0

Internet SECRETS™
by John Levine & Carol Baroudi

ISBN: 1-56884-452-2
$39.99 USA/$54.99 Canada
Includes software.

Network Security SECRETS™
by David Stang & Sylvia Moon

ISBN: 1-56884-021-7
Int'l. ISBN: 1-56884-151-5
$49.95 USA/$64.95 Canada
Includes software.

PC SECRETS™
by Caroline M. Halliday

ISBN: 1-878058-49-5
$39.95 USA/$52.95 Canada
Includes software.

IDG BOOKS WORLDWIDE

Here's a complete listing of PC Press Titles

Title	Author	ISBN	Price
BBS SECRETS™	by Ray Werner	ISBN: 1-56884-491-3	$39.99 USA/$54.99 Canada
Creating Cool Web Pages with HTML	by Dave Taylor	ISBN: 1-56884-454-9	$19.99 USA/$26.99 Canada
DOS 6 SECRETS™	by Robert D. Ainsbury	ISBN: 1-878058-70-3	$39.95 USA/$52.95 Canada
Excel 5 For Windows® Power Programming Techniques	by John Walkenbach	ISBN: 1-56884-303-8	$39.95 USA/$52.95 Canada
Hard Disk SECRETS™	by John M. Goodman, Ph.D.	ISBN: 1-878058-64-9	$39.95 USA/$52.95 Canada
Internet GIZMOS™ For Windows®	by Joel Diamond, Howard Sobel, & Valda Hilley	ISBN: 1-56884-451-4	$39.99 USA/$54.99 Canada
Making Multimedia Work	by Michael Goodwin	ISBN: 1-56884-468-9	$19.99 USA/$26.99 Canada
MORE Windows® 3.1 SECRETS™	by Brian Livingston	ISBN: 1-56884-019-5	$39.95 USA/$52.95 Canada
Official XTree Companion 3rd Edition	by Beth Slick	ISBN: 1-878058-57-6	$19.95 USA/$26.95 Canada
Paradox 4 Power Programming SECRETS™, 2nd Edition	by Gregory B. Salcedo & Martin W. Rudy	ISBN: 1-878058-54-1	$44.95 USA/$59.95 Canada
Paradox 5 For Windows® Power Programming SECRETS™	by Gregory B. Salcedo & Martin W. Rudy	ISBN: 1-56884-085-3	$44.95 USA/$59.95 Canada
PC World DOS 6 Handbook, 2nd Edition	by John Socha, Clint Hicks & Devra Hall	ISBN: 1-878058-79-7	$34.95 USA/$44.95 Canada
PC World Microsoft® Access 2 Bible, 2nd Edition	by Cary N. Prague & Michael R. Irwin	ISBN: 1-56884-086-1	$39.95 USA/$52.95 Canada
PC World Word For Windows® 6 Handbook	by Brent Heslop & David Angell	ISBN: 1-56884-054-3	$34.95 USA/$44.95 Canada
QuarkXPress For Windows® Designer Handbook	by Barbara Assadi & Galen Gruman	ISBN: 1-878058-45-2	$29.95 USA/$39.95 Canada
Windows® 3.1 Configuration SECRETS™	by Valda Hilley & James Blakely	ISBN: 1-56884-026-8	$49.95 USA/$64.95 Canada
Windows® 3.1 Connectivity SECRETS™	by Runnoe Connally, David Rorabaugh & Sheldon Hall	ISBN: 1-56884-030-6	$49.95 USA/$64.95 Canada
Windows® 3.1 SECRETS™	by Brian Livingston	ISBN: 1-878058-43-6	$39.95 USA/$52.95 Canada
Windows® 95 A.S.A.P.	by Dan Gookin	ISBN: 1-56884-483-2	$24.99 USA/$34.99 Canada
Windows® 95 Bible	by Alan Simpson	ISBN: 1-56884-074-8	$29.99 USA/$39.99 Canada
Windows® 95 SECRETS™	by Brian Livingston	ISBN: 1-56884-453-0	$39.99 USA/$54.99 Canada
Windows® GIZMOS™	by Brian Livingston & Margie Livingston	ISBN: 1-878058-66-5	$39.95 USA/$52.95 Canada
WordPerfect® 6 For Windows® Tips & Techniques Revealed	by David A. Holzgang & Roger C. Parker	ISBN: 1-56884-202-3	$39.95 USA/$52.95 Canada
WordPerfect® 6 SECRETS™	by Roger C. Parker & David A. Holzgang	ISBN: 1-56884-040-3	$39.95 USA/$52.95 Canada

IBM™

IBM PRESS

IDG BOOKS WORLDWIDE

இப் புத்தகங்கள் மிகவும் நல்லவை
(way cool)

9/19/95

OS/2® Warp Internet Connection: Your Key to Cruising the Internet and the World Wide Web

by Deborah Morrison

OS/2 users can get warped on the Internet using the OS/2 Warp tips, techniques, and helpful directories found in *OS/2 Warp Internet Connection*. This reference covers OS/2 Warp Internet basics, such as e-mail use and how to access other computers, plus much more! The Internet gets more

complex every day, but for OS/2 Warp users it just got a whole lot easier! Your value-packed disk includes 10 of the best internet utilities to help you explore the Net and save money while you're on-line!

EXPERT AUTHOR PROFILE
Deborah Morrison (Raleigh, NC) is an award-winning IBM writer who specializes in TCP/IP and the Internet. She is currently the editor-in-chief of IBM's *TCP/IP Connection* quarterly magazine.

ISBN: 1-56884-465-4
$24.99 USA/$34.99 Canada
Includes one 3.5" disk

Available: Now

Official Guide to Using OS/2® Warp

by Karla Stagray & Linda S. Rogers

IDG Books and IBM have come together to produce the most comprehensive user's guide to OS/2 Warp available today. From installation to using OS/2 Warp's BonusPak programs, this book delivers valuable help to the reader who needs to get up and running fast. Loaded with working examples, easy tips, and operating system concepts, *Official Guide to Using OS/2 Warp* is the only official user's guide authorized by IBM.

EXPERT AUTHOR PROFILE
Karla Stagray and Linda Rogers (Boca Raton, FL) both have a unique understanding of computer software and hardware. As award-winning IBM writers, Stagray and Rogers have received Society of Technical Communicators awards for various endeavors.

ISBN: 1-56884-466-2
$29.99 USA/$39.99 Canada

Available: Now

OS/2® Warp Uncensored

by Peter G. Magid & Ira H. Schneider

Exploit the power of OS/2 Warp and learn the secrets of object technology for the Workplace Shell. This all new book/CD-ROM bundle, for power users and intermediate users alike, provides the real inside story—not just the "what," but the "how" and "why" — from the folks who designed and developed the Workplace Shell. Packed with tips and techniques for using IBM's REXX programming language, and the bonus CD includes new bitmaps, icons, mouse pointers, REXX scripts, and an Object Tool!

EXPERT AUTHOR PROFILE
Peter G. Magid (Boca Raton, FL) is the User Interface Design Lead for the Workplace Shell and has over 12 years of programming experience at IBM. He is a graduate of Tulane University, and holds a B.S. degree in Computer Science.

Ira H. Schneider (Boca Raton, FL) has focused on enhancements to the Workplace Shell and has over 25 years of experience with IBM. He has held numerous lead programming positions within IBM and graduated from Northeastern University with a B.S. degree in Electrical Engineering.

ISBN: 1-56884-474-3
$39.99 USA/$54.99 Canada
Includes one CD-ROM

Available: Now

OS/2® Warp FAQs™

by Mike Kaply & Timothy F. Sipples

At last, the ultimate answer book for every OS/2 Warp user. Direct from IBM's Service Hotline, *OS/2 Warp FAQs* is a comprehensive question-and-answer guide that helps you optimize your system and save time by putting the answers to all your questions right at your fingertips. CD includes FAQs from the book in an easy-to-search format, plus hard-to-find device drivers for connecting to peripherals, such as printers.

EXPERT AUTHOR PROFILE
Mike Kaply (Boca Raton, FL) is currently on the OS/2 Help Manager Development Team at IBM in Boca Raton, Florida. He holds a B.S. degree in Mathematics and Computer Science from Southern Methodist University.

Timothy F. Sipples (Chicago, IL) is an OS/2 Warp specialist from IBM. He has written for *OS/2 Magazine* and was named "Team OS/2er of the Year" by *OS/2 Professional*.

ISBN: 1-56884-472-7
$29.99 USA/$42.99 Canada
Includes one CD-ROM

Available: September 1995

OS/2® Warp and PowerPC: Operating in the New Frontier

by Ken Christopher, Scott Winters & Mary Pollack Wright

The software makers at IBM unwrap the IBM and OS/2 mystique to share insights and strategies that will take business computing into the 21st century. Readers get a long, hard look at the next generation of OS/2 Warp for PowerPC.

EXPERT AUTHOR PROFILE
Ken Christopher (Boca Raton, FL) is Program Director of Development for OS/2 for Power PC. He has been a key player in the development on OS/2 Warp.

Scott Winters (Boca Raton, FL) is lead architect of OS/2 for the PowerPC. He has been instrumental in the development on OS/2 Warp on the PowerPC platform.

Mary Pollack Wright (Boca Raton, FL) is currently the technical editor for the OS/2 Techinical Library. She has been part of the OS/2 team since 1985. Her technical articles on OS/2 have been published in the *OS/2 Developer* magazine and *OS/2 Notebooks*.

ISBN: 1-56884-458-1
$29.99 USA/$39.99 Canada

Available: September 1995

Order Center: **(800) 762-2974** *(8 a.m.–6 p.m., EST, weekdays)*

Quantity	ISBN	Title	Price	Total

Shipping & Handling Charges				
	Description	**First book**	**Each additional book**	**Total**
Domestic	Normal	$4.50	$1.50	$
	Two Day Air	$8.50	$2.50	$
	Overnight	$18.00	$3.00	$
International	Surface	$8.00	$8.00	$
	Airmail	$16.00	$16.00	$
	DHL Air	$17.00	$17.00	$

*For large quantities call for shipping & handling charges.
**Prices are subject to change without notice.

Ship to:

Name _____

Company _____

Address _____

City/State/Zip _____

Daytime Phone _____

Payment: ☐ Check to IDG Books Worldwide (US Funds Only)

☐ VISA ☐ MasterCard ☐ American Express

Card # _____ Expires _____

Signature _____

Subtotal _____

CA residents add
applicable sales tax _____

IN, MA, and MD
residents add
5% sales tax _____

IL residents add
6.25% sales tax _____

RI residents add
7% sales tax _____

TX residents add
8.25% sales tax _____

Shipping _____

Total _____

Please send this order form to:

IDG Books Worldwide, Inc.

7260 Shadeland Station, Suite 100

Indianapolis, IN 46256

*Allow up to 3 weeks for delivery.
Thank you!*

Yahoo!

Installing and Using the CD-ROM

See instructions on back of this sheet.

Installing and Using the CD-ROM

Windows

To install Quarterdeck Mosaic on a Windows machine:

1. Insert the CD-ROM into the drive.

2. Select your CD-Rom drive and open the QMOSAIC folder.

3. Double-click on INSTALL.EXE.

4. Follow the dialog boxes to install Quarterdeck Mosaic.

To run Yahoo! Unplugged on a Windows machine:

The CD-ROM presentation of Yahoo! Unplugged works like a Web page on your computer. It must be viewed in a Web browser. If you are using Quarterdeck Mosaic, open the file YAHOOUN.HTM on the CD.

If you are using a browser other than Quarterdeck Mosaic, such as

Netscape, choose Open⇨File from the File Menu and open the file YAHOOUN.HTM.

PC System Requirements:

- PC with 386SX/25 or higher

- Windows 3.1 or higher

- 4MB RAM

- 256 colors

- 640 x 480 monitor resolution or higher

- Double speed CD-ROM drive

Mac

To install Quarterdeck Mosaic on a Macintosh:

1. Insert the CD-ROM into the drive.

2. Double-click on the file QMosaic for Mac.

To run Yahoo! Unplugged on a Macintosh:

The CD-ROM presentation of Yahoo! Unplugged works like a Web page on your computer. It must be viewed in a Web browser. If you are using Quarterdeck Mosaic, open the file YAHOOUN.HTM, located on the CD.

If you are using a browser other than Quarterdeck Mosaic, such as Netscape, choose Open⇨File from the File Menu and open the file YAHOOUN.HTM.

Mac System Requirements:

- Color Macintosh

- 8MB RAM

- System 6.05 or later

- Double speed CD-ROM drive

Tips on searching   History of Yahoo!   Guided tours of Yahoo!

Browse Yahoo! on CD   Go to Animated Design home page   Go to this book's home page on the Web

Go to Yahoo! on the Web

Go to IDG Books home page on the Web

IDG BOOKS WORLDWIDE REGISTRATION CARD

RETURN THIS REGISTRATION CARD FOR FREE CATALOG

Title of this book: Yahoo! Unplugged: Your Discovery Guide to the Web

My overall rating of this book: ❏ Very good [1] ❏ Good [2] ❏ Satisfactory [3] ❏ Fair [4] ❏ Poor [5]

How I first heard about this book:

❏ Found in bookstore; name: [6] _____ | ❏ Book review: [7]
❏ Advertisement: [8] | ❏ Catalog: [9]
❏ Word of mouth; heard about book from friend, co-worker, etc.: [10] | ❏ Other: [11]

What I liked most about this book:

_____

_____

What I would change, add, delete, etc., in future editions of this book:

_____

_____

Other comments:

_____

Number of computer books I purchase in a year: ❏ 1 [12] ❏ 2-5 [13] ❏ 6-10 [14] ❏ More than 10 [15]

I would characterize my computer skills as: ❏ Beginner [16] ❏ Intermediate [17] ❏ Advanced [18] ❏ Professional [19]

I use ❏ DOS [20] ❏ Windows [21] ❏ OS/2 [22] ❏ Unix [23] ❏ Macintosh [24] ❏ Other: [25]_____
(please specify)

I would be interested in new books on the following subjects:
(please check all that apply, and use the spaces provided to identify specific software)

❏ Word processing: [26] | ❏ Spreadsheets: [27]
❏ Data bases: [28] | ❏ Desktop publishing: [29]
❏ File Utilities: [30] | ❏ Money management: [31]
❏ Networking: [32] | ❏ Programming languages: [33]
❏ Other: [34]

I use a PC at (please check all that apply): ❏ home [35] ❏ work [36] ❏ school [37] ❏ other: [38] _____

The disks I prefer to use are ❏ 5.25 [39] ❏ 3.5 [40] ❏ other: [41]_____

I have a CD ROM: ❏ yes [42] ❏ no [43]

I plan to buy or upgrade computer hardware this year: ❏ yes [44] ❏ no [45]

I plan to buy or upgrade computer software this year: ❏ yes [46] ❏ no [47]

Name: _____ Business title: [48] _____ Type of Business: [49] _____

Address (❏ home [50] ❏ work [51]/Company name: _____)

Street/Suite# _____

City [52]/State [53]/Zipcode [54]: _____ Country [55] _____

❏ **I liked this book!** You may quote me by name in future
IDG Books Worldwide promotional materials.

My daytime phone number is _____

IDG BOOKS
THE WORLD OF COMPUTER KNOWLEDGE

☐ **YES!**

Please keep me informed about IDG's World of Computer Knowledge.
Send me the latest IDG Books catalog.